'This wonderful book provides a lucid overview of the main [...] offers useful distinctions and key insights directly relevant to the array of case studies included in this timely volume.'

– Daryl Koehn, *Managing Director, Institute of Business and Professional Ethics, DePaul University, USA*

'This book adopts a person-centred approach that fits very nicely with the nature of the firm and the identity and role of business leaders. Companies are made up of people, their success depends on the quality of their people, and managing organizations is mainly about managing people. Furthermore, many crucial points regarding leadership and ethics in organizations are central to this book, such as respect for each person, the proper use of power, the role of values and mission statements in successful firms, and organizational designs that not only are effective but also contribute to the personal and professional growth of those involved in the organization.'

– Jordi Canals, *Professor and Former Dean of IESE Business School, Spain*

'This outstanding third edition of *Business Ethics in Action* offers a fresh and thoughtful perspective on the most urgent moral challenges facing companies and business leaders, taking a unique person-centred approach pioneered and perfected by the author through the decades, as few others have done. Teachers and students alike have a little treasure in their hands.'

– Giancarlo Ianulardo, *University of Exeter, UK*

'Domènec Melé skillfully integrates a philosophical approach combining virtue, responsibility, moral insight and sound judgement, with a practical analysis of real-world business dilemmas. This combination makes the book an invaluable resource for students and educators in the field of business ethics.'

– Alexander Pepper, *London School of Economics, UK*

'The new edition of this excellent book embellishes and updates material, making it indispensable to those interested in getting a clear and actionable account of a complex and globally important subject. Melé's rare expertise combines theological insight, ethical theory and practical business management to give the reader an ethics "tour de force". I strongly recommended this book to all who wish to gain a first-rate actionable knowledge of Business Ethics.'

– David Coldwell, *University of the Witwatersrand, South Africa*

'Melé draws on considerable classroom experience to enhance the detail and depth of knowledge in this latest edition of *Business Ethics in Action*. The book offers students a multitude of paths, combining detailed introductions to foundational theories of ethics with opportunities for reflection, and each chapter presents engaging scenarios of persons and organisations striving for a better business world. The nuanced and practical orientation of this book will appeal to instructors and students alike.'

– Laura Mitchell, *University of York, UK*

Business Ethics in Action

Managing Human Excellence

Third Edition

Domènec Melé

BLOOMSBURY ACADEMIC
LONDON · NEW YORK · OXFORD · NEW DELHI · SYDNEY

BLOOMSBURY ACADEMIC
Bloomsbury Publishing Plc, 50 Bedford Square, London, WC1B 3DP, UK
Bloomsbury Publishing Inc, 1359 Broadway, New York, NY 10018, USA
Bloomsbury Publishing Ireland, 29 Earlsfort Terrace, Dublin 2, D02 AY28, Ireland

BLOOMSBURY, BLOOMSBURY ACADEMIC and the Diana logo are
trademarks of Bloomsbury Publishing Plc

First published in Great Britain 2009
Second edition published 2019
This edition published 2026

Copyright © Domènec Melé, 2009, 2019, 2026

Domènec Melé has asserted his right under the Copyright, Designs and
Patents Act, 1988, to be identified as Author of this work.

For legal purposes the Acknowledgements on p. xxi constitute an
extension of this copyright page.

Cover design: Paul Smith
Cover image © iStock

All rights reserved. No part of this publication may be: i) reproduced or transmitted in
any form, electronic or mechanical, including photocopying, recording or by means of
any information storage or retrieval system without prior permission in writing from the
publishers; or ii) used or reproduced in any way for the training, development or operation
of artificial intelligence (AI) technologies, including generative AI technologies. The rights
holders expressly reserve this publication from the text and data mining exception as per
Article 4(3) of the Digital Single Market Directive (EU) 2019/790.

Bloomsbury Publishing Plc does not have any control over, or responsibility for, any
third-party websites referred to or in this book. All internet addresses given in this
book were correct at the time of going to press. The author and publisher regret
any inconvenience caused if addresses have changed or sites have ceased
to exist, but can accept no responsibility for any such changes.

A catalogue record for this book is available from the British Library.

A catalog record for this book is available from the Library of Congress.

ISBN: HB: 978-1-3504-3867-5
PB: 978-1-3504-1464-8
ePDF: 978-1-3504-3865-1
eBook: 978-1-3504-3868-2

Typeset by Integra Software Services Pvt. Ltd.
Printed and bound in Great Britain by Bell and Bain Ltd, Glasgow

For product safety related questions contact productsafety@bloomsbury.com.

To find out more about our authors and books visit www.bloomsbury.com
and sign up for our newsletters.

Contents

List of Figures — xii
List of Tables — xiii
Table of Cases — xiv
Preface — xvi
Acknowledgements — xxi

Part I Foundations of Business Ethics

1 Introducing Business Ethics — 3
Overview — 3
Chapter Aims — 3
Historical Case #1 – The Enron collapse — 4

SECTION A. What is Business Ethics About? — 6
1.1 Antecedents and contemporary developments of business ethics — 6
1.2 Is business ethics profitable? — 8
1.3 Why companies engage in business ethics — 10
1.4 Normative vs. behavioural business ethics — 12
1.5 Scope of business ethics and ethical analysis — 13
Business Ethics in Action #1 – The Johnson & Johnson Credo and the Tylenol affair — 16

SECTION B. Introducing Ethics — 19
1.6 The human experience of morality — 19
1.7 Ethics as a systematic approach to morality — 20
1.8 Common insights of morality worldwide — 22
1.9 Subjective and social values vs. objective ethical values — 24
1.10 Goods, principles, and virtues — 25
Case Study #1 – Iam's dilemma — 28
Notes — 29

2 Ethical Foundations for Business Ethics — 33
Overview — 33
Chapter Aims — 33
Historical Case #2 – The controversial launch of the space shuttle *Challenger* — 34

SECTION A. Ethical Approaches: An Overview ... 36
2.1 Development of ethical theories: A concise historical view ... 36
2.2 Frequent ethical approaches for business ethics ... 39
2.3 Discussing ethical approaches in business ethics ... 48
2.4 Searching for a complete ethical theory ... 60
Business Ethics in Action #2 – The person-centred vision of François Michelin ... 63

SECTION B. Essentials of Aristotelian-Personalist Ethics ... 65
2.5 The human person – inherent dignity, innate rights and the pursuit of human fulfilment ... 65
2.6 Moral goods (ethical values) and the common good ... 68
2.7 Basic ethical principles ... 73
2.8 Fundamental virtues ... 82
Case Study #2 – A labour accident ... 87
Notes ... 88

Part II Individual Involvement in Business

3 Understanding Moral Responsibility ... 97
Overview ... 97
Chapter Aims ... 97
Historical Case #3 – The Volkswagen diesel emission test scandal ... 98

SECTION A. Concepts and Scope of Moral Responsibility ... 100
3.1 Responsibility, accountability and liability ... 100
3.2 For what is one responsible? ... 102
3.3 Modifiers of moral responsibility ... 103
3.4 Are we responsible for consequences? ... 105
3.5 Forms of individual responsibility ... 108
Business Ethics in Action #3 – Enrique Shaw: A responsible manager ... 111

SECTION B. Personal Responsibility within the Organization ... 113
3.6 Organizational influence on individual moral responsibility ... 113
3.7 Material cooperation with wrongdoing ... 114
3.8 Personal responsibility in whistleblowing ... 116
Case Study #3 – TEPCO and the Fukushima tsunami ... 118
Notes ... 119

4 Ethics in Decision-Making ... 121
Overview ... 121
Chapter Aims ... 121
Historical Case #4 – Bernard L. Madoff: Deciding on a financial model ... 122

SECTION A. The Ethical Dimension of Decision-Making	124
4.1 Elements of moral behaviour	125
4.2 Practical wisdom in formulating moral judgements	127
4.3 Full rationality in decision-making	130
4.4 Evaluative criteria in decision-making	132
Business Ethics in Action #4 – Malden Mills: An unusual decision	136
SECTION B. Making Moral Judgements in Decision Making	138
4.5 The Triple Font of Morality approach for making moral judgements	138
4.6 The Principle of Double Effect	142
4.7 Solving ethical dilemmas	144
Case Study #4 – Junseo's promotion	147
Notes	148

5 Frequent Misbehaviours and Irregular Payments — 151

Overview	151
Chapter Aims	151
Historical Case #5 – Siemens: Accusations of bribery hit the company	152
SECTION A. Misbehaviours in Business and Finance	154
5.1 Some basic requirements of good behaviour	154
5.2 Business contracts – infringement and other misbehaviours	159
5.3 Misappropriation and fraud	162
5.4 Violation of trade secrets	165
5.5 Moral hazard and conflict of interests	166
5.6 Money laundering and tax evasion	168
5.7 Insider trading	170
Business Ethics in Action #5 – The Anti-Corruption Compliance Programme of ENI	172
SECTION B. Irregular Payments in Business	173
5.8 Bribery, extortion and other irregular payments	173
5.9 Morality of bribery and extortion	175
5.10 Damages of corruption and the fight against corruption	178
Case Study #5 – Preparing the Christmas sales campaign	183
Notes	184

6 Moral Character in Leadership — 187

Overview	187
Chapter Aims	187
Historical Case #6 – Leadership shift in Arthur Andersen	188
SECTION A. Relevance of Character in Leadership	191
6.1 Leading organizations: Authority, not just power	191

	6.2 Moral character and spirituality in leadership	193
	6.3 Relational leadership and ethics	195
	Business Ethics in Action #6 – TD Industries: Developing a servant leadership culture	198
	SECTION B. Relevant Virtues in Leadership	200
	6.4 Integrity as integration of virtues	200
	6.5 Wisdom in leadership	202
	6.6 Virtues for a good treatment	203
	6.7 Virtues for trustworthiness	206
	6.8 Self-mastery virtues	207
	Case Study #6 – United Laboratories: Leadership and values	211
	Notes	213

Part III Organizational Business Ethics

7 Free Market Economy and the Business Company — 221

Overview — 221
Chapter Aims — 222
Historical Case #7 – Lehman Brothers and the subprime crisis — 222

SECTION A. Business in the Free Market Economy — 224
7.1 The ethical dimension of the market economy — 225
7.2 Acceptable capitalism and the role of the government — 227
7.3 Governmental regulations of economic activities — 228
Business Ethics in Action #7 – AES Corporation: A values-driven company — 231

SECTION B. Nature and Purpose of the Business Company — 233
7.4 The company, a social institution and a community of persons — 234
7.5 Views of the purpose of the business company — 237
7.6 The common good as reference for the purpose of business — 245
7.7 The purpose of the company: Serving people through a dual mission — 247
7.8 The purpose of each company and 'purpose-driven companies' — 252
Case Study #7 – Suicides in France Télécom — 253
Notes — 255

8 The Right Use of Power in Business — 263

Overview — 263
Chapter Aims — 263
Historical Case #8 – Building up the Parmalat holding — 264

SECTION A. Managing Power Ethically — 267
8.1 Power within the business company — 267
8.2 Responsible use of power — 269

8.3 'Human Quality Treatment' in managing people — 272
8.4 Responsibility and virtues in managerial work — 275
8.5 Stewardship in managing corporate resources — 278
8.6 International standards for managing business responsibly — 280
Business Ethics in Action #8 – Mondragón Corporation:
The inclusive participatory company model — 285

SECTION B. Ethics in Corporate Governance — 287
8.7 Corporate governance for the common good — 287
8.8 Good ethical practices of corporate governance — 289
8.9 The question of executive compensation — 292
8.10 Power and responsibility of shareholders — 293
Case Study #8 – Recovering a company in crisis — 294
Notes — 295

9 Institutional Ethics and Organizational Ethical Culture — 299
Overview — 299
Chapter Aims — 299
Historical Case #9 – Cambridge Analytica operational techniques — 300

SECTION A. Institutionalizing Ethics into the Company — 302
9.1 Institutional statements — 304
9.2 Codes of business conduct — 307
9.3 Integrity and compliance programmes — 310
Business Ethics in Action #9 – Bill George's business vision — 313

SECTION B. Ethics in Organizational Culture, Strategy and Structures — 316
9.4 Organizational culture — 316
9.5 Factors in building an ethical organizational culture — 319
9.6 The ethical dimension of strategy — 320
9.7 Ethics in organizational structure and the informal organization — 321
9.8 Ethical principles in designing organizations — 323
Case Study #9 – La Fageda: A social enterprise facing a problem — 326
Notes — 327

10 Ethics in Managing Work and Technology — 333
Overview — 333
Chapter Aims — 334
Historical Case #10 – Questionable labour practices at Uber — 334

SECTION A. Managing Work Ethically — 338
10.1 Human work and its inherent dignity — 338
10.2 Labour rights — 341
10.3 Exploitative labour — 346
10.4 Violence and harassment at the workplace — 349

10.5 Diversity in the workplace: Unfair discrimination and justice — 350
10.6 Decent work, meaningful work and developmental work — 354
Business Ethics in Action #10 – Surgikos: From a *maquiladora* to a cellular manufacturing system — 358

SECTION B. Ethics in Managing Technology, IT and AI — 361
10.7 Technology as ally of work and instrumental for the common good — 361
10.8 Ethical issues in developing, implementing and using technology — 363
10.9 Ethical issues in using information technology — 366
10.10 Ethics in artificial intelligence — 369
10.11 The interaction between humans and technology — 372
Case Study #10 – Using AI in a hiring process — 375
Notes — 376

11 Ethics in Sales and Marketing — 381

Overview — 381
Chapter Aims — 381
Historical Case #11 – Sanlu: The melamine-tainted milk — 382

SECTION A. Consumer Rights and Authentic Service — 384
11.1 Consumer rights — 384
11.2 Providing authentic service to customers — 386
11.3 Ethics in market and marketing research — 389
Business Ethics in Action #11 – Bimbo: Responsible marketing of a responsible company — 391

SECTION B. Ethics in Marketing — 393
11.4 Marketing and consumerism — 393
11.5 Ethical issues regarding the product — 394
11.6 Fair price and abuses in pricing — 396
11.7 Promotion of the product: Advertising ethics — 399
11.8 Ethics in placement of the product — 402
11.9 Ethics in e-commerce — 403
Case Study #11 – Solving a problem in commercial activity — 404
Notes — 405

Part IV Societal Business Ethics

12 Business Responsibility and Relationships in Society — 409

Overview — 409
Chapter Aims — 409
Historical Case #12 – Responsibilities in the Bangladesh factory disaster at Rana Plaza — 410

SECTION A. The Social Responsibility of Business	412
12.1 Criticisms and responses to the social responsibility of business	413
12.2 Individual or corporate responsibilities?	415
12.3 Mainstream approaches to the social responsibility of business	416
12.4 Sustainability and CSR	419
12.5 Ethical principles for CSR	420
Business Ethics in Action #12 – Stormberg AS: A responsible SME	423
SECTION B. Societal Relationships of Business	424
12.6 Corporate relationships with governments	424
12.7 Corporate responses to social demands and cooperation with NGOs	427
12.8 Corporate accountability: Auditing and reporting	428
Case Study #12 – Interquim: Involving employees in social responsibilities	431
Notes	433

13 Ecological Responsibilities and Sustainable Development

	437
Overview	437
Chapter Aims	437
Historical Case #13 – Shell Africa: Environmental legacy, problems and prospects	438
SECTION A. Ecological Responsibility of Business	441
13.1 Natural resource depletion and diversity loss	441
13.2 Pollution, waste and climate change	444
13.3 The human–nature relationship, ecological ethics and integral ecology	446
13.4 Precautionary and proactive business actions	449
13.5 Waste management and product stewardship	452
Business Ethics in Action #13 – Patagonia, Inc.: 'Doing good while doing well'	453
SECTION B. Business and Sustainable Development	455
13.6 Sustainable development and circular economy	455
13.7 The ESG criteria and socially responsible investing	458
13.8 Multinational and transnational corporations in a global world	460
13.9 Supply chain and offshore outsourcing	464
13.10 Integrating responsibility and sustainability into the organization	466
Case Study #13 – Botnia: A controversial paper pulp factory	467
Notes	469

Afterword	472
Index	476

Figures

1.1	Ethical analysis of business situations	15
1.2	Motivations for good behaviour in business	20
1.3	Overlapping legality and morality	21
2.1	Interconnection of goods, principles and virtues	62
2.2	Connection of the four cardinal virtues	86
3.1	Forms of individual moral responsibility	108
4.1	Effects of the business action	133
4.2	Triple evaluative criteria for decision-making	134
4.3	The triple font of morality	140
5.1	Bribe and extortion in the business context	176
6.1	Leader integrity as the integration of virtues	202
7.1	Regulatory frame of the firm's manager	230
7.2	The common good-based multi-ends: Framing a dual corporate mission	251
8.1	Levels of Human Quality Treatment	273
9.1	Observable manifestations and hidden elements of organizational cultures	317
9.2	Gap between desired and existing organizational cultures	318
13.1	Integrating responsibility and sustainability into the firm	467

Tables

1.1	Analytical levels of business ethics	14
2.1	Main ethical theories proposed for business ethics	40
2.2	Praises and criticisms of ethical approaches employed in business ethics	48
2.3	Basic ethics principles in Aristotelian-personalist ethics	74
2.4	Basic moral goods, principles and virtues	83
4.1	Psychological components of moral behaviour	125
5.1	Key international and regional conventions against corruption	181
7.1	The common-good-oriented intrinsic ends of the company	249
8.1	International standards for responsible business	282
8.2	The Equator Principles	284
8.3	Recommended good practices in corporate governance	290
9.1	Medtronic mission statement	305
9.2	Common corporate values	306
12.1	Criticisms and responses on business social responsibility	413
13.1	Current ecological problems and business challenges and responsibilities	442

Cases

HISTORICAL CASES

1	The Enron collapse	USA
2	The controversial launch of the space shuttle *Challenger*	USA
3	The Volkswagen diesel emission test scandal	Germany
4	Bernard L. Madoff: Deciding on a financial model	USA
5	Siemens: Accusations of bribery hits the company	Germany
6	Leadership shift in Arthur Andersen	USA
7	Lehman Brothers and the subprime crisis	USA
8	Building up the Parmalat holding	Italy
9	Cambridge Analytica operational techniques	UK
10	Questionable labour practices at Uber	USA
11	Sanlu: The melamine-tainted milk	China
12	Responsibilities in the Bangladesh factory disaster at Rana Plaza	Bangladesh
13	Shell Africa: Environmental legacy, problems and prospects	Nigeria

BUSINESS ETHICS IN ACTION

1	The Johnson & Johnson Credo and the Tylenol affair	USA
2	The person-centred vision of François Michelin	France
3	Enrique Shaw: a responsible manager	Chile
4	Malden Mills: An unusual decision	USA
5	The Anti-Corruption Compliance Programme of ENI	Italy
6	TD Industries: Developing a servant leadership culture	USA
7	AES Corporation: A values-driven company	USA
8	Mondragón Corporation: The inclusive participatory company model	Spain
9	Bill George's business vision	USA
10	Surgikos: From a *maquiladora* to a cellular manufacturing system	Mexico
11	Bimbo: Responsible marketing of a responsible company	Mexico
12	Stormberg S/A: A responsible SME	Norway
13	Patagonia, Inc.: 'Doing good while doing well'	USA

CASE STUDIES

1	Iam's dilemma	Vietnam
2	A labour accident	Southern Europe
3	TEPCO and the Fukushima tsunami	Japan
4	Junseo's promotion	South Korea
5	Preparing the Christmas sales campaign	Latin America
6	United Laboratories: Leadership and values	Philippines
7	Suicides in France Télécom	France
8	Recovering a company in crisis	Latin America
9	La Fageda: A social enterprise facing a problem	Spain
10	Using AI in a hiring process	Australia
11	Solving a problem in commercial activity	Latin America
12	Interquim: Involving employees in social responsibilities	Colombia
13	Botnia: A controversial paper pulp factory	Uruguay/Argentina

Preface

As in the first edition of this work, I would like to begin with a personal anecdote, if I may. Once, long ago, while travelling to a conference in the United States, I was reading a book on business ethics. Beside me was a man who was surreptitiously glancing at my book. My travelling companion, a businessman as I later learned, eventually spoke:

'You seem interested in business ethics. Are you?'

'Yes, I am,' I answered. 'In fact, I teach business ethics at a business school.'

His response was quick and very frank:

'Oh! This is really important; there's so much corruption nowadays. Look, in my father's time, a contract was just a page and a handshake. Now, a contract is a tome, and each new one contains more and more clauses. Great for lawyers, who charge a fortune.'

I replied:

'You're right. Cases of deception, fraud, or manipulation, and abuses of good faith led people to lose trust, which in turn brings about increasingly complex mechanisms of control. The higher the level of ethical behaviour, the lower the cost of control.'

I continued:

'However, I disagree with those who think business ethics is only about corruption. Certainly, corruption and misconduct are part of ethics, and we can learn proper conduct by examining wrongdoing. But I believe ethics is much more than just a set of rules to avoid corruption or a set of minimum standards to support the law, or even to go beyond it in some respects. As many others, I believe that ethics serves as a guide to human freedom, orienting it toward the good life. As such, it is fundamentally concerned with human excellence.'

My companion seemed a little surprised, and we continued our conversation until the plane landed.

This anecdote reflects the first key characteristic of this book: providing a compass for managing human excellence in business, as highlighted in the subtitle, not merely for avoiding misconduct. From this perspective, business ethics is not only about determining acceptable or unacceptable actions and solving dilemmas but also, and most importantly, about improving ethical conduct in business and inspiring excellent practices in organizations, management and corporate governance – practices that foster trust and high-quality human performance in business relationships.

A second characteristic of the book is the Aristotelian–Personalist approach to ethics, which serves as the theoretical foundation for business ethics. Aligned with Aristotle's virtue ethics, this approach takes seriously the human capacity to develop good character traits – traditionally called 'virtues' – through action, and how these influence good behaviour and lead to human flourishing. Personalism, or more properly 'Personalist Philosophy,' in versions compatible with Aristotelian realism, is the second philosophical pillar of this approach. In personalism, central to the theory is the recognition of the human being as a whole, the common equality of all humans and, at the same time, the uniqueness of each individual. Personalism stresses human dignity and innate human rights, endowed with relationality and sociability, as well as autonomy and self-determination, oriented towards personal growth – although in different ways, depending on the uniqueness of each person. In this way, personal moral responsibility is emphasized. As in the Aristotelian tradition, personalism highlights that every human action influences a person's character, contributing to or detracting from human flourishing. This flourishing, and the subsequent human fulfillment, requires avoiding harm to others and respecting the environment, but also, and more importantly, doing good to people and caring for 'our common home'. Thus, human flourishing is associated with concern for others, justice, care and promoting a culture of mutual harmony and cooperation.

A third characteristic is the integration of human goods (human flourishing), norms and virtues, overcoming the conventional principles-versus-virtues dichotomy or the exclusive focus on actions, consequences, or agents. The Aristotelian–Personalist approach does not limit ethics to principles and their associated duties or to virtues as character traits disconnected from the human good or universal principles. Consequences of actions are also considered through practical wisdom – Aristotle's phronesis – a crucial virtue for moral discernment.

Another characteristic of this book is that it has been written from an international perspective expressed in both theoretical contents and the case studies included, that originate from around the world. The ethical approach employed here aligns well with many common moral intuitions, and many of the issues studied have relevance in most countries. This fourth characteristic is intended to make the book useful across different cultures, perhaps with certain adaptations. The international perspective is further reinforced by introducing standards for business ethics and corporate social responsibility proposed by recognized international organizations, such as the United Nations (UN), the International Labour Organization (ILO), the Organization for Economic Co-operation and Development (OECD) and others.

A fifth characteristic is the potential audience of this book, which assumes its intended readers will be people involved in business, including those preparing to become managers, business executives and consultants. The book generally focuses on managerial work, including aspects relevant to managerial decision-making, organizational design and managing the relationship between business and society. However, we believe it will provide useful perspectives not only for managers but also for anyone involved in business, from those in corporate governance to supervisors and employees.

Considering the potential audience, a sixth characteristic is that discussions are concise, accessible to the intended readers, and practical. Concision is important given the vast development of business ethics, especially since the late 1970s. The aim is not to discuss in depth every specific ethical issue that might arise in operations, marketing, finance, accounting, information technology and other business areas. However, the book presents what, in my view and after a careful exploration, are the most relevant themes in these areas. As for accessibility, the book assumes that readers do not need any prior background in ethics or philosophy to follow the discussions. A few bibliographical references are included in each chapter for further study if needed. The practical orientation – reflected in the title *Business Ethics in Action* – is evident in the style, with short examples interspersed in the main text and real business cases. This practical focus is still compatible with a solid conceptual foundation, as it is often said that 'there is nothing more practical than a good theory'.

Finally, the seventh characteristic is the balance between clarity and rigour, avoiding erudite but superfluous elaboration. The book has been written with a restricted vocabulary and includes illustrative examples, as well as figures and tables to clarify and aid in the discussion. Occasionally, a brief historical overview is provided to help readers learn from the past, understand where we are coming from and compare current situations with their antecedents.

Innovations of the third edition of **Business Ethics in Action** introduces significant revisions, updating information and expanding on certain topics. It also includes additional case studies, some of which address recent, significant ethical issues.

This edition faces new challenges in business. One of these concerns artificial intelligence (AI) and the exponential automation of processes, which are often linked to societal biases, discrimination, and job displacement. Other key challenges include growing sensitivity to environmental ethics and sustainability, respect for human dignity and diversity, emerging aspects of corporate social responsibility, transparency and accountability, labour practices and ethical supply chains, and ethical considerations in marketing and consumer protection.

Beyond these concerns – which require the prevention of unethical behaviours – this book, as in previous editions, emphasizes the promotion of human excellence and the development of humanistic companies where the human person remains central.

In practical terms, this edition introduces several new features compared to the previous one, specifically:

Now, each chapter begins with an overview that provides a rationale for the relevance of the topic to be addressed, along with a brief summary of the main themes to be discussed. This aims to offer readers a general understanding of the chapter's content from the outset. As in the second edition, this introduction is complemented by a reviewed list of learning aims, helping to frame the chapter's objectives and guide the reader's focus.

Greater emphasis has been placed on business ethics case studies, with some entirely new cases and others updated. The book now includes thirty-nine case studies, three per chapter, featuring scenarios set in various countries and contexts to provide a global perspective. The increased focus on case studies has not diminished the commitment to presenting theoretical aspects with clarity and rigour.

Each chapter opens with a Historical Case in business ethics. Thus, the introductory case from previous editions has been replaced by challenging and well-known corporate examples – often involving corporate or financial scandals – which can now be considered 'classics'. These cases provide evidence of the consequences of unethical behaviour. As in earlier editions, they are designed to engage students and encourage them to read the chapter for deeper insights into the issues presented.

A case study highlighting good ethical practices, titled 'Business Ethics in Action,' has been included approximately halfway through each chapter. This is accompanied by a brief commentary linking the case to key concepts discussed in the chapter. In addition, each chapter continues to conclude with a case study for class discussion or an assignment suitable for independent work.

Minor modifications have been introduced, including changes to some section titles and topics. Certain sections have been condensed, others expanded, and some reorganized to enhance their pedagogical impact. Each chapter remains divided into two related parts – A and B – as in the second edition, allowing greater flexibility in structuring teaching sessions.

Two new parts have been added. One presents a comprehensive overview of ethical theories, now integrated into the main body of the book (Chapter 2, Part A), rather than included as an appendix, as in the second edition. This offers the opportunity to explore the mainstream ethical theories that have been proposed as foundations for business ethics, examining both their strengths and weaknesses. The section also provides the rationale for the Aristotelian-Personalist ethical approach proposed in Chapter 2, Part B, which integrates goods (ethical values), principles (norms) and virtues (moral traits of character). The other new part (Chapter 10, Part B) addresses the ethical management of emerging technologies, including AI. Additionally, some existing sections have been expanded – for instance, the one devoted to corporate ecological responsibility and the role of businesses in sustainable development.

Several new examples drawn from business practice have been introduced to illustrate theoretical explanations and concepts more vividly.

New tables have been added to various chapters, aiming to support the reader in following the text and providing concise summaries of the main points discussed.

The entire text has been thoroughly revised to clarify, expand or refine descriptions and explanations where necessary. This includes critical arguments on moral relativism and discussions surrounding Environmental, Social, and Governance (ESG) criteria, among others.

Bibliographical references have been updated to facilitate further reading, while retaining those deemed valuable for the book's overall presentation.

Lastly, to keep the text concise, two elements from the second edition have been removed: chapter summaries, which can now be easily generated using AI, and key term lists, which can be compiled independently as part of personal study.

The book is structured into four parts, containing a total of thirteen chapters, each divided into two parts. Part I focuses on the foundations of business ethics, beginning with an introduction to business ethics and basic ethical concepts (Chapter 1), followed by a discussion of the ethical foundations of business ethics (Chapter 2).

Part II explores various aspects of individual involvement in business ethics. It begins with a discussion of personal moral responsibility within organizations (Chapter 3) and how to make moral judgements in decision-making (Chapter 4). It then addresses common ethical issues in business and finance, including the morality of questionable payments often encountered in business (Chapter 5). The final chapter of this part examines the role of character in leadership (Chapter 6).

Part III delves into organizational business ethics. It begins with an overview of the market economy, discussing the purpose of the firm and its ethical implications (Chapter 7). This is followed by an examination of the proper use of power within organizations, focusing on the ethical aspects of management and corporate governance (Chapter 8). The next chapter covers general aspects of organizational ethics (Chapter 9). This part concludes with two chapters dedicated to ethics in managing human work and technology, including AI (Chapter 10), and ethics in sales and marketing (Chapter 11).

Finally, Part IV addresses societal business ethics, with a particular focus on corporate responsibility and sustainability. It begins by discussing corporate social responsibility, sustainability, corporate accountability, and the relationship between business and society (Chapter 12). The final chapter focuses on the ecological responsibility of businesses and their role in sustainable development in a global context (Chapter 13).

In the middle of each chapter, there is a commented case highlighting exemplary aspects to illustrate business ethics in action. At the end of each chapter, there is another case study, focusing on managerial situations that require detailed analysis and decision-making, generally related to concepts discussed in the current and previous chapters. We hope these innovations will be valuable for both teachers and students, enabling them to deepen their knowledge and reflect on the fundamental bases of business ethics, which this work aims to present.

Domènec Melé
8 August 2025

Acknowledgements

The first words of this new edition are an expression of gratitude – to the many colleagues in business ethics who have adopted or recommended this work for their classes and to the students who have used it. Not infrequently, some of them have written to me, sharing their appreciation and suggesting points for improvement. I am also grateful to Bloomsbury Academic, which acquired the publishing rights to this book, encouraging me to prepare and publish an updated and expanded version. After months of work, it has finally been completed.

The author is also deeply grateful to several reviewers for their thoughtful suggestions, as well as to many colleagues for their constructive comments, particularly Kleio Akrivou, Antonio Argandoña, Joan Fontrodona, Álvaro Pezoa, Marion Prats, Kemi Ogunyemi, Antonino Vaccaro, Sébastien Fosse, and Javier Zamora. Their contributions have undoubtedly improved the book in many respects, as have the insights from students at the IESE Business School and participants in programmes and seminars in various countries.

The author would also like to thank Prof. Jordi Canals, former Dean of the IESE Business School, for suggesting that I write this book and for writing the Foreword to the first edition (2009), and the current Dean of this business school, Prof. Franz Heukamp, for his continued support of my work.

Part I

Foundations of Business Ethics

1
Introducing Business Ethics

I do not think we have psychological, ethical and economic problems. We have human problems with psychological, ethical and economic aspects, and as many as you like, legal often.[1]

MARY PARKER FOLLETT (1868–1933), pioneer in management thought

Overview

Business ethics considers the moral dimension of business and is now a well-established discipline, often grouped with related fields such as management, operations, accountability, corporate responsibility, sustainability, and good governance. Many companies have incorporated business ethics and related concepts, motivated either by a genuine sense of responsibility or in response to social pressure and public concern, aiming to mitigate risks or enhance corporate reputation.

Section A of this chapter begins by presenting the recent historical development of business ethics and exploring corporate motivations for adopting ethical practices. It also discusses the relevance of business ethics and examines the outcomes of ethical corporate behaviour.

Section B delves into the concept of ethics, which obviously is central to business ethics, reflecting on the role of ethics as a guide for human conduct and human activities, including business. Additionally, it outlines the scope of business ethics and distinguishes between normative and behavioural ethics.

Chapter Aims

After reading this chapter you should be able to:

- Explain how the current interest in business ethics emerged.
- Describe how and why business ethics and related concepts are integrated into companies.
- Provide arguments about the possible link between ethics and economic performance.
- Highlight the scope of business ethics.
- Distinguish between normative and behavioural business ethics.
- Introduce a deeper understanding of morality and ethics.
- Reflect on the role of ethics as a guide for human conduct.
- Clarify some basic ethical concepts.

Historical Case #1

The Enron collapse[2]

Enron was established in 1985 as a traditional pipeline company distributing natural gas. Energy liberalization in the United States created a new business environment, and under the leadership of CEO Kenneth (Ken) Lay, Enron took on a new role.

Enron took the opportunity to change into a commodity trader, buying and selling natural gas. As deregulation caused disparities in gas prices, Enron guaranteed long-term supply to its clients at a fixed price.

By 1995, Enron had become the leading company in its sector. Soon after, it expanded its intermediary services and began acting as a broker. The mediation risks previously borne by the clients – who were insured against interest rate movements, unpaid credits, meteorological conditions, and so on – were now assumed by Enron. The company relied heavily on buyers and sellers, and required quick access to credit markets. Since Enron rarely had liquidity, it was often forced to turn to banks. Enron introduced a technique called 'mark-to-market accounting', an accounting practice permitted by US law that involves recording the value of an asset to reflect its current market levels. Enron applied this practice to contracts that were lasting up to twenty years.

Company turnover rose so impressively that, by the end of 2000, Enron was one of the largest firms in North America in terms of sales. *Fortune* magazine named Enron 'America's Most Innovative Company' for five consecutive years between 1996 and 2000. However, behind this facade, its debt was soaring disproportionately to its equity. With such high debt levels, Enron struggled to maintain a good credit rating.

In 1997, Enron began exploring new markets, believing that the solution to its debt problem was to invest abroad in power plants, internet companies, fibre optics and other ventures. However, many of these investments did not meet expectations. The failure of these new businesses and the negative developments in energy markets affected Enron's profits and growth, making it difficult to maintain a good credit rating and share price.

At this point, some senior Enron managers began introducing dubious practices. These operations were led by Andrew Fastow, Enron's executive vice-president and CFO. Another key figure was Jeffrey (Jeff) K. Skilling, who was promoted to president and chief operating officer of Enron in 1997. Fastow set up a complex network of supposedly independent partnerships known as 'special purpose entities' (SPEs) to hedge the value of certain assets, take on current and future debts and carry out transactions – especially asset sales – in a covert manner. These SPEs, of which there were about 3,000, were small, with Enron's participation at less than 3 per cent. Fastow and certain acquaintances provided most of the capital to create these entities. Enron avoided consolidation through a loophole in accounting rules, which allowed a company to avoid consolidation if an outside party held an equity investment in the SPE equal to 3 per cent of its total assets. Fastow raised capital from relatives, friends and acquaintances. Additionally, with heavy pressure to find new contracts, especially at the end of each quarter, traders were under immense strain.

In August 2000, Enron reached its peak with a share price of US$90.56. However, the bursting of the internet bubble in mid-2000 led Enron's stock price to tumble. By early 2001, the company's shares on Wall Street had plummeted from US$85 to US$30 as rumours spread about fraudulent accounting techniques, endorsed by its auditor, the then-prestigious firm Arthur Andersen. Allegations of bribery and influence peddling to obtain contracts in developing countries also surfaced.

In October 2001, Enron revealed third-quarter losses of US$618 million and announced a reduction in shareholder equity of US$1.2 billion, which pushed the share price even lower. Eventually, the true situation became known, and Enron's stock dropped to around US$0.30. Unable to repay its loans, Enron filed for bankruptcy protection, and, on 2 December 2001, Enron's assets were liquidated and its last remaining businesses were sold. Prior to bankruptcy, Enron employed approximately 20,000 staff.

Enron had a detailed sixty-four-page 'Code of Ethics' and a set of corporate values, which included respect, integrity, communication and excellence. However, in practice, the supreme value was the bottom line. According to former employees, the climate at Enron was characterized by arrogance, greed, corruption and ruthlessness.

Ken Lay sold large amounts of company shares between September and October 2001 while encouraging his employees to buy stock, claiming that the decline in prices was an opportunity for the future.

Following the fall of Enron and intense public debate, the Sarbanes–Oxley Act was enacted in the United States in 2002. This law introduced stringent measures to prevent situations like Enron's and was the most significant change in US securities legislation since the early 1930s. Although Sarbanes–Oxley increased transparency in corporate accounting practices, some critics argue that compliance is costly for companies, especially small and medium-sized enterprises.

Ken Lay, Andrew Fastow, Jeff Skilling and other former Enron executives were found guilty of fraud. On 5 July 2006, Lay died suddenly of a heart attack at his Colorado residence while awaiting sentencing. He had earlier accepted responsibility for Enron's collapse and admitted that the company had taken excessive risks and that their internal controls had failed.

Questions

1. Do you think that the strategies of the CFO, Andrew Fastow, to maintain the credit rating and the share price were morally correct? Why or why not?
2. Do you think the Enron scandal was due solely to deficiencies in US law? Explain your view.
3. Who is responsible for the Enron scandal?
4. How did this case challenge or affirm your ethical views?
5. What lessons will you apply in your own professional future?

SECTION A. WHAT IS BUSINESS ETHICS ABOUT?

There is no single definition of 'business ethics', although many understand it as morality in business, highlighting the distinction between right and wrong or good and bad behaviour. Business ethics is generally connected to sets of values, moral principles, and norms that govern the actions and behaviour of people in business contexts, along with traits of character, termed 'virtues', that promote good behaviour. It involves considering the ethical dimension of actions, practices, policies, and strategies within the business environment, and striving for responsible and morally upright behaviour.

As an initial approach, it can be said that business ethics is related to a set of familiar concepts in business, including integrity, transparency, accountability, respect for people's rights, fair treatment of employees, social and environmental responsibility, moral competence in management and leadership, contribution to sustainability, compliance with legal and regulatory requirements, and moral standards adopted by companies, among others. It involves the ethical evaluation of decisions and the impact of business activities on groups related with the company – usually termed 'stakeholders' – including customers, employees, investors, suppliers, communities and the environment. Ethical behaviour in various roles in business – employees, supervisors, managers and directors of the corporate board – and their respective traits of character are also key components of business ethics.

A tentative definition of business ethics could be a specific field of ethics focused on business activity carried out by people working within business organizations or acting on behalf of their respective organizations.

Ethics is inherent to all human actions. For this reason, business, as a human activity, is inseparable from ethics. This is what Mary Parker Follett, a brilliant pioneer of management thought, emphasized: we do not have separate psychological, ethical and economic problems in business. Instead, 'we have human problems with psychological, ethical, and economic aspects, and as many legal aspects as you like.'[3]

1.1 Antecedents and contemporary developments of business ethics

Ethics in business is scarcely new. Abundant references to moral aspects of business can be found in religious traditions. Some moral philosophers consider several aspects of business within the realm of justice. Nevertheless, over the past 200 years, influential streams of thought have regarded business as belonging exclusively to the economic domain, and therefore as an amoral activity. For generations, some practitioners have echoed the well-known expression 'business is business', reflecting this presumed amorality – or even the subordination of ethics to profit.

In spite of this dominant view, a sense of morality has always persisted in many businesspeople and executives. Many corporations have been built with a strong ethical framework – HP, IBM and

Medtronic, for example. Johnson & Johnson launched its now famous 'Credo', with a set of ethical values and principles for business conduct, in 1942 (see Business Ethics in Action #1, below). Other companies developed codes of conduct, one of which dates to 1913.[4] Moreover, since at least the 1950s, many scholars and practitioners have taken an interest in social issues and corporate social responsibility (CSR).[5]

Some communities have also, historically, promoted ethics in investing. Thus, in the middle of the eighteenth century, the Quakers prohibited its members from participating in the trade of enslaved people – the buying and selling of humans.

It was not until the 1970s that business ethics as we know it today became a strong movement, with an influence evident from both academics and business practitioners. The movement of business ethics, beginning in the middle of 1970s, was triggered by business scandals, misbehaviours and corruption in which business executives were involved. However, over time, business ethics has been recognized for its positive potential, as a guide for moral excellence and an essential component of good management.

At the beginning of the twenty-first century, a new demand for business ethics emerged due to a series of now well-known business scandals. The financial crisis of 2008, the subsequent fall of Lehman Brothers Holdings Inc. and the manipulation of LIBOR – the London Inter-Bank Offered Rate upon which trillions of financial contracts rest – discovered in 2012, created a new demand for business ethics.

As the century advances, ethics-related demands of business involve concerns for environmental issues such as global warming and climate change, for social and ethical problems associated with globalization – including poor working conditions in certain regions or countries and responsibility in the supply chain – and for problems with immigration and the integration of socially excluded groups, among others. In addition, certain voices advocate the development of a more humanistic approach to management.[6]

Since the turn of the century, there has been renewed interest in *social responsibility of business* (12, A), often termed *corporate social responsibility* and *ecological responsibilities* (13, A). At the same time, there has been growing social demand for *corporate accountability* (12.8) in social and environmental issues, in addition to the traditional financial reporting. In this context, business writer John Elkington[7] coined the term 'Triple Bottom Line' (TBL or 3BL) as an accounting framework that incorporates three parts: social, environmental (or ecological) and economic. Today, in some countries, reporting on the non-financial impacts of business is even mandatory.

In recent decades, other concepts connected to business ethics have been introduced into the corporate world, stressing the idea that business is not merely an economic entity, but also a part of the society at large and should therefore contribute to societal good beyond what is required by law. In this way, business enterprises do not appear as isolated groups whose only concern is making money, but as institutions trying to work hand-in-hand with citizens, governments and social organizations in order to build a good society, even on a global scale.

Another popular notion is that of *sustainability* (12.4), which, simply put, refers to concern for future generations. Business can contribute to sustainability and some companies are now in line with the United Nations' calls for sustainable development. With the Sustainable Development Goals (SDGs) for 2030 (13.6), the United Nations has not only challenged governments, business corporations and other institutions to eradicate poverty and hunger but also has proposed goals more directly related to business, such as decent work and economic growth, gender equality, responsible consumption and production, climate action and partnership. Beyond sustainability, another concept with strong ethical content is that of the *circular economy* (13.6), which requires innovation as to how to confront waste and obsolete products.

Ethics in investing is another field in which ethics and social causes are integrated to mere financial investing. In this regard, several concepts have been considered, including *social investment, sustainable, socially conscious, and 'green' ethical investing or impact investment* – using money and investment capital for positive social results – and what is probably the more comprehensive: *Socially Responsible Investing* (SRI).

Currently the *ESG criteria* (an acronym for environmental, social and corporate governance) (13.7) is used by investors to assess the sustainability and ethical impact of an investment in a company or organization, based on a set of issues and corporate practices related to the environment, its impact on society and the quality of its governance structure.

Other business practices that have been introduced in some companies (13, B) include the integration of marginalized or excluded people and communities in the value chain of a company (*inclusive businesses*), providing affordable and accessible products and services for the population at the bottom of the socioeconomic scale (*base of the pyramid business*), adoption of measures to ensure that suppliers and business partners comply with ethical, social and environmental standards (*responsible management of the supply chain*), and creating values for groups related to the company, not just shareholders (*value creation*).

Last but not least, some companies have redefined the *purpose of the company* beyond maximization of shareholder value, focusing on those interrelated with the company.

1.2 Is business ethics profitable?

A frequently asked question is whether ethics in business leads to profits or whether ethics and profits are irreconcilable enemies. In colloquial terms, the questions are: Does ethics pay? Is business ethics profitable? A different question, which will be treated below, asks whether business ethics should only be considered when it is found to be profitable.

Some people enthusiastically proclaim that 'good ethics is good business'. Others, however, are more sceptical about the profitability of business ethics, or believe that ethics does not always pay. A third group sits between the two aforementioned viewpoints, holding that the 'ethics pays' argument might be valid if one takes a broader view and looks to the long-term effects.[8] In the short term, unethical behaviours – such as abusive labour contracts, fraud, bribery and polluting – can lead to profits more readily than acting with fairness does. However, such conduct risks losing trust in the business, aside from legal penalties. If a public scandal ensues, the loss of reputation can be dramatic; drastic action, as well as the investment of much time and money, might be necessary to recover the credibility and trust lost.

There is increasing evidence that business ethics and related concepts are associated with positive outcomes, which contribute to good performance. Among them are the following:

- *Generation of trust and credibility*: Trust is a subjective belief or confidence in the reliability and intentions of someone or something. It is created through conversation and dialogue and through various forms of behaviour by which individuals exercise their duties.[9] For instance, research shows that a salesperson's ethical behaviour leads to greater customer satisfaction as well as trust in, and loyalty to, the firm that the salesperson represents.[10] Within organizations, perceptions of a leader's integrity and fairness are key determinants of trust.[11] Thus, trust is closely related to ethics.[12] Credibility focuses on the objective side of behaviour; it refers to an objective assessment of the believability and trustworthiness of a person, organization or information. Credibility is acquired through a gradual process that involves building trust by demonstrating ethics, as well as expertise. The conclusion is that ethical behaviours tend to generate trust and credibility, and both elements are crucial to good business performance.[13]
- *Risk mitigation*: Since the 1960s there have been those who argue that companies that do not take responsibility for their power will ultimately lose it,[14] and this is a risk. In recent decades, risks have increased due to tightening regulatory obligations, demands for transparency from investors and public opinion, and greater pressures – particularly on large corporations – from non-governmental organizations and the mass media. Misbehaviours are often also illegal and therefore entail the risk of fines, which can be extremely costly. Ethical behaviour helps minimize legal, financial and reputational risks for businesses.
- *Corporate reputation and brand enhancement*: Reputation refers to the opinion people hold about a person, a brand, a company or any other institution. Corporate reputation specifically focuses on the evaluation of a company by the public and significantly by people related to the company. Ethical behaviour, as noted, along with other factors, such as a good corporate governance, builds trust and credibility, which are closely related to corporate and brand reputation. Building up a positive reputation and enhancing brand image are valuable as they attract customers to products, investors to securities and employees to jobs, therefore constituting a competitive advantage, differentiating the business from competitors. This can result in increased sales, market share and long-term profitability. When the company's image has been damaged by a business scandal, a common reaction is to introduce ethical programmes, generally focused on compliance (9.3). These include codes of ethics, employee training, ethics committees, direct lines for consultations, sanctions, and so on. This has been the case in firms such as Lockheed, Nike, Tyco, Boeing and many others, after notorious scandals involving company misbehaviours.
- *Satisfying social expectations* (*licence to operate*): Society and groups interrelated with a company, including stakeholders, employees, customers, investors, communities and regulatory bodies, often expect companies to operate ethically and contribute positively to society. Meeting these social expectations can avoid potential backlash or reputational damage and, in positive terms, obtaining a 'licence to operate', which is necessary for the company to survive.[15]
- *Improvement of company relationships*: Beyond social expectations, business ethics is particularly important in improving relationships with people interrelated to the company

(often termed 'stakeholders').[16] Ethical behaviour can lead to the improvement of reciprocity, cooperation, loyalty and other trust-related behaviours of people interrelated with the company. Strong relationships are particularly important during challenging times, and can even provide access to resources, opportunities for partnerships and overall business stability.

- *Customer satisfaction and loyalty*: Some ethical practices in marketing, such as delivering high-quality products and services, being transparent in business operations and treating customers fairly, contribute to customer satisfaction. This satisfaction will likely lead to both new customers and repeat-purchase customers, as they become and remain attracted to the product, brand or company with true consumer loyalty.
- *Employee engagement and retention*: The impact of business ethics can be particularly significant on employee morale and motivation. It also serves recruitment, attracting talented people who appreciate the firm's sense of responsibility. Remuneration alone may not be enough to attract and retain good employees who are looking for meaningful work. A company who promotes fairness, respect and integrity attracts and retains talented employees.
- *Innovation and creativity*: An ethical business environment encourages employees to think creatively and innovatively. This environment may entail consideration for people working in the company, listening and valuing their ideas and capacity of initiative. Such a consideration would lead them to a more collaborative attitude, contributing with their skills and knowledge to improve products, processes and services.
- *Access to capital and investment opportunities*: Ethical reputation and a commitment to CSR can help businesses to access capital and investment opportunities, as well as opportunities for partnerships and collaborations. In recent years there has been an increasing recognition among investors and financial institutions that ethical and sustainable practices are crucial for long-term business success. In this sense, investors and financial institutions are increasingly considering ESG factors when making investment decisions.
- *Long-term sustainability*: Ethical behaviour promotes long-term sustainability by fostering responsible and mindful practices that consider the needs of the present and future generations facing issues such as climate change, resource scarcity and social inequality.

1.3 Why companies engage in business ethics

The 'business case' vs. the 'moral case'

Regarding the question of whether ethics is profitable, some may feel uncomfortable, especially when profitability is presented as the sole reason for being ethical. Ethics concerns what is right or wrong, or good or bad, from a moral standpoint. It is not merely a tool for generating profits but has intrinsic value. In other words, good management should act ethically because it is the right thing to do, not simply because it is profitable.

In practice, two motivations for implementing ethical practices can be identified. They are known respectively as the 'business case', and the 'moral case'. In the *business case* the motivation for implementing business ethics and other related concepts, such as CSR and sustainability, is *exclusively* economic self-interest, to cope with social pressures or to gain reputation, while in the moral case the driver is moral responsibility. It is argued that acting ethically can deliver tangible benefits and value to a company in terms of profits and public image, which is ultimately expressed in the bottom line.

The *moral case* derives from the understanding that businesses need to do the right thing and contribute to the society in which they belong. While the business case for engaging with business ethics relates exclusively to the profit motive, here there is a commitment to respond to a moral duty. Firstly, to avoid misbehaviours, and then to positively contribute to society.

The moral case does not ignore possible good economic consequences of a good business behaviour but deems the moral motive more important than the importance of the positive economic consequences of such behaviour.

The business case raises the problem of credibility. While numerous companies have implemented business ethics, corporate social responsibility or sustainability practices, many wonder if these respond to a real commitment or is just a catchphrase or public relations technique. Some companies that show apparent ethical commitment, presumably due to external pressures, do little to foster ethical behaviour within their organizations. This might be the case in Enron.[17] Other companies, however, focused on the 'moral case', are active both in showing external commitment and in promoting ethical practices.

Indeed, acting for the business case can easily lead to slipping into hypocritical and even unethical positions. When the goal is developing a good image and reputation, ethical behaviour can be fictitious. This is what happens with so-called 'greenwashing', which involves creating an illusion of ecological responsibility or disseminating misleading information about how a company's products are environmentally sound. In the moral case, managers try to do things well as it is the right thing to do, not just to foster a good image. This sincere attitude, as noted, is not necessarily in opposition to the commercial benefits, but when economic and moral motive conflict, the priority is morality.

There are some arguments questioning whether ethics pays. Some ethical behaviour can entail additional costs or the loss of a contract. Investing in worker safety could lead to a loss in competitiveness if one's rivals fail to do likewise. Laws and their enforcement can help to prevent such situations but, if this is not the case, managers should do their best in the circumstances. Competent managers will seek to run businesses that are both ethical and profitable. With imagination, they can find alternative means of solving difficult problems.

Business ethics – often understood in terms of CSR – brings about outcomes which can impact the financial performance of a company.[18] Numerous researchers have sought correlations between corporate ethics financial performance and the correlation between ethical leadership or ethical cultures and significant variables related to performance, such as employee morale, reduction of misconduct and business performance.[19] Most of them, although not all, confirm the existence of a positive relationship between the two variables.

Some years ago, Lynn Sharp Paine of Harvard Business School noted that more and more companies are launching ethics programmes, values initiatives and community involvement activities based on the belief that 'ethics pays'.[20] Paine also pointed out that many corporate initiatives, rather than aiming directly at profitability through ethics, focus on enhancing corporate reputation or becoming more responsive to the needs and interests of their various stakeholders.[21]

However, she finds the motto 'ethics pays' is 'troubling as a guiding principle for business leaders in the twenty-first century. In suggesting that ethics must be legitimated by economics, it devalues ethics as an independent point of reference on the quality of life and society.'[22]

In some cases, however, ethics may not bring financial return.[23] In such cases, managers with integrity behave ethically; profits cannot come at any price. Even when ethical behaviour does not pay off in economic terms, it pays off personally, because, in acting wrongly, an individual harms his or her own integrity, becoming worse as a human being. This was suggested by Socrates more than 2,400 years ago in the words: 'Seeing then that there are these two evils, the doing injustice and the suffering injustice – and we affirm that to do injustice is a greater, and to suffer injustice a lesser evil.'[24] This is because an individual harms his or her own integrity by acting wrongly. This is not the case for suffering injustice. Similarly, in the Gospel, Jesus Christ said: 'For what shall it profit a man, if he shall gain the whole world, and lose his own soul?'[25]

In business, as in other areas of life, there can arise a tension between 'having more' (money, power or the like) and 'being better' as a human being; that is, between *external goods* (what one owns) and internal goods (what one is in terms of human quality). Facing this dualism, virtuous people resolve the tension in favour of *internal goods*. We will return to this point below (1.10).

1.4 Normative vs. behavioural business ethics

In dealing with business ethics, an important distinction between normative and behavioural business ethics must be made. *Normative business ethics* proposes rational principles and norms, along with virtues for good behaviour. It is therefore *prescriptive*; it is not about what people do, but what they ought to do.

Behavioural business ethics describes ethical aspects of people's behaviour in the business context. Studies on behavioural business ethics may focus on different psychological, organizational or situational factors and their possible influence on behaviour or decision-making.[26] There are countless studies about the real behaviour of people in organizations[27] and journal special issues.[28] Behavioural business ethics is therefore *descriptive*. It describes behaviours by studying a certain sample, but does not reveal whether such behaviour is 'right' or 'wrong'. Like any experimental science, it is based on empirical data that is interpreted by explanatory hypotheses. This would be the case, for example, with an experiment conducted to study the correlation of age or gender in lying. The hypothesis that the elderly and women are more likely to tell the truth than the young or men might be confirmed for one sample but can also appear irrelevant with another.

In spite of its limitations, behavioural business ethics serves to tell what actually happens in firms, but it would be a great error to adopt its findings (descriptions of what people do) as a normative guide (prescription of what people should do).

The distinction between normative and behavioural business ethics does require radical separation. In practice, normative business ethics can be used to formulate hypotheses or to evaluate codes of conduct or real behaviours in a certain collective, while behavioural business ethics can help businesses reflect on the effectiveness of the corporate guidelines implemented.

This book focuses on normative business ethics. However, some references to behaviours will be made, particularly in the cases presented in 'Business Ethics in Action' boxes, in addition to some evaluative comments from the normative ethics perspective.

1.5 Scope of business ethics and ethical analysis

Micro-, meso- and macro- business ethics

Insofar as business ethics deals with ethics in business activity, several analytical levels can be considered, depending on the focus adopted: *micro-business ethics* (focused on the individual within the organization), *meso-business ethics* (focused on the ethical conduct and responsibilities of the organization as a whole and those who rule it) and *macro-business ethics* (focused on the broader societal, economic and global implications of business activities). These basic categories can be detailed as follows (see Table 1.1):

1. *Micro-business ethics* focuses on the individual involvement in business, including personal *ethical behaviour and individual moral judgements for decision-making* within the business context. This makes sense since businesses consist of individuals with personal responsibility and specific roles or functions that carry responsibilities toward others, and, foremost, moral responsibility to one's own conscience. This requires making moral judgements during decision-making. While companies are often seen as cohesive entities, it is ultimately individuals, with their moral competencies, who make decisions, interact with others, and are aware of the human, social and environmental consequences of their actions. An important aspect of micro-business ethics *is manager ethics*, which refers to the moral principles, virtues and responsibilities that guide those in managerial roles when leading people, making decisions, and organizing work. *Leadership ethics* is another key aspect, inspiring, motivating and influencing others to achieve common goals with an ethical vision. *Entrepreneurship ethics* can also be included, as it involves striving to create businesses that provide value while adhering to ethical principles.
2. *Meso-business ethics* refers to organizational ethics, understood as the ethical dimension of a business organization as a whole and the proper use of power within it, including by executives and members of corporate governance, such as boards of directors, executive committees and other oversight bodies. Organizational ethics typically includes *institutional statements* defining the identity and purpose of the company, its corporate values, and other ideals that promote ethical behaviour, fostering trust, credibility and reputation. It also encompasses ethics in strategies and organizational structures, involving objectives, systems, procedures and rules. A crucial element at this level is *organizational culture*, viewed from an ethical perspective, which is shaped by ethical leadership and other factors, along with *ethical training* within the company.

3   *Macro-business ethics* covers the broad field of *business-societal relationships* and the *social and environmental impacts of business*, as well as the global implications of business activities. This entails *social and ecological responsibility* of the business as well as sustainability, including businesses' contribution to addressing social issues, supporting community development and engaging in philanthropic activities. Also important are the *interactions with society* and the relationships between *businesses and governments*, including concerns around lobbying, political contributions and engagement with government entities to ensure transparency and avoid corruption. Macro-business ethics also considers the responsibilities of businesses operating globally, such as addressing human rights issues in vulnerable areas and mitigating environmental impacts. Macro-business ethics also considers how businesses can contribute to *sustainable development*, both locally and globally, and act *as ethical leaders in society* by promoting responsible practices, setting industry standards and serving as role models for ethical conduct.

These levels of analysis are valuable for studying various aspects of business ethics and addressing ethical considerations across the different scopes and contexts within the realm of business.

Ethical analysis of business situations

Business processes and behaviours require an ethical evaluation. In some cases, the evaluation does not pose special difficulties, while other situations can be more problematic.[29]

Table 1.1 Analytical levels of business ethics

Level	Specification	Matters addressed
Micro-business ethics (Focuses on individual ethical behaviour)	Individual involvement in business	– Personal moral responsibility – Moral competences – Moral judgements – Ethical conduct and misbehaviours – Ethical decision-making – Management ethics – Leadership ethics – Entrepreneurial ethics
Meso-business ethics (Focuses on the organization as a whole)	Organizational ethics	– Right use of power – Institutional statements – Ethics in strategies – Ethics in organizational structures – Corporate governance – Organizational culture
Macro-business ethics (Focuses on the broader societal, economic, and global implications of business activities)	Societal and ecological business ethics	– Social and ecological responsibilities of business – Sustainability – Business and government relations – Global business ethics – Sustainable development

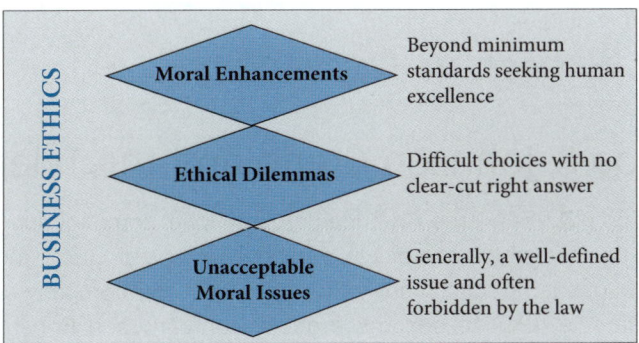

Figure 1.1 Ethical analysis of business situations

At the beginning of the business ethics movement this evaluation focused on ethically acceptable and non-acceptable actions taken when solving ethical dilemmas. Today, however, many understand that this is a narrow view of ethics; rather than simply highlighting forbidden actions, ethics focuses on promoting moral excellence and therefore on improving the human and moral quality of business. Thus, in analysing business situations three types of judgements can be considered 'unacceptable ethical issues', 'ethical dilemmas' and 'moral enhancements' (Figure 1.1).

- *Unacceptable moral* issues: These are actions that are well-defined and clearly contradict ethical standards. Examples include stealing company property, engaging in commercial fraud or illegally disposing of toxic waste. Such actions are often labelled with specific terms, like fraud, bribery or embezzlement, and are explicitly prohibited in most legal and ethical frameworks.
- *Ethical dilemmas*: These arise when a decision-maker faces a difficult choice with no clear-cut right answer. For example, deciding whether to accept a higher-paying job that would support one's family but require frequent travel, reducing time with one's children. Ethical dilemmas may also occur when one must choose between two or more alternatives, each of which seems ethically undesirable, or when conflicting duties must be balanced.
- *Moral enhancements*: Some situations may be morally acceptable but can be improved from an ethical standpoint. Every human action has a moral dimension, as it affects others either positively or negatively. Business ethics encourages the pursuit of higher standards in serving others. For instance, while treating customers fairly is the minimum standard when selling a product, striving for a higher standard – such as demonstrating kindness, empathy and a genuine effort to understand their needs – can enhance the overall service and create a more ethical business environment.

In summary, business ethics offers guidelines for assessing the acceptability of actions, resolving ethical dilemmas and inspiring moral improvements. This is achieved by striving for ethical excellence in any given situation.

Business Ethics in Action #1

The Johnson & Johnson Credo and the Tylenol affair

Johnson & Johnson (J&J) is a large American multinational company founded in 1886 that develops medical devices, pharmaceuticals, personal hygiene products and other consumer and biotechnology goods, among many others. In 1943 the company was preparing for its initial public offering (IPO) to become a public company and Robert Wood Johnson, chairman of J&J and a member of the Company's founding family, crafted what would be called 'Our Credo', following the principles set down by its founder, General Robert Johnson. This is the text of this document:[30]

'Our Credo'
We believe our first responsibility is to the doctors, nurses and patients,
to mothers and fathers and all others who use our products and services.
In meeting their needs everything we do must be of high quality.
We must constantly strive to reduce our costs
in order to maintain reasonable prices.
Customers' orders must be serviced promptly and accurately.
Our suppliers and distributors must have an opportunity
to make a fair profit.
We are responsible to our employees,
the men and women who work with us throughout the world.
Everyone must be considered as an individual.
We must respect their dignity and recognize their merit.
They must have a sense of security in their jobs.
Compensation must be fair and adequate,
and working conditions clean, orderly and safe.
We must be mindful of ways to help our employees fulfil
their family responsibilities.
Employees must feel free to make suggestions and complaints.
There must be equal opportunity for employment, development
and advancement for those qualified.
We must provide competent management,
and their actions must be just and ethical.
We are responsible to the communities in which we live and work
and to the world community as well.
We must be good citizens – support good works and charities
and bear our fair share of taxes.
We must encourage civic improvements and better health and education.
We must maintain in good order
the property we are privileged to use,
protecting the environment and natural resources.
Our final responsibility is to our stockholders.

Business must make a sound profit.
We must experiment with new ideas.
Research must be carried on, innovative programs developed
and mistakes paid for.
New equipment must be purchased, new facilities provided
and new products launched.
Reserves must be created to provide for adverse times.
When we operate according to these principles,
the stockholders should realize a fair return.

People working in J&J are encouraged to make decisions inspired by the philosophy embodied in the Credo. In practice, people from J&J have made countless decisions inspired by the Credo guidelines, including in situations of crisis management such as that of the Tylenol affair, now a well-known case study of business ethics.

Tylenol was a popular painkiller in the US and in other countries. In 1982 the sudden death of seven people after having taken Extra-Strength Tylenol brand capsules caused great alarm among the executives of McNeil Consumer Products, a division of J&J. It was proved that Tylenol capsules contained cyanide. Within a few days of the incident, the recall of all Extra-Strength Tylenol was made. In addition, the company offered to exchange Tylenol capsules for Tylenol tablets. This operation cost US$100 million.

Such a huge operation was mounted despite the company having no real knowledge of the extent of the contamination and consequently being unable to ensure that no one else would be poisoned. As the investigation proceeded, it was discovered that the contamination was caused by outsiders, probably at some part of the distribution process. But it was sure that the contamination was not during the production process, or from any other internal operation.

A decision from the top to recall all contaminated medications was seen as the responsible thing to do. Moreover, many believe that this decision was guided by the principles on which Johnson & Johnson was founded, and mainly by the first article: 'Our first responsibility is to the doctors, nurses and patients, … '

J&J received recognition for having acted quickly and honestly during the crisis and therefore was able to preserve its good name and reputation, putting its Tylenol-acetaminophen business back on track.

During a TV talk-show, Mr James E. Burke, CEO of J&J during the Tylenol crisis, explained that the widespread disposition to view Johnson & Johnson favourably was a result of the high level of public trust built and handed down as a legacy of previous managers. Burke says: 'All of the previous managers who built this corporation handed us, on a silver platter, the most powerful tool you could possibly have' – trust.[31]

* * *

When business ethics was not in the mainstream of business management, J&J launched its famous Credo (Creed), now world famous and translated into many languages and disseminated wherever this multi-national company operates around the world.

The Credo of Johnson & Johnson outlines the company's core values, but, more importantly, it expresses a hierarchy of commitments towards people to whom J&J have a responsibility. It is made clear that the first responsibility and main priority is not making profits but being responsible towards its customers, employees, communities and, finally, stockholders. All of that without ignoring concern for innovation, reducing costs and making profits: 'Business must make a sound profit', says the Credo. According to Johnson & Johnson, ethics and profits are not two independent matters. The current presentation of the Credo reads: 'Our Credo is more than just a moral compass. We believe it's a recipe for business success. The fact that Johnson & Johnson is one of only a handful of companies that have flourished through more than a century of change is proof of that.'[32] The J&J Credo presents a list of good practices, showing commitment to acting responsibly and ethically in many aspects of its business operations. This list is an important guideline for decision-making and responding to emerging problems.

Putting the needs of customers first, specifically their health and safety, was particularly noteworthy in the Tylenol affair. When Tylenol products were tampered with, resulting in several deaths, J&J faced a significant crisis. The quick and unanimous response of the whole company to solve the problem shows an effective commitment of the company to its customers. J&J executives and employees immediately prioritized public safety over financial considerations by recalling all Tylenol products from store shelves, while working closely with law enforcement. J&J had a good reputation, and the expensive recalling enhanced this further.

The management of the Tylenol crisis made clear the importance of prioritizing customer safety and well-being over immediate financial considerations, although in the long term the company's bolstered reputation may have compensated the recalling costs. Crises and other difficult situations are a real test of the sincerity of corporate values, and the Tylenol case shows that Johnson & Johnson acted consistently with the corporate values.

It is also worth mentioning that J&J's response emphasized the importance of transparency, open communication and taking decisive action during a crisis; these are embedded aspects of ethical values which contribute to building trust.

A central point in the case is the relevance of trust in sustaining a company's reputation. By acting swiftly, taking responsibility and implementing improved safety measures, J&J rebuilt trust and enhanced its reputation. The CEO of J&J had built considerable public trust over the years and considered maintaining this trust. The connection between ethical behaviour and trust is clear in the J&J philosophy. Currently, J&J's corporate ethical behaviour and corporate reputation are generally praised. However, nobody is perfect, and in its long history J&J has occasionally faced lawsuits of its own.[33]

Last but not least, something which is not often mentioned in the case is the lasting impact the Tylenol incident had on the pharmaceutical industry and regulatory rules. It led to the introduction of tamper-evident packaging and stricter safety measures, setting new industry standards for consumer product safety.

SECTION B. INTRODUCING ETHICS

Naturally, business ethics is grounded in a clear understanding of ethics itself. In this section, we will provide an introductory overview of ethics, aiming to shed light on its key concepts and relevance to the business world.

1.6 The human experience of morality

The root of ethics is the human experience of morality. When a business scandal appears on the front page of the *Financial Times* or the *Wall Street Journal*, readers usually blame those who have taken advantage of their position for personal enrichment, or who have been negligent in provoking an accident or have abused others in some way. This makes it clear, among many other common experiences, that human beings have a certain sense of morality and capacity for moral judgements.

Language also bears witness to a certain human capacity that permits us to evaluate human behaviour. Every language is full of words with moral connotations. We approve or criticize behaviours, employing terms such as good and bad, right and wrong, fair and unfair, praiseworthy and blameworthy, responsible and irresponsible, rights and duties, licit and illicit, etc. Drawing from this evidence, a notion of *moral agency* emerged, understood as the capacity of a person to make ethical judgments and be responsible for their actions.

Although moral agency is inherent to the human condition, some people have a more cultivated moral sense than others, just as one can cultivate their innate logical and aesthetics capacities. Moral development has been widely studied through a multitude of theoretical lenses, but there is wide agreement that family, schooling, religion, cultural environment and study exert a significant influence on the moral development of each person. However, a crucial element of personal moral development is one's own behaviour followed by personal reflection, which shapes the character, as ancient thinkers – particularly Aristotle – pointed out. When a person acts well, the internal moral sensibility increases and improves the ease of acting well in subsequent actions. In contrast, if one persistently avoids evaluating what is right, or consciously acts in a wrong way, personal moral sensitivity and the disposition for good behaviour will decrease.

Motivations for ethical practices in business

People can have different motivations for good behaviour in business (Figure 1.2). Sometimes, honesty or other ethical behaviours respond to utilitarian motives such as eluding punishments, escaping from legal risks or obtaining a good image. Other motives include wanting to feel satisfied with oneself by partaking in 'good' behaviour, and therefore avoiding the guilt often felt once you've done something 'wrong'. Other motives can be moral in nature, such as a desire to help (or at least not hurt) others and to contribute to creating a good society, and – related to this – willingness to become a better person (personal moral growth). Finally, some people can bear religious or spiritual motivation, connected to divinity or to some transcendence.

Figure 1.2 Motivations for good behaviour in business

1.7 Ethics as a systematic approach to morality

Personal experience of morality is structured and systematized through ethical theories. Thus, we can define ethics is a systematic approach to morality, which permits one to verify personal views and to evaluate the morality of human actions and the corresponding behaviour.

The rational approach to morality, or *moral philosophy*, is a long tradition. It was started by Socrates (470–399 BCE) and followed by Plato (around 425–348 BCE) and Aristotle (384–322 BCE), who reflected on morality and proposed rational ethics. Over time, philosophers have made a great effort to develop theories of ethics using similar or different rational perspectives. In addition, religions propose norms for good behaviour, encourage moral virtues and provide guidelines to believers, as do some non-religious wisdom traditions. Moral theology – a systematic and rational development of religious faith – also presents ethics as a consistent system of morality.

Both religious ethics and moral theology deserve consideration and, in a global world where religion is salient for many, deserves consideration especially for those who manage businesses and organizations in a plural society and in a global context.[34] However, it is not the aim of this book to develop religious or theological perspectives to business ethics, but only to develop a rational approach acceptable beyond the realms of any particular faith.

The question regarding the relationship between rational ethics and religious ethics is not new. In Socrates' time, it was commonly accepted that moral obligation came from the gods. Socrates, despite being a religious man, defended the position that reason can understand what is morally good, and that gods only command what is good.[35] In other words, Socrates held that there are standards of goodness that can be known by human reason.

The word *ethics* comes from the Greek *ethos*, meaning 'custom' or 'habit', something belonging to character, and the ethical thought of these philosophers refers to the good traits of character acquired through good behaviour. They termed these traits *areté*, denoting excellence, later translated as *virtue*. Virtue is still a key concept in ethics, but there are at least two more, values, connected to both goods, and principles, as will be discussed below (1.10).

Legality vs. morality

Legality refers to external standards imposed upon citizens, social groups or institutions, including businesses. It derives from laws, regulations and rules enacted by the legal system and enforced by a governing authority, often with sanctions, including fines, imprisonment or other legal penalties. Laws have a specific scope and jurisdiction and therefore can vary from one country or jurisdiction to another.

Legality, through laws and other regulations, sets out minimum standards of behaviour for living together in harmony, which frames the content of legal responsibility. This contrasts with morality, which refers to what is right or wrong, or good or bad, and leads to a set of values and system of principles, with subsequent norms of conduct.

Morality involves self-reflection and an individual's own judgement of what is right or wrong, along with principles of morality. Morality affects one's own conscience, although others can also perceive moral wrongdoings.

Moral norms are not enacted by any civil authority, like the law, but by rational reflection or from moral leaders of a community. Moral violations may lead to feelings of guilt, shame, social condemnation or an inner sense of religious disapproval, but there are no external sanctions associated to breaching such norms.

Morality is more universal than legality, aiming to establish principles and values that transcend cultural and geographical boundaries, although people and cultures can hold particular moral beliefs and practices.

However, morality is wider in its requirement than legality – which, as noted, is limited to minimum standards – while morality involves positive precepts oriented to doing as much good as possible in all situations. However, legality and morality can overlap, especially in moral negative precepts – for instance, stealing or murder. In addition, morality can give support to legality, although laws can also respond to ideologies or social claims not consistent with ethics. Thus, some legal norms can be born out of the ethical realm because they are morally neutral or even contrary to ethics.

In summary, although legality and morality can intersect and overlap in certain instances (Figure 1.3), they are distinct concepts that operate on different levels and have different foundations. Morality does not derive from legality, while it would be desirable that legality was inspired on morality. In practice, many regulations in business and in other fields have been enacted after notorious moral misbehaviours.

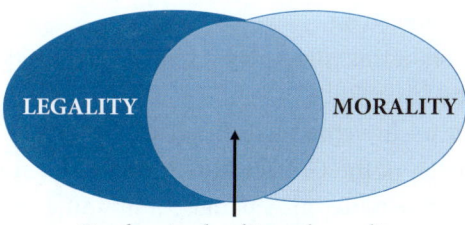

Figure 1.3 Overlapping legality and morality

Ethics vs. moral judgements

Moral judgements are about particular situations or events occurring under specific circumstances, while ethics presents rational foundations for making sound moral judgements. Consider, for instance, the case of selling a children's toy that is decorated with toxic paint. A moral judgement would be: 'It is unfair to sell this product.' This is the result of the following implicit ethical reasoning: 'It is unfair to sell this product because it is unsafe, and people have the right to buy safe products.' Deliberation could follow regarding the idea that everyone has the right to avoid danger to health and that life is a universal human value deserving of respect. Ethics provides these kinds of grounds for making moral judgements.

Moral judgements sometimes arise from feelings of approval or rejection. Feelings can make one aware that something is wrong; however, they do not guarantee sound judgement. For instance, if you are a manager, your decision to fire somebody who has committed numerous serious breaches may make you feel bitter, especially if you are sympathetic towards the individual. Nonetheless, from an ethical perspective, it would be the right thing to do.

1.8 Common insights of morality worldwide

When considering ethics, we have to consider cultural diversity. In the global business environment, companies often operate across multiple countries, and each country is likely to have citizens with numerous different beliefs and values. However, within this variety of beliefs and values one can often find common insights of morality in people from different countries, cultures and religions, which suggests a certain shared sense of morality. Let us review some of these insights or intuitions, which cannot be ignored.

The Golden Rule

The so-called Golden Rule expresses a fundamental maxim for living on friendly terms with others and can be formulated in colloquial terms as 'put yourself in the place of the other' or 'treat others as you would like to be treated'. A more accurate developed articulation might read: 'treat others only as you would be willing to be treated in an identical situation'. For instance, if you are a salesperson, consider how you would like to be treated as the buyer; if you are the supervisor, put yourself in the shoes of your subordinate; and so on.

The negative formulation of this rule – 'never impose on others what you would not choose for yourself' – is known as the Silver Rule.

The Golden Rule appears in some form in all of the great religious and ethical traditions. Although not in every religion, the Golden Rule is the cornerstone of morality.[36] This common maxim, which is formulated in numerous separate communities, suggests a natural human capacity to discover this basic principle of morality, which permits humans to live together in a harmonious and peaceful way.

Neighbourly love/benevolence

Neighbourly love, present in many religions and wisdom traditions, means to be friendly with your neighbour. It refers to treating one's neighbours with benevolence, understood as goodwill for doing good. Of course, the first prescription is not harming the neighbour. The second requires extending goodwill, support and understanding to people, especially those who live in proximity to us or are part of one's own community.

In Judaism its prescript is 'you shall love your neighbour as yourself' and in Christianity loving one's neighbour is central and extended to all people, evidenced by the teachings of Jesus Christ and the parable of the Good Samaritan, a story in which a person from a despised group helps a stranger in need. Loving one's neighbour is agapic love, often associated with unconditional and selfless love. In the Christian tradition, loving one's neighbour as oneself encompasses all other ethical norms in how people should relate to one another.[37] The importance of treating neighbours with kindness and respect can be found in other religions, as Templeton[38] has shown. Islamic teachings emphasize the importance of treating neighbours with kindness and respect. Buddhism preaches *mettā* or loving-kindness, which promotes benevolence, compassion and goodwill towards all beings, including one's neighbours. The Hinduist concept of *karuna* promotes compassion and empathy, and encourages individuals to extend kindness, mercy and understanding to others. Neighbourly love in Confucianism is expressed through the concept of *ren*, often translated as benevolence or humaneness.

Common values among religions

In addition to the Golden Rule and neighbourly love, there are many other common values among religions. The Interfaith Declaration, composed in the capital of Jordan by theologians, academics and prominent business figures in 1993, identifies four key concepts or principles presented in Judaism, Christianity and Islam: (1) justice (fairness); (2) mutual respect (love and consideration); (3) stewardship (trusteeship); and (4) honesty (truthfulness).[39] Dalla Costa[40] suggests that five core values (norms) emerge from two other religious declarations – 'The Declaration of the Parliament of the World's Religions' (1993) and 'The Tie That Binds' (1991) – which are not dissimilar: respect life, be fair, be honest, strive for justice and honour the environment.

Moses and Lewis[41] also identified values common to most great world religions and wisdom traditions. They include respect for persons (Golden Rule), following one's conscience, beneficence and avoidance of malice, justice, equity, truthfulness, honesty, caring, mercy (compassion), generosity, hospitality, peace, unity of humanity, stewardship, wealth sharing, magnanimity and moderation.

Globally recognized positive character strengths

Psychologists Peterson and Seligman[42] sought to identify common character strengths (virtues) by studying globally influential religious and philosophical traditions. The authors found six encompassing virtues – wisdom, courage, humanity, justice, temperance (moderation) and transcendence – which frame twenty-four character strengths. Although this work has some limitations and the names used could be refined, it provides interesting findings, which, at least in an exploratory way, suggests a clear convergence on what is understood as virtues and character strengths, and a non-arbitrary foundation for these virtues, albeit one rooted in the human condition.

Human dignity and innate rights

Human dignity refers to the inherent worth and value of every human being, simply by virtue of being human, regardless of his or her individual characteristics, circumstances or societal roles. Closely related to human dignity is the idea that all human individuals possess fundamental innate rights and deserve to be treated with respect, fairness and compassion.

Human dignity is often considered to be a universal ethical value. Although this notion is not present in every cultural tradition, you often find other equivalent ideas highlighting the importance of respecting every human being.[43] However, difficulty arises due to nuances in the interpretation and the expression 'human dignity' and 'human rights.' Still, there is a consensus on accepting these concepts in order to promote peace and harmony as the *Universal Declaration of Human Rights*,[44] approved by the General Assembly of the United Nations in 1948, points out at the beginning of its Preamble: 'Whereas recognition of the inherent dignity and of the equal and inalienable rights of all members of the human family is the foundation of freedom, justice and peace in the world.'

The idea of 'human rights' appeared within the humanism of Western civilization, with its profound Judeo-Christian roots. But basic human rights can also be found in ancient civilizations – such as the Persian Empire in the sixth century BCE under Cyrus the Great, in the Maurya Empire of ancient India in the third century BCE, and in the Early Islamic Caliphate in the seventh century CE – although without the label 'human rights'.[45] Democratic societies in Asia, such as those of the Hindus, have a long tradition of respect for individual rights.[46]

1.9 Subjective and social values vs. objective ethical values

Values can refer to subjective or individual values, social values and objective ethical values. *Subjective values* can be defined as fundamental individual beliefs or preferences about what is important and meaningful to us as individuals or as a society. These values guide individual aspirations, attitudes, choices and behaviours. They are closely related to the aim or purpose of an action. Individual values shape individual goals and motivate us to achieve such goals. They can entail moral content but can also refer to something valuable for any other reason, including economic self-interest, ambition for power or pleasure. *Social values*, however, are shared convictions on what is important, accepted and recognized by a larger group or society. Individual values can change over time due to learning experiences, influence of cultural sensibilities, means of communication, new knowledge and personal reflection. Social values can also change accordingly with people belonging to a group or society.

In contrast, *objective ethical values* are considered universally valid and applicable regardless of personal preferences or opinions. Ethical values go beyond immediate gratification and individual desires. They can be discovered through the human capacity for self-transcendence that leads one to moving beyond one's self-centred concerns and personal interests to connect with something larger than oneself. For example, the values of respecting a person's dignity, acting with fairness, equity and truthfulness and serving others. Thus, ethical values are discovered rather than created. These values can be assumed by persons and become subjective values and social values.

Individual values can share (objective) ethical values or not. An honest person would hold quite different values from those of a serial embezzler. Despite this evidence, some people adopt the position that only personal values or 'moral opinions' are relevant, putting aside any objective ethics and instead adopting a position of moral relativism. This position, called *subjectivism*, makes dialogue on morality difficult because of a lack of any objective ethical reference.

In practice, subjectivism is difficult to hold, especially when one is a victim of a clear abuse of power or other unfair treatment, such as living under tyranny. In such situations, the victim generally proclaims a right to fair treatment. A subjectivist cannot coherently claim any objective right, other than the right to an opinion.

Another form of moral relativism is social or *cultural relativism*, which only accepts values widely shared by members of groups and communities or within a common cultural environment. Some personal values might be similar, or even identical, to the social values of groups or communities to which the individual belongs.

Ethics is distinct from cultural values. The latter concerns descriptions (what *is*) of a social group's beliefs and values, but not prescriptions (what *ought to be*) derived from a rational reflection. Some cultural values are fully compatible with ethical principles, but others are not. Think of a social environment which has 'values' that lead it to be tolerant of inhumane working conditions, corruption, a lack of respect for minority rights or scant concern for environmental issues.

1.10 Goods, principles, and virtues

Moral goods (ethical values)

The notion of moral good or intrinsic good, with a long tradition going back to ancient Greek philosophy, refers to the goal of an action which is valuable in and, of itself, independent of any further consequences because it contributes to human fulfilment. Moral goods are related to internal goods (1.3), which make one better, in contrast with owned external goods, which refer to having more money, power, etc. Values express the significance or worth of goods, highlighting why they are desirable or estimable.

Moral goods assumed as motives for acting become moral values (also termed ethical values), a source of motivation (moral motivation), which initiates, guides and maintains ethics-oriented behaviours. In other words, moral goods appear as valuable for acting and therefore expressing ethical values.

The concept of moral goods differs from the notions of useful and pleasant goods, which can also be motives for acting. *Useful goods* refer to objects, possessions or actions that serve for a certain end. A computer, a car and money are examples of useful goods. They can favour human activity or well-being, but they do not make one a better person. *Pleasant goods* are those that bring about physical or psychical pleasurable experiences or sensations. They can include feelings of enjoyment, comfort or sensory satisfaction. Examples of pleasant goods include delicious food, beautiful artwork, meaningful work, enjoyable leisure activities or receiving praise.

Both useful goods and pleasant goods can enhance human well-being, though they do not necessarily have a direct moral dimension related to human fulfilment, as previously noted. However, they can serve as a means to achieve excellent goods or favour them. For instance, acquiring money can be a means to support a noble cause. In this sense, useful and pleasant goods can act as instrumental goods in the pursuit of intrinsic or excellent goods. It's also worth noting that a single aim can encompass more than one type of good. For example, certain work can be useful (profitable), pleasant (enjoyable) and moral (honestly serving people's needs).

All types of goods – useful, pleasant and moral – can be described as values – something important, worthwhile or desirable – because of the existing correspondence between goods and values. Moral good or the associate values serve as the foundation for moral judgements and guide individuals' attitudes and choices, good or bad, in terms of ethics.

Moral principles (ethical norms/moral duties)

Moral or ethical principles (or simply 'principles') are understood as standards or norms of right and wrong, indicating moral duties. Principles can be accepted by an individual or by a social or religious group (rules of corporate compliance, deontological professional codes or the Ten Commandments in the Judeo-Cristian tradition, for instance). Principles can also come from recognized institutions, such as the United Nations' Global Compact's[47] 'Ten Principles' of business conduct. These principles come from personal beliefs, cultural or religious traditions, or through the recognition of certain established principles.

Sometimes principles are very generic, such as 'treat others the way you want to be treated' (the so-called 'Golden Rule') or 'give to each one his or her own right' (Principle of Justice), while others are more specific norms, often derived from generic principles. Thus, 'always help other people' is a way to practically use the Golden Rule and 'do not lie', 'do not steal' and 'keep legitimate secrets' are specifications of the Principle of Justice.

Within an ethical system, moral principles are closely related to ethical values and moral goods. Thus, the Golden Rule is a principle which entails the intrinsic value of each person. Principles translate abstract ethical values into specific norms of conduct, making possible the embodiment of values in action. Thus, the principle (or duty) of justice, with several derived norms, makes operative the value of justice. In other words, ethical values grant the foundation and motivation for the development and application of principles, while principles provide a framework for individuals or societies to behave consistently with ethical values.

Moral virtues

According to Aristotle[48] virtues are stable dispositions or habits (*hexis*, in Greek) with a sense of excellence. He distinguishes two types of virtues: intellectual and moral virtues. *Intellectual virtues* contribute to effective and responsible intellectual engagement. They refer to inquiring about the truth of reality, critically analysing information, making sound judgements and engaging in productive intellectual endeavours, problem-solving and decision-making. There is an intellectual virtue, termed *practical wisdom* (*phronesis*, in Greek), which is particularly relevant in ethics. This virtue reinforces the rational capacity, termed '*practical reason*', which evaluates the most convenient in each situation considering life in its integrity.

Moral virtues, often also termed human virtues, are traits or qualities that reflect good moral character. Some of these virtues foster good relational behaviour. One example of these virtues is truthfulness, which favours communicating in accordance with the truth, or at least, what one believes is truth. Other moral virtues moderate our emotions and desires. For instance, courage may moderate feelings of fear while restraining overconfidence, placing it in the middle of two opposed extremes, cowardice and rashness; a right means determined with practical wisdom in each situation.

Virtues are acquired by *repetition of deliberate good actions*, which enable persons to act in morally upright ways and make virtuous choices. Acquiring moral virtues requires knowing the right thing to do, favouring practical wisdom, and engaging our emotions and feelings correctly. Thus, virtues are not mere routines acquired through a 'mechanical' repetition of actions, but through a repetitive, conscious and free election of what is good. Aristotle compares acquisition of virtues with developing skills:

> Men become builders by building and lyreplayers by playing the lyre; so too we become just by doing just acts, temperate by doing temperate acts, brave by doing brave acts.[49]

Moral virtues are closely related to moral goods (ethical values), since these goods are the results of said virtues. In this sense, virtues provide a practical expression of values and associated principles by shaping an individual's moral character and contributing to the cultivation of an ethical and virtuous life.

To sum up, moral goods provide valuable ends (motives) for acting (doing good). Moral principles, and subsequent norms, are required to produce goods and provide guidelines for good behaviour, which in turn develop human virtues. Virtues give interior strength for recognizing and achieving goods and therefore helping humanity to flourish. The knowledge of principles and norms accumulated over time by wise people can be the starting point for educating ethical beginners in a virtuous life.

Case Study #1

Iam's dilemma[50]

Iam is twenty-five years old, married and has a child. A year ago, she accepted a position offered by Pest Control, S.A. (CPSA), a Vietnamese decontamination company. Despite her qualifications – a university degree, fluency in English and administrative experience – she was only offered an internship.

The responsibilities of her position were varied, as the company was small, and everyone had to share the workload. This allowed her to observe several situations that raised concerns. One of these involved employment contracts. After reaching the maximum legal period for an internship, contract renewals were processed through one of the three other companies owned by CPSA's partners. Two of these companies were 'ghost' companies, existing only as names in the Companies Registrar, with no physical presence. These continuous short-term renewals kept the workers in a state of ongoing precariousness, while the firm benefitted from government subsidies for such contracts.

Iam also noticed that certain sums of money (which, according to her calculations, could amount to 10 per cent of production) were stored directly by distributors in a metal box, without being recorded in the accounts. A similar practice occurred during payroll: workers received a sealed envelope with part of their salary, while the remaining portion was transferred by bank. The workers did not complain, as they paid less in income tax this way.

A third concern was the improper storage of substances used for insect extermination. More than once, Iam had to close her office door because of the foul odour emanating from the storage room. She wondered whether it might pose a health risk to the workers.

Fed up with the situation, Iam considered leaving her job. Although the salary was helpful for her family, it was not essential, as her husband earned enough to support them. She also considered reporting the situation to the authorities, but she had doubts. She worried that reporting could lead to repercussions, which might endanger the company's survival and leave many workers, who relied on their income, without jobs.

Questions

1. Which aspects of the case do you believe violate basic ethical principles such as justice, dignity, or honesty? How did you personally respond to those situations?
2. What do you think of the CPSA managers' behaviour?
3. What advice would you give Iam facing both care for her well-being and commitment to justice and responsibility?

Suggestion

These questions invite you to think deeply about your own ethical responses. However, personal feelings alone are not enough. A well-grounded reflection connects your perspective with universal ethical values such as respect for human dignity, justice, honesty, and the protection of the vulnerable.

Notes

1. M. P. Follett, *Dynamic Administration: The Collected Papers of Mary Parker Follett*, ed. by H. C. Metcalfy and L. Urwick (New York and London: Harper & Brothers, 1940), p. 184.
2. Sources: B. McLean and P. Elkind, *The Smartest Guys in the Room: The Amazing Rise and Scandalous Fall of Enron* (London: Penguin Books, 2004); W. Norman, 'What can the Stakeholder Theory Learn from Enron?', *Zeitschrift für Wirtschafts- und Unternehmensethik*, vol. 5, no. 3, 2004, pp. 326–36; R. R. Sims and J. Brinkmann, 'Enron Ethics (Or: Culture Matters More than Codes)', *Journal of Business Ethics*, vol. 45, no. 3, 2003, pp. 243–56; D. Windsor, 'Enron Corporation', in R. W. Kolb (eds), *Encyclopedia of Business Ethics and Society* (Thousand Oaks, CA: Sage, 2018), pp. 1138–42.
3. Follett, *Dynamic Administration*, p. 184.
4. M. E. Oliverio, 'The Implementation of a Code of Ethics: The Early Efforts of One Entrepreneur', *Journal of Business Ethics*, vol. 8, no. 5, 1989, pp. 367–74.
5. R. E. Frederick, *Corporation, Be Good! The Story of Corporate Social Responsibility* (Indianapolis, IN: Dog Ear Publishing, 2006); and A. B. Carroll, 'Corporate Social Responsibility: A Historical Perspective', in M. J. Epstein and K. O. Hanson (eds), *The Accountable Corporation: Corporate Social Responsibility* (Westpoint, CT: Praeger Publishers, 2006), pp. 1–30.
6. D. Melé, 'The Challenge of Humanistic Management', *Journal of Business Ethics*, vol. 44, no. 1, 2003, pp. 77–88; H. Spitzeck, M.M. Pirson, W.W.W. Amann, S. S. Khan and E. V. Kimakowitz (eds), *Humanism in Business: Perspectives on the Development of a Responsible Business Society* (Cambridge: Cambridge University Press, 2009); and E. V. Kimakowitz, M. Pirson, H. Spitzeck, C. Dierksmeier and W. A. Mann (eds), *Humanistic Management in Practice* (New York: Palgrave-Macmillan, 2011).
7. J. Elkington, *Cannibals with Forks: Triple Bottom Line of 21st Century Business* (Stoney Creek, CT: New Society Publishers, 1997).
8. This is, for instance, the position of L. S. Paine, *Value Shift* (New York: McGraw-Hill, 2003).
9. For development of this point, see G. G. Brenkert, 'Trust, Morality and International Business', *Business Ethics Quarterly*, vol. 8, no. 2, 1998, pp. 293–17.
10. See S. Román, 'The Impact of Ethical Sales Behaviour on Customer Satisfaction, Trust and Loyalty to the Company: An Empirical Study in the Financial Services Industry', *Journal of Marketing Management*, vol. 19, no. 9/10, 2003, pp. 915–39.
11. See, for instance, M. C. Clark and R. L. Payne, 'Character-Based Determinants of Trust in Leaders', *Risk Analysis: An International Journal*, vol. 26, no. 5, 2006, pp. 1161–73.
12. See L. T. Hosmer, 'Trust: The Connecting Link Between Organizational Theory and Philosophical Ethics', *Academy of Management Review*, vol. 20, no. 2, 1995, pp. 373–97.
13. See J. M. Hagen and S. Choe, 'Trust in Japanese Interfirm Relations: Institutional Sanctions Matter', *Academy of Management Review*, vol. 23, no. 3, 1998, pp. 589–600.
14. This was especially emphasized by K. Davis and R. L. Blomstrom, *Business and its Environment* (New York: McGraw-Hill, 1966).
15. P. J. DiMaggio and W. W. Powell, *The New Institutionalism in Organizational Analysis* (Chicago: University of Chicago Press, 1991).
16. K. MacMillan, K. Money and S. Downing, 'Successful Business Relationships', *Journal of General Management*, vol. 26, no. 1, 2000, pp. 69–83.

17. See Historical Case #1.
18. J. D. Margolis and J. P. Walsh, 'Misery Loves Companies: Rethinking Social Initiatives by Business', *Administrative Science Quarterly*, vol. 48, no. 2, 2003, pp. 268–305; F. Alshannag, M. Y. A. Basah and K. F. Khairi, 'The Relationship Between Corporate Social Responsibility and Corporate Financial Performance: A Survey of Literature', *International Journal of Business & Administrative Studies*, vol. 3, no. 1, 2017, pp. 8–14.
19. L. K. Trevino and K. A. Nelson, *Managing Business Ethics: Straight Talk about How to Do It Right* (Hoboken, NJ: John Wiley & Sons, 2016), who emphasizes the positive impact that ethical leadership and culture have on employee behaviour, customer trust and overall company performance. By the same token, a national survey on labour in the USA in 2013, linked ethical cultures to improved employee morale, reduced misconduct and enhanced business performance: https://magazine.ethisphere.com/2013-national-business-ethics-survey-of-the-u-s-workforce/. (Accessed on 30 October 2024).
20. L. S. Paine, 'Does Ethics Pay?', *Business Ethics Quarterly*, vol. 10, no. 1, 2000, pp. 319–30.
21. Paine, 'Does Ethics Pay?'
22. Paine, 'Does Ethics Pay?', p. 329.
23. A. Bhide and H. H. Stevenson, 'Why be Honest if Honesty Doesn't Pay?', *Harvard Business Review*, vol. 68, no. 5, 1990, pp. 121–9. These scholars provide examples showing that ethics does not always pay off in economic terms.
24. See *Gorgias*, 8, in *Plato in Twelve Volumes* (Cambridge, MA and London: Harvard University Press & William Heinemann, 1967).
25. Bible, Mk 8:36.
26. See a bibliographical review on the influence of personal and situational factors in decision-making in M. J. O'Fallon and K. D. Butterfield, 'A Review of the Empirical Ethical Decision-Making Literature: 1996–2003', *Journal of Business Ethics*, vol. 59, no. 4, 2005, pp. 375–413; J. L. Craft, 'A Review of the Empirical Ethical Decision-Making Literature: 2004–2011', *Journal of Business Ethics*, vol. 117, no. 2, 2013, pp. 221–59; and K. Lehnert, Y.-h. Park and N. Singh, 'Research Note and Review of the Empirical Ethical Decision-Making Literature: Boundary Conditions and Extensions', *Journal of Business Ethics*, vol. 129, 2015, pp. 195–219.
27. See a review of the first years of this discipline in L. K. Treviño and G. R. Weaver, 'Behavioural Ethics in Organizations: A Review', *Journal of Management*, vol. 32, no. 6, 2006, pp. 951–90.
28. See, for instance, M. S. Mitchell, S. J. Reynolds and L. K. Treviño, 'The Study of Behavioural Ethics within Organizations: A Special Issue Introduction', *Personnel Psychology*, vol. 73, no. 1, 2020, pp. 5–17.
29. On this point see, for instance, B. L. Toffler, *Tough Choices: Managers Talk Ethics* (New York: John Wiley and Sons, 1986), p. 20.
30. https://www.jnj.com/credo/. (Accessed on 30 October 2024).
31. Phil Donahue interview with Mr James E. Burke, quoted by Paine, 'Does Ethics Pay?'
32. https://www.jnj.com/credo/. (Accessed on 30 October 2024).
33. This is the case of a specific product accused of causing ovarian cancer, mainly in the second decade of the twenty-first century. Lawsuits referred to talc-based powder for babies contaminated with asbestos, a known carcinogen commonly found in places where talc is mined. The company announced that it would stop making talc-based powder by 2023 and replace it with cornstarch-based powders.

34. See Melé, D. 2006. 'Religious Foundations of Business Ethics.' In M. J. Epstein & K. O. Hanson (Eds.) *The Accountable Corporation*: 11–43. London: Praeger Publishers, 2006, for an overview on religious approaches to business ethics.
35. This dilemma arose from a dialogue between Socrates and Euthyphro, known as the 'Euthyphro Dilemma'. Literally, the question was formulated as follows: 'Is the pious loved by the gods because it is pious, or is it pious because it is loved by the gods?' (Plato, *Euthyphro*). The dilemma has been revived over time and is still alive today. Some people only accept ethics based exclusively on religious precepts, while others reject any ethics that has any connection with religion.
36. N. Cofnas, 'The Golden Rule: A Naturalistic Perspective', *Utilitas*, vol. 34, no. 3, 2022, pp. 262–74. This author reviews the Golden Rule in several religions and ethical traditions and argues that while the Golden Rule – do unto others as you would have them do unto you – appears in some form in all of the great religious and ethical traditions, this rule is the cornerstone of morality only in Christianity.
37. Bible, Mt. 22:40; Rom. 13:9.
38. J. Templeton, *Agape Love: Tradition in Eight World Religions* (Radnor, PN: Templeton Foundation Press, 1999).
39. S. Webley, 'The Interfaith Declaration: Constructing a Code of Ethics for International Business', *Business Ethics: A European Review*, vol. 5, no. 1, 1996, pp. 52–4; S. Webley, 'The Interfaith Declaration: Context, Issues and Problems of Application of a Code of Ethics for International Business among those of Three Major Religions', in B. N. Kumar and H. Steinmann (eds), *Ethics in International Management* (Berlin and New York: Walter de Gruyter, 1998), pp. 439–54.
40. J. Dalla Costa, *The Ethical Imperative: Why Moral Leadership is Good Business* (Toronto: HarperCollins, 1998).
41. J. Moses, *Oneness: Great Principles Shared by All Religions* (New York: Ballantine, 2001); C. S. Lewis, *The Abolition of Man* (London: Collins & Sons, 1944 [2010]): in this classic book Lewis argues on the importance and relevance of universal values in contemporary society.
42. C. Peterson and M. Seligman, *Character Strengths and Virtues: A Handbook and Classification* (Washington, DC: American Psychological Association, 2004), especially the chapter 'Universal Virtues? Lessons From History', pp. 33–52.
43. D. Koehn and A. Leung, 'Dignity in Western versus in Chinese Cultures: Theoretical Overview and Practical Illustrations', *Business & Society Review*, vol. 113, no. 4, 2008, pp. 477–504.
44. https://www.un.org/en/universal-declaration-human-rights/. (Accessed on 30 October 2024).
45. M. Ishay, *The History of Human Rights: From Ancient Times to the Globalization Era* (Berkeley: University of California Press, 2008).
46. On this point, see A. Sen, 'Democracy as a Universal Value', *Journal of Democracy*, vol. 10, no. 3, 1999, pp. 3–17.
47. https://unglobalcompact.org/what-is-gc/mission/principles. (Accessed on 30 October 2024).
48. Aristotle, *Nicomachean Ethics*. Translated by W. D. Ross, rev. by Lesley Brown, http://classics.mit.edu/Aristotle/nicomachaen.html. (Accessed on 30 October 2024).
49. *Nicomachean Ethics*, 2, c. 1.
50. All names and places are fictitious.

2
Ethical Foundations for Business Ethics

... the plain person often unsystematically asking: 'What is my good?' and 'What action will achieve it?' And the moral philosopher systematically enquiring 'What is the good for human beings? What kind of actions will achieve the good.'[1]

ALASDAIR MACINTYRE (1929–2025), Scottish-American moral philosopher

Overview

Taking business ethics seriously requires a strong foundation, which, in turn, calls for a well-grounded ethical theory. Since Socrates initiated rational reflection on morality in the fifth century BCE, numerous ethical theories have been proposed. This presents both a challenge and an opportunity for critical analysis and a deeper understanding of what constitutes a sound ethical theory.

Section A of this chapter critically examines the most relevant ethical theories, particularly those currently applied in business ethics. Some theories focus primarily on principles and duties, others on virtues, and a third group emphasizes goods or values – each understood in different ways. A common issue among many of these theories is their fragmentation and incompleteness.

Section B proposes a return to ethics in its 'nascent state', viewing it as a guide for personal freedom aimed at human fulfilment. An approach is presented as being rooted in the Aristotelian tradition and enriched by modern Personalist philosophy. It argues that human fulfilment requires respecting human dignity and rights – including the identity of others – and practising benevolent behaviour, which entails justice, care, and a spirit of service toward persons and the common good. This approach integrates goods (ethical values), norms (principles), and virtues in an interconnected way. The chapter concludes by presenting key ethical principles and fundamental virtues.

Chapter Aims

After reading this chapter you should be able to:

- Understand how ethical theories have emerged and developed over time.
- Provide an overview of relevant ethical approaches in business ethics.

- Discuss the strengths and weaknesses of different approaches.
- Understand why a complete ethical framework should include goods, norms and virtues as mutually interrelated components.
- Reflect on the necessity of viewing ethics as oriented towards human excellence.
- Discuss the ethical relevance of human dignity and human fulfilment (or flourishing).
- Be familiar with an ethical approach that integrates goods (ethical values), principles (moral norms) and virtues (moral traits of character).
- Deliberate on the nature of real goods and their connection with norms and virtues.
- Understand the role and content of key ethical principles.
- Acquire knowledge of the fundamental moral virtues and their significance in business ethics.

Historical Case #2

The controversial launch of the space shuttle *Challenger*[2]

Morton Thiokol Inc., an American corporation concerned with rocket and missile propulsion systems, was involved in the launching of the space shuttle *Challenger*, as a contractor of the National Aeronautics and Space Administration (NASA). The craft of the space shuttle *Challenger* was built by Rockwell International's Space Transportation Systems Division in Downey, California, while Morton Thiokol manufactured the O-rings rubber seal on the shuttle's booster rockets.

Unfortunately, this shuttle exploded seventy-three seconds after being launched at Kennedy Space Center, in Florida, USA on the 28th of January 1986; it disintegrated, resulting in the death of all seven crew members. This was the first time a shuttle had been destroyed in flight, after nine successful NASA space missions. The data showed that the O-rings didn't seal properly in cold temperatures, and this was the coldest launch ever. It was known that the seals had not been tested at temperatures below 50°F.

Bob Ebeling was one of the five engineers working for contractor Morton Thiokol in the launching of the *Challenger*. Thirty years after the explosion and less than three months before he passed away, Ebeling remembered the facts on the US National Public Radio (NPR). He confessed that he had been swamped by his own grief and guilt over the catastrophe he had failed to stop. Ebeling retired soon after the *Challenger* explosion. He suffered deep depression and was never able to shed the burden of guilt.

Ebeling and the four other engineers had tried to delay the launch. They had concerns about whether the rubber O-rings on the shuttle's booster rockets would seal properly in the freezing temperatures. Ebeling had authored an urgent memo to Allan McDonald, his boss and Morton Thiokol's representative at the Kennedy Space Center. Ebeling detailed the problems with the rings. The subject line of this report read bluntly, 'Help!' He told McDonald that the rocket-seal taskforce needed more resources. According to a presidential commission's 1986 report, the accident was signed off with the words 'This is a red flag.'

The launch date – already delayed once because of wind conditions – was approaching, with temperatures forecast at about 30°F (around 0°C). On the afternoon before the *Challenger* was due to be launched, Ebeling called McDonald warning him that the cold could be disastrous for the launch for several reasons, including the shuttle booster recovery, the presence of ice in the booster support, and the seals. Six hours of teleconferences between Morton Thiokol engineers and executives and officials with NASA were to follow. Ebeling wasn't involved in these discussions, but McDonald, along with engineers Arnold Thompson and Roger Boisjoly, argued emphatically for a delay, although their managers and NASA overruled them. Finally, Morton Thiokol signed off on the launch over the objections of the engineers.

Ebeling recalled that 'there was more than enough [NASA officials and Thiokol managers] there to say, "Hey, let's give it another day or two," but no one did'. The night before the tragedy he told his wife Darlene, 'It's going to blow up.'

'I was one of the few that was really close to the situation,' Ebeling also recalled. 'Had they listened to me and wait[ed] for a weather change, it might have been a completely different outcome.' He added that NASA ruled in favour of the launch because 'they had their mind set on going up and proving to the world they were right, and they knew what they were doing. But they didn't.'

The US President Ronald Reagan was set to deliver the State of the Union address that evening and reportedly planned to tout the *Challenger* launch. NASA executives wanted to launch the *Challenger* with no delay; it was a matter of prestige. The space shuttle programme had an ambitious launch schedule that year and NASA wanted to show it could launch regularly and reliably.

Hundreds of people who listened to that interview with Ebeling on the radio disagreed with his blaming of himself. Among them was Allan McDonald, Ebeling's boss, who said to NPR a month later:

'I called [Ebeling] up and told him, "You know, to me, my definition of a loser is somebody that really doesn't do anything, but worse yet, they don't care …" I said, "You did something, and you really cared. That's the definition of a winner."'

After the *Challenger* tragedy, NASA cancelled space flights for two years and implemented technical modifications, along with strict regulations regarding quality control and safety within the space shuttle programme.

Questions

1. What criteria were considered in deciding to launch the *Challenger* on 28 January 1986? If you were one of the decision-makers, what would have helped you stay true to your ethical obligations?
2. Can you identify any ethical principles (or the lack thereof) in Morton Thiokol's decision to approve the launch despite the objections of the engineers?
3. What virtues, or lack of them, did Bob Ebeling, his boss Allan McDonald and Morton Thiokol's representative at the Kennedy Space Centre demonstrate?
4. Why do you think Bob Ebeling still felt such guilt over the explosion thirty years later? Does that make sense to you? Why?

SECTION A. ETHICAL APPROACHES: AN OVERVIEW

2.1 Development of ethical theories: A concise historical view

Philosophical reflection has brought about several ethical theories. An overview of the historical development of ethical thought will help us to understand when and why different theories appeared, as well as their current relevance.

Ancient and medieval periods: Centrality of human fulfilment and virtues

As noted (1.8), ethical reflection was systematically developed in *Ancient Greece*, beginning with *Socrates* (c. 470–399 BCE), followed by his student *Plato* (c. 427–c. 347 BCE) and later *Aristotle* (384–322 BCE). These three thinkers are known as Socratic Philosophers. In the early discussions on the subject, Socrates challenged the *Sophists,* a group of thinkers who used rhetoric to persuade others to achieve their own interests – regardless of whether these were just, as in lawsuits. The Sophists charged exorbitant fees to teach these skills, enabling their clients to succeed in Athens' highly litigious society. Socrates opposed this approach, advocating instead for a rational search for *moral good*.

Consistently, Socrates and the other Socratic philosophers linked moral good with human life as a whole, emphasizing each individual's capacity and responsibility to act towards the *telos* (end) of human existence. This teleological orientation led them to define the ultimate goal of human life as *eudaimonia*, often translated as 'human flourishing' in the sense of 'human fulfilment', and also as 'the good life'. *Human flourishing* refers to the plenitude of capacities distinctively human – accompanied by inner happiness – and is closely associated with *virtues* (1.10), understood as the excellent dispositions necessary to achieve human fulfilment. *Virtues* are, therefore, central to Socratic tradition.

According to Socrates and his student Plato, virtue is tied to the recognition of the good, as a virtuous person naturally desires to do good and such a knowledge is the essence of human morality. Plato identified four fundamental virtues: *practical wisdom* (or prudence); *justice; fortitude* (related to courage, patience); and *temperance* (understood as moderation). These virtues guide individuals towards knowing and doing what is good.

Aristotle disagreed with Socrates and Plato, arguing that merely knowing what is good does not necessarily lead to good behaviour. Instead, virtuous action requires not only intellectual understanding of what is good but also strength of moral character. In this sense, Aristotle distinguishes between *intellectual virtues*, which support rational understanding of reality, and *moral virtues*, which provide the strength of character to regulate emotions and *sense of responsibility*, as readiness to be accountable for choices and to fulfil moral obligations.

Among the intellectual virtues, *wisdom* (deep knowledge of the world) and *practical wisdom* (*phronesis* in Greek), which promotes sound judgement, are key. Aristotle's *moral virtues*, including what is good, are those that help persons endure pain and hardship in pursuit of challenging goods, as well as those that foster balance and inner harmony. Virtues such as *justice*, *honesty and friendliness* enable harmonious social living and mutual friendship.

According to Aristotle, moral virtues represent the 'golden mean' between excess and deficiency in relation to an action or emotion. This balance is not mathematical but is determined by practical wisdom, as a wise person would judge in each situation. For example, good temper lies between apathy (deficiency) and irascibility (excess).

The *Stoics* were another school of ancient ethical thought proposed by *Zeno of Citium* (c. 334–262 BCE), *Lucius Annaeus Seneca* (c. 4 BCE–65 CE) and *Marcus Aurelius* (121–180 CE), among others. Stoic ethics essentially views virtue as the *willpower* to live in accordance with rationality. A quite different moral approach in Ancient Greece is that of *Epicurus* (341–270 BCE), who also focused on the ultimate goal of human life, but he believed that this was pleasure (*hêdonê* in Greek) rather than human fulfilment – although not pleasure based on immediate gratification, but instead, pursuing rational pleasure, including that provided by friendship, inner tranquillity and the absence of pain. This contrasts with some forms of modern *hedonism* usually related to immediate sensorial pleasure. Epicurean hedonism makes it less of a moral system and more of a personal philosophy of well-being. This does not entail a sense of responsibility towards others, only individual satisfaction, and neither prescribe absolute moral duties (such as honesty, justice or respect for people).

Virtues were also central to *Eastern wisdom traditions*, particularly *Confucianism* and *Buddhism*, which emphasized ethical cultivation and harmonious living. The *Judeo-Christian* tradition focused on *moral norms*, including the famous Ten Commandments, and virtues. *Self-giving love* (*agape*) is central to Christian ethics, serving both as a moral principle and a virtue – one that encompasses all other virtues.

In the thirteenth century, *Thomas Aquinas*, at the University of Paris, integrated Aristotelian ethics into Christian thought. He emphasized virtues informed by self-giving love and connected them to moral law, which he saw as derived from rational knowledge of human nature. He defends the existence of a *Natural Moral Law*, accessible by the human reason, at least in its more basic requirements, which is consistent with the *Ten Commandments* (Decalogue) in the Judeo-Christian tradition.

However, in the fourteenth century, *William of Ockham* introduced *theological voluntarism*, which rejected the rational search for morality and instead reduced ethics to divine commandments – a view known as the *Divine Command Theory*. Over time, as secularism expanded, theological voluntarism evolved into broader forms of voluntarism, assigning greater importance to the will (*voluntas* in Latin) over intellect in ethical behaviour. Divine commandments were replaced by social norms.

Ethics in the Enlightenment: Moral sentiments and rationalism

During the Renaissance, a period of intellectual development emerged, leading to a cultural movement known as the *Enlightenment*, from the late seventeenth century to the early nineteenth century, along with the so-called *Philosophical Modernity*. This movement rejected any authority that could not be justified by reason and, therefore, discarded voluntarism. The *Scottish Enlightenment* developed an ethical system that emphasized the role of *moral sentiments*, the intuition of good, and the feeling of responsibility in addressing each situation. Prominent advocates of this approach included *David Hume* (1711–76) and *Adam Smith* (1723–90). Moral distinctions were no longer derived from reason but rather from feelings of approval (esteem, praise) and disapproval (blame). Smith introduced the concept of considering what an *impartial spectator* would feel when observing a particular character trait or action. Additionally, Smith assumed *Stoic virtues*.

Another ethical perspective is that of the British philosopher *John Locke* (1632–1704), who argued that moral order is inherent in human nature and can be intuitively discovered through reason. He emphasized the existence of *natural rights*, such as life, liberty and property, viewing them as self-evident and originating from God. Previously, *Francisco de Vitoria*[3] (1483–1546) and other members of the School of Salamanca (Spain and Portugal), had already defended native Indians as humans and deserving of respect, along with the existence of certain natural rights, mentioning both rights related to the body (right to life, to property) and to the spirit (right to freedom of thought, dignity).

Returning to Epicurean ideas, *Jeremy Bentham* (1748–1832) developed *utilitarianism*, arguing that morality is determined by pleasure and pain – actions should maximize pleasure and minimize pain. He proposed the core principle: 'The greatest happiness of the greatest number is the measure of right and wrong.' Later, *John Stuart Mill* (1806–73) refined utilitarianism, introducing distinctions between higher and lower pleasures and emphasizing individual rights within the utilitarian framework.

Continental Enlightenment focused on establishing *universal principles* of morality to determine which actions are ethically acceptable, setting sentiments and virtues aside. Theories based on principles begin with rational evidence (an *a priori* element of reason) as the fundamental reference for evaluating whether an action is ethically acceptable. In this line of thought, Immanuel Kant (1724–1804) is outstanding.

Postmodernity: Criticism of universal principles and emphasis on particular situations

The universal-principles approach rooted in Modernity has faced criticism since the mid-nineteenth century, giving rise to a heterogeneous philosophical movement known as *Postmodernity*. Postmodernist thinkers typically reject the idea of absolute, universal foundations for ethics, favouring a perspective that considers ethics context-dependent and culturally constructed.

Some postmodernist authors go further, rejecting the very possibility of formulating morally right or wrong judgements – a view known as *moral nihilism*. One of the best-known thinkers in this line is *Friedrich Nietzsche* (1844–1900), who advocated for values rooted in individual will and creativity. *Jean-Paul Sartre* (1905–80) argued that individuals are radically free to create their own values and meanings through their choices and actions. *Michel Foucault* (1926–84) emphasized the role of power and social structures in shaping morality, viewing ethics as interwoven with social, political and cultural influences rather than rooted in objective principles. The question which arises is whether, despite the influence of social structures, we must still reflect on what is ethically correct and which social structures favour human flourishing.

Some postmodernists also emphasize the role of language in constructing meaning. *Emotivism*, an ethical theory associated with Alfred J. Ayer (1910–89), holds that moral judgements are merely expressions of the speaker's emotions and often depend on individual circumstances. Emotivism has been criticized, arguing that it fails as a moral philosophy because it reduces ethics to subjective preferences and undermines the possibility of rational moral discourse.[4]

On the positive side, Postmodernity has drawn appropriate attention to particular situations, highlights specific issues, and considers the unique context of each case. However, it has been criticized for falling short of presenting a coherent and comprehensive ethical approach for human behaviour, as well as a framework for dialogue grounded in universal principles. Rather than offering a systematic reflection on morality, in Postmodernity, many authors tend to support subjective perspectives, social values or context-dependent norms, placing them within moral relativism – a stance that presents significant challenges (see 1.9).

In the twentieth century, critiques of both Modernity and Postmodernity spurred a renewed interest in *virtue ethics*, going back to Aristotle. Among those advocating this shift were Elizabeth Anscombe,[5] who disagreed with modern moral philosophy for various reasons, including its neglect of the moral agent, and Alasdair McIntyre,[6] who was critical of the 'Enlightenment Project' and emotivism. These and other thinkers contributed to a revival of virtue ethics, now considered a mainstream approach alongside principle-based theories and issue-focused ethics.

Alongside the revival of virtue ethics, an ethics of care has also emerged, introduced by Carol Gilligan.[7] *Care ethics* centres on relational and empathetic approaches, prioritizing the specific needs of individuals and the interdependencies in caregiving and community contexts.

2.2 Frequent ethical approaches for business ethics

Contemporary moral philosophy is characterized by a plurality of ethical systems, including both historical traditions and emerging perspectives that respond to globalization, the need for global social justice, environmental crises, responsibility for future generations and respect for the non-human world.

At the same time, business scandals, acts of terrorism, the destructive potential of advanced weapons, the risks of totalitarian uses of technology, and the urgent need for sound ethical principles have heightened awareness of ethical considerations. The growing interest in bioethics and business ethics in the latter part of the twentieth century may have contributed to this renewed focus on principles, human rights, consequences and virtues.

A comprehensive discussion of each ethical theory or approach is beyond the scope of this book; however, a brief overview of the most common approaches will be outlined here, followed by a critical discussion of the mainstream ethical systems applied in Business ethics (2.3).

In summary, contemporary ethical approaches can be categorized into the following groups (Table 2.1):

Table 2.1 Main ethical theories proposed for business ethics

	Ethical theories	**Main proponents**
Deontologism	Kantian ceontologism	I. Kant
	Common-sense intuitionism	D. Ross
Consequentialism	(Act) Utilitarianism	B. Betham, J. S. Mill
	(Rule) Utilitarianism	R. Brandt, R. Hooker
	Ethical egoism (and enlightened self-interest)	A. Rand
Virtue ethics	Eudaemonist virtue ethics	Aristotle, A. MacIntyre
	Stoic virtue ethics	Zeno of Citium, L. A. Seneca, Marcus Aurelius and others
	Religious and wisdom-based approaches to virtue ethics	Abrahamic religions (Judaism, Christianity and Islam)
		Eastern Religions/Wisdoms (Confucianism, Buddhism and Hinduism)
	Positive organizational virtue ethics	K. S. Cameron, D. S. Bright and A. Caza
	Relativist virtue ethics	Several proponents with scarce acceptance
Contractualism and procedural ethics	Moral by agreement	D. Gauthier
	Integrative social contract theory	T. Dunfee, T. Donaldson
	Discourse ethics	J. Habermas, K.-O. Apple
	Justice theory as fairness	J. Rawls
Natural law, human rights and capabilities approach	Realistic Natural Law (and virtues)	T. Aquinas, J. Maritain
	Human rights theories	F. de Vitoria, H. Grotius (ontological)
		J. Locke (rationalist)
		Declarations of Human Rights (consensual)
	Capabilities approach	A. Sen, M. Nussbaum
Care ethics	Care ethics	C. Gilligan, N. Noddings
Personalist ethics	Dialogue philosophy-based ethics	M. Buber, E. Levinas
	Ontological personalist ethics	J. Maritain, R. Spaemann, L. Polo
	Phenomenological (ontological) ethics	M. Scheller, D. von Hildebrand, K. Wojtyla

Deontologism

This category embraces ethical systems based on moral duties. Immanuel Kant, mentioned above (2.1), is probably the most popular deontologist author.

- *Kantian ethics* is a duties-based ethical approach based on the human capacity to discover rational principles that are known to be true, in order to decide ethically. Kant assumes that there is a very basic principle, which he called 'categorical imperative', which should be the basis for universal moral law. He presented three different possible formulations of the categorical imperative. It seems that the third formulation of the categorical imperative is the most comprehensive and establishes that each subject must follow maxims that could become universal norms. In Kant's words, this formulation entails the idea of the will of every rational being as a universally legislating will.[8] For instance, stealing is not allowed since the proposition 'it is permissible to steal' would be impossible to universalize for civilized persons living together. The two other formulations of the Categorical Imperative are also relevant, particularly the second, known for its focuses on human dignity – 'act in such a way that you treat humanity, whether in your own person or in the person of any other, always as an end and never simply as a means'.[9] In relation to this, Kant argues that all things have a price when people have dignity, that is, an intrinsic and incommensurable value.
- *Common-sense intuitionism* or *prima-facie duties*, is another deontological approach. It was proposed by the Scottish philosopher W. David Ross,[10] who presents a set of moral duties that are binding or incumbent upon us 'at first glance' (*prima facie* in Latin). These duties, which include fidelity, non-injury, beneficence, reparation, gratitude and justice, are not absolute, but they carry moral weight and serve as prima facie reasons for action.

Consequentialism

Consequentialism is the generic category of ethical theories based on consequences. It proposes to evaluate the rightness or wrongness of one's action by balancing the good and bad consequences of said action. The oldest form of consequentialism comes from Chinese philosophy and dates to the fifth century BC. This is the *Mohist consequentialism*, also known as *State consequentialism*, which considers a plurality of intrinsic goods taken as constitutive of human welfare, including order, material wealth and increase in population.

- *Utilitarianism (Act and Rule)*: Utilitarianism is the most common form of consequentialism. Unlike *Mohist consequentialism*, utilitarianism only considers utility (satisfaction) as the sole good and evaluates consequences with this criterion in mind. Utilitarianism balances consequences through the so-called utilitarian principle, which states that an action is right when it achieves 'the greatest happiness of the greatest number'[11] on calculation of the consequences of the action. Those who defend the theory hold that the utilitarian principle has stronger intuitive grounding than Kant's reliance on reason. In addition, utilitarianism can better explain why certain actions are right or wrong than Kantianism.[12]

The main proponents of utilitarianism were Jeremy Bentham (1748–1832) and John Stuart Mill, mentioned above. According to the former, who took a completely hedonistic evaluation of the consequences of the action, a right action is one that equals the greatest sum of pleasure and the least sum of pain in those affected by the action.[13] Mill also followed a utilitarian principle but presented a wider vision about the goods to be evaluated. In Mill's view, higher pleasures are associated with the mind and lower ones with the body. Each of these must be considered and evaluated.[14]

An example of applying utilitarianism would be a manager who invites himself to visit a sick collaborator in hospital the following weekend, sacrificing other plans. His decision to do so is not out of any sense of friendship, neighbourly love or notion of duty, but for reasons of utilitarian calculation. The action will be right if the cumulative satisfaction of everybody involved in this action (the collaborator, his or her relatives and the manager him- or herself) is higher after the visit and all end up feeling better. The net gain for the manager can be calculated by offsetting the opportunity cost of renouncing his other plans for the weekend against his desire/satisfaction and other benefits.

In utilitarianism, a right decision requires a measurement of pleasure and pain and making an arithmetical calculation, before applying the utilitarian principle. This presents the serious difficulty of measuring pleasure and pain, which are subjective. In the face of this difficulty, and to make utilitarianism easier to apply, a different approach was suggested, consisting of replacing the analysis of each act (*act utilitarianism*) with a set of rules (*rule utilitarianism*) for actions that never favour general happiness (for example, slavery or child labour).[15]

In addition to utilitarianism, other forms of consequentialism are sometimes mentioned:

- *Ethical egoism*: This proposes individuals should act in their own self-interest, as it is morally right for them to prioritize their own well-being. Some add acting in self-interest by being attentive to both immediate and mediate consequences. The American writer Ayn Rand defended ethical egoism and even proposed selfishness as a virtue.[16]
- *Enlightened self-interest* is a related concept where individuals pursue self-interest but consider the long-term impacts on others, often acting in a way that benefits others to ultimately serve themselves. In the business context, this means doing good not for the intrinsic worth of doing so, but exclusively because doing good will have good (utilitarian) consequences.

Virtue ethics

Virtue ethicists insist that being a virtuous person, rather than applying ethical principles, is the best approach to business ethics. Virtue ethics is now widely present in business ethics and many scholars adopt it, although from different standpoints.[17] Most of them are rooted in the Aristotelian tradition, but there are other approaches:

- *Eudemonistic virtue ethics*: This is a Neo-Aristotelian approach to virtue ethics, which defines virtues by how they contribute to human fulfilment (*eudaimonia*). This approach has been discussed earlier in this chapter (2.1). Other forms of virtue ethics are also eudemonistic, as they are oriented towards human flourishing, though with some distinct nuances and particularities.

Along with other moral virtues, which shape the moral character, virtue ethics in the Aristotelian tradition stresses *practical wisdom*, the virtue of good discernment (mentioned at 2.1), which reinforces human capacity for making sound moral judgements[18] in each situation, and in determining the 'golden mean' of each virtue, placing it between two extreme vices, one by excess and another by defect.

Alasdair MacIntyre (1929–2025) is one of the most influential contemporary ethicists advocating for a return to Aristotelian virtue ethics grounded in community and tradition, facing the current fragmentation of moral discourse in the modern world. He emphasizes the importance of virtues in the context of practices, traditions and communities, arguing that virtues are essential for achieving the 'internal goods' of practices (activities that have inherent value) and for living a fulfilling, meaningful life.

- *Stoic virtue ethic*: Like Aristotelian virtue ethics, Stoicism emphasizes the role of virtue in achieving a good life, but the two traditions differ in their understanding of virtue. Among other differences, Stoic virtues aim ultimately at freedom from passions (*apatheia*) and living in accordance with nature and reason, while Aristotle, as noted, focuses on human fulfilment (*eudaimonia*) through the cultivation of virtues. Additionally, virtue in Stoicism is absolute and binary – one is either virtuous or not. In contrast, in the Aristotelian tradition, virtue is a character trait developed over time through virtuous behaviour. It is applied situationally, seeking the 'golden mean' between excess and deficiency.
- *Religious and wisdom-based approaches to virtue ethics*: Virtues play a central role in many religious and wisdom traditions, including the Abrahamic religions (Judaism, Christianity and Islam) and Eastern traditions (Confucianism, Buddhism and Hinduism). The Abrahamic religions emphasize universal human virtues such as concern for others, self-discipline and moral integrity, along with specific virtues oriented towards one's spiritual relationship with God. In Eastern traditions: *Confucianism* promotes benevolence, righteousness, trustworthiness, honesty, and the pursuit of moral and intellectual excellence, *Buddhism* emphasizes compassion, wisdom and the path to overcoming suffering, and *Hinduism* focuses on *dharma* (moral duty), self-discipline and self-realization. Despite differences in doctrine, religious and wisdom traditions share a common emphasis on virtues as essential for ethical living and spiritual growth.
- *Positive organizational virtue ethics*: The origin of this approach is the movement of Positive Organizational Scholarship (POS), which focuses on understanding the factors that contribute to human fulfilment – understood in terms of psychological well-being – in organizations.[19] Frequently, POS scholars invoke virtue as a foundational concept for this approach. However, although the idea is present, there are concerns about the grounding of POS, particularly due to the possibility of a superficial understanding of virtue. This issue has been recognized, and some scholars have made efforts to address it.[20]
- *Relativist virtue ethics approaches*: The heyday of virtue ethics has favoured the emergence of various theories that deviate from the Aristotelian tradition[21] and often involve moral relativism. In practice, they have had very little implementation in business ethics. Among them are the *rule-based virtues*, which understand virtues as mere dispositions to act in conformity with certain given moral norms or duties. Others talk of *contextual virtue ethics*

and defend that a trait of character is a virtue when the individual's community applauds it as admirable.[22] The problem is that some 'virtues' that are accepted as such in a particular society would be dubious examples of human excellence in another. Other approaches consider the differing definitions of virtues, including good motivations (*agent-based virtue ethics*), personal evaluation of other people and the desire to imitate their traits of character (*exemplarist virtue ethics*) and the personal conception of the virtues related to a certain field, such as avoiding damage or concern for others (*target-centred virtue ethics*).[23]

Contractualism and procedural ethics

Contrasting with deontologism and other ethical system based on substantive norms, contractualism and Procedural Ethics are based on consensus of people. *Contractualism* defines ethical validity by whether rational individuals would agree to the principle, while *procedural ethics* defines ethical legitimacy through a deliberative process to reach a fair agreement, independent of individual agreements. These approaches are mainly, but not exclusively oriented to politics, although they have also been applied to Business Ethics. In contractualism a just law is one that people would rationally agree to, while in Procedural Ethics, a law is considered just if it has passed a fair legislative process, even if people disagree with it. These understandings of ethics can be found in the following systems, among others:

- *Morals by agreement*, proposed by David Gauthier,[24] is clearly contractualist. This author argues that morality emerges from rational self-interest. He suggests a universal rational bargain, in which all individuals agree to limit their pursuit of self-interest by acting according to principles that would yield optimal benefits for all. In this framework, rational individuals would choose to act morally because cooperation is beneficial in the long run. Thus, morality would be a strategic form of self-interest for long-term success rather than a set of imposed duties.
- *Integrative social contracts theory* (ISCT) is another form of contractualism, developed by Dunfee and Donaldson.[25] This approach distinguishes two types of norms: *hypernorms* arising from a universal consensus (universal declarations of human rights, communality among religions, international agreements and so on) and *authentic norms*, taken from particular communities. The norm should be harmonized, with priority given to hypernorms to ensure ethical consistency across different cultural contexts.
- *Discourse ethics* is a procedural ethics approach which assumes that a just process ensures a just outcome. It is based on the theory of communicative action, proposed by German philosopher Jürgen Habermas[26] and further developed by Karl-Otto Apel.[27] Discourse Ethics proposes a communicative exchange process to promote understanding between the participating parties to reach a consensus as to what should be done. A key point is that moral norms are only valid if they could gain the acceptance of all affected in a rational discourse, under conditions of equality and freedom. What is right or just emerges from open communication, where participants aim for mutual understanding rather than persuasion or domination.

- *Justice as fairness* proposed by John Rawls[28] presents a conception of fairness understood as impartiality. Justice is based on two main principles: liberty and equality; the second is subdivided into fair equality of opportunity and the difference principle. This approach is primarily classified as a contractualist theory with procedural elements. *Rawls' theory of justice* focuses on the problem of the socially-just distribution of goods. Taking some elements of Kant and the political concept of 'social contract', Rawls proposes rules of fairness as a procedural approach to justice based on a hypothetical veil of ignorance.

Natural law, human rights and capabilities approach

These ethical approaches, while different, share key humanistic concerns related to respect for people, and of justice, and related moral obligations.

- *Natural law theory*: This is rooted in ancient Greek and Roman thinkers, particularly Cicero, and developed in the medieval period by Thomas Aquinas, connected with a theory of virtues. It has been taken up by modern philosophers, such as Jacques Maritain. Natural law traditions[29] assume moral norms are derived from the objective nature of things and suggest that the very basic rules of good behaviour can be recognized by every person simply in virtue of being rational, beyond the existence of social conventions. Aquinas presented a *realistic natural law* discoverable by reason from innate human tendencies and provides a moral order that applies to all humans. Natural Law has been applied to business ethics.[30] Contrasting with Aquinas, John Locke held a *rationalistic natural law*, as discussed next.
- *Human rights theories*: The idea that a natural moral law can be discovered influenced thinkers like Francisco de Vitoria, Hugo Grotius and John Locke, who helped shape modern human rights philosophy. *Francisco de Vitoria*, aligned with Aquinas' realistic natural law, proposed an ontological perspective, arguing that all humans, including Indigenous peoples, have inherent rights given by natural law, and ultimately by God, author of the human nature. Vitoria influenced later legal frameworks on sovereignty, human rights and international law.

  Hugo Grotius adopted a secularized natural law theory, arguing that there are innate rights, intrinsic to human nature, which exist independently of divine command and government. Influenced by Grotius, and very influential in the subsequent conception of human rights, was *John Locke*. He believed that there are self-evident rights innate in every human individual placed by God in the human mind.[31] In this way, Locke held a rationalistic view of natural law. He held that the rights to life (right to self-preservation), liberty (right to freedom and self-rule) and property (right to own and use private resources) are basic natural rights that precede the establishment of civil society, and claimed that others should respect these rights.[32]

  Today, human rights are widely recognized and enforced through international institutions, treaties and legal mechanisms that aim to protect individual dignity, freedom and justice worldwide. A milestone was *The Universal Declaration of Human Rights* (UDHR, 1948) adopted by the United Nations (UN) after the Second World War.
- *Capabilities approach*: This perspective, developed by economist Amartya Sen and philosopher Martha Nussbaum,[33] is a human-centred ethical framework that evaluates morality based on

people's real freedoms and opportunities to achieve a dignified life. Ethics is thus understood as justice and related to the goal of improving access to the tools people use to live a fulfilling life. Sen advocates for freedoms and the removal of obstacles to human development, arguing that capabilities should be determined contextually. On her part, Nussbaum establishes ten essential capabilities and argued that justice requires institutions to guarantee fundamental capabilities.

The capabilities approach and human rights theory share many common goals but differ in their respective approach. While human rights theory provides legal protections, ensuring that people are entitled to rights (e.g. the right to free speech, education and healthcare), the capabilities approach focuses on real freedoms – ensuring that people can actually exercise their rights (e.g. having access to education, not just a formal right to it).

The capabilities approach also has measurement challenges, since assessing capabilities and their influence on well-being is complex and subjective, and conflicts among capabilities can exist. In addition, the definition of 'capabilities' varies across cultures and has the risk of overlooking immediate needs, and its practical application entails complexity.

Care ethics

Care ethics is a relationship-focused approach centred on *interpersonal relationships* and on providing attention and care to others as the key reference of morality. Care ethics can be seen as a sentiment-based approach, although it is often considered part of the virtue ethics field, because care for others is taken as a permanent disposition and, therefore, as a moral habit.

In the early days, scholars termed this approach 'feminist ethics' as it began within feminist circles in the late 1970s and early 1980s.[34] The starting point was contrasting male and female moral attitudes, assuming that the former emphasizes justice and rights, while the latter focuses on care and on how to respond to other people's needs, which favours interpersonal relationships. However, care ethics is now understood as an ethical theory for all, not only for women. It takes connectedness with others and the obligation to respond to the specific situations of people in need and the vulnerable as its central features.

Proponents of care ethics are generally critical of views of ethics focused on solving 'ethical problems' by applying universal and abstract rules, which can breed moral blindness or indifference towards those in need.[35] The key question for them is the recognition of human need and vulnerability, and personal engagement in a network of interdependences with others, which demands responsibility for promoting well-being.

Personalist ethics

Personalist ethics is a philosophical approach that places the human person at the centre of moral reflection, emphasizing the value and moral worth of each individual. This ethical approach is rooted in personalist philosophy, also known as personalism,[36] which developed from the mid-twentieth century. This philosophy emphasizes the importance of the human person as both an individual and a relational being, endowed with inherent dignity and called to personal growth. It also highlights the uniqueness and moral responsibility of each person. Personalist ethics emerged as a response to impersonal ethical systems (e.g. utilitarianism, Kantian formalism) and seeks to integrate relational, existential and humanistic elements into ethical thinking.

There are several streams of thought within personalist ethics, which are not necessarily incompatible with each other.

- *Dialogue-based ethics, also called 'ethics of encounter' and 'relational ethics'*: This philosophical approach emphasizes the worth of the induvial (person), the relevance of the encounter to persons, of inter-personal dialogue in moral life and responsibility to the other. In this regard, Martin Buber (1878–1965)[37] focuses on genuine relationships ('I–Thou') rather than impersonal rules. In his approach, Buber distinguishes between two types of human interactions: 'I–Thou' and 'I–It.' In an 'I–Thou' relationship, individuals engage with others in a genuine, mutual and respectful way, seeing the other person as a unique and whole being. In contrast, 'I–It' relationships treat others as objects or means to an end. Buber's ethics emphasizes the importance of authentic, reciprocal relationships in achieving moral and spiritual life, with true ethics emerging from these deep, personal encounters. Within the philosophy of dialogue-based ethics is Emmanuel Levinas (1906–95),[38] whose views are notably different from Buber. Levinas holds that our primary moral obligation is not to a set of rules, but directly to other people in discovering our responsibility in encounters with the other. Last, but not least, Gabriel Marcel (1889–1973) deserves mention, for adopting an existentialist perspective, suggesting that ethics is about authentic presence, fidelity and intersubjective relationships.
- *Ontological personalist ethics*: This ethics is grounded in the being of the person, not just in actions, duties or consequences, and considers that ethical life involves acting in accordance with one's nature and rational freedom. It defends the ontological (metaphysical) roots of human dignity and the relevance of relationships for human flourishing, since persons exist in community and relation with others and with the transcendent. Aligned with Aquinas' ideas this emphasizes the intrinsic dignity of the person and their calling to personal growth, flourishing as a human being. Significant authors in this stream are Jacques Maritain (1882–1973), who synthesized Thomistic metaphysics with modern personalism, grounding human dignity in natural law and divine order, Robert Spaemann[39] (1927–2018), who defends the objective dignity of the person against modern utilitarianism and scientism, and presented an ethical approach building a bridge between Aristotle's eudaimonism and Kantian universalism, and Leonardo Polo[40] (1926–2013), who proposed a 'transcendental anthropology' in which human freedom is crucial, but understood as more than mere autonomy. The person has a radical openness to truth, to others and to transcendence, and ethical life is about self-giving, not self-centred autonomy. Following this approach, *personalist virtue ethics has been proposed.*[41]
- *Phenomenological-ontological personalist ethics*: Authors of this stream employ phenomenology (the study of internal experience) to understand moral values and human dignity. Among them, Max Scheler[42] (1874–1928), who opposed objective ethical values to

the Kantian formalism and emphasized that persons have an inherent worth beyond utility, and Dietrich von Hildebrand[43] (1889–1977), who highlighted the heart's role in moral intuition. Some authors combine ontological ethics, mainly drawing from Thomas Aquinas and phenomenology. One is Edith Stein (1891–1942), whose thought integrates human dignity, empathy, moral development[44] and the call to transcendence, and Karol Wojtyla[45] (1920–2005), who combines Thomistic ethics and phenomenology.

2.3 Discussing ethical approaches in business ethics

Among the ethical approaches mentioned in the previous section, three mainstream theories are commonly presented as foundational to business ethics: *Kantian ethics*, *utilitarianism* and *virtue ethics* – especially in the Aristotelian tradition. Other approaches, such as *contractualism*, *procedural ethics*, *human rights*, *personalist ethics* and *care ethics*, are also employed in specific areas of business ethics. These frameworks have received both praise and criticism, which will be discussed concisely in this section (see Table 2.2).

Table 2.2 Praises and criticisms of ethical approaches employed in business ethics

Ethical approach	Praises	Criticisms
Kantian ethics	– Promotes moral consistency avoiding moral relativism. – Encourages moral duty over personal gain. – Establishes universal moral laws. – Pushes respect for human dignity.	– Formalism and lack of practical guidance. – Rigidity and lack of context-sensitivity and concern for consequences. – Neglect of emotions and moral character. – Narrow view of moral motivation. – A biased view of human autonomy.
Utilitarianism	– Provides an impartial principle. – Overcomes the rigidity of deontological principles. – Introduces the relevance of consequences. – Offers a tool for policymakers based on balancing interests of people affected.	– Questionable hedonistic evaluative criteria. – Difficulty to measure consequences. – Unethical means can be justified for good ends. – Justice and human rights may not always be respected.
Virtue ethics	– Focuses on human flourishing (*eudaimonia*). – Seeks to promote the moral character of the agent. – Considers context and consequences in addition of a few moral absolutes. – Recognizes the importance of emotions guided by practical wisdom. – Emphasizes moral education and human development.	– Lack of clear guidance for moral decision-making. – The 'golden mean' of virtues can be vague. – Necessity of a long moral development to make sound ethical judgments. – Different conceptions of good life. – Diversity of cultural assessments of virtues. – Possible conflicts in virtue-based judgements.

Ethical approach	Praises	Criticisms
Contractualism	– Facilitates consensus in pluralistic societies. – Aligns with enlightened self-interest.	– Ethics is treated as merely a product of negotiated agreements. – Neglects moral obligations that extend beyond mutual advantage.
Procedural ethics	– Provides a way to reach minimal common ethical agreements. – Introduces principles of impartiality beyond simple consensus.	– Primarily political rather than ethical. – Lack of moral substance. – Dependence on consensus. – Potential for inequality. – Inadequate in emergencies. – Ambiguity in implementation. – Risk of relativism and cultural limitations. – Neglect of virtue and character. – Difficulty of practical implementation.
Human rights	– Protect human dignity, essential equality and innate rights. – Provide universal moral standards. – Safeguard individuals from government and corporate abuses. – Serve as a foundation for international law and justice. – Promote social and democratic progress.	– Human rights are based more on consensus than on sound philosophical foundations. – Rights-based ethics overlooks moral duties and responsibilities. – Human rights reflect Western values rather than true universality. – Difficulties in enforcement and selective application. – Human rights rhetoric is sometimes used to justify political actions.
Care ethics	– Providing an alternative to impersonal ethics. – Emphasis on relationships. – Attention to the specific context of each situation. – Consideration of the moral importance of empathy, compassion and responsiveness. – Support for vulnerable groups.	– Lack of universal norms. – Risk of partiality. – Underdeveloped structural analysis. – Limited applicability in certain business contexts.
Personalist ethics	– The intrinsic value and dignity of every human being. – Consideration of the wholeness of the human person. – Emphasis on personal moral responsibility and concern for the common good. – Foundation for human rights. – Combination of rationality, sensibility and virtues. – Prominence of both personal freedom and solidarity. – Consideration of consequences and contextual circumstances. – Integration of universal principles with virtue ethics. – Inclusion of care and a sense of service. – Integration of spiritual and transcendent dimensions.	– Conceptually ambiguous. – Anthropocentrism. – Lack of objective norms and risk of subjectivism. – Inadequate treatment of social structures.

Kantian ethics

The Kantian approach has been employed in business ethics as a basis for ethical reasoning in decision-making,[46] and even as a foundation for textbooks in both business and management ethics.[47] Through the categorical imperative, Kantian ethics establishes a moral system, based on duty and universal principles, offering several advantages:

- *Promotes moral consistency*: Establishes clear and absolute duties and avoids moral relativism.
- *Encourages moral duty over personal gain*: Actions such as theft, lying and deception are universally forbidden, while keeping promises is always required.
- *Establishes universal moral laws*: Moral actions apply to all people in all situations.
- *Pushes respect for human dignity*: A strong duty in Kantian ethics is treating persons as ends in themselves, not mere means to an end.

Despite its strengths, Kantian ethics faces several objections:

- *Formalism and lack of practical guidance*: Kantian ethics provides abstract moral principles (maxims) but does not specify concrete actions or values. Individuals are expected to determine ethical actions themselves, guided by impartiality and universal reasoning, but without predefined moral content. This leaves moral agents without practical guidance in specific situations.
- *Rigidity and lack of context-sensitivity and concern for consequences*: Kantian ethics is absolute and allows no exceptions, which can lead to harmful moral duties. It can be objected that some situations may require balancing competing values and context, rather than rigid adherence to universal principles. Thus, if a company must downsize, Kantian ethics does not consider the consequences, focusing only on following an absolute moral rule.
- *Neglect of emotions and moral character*: Kant focuses only on rational duty, emphasizing the agent's goodwill in fulfilling moral law. This goodwill is developed through rational reasoning. Thus, he rejects the role of emotions and character development. Critics argue that moral behaviour is not just about reasoning but also about empathy for others and virtue.
- *Narrow view of moral motivation*: The only morally acceptable motivation in Kantian ethics is duty for duty's sake. Thus, in business, an action motivated by a desire to gain trust or build a good reputation would have no moral worth – because the agent is not acting purely out of duty. This position raises the question – Why can't duty and practical benefits work together? Shouldn't trust and duty be complementary rather than mutually exclusive?
- *A biased view of human autonomy*: Kant's categorical imperative assumes that moral law is self-imposed by rational agents rather than discovered through human nature or divine law. This differs from the pre-Kantian view of Aristotle and Aquinas, who saw human autonomy as the ability to discover moral laws that lead to human flourishing. Furthermore, Kant's version of autonomy replaces God as the moral legislator, making human reason the origin of moral law.

Utilitarianism

Utilitarianism is used in public policy, economics, and healthcare, influencing decisions in areas like cost–benefit analysis, balancing interests in environmental protection and in making regulations. Deciding in favour of the interests of the majority can be useful. However, this is not a guarantee of justice and respect for human rights. Some scholars and practitioners support and apply utilitarianism in business ethics.[48]

Among the strengths generally presented for utilitarianism are the following:

- *Promotes overall well-being*: This entails seeking satisfaction for the majority and minimizing suffering. In this sense it focuses on greatest societal benefit, even if it imposes minor inconveniences. One strength of this theory is its *concern for consequences of the action* for those affected by the action, and, therefore, it seeks to maximize the satisfaction of the majority.
- *Provides an impartial principle*: The utilitarian principle – the greatest happiness for the greater number – is applcable to everybody, preventing bias or favouritism.
- *Overcomes the rigidity of deontological principles*: such as the universal prohibition of not lying. However, some deontologists distinguish lying from legitimate defence by hiding the truth in extreme situations, for instance in keeping legitimate secrets or to protect people facing unjust aggressors.
- *Introduces the relevance of consequences*: Consequences can play a significant role in analysing the morality in decision-making.
- *Offers a tool for policymakers based on balancing the interests of people affected*: This can help to make decisions in areas related to welfare.

Utilitarianism has also received criticism and become problematic for several reasons:

- *Questionable hedonistic evaluative criteria*: This is a crucial problem. Usually, the criterion employed for evaluating consequences is pleasure, satisfaction or something useful. This is a hedonistic approach rather than one consistent with human flourishing.
- *Difficulty to measure consequences*: In many situations, it may not be easy to measure all the consequences of an action. The problem is even greater when calculating the subsequent consequences deriving from the action's primary effect. Thus, the immediate effect of a lay-off is unemployment, but this can cause depression, family problems, demoralization of people within the organization and so on.
- *Unethical means can be justified for good ends*: This introduces a problematic evaluation of some ethical dilemmas. While a deontological approach considers unacceptable certain actions such as lying and breaking promises, consequentialism would accept that the balances of consequences is positive. However, if unethical means can be justified for good ends, the whole system of morality is at risk.
- *Justice and human rights could not be respected*: Seeking happiness or satisfaction for the majoriy can lead to a lack of respect for minorities and there may even be a violation of human rights. In such cases, individuals can be harmed for the sake of the majority.

The main argument is that utilitarianism considers the social benefits of business activity, along with consideration of the negative social consequences of managerial decisions.[49] However, *utilitarianism* posits difficult questions in a business context. How should we evaluate right action regarding safety in the workplace? How can we compare the value of human life with economic costs? Should we sell substandard or unsafe products to a relatively small number of ignorant people for the sake of profits that would benefit the whole organization and thus serve many people? Should we lie or provide misleading information if doing so benefits a large majority?[50]

Regarding *ethical egoism*, we can add that *ethical egoism* can promote *selfishness* and disregard for others' well-being, potentially leading to harmful actions that ignore or undermine the welfare of society, which is contrary to the common sense of morality. In addition, this approach undermines social harmony. If everyone acted in self-interest alone, *social cohesion and mutual trust* could deteriorate, as individuals would be less inclined to help others unless it benefited them personally.

Virtue ethics

Virtue ethics, as noted, emphasizes character, moral excellence, and the development of virtues as the foundation of ethical life. This provides an alternative approach contrasting with deontology (Kantian ethics) or consequentialism (utilitarianism), which respectively focus on duties and outcomes. Aristotle's ethics shaped modern virtue ethics, moral philosophy, and political theory. As noted (2.1), in the past few decades, virtue ethics has grown in popularity, and several scholars have presented neo-Aristotelian approaches to business ethics.[51] Macintyre's thought, in the Aristotelian tradition, has also been applied to business ethics.[52] Stoic ethics remains popular today mainly in self-help, resilience training, and modern mindfulness, while its use in business ethics is quite limited.

The main strengths of virtue ethics in the Aristotelian tradition are these:

- *Focuses on human flourishing (eudaimonia)*: Virtue ethics entails moral evaluation of the actions; however, this is not just about right and wrong actions, but about living a meaningful, fulfilling life. In this sense, being a person with moral qualities is not just about following rules, but about becoming a person with integrity as a human being.
- *Seeks to promote the moral character of the agent*: This is not just about making tools available for evaluating particular actions. Virtues shape an individual's character, providing stable dispositions for good behaviour. Thus, a just person does not simply act with justice in one situation but also has a permanent disposition of acting with justice. The same can be said of an honest, generous or courageous person of acting in accordance with these virtues.
- *Considers context and consequences*: Virtues are placed in the 'golden mean' between two extreme vices: excess and deficiency – courage, for instance, between cowardice and rashness– and this should be determined in each situation. This takes the place of the virtue of practical wisdom, which provides capacity for good judgement when considering context and foreseeable consequences.

- *Recognizes the importance of emotions that are guided by practical wisdom*: Thus, emotions are neither unreliable, unlike Kantian ethics, nor are they the exclusive driver of good behaviour.
- *Emphasizes moral education and human development*: Aristotle saw moral development as a lifelong process learned through practice, role models and community, not only in being able to apply rules.

Critics of virtue ethics claim several weaknesses:

- *Lack of clear guidance for moral decision-making*: Unlike Kantian ethics, which provides universal moral rules, or utilitarianism, which focuses on calculating happiness, virtue ethics lacks specific ethical rules for action. The typical response from virtue ethicists is that virtuous individuals know how to act with justice, generosity, courage, etc., in each situation based on his or her moral character and experience.
- *The 'golden mean' of virtues can be vague*: The idea that virtue lies between two extremes can be unclear in complex moral situations. For instance, what is the 'mean' between arrogance and self-deprecation? Different people may disagree on where the appropriate balance – or the virtuous mean – lies. However, this challenge was already anticipated by Aristotle, who argued that the golden mean is what a wise person would determine in a given situation.
- *Necessity of a long moral development to make sound ethical judgements*: Virtue ethics requires a long-term process of moral development, rather than serving as a quick decision-making tool. To develop practical wisdom, individuals must cultivate virtues over time. Those who lack strong moral character and practical wisdom may need to seek guidance from wise individuals when faced with ethical dilemmas. However, practical wisdom can serve as a guiding path for young or less virtuous individuals, through maxims or norms, helping them in their moral and ethical development.
- *Different conceptions of good life*: The concept of the *good life* can differ depending on the person, making it an inappropriate ethical reference point. Aristotelians might respond by acknowledging that, while individuals can indeed have their own views of the good life, certain aspects of human fulfilment, such as justice, honesty and generosity, are easily recognizable and understandable to ordinary people.
- *Diversity of cultural assessments of virtues*: Different cultures may prioritize certain virtues over others. Some cultures may value justice over courage, while others may prioritize solidarity over self-interest. This has led to the argument that virtue ethics is culturally dependent, unlike human rights or deontological ethics, which claim universality. However, the key reference point for virtue ethics should not be social preferences but rather the contribution of virtues to human flourishing in accordance with human nature. Additionally, there is evidence of a core set of fundamental virtues, with some cultural variations, that are shared across major religious and philosophical traditions worldwide.
- *Possible conflicts in virtue-based judgements*: A common example of virtue conflict is whether a leader should fight for justice at all costs (courage) or prioritize peace and compromise (moderation). Similarly, one may face a conflict between loyalty to one's company and loyalty to one's family. In such dilemmas, practical wisdom can help harmonize conflicts. Practical wisdom recognizes the relational nature of persons and the differing significance

of their bonds, as well as how properly lived relationships contribute to personal growth.[53] If uncertainty remains, advice from wise people can aid in situations of doubt.

Contractualism

Contractualist ethics emphasize the importance of reaching consensus in a pluralistic society, where individuals hold diverse values and beliefs, rather than focusing on specific substantive norms, duties or outcomes.

Contractualism is praised because it:

- *Facilitates consensus in pluralistic societies*: Contractualist views, such as Gauthier's *Morals by Agreement*, illustrate how social cooperation can be built through rational agreement. Similarly, procedural ethics emphasize the necessity of reaching consensus to resolve social conflicts while ensuring fair and impartial decision-making processes.
- *Aligns with enlightened self-interest*: This resonates with certain business mindsets that prioritize mutual advantage and operate under a notion of the 'social contract'.

Criticisms of contractualism include:

- *Ethics is treated as a product of negotiated agreements*: This reflects an individualistic perspective, portraying individuals primarily as self-interested agents rather than members of a moral community. In doing so, contractualism overlooks broader dimensions of morality. Ethics is not solely based on rational agreement – it also involves intrinsic values, virtues, emotions, and duties that cannot always be reduced to contracts.
- *Neglects moral obligations beyond mutual advantage*: Contractualism does not adequately account for ethical duties towards those who cannot reciprocate – such as the vulnerable, the disadvantaged or future generations.

Procedural ethics

Procedural ethics, and in particular discursive ethics have been considered as a foundation for business ethics[54] to reach agreements for issues, which permit a dialogue between all people involved. The legitimacy of moral norms arises not from authority, tradition or outcomes, but from the process of mutual agreement. In other words, ethical validity is not based on discussing what is really good, trying to understand or apply substantive moral norms, but on arguments judged as rational.

Discursive ethics and other procedural ethics are praised because they:

- *Provide a way to reach minimal common ethical agreements*. This can aid in resolving social issues, while remaining compatible with more demanding personal ethics.
- *Introduce principles of impartiality beyond simple consensus*: This involves injecting rationality into the factual agreements proposed by contractualist frameworks.

Common objections to procedural ethics include:

- *Primarily political rather than ethical*: Proceduralism was originally conceived as a political strategy for reaching consensus, rather than a true ethical theory grounded in moral philosophy.
- *Lack of moral substance*: By focusing solely on agreement, procedural ethics can lead to a 'value-neutral' stance, offering little guidance on what is morally right or wrong. In practice, this may allow morally questionable actions to be accepted if they follow agreed-upon procedures, bypassing deeper ethical evaluation.
- *Dependence on consensus*: The requirement for agreement can cause decision paralysis or lead to compromise solutions that fail to address the ethical complexities of a situation – especially in cases involving deeply rooted moral conflicts.
- *Potential for inequality*: Although theoretically all participate independently of their power and status, in practice, outcomes reached via procedural ethics may favour those with greater influence or resources, undermining the fairness that the approach seeks to promote.
- *Inadequate in emergencies*: Procedural ethics rely on deliberation, which can be too slow or impractical in urgent situations such as crises or emergencies.
- *Ambiguity in implementation*: Without clear guiding principles, procedural ethics can result in inconsistency or subjectivity, especially in complex or rapidly changing environments.
- *Risk of relativism and cultural limitations*: Emphasizing process over moral content may lead to ethical relativism. Moreover, what is considered consensual in one cultural context may not be acceptable in another, limiting cross-cultural applicability.
- *Neglect of virtue and character*: Like some forms of deontological ethics, procedural approaches often overlook the character and virtues of the individuals involved – elements central to many ethical traditions and crucial to understanding human behaviour.
- *Difficulty of practical implementation*: Achieving consensus on ethical matters is often challenging, except in limited situations where mutual agreement is relatively straightforward. Focusing on Rawls' theory of justice, Michael Sandel criticized its lack of realism, arguing that we are, by nature, 'encumbered' – that is, embedded in relationships and identities that make it impossible to adopt the hypothetical *veil of ignorance*. For example, our ties to family cannot simply be abstracted away. In response, Rawls clarified that his theory of justice was not a *metaphysical* theory but a *political* one – intended to guide fair agreement within democratic societies, not to represent an idealized ethical detachment.

Human rights

Human rights are often considered a relevant ethical approach that upholds human dignity, freedom and justice for all persons. Human rights in business are promoted by relevant international organizations, including the United Nations, presenting to companies the obligation to respect, protect and promote fundamental human rights in their operations, supply chains and corporate policies. This includes workers' rights, environmental responsibility, consumer protection and corporate social responsibility. While many argue that businesses should uphold human rights as a moral and legal duty, others challenge the extent and practicality of corporate human rights obligations.

To a great extent, human rights are widely applauded because they:

- *Protect human dignity, essential equality, and innate rights*: Both dignity and equality promote morality by ensuring that all individuals are treated with respect and fairness, regardless of nationality, race, gender or social status. Human rights are innate, existing prior to any legislation or government concession.
- *Provide universal moral standards*: Applicable to all people, countering cultural relativism. This ensures the prohibition of practices such as slavery and torture while promoting personal freedom.
- *Safeguard individuals from government and corporate abuses*: Prevent oppression and exploitation through laws against forced labour and discrimination, thereby holding governments and businesses accountable.
- *Serve as a foundation for international law and justice*: Foster dialogue on common ethical principles to ensure fair treatment of individuals and nations.
- *Promote social and democratic progress*: Encourage societies to evolve ethically, advocating for minority rights, gender equality, freedom of expression and protection for individuals with disabilities.

Critics express concerns or openly argue against human rights for several reasons:

- *Human rights are based more on consensus than on sound philosophical foundations*: This can allow for the introduction of questionable rights or ambiguous interpretations. The challenge lies in providing a solid foundation for human rights while ensuring careful scrutiny of interpretations and the addition of new rights.
- *Rights-based ethics overlooks moral duties and responsibilities*: While individuals have rights, they also have moral obligations. In other words, rights-based ethics is incomplete as a moral system because it focuses primarily on individual rights, sometimes neglecting duties to the community, family or nature. This also applies to business ethics. However, the counterargument is that rights and responsibilities should be complementary, not conflicting.
- *Human rights reflect Western values rather than true universality*: Some cultural traditions define dignity and rights differently, challenging the universality of human rights. The key issue is how to develop arguments grounded in the common biological and ontological human condition while allowing for cultural adaptability without compromising the core meaning of human rights.
- *Difficulties in enforcement and selective application*: Some argue that, for human rights to be effective, they must be legally codified, which is not always easy to achieve. Additionally, human rights laws are not always enforceable, leading to inconsistent application. Supporters counter that human rights should remain an aspirational ideal, even if enforcement is imperfect.

- *Human rights rhetoric is sometimes used to justify political actions*: Some nations use human rights as a political tool to pressure other countries while ignoring their own violations. However, this argument does not invalidate human rights as an ethical necessity – the existence of abuses in their application does not undermine their fundamental moral value.

Care ethics

Some work has been done in applying care ethics to specific business issues, particularly in contexts where justice alone appears insufficient – for instance, in crisis management[55] or within social enterprises. However, further research and practical initiatives are still needed to develop truly *caring organizations*. Strengths of care ethics include:

- *Providing an alternative to impersonal ethics*: Care ethics offers a more humane framework for leadership and corporate social responsibility, in contrast to universal, abstract and individualistic ethical models.
- *Emphasis on relationships*: Care ethics places crucial importance on interpersonal relationships as a key element in moral decision-making. It considers the effects of decisions on employees, customers, communities and other stakeholders – going beyond purely profit-driven motives.
- *Attention to the specific context of each situation*: Unlike rule-based approaches, care ethics emphasizes the relevance of situational factors and concurrent circumstances. This leads managers toward flexible responses rather than rigid policy enforcement, fostering human-centred decision-making.
- *Consideration of the moral importance of empathy, compassion and responsiveness*: These emotional and relational dimensions can humanize interactions that might otherwise be dominated by instrumental logic – particularly in leadership, people management, customer service and conflict resolution.
- *Support for vulnerable groups*: Care ethics prioritizes attentiveness to vulnerability and dependency, encouraging inclusive and equitable practices.

However, associated with these strengths are also several commonly noted weaknesses:

- *Lack of universal norms*: Care ethics lacks universally applicable rules or principles, which can be problematic in large organizations where standardized policies are necessary for consistency and fairness.
- *Risk of partiality*: Emphasizing empathy and close relationships can compromise impartiality in contexts requiring fairness and equal treatment – such as hiring, promotion or disciplinary processes. This may result in favouritism or nepotism.
- *Underdeveloped structural analysis*: By focusing primarily on interpersonal relationships, care ethics may underemphasize broader institutional or systemic issues such as power structures, problematic global supply chains or exploitative economic systems.

- *Limited applicability in certain business contexts*: Care ethics may be insufficient or difficult to apply in highly competitive or adversarial sectors (e.g. litigation, finance or sales), or when addressing conflicts between multiple stakeholders with opposing interests.

Undoubtedly, care ethics expands the moral scope beyond the limits of justice. Yet, one might ask why it is so often presented as an alternative or opposition to justice. The underlying question remains: *Are care and justice truly opposites – or could they, in fact, be complementary?*

Personalist ethics

Proposals related to business ethics, drawing from different personalist philosophers, have been presented.[56] However, a comprehensive application of personalist ethics to business practice is still pending. As mentioned, there are different forms of personalist ethics (2.1), but some plausible commonalities can be identified in many of them. These include:

- *The intrinsic value and dignity of every human being*: Unlike utilitarianism, which measures morality by hedonistic happiness, personalism affirms that human dignity is inviolable, regardless of utility. In practical terms, this requires not only avoiding treating humans as mere means but also actively assuming responsibility towards others. This unconditional respect for each human person echoes the Kantian second formulation of the categorical imperative, though personalism is grounded in a different philosophical tradition that offers a broader scope.
- *Consideration of the wholeness of the human person*: This includes both individual and relational-social dimensions, as the starting point for ethical reflection. Personalism considers not only rationality but also the emotion, relationships, spirituality and social aspects of human existence.
- *Emphasis on personal moral responsibility and concern for the common good*: Personalist ethics encourages individuals to act as moral agents with a deep sense of responsibility towards others, the environment and society. The common good is central to its social ethics.
- *Foundation for human rights*: Personalist ethics provides a sound ethical basis for universal human rights and social justice. It supports the view that human rights are intrinsic, not merely social constructs.
- *Combination of rationality sensibility and virtues*: Personalist ethics recognizes that ethical decisions are shaped not only by rational analysis but also by empathy, relational understanding and the cultivation of virtues.
- *Prominence of both personal freedom and solidarity*: Personalist ethics fosters a balance between communal support and respect for individual autonomy, offering guidance for building communities that goes beyond mere organizational structures.
- *Consideration of consequences and contextual circumstances*: Drawing on the importance of practical wisdom, personalist ethics considers the particularities of each situation, avoiding the rigid, rule-based morality often associated with Kantian formalism.

- *Integration of universal principles with virtue ethics*: Seeks to overcome the dichotomy between duty-based universal principles and the virtues that shape moral character.
- *Inclusion of care and a sense of service*: These are central principles and virtues of personalist ethics.
- *Integration of spiritual and transcendent dimensions*: Some personalists, such as Maritain and Wojtyla, argue that human dignity is rooted in transcendence, with God as the ultimate source of moral law. In this regard, Catholic Social Teaching is often associated with personalist ethics.

Despite its strengths, personalist ethics has been subject to several criticisms. Among them the following:

- *Conceptually ambiguous*: Since it encompasses various theories, personalist ethics can appear conceptually ambiguous. For example, dialogue-based ethics differs from ontological personalism, which in turn differs from phenomenological-ontological approaches. This ambiguity can be addressed either by focusing on a specific strand or by drawing from compatible elements across different approaches.
- *Anthropocentrism*: Critics argue that personalism prioritizes human dignity above all else and fails to provide sufficient moral consideration for non-human animals or the natural environment. In contrast, ecological ethics often embraces biocentrism (valuing all forms of life equally) or deep ecology (viewing humans as part of a broader ecosystem). Personalists may respond by emphasizing the superior dignity of humans while still recognizing the intrinsic value of non-human beings and the importance of environmental protection – both of which are acknowledged in several personalist frameworks.
- *Lack of objective norms and risk of relativism*: By placing strong emphasis on personal moral responsibility, personalist ethics is sometimes seen as leaning towards subjectivism, a form of relativism. While this is a legitimate concern, personalism defends objective values such as dignity, from which norms can be derived. Moreover, practical wisdom, including guidance from morally wise individuals, can help prevent ethical relativism.
- *Inadequate treatment of social structures*: Some critics argue that personalist ethics focuses too much on interpersonal relationships (e.g. the 'I–Thou' dynamic) and not enough on analysing systemic issues, such as institutional injustice, systemic racism or corporate misconduct. The frequent emphasis on interpersonal ethics by personalist authors does not, however, exclude concern for the common good or structural critique. In business ethics, the challenge remains to develop more robust guidance for navigating institutional and economic complexities.

All things considered, personalist ethics appears promising for business ethics. It highlights the unconditional dignity of every human being and the importance of moral flourishing, which involves cultivating virtues and doing good for others. Combining personalism and virtue ethics is possible.[57] Furthermore, the main objections to personalist ethics can be addressed or mitigated. In Section B of this chapter, the essentials of an Aristotelian-personalist ethics approach will be presented, combining elements of personalism and Aristotelian virtue ethics.

2.4 Searching for a complete ethical theory

The existence of so many ethical theories (Table 2.1), all of them with strengths and weaknesses, can be perplexing. Besides multiplicity, each theory has its own assumptions (metaethics) and adopts different focuses; some on goods achieved with the action (consequentialism), others on principles or norms to evaluate the action (deontologism), and a third group centred on virtues which foster good behaviour (virtue ethics). Some theories focus on universal principles, while others take the singularity of each situation as their focal point. A third problem is that not every ethical theory covers the personal, organizational and societal dimensions of business ethics (1.5), which introduces a reductionist view of business because of the narrow view of the underlying ethical theory. Despite these difficulties, business ethics requires sound ethical theory.

Are ethical pluralism or pragmatist ethics the solution?

Some have tried to solve the problem of the multiplicity of theories, suggesting that every theory about what is 'right' and 'wrong' (moral norms) is worthy of respect, even though they may be incompatible and/or incommensurable (*Theory of Moral Pluralism*). Under this perspective, the solution would be to apply several theories or applying one of them to certain situations and other theories to different situations. However, this allows us to ignore some theories and the criticisms that have been made against them. It also introduces the problem of which theory to choose in the case of obtaining contradictory results. In addition, this 'moral pluralism', which ultimately is a form of relativism, favours opportunism by opening the door to choosing the theory that better justifies one's own interests.

Other proposals come from *pragmatist ethics*,[58] a view that one deliberates without adopting any specific ethical theory nor making any reference to moral truths. Rather it focuses on social acceptability, which changes over time and depends on each society. However, diverse theories may be considered since each of them presents certain relevant ethical aspects (duties involved, foreseeable consequences, virtues applicable, sensibility of people's needs and so on) without full acceptance of any particular one. In the field of business ethics, a pragmatist approach could be combining different theories 'with personal, cultural, psychological, cognitive, and context related factors for ethical decision-making.'[59]

Pragmatists are correct in highlighting the incompleteness of most current ethical theories. However, it is questionable whether the best solution is to rely on personal opinion by combining various theories, each with different philosophical foundations, or by accepting social approval as the sole criterion of morality. Although pragmatic ethics does not explicitly present itself as relativistic, in practice it often leads to moral relativism (1.9).

Supporters of these two positions may consider themselves open-minded people and even accuse those favouring a particular theory of being partisan. However, a truly open-minded person, after listening to different proposals, tries to discern and seek the best theory and, as much as possible, the moral truth.

When reflecting on the history of ethical thought and sound ethical theory, a key question arises: Is ethics solely about applying principles to determine the 'right action' or is it about identifying a 'good action' that enhances the moral quality of the acting individual? In other words, is ethics focused on principles or virtues? Alternatively, one might wonder whether both principles and virtues are integral aspects of ethics.

'Right action' vs. 'good action'

The goal of the theories based on rationalistic principles, such as Kantianism or utilitarianism, also termed 'rule ethics', is to evaluate what a *right action* is. In contrast, 'virtue ethics', in the Aristotelian tradition, is centred on achieving *human good* and ultimately human excellence through *virtues*. In the latter approach, the focus is not on the right action, according to certain rules, but on the *good action*, which contributes to human excellence.

Deliberation on the 'good action' requires 'practical wisdom' – a crucial virtue in Aristotelian ethics (2.1), which helps one to discern what is good, beyond rules, by considering each situation independently, as they are often not 'black or white'. In practice, people may use this wisdom, even ignoring its name. Empirical research shows that in the everyday activity of organizations, which includes many particular situations, moral reasoning is based more on practical wisdom than on theories or codes of conduct.[60]

Another important distinction relates to who determines the morality of an action. There is *third-person ethics* (associated with rule-based ethics) and *first-person ethics* (associated with virtue ethics).[61] In third-person ethics, ethical experts determine what is morally correct, for example, by evaluating the consequences of an action in utilitarian terms and calculating the greatest good for the greatest number (2.2). In contrast, first-person ethics involves the agent making the moral judgement, guided by practical wisdom and possibly advised by a wise person. First-person ethics, therefore, relies on personal judgement for each specific action – what some traditions refer to as a 'moral judgement of conscience' or simply 'conscience'. We will return to this theme later in this book (4.2).

Ethical principles and codes can serve as guidelines and are very useful for alerting less virtuous people against forbidden actions, but the immediate norm of morality is one's own wise judgement. Notice that first-person ethics is different from subjectivism (1.9), which refuses any objective ethics.

Towards a complete ethical theory

Another question regards the incompleteness of many ethical theories. Deontologism, as noted (2.2), focuses only on principles and disregards the consequences of the human action, while utilitarianism and other consequentialisms emphasize consequences and forget personal duties. On its side, utilitarianism includes a principle (the greater happiness for the greater number) and the consideration of goods (consequences) of the action (although reduced to utilitarian goods). Care ethics leaves out universal principles as well as most virtues, and reduces ethics to care and maintaining relationships.

Apart from incompleteness regarding principles and goods, these theories ignore the role of the agent's character and therefore the role of virtues understood as good stable dispositions of the character. Virtue ethics, obviously, includes virtues and often human goods required for human fulfilment, but principles are not generally considered.

In conclusion, we can affirm that certain ethical theories exhibit incompleteness, and, as several thinkers have pointed out, ethics encompasses goods, norms and virtues. In this regard, Koslowski asserts that 'ethical theory aims at the theory of virtues, the theory of goods, and the theory of duties'.[62] Similarly, Polo emphasizes that 'a complete ethics must include goods, norms, and virtues'.[63] MacIntyre agrees, adding that "virtues, rules and goods must be understood in their mutual relationship".[64]

This mutual connection can be understood by taking goods (ethical values) as the starting point, with virtues facilitating the achievement of these goods (as the ends of virtues), while moral principles express the moral duties required to act in accordance with these goods. By adhering to principles (norms), individuals develop virtues, and goods help define the content of those virtues. In turn, virtues strengthen principles, and principles guide behaviour towards the realization of goods (see Figure 2.1).

In summary, a complete ethical theory must integrate goods, principles and virtues in their mutual relationship. In Section B, it will be suggested that this aim can be achieved outlining a particular approach.

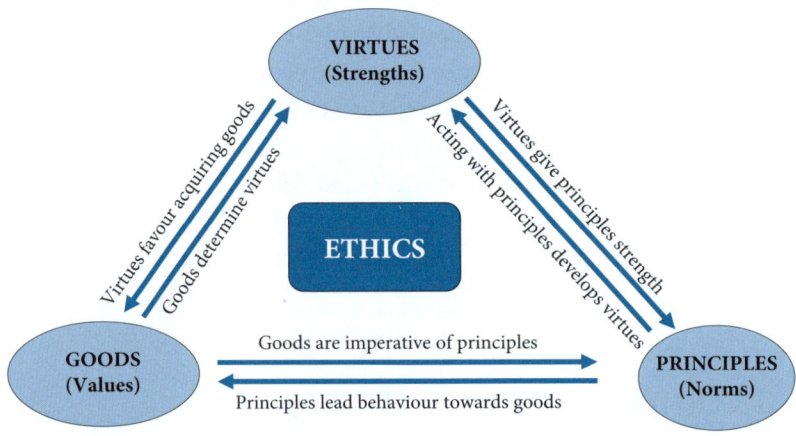

Figure 2.1 Interconnection of goods, principles and virtues

Business Ethics in Action #2

The person-centred vision of François Michelin[65]

The French company Michelin has its origins in a small factory established in 1832 to produce vulcanized rubber products for the manufacture of seals, belts, valves and pipes that could be used in agricultural machinery. Once an English cyclist came to Clermont-Ferrand, a French village, looking for a rubber patch to repair a tyre. Jules Michelin, a member of the owning family, made the repairs in two hours and then suddenly thought about the need for tyres in general. Six months afterwards, he invented the tyre that could be dismounted and changed in a few minutes.

Many years later, in 1946, there was another great innovation in Michelin: the radial. It was born out of the difficulties experienced with the standard tyre, with which cars could go no faster than 80 miles per hour without suffering a blow-out. The radial gives three times more mileage than a conventional model, allows a reduction in fuel consumption and gives a more comfortable ride. Its invention was thanks to Marius Mignol, a Michelin employee who had joined the company as a typist in the printing department. Within the company, Mignol's creativity and talent were appreciated, and he was promoted to technical functions.

Today, Michelin Group is a global company. François Michelin (1926–2015), the great-grandson of Jules, was at the helm of Michelin for over half a century and then became honorary president of the company. He has a particular 'business philosophy' – inherited, in part, from his family understanding that a factory 'conjures up notions of machines, things that are produced, and, most importantly, men and women who are employees, customers and shareholders'.[66] Moreover, he states that property is unappropriate when it is not at the service of people.

François' vision is that every human being is unique and unrepeatable. It is not his or her job or job title but being a person that determines who he or she is. He believes that a manager must treat all of his workers individually and with great respect, just as his grandfather used to do, addressing a worker as 'Sir'. François underlines that 'the most important aspect of the human being is that he is self-teachable'.

François Michelin has great confidence in the human person:

> All that man asks for is to be allowed to surpass himself and become what he is. As soon as you give him the means to do so, you acknowledge all the glorious splendour of his humanity. Any man that you can look at straight in the face, regarding him as a unique individual who is free and responsible, blazes forth like a light as dazzling as the sun. When I think of everything that could be accomplished if one could release all the energy found in human beings![67]

Meanwhile, every action in business remains a reflection of the freedom and responsibility of the person who performs it. Michelin reminds us of the Golden Rule, according to which one should not do to others what one would not want done to oneself. Being a Christian,

Michelin often recalls that human beings have been created in the image and likeness of God, which provides every individual with an incomparable dignity: the dignity of being a person. This is why one of the elements that differentiates the company is their emphasis on the individual treatment of workers, listening to them and to their deepest motivations, giving them the opportunity to develop talents inside and outside the plant. He points out that people have all the means to better themselves or to destroy themselves,[68] and he believes that work gives each person the opportunity not only to build certain goods but also to grow themselves as human beings.

One of the company's most important characteristics is the importance of fair treatment for the customer. Transactions between a producer and buyer have to respect a code of ethics. A person has no right to lie – François underlines – and you should always be asking yourself if what you are doing is good. 'Truth is greater than you are.'[69] Acting on the truth is, however, insufficient. According to François, it is also necessary to love and accept other people as they are. Passing that message on to the generations to come is one of his keenest desires.

François Michelin's approach to business entails treating employees and customers with respect and promoting the personal growth of his staff. He spoke of 'the sanctity of fair treatment for the customer' and implemented ethical norms through a code, not in a formal or cold manner, but with an emphasis on honesty: 'no right to lie', he used to say. At the same time, he advocated for practical wisdom, advising, 'if you are not always asking yourself if what you are doing is good, you slip'.

Today, Michelin manufactures and sells tyres for all kinds of vehicles in more than 170 countries and accounts for 70 per cent of the replacement tyre market. Behind the success of the radial, which established Michelin as the most important tyre producer in the world, constant innovation and development are always in focus. One of the latest advances of Michelin are tyres integrated in digital systems; another, the development of a complete coherent pressure monitoring system – the *EnTire Solution*.

Another frequent saying of François was, 'The means to an end are as important as the end itself.' Aligned with this spirit, the corporate website[70] presents Michelin's corporate values, emphasizing 'the way of reaching our goals is just as important as the results themselves' and adds, that Michelin is attached to values of respect, shared by all, which are set out in multiple pillars:

- *Respect for clients*: Innovate relentlessly for the success of our customers and set our priorities accordingly.
- *Respect for people*: Care for every person inside and outside our company and earn their trust through our integrity.
- *Respect for shareholders*: Strive to earn and keep shareholders' trust and act to create sustainable shareholder value.
- *Respect for the environment*: Act for the sustainable development of our partners, the society and the planet.
- *Respect for facts*: Utilize facts to learn, honestly challenge our beliefs and guide our actions with agility.

* * *

> François Michelin's vision embodies a profound understanding of the human being, recognizing the intrinsic dignity and uniqueness of every employee, each of whom deserves to be treated individually and with great respect. He had immense confidence in his employees, acknowledging that the most important aspect of a person is their capacity to self-learn and grow within the company. This vision likely contributed significantly to Marius Mignol's invention, which was crucial for Michelin.
>
> Michelin's philosophy also emphasizes the role of property and the purpose of the company. Property, in his view, has value when it serves people. The factory is not merely a capital asset owned by shareholders but a union of people and resources, where individuals are central – not reduced to mere 'human resources'.
>
> This anthropological vision was passed down to him by his father and grandfather and was further reinforced by his Christian faith, which teaches that human beings are created in the image and likeness of God, giving every individual unparalleled dignity.
>
> While certain principles and ethical norms guided François's leadership, his consistent exemplary behaviour over many years suggests that he was a truly virtuous person.

SECTION B. ESSENTIALS OF ARISTOTELIAN-PERSONALIST ETHICS

Facing the problems of some ethical theories discussed in Section A, and the necessity of a complete ethical theory with interrelated goods (values), virtues (strengths) and principles (norms), this section presents the ethical approach recommended in this book. It integrates the Aristotelian virtue ethics tradition (2.1) with modern personalist philosophy,[71] developed by various authors under the concept of 'personalism'.[72] Though there are nuances, these perspectives are centred on the notion of the person, emphasizing the wholeness and uniqueness of each individual, who is endowed with inherent dignity and a calling to flourish as a human being. As we will discuss, this approach entails the integration of goods, principles and virtues, all centred around the goal of personal growth in human excellence as the ultimate aim of ethics.

We begin this section with a brief presentation of the notion of the person and the inherent human dignity of every human being. This is followed by an exploration of how human goods, moral principles and virtues are mutually connected.

2.5 The human person – inherent dignity, innate rights and the pursuit of human fulfilment

Reflection on the human being, as that on morality, began in Ancient Greece and has continued over time. Aristotle defined the human being as an animal who possesses reason (logos) and sociability. Being 'animal' entails *corporeity*, identified as a body, with analogies of highly evolved animals, but also 'rational' expressing a spiritual element called *soul* by Aristotle and other ancient Greek philosophers.[73] This spiritual element is inferred from certain human characteristics that seem irreducible to matter. These include self-consciousness – the ability to reflect on oneself and one's actions; the possession of abstractive cognition – the ability to grasp abstract concepts beyond the material world; and conscious self-determination – the capacity to choose freely and direct one's actions according to moral principles or rational thought.

Moreover, the human being is marked by the capacity for benevolence, including gift-love, an ability to give selflessly and form deep relationships, which surpasses biological or survival instincts. Lastly, humans have an inherent search for meaning, a willingness to explore and understand the purpose of existence, transcending mere material satisfaction. These qualities described underline the spiritual dimension of human existence, suggesting that humans are not only physical beings but are also oriented towards transcendence.

Current cognitive psychology uses the term mind, which bears similarities to the concept of the soul, though not with the same meaning as that used by ancient and medieval philosophers. The mind refers to a set of cognitive faculties, including consciousness, mental perception, thinking, judgement and language. In addition, cognitive psychology often refers to the human psyche, which encompasses both the cognitive and affective dimensions of human experience, acting as an intermediate element between the brain and the spirit.

The notion of 'human person'

Thus, the human being can be understood as body, mind and spirit into a unified whole in a *psychosomatic-spiritual unity*. This concept acknowledges that human experiences and actions arise from the complex interaction between the physical, mental and spiritual aspects of our existence. The psychosomatic-spiritual unity, expressing human-wholeness, is included in the notion of person, although this notion is richer than that.

The roots of the notion of person can be traced back to Greco-Roman antiquity, denoting the singularity of each human individual. In the Middle Ages, 'person' was seen as a *rational subsisting being*,[74] that is, as an individual entity with their own distinct 'being' (real existence), endowed with rationality, which encompasses the capacity for abstract understanding, reasoning, self-awareness, establishing conscious relationships and making deliberate choices. Modern philosophy lost the notion of 'person' as a being, emphasizing the self as individual consciousness and self-awareness. However, contemporary personalism has recuperated and even expanded the notion of person as a *subsisting being*. Additionally, some personalist authors[75] have incorporated *subjectivity* as a key feature of the person. Subjectivity embraces oneself as a subject with inner experiences, thoughts, feeling and intimacy, which is close to self-awareness, central to modern philosophy.

Personalism emphasizes that every person is someone unique and irrepressible; not 'something' but 'someone',[76] neither an anonymous subject nor just a simple individual of the human species, but one with a rich inner life, social links and a biography. In short, the person is not a 'what' but a 'who'.[77] This perspective, which entails personal freedom along with relationability and sociability, contrasts with other philosophical anthropologic approaches in which the individual is diluted to a collective or is reduced to someone who possesses interests and preferences, as given ends, and rationality to optimized means of these ends.

Intrinsic human dignity and innate rights

Human dignity refers to the intrinsic worth of each human being, regardless of external factors such as social status, accomplishments or physical abilities. Human dignity has been emphasized from the Middle Ages to our present day. Aquinas affirmed that 'the name «person» was given to signify those who held high dignity'.[78] In the Renaissance, human dignity is especially highlighted.[79] In the eighteenth century, the philosopher Immanuel Kant emphasized that things have a price, while persons have dignity.[80] Kant grounds such dignity in human autonomy, in the fact that a person gives ends to him- or herself, and so belongs to the 'the kingdom of ends'. Nowadays, the *Universal Declaration of Human Rights* states that all human beings are born equal in dignity.[81]

Personalist philosophers strongly emphasize the intrinsic human dignity of every person, but not only based on autonomy, like Kant, or because of human's physical or cognitive abilities but from radical features of the person, including self-determination, personal knowledge, self-transcendence and capacity for benevolent behaviour. They emphasize the great worth of the person and an intrinsic value superior to all earthly things. This is an *ontological dignity* – rooted in being human – and therefore independent of sex, state, age or condition. A dignity, which cannot be lost.

Theological perspectives reinforce philosophical arguments. Thus, in the Judeo-Christian tradition, human dignity is seen as a reflection of being made in the image of God called to a transcendent destiny beyond mere material existence. In Islam, the Qur'an describes human beings as *khalifas* (stewards) of the earth, giving each person a unique dignity tied to his or her moral responsibilities.

Human *ontological dignity* contrasts with other forms of dignity like *dignity of the office*, conferred by certain relevant positions within society (judges, presidencies, etc.) or *moral dignity*, derived of from exemplary behaviour. This latter can be eroded by bad behaviour or by committing crimes, while the ontological dignity remains.

As noted in the previous chapter (1.8), human dignity is often considered to be a universal and crucial ethical value in the sense of honouring and respecting every human being, along with a set of rights – human rights closely connected to human dignity.[82] Human rights are *innate* and exist independently of any legal framework because they are inherent to the person. Innate rights remain inviolable and inalienable, even when they are disregarded or violated by governments or communities. Just as with human dignity, human rights are intrinsic to every person and are essential in establishing social harmony and peace. We will return to human rights below (2.7).

The pursuit of human fulfilment

Persons, in their corporeality, undergo physical development when they receive appropriate nourishment. However, the development of the whole human being cannot be reduced to just the physical aspect. Humans can learn through education and action, developing stable dispositions that influence behaviour. These stable dispositions or *habits* are known as *virtues*, and they are oriented towards the development of the noblest human capacities, including intellect and will, as well as the moderation of the affective sphere. The necessity for such development is felt as an internal experience – an inner calling to grow and achieve fulfilment as a human being. Thus, the concept of human fulfilment emerged.

Human fulfilment, often asimilated to human flourishing,[83] refers to the realization of human potential in areas unique to human beings. Aristotle describes human fulfilment, or *eudaimonia*, as the ultimate end (*telos*) of human life, characterized by a sense of deep joy or inner happiness. According to Aristotle, eudaimonia is achieved through virtuous activity in accordance with reason, cultivated over the course of a complete life. Aristotle also emphasizes the importance of friendship (*philia*) as an essential element of a good life, particularly in the form of mutual goodwill and shared virtues between friends.

In the Middle Ages, Aquinas, integrating Aristotelian thought with Christian theology, viewed love as the highest virtue, essential for both divine and human flourishing. Some contemporary scholars and philosophers also emphasize benevolence and love as crucial components of human flourishing, extending and complementing Aristotle's original framework.

Personalist philosophers, generally speaking, acknowledge the importance of *human fulfilment* (the orientation of human life toward an ultimate end) from the perspective of benevolence and love. However, their focus remains on the person, emphasizing *personal growth* – that is, human flourishing as achieved by each person.

After this brief introduction to the concept of the person, along with the inherent dignity and the pursuit of fulfilment, let us now turn to the understanding of moral goods, principles and virtues.

2.6 Moral goods (ethical values) and the common good

The notion of moral good was crucial in the first ethical reflection of Greek philosophers, along with virtues (2.1). According to Aristotle, the notion of 'good' can be identified with the end pursued by an action – not necessarily understood in moral terms. In other words, every human action is carried out to achieve a certain aim, which appears as 'good', something attractive or interesting for some reason. Thus, goods become motives for acting. Since a good can be recognized as a value for the agent, goods can also be termed 'values' (1.10) – a term introduced by modern psychology.

Aristotle identified three different types of desirable goods: *useful, pleasant* and *honest* or *moral* goods. In the economic sphere, when talking about goods, they are typically understood as useful goods, while in ethics, the focus is on moral goods. However, all these types of goods are present in human life – and, of course, in business.

Real goods vs. apparent goods

As MacIntyre points out, 'for an Aristotelian view, the questions posed by the moral philosopher and the questions posed by the plain person are to an important degree inseparable'. He adds that a reflective person will move beyond the instant attraction of a good and question whether the aim of their action will *really* be good. This question about the good of one's action leads to a rational inquiry: 'What is really good for me, as a human being and beyond my desires?' This in turn leads to a more philosophical question: 'What is the good, as such, for human beings, as such?'[84]

Recognizing what is *truly good* as the end of an action is indeed a crucial question in ethics – and for human life. According to Aristotelian ethics (2.2) human excellence and human fulfilment (*eudaimonia*) (2.1) are the highest good. All other goods should refer to that ultimate end. This can be understood by considering that the excellence of a thing consists of whatever traits or qualities enable it to perform its function well. For example, the excellence of a knife is whatever enables it to cut effectively. Similarly, the highest human good is living in accordance with what fulfils one's potential as a human being – endowed with intellect and free will and accompanied by the affective sphere that includes feelings and emotions.

Business actions generally involve goods for the agent, which can simultaneously be *useful* (economic results), *pleasant* (satisfaction) and *moral* (contribution to human fulfilment). These goods can be mutually compatible and present in the same action. For instance, one may work in an honest activity (moral good), enjoy the work (pleasant good) and earn money for it (useful good). The problem arises when obtaining useful or pleasant goods conflicts with a moral good. In such cases, the aim of the action is merely an *apparent good*, not a *real good* for the person.

Conflicts between *moral goods* (*ethical values*) and other types of goods (*values*) are inherent to human life, and business is no exception. Often, businesses may be profitable but immoral. While one option is to follow spontaneous desire without reflection, this is not necessarily the best choice.

When faced with different types of goods, it is reasonable to establish a hierarchy of goods (or values). Humans possess *self-governance*, which involves ordering goods. A right self-governance gives pre-eminence to moral goods over useful and pleasant ones when a conflict arises. However, it is often possible to find ways to harmonize different types of goods. Ethics, in essence, provides guidelines that give *priority to moral goods* over other types of goods. For a responsible person, a right self-governance comes before self-determination in decision-making.

Practical reason (1.10), oriented to evaluate what is most convenient in each situation considering life in its integrity – reinforced by the virtue of *practical wisdom* (2.1, 2.8) – plays an important role in discerning real goods from apparent goods.

Basic goods for the person

From this perspective, three basic types of goods – encompassing many others – can be identified, each contributing to human excellence. These goods correspond respectively to the intellect, the will and the whole life: (1) *truth* (pertaining to the intellect); (2) *benevolence* (pertaining to the will); and (3) *fully human life,* involving the person as a whole, harmonizing impulses, emotions and desires with rational faculties.

Truth

Truth as a moral good refers to the idea that truthfulness – both in knowing and expressing the truth – is a fundamental element of ethical behaviour. According to a classical definition originating in the Middle Ages, truth is the correspondence between reality and the intellect (*adæquatio rei et intellectus*). This definition implies that recognizing, acknowledging and acting in accordance with the truth is essential for aligning one's actions with the reality of the world and other beings. Acting truthfully allows one to live authentically and honestly, which forms the basis for many moral interactions.

Humans are naturally inclined to seek knowledge, and the human intellect, in exploring the world and oneself, strives to discover truth – that is, to attain an accurate understanding of reality. Achieving this requires a sincere attitude, with the goal of understanding and describing reality as accurately and objectively as possible. Recognizing truth is a good achieved when the intellectual perception of reality corresponds to what truly exists.

Recognizing truth enables individuals to align their actions with reality, leading to informed decision-making and a deeper understanding of life. As with any other good, truth is presented as an aim – the pursuit of correct knowledge of reality, avoiding falsehoods.

The recognition of truth involves understanding both particular and universal truths (theoretical knowledge), and knowing how to act in particular situations (practical knowledge). This dual understanding allows us to discern what is truly good and directs our choices towards it.

Beauty is another good that could be included in this category, though it transcends pure knowledge since it also involves emotional elements.

In a certain sense, all goods (as discussed below) involve walking in truth. In other words, the recognition of truth allows one to act in accordance with what is known to be true.

Benevolence

Benevolence as a moral good refers to the right aim of the will in treating others – whether persons, animals, plants, ecosystems or the divine – in accordance with their objective identity.[85] Derived from the Latin *bene* (good) and *volere* (to wish), benevolence expresses a goodwill that is not merely reduced to feelings of kindness, good intentions, or moral duty but instead reflects the proactive wish to do good, treating others properly in accordance with their according to their respective being (ontological nature). In this way, benevolence is the orientation of a properly directed self-determination, guiding human autonomy. It is important to insist that benevolence refers not to feelings but to the will, making it a form of *rational benevolence*.

Regarding *human beings*, benevolence firstly requires the recognition of others as persons – like oneself – endowed with inherent human dignity and innate human rights, and acting with *justice* respecting dignity and human rights. It also implies fairness in exchanges and actions, characterized by *reciprocity*. In a broader sense, benevolence entails generosity and concern for the well-being and personal growth of others. It can extend to *love of benevolence*, which is expressed through giving without expecting anything in return, although a benefit may occur. Benevolence, often accompanied by self-denial, is widely regarded as the noblest form of human relationship.

While exchange and reciprocity are based on the principle of *quid pro quo* – 'giving something in return for something' – the love of benevolence involves giving 'for the sake of the other', as noted, without expecting anything in return. The former follows the 'logic of interest', whereas the latter follows the 'logic of gift'.

Other moral goods or ethical values can be included within the basic good of benevolence. These, apart from justice, include *honesty*, *kindness*, *compassion* (mercy), *care* and *generous service* for the welfare and personal growth of others, as well as solidarity and friendship. *Beneficence* is another expression of benevolence, involving generous giving to those who are vulnerable, marginalized or in need.

Love of benevolence also extends to one's relationship with the *divine*. Recognizing God as the Supreme Being and Creator, as in the Abrahamic religions, entails worship, spirituality and religious practices. In this context, benevolence involves doing good to oneself for inner enrichment while also recognizing and receiving love from God, establishing a deep connection with the divine.

Recognition of the truth concerning *non-rational beings* also has implications for benevolence. For example, recognizing the identities of animals obligates us to avoid cruelty and promote animal welfare. We will return to this point in our discussion of ecological ethics in Chapter 13.

Fully human life

Human life as a moral good refers to the recognition of fully human life as possessing inherent worth and dignity, making it the foundation of ethical considerations. Human life is valued not just for its utility or for the experiences it enables, but also for the intrinsic value that comes from being human and participating in human dignity. Human life is a primary good which gives support to others.

Being rational and spiritual beings, a fully human life involves not only the biological aspect but also, and mainly, exercising our rational capacity to guide and govern vital impulses and emotions. These natural impulses (e.g. desire for food, comfort or pleasure) and emotional responses (e.g. anger, fear, joy) are part of human life, but without self-mastery, they can dominate and detract from true flourishing as a human being.

The good of fully human life emphasizes the importance of respecting and protecting the sanctity of human life, preventing harm or suffering and promoting the possession of what is necessary for a dignified life, the well-being and fulfilment of persons, along with a responsible transmission of life. Upholding the value of life involves prioritizing the preservation of life, promoting health and safety, and fostering conditions that enable persons and communities to thrive.

Animal life is also valuable, and thus requires us to prevent harm or suffering, and promote welfare in animal life. Some even think that respect for life requires avoiding using animals as food. However, this is questionable. Animals are part of an ecological chain. Some animals use others as a food, and it seems that humans can also employ animals for their sustenance.

Self-mastery refers to the ability to govern oneself by controlling emotions, impulses and desires, in order to align one's actions with reason and goodwill. It involves both the strength to endure difficulties and the moderation of the attraction to pleasure, helping persons maintain balance and act in accordance with their rational nature.

Self-mastery brings together the rational (intellectual) and affective (emotional) aspects of the human person. By governing emotions and desires with reason, self-mastery creates internal harmony, allowing individuals to act in accordance with higher goals. It ensures that impulses and feelings do not overwhelm judgement, in pursuing the truth, and favours acting with benevolence.

Through self-mastery, a person can maintain balance in work, relationships and personal development, achieving a life that is not dominated by fleeting emotions or desires, but is guided by thoughtful and virtuous choices.

Together, these three goods – recognition of truth, benevolence and self-mastery – form a comprehensive framework of goods for human excellence. Each plays a crucial role in fulfilling a person's rational nature and leads to eudaimonia, the highest goal of human life. The pursuit of truth sharpens the intellect, benevolence builds moral relationships, and self-mastery ensures harmony between reason and emotion, enabling individuals to live well-rounded, virtuous lives.

The common good

The concept of *the common good* appears upon considering the social dimension of the person and how people live and act in a collaborative manner within communities, establishing either more or fewer lasting ties.[86] The common good refers to goods shared by those who are united in some way or belong to a community. In short, it can be defined as the good of all of us.

Some examples may clarify the notion of common good. A society without epidemics, with unpolluted air, living in a peaceful manner, with social cohesion and a good educational system is a society enjoying conditions of common good; as such, these are shared goods from which all can benefit. If we consider a small society, like the family, we can recognize shared goods, such as having an atmosphere of harmony, mutual respect, understanding and concern for one another. In business firms, common goods are, for example, having a culture of commitment, cooperation, a good work climate and a favourable financial situation. At an international level, neighbourly relations among nations, free-flowing communications and agreements on sustainable global development are also expressions of shared goods.

The idea of 'common good', as susceptible to being shared by each and every one of the members of the social body, was originally supported by Plato and Aristotle as a crucial reference for good governance. Although the idea is typically applied to society as a whole, each human community, including the business company, has a specific common good that can be recognized as such. The political community has a more complete common good than smaller communities, which focus only on partial aspects. In the current global world, in which people are highly interconnected, there is also a universal common good.

All members of the community share the common good, although the effective participation depends on the particular needs of each person. Thus, for example, a system of legal guarantees in a country is a common good shared by all citizens, although a subject is a beneficiary of this good only when he or she enters into a judicial process. Similarly, having a good healthcare system is a common good but people have an effective participation only when they are ill.

The common good means shared goods that are directly or indirectly necessary or convenient for human fulfilment. We call this 'person-based common good' since it includes the good of all persons and of the whole person. This understanding differs from others, which reduces the common good to a particular aspect – commonwealth (shared wealth), public interest (prosperity or welfare) or interest of the majority.

2.7 Basic ethical principles

Ethical principles are moral imperatives that leads us to good behaviour. Among these principles, the so-called first principle of practical reason, and others related to it will be discussed next (Table 2.3).

The first principle of practical reason

Since medieval times, an innate human habit, termed *synderesis*,[87] has been identified. This habit introduces a moral command to act in accordance with what is known to be good. In essence, this commandment is as simple as: 'evil must be avoided, good must be done'. More precisely, it has been formulated as: 'good is to be done and pursued, and evil is to be avoided',[88] which is referred to as the *first principle of practical reason*. This is considered the fundamental commandment for correct ethical behaviour, guided by practical reason, which seeks to act in a way that takes life in its integrity (1.9).

Though this principle is quite general, it serves as a crucial connection between goods and principles – and, by extension, the ethical norms and duties derived from these moral principles. Once someone recognizes what is good, the moral imperative that arises within their conscience is to 'do it' and, consequently, to avoid evil. For instance, if one knows that justice is good, the imperative becomes: 'do justice' – that is, act justly by giving each person their due. Similarly, if one understands that stealing is evil (as it contradicts justice), the moral norm is to 'avoid stealing'.

Considering the basic goods discussed earlier (2.6), the first principle of practical reason entails three moral imperatives:

- Seeking the truth, including the moral truth: what is the *good* in terms of human excellence and acting accordingly. This involves rationally discerning *what is truly good*, as opposed to apparent goods (2.6), through an open attitude towards reality, trying to understand the identity of each being, and what behaviour is appropriate to each identity and situation.
- Determining *what benevolence entails* in each situation and *acting* with genuine benevolence.
- Recognizing the importance of *preserving and self-mastering* one's own life and making decisions aligned with this understanding.

Table 2.3 Basic ethics principles in Aristotelian-personalist ethics

Ethical Principle	Formulation
The first principle of practical reason	Good is to be done and pursued, and evil is to be avoided.
The personalist principle	Persons should be treated with respect, never as a mere means to an end, and even with an ordered rational benevolent love, in terms of care and friendly service.
The common good principle	Every social or economic system, institution, community or social activity finds its moral legitimacy for its contribution to the common good – the good of all persons and of the whole person.
The solidarity principle	Groups and persons ought to contribute to the common good of the community in accordance with their respective capacity and avoid anything contrary to this good.
The subsidiarity principle	A larger and higher-ranking body should not exercise functions that could be efficiently carried out by a smaller and lesser body; rather, the former should support the latter and coordinate its activities, always towards the common good.
The participation principle	Those who belong to a community have the right and duty to be heard and participate, in some direct or indirect way, in decisions regarding the community in matters related to their life and situation.
The stewardship principle	Human activity should be harmonized by respecting the environment and caring for it as responsible stewards.
The self-mastering principle	One's desires, emotions and impulses must be governed aligning one's actions with practical wisdom (*phronēsis*) and the ongoing pursuit of virtue.

Next, we will explore more specific principles, beginning with a focus on benevolence towards others.

The personalist principle

The *good of benevolence* involves the imperative of *acting with benevolence*, which can be specified though various principles, some of which are highly relevant for business ethics. Among them is the personalist principle, some basic principles for social life and the stewardship principle, which will be discussed next.

Considering the intrinsic dignity of the human person, benevolence, as previously noted (2.6), entails treating people with respect, in accordance with their dignity, and never as 'mere means', but goes even further than that. Karol Wojtyla, a prominent personalist philosopher, affirms: 'The person is the kind of good which does not admit of use and cannot be treated as an object of use and as such the means to an end,' and adds: 'A person is an entity of a sort to which the only proper and adequate way to relate is love.'[89]

This firstly requires interacting with people in a respectful way – never treating any person as an object of use – by recognizing their human dignity and innate rights. But it doesn't stop there. According to Wojtyla, the most appropriate way to engage with persons is through love. In this context, love means wanting to do good to another, and this is referred to as 'love of benevolence', particularly when a certain proximity exists. Love of benevolence involves a generous attitude of doing good to others, often accompanied by care and a friendly attitude of service. This is not a self-centred or possessive love, nor is it a sentimental love. Instead, it is a love grounded in the recognition of the person as another 'I', connected to oneself through specific relationships, such as peers in a team, co-workers in the same company or collaborators.

While every person deserves respect for their dignity and rights, love of benevolence can vary in intensity and follow a certain order, reflecting the practical impossibility of loving everyone in an effective way. Following these considerations, the 'personalist principle' can be enunciated in these terms:[90]

Persons should be treated with respect, never as a mere means to an end, and even with an ordered rational benevolent love, in terms of care and friendly service.

The personalist principle shows certain similitude with the second formulation of the Kantian imperative, which commands treating people as an end and never simply as a means (2.2). However, there are two great differences from the Kantian approach. Firstly, it is not derived from an aprioristic formal formulation, like Kant, but by observation of the reality of the human being and the internal experience of the human condition. Secondly, the personalist principle is not limited to respect; it also includes rational benevolent love.

In the personalist principle, as in Wojtyla's formulation, two aspects can be distinguished: one negative and another positive. The first *proscribes* using people as a mere means to an end, while the second *prescribes* a disposition of doing good. Notice that the negative aspect uses – as Kant did – the adjective 'mere'. This is essential since people can be means or resources to obtain certain ends but not 'mere' means. Thus, workers are human resources or assets in the production process, and customers are the means by which to obtain incomes. However, both workers and customers are much more than this; they are persons and consequently deserve to be treated with respect and never as 'mere' resources or simple means but, rather, in a respectful way. In business argot, the term 'human resources' is still often used, but this brings the risk of forgetting that people are not 'mere' resources. That is why, in some companies, employees are referred to as persons or collaborators, denoting dignity.

The personalist principle promotes relations of reciprocity, in which people give and receive or even only receive, and this brings about links and networks, including those generated within business organizations.[91]

Respect for people and their rights

The first requirement of the personalist principle is to treat people with respect. This involves acknowledging the dignity and rights of each person – whether acquired or innate – regardless of their background, origin, opinions or behaviour. Every person deserves to be treated with consideration, fairness and kindness.

Respect for rights includes both innate and acquired rights. Innate rights, as noted previously (2.5), belong to the person and are closely connected to human dignity. Acquired rights can stem from agreements (such as *contractual rights* and other exchange-based rights), while other rights are *received* (such as those granted to citizens of a country).

Recognizing human beings as persons also includes respect for what they *legitimately possess*, including life, body, reputation, privacy, property, freedom of movement and anything else related to basic human needs. In the business context, this particularly includes respect for the life and physical integrity of those involved in the company, which requires the provision of safe working conditions.

Respecting others also requires *truthfulness* in both words and actions, as well as using polite and kind language in communication. It is ethically unacceptable to deceive people through *lies, false promises, unfounded expectations or inaccurate statements.*

Closely related to truthfulness is the ethical duty of *honouring one's word* – fulfilling commitments and agreements, and being reliable in both personal and professional relationships. Trust is built upon the words of others, and failing to honour one's word is a failure to give people the respect they are due.

In a more negative vein, respectful treatment means *avoiding exploitation* or *manipulation* of people. People must never be treated as objects or property (such as in slavery) or used for selfish purposes (exploitation). Treating people as mere instruments for personal gain (manipulation) is ethically unacceptable.

Respectful treatment involves avoiding any form of mistreatment, whether towards individuals or groups. It is unacceptable to insult, humiliate, slander, blackmail or engage in other harmful behaviours such as discrimination, gossip or belittling others. Additionally, sexual and psychological *harassment*, as well as coercing someone to act against their conscience, are equally unacceptable.

Moreover, respect entails avoiding *indifference* towards people around us. Instead, individuals deserve to be actively listened to, with their ideas and concerns given consideration. Both physical and emotional boundaries should be respected, and *diversity* in perspectives, cultures and experiences should be valued.

The personalist principle in its requirement for respect is closely tied to the virtues of justice and truthfulness (5.1).

The first requirement of the personalist principle is treating persons with respect. This refers to acknowledging the dignity and rights of each person – including both acquired and innate rights – regardless of their background, origin, opinions or behaviour. All people deserve to be treated with consideration, fairness and kindness.

Respect for rights includes both acquired and innate rights. Some rights are acquired through agreements (for example, contractual rights and other exchange-based rights), others are received (for example, rights inherent to citizens of a country), while others, called '*human rights*', are innate and before any legal formulation, since they are inherent to the person. They remain inviolable and inalienable, even when dismissed or trampled on by governments or by a community.

The recognition of human beings as persons includes respect for *whatever persons legitimately possess*, including life, body, reputation, privacy, property, freedom of movement and anything else related to basic human needs. Particularly important in the business context are respect for life and physical integrity of people involved in the company, which require *safe working conditions*. As with human dignity, human rights are intrinsic to every human being. Human dignity and human goods provide a sound basis for determining human rights.[92]

In business, the personalist principle requires that every person be recognized as a free agent, endowed with intrinsic worth and capable of self-determination, inseparable from moral responsibility. Human beings must never be reduced to mere utility, social status or function; they cannot be instrumentalized, exploited or sacrificed for utilitarian purposes. Economic goals, technical efficiency or policy decisions – though necessary for organizational success – must never override the fundamental dignity of the person. Accordingly, technologies, management practices and institutional arrangements are legitimate only insofar as they foster the authentic flourishing of the human person.

This principle implies that human dignity must be the guiding criterion for all decisions – whether in interpersonal relations, organizational policies or broader political and economic strategies. Business activity, therefore, cannot be limited to productivity and profit; it must also be concerned with the conditions that enable persons to grow and thrive. Such growth must be understood in its full breadth: physical well-being, intellectual development, moral integrity, spiritual depth and relational capacity. To restrict human development to material or technical dimensions alone would be to impoverish its meaning.

Furthermore, organizational structures – like any social, political or economic system – exist to serve persons, not the other way around.

Rational benevolent love: care and friendly service

On the positive side, the personalist principle requires rational benevolent love, which seeks other people's good and leads to acting in favour of other people's needs. This firstly entails care and compassion, an awareness that we are interdependent beings, and that people are vulnerable, experience needs and have legitimate interests. *Care* involves being attentive to other people's needs, especially those around us, acting with conscientious effort to support them, and seeking effective ways to help them, especially those subject to one's power. Acting with care fosters relationships and connectedness to one another.[93] Love of benevolence is expressed mainly as service, and this requires a permanent attitude of *friendly service*.

While the requirements of the personalist principle to respect people are very specific, other aspects of rational benevolent love, such as care and friendly service, are quite open and cannot easily be expressed in rigid norms. Practical wisdom (the section above) is essential in order to determine the best course of action in each situation.

One criterion is to prioritize people closest to oneself, considering those belonging to the same community and those others who have more relational proximity. Thus, in the case of managers, they have more obligation to care for people involved in their organization than for others outside it. This is a criterion of common sense. It does not seem logical to be negligent with one's family in order to care for strangers or to pass the only life vest available in a shipwreck to a stranger when one's son is also drowning. Another criterion is giving priority to the peremptory needs of those in interdependence with oneself.

To sum up, in business companies, the personalist principle is expressed, to a great extent, through respecting, caring and serving people. This principle, beyond its high ethical value, would promote trust, strengthen relationships and foster a positive social environment where everyone feels valued.

Social ethics principles

Persons belong to a set of communities, such as family, company, neighbourhood, religious and cultural associations, and society at large. The moral imperative of doing good – acting with goodwill and love of benevolence – also applies to society and particular communities. Drawing from personalist philosophy, some principles can be proposed.

The common good principle

This principle turns around the notion of the common good, previously introduced above. It involves the conviction that each person or group that forms part of a community is interdependent with the whole, and the whole should not be an obstacle to personal fulfilment. On the contrary, every community should remain at the service of those who make it up, and to society at large, to favour human fulfilment. Drawing from this, the common good principle can be formulated as follows:

> *Every social or economic system, institution, community, or social activity finds its moral legitimacy for its contribution to the common good—the good of all persons and of the whole person.*

This is the supreme principle for governance of communities, establishing common goals and a higher criterion by which to judge particular interests that might conflict. Consequently, the common good principle requires subordinating one's own interests to the common good if any conflict arises. This means, for instance, that a CEO's particular interest in amassing more power by making acquisitions of other companies has to be subordinate to the good of the company as a whole. A merger might be good for the company, but under certain circumstances it may not be (for instance, if the operation requires an unreasonable burden of debt).

Notice that a person-based common good includes respect for human dignity and human rights as two essential elements. Thus, it would be a misinterpretation of the principle of the common good to exclude such respect on account of any supposed 'higher' common interest. This precludes the common good being used as a pretext for 'totalitarian' positions in which human rights are not respected.

The common good entails 'instrumental goods' and 'intrinsic' or 'excellent goods' that are essential to human fulfilment. These goods are present in 'an ensemble of conditions which enhance the opportunity of fulfilment for all members of a community'.[94] Three types of external conditions contribute to the common good:

- *Socio-cultural values*: These enable people to live together respectfully, fostering tolerance, cooperation, civic friendship and solidarity. Key values include full respect for human dignity and innate human rights, freedom and justice.
- *Social well-being and community development*: These are external conditions that support people in living with dignity, including socio-economic factors for human development. Access to health, education, culture and religious goods is essential, along with a sustainable habitat that considers the needs of current and future generations. Economic growth should serve humanity, not the reverse.
- *Living in social harmony and peace, with the stability and security of a just social order*: This requires responsible authority, fair laws, guarantees of fair trials, equitable evaluations and institutions that prevent corruption while maintaining social cohesion and harmony.

The specific determination of what contributes to the common good in each community depends on circumstances. It must be discovered with practical wisdom and also, frequently, through sincere social dialogue. The final decision on particular aspects of the common good within a community is the job of those who rule it, but it must always respect human dignity and human rights.

Closely related to the common good principle are several other key principles. In terms of social life, the principles of solidarity, subsidiarity and participation are particularly important. Regarding environmental care with a sense of sustainability, the stewardship principle plays a central role.

The solidarity principle

The solidarity principle refers to the obligation to contribute to the common good and can be formulated as follows:

> *Groups and persons ought to contribute to the common good of the community in accordance with their respective capacity and avoid anything contrary to this good.*

All members of a community share the common good, but at the same time community members promote shared good. The common good is fostered when members of the community are receptive to ways of contributing to the community's improvement, to the benefit of everyone, including themselves, and have special concern for the weakest and most vulnerable.

Since collaboration is necessary for social life, it is rational to hold that ethics requires, as a duty, that every member of a community collaborates towards the common good and never damages it. On the contrary, it is not acceptable behaviour to take advantage of the common good for personal interest without any contribution (this is what is called the 'free rider problem'). The specific contribution required is not equal for all; it depends on the capacities of each member.

The subsidiarity principle

While solidarity emphasizes the sociability of the human being, subsidiarity centres on freedom and on the necessity of respecting and favouring individual talents and initiative to contribute to the common good of the community. In practical terms, subsidiarity requires, for instance, that a large organization should not take over what a smaller organization can do by itself but should give support to smaller groups or organizations or even individuals to develop their potential. This leads us to formulate the *subsidiarity principle* as:

> *A larger and higher-ranking body should not exercise functions that could be efficiently carried out by a smaller and lesser body; rather, the former should support the latter and coordinate its activities, always towards the common good.*

The principle of subsidiarity not only respects freedom and fosters initiative through the achievement of common goals, but it also ensures diversity within the organization, without submitting each individual to a grey uniformity. At the same time, this ethical principle favours developing one's own talents and not making others feel like passive elements of the whole. Moreover, the subsidiarity principle, as noted, favours conditions where workers can put their talents to use at the service of the common good of the firm.

The participation principle

Humans are members of communities and are directly or indirectly affected by decisions made for and about the society they belong to. In addition to the duty of building up the community (solidarity) and respecting people's initiative (subsidiarity), those who are members of a community should be heard and, in some way, contribute to making sound decisions for the life of the community. The *participation principle* can be formulated as:

> *Those who belong to a community have the right and duty to be heard and participate, in some direct or indirect way, in decisions regarding the community in matters related to their life and situation.*

The participation principle takes the existence of the differentiated goals and interests of people within a community into consideration and can favour ways of integrating these differences.

This principle, like the others, is not a rigid norm but a guide for reflection. Any application should consider the concurrent circumstance and possible consequences with practical wisdom.

The stewardship principle

Human goods entail an appropriate relationship with nature (13, A). However, the sensibility for this issue has not always been high. In fact, many generations have considered the natural environment a mere raw resource for the creation of wealth. A different perspective is to see nature as being endowed with beauty and a rich biodiversity, with a multiplicity of identities and significant interconnectedness with a notable order. The ancient Greeks coined the expression 'cosmos' precisely to designate this order of nature.

Human beings are part of material nature, although, because of their spiritual dimension, they possess dignity and transcend it. But that does not mean that material nature deserves no more consideration than as a simple raw material. Transcending material nature does not give us the right to believe ourselves to be owners of the planet, to use nature despotically or even to consider the natural environment as a mere object to be used, with no further reflection. Each natural identity – animals, plants and even non-living beings – deserves consideration in itself. Furthermore, humans and the rest of the planet are interconnected within a large ecosystem.

A consequence of this is that we should try to harmonize productive activities with a delicate respect for each non-human identity and a caring attitude towards the 'common home', to use the celebrated expression of Pope Francis.[95] In other words, our rationality should not be used to destroy the planet, but to serve as its caretakers. We have received the Earth, and we should pass it on well conserved for future generations.

Human activity requires caring for the environment by assuming a sense of responsibility as stewards of the Earth. This is the foundation of the *stewardship principle*, which can be formulated as follows:

> *Human activity should be harmonized by respecting the environment and caring for it as responsible stewards.*

Like other principles, it has a prohibitive aspect, regarding respect – avoiding damage to the environment – as well as the positive aspect of respecting and caring for the Earth.

The self-mastering principle

Finally, the good of fully human life, requires self-mastery over one's own existence, including the psychosomatic aspects. This means caring for one's body and exercising self-control over feelings, emotions and impulses – crucial parts of the human condition. In this sense, self-mastery (*enkrateia* in Greek) can be defined as the ethical principle that entails *governing one's desires, emotions, and impulses through reason, thereby aligning one's actions with practical wisdom and the ongoing pursuit of virtue.*

When moderated and balanced appropriately, these elements help to mature one's personality, promote benevolent actions and foster personal growth, while also favouring living together with harmony and achieving professional goals.

On the contrary, lack of self-mastery (*enkrateia* in Greek) can have bad consequences for living together. Industrial psychology describes toxic emotions as dominant affective states that are harmful to oneself or others. For instance, behaviours driven by excessive aggressiveness or furious anger can have disastrous consequences. Such behaviours may harm others, create a toxic work environment, and lead to feelings of guilt and remorse. In addition to these impulses, many other relevant feelings, emotions and spontaneous desires can influence behaviour.

Two types of spontaneous impulses can be identified. One group of impulses arises in the face of *obstacles or difficulties*. These can provoke feelings of fear in the face of uncertainty, failure, discouragement when confronted with challenges, anguish, sadness, melancholy, shame over past actions, dissatisfaction with work or guilt. In such situations, self-mastery requires fortitude to resist and overcome adversities, face the future with courage, and manage the emotions generated by these difficulties.

Another group of impulses is directed towards objects perceived as *pleasurable*, such as food, drink, sex and comfort. Others might involve less material desires, such as the pursuit of material possessions, power, praise or rewards. Attachment to one's ego can manifest as vanity, arrogance or a desire for ostentation. Negative emotions like jealousy, envy, resentment and hatred or a desire for revenge can also arise.

Self-mastery as a principle of action is, therefore, essential for controlling impulses and emotions like anger, resentment, and hatred, or the desire for revenge. In the workplace, impulses like laziness, seeking comfort, or curiosity can lead to prioritizing what is desirable in the moment rather than what should be done. In a positive sense, self-mastery drives individuals to act with courage and bravery, enabling them to pursue valuable tasks even when it comes at a personal cost.

Certain emotions and impulses, like hatred or the desire for revenge, are inherently harmful because they oppose human dignity and benevolence. However, other emotions can serve a positive role by bringing awareness to a situation. For example, fear can alert us to danger, sadness can highlight failure, and shame or guilt can reflect a recognition of having done something wrong.

As will be discussed, a set of virtues reinforces the capacity for self-mastery, while the virtue of practical wisdom ensures a balance between excess and deficiency in impulses and emotions.

2.8 Fundamental virtues

As previously noted (1.7), virtues are stable dispositions that favour good behaviour, that is, acting in accordance with moral goods. Virtues are acquired over time by acting well; they are learning by doing. Humans learn, not only by trial and error like the animals, but also by doing things in a rational way. Thus, we acquire technical abilities (human skills) and also moral habits (virtues), which forge our own character.

Virtues, in shaping the character, favour the achievement of goods, and thus contribute to human fulfilment. Virtues, on one hand, support a moral response to desires, emotions and other affective states. On the other hand, virtues reinforce our will to moderate desires based on apparent goods and pushing one towards real goods. Virtues are related with basic goods and principles as summarized in Table 2.4.

Some virtue ethics theories, as already noted (2.4), define virtues in different ways, including what is valued by the social environment. This is not the case for the theories which follow the Aristotelian tradition. Virtues are habits, which push us to achieve moral goods and human fulfilment.

Virtues are closely related to goods, and three groups of virtues can be distinguished in correspondence with the basic good (Table 2.4): *intellectual virtues*, among them wisdom and practical wisdom, *relational virtues* related to benevolence, and *self-mastery virtues*, which moderate psychosomatic tendencies.

Table 2.4 Basic moral goods, principles and virtues

Human endowments	Moral goods	Moral principles	Moral virtues
Intellect (related to abstractive and discursive knowledge)	Truth	Seeking what is good in terms of human excellence and acting accordingly.	Intellectual virtues (wisdom and practical wisdom, among others)
Will (related to self-determination)	Benevolence	Determine what benevolence entails in each situation and acting with genuine benevolence. – The personalist principle – Principles for social life – The stewardship principle	Relational virtues (benevolence, including justice, care and friendly service, and others)
Psychosomatic endowments (related to corporeity and affectivity)	Fully human life	Preserving and self-mastering one's own life in pursuit of a well-rounded human life.	Self-mastery virtues (fortitude and temperance)

Motivation and virtues

Practical reason (2.1, 2.6) provides a *moral-rational motivation* for what is convenient, and the most convenient thing is to achieve human fulfilment. However, the human being possesses not only reason but also feelings, emotions, sentiments and bodily needs that stimulate desires, which can aim for apparent goods (2.6). These latter desires generate *spontaneous motivation*, which can conflict with rational motivation. Free will, in its self-determination, permits one to decide whether to respond to a spontaneous motivation or to choose among several alternative courses of action.

It is in the context of the tension between rational and spontaneous motivations where virtues – strengths of character for good behaviour – play a relevant role. As Aristotle pointed out (2.1) there are virtues that reinforce intellect (intellectual virtues), while others reinforce the will to achieve human goods (moral virtues).

Focusing on the latter, we can add that at the root of spontaneous motivations there are natural tendencies or inclinations. Virtues reinforce the will, moderating these tendencies. Drawing from Aristotle and Aquinas, we can distinguish three basic natural tendencies. One is the tendency to possess (self-interest), which is quite evident, and also the tendency to share what one possesses, which emerges in certain situations. In addition, in the human being – and in animals too, but in a different way – there are two more basic inclinations: the inclination to fight to achieve valuable things and the inclination towards that which produces pleasure. Different inclinations, feelings and desires, described in relation to the principle of self-mastering (2.7) can be included in these two groups.

Wisdom and practical wisdom

Wisdom, greatly appreciated in ancient times, is an intellectual virtue or stable disposition that reinforces theoretical reason in its intellectual recognition of reality. It helps to recognize the world and the self and also to abstract concepts from reality.

Another crucial intellectual virtue is *practical wisdom* (*prudence* in classic nomenclature), which aids practical reason in determining the right thing to do in each situation and the right treatment of people and the natural environment, serving them and not causing them any damage. Practical wisdom is a central aspect of moral character since it has a driving role among moral virtues, determining the right means between two extremes, one being excess and the other deficit, as will be discussed next. Due to the relevance of practical wisdom on moral virtues, it is often included as a moral virtue, although properly, as noted, it is an intellectual one.

Wisdom and practical wisdom are acquired by each individual through reflective learning from one's own experience and also from education, by acknowledging wisdom accumulated over time, often in form of codes, precepts or sapiential maxims.

Relational virtues

The tendency to possess is moderated by 'relational virtues', which facilitate the achievement of goods regarding relation. The most elemental virtue for living in harmony is *justice*, which moves one to respect others, giving them their due. Closely related to justice and, like justice, extremely important in business is *truthfulness* or *honesty*, also related to the good of the truth, which refers to the truth in behaviour, as noted above (2.7).

Justice and truthfulness are necessary but not wholly sufficient in encouraging people to live together in harmony and in a friendly way. People have needs for their life and are called to achieve full development, which can require acting with reciprocity and a sense of cooperation. Sometimes people suffer, and others can contribute to remedying such distress. Recognizing that others are like oneself leads the person to do good by giving others more than what is strictly due. This behaviour is facilitated by virtues such as compassion, care and a sense of service, among others. These and other relational virtues are included in benevolence and considered as a virtue related to the good of benevolence (2.7).

Benevolence as a habit of goodwill and love of benevolence is a virtue that encompasses all other relational virtues. Notice that benevolence, in this sense, is not a mere sentiment, but a virtue driven by practical reason (1.10) – in this sense we can call it *wise benevolence* – and love of benevolence is an affective and rational disposition of 'wanting to do good'. Notice that benevolence entails doing good to others while improving one's own excellence or human fulfilment.

It might sound odd talking of benevolence, compassion, care and so on in the business context, but it should not. It is understandable, since in Western culture, for three centuries at least, justice has been considered the only ethical obligation in business. However, benevolence is an ethical requirement in most common moral, as well as in many religious and wisdom, traditions, as has been pointed out (1.9).

The basic good of benevolence, as noted (2.7) also includes dealing correctly with nature and with divinity, and this entails specific virtue, which we will not consider here, although some ecological virtues will be mentioned later in this book (13.2).

Self-mastery virtues

These virtues foster the practice of preserving and self-mastering one's own life. Inclinations to fight for valuable things and to seek that which produces pleasure require the virtues of self-mastery (2.8). A group of these virtues is included under the basic virtue of *fortitude* (often known as courage), while others fall within *temperance* or *moderation*.

Fortitude enables us to confront difficulties, dangers and pain in pursuit of the good. This virtue moderates – either by increasing or decreasing – the inclination to engage in struggle. It represents the mean between the extremes of recklessness (too much bravery) and cowardice (too little bravery). Fortitude is not only about physical courage but also involves spiritual courage to endure suffering for the sake of a greater good. Fortitude includes, among other virtues: *courage*, or the ability to face fears and hardships; *patience*, which provides the capacity to endure suffering without giving in to despair or frustration; and *magnanimity*, referring to the aspiration for great things in a noble manner.

The second key virtue is *temperance* (also termed *moderation*), which regulates the inclination to seek pleasure – especially those associated with bodily appetites like food, drink and sexual desire – but also self-complacency, arrogance and an immoderate passion for money, power or social recognition. Temperance is the mean between self-indulgence and insensibility (the lack of any desire for pleasure). Temperance, along with virtues such as self-control in governing one's impulses and desires, sobriety and humility, contributes to inner harmony.

Both fortitude and temperance contribute to one's capacity to act with benevolence. In organizations, these virtues help individuals overcome toxic emotions and foster the development of mature individuals and a humanistic culture.

Cardinal virtues and the unity of the virtues

Traditionally, in Western culture, four virtues are considered to be fundamental: justice, fortitude, temperance and practical wisdom (prudence). In this context, justice is understood in a broad sense as 'uprightness in dealing with others' and includes strict justice, compassion, religiosity and any other relational virtue. In this sense, and following our approach, it would be more appropriate to talk of benevolence, including justice and any other relational virtue.

These four fundamental human virtues are often called 'cardinal virtues' (from the Latin *cardo*, 'hinge') because they are like the hinge upon which the door of human excellence swings. Contemporary scholars have emphasized and developed aspects of these virtues.[96] Other virtues for human fulfilment can be included within these four. In Eastern traditions, similar virtues are also recognized as expressions of human excellence,[97] as noted previously (1.9).

All of these virtues provide for a right compromise between two vicious extremes.[98] Thus, courage negates cowardice and also precludes temerity. In practice, these virtues require the determination of the 'golden mean' between two extremes. In other words, to become moderate, courageous and just, it is necessary to know what 'the moderate', 'the courageous' and 'the just' actions are in every particular situation. This requires an intimate knowledge of each situation and a sense of the human goods acquired by previous actions. This is precisely the role of practical wisdom, which helps us to find the golden mean of the operative moral virtues (justice, fortitude, temperance and other comprised virtues) and, consequently, the right thing to do in each situation. Practical wisdom therefore has a driving role among the operative moral virtues. It is a cognitive virtue because it belongs to the cognitive sphere but also a moral virtue because it is essential for good behaviour.

According to Aristotle[99] and other outstanding scholars, there is *unity of the virtues* when they are fully developed. Let us explain that with the help of Figure 2.2, which schematizes the connection between the four cardinal virtues.

Moral virtues are connected in their 'perfect state',[100] that is, when they are highly developed. Justice (we may say 'benevolence') requires both great courage for doing what is right and also moderation to avoid pleasant situations that would prevent one's acting with justice. Similarly, courage is not virtuous if it is without rectitude of giving to each what is due (justice), moderation (self-control) and discernment (practical wisdom). The same applies to the other operative cardinal virtues. Exercising every virtue favours the development of practical wisdom, as it requires the determination of the 'golden mean'. Thus, practical wisdom and the other moral virtues stand in mutual need of one another and, if one virtue is lacking, the others will not be fully present either.[101] However, when virtues are not fully developed, some might be better developed than others. Virtues at a low degree of development can prevent good conduct. For instance, a person with a lack of courage may find it difficult to act with justice, even if they have a well-developed sense of justice.

Historically, there has been a progressive accumulation of practical wisdom and recorded maxims that can be useful for spurring human action and ethical principles (2.8).

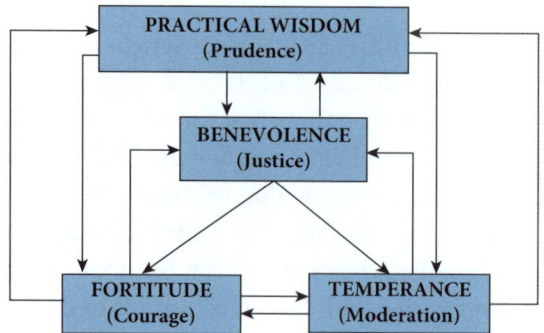

Figure 2.2 Connection of the four cardinal virtues

Case Study #2

A labour accident

A petroleum refinery plant in a Southern European country was proud of the low level of labour accidents they had and, for that reason, paid bonuses to its employees. Nevertheless, over the years, safety standards began to fall, especially among workers who were not employees of the company but, rather, employees of subcontracted companies. These workers mainly carried out maintenance tasks under the supervision of the chief maintenance engineer from the refinery or one of his technicians. They received minimum instruction for each assigned task.

One day, in the course of usual maintenance operations, work was due on the atmospheric distillation tower. It was necessary to replace a heat exchanger, a delicate operation that requires rapid execution in order to avoid gas leaks. The head of the maintenance department chose two employees from a subcontracted company who had previously carried out routine operations but had never replaced a heat exchanger. After a short training session that same morning, and accompanied by a supervisor, the operation began. In the course of the substitution, they unwittingly altered the positioning of a pipe connection, which resulted in the pipe sliding and the violent emission of the liquid that flowed through it, producing a 'blow torch effect' that burned both workers and caused superficial wounds to the supervisor. One of the workers died instantly, the second a few hours later in hospital.

It was necessary to deal with journalists who were waiting for information on the causes and other details of the explosion. The general manager of the refinery knew that journalists could either assuage an incident or stoke a climate of hostility towards the company.

Questions

1. Does anyone have responsibility for the accident described or was it something that could not have been anticipated?
2. Imagine you are the head of maintenance. With the knowledge and pressure you'd be under in a real refinery setting, how would you have made the decision about assigning this task? What would have helped you make a safer choice?
3. What would you do if you were the general manager of this plant, regarding the official statement? What moral criterion would you employ? Is this criterion consistent with any ethical approach, virtue or principle discussed in this chapter?
4. What would you recommend doing to avoid similar accidents in the future?

Notes

1. A. MacIntyre, 'Plain Persons and Moral Philosophy: Rules, Virtues and Goods', *American Catholic Philosophical Quarterly*, vol. 66, no. 1, 1992, p. 3. Reprinted in K. Knight (ed.), *The MacIntyre Reader* (Cambridge: Polity Press, 1998), pp. 136–52.
2. Sources: T. J. Radin, 'The *Challenger* Disaster', in R. W. Kolb (ed.), *Encyclopedia of Business Ethics and Society*, vol. 1, pp. 418–19 (Los Angeles: Sage, 2016); '30 Years After Explosion, *Challenger* Engineer Still Blames Himself', *National Public Radio, USA*, online, 23 January 2016, https://www.npr.org/sections/thetwo-way/2016/01/28/464744781/30-years-after-disaster-challenger-engineer-still-blames-himself; S. Kaplan, 'Finally Free from Guilt over *Challenger* Disaster, an Engineer Dies in Peace', *The Washington Post Online*, 22 March: https://www.washingtonpost.com/news/morning-mix/wp/2016/03/22/finally-free-from-guilt-over-challenger-disaster-an-engineer-dies-in-peace/; Britannica, '*Challenger* Disaster': https://www.britannica.com/event/Challenger-disaster. (Accessed on 30 October 2024).
3. F. De Vitoria, *Derechos y deberes entre indios y españoles en el Nuevo Mundo según Francisco de Vitoria* (The rights and obligations of Indians and Spaniards in the New World according to Francisco de Vitoria). Reconstructed by Luciano Pereña Vicente. (Salamanca: Cátedra V Centenario, 1992).
4. A. MacIntyre, *After Virtue* (New York: Bloomsbury Academic, 2013 [1981]).
5. E. Anscombe, 'Modern Moral Philosophy', *Philosophy*, vol. 33, 1958, pp. 1–19.
6. MacIntyre, *After Virtue*.
7. C. Gilligan, *In a Different Voice: Psychological Theory and Woman Development* (Cambridge, MA: Harvard University Press, 1982).
8. I. Kant, *Groundwork of the Metaphysics of Morals*. Translated by James W. Ellington, 3rd ed. (Indianapolis, IN: Hackett, 1993 [1785]), p. 43.
9. Kant, *Groundwork*, p. 36.
10. W. D. Ross, *The Right and the Good*, ed. Philip Stratton-Lak (New York: Oxford University Press, 1930 [2002]).
11. This sentence is attributed to Francis Hutcheson, a British eighteenth-century philosopher.
12. D. Miller, *John Stuart Mill: Moral, Social, and Political Thought* (Hoboken, NJ: John Wiley & Sons, 2013).
13. J. Bentham, *An Introduction to the Principles of Morals and Legislation* (Oxford: Clarendon Press, 1780 [1996]).
14. J. S. Mill, *Utilitarianism*, ed. (Indianapolis, IN: Hackett Publishing, 1863 [2001]).
15. R. B. Brandt, *A Theory of the Good and the Right* (Oxford: Clarendon Press, 1979); and B. Hooker, 'The Collapse of Virtue Ethics', *Utilitas*, vol. 14, no. 1, 2002, pp. 22–40.
16. A. Rand, *The Virtue of Selfishness* (New York: New American Library, 1964).
17. Some of them are included in A. J. G. Sison, G. R. Beabout and I. Ferrero (eds), *Handbook of Virtue Ethics in Business and Management* (Dordrecht: Springer, 2017).
18. On this point, see E. M. Hartman, 'Can We Teach Character? An Aristotelian Answer', *Academy of Management Learning & Education*, vol. 5, no. 1, 2006, pp. 68–81.
19. K. S. Cameron and G. M. Spreitzer (eds), *Handbook of Positive Organizational Scholarship* (New York: Oxford University Press, 2012).
20. D. S. Bright, J. Stansbury, M. M. Alzola and J. M. Stavros, 'Virtue Ethics in Positive Organizational Scholarship: An Integrative Perspective', *Canadian Journal of Administrative Sciences*, vol. 28, no. 3, 2011, pp. 231–43.

21. See discussion in M. Alzola, 'Virtuous Persons and Virtuous Actions in Business Ethics and Organizational Research', *Business Ethics Quarterly*, vol. 25, no. 3, 2015, pp. 287–318.
22. Thus, Robert Solomon defines virtue as 'a pervasive trait of character that allows one to "fit into" a particular society and excel in it', *Ethics and Excellence: Cooperation and Integrity in Business* (New York: Oxford University Press, 1992), p. 107.
23. R. Hursthouse and G. Pettigrove, 'Virtue Ethics', in E. N. Zalta and U. Nodelman (eds), *The Stanford Encyclopedia of Philosophy*: https://plato.stanford.edu/archives/win2022/entries/ethics-virtue/: 2022. (Accessed on 30 October 2024).
24. D. Gauthier, *Morals by Agreement* (Oxford: Oxford University Press, 1987).
25. T. Donaldson and T. W. Dunfee, 'Towards a Unified Conception of Business Ethics: Integrative Social Contracts Theory', *Academy of Management Review*, vol. 19, no. 2, 1994, pp. 252–84, and *Ties That Bind: A Social Contracts Approach to Business Ethics* (Boston: Harvard Business School Press, 1999).
26. J. Habermas, *Moral Consciousness and Communicative Action* (Boston, MA: MIT Press, 1983 [1990]). Discourse ethics has been applied to business ethics by some scholars, including H. Steinmann and A. Löhr, *Gundlagen der Undernehmensethik* (Stuttgart: Schäffer-Poeschel, 1994).
27. K.-O. Apel, *Selected Essays: Ethics and the Theory of Rationality* (Cambridge: Humanity Books, 1996).
28. J. Rawls, *A Theory of Justice* (Oxford: Oxford University Press, 1971 [1999]).
29. M. Murphy, 'The Natural Law Tradition in Ethics', in E. N. Zalta (ed.), *The Stanford Encyclopedia of Philosophy* (Redwood City, CA: Stanford University Press, 2019).
30. M. Velasquez and F. N. Brady, 'Natural Law and Business Ethics', *Business Ethics Quarterly*, vol. 7, no. 2, 1997, pp. 83–107; and M. Aßländer, 'Honorableness or Beneficialness? Cicero on Natural Law, Virtues, Glory, and (Corporate) Reputation', *Journal of Business Ethics*, vol. 116, no. 4, 2013, pp. 751–67.
31. A. J. Simmons, *The Lockean Theory of Rights* (Princeton, NJ: Princeton University Press, 1992).
32. J. Locke, *The Two Treatises of Civil Government*, ed. Richard Ashcraft (London: Routledge, 1989 [1689]).
33. A. Sen, 'Well-Being, Agency, and Freedom', *Journal of Philosophy*, vol. 82, no. 4, 1985, pp. 169–221; and M. C. Nussbaum, *Women and Human Development: The Capabilities Approach* (New York: Cambridge University Press, 2000).
34. Gilligan, *In a Different Voice* and N. Noddings, *Caring: A Feminist Approach to Ethics and Moral Education* (Berkeley: California University Press, 1984).
35. Cf. C. Gilligan, 'Moral Orientation and Moral Development', in E. F. Kittay and D. T. Meyers (ed.), *Women and Moral Theory* (Totowa, NJ: Rowman & Littlefield, 1987), p. 24.
36. J. M. Burgos, *An Introduction to Personalism* (Washington, DC: The Catholic University America Press, 2018).
37. M. Buber, *I and Thou* (New York: Simon and Schuster, 1923 [1996]).
38. E. Levinas, *Totality and Infinity: An Essay on Exteriority* (Pittsburgh, PA: Duquesne University Press, 1961 [1969]).
39. R. Spaemann, *Happiness and Benevolence* (Notre Dame, IN: Notre Dame University Press, 2000 [1989]), and *Basic Moral Concepts* (London: Routledge, 1982 [1990]).
40. L. Polo, *Ética: hacia una versión moderna de los temas clásicos* (Madrid: Unión Editorial, 1996). English translation: *Ethics. A Modern Version of Its Classics Themes* (Manila: Sinag-Tala Publishers, 2008).

41. D. Melé, 'Integrating Personalism into Virtue-Based Business Ethics: The Personalist and the Common Good Principles', *Journal of Business Ethics*, vol. 88, no. 1, 2009, pp. 227–44; K. Akrivou, J. V. Orón and G. Scalzo, *The Inter-Processual Self: Towards a Personalist Virtue Ethics Proposal for Human Agency* (Newcastle upon Tyne: Cambridge Scholars Publishing, 2018).
42. M. Scheler, *Formalism in Ethics and Non-formal Ethics of Values: A New Attempt Toward the Foundation of an Ethical Personalism*, translated by M. S. Frings and R. L. Funk (Evanston, IL: Northwestern University Press, 1913–16 [1973]).
43. D. von Hildebrand, *Ethics*. Introduction by John F. Crosby (Steubenville, OH: Hildebrand Press, 2020).
44. D. Moran, 'The Personalistic Attitude: Edmund Husserl and Edith Stein on Empathy as the Intuition of the Person as Value', in M. Englander and S. Ferrarello (eds), *Empathy and Ethics* (New York and London: Rowman & Littlefield, 2022), pp. 83–110.
45. K. Wojtyla, *Love and Responsibility*, translated by H. T. Willets (San Francisco, CA: Ignatius Press, 1993 [1960]), *Mi visión del hombre. Hacia una nueva ética* (Madrid: Palabra, 1997). See also Ioannes Paulus II, *I fondamenti dell'ordine etico* (Bolonia: CSEO, 1989).
46. See, for example, R. T. De George, *Business Ethics* (Boston, MA: Pearson, 2009); and M. G. Velasquez, *Business Ethics: Concepts and Cases* (Upper Saddle River, NJ: Prentice Hall, 2001).
47. N. E. Bowie, *Business Ethics: A Kantian Perspective* (Cambrige: Cambridge University Press, 1999 [2017]).
48. See a review in M. Snoeyenbos and J. Humber, 'Utilitarianism and Business Ethics', in R. E. Frederick (ed.), *A Companion to Business Ethics* (Oxford: Blackwell, 2002), pp. 17–29.
49. A. Gustafson, 'In Defense of a Utilitarian Business Ethic', *Business & Society Review*, vol. 118, no. 3, 2013, pp. 325–60.
50. For further discussion of utilitarianism see, for example, J. J. C. Smart and B. Williams, *Utilitarianism: For and Against* (Cambridge: Cambridge University Press, 1973); C. Taylor, 'The Diversity of Goods', in A. Sen and B. Williams (eds), *Utilitarianism and Beyond* (Cambridge and Paris: Cambridge University Press and Maison des Sciences de l'Homme, 1982), pp. 129–44; and J. Finnis, *Fundamentals of Ethics* (Oxford: Clarendon Press, 1983). The latter even questions whether utilitarianism is truly an ethical theory or merely a political one.
51. Among the pioneers, R. C. Solomon, *Ethics and Excellence: Cooperation and Integrity in Business* (New York: Oxford University Press, 1992); D. Koehn, 'A Role for Virtue Ethics in the Analysis of Business Practice', *Business Ethics Quarterly*, vol. 5, no. 3, 1995, pp. 533–9; E. M. Hartman, *Organizational Ethics and the Good Life* (New York and Oxford: Oxford University Press, 1996) and 'The Role of Character in Business Ethics', *Business Ethics Quarterly*, vol. 8, no. 3, 1998, pp. 547–59.
52. G. Moore, *Virtue at Work: Ethics for Individuals, Managers, and Organizations* (Oxford: Oxford University Press, 2017).
53. This way of understanding practical rationality considers 'Inter-Procedural Self', which emphasizes the relational dimensions of the self and its contribution to human flourishing. This stands in contrast to the narrower view of the 'autonomous self', in which the self is seen as a bounded, self-contained individual, capable of making choices independent of external influences and disconnected from human flourishing (K. Akrivou and G. Scalzo, 'In Search of a Fitting Moral Psychology for Practical Wisdom: Exploring a Missing Link in Virtuous Management', *Business Ethics, the Environment & Responsibility*, vol. 29, S1, 2020, pp. 33–44).

54. T. Beschorner, 'Ethical Theory and Business Practices: The Case of Discourse Ethics', *Journal of Business Ethics*, vol. 66, no. 1, 2006, pp. 127–39.
55. S. Simola, 'Ethics of Justice and Care in Corporate Crisis Management', *Journal of Business Ethics*, vol. 46, no. 4, 2003, pp. 351–61.
56. For instance, focusing on Martin Buber, R. Beavers, D. Daniels and A. Erisman, 'Technology and Non-interpersonal Relationships', *Journal of Biblical Integration in Business*, vol. 1, no. 1, 2020, pp. 21–9; on Immanuel Levinas, C. Rhodes, *Disturbing Business Ethics: Emmanuel Levinas and the Politics of Organization* (London: Routledge, 2019); on Jacques Maritain, A. Acevedo, 'Personalist Business Ethics and Humanistic Management: Insights from Jacques Maritain', *Journal of Business Ethics*, vol. 105, no. 2, 2012, pp. 197–219; on Karol Wojtyla, Melé, 'Integrating Personalism into Virtue-Based Business Ethics'; and on Leonardo Polo, G. Scalzo, K. Akrivou and M. J. Fernández González, 'A Personalist Approach to Business Ethics: New Perspectives for Virtue Ethics and Servant Leadership', *Business Ethics, the Environment & Responsibility*, vol. 32, suppl. no. 1, 2003, pp. 145–58.
57. Melé, 'Integrating Personalism into Virtue-Based Business Ethics'.
58. Mainly that proposed by J. Dewey, 'Moral Theory and Practice', *International Journal of Ethics*, vol. 1, no. 2, 1891, pp. 186–203.
59. A. Crane and D. Matten, *Business Ethics* (Oxford: Oxford University Press, 2007), p. 120.
60. D. Nyberg, 'The Morality of Everyday Activities: Not the Right, But the Good Thing to Do', *Journal of Business Ethics*, vol. 81, no. 3, 2008, pp. 587–98.
61. G. Abbà, *Quale impostazione per la filosofia morale? Ricerche di filosofia morale – 1* (Rome: LAS, 1996).
62. P. Koslowski, 'The Ethics of Banking: On the Ethical Economy of the Credit and Capital Market, of Speculation and Insider Trading in the German Experience', in A. Argandoña (ed.), *The Ethical Dimension of Financial Institutions and Markets* (Berlin: Springer-Verlag, 1995), p. 183.
63. Polo, *Ética*, p. 114.
64. MacIntyre, *After Virtue*.
65. Sources: F. Michelin, *And Why Not? Morality and Business* (Maryland, MD: Lexington Books, 2003); C. Védrine, 'Transmitting the Spirit', in *The Spirit of Capitalism According to the Michelin Company*, Palgrave Studies in Urban Anthropology (London: Palgrave Macmillan, 2019), pp. 111–49; Grand Témoin: François Michelin (several videos with interviews to François Michelin, in French).
66. Michelin, *And Why Not?*, p. 1.
67. Michelin, *And Why Not?*, p. 78.
68. Michelin, *And Why Not?*, p. 20.
69. Michelin, *And Why Not?*, p. 80.
70. https://www.michelin.com/en/group/purpose-values; https://www.youtube.com/watch?v=Py-75kcqLC8. (Both accessed on 30 October 2024).
71. For a seminal approach, seeking combining virtue ethics and personalism, see Melé, 'Integrating Personalism into Virtue-Based Business Ethics'. The term 'personalist virtue ethics' has been used by Scalzo, Akrivou and Fernández González, 'A Personalist Approach to Business Ethics', pp. 145–58.
72. See: J. M. Burgos, *An Introduction to Personalism* (Washington, DC: The Catholic University America Press, 2018); and J. M. Burgos and D. Melé, 'Personalism', in D. C. Poff and A. C.

Michalos (eds), *Encyclopedia of Business and Professional Ethics* (Cham: Springer, 2023), pp. 1454–59.
73. Aristotle himself wrote a treatise devoted to the soul.
74. Thomas Aquinas, taken from a previous medieval definition of person, affirms that 'person is an individual substance of a rational nature', *Summa Theologiae* (London: Burns Oates and Washbourne, 1981 [1273]), I, q. 29, a. 1, ob. 1.
75. Among them, K. Wojtyla,*The Acting Person: A Contribution to Phenomenological Anthropology*. Translated by Andrzej Potocki and edited by Anna-Teresa Tymieniecka Dordrecht, Netherlands: D. Reidel Publishing Company, 1969[1979].
76. This is especially stressed by Spaemann, *Happiness and Benevolence*.
77. Spaemann, *Happiness and Benevolence*.
78. Aquinas, *Summa Theologiae*, I, q.29, a.3 ad 2.
79. G. Pico Della Mirandola, *Oration on the Dignity of Man*, eds Francesco Borghesi, Michael Papio and Massimo Riva (Cambridge: Cambridge University Press, 1486 [2012]).
80. 'In the kingdom of ends everything has either a *price* or a *dignity*. What has a price can be replaced by something else as its *equivalent*; what on the other hand is above all price and therefore admits of no equivalent has a dignity.' (Kant, *Groundwork*, 4:435).
81. https://www.un.org/en/about-us/universal-declaration-of-human-rights, art. 1. (Accessed on 30 October 2024).
82. T. D. Williams, *Who is My Neighbor? Personalism and the Foundations of Human Rights* (Washington, DC: Catholic University of America Press, 2005).
83. Both human fulfilment and human flourishing translate to *eudaimonia.* In the last decades human flourishing has become popular, and using this expression as human fulfilment or human excellence is fine, but a little confusing, because, in positive psychology, flourishing is understood as a psychosomatic state where persons experience well-being, happiness, and psychological resilience, while the moral dimension is not mentioned. While in the Aristotelian tradition, as noted in the main text, *eudaimonia* refers to *flourishing* as human plenitude. On positive psychology see, for instance, M. Seligman, *Flourish: A New Understanding of Happiness and Wellbeing: The Practical Guide to Using Positive Psychology to Make You Happier and Healthier* (London: Free Press, 2011).
84. MacIntyre, *After Virtue*, p. 3.
85. See Spaemann, *Happiness and Benevolence*; and Melé, 'Integrating Personalism', Chapter 4.
86. The roots of the 'common good' concept can be found in Aristotelian–Thomistic thought: A. J. G. Sisón and J. Fontrodona, 'The Common Good of the Firm in the Aristotelian–Thomistic Tradition', *Business Ethics Quarterly*, vol. 31, no. 2, 2012, pp. 211–46; and K. Akrivou and A. J. G. Sison (eds), *The Challenges of Capitalism for Virtue Ethics and the Common Good: Interdisciplinary Perspectives* (Northampton: Elgar, 2016). In recent times, it has been especially stressed by J. Maritain, *The Person and the Common Good*, translated by John J. Fitzgerald (New York: George Schribner's Sons, 1947) and *The Person and the Common Good* (Washington, DC: Chicago University Press, 1951; Chicago: Catholic University Press, 2015); and by Catholic social thought (see Pontifical Council for Justice and Peace, *Compendium of the Social Doctrine of the Church*, Chapter 4 (Vatican City: Libreria Editrice Vaticana, 2004). Also available at: http://www.vatican.va/roman_curia/pontifical_councils/justpeace/documents/rc_pc_justpeace_doc_20060526_compendio-dott-soc_en.html. (Accessed on 10 June 2025); and T Bertone, *L'Etica del bene comune nella dottrina sociale della Chiesa* (Vatican City: Librería Editrice Vaticana, 2007).

87. According to Thomas Aquinas (*Summa Theologiae*, I, q. 79, a.12), '«synderesis» is said to incite to good, and to murmur at evil, inasmuch as through first principles we proceed to discover, and judge of what we have discovered'.
88. Aquinas, *Summa Theologiae*, I–II, q. 94, a. 2.
89. Wojtyla, *Love and Responsibility*, p. 41.
90. The personalist principle proposed here is similar to the 'Personalistic Norm' presented by Karol Wojtyla, who affirms: 'The person is the kind of good which does not admit of use and cannot be treated as an object of use and as such the means to an end' and adds: 'A person is an entity of a sort to which the only proper and adequate way to relate is love' (Wojtyla, *Love and Responsibility*, p. 410).
91. This point, drawing from Macintyre, has been developed by C. Bernacchio, 'Pope Francis on Conscience, Gradualness, and Discernment: Adapting Amoris Laetitia for Business Ethics', *Business Ethics Quarterly*, vol. 29, no. 4, 2019, pp. 437–60.
92. J. Finnis, *Natural Law and Natural Rights* (Oxford: Clarendon Press, 1986); Williams, *Who is My Neighbor?*; and M. J. Adler, 'Real Goods Make Real Rights', in *The Time of Our Lives: The Ethics of Common Sense* (New York: Fordham University Press, 1996 [1970]), pp. 139–52.
93. Cf. P. M. Linsley, 'Application of an Ethics of Care to Business', in A. J. G. Sison, G. R. Beabout and I. Ferrero (eds), *Handbook of Virtue Ethics in Business and Management* (Dordrecht: Springer, 2017), pp. 307–19.
94. Finnis, *Natural Law and Natural Rights*, p. 165.
95. Francis, '*Encyclical-Letter "Laudato si"*, on the Catholic vision of the ecology', 2015: http://w2.vatican.va/content/dam/francesco/pdf/encyclicals/documents/papa-francesco_20150524_enciclica-laudato-si_en.pdf. (Accessed on 30 October 2024).
96. The cardinal virtues were first introduced by Plato. The Bible also mentions them (Wis. 8:7). The Roman emperor-philosopher Marcus Aurelius emphasized them and stressed their comprehensive character in his book *Meditations* (London: Penguin, 2006), pp. 3, 6. Subsequently, the cardinal virtues were also adopted by Christian authors, such as St Ambrose, St Augustine of Hippo and St Thomas Aquinas. Some modern authors have resumed the subject. Among them, J. Pieper, *The Four Cardinal Virtues: Prudence, Justice, Fortitude, Temperance* (Notre Dame, IN: University of Notre Dame Press, 1966); P. T. Geach, *The Virtues* (Cambridge: Cambridge University Press, 1977); and P. Jaroszynski and M. Anderson, *Ethics. The Drama of the Moral Life* (originaly published in Polish under the title: *Etyka: dramat zycia moralnego* in 1992) (New York: St Paul, 2003).
97. C. Peterson and M. Seligman, *Character Strengths and Virtues: A Handbook and Classification* (Washington, DC: American Psychological Association, 2004).
98. On this point, see *The Nicomachean Ethics*, lib. 2, c. 6.
99. *The Nicomachean Ethics,* lib. 6, c. 13.
100. Aquinas, *Summa Theologiae*, I–II, q. 65, a. 1.
101. For a further discussion of Aristotle's position on the unity of virtues, see G. J. Hughes, *Aristotle on Ethics* (London: Routledge, 2001), pp. 109–16.

Part II
Individual Involvement in Business

3
Understanding Moral Responsibility

… it is in our power to be virtuous or vicious.[1]

ARISTOTLE (284–322 BCE), Greek Philosopher

Overview

Responsibility refers to the obligation to act correctly, fulfil duties, and be accountable for one's actions and their consequences. Moral responsibility is a central topic in ethics and, consequently, in business ethics.

Section A of this chapter discusses several key concepts related to moral responsibility, including its boundaries, extent and applications. A core concept concerns the foundation of responsibility in the human capacity for deliberation and free choice. Because of this, responsibility can be diminished or affected by a lack of knowledge regarding the action and its morality, or by imperfect consent of the will in making a decision. Four forms of personal moral responsibility are explored: two involving the commission or omission of individual actions, and two related to influencing or cooperating in the actions of others.

Section B focuses on personal responsibility within organizations. It begins by discussing responsibility under obedience and various organizational factors that influence individual responsibility. It then examines cooperation with wrongdoing without approval or under necessity (material cooperation with wrongdoing), and addresses personal responsibility in reporting illegal, immoral or fraudulent activities within an organization (whistleblowing).

Chapter Aims

After reading this chapter you should be able to:

- Understand the different meanings of responsibility.
- Distinguish between responsibility, accountability and liability.
- Discuss what we are responsible for and to whom.
- Understand the criteria for ascribing responsibility.
- Consider to what extent individuals within an organization bear responsibility.
- Distinguish between four forms of individual moral responsibility.
- Differentiate between direct and indirect voluntary action.

- Analyse the responsibility for the collateral consequences of one's actions.
- Evaluate the responsibility in influencing and collaborating in others' actions.
- Discuss whether, in certain situations, cooperating in wrongdoing can be acceptable.
- Understand whistleblowing and the conditions for its moral appropriateness.

Historical Case #3

The Volkswagen diesel emission test scandal[2]

In 2007, Martin Winterkorn, CEO of the German automaker Volkswagen Group (VW), launched an ambitious plan, termed 'Strategy 2018', with four main goals: (1) to become a leader in customer satisfaction and quality through intelligent innovations and technologies; (2) to increase unit sales by more than ten million vehicles a year; (3) to get a sustainable return on sales before tax of at least 8 per cent; and (4) to become the top employer across all branches and build a first-class team. The overall goal of 'Strategy 2018', in the words of this report, was to 'position the Volkswagen Group as a global and environmental leader ... The best automaker in the world by 2018.'

The goals were commendable, but a problem emerged in 2005 when the US Environmental Protection Agency (EPA) imposed the toughest-ever emission standards on the automobile industry. The engineers at VW were unable to meet the US benchmark on time with the technology available and the budget allocated. They had to make an imaginative decision.

In designing 'turbocharged direct injection' (TDI) diesel engines, three variables come into play: power, fuel efficiency and the cleanliness of the emissions. It is not possible to optimize these three at the same time. A good power/fuel consumption ratio entails more pollution, and reducing pollution means less power or more fuel consumption. In practice, a trade-off of the three variables is required.

One way to meet the high standards of US regulation on emissions would be to optimize the power/fuel ratio and then calculate how to keep the emissions below the level permitted in order to pass the emission tests. These tests were usually carried out in a laboratory, not on the road. Their solution was to equip the engine with a *defeat device* software that turned on its pollution control systems during testing (decreasing the power/fuel ratio) but largely disabled them when the vehicle was actually on the road. This software was supplied for internal tests during the fabrication process by Bosch, a German firm, which allegedly warned VW not to use its software illegally. The software controls the combustion in such a way that it detects when the vehicle is being subjected to a test (via an algorithm based on steering movements, uniformity of the gear, wheel movements and so on).

In 2007, VW announced new clean diesel cars, and for several years nobody complained. Things started to change when, in 2014, the independent body International Council on Clean Transportation (ICCT) commissioned a study on the emission of diesel cars. John German, co-leader of the US branch of the ICCT, said they chose to put US vehicles through on-the-road tests because their emission regulations are more stringent than those in the European Union.

A group of scientists at West Virginia University submitted a proposal to the ICCT, and John German awarded them a US$50,000 grant for a study that involved tests on three diesel cars, comparing lab findings and road measurements. The study found that the test subjects exceeded US emissions limits by 5–35 per cent, although they did not identify the defective device. The findings were published after they were presented at a public forum in May 2014 and came to the attention of the EPA.

The environmental agency repeated the tests and contacted VW for an explanation of excessive (NO_x) emissions. VW alleged a 'technical error' and ordered a voluntary recall of TDI cars, but the EPA was not satisfied. On 3 September 2015, it threatened not to certify 2016 diesels, to which VW responded by admitting their use of software programmed to cheat testing.

On 18 September, the EPA issued VW a notice of violation of the Clean Air Act. The agency had found that VW had intentionally programmed TDI diesel engines to activate their emissions controls only during laboratory emissions testing. This had allowed the vehicles to meet US standards during regulatory testing but emit up to forty times more NO_x in real-world driving. Two days later, VW publicly recognized the deceit and apologized for it. On the first trading day after the news broke, the VW share price fell 20 per cent. When, on 22 September, the company announced spending US$7.3 billion to cover the costs of the scandal, stock dropped another 17 per cent.

The following day, CEO Winterkorn resigned. A few days later, Heinz-Jakob Neußer, the head of brand development, was suspended, along with two other engineers, Ulrich Hackenberg and Wolfgang Hatz, Head of Research and Development of two VW brands (Audi and Porsche respectively). They were considered among the best engineers in the global auto industry. Later, an external investigator employed by Volkswagen revealed that fifty members of staff had confessed that they were fully aware of the emission-rigging activity.

Between 2009 and 2015, VW deployed the defeat device in about 11 million cars worldwide, including 500,000 in the United States. The real spending on rectifying the emissions issues and on projected refit costs for the affected vehicles as part of a recall campaign amounted to US$18.32 billion.

On 25 September 2015, Matthias Müller was appointed CEO of VW. He faced great challenges and had to make significant decisions.

Questions

1. What types of criteria were used to make the decision to deploy the defeat device?
2. Imagine you are part of VW's leadership team in 2015. What internal and external pressures would you be facing, and how might they influence your response to the scandal?
3. Think about accountability. In a large organization, how should responsibility be distributed when unethical practices are uncovered? What principles guide your reasoning?
4. What challenges did Mr Müller face on 25 September 2015? What decisions would you have made if you were him?

SECTION A. CONCEPTS AND SCOPE OF MORAL RESPONSIBILITY

The concept of responsibility is tied to the ability to answer for one's own actions. The word 'responsibility' derives from the Latin *respondere*, meaning 'to respond', and refers to the human capacity to act through free will, rather than as a 'mechanical response' to internal or external stimuli. In other words, responsibility presupposes free will.[3]

Responsibility, therefore, only applies to 'human acts', understood as conscious acts involving deliberation and free choice. These are distinct from other actions that occur in humans without the consent of the will, such as physiological or reflex actions.

Being aware of one's authorship of a particular act or behaviour can evoke feelings of guilt or shame, or, alternatively, happiness and pride. These emotions may arise from one's personal perception of an action in light of moral standards or from observing the reactions of others. However, feeling guilt or pride for an action does not necessarily imply actual responsibility in the objective sense of being accountable for good or bad actions. Some individuals are more sensitive to feelings of guilt or shame than others, and emotional impacts or certain psychological dispositions may heighten these emotions.

In this chapter we will focus on objective moral responsibility, particularly in the context of business. Since Aristotle, philosophical reflection on moral responsibility has a long history. Our aim here is to provide a few basic yet practical insights for use in business ethics.

3.1 Responsibility, accountability and liability

Let us begin by distinguishing three related concepts: responsibility and its different meanings, accountability and liability.

Responsibility

In business, as in other contexts, responsibility can have different meanings, although each of these has to do with giving answers or being answerable for actions.

Responsibility as a virtue

When we call someone a 'responsible person' or remark that someone 'conducts themselves responsibly', we refer to a positive character trait. A responsible person is one who acts after deliberation over his or her deeds considering what should be done and foreseeable consequences of the action. Being responsible is a sign of moral maturity and is closely related to trustworthiness.

Responsibility as obligation

In this case, responsibility involves an entrusted or assigned activity, or a duty or job inherent in a position. For example, in a workplace environment, we may say 'she is responsible for logistics'. Within organizations, managers and employees bear certain responsibilities and have to answer for their compliance. In a broad sense, this duty can also be understood as self-assumed in response to one's awareness of the needs of one's peers and of how such needs might be met.

Responsibility as attribution

This refers to the cause or condition of assigning or imputing an action or its consequences to someone. For instance, when we say, 'He is responsible for this fraud', or 'He is responsible due to negligence', we are attributing responsibility. This understanding also indicates who must compensate for damages caused by misbehaviour. Attributing responsibility can refer to different fields:

- *Moral responsibility*: This concerns the evaluation of an action's moral quality, determining whether it is good or bad, right or wrong. In addition to external judgement, persons possess an 'internal judge', known as the moral conscience (4.2), which can lead to feelings of joy or remorse based on one's actions. Some philosophers – and most religious traditions – assert that we are ultimately responsible to God, the author of moral law and the supreme judge.
- *Legal responsibility*: As members of a structured society, we are bound by laws and regulations set by public authorities. Legal responsibility entails answering to these authorities, including courts, regarding compliance with or violations of the law. In the legal field, therefore, responsibility is only mentioned in connection with offences or crimes to determine guilt,[4] whereas in ethics it refers to all manner of human actions, good or bad, meritorious or blameworthy. In ethics, it is known as 'moral responsibility'.
- *Social responsibility*: This involves being accountable for the impact of one's actions on society, or specific social groups. Social responsibility requires, at minimum, not causing harm to others, and, in a broader sense, taking actions that benefit society and promote well-being. In business, this is referred to as *corporate social responsibility* (12, A), which focuses on an organization's obligations to society, particularly to the groups directly affected by its activities.
- *Ecological or environmental responsibility*: This refers to the obligation to respect and protect the environment (13, A).

Accountability

Accountability is closely related to responsibility but has a narrower meaning, especially in the business world. It refers to being open to judgement by one's peers or by society as a whole.

Accountability often involves providing written or verbal explanations or justifications for one's actions.

While accountability focuses on explaining actions, responsibility emphasizes who is the author of those actions. Although these terms are sometimes used interchangeably, they are distinct. For example, managers can delegate responsibilities to others, but they retain accountability for the tasks they have assigned. Similarly, while one can debate who is responsible for a fraud within a company, the company as a whole remains accountable.

This version improves readability, provides clearer definitions, and maintains the original meaning while enhancing the flow of ideas.

Liability

Liability can be defined as 'the fact that someone is legally responsible for something'.[5] This refers to the responsibility of fulfilling one's legal obligations. In business, for example, we speak of 'product liability' and 'accounting liability'. *Product liability* refers to the responsibility a person or company must assume for any injuries caused by their product. This responsibility is borne by those who make the product available to the public, including manufacturers, distributors, suppliers and retailers. *Accounting liability* refers to obligations arising from past transactions or events, the settlement of which may result in the transfer or use of assets, provision of services, or other economic benefits in the future.

3.2 For what is one responsible?

The human being is endowed with *self-possession* and *self-determination*.[6] Self-possession means that the person is the owner of his or her acts. As Aristotle says, 'man is a moving principle of actions'.[7] Self-determination expresses the human capacity to make responsible choices, which includes deciding to act or not or to follow one course of action or another. Both elements are fundamental to individual responsibility.

Some speak as if one were responsible for only the *consequences* of an action, but this is simplistic. One is responsible if one assumes one's own freely performed action and its consequences. Carlos Llano identified four types of responsibility.[8] Two of these refer to the action itself: antecedent and consequent responsibility. Two others, termed congruent and transcendent, refer to a comprehensive vision of one's own life.

- *Antecedent responsibility*: It would be irresponsible to lack sound reasons for one's actions. In this sense, there is an antecedent responsibility that consists of acting only after possessing proper justification.
- *Consequent responsibility*: It would also be irresponsible to fail to own up to the consequences of one's actions, seeking to attribute them to someone else. The question arises: for which

consequences is one responsible? This is a complex matter and one we will return to below (3.4).
- *Congruent responsibility*: This regards being congruent with one's vision of life. It refers to a 'vital' attitude of acting consistently and in harmony with what one is (or would like to be). This responsibility can be especially relevant under the pressure of circumstances, such as awaking to the reality of being surrounded by people in need, noticing a chance to contribute to solving important problems, or deciding to impact a political or social situation.
- *Transcendent responsibility*: This derives from discovering a personal calling or 'vocation' to carry out a certain mission in the world. This calling includes, firstly, personal growth as a human being. We should not forget that human actions have internal effects on the subjects who perform them. Agents develop themselves, acquiring virtues and vices through their actions. There is a more specific sense of professional vocation that can be strong in doctors, nurses or teachers, but in a certain sense any noble human work, including management, amounts to a calling.[9] Frequently this calling, and the corresponding responsibility, are connected with transcendence and divinity. Thus, it is called *transcendent* responsibility.

3.3 Modifiers of moral responsibility

Certain elements can modify the degree of moral responsibility of an action. The concept of *voluntariness* can be useful to explain this. Voluntariness refers to the responsibility assumed for voluntary actions, that is, those entailing a rational choice made of a person's free will, as opposed to being made as the result of coercion or duress. Voluntariness therefore requires rational knowledge of the action and the agent's inner consent to performing it. These two elements – knowledge and consent – determine moral responsibility for a human action. As a consequence, establishing the degree to which an action can be ascribed to an agent requires evaluating to what extent an act proceeds from the agent's own understanding and free decision.

Voluntariness is complete or perfect when the agent has full knowledge and gives total consent when performing an action. However, if knowledge or consent is for some reason diminished, the voluntariness is incomplete, and the responsibility partial. The following factors can modify the degree of an agent's voluntariness and therefore his or her responsibility.

Modifiers of knowledge

The agent might suffer from a lack of knowledge of some material or ethical aspect of the action. One who pays for something with counterfeit currency is most probably aware that it is wrong to do so (knowledge of the ethical norm); however, the person might not realize that the currency is false (ignorance of a relevant material aspect).

We can distinguish three types of ignorance or lack of awareness: the invincible, the vincible and the intentional:

- *Invincible ignorance*: This is when ignorance cannot be overcome by reasonable means (relatively easy investigation, asking an expert when there is a suspicion that something is wrong, and so on). Invincible ignorance or lack of awareness eliminates the voluntariness of an action. Therefore, an action preceded by invincible ignorance is not morally ascribable to the agent.
- *Vincible* or *avoidable ignorance*: This refers to a person being able to overcome such ignorance by applying reasonable diligence in the given set of circumstances. For instance, in the case of unwittingly using a food additive that is prohibited because it is carcinogenic. This lack of knowledge originates in a person's negligence or lack of interest in personal training, in the failure to ask for advice, or in the failure to pay enough attention. When ignorance or lack of awareness is avoidable, these actions are morally imputable. Guilt increases in proportion to negligence, recklessness or the demonstrable lack of concern about an action's seriousness.
- *Intentional ignorance*: In some cases, the ignorance or lack of awareness is purposeful. This occurs when someone wilfully avoids finding out what his or her responsibilities are or overlooks them in order to evade them. This attitude leads to the intentional avoidance of knowing those things one is obliged to know. It might be due to a particular interest (generally economic). Purposeful ignorance is not only ascribable to the agent, but is morally more serious than avoidable ignorance, because it is the consequence not merely of convenience or negligence but also of a lack of moral rectitude.

Modifiers of consent

Some actions may lack full voluntariness due to a partial or complete absence of consent of the will. It is worth noting that *experiencing a feeling* and *giving consent* are not the same. Feelings arise spontaneously or in response to external stimuli, but consent does not occur until these feelings are freely accepted or 'owned'. For example, an action against our interests may cause *feelings of aversion* or resentment towards the person responsible. However, this differs from *wanting to hate*, which is a deliberate, free act that transforms spontaneous hatred into a consented or accepted feeling.

Several factors can affect the voluntary nature of an action, leading to a partial or complete absence of consent:

- *Mental or physical factors*: The use of reason can be impaired by various causes, including mental illness and other diseases. In such cases, voluntariness may be limited or even absent. Acting while intoxicated or under the influence of drugs also diminishes free will, although the initial decision to be under such influence might have been voluntary.
- *Presence of force*: This occurs when violence or psychological coercion (more rarely, physical coercion) is used to compel someone to act against their will. If the victims of force do not internally consent, they bear no responsibility. If they consent reluctantly, responsibility is reduced but not entirely eliminated.
- *Strong emotions*: Emotions involve a mental and physiological state that can greatly intensify actions. Anger or rage can play a significant role in some situations, as can fear. Expressions such as 'he was blinded by anger' or 'she fell into a fit of rage' indicate actions driven by

intense emotions. The moral responsibility of a person influenced by anger depends on the extent to which the anger was willed. For instance, spontaneous anger upon being insulted lessens voluntariness and, consequently, responsibility. In some cases, a strong emotion can lead to a complete loss of control, precluding moral responsibility. However, one can also nurture anger voluntarily by dwelling on past insults or humiliations, which can increase voluntariness in subsequent actions.

- *Intellectual fear*: This refers to a rational awareness of a potential harm and a desire to avoid it by deliberate means. Intellectual fear can be seen, for example, when someone falsifies a document out of fear of losing his or her job, or lies to avoid disgrace. Intellectual fear differs from emotional fear; the former involves acting from fear, while the latter is acting with fear. Although intellectual fear may accompany emotional fear, it is conceptually distinct. Intellectual fear does not eliminate voluntariness, but it can diminish it, reducing the associated moral responsibility.
- *Habits*: Established character dispositions create a fixed tendency or typical behaviour, for better or worse. Habits are acquired through repeated actions and influence how tasks are performed. Actions performed out of habit occur easily, often with minimal deliberation. For example, some people lie frequently without conscious awareness, having developed the habit early on. Others may neglect duties due to habitual laziness. There is responsibility in the voluntary acquisition of habits. For any specific action, voluntariness depends on the level of awareness and the effort made to break an existing pattern.
- *Sociological factors*: These relate to cultural and social environments, customs, and, sometimes, genuine pressures from the immediate work environment. To some extent, these factors may diminish responsibility, although they rarely eliminate it entirely. We will revisit this point within the organizational context in Section B of this chapter.

Detailed analysis of factors that can modify the consent of the will is beyond the scope of this work. Each situation has its own variables and, in some cases, may require the insights of specialists.

3.4 Are we responsible for consequences?

Returning to the question of consequences introduced above (3.2), we may ask: is the agent responsible only for the immediate and desired consequence of an action? Is there any responsibility for unintended but foreseeable consequences? What about possible yet improbable consequences? Is one responsible for every effect of an action, including those that were impossible to foresee? To what extent is one responsible for a chain of events resulting from an action when other causes may also have contributed?

In addressing these questions, two extreme positions can be identified:

- *Universal responsibility*: Advocates of this view argue that, since people continually interact with others and are all in a state of global interdependence, we are collectively responsible for everything that happens in the world.

- *Very narrow responsibility*: At the opposite extreme, this view holds that one is responsible only for the immediate and intentional (desired) consequences of an action. This perspective implies that unintended consequences associated with an action are beyond one's responsibility. This would be the stance of a manager who disregards the effects on a neighbourhood caused by a factory producing foul odours, noise and dust. Fortunately, there is growing awareness of these unintended yet foreseeable *collateral* or *secondary effects*, as they are commonly called.

Direct and indirect voluntary action

Determining responsibility for secondary effects can be complex, but it is an important issue and we will now consider it in detail. To analyse responsibility for consequences, we begin by distinguishing between direct and indirect voluntary actions:

Direct voluntary actions

An action is directly voluntary when someone decides to perform or refrain from an action to achieve something desired, or as a means to an end. Many business actions are directly voluntary. This includes, for example, a manager setting a strategy, expanding a business, knowingly omitting certain workplace safety measures, forging a commercial document or consciously failing to make a payment.

Indirect voluntary actions

These occur when someone consciously, on their own initiative, performs an action (or permits an omission) that causes something undesirable but foreseeable (at least vaguely) and avoidable. Intentionality is 'indirect' when one knows that a particular event may result from a given act or that foreseeable harm may arise through negligence or recklessness. Such actions are also termed 'voluntary in the cause'.

A classic example of an indirectly voluntary action is a driver who injures someone while intoxicated. In business, an illustrative example would be an employee injured due to a failure to take reasonable precautions, or an accident involving a consumer resulting from inappropriate product use when proper instructions were not provided by the manufacturer. In these cases, there is no present consent of the will, but there is consent to the cause that leads to such accidents.

Having made this distinction, we can better address the issue of foreseen but unintended consequences. Agents pursue specific goals, but these goals are often accompanied by other outcomes, referred to as collateral or secondary effects, as noted. This terminology is fitting because these effects are associated with the primary outcomes – the intended goals. Notice that the term 'secondary effects' does not imply that these outcomes are unimportant but rather that the intention to bring them about is indirect or secondary.

Criteria to evaluate collateral effects

Responsibility for collateral or secondary effects primarily depends on the *capacity to foresee and prevent them*. Additional factors include the *seriousness of the wrongdoing* involved and the *causal proximity* between the action and its consequences. Thus, several criteria can help determine responsibility for an action's consequences:

Foreseeability and preventability

Every agent is responsible for *reasonably predictable consequences* of an action that can be readily *prevented or avoided*. There is indirect voluntariness for foreseeable effects on people and the natural environment because the agent is aware they may be associated with the action. Such predictable consequences are assessed through one's own experience, by seeking appropriate advice, and by considering what generally occurs in similar situations. Therefore, managerial decisions must account for foreseeable secondary effects, whether they are largely or minimally avoidable. This consideration raises ethical questions, particularly when the secondary effects are negative. We will return to this point later.

Capacity to avoid negative secondary effects

The greater the *capacity to avoid negative secondary effects*, the greater the responsibility to do so. For example, some medicines produce side effects; if these can be mitigated by adding another ingredient, there is a responsibility to introduce it. Similarly, industries such as mining and construction, with extensive experience in handling industrial accidents, have a duty to draw on this knowledge and implement preventative measures, such as proper training, job-specific precautions, appropriate monitoring and prohibition of alcohol in the workplace. Responsibility is diminished in sectors where experience with accidents is limited or where incidents are inherently more challenging to prevent.

Seriousness of consequences

The more *serious the potential consequences* of an action, the greater the responsibility to implement preventive measures, even if the likelihood of occurrence is remote. For example, a machinery manufacturer should anticipate potential injuries to operators and incorporate safety features to mitigate these risks. When lives are at stake, precautions must be stringent. Similarly, in the food industry, the responsibility for quality control is heightened, as consumer health is at risk, particularly with products directly affecting well-being.

Causal proximity

Responsibility increases with the causal proximity, understood as the link between the action and its consequences. Consequences often lead to further effects, creating a chain of events. Immediate consequences have a closer causal connection to the action, whereas more remote effects involve actions beyond the control of the original agent, often relying on the decisions of others. For instance, there is close causal proximity between an industrial accident and inadequate safety precautions, while the causal proximity between a traffic accident and the brewery that produced the alcohol consumed by a driver is negligible. However, a closer causal link could exist if the brewery used highly persuasive advertising to encourage excessive consumption.

3.5 Forms of individual responsibility

Four forms of moral responsibility can be distinguished: two due to the individual actions themselves and two by virtue of contributions to the actions of others (see Figure 3.1).

Responsibility for commission of actions

Responsibility for performing a voluntary action is commonplace (for example, selling a product, requesting or approving an advertising campaign, committing fraud and so on). Every directly voluntary act is ascribable to its author or agents since it is the result of deliberation and free choice. As noted, when someone performs an act, he or she becomes personally responsible for it and for its reasonably foreseeable and avoidable consequences.

Responsibility for omission of actions

An omission, in the ethical sense, takes place when one fails to perform a feasible action despite an obligation to do so. For example, failure to establish the necessary rules to protect worker health or to provide the required resources for safety and hygiene in the workplace would be acts of omission by the manager. Consequently, to the extent that an action could and should have been carried out, the individual is guilty of omission.

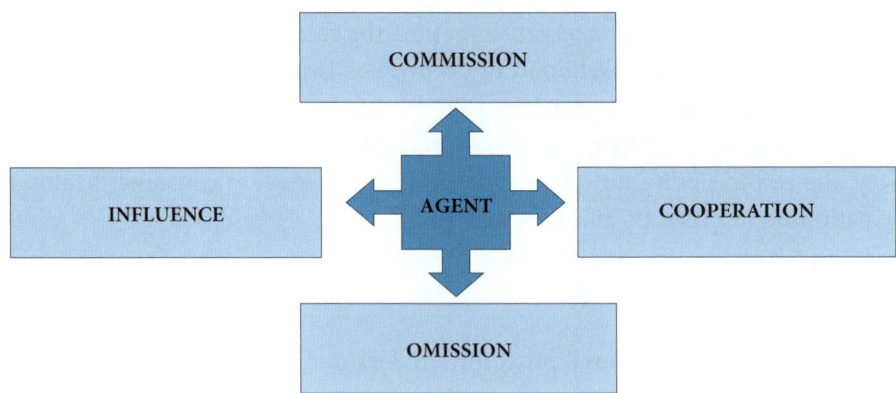

Figure 3.1 Forms of individual moral responsibility

An omission can be fully deliberate; that is, with direct intentionality. This occurs when someone omits something knowingly while being perfectly aware of the obligation to act – when one can act but does not. Full responsibility attaches to such conscious omission. This responsibility or guilt can be greater if the omission was premeditated or made with real malice.

There are other types of omission, more frequent in business life, that do not involve direct intentionality. These occur when someone fails to perform a feasible action due to lack of awareness of the situation or lack of consciousness of the obligation. These omissions can fall under the headings of negligence or recklessness:

- *Negligence*: This entails a failure to act with the prudence that a reasonable person would exercise under the same circumstances. For instance, maintaining obsolete equipment through a lack of interest in staying abreast of technological innovations or losing a contract due to inadequate attention to the correct preparation of a tender.
- *Recklessness*: This is conduct characterized by a conscious and dangerous disregard of others' safety or well-being, resulting in the creation of an obvious and substantial risk of harm (safety in industrial facilities, in driving and so on).[10] Recklessness can also be present in behaviours driven by an intemperate activism, for example, or running excessive risks without carrying out a serious study or seeking adequate advice.

Responsibility increases in proportion to the degree of negligence, recklessness or lack of concern demonstrated along with the seriousness of the omission (for example, the responsibility is greater when human lives, as opposed to material goods, are at stake).

Responsibility for influencing the actions of others

In acting or in failing to act, one can induce others to act in a certain sense. Employees rarely lose responsibility completely within the organization, as will be discussed in Section B, but they are often largely influenced by the actions of their managers and co-workers.

One way to induce people to act is by *persuasion*. This can be done in various ways, including *giving advice* and *praising* or *criticizing* someone's decisions and actions. People whose position or profession gives them special influence over an action have an added responsibility. Consultants, lawyers and others with experience or prestige fall into this category.

Inducement to wrongdoing can take the form of advice with no moral consideration whatsoever (*impulsive advice*) or advice that denies the immorality of the act and persuades the person that the act is actually good (*doctrinal advice*), which is even more serious. Those who induce others to do wrong through advice or persuasion are responsible for the action regardless of whether they acted in bad faith, with invincible ignorance, or with serious negligence.

Acting as a *role model* is another significant means of influence. Someone who behaves well *sets a good example*. People who behave poorly set a bad example. It is well known that people are influenced by the thoughts expressed by others in their social environment and by their actions, even in the absence of explicit advice or attempts at persuasion. We have a natural tendency to try to emulate the achievements of others and to imitate some aspects of their lives. We often adopt certain people as role models of conduct. The responsibility for setting a good or bad example depends largely on the level of recognition or authority of the one who influences and on the personality of the 'influence'.

Any inducement to misbehaviour in others is termed 'scandal' (in a moral sense) – etymologically, a 'stumbling block'. In its common sense, scandal usually means an apparent violation of morality or propriety; in a moral sense, it is closer to the original meaning in that it leads one to stumble and fall. It could be defined as an attitude or behaviour that leads others into wrongdoing or an impediment that prevents others from improvement.

Sometimes, giving good examples or scandals is *direct*; that is, deliberate and intentional attempts to influence others. Sometimes, however, they are *indirect*; their purpose is not to induce others to act, though some imitation might be foreseen. In direct scandal, there is full guilt.

However, an indirect scandal is not always imputable. This occurs, for example, when someone praises another and that is interpreted as an act of flattery to obtain certain favours, when it is not the case. If it is foreseeable that indirect scandal might occur, reasonable means should be taken to prevent it. In this example, reasons for giving the praise should be explained in order to prevent misinterpretation.

Responsibility for cooperation in the actions of others

In business, people often perform actions in cooperation with others. Manufacturers cooperate with salespeople and vice versa; designers cooperate with manufacturers; investors cooperate with the enterprises in which they invest; suppliers cooperate with the activity of their clients through the products or services they provide; buyers cooperate with the activity of the company that sells to them; advertising agencies cooperate by providing economic support to the media in which their advertisements are placed; and so on. Ethical issues can arise in certain cases of cooperation. For instance, when a manager gives in to the wishes of a corrupt politician or civil servant who asks for a commission to 'speed up' matters, when someone acts as a supplier to a company that carries out questionable activities, or when an employee in an organization decides to sponsor depraved television programmes.

In cooperating with others' actions, one shares in them – including in their morality – to some extent. Cooperation with good actions should be fostered, and corporation in wrongdoing avoided. However, sometimes people are under heavy pressure to participate. This often produces delicate situations that require further considerations to analyse cooperating in wrongdoing. We will return to this point (3.7).

Business Ethics in Action #3

Enrique Shaw: A responsible manager[11]

In 1961, Enrique Shaw was forty years old and, for three years, he had been the Managing Director of *Cristalería Rigolleau* (CR), an Argentine company of family origin dedicated to the glass industry, with 3,400 employees and its main facilities located in Berazategui, in the south, from Buenos Aires. At this time, Argentina was stuck in a deep social and economic crisis with consequences for CR, who had experienced a drop in demand for its products. In May of 1961, León Fourvel Rigolleau, grandson of the company's founder and Enrique's uncle, died. In June, quite unexpectedly, several shareholders sold 40 per cent of the CR shares to *Corning Glass Works* (*Corning Inc.*, since 1989), an important company in the sector with headquarters in New York, and, in this way, *Corning Glass Works* took control of CR. A few weeks later this company made the decision to eliminate 1,200 jobs and this was communicated to Enrique so that he should proceed to implement the decision. Enrique did not think it was a good decision, all things considered, and wondered what he could or should do. Enrique knew the glass sector and the company, where he had worked since he was twenty-five years old, well. He also knew Corning Glass Works, where he spent almost a year before joining CR in order to become familiar with glass production and, above all, with the manufacture of 'Pyrex' glass pieces that are resistant to high temperatures. He was sent there by relatives who were related to the family that owned CR. His management training included participation in a Harvard programme at a time when this was not common in Argentina. Along with this professional preparation, Enrique had deep ethical and religious convictions. He was a devoted and committed Catholic who knew and understood Catholic social teachings very well, which favoured a deep humanistic vision of the company, the relevance of each person, each endowed with great dignity, and the value of work, not only in terms of earning a living, but also as a source of meaning and personal development. He had also promoted an association of Christian managers in Argentina.

Shaw understood that his responsibility could not be reduced to solving an economic problem, nor isolated from the identity of the company and its purpose, in which he saw a triple dimension: economic, human and social. According to Shaw, the economic purpose was to produce goods or services to satisfy authentic human needs and provide adequate remuneration for the various categories of people who make the existence of the company possible. The human purpose is to constitute a human community of work, which would unite and develop those who formed it. The social purpose (Shaw termed it 'public') is to contribute to the good of the community of which it is a part (common good). He concluded that 'these three purposes are combined with each other, and any decision by company managers must take *them all* into account; a balance, a *harmony*, is seriously necessary in the *simultaneous* consideration of all of them' [italics in original].[12]

He believed that unemployment was a serious human harm and was only acceptable when there was no other viable alternative. He had applied this idea in his management at times of decreased demand, giving the affected workers other occupations within the company or, on another occasion, helping to create an autonomous company for workers in a section – specifically carpentry – that was not necessary for the company. However, with Corning's decision it was no longer up to him alone.

Thus, as he believed that dismissing people should be the very last solution, he wondered whether he could propose to the board of directors that they reconsider their decision, or whether he could offer sound arguments for an alternative solution to avoid or decrease downsizing.

Enrique had three alternatives. The first was simply to lay off the 1,200 employees, something that he deeply disliked and that he was not willing to do because he thought it was not the only possible solution. The second was to present his resignation from his position. That would be particularly hard since he had a large family, with nine children. In addition, he had also been diagnosed with cancer that, at the moment, did not prevent him from working, but was progressing. The third alternative was to prepare a reasoned strategic plan and negotiate it as an alternative to the downsizing with Corning's senior executives. He opted for the latter and took a plane to New York. The strategic plan included three points: (1) diversifying production to respond to the growth of plastic and, in this way, moving employees from glass to plastic jobs; (2) reassign any excess personnel to useful tasks and retain qualified workers for a later time, when the purchase orders would flow in again, without having to pay severance packages; and (3) attempt to reconvert those sectors in the glass production process that had become obsolete because of technological changes, or to train those employees so that they could outsource services outside of the factory. This strategy was meant to somewhat modernize the company, both in terms of manufacturing processes and staff training, as well as attracting trade agreements with other large, foreign companies. Enrique presented this proposal adding that 'if they fired even one employee, he would quit'. The plan was eventually accepted, no employees were fired, and the company moved forward. Enrique's cancer took him to the grave just a year later.

* * *

Enrique Shaw managed with an extreme sense of responsibility, not only avoiding wrongdoing but also imagining better alternatives. This is real ethical behaviour. Shaw understood that ethics is more than applying a set of rules. It requires a coherent vision of the company and people.

Additionally, the reaction of employees, as you can imagine, was outstanding. Employees were extremely happy when they knew that Shaw's plan was accepted. Furthermore, employees gave a positive response in the final stages of Shaw's illness, when, faced with the need to receive blood transfusions to stay alive, approximately 260 – mostly workers at the Rigolleau – were willing to donate their blood for that purpose.

SECTION B. PERSONAL RESPONSIBILITY WITHIN THE ORGANIZATION

3.6 Organizational influence on individual moral responsibility

In regard to the responsibility of individuals within an organization, the Milgram experiment on the influence of people with authority over others is often considered. Although this experiment has been quite controversial, it is at least illustrative of the problem of the influence on persons within an organization.

The Milgram experiment

In the 1960s, psychologist Stanley Milgram conducted an experiment to explore whether people would obey orders, even if it meant harming another person.[13] He recruited forty volunteers for what they believed was a learning study. An actor played the role of a 'student', while the volunteers were the 'teachers', instructed to administer increasingly stronger electric shocks for incorrect answers. Though the shocks were simulated, participants believed they were real. Despite the student's protests and eventual silence, 65 per cent of the volunteers continued administering shocks beyond 400 volts, following the authority figure's orders. Milgram's findings suggested that people would obey authority, even at the cost of harming others.

More recently, experts have questioned the validity of the studies, suggesting that participants may have been coerced and that some likely recognized the student was only pretending to be shocked. Despite these criticisms, some replications indicate that people are still surprisingly prone to following authority, even when it conflicts with their moral conscience.

Despite its limitations, Milgram's experiment raises the question of whether people truly lose responsibility when working for an organization. A first, obvious observation is that in the context of the Milgram experiments, 35 per cent of participants did not obey orders. This could be because people with greater ethical sensitivity and stronger character are less likely to obey orders that conflict with their conscience. A second insight comes from personality psychologists, who emphasize the relevance of personal freedom and personality traits, even in organizational settings, and criticize laboratory experiments for being too removed from real-world contexts.[14]

People's moral character and personal responsibility

Some social psychologists emphasize the influence of the organizational context on personal behaviour to such an extent that individuals within organizations are viewed as automatons, with their character and personal traits deemed irrelevant in explaining their actions.[15] In contrast, personality psychologists argue for the significance of personal freedom and personality traits, even within organizational settings, and they criticize laboratory experiments for being too far removed from real-world contexts.[16] Similarly, many scholars in business ethics defend the importance of moral character in explaining individual behaviour within organizations.[17] This does not imply, however, that organizational conditions have no influence on the people involved.

In practice, individuals exhibit varying degrees of susceptibility to situational pressure from their organizations, which can make moral conduct more or less difficult for each person.[18] Indeed, organizational pressure is one of the social factors that can modify responsibility (3.3), reducing voluntariness and blame for an employee who is compelled to commit wrongdoing, especially in cases where the individual has limited decision-making authority and refusing to follow orders could result in serious consequences.

However, it is generally untrue that an individual within an organization has no choice but to obey when pressured to act unethically. In many cases, an employee can report such pressures to superiors or external entities with the power and willingness to take corrective action – this is known as whistleblowing (discussed further later in 3.9). In other situations, a manager or employee who is pressured to act unethically or cooperate in wrongdoing may raise an objection of conscience or, as a last resort, leave the company. There are also cases where an individual's cooperation with others' actions within an organization constitutes 'material cooperation with wrongdoing', which may be acceptable under certain conditions, as we will explore further.

Various organizational factors can influence individual behaviour, for better or for worse, although it is important to remember that personal responsibility is rarely entirely lost. Several organizational factors have been identified as influential over individual behaviour, including: (1) the leader's values and character; (2) the vision and exercise of power; (3) corporate control systems; (4) internal networks of influence; (5) organizational culture; (6) internal and competitive pressures: and (7) external influences. A comprehensive framework of interrelated organizational factors, termed the *organizational moral structure*, has been proposed[19] to explain how these factors condition, incite or influence moral or immoral behaviour within organizations.

3.7 Material cooperation with wrongdoing

A relevant problem regarding people in organizations is to evaluate whether or not it is acceptable to cooperate in other people's wrongdoing, including situations in which there is a strong need to cooperate. For instance, does a marketing manager who gives support to a morally bad TV programme, with a large audience, or contracts space for an advertisement during this programme, have any responsibility? What about an employee who is required to participate in a fraud, although in a very indirect way? Is a salesperson responsible for accepting the giving of a commission to the head purchaser of a company if there is no other way to sell a certain product?

To address this problem, it is, firstly, important to distinguish between formal and material cooperation with wrongdoing:

- *Formal cooperation in wrongdoing*: This occurs when a person explicitly approves of another's action or shares the principal agent's intention, either for its own sake or as a means to some other goal. This is what happens, for instance, when a manager agrees to a fraud proposed by his boss and cooperates in carrying it out. Formal cooperation in wrongdoing involves guilt as complete voluntariness is present. It is therefore never acceptable.
- *Material cooperation with wrongdoing*: This form of cooperation is present when one *disapproves* of the other's action but cooperates out of *real necessity* (for instance, to avoid being fired). The first responsibility here is to seek to avoid such cooperation. In some situations, the principal agent might even be persuaded to switch to an acceptable course of action, one in which the secondary agent could collaborate without misgivings. If the agent might be open to such a change, the first responsibility is to try to instigate it.[20]

With material cooperation with wrongdoing, there is *voluntariness in the cause* (3.4) but not in the effects. The agent tolerates or suffers undesirable consequences associated with the action because of the need to obtain a good or avoid a harm. What has been said above regarding responsibility for consequences (3.4) is therefore fully applicable to material cooperation with wrongdoing.

Responsibility in material cooperation with wrongdoing

Material cooperation in business and other fields involves several considerations. One key factor is the *causal proximity* of the cooperation, allowing us to distinguish between *immediate* and *non-immediate material cooperation*. Another important factor is the *seriousness of the wrongdoing* involved, and a third is the *necessity of cooperation* under the given circumstances.

Immediate material cooperation

Immediate material cooperation occurs when the cooperator's involvement has *close causal proximity to the principal agent's actions*, and the principal action cannot proceed without this cooperation. For example, consider an accountant who, under pressure from a supervisor, assists in creating a misleading financial report, even though no documents are falsified. When the cooperation involves a gravely unethical action, such as violating the right to life or preparing weapons for a terrorist group, the responsibility and moral culpability are significant. In such cases, immediate material cooperation is never acceptable.

In less severe instances, the proportionality between the necessity of cooperation and the gravity of the wrongdoing becomes relevant. For instance, consider a sales manager who is required by the client's purchasing director to pay a 'commission' under the threat of losing a sale. In this case, the manager's immediate cooperation with the client's illicit action may involve guilt due to causal proximity. However, in extreme circumstances, where maintaining one's job or ensuring the survival of the business is at stake, immediate material cooperation might be temporarily justified while seeking alternatives, provided that no grave ethical violations are involved. This topic will be revisited in our discussion on extortion (5.8).

Non-immediate material cooperation with wrongdoing

Non-immediate material cooperation occurs when the cooperator does not condone the principal agent's actions, and the cooperation has limited causal proximity or is not essential for the action to occur. For instance, a clerk might, under instruction, retrieve documents that will later be used to create a misleading report. In the earlier example, an employee tasked with preparing the commission payment under orders provides another example of remote cooperation with an illicit act. While non-immediate material cooperation is less morally troubling than immediate cooperation, it, too, should be avoided if possible.

Criteria for material cooperation in wrongdoing in extreme situations

Material cooperation with wrongdoing might be morally justifiable and may not entail guilt if certain criteria are met:

- *No viable alternatives to cooperation exist*: Includes a sincere belief that the wrongdoer cannot be persuaded to take an ethical course of action.
- *The cooperator's action is not intrinsically wrong*: Otherwise, it would constitute both cooperation and an independently objectionable act.
- *No endorsement of the principal agent's action is present*: This is a necessary condition for material (as opposed to formal) cooperation.
- *There is a proportionately serious reason for cooperating*: Includes protecting an important good or preventing significant harm. The graver the wrongdoing and the closer the cooperation, the more serious the justification required.

Additionally, it may be prudent to clarify one's reasons for cooperating to avoid misunderstandings. Regular review of the situation is also recommended to evaluate if alternative actions become feasible over time.

3.8 Personal responsibility in whistleblowing

The term 'whistleblowing' has its origins in the practice of English metropolitan police officers (*bobbies*) who would blow their whistles when they observed a crime. In business ethics, it means revealing illegal, immoral or fraudulent activity within an organization by a current or former employee, either within the organization ('internal whistleblowing') or publicly ('external whistleblowing').[21] The wrongdoing might have to do with corrupt practices, adulteration of foods, health or safety violations, blatantly unlawful conduct, fraud and so on – circumstances that generally have a considerable effect on the public interest.

Whistleblowing, as with any other ethical action, requires rectitude. This means that one needs to be revealing the wrongdoing on moral grounds and not, for instance, for revenge.

External whistleblowing conduct is contrary to the common good or public interest of people or entities that have the power and, presumably, the willingness to take corrective action. These entities might be governmental or watchdog agencies, local authorities or law enforcement agencies. Sometimes, the mass media can also be an appropriate channel for whistleblowing.

Internal whistleblowing can include similar issues or any other irregularity. Some companies have institutionalized channels to report misconduct, with the opportunity for anonymity. These channels can include ombudsmen, ethical or compliance officers and complaint hotlines.

Whistleblowing has its ethical justification in the moral duty to avoid wrongdoing and to contribute to the common good. Covering up wrongdoing when it could be prevented entails responsibility for cooperation – by omission – in wrongdoing (3.7).

Some people bear more responsibility than others due to their organizational position, role or expertise on a topic. For instance, a company physician has more responsibility for whistleblowing about a lack of protection of workers' health than does a financial officer, who also knows the facts.

Because of its negative effects, whistleblowing should be the last resort. These effects include personal inconvenience, risk of retaliation against the whistleblower and the possible loss of the organization's reputation.

There are several criteria for analysing the extent to which one might be obliged to become a whistleblower:

- *Whistleblowing should be done with uprightness*: Never do it as an act of revenge or with the intention of damaging a person or the organization to which one belongs or has belonged.
- *Whistleblowing should relate to an issue of sufficient moral importance*: For instance, when covering up an issue would affect people's health or bring about serious economic damages.
- *One should possess relevant information before blowing the whistle*: This does not mean possessing absolute certainty, as if one were proving a crime at a trial, but at least sufficient clues to initiate an investigation.
- *All ordinary channels should be explored within the organization*: Regarding misconduct, all possibilities should be exhausted before undertaking any external whistleblowing, which could damage the organization. However, in some cases, such as a real risk of retaliation against the whistleblower, or urgency, public whistleblowing could be recommended.
- *One must have reasonable grounds for believing whistleblowing would be effective*: This requires foreseeing that those charged with preventing or punishing misconduct will act effectively.
- *One should choose the best way to blow the whistle*: Achieving recourse vis appropriate agencies is often preferable to going to the media. A question that arises is whether whistleblowing is in conflict with the employee's duties of loyalty to the firm. There is no doubt that employees

bear duties of loyalty in serving the legitimate interests of their company and in keeping the secrets and confidential information that they know by virtue of working there. However, loyalty is not a virtue if it means adherence to illegitimate interests or faithfulness to illegitimate commitments.[22] Whistleblowing favours the common good and does not work against any legitimate commitment. A whistleblower who acts uprightly is being loyal to the moral good as well as to his or her employer.

In order to protect higher goods and avoid retaliation, whistleblowers should be protected, and many countries have taken steps to ensure this protection. In addition, there is significant awareness and protection from false accusations both in legislation and within organizations.

Case Study #3

TEPCO and the Fukushima tsunami[23]

On 11 March 2011, following the largest earthquake in Japan's recorded history and the resulting tsunami, a dramatic accident occurred at the Fukushima nuclear power plant. The accident had serious consequences for the plant, which was forced to close, and, more importantly, for the people exposed to radiation. The blast occurred as Tokyo Electric Power Company (TEPCO) was working desperately to reduce pressure in the core of a reactor at the forty-year-old plant, located 240 km (150 miles) north of Tokyo.

TEPCO, the operator of the plant, later admitted that it may have failed to accurately report cracks in its nuclear reactors during the late 1980s and 1990s. TEPCO was suspected of falsifying twenty-nine safety repair records. In 2002, the company had already admitted to falsifying safety reports, leading to the shutdown of all seventeen of its boiling-water reactors, including those at Fukushima, for inspection.

More than a decade later, the exclusion zone around the plant remains, and many residents have not returned. Authorities estimate that it may take up to forty years to complete the decontamination work, which has already cost Japan trillions of yen.

Questions

1. Was this incident completely unforeseeable, or do some bear responsibility? If so, who and why?
2. Imagine you were a mid-level TEPCO engineer who had known about safety problems in the 1990s but felt unable to speak up. Looking back after the Fukushima disaster, how would you reflect on your role and responsibility? What would you wish you had done differently, and why?
3. If you were been part of TEPCO's leadership team, what actions would you could take to show real accountability to the communities affected by the disaster? Which action would be hardest for you to take, and why?

Notes

1. Aristotle, *The Nicomachean Ethics*, translated by David Ross (Oxford and New York: Oxford University Press, [1925] 1980), lib. 3, c. 5.
2. Sources: B. Blackwelder, K. Coleman, S. Colunga-Santoyo, J. S. Harrison and D. Wozniak, 'The Volkswagen Scandal', *Robins Case Network* (Robins School of Business, University of Richmond, 2016); J. C Jung and S. B. A. Park, 'Case Study: Volkswagen's Diesel Emissions Scandal', *Thunderbird International Business Review*, vol. 59, no. 1, 2017, pp. 127–37; C. Rhodes, 'Democratic Business Ethics: Volkswagen's Emissions Scandal and the Disruption of Corporate Sovereignty', *Organization Studies*, vol. 37, no. 10, 2016, pp. 1501–18; N. Mansouri, 'A Case Study of Volkswagen Unethical Practice in Diesel Emission Test', *International Journal of Science and Engineering Applications*, vol. 5, no. 4, 2016: https://www.researchgate.net/publication/303797234_A_Case_Study_of_Volkswagen_Unethical_Practice_in_Diesel_Emission_Test. (Accessed on 30 October 2024).
3. See a broader discussion of freedom and responsibility in H. Bok, *Freedom and Responsibility* (Princeton, NJ: Princeton University Press, 1959).
4. Legal studies, apart from this responsibility, also consider 'civil and administrative responsibility'.
5. https://dictionary.cambridge.org/es/diccionario/ingles/liability. (Accessed on 30 October 2024).
6. See, for instance, J. F. Crosby, *The Selfhood of the Human Person* (Washington, DC: Catholic University of America Press, 1996).
7. Aristotle, *Nicomachean Ethics*, lib. III, c.1.
8. C. Llano, *El empresario ante la responsabilidad y la motivación* (México: McGraw Hill – IPADE, 1991), pp. 69–146.
9. See M. Novak, *Business as a Calling – Work and the Examined Life* (New York: Free Press, 1996).
10. In law *reckless* or *wanton negligence* is when actions are taken that would be classified as crimes, if they have been performed with malice.
11. Sources: Adolfo Critto (ed.), *Enrique Shaw, notas y apuntes personales*, 2nd ed. (Buenos Aires: Claretiana, 2002); M. Paladino, 'Enrique Shaw: decisión en tiempos de crisis. ¿Hasta dónde influyen los valores en la decisión?', s.d. https://empresa.org.ar/wp-content/uploads/2023/10/CASO-ENRIQUE-SHAW-a-IAE-1.pdf. Accessed on 30 October 2024; and S. Crito de Shaw and H. Rocha, 'Redescubrir la misión de la empresa: Una entrevista a Enrique Shaw', *IAE Revista Alumni*, 8 May 2017: https://www.iae.edu.ar/revista-alumni/redescubrir-la-mision-de-la-empresa-una-entrevista-a-enrique-shaw/; ACDE (Asociación Cristiana de Dirigentes de Empresa), 'Enrique Shaw biografía', https://enriqueshaw.com/wp-content/uploads/2019/03/Biografia_Enrique_Shaw.pdf (Accessed on 30 October 2024).
12. E. Shaw, '… *Y Dominad la Tierra*'. Mensajes de Enrique E. Shaw compilados por Fernán de Elizalde (Buenos Aires: Asociación Cristiana de Dirigentes de Empresa (ACDE), 2010), p. 97.
13. S. Milgram, *Obedience to Authority* (New York: Harper and Row, 1974).
14. See a deeper discussion on this point in S. Soloman, 'Victims of Circumstances?', *Business Ethics Quarterly*, vol. 13, no. 1, 2003, pp. 43–62.
15. Among them, G. Harman, 'The Non-existence of Character Traits', *Proceeding of the Aristotelian Society*, vol. 100, 2000, pp. 223–6. He argues that character traits do not exist. Doris adds that personality traits make no significant contributions to predicting and explaining behaviour (J. Doris, *Lack of Character: Personality and Moral Behavior* (New York: Cambridge University Press, 2002), p. 28).

16. See a deeper discussion on this point in Solomon, 'Victims of Circumstances?'
17. Apart from Solomon, 'Victims of Circumstances?', R. F. Card, 'Individual Responsibility within Organizational Contexts', *Journal of Business Ethics*, vol. 62, no. 4, 2005, pp. 397–405; and M. Alzola, 'Character and Environment: The Status of Virtues in Organizations', *Journal of Business Ethics*, vol. 78, no. 3, 2008, pp. 343–57, among others.
18. See D. Comer and G. Vega, 'Using the PET Assessment Instrument to Help Students Identify Factors that Could Impede Moral Behavior', *Journal of Business Ethics*, vol. 77, 2008, pp. 129–45.
19. P. Roszkowska and D. Melé, 'Organizational Factors in the Individual Ethical Behaviour. The Notion of the "Organizational Moral Structure"', *Humanistic Management Journal*, vol. 6, no. 2, 2021, pp. 187–209: https://link.springer.com/content/pdf/10.1007/s41463-020-00080-z.pdf.
20. This could be the case of large corporations cooperating with the wrongdoing of a contractor somewhere along their supply chain (13.8).
21. See M. P. Miceli and J. P. Near, *Blowing the Whistle: The Organizational and Legal Implications for Companies and Employees* (New York: Lexington Books, 1992).
22. Three different categories of loyalty can be distinguished: 'utilitarian loyalty', 'emotional loyalty' and 'virtuous loyalty' (D. Melé, 'Loyalty in Business: Subversive Doctrine or Real Need?', *Business Ethics Quarterly*, vol. 11, no. 1, 2001, pp. 11–26).
23. Sources: 'Fukushima Disaster: What Happened at the Nuclear Plant?', *BBC News*, 23 August 2023: https://www.bbc.com/news/world-asia-56252695; 'Japan's nuclear power operator has checkered past', *Reuters World News*, 12 March 2011: https://www.reuters.com/article/world/us/japans-nuclear-power-operator-has-checkered-past-idUSTRE72B1B4/. (Accessed on 30 October 2024); J. Choi and S. Lee, 'Managing a Crisis: A Framing Analysis of Press Releases Dealing with the Fukushima Nuclear Power Station Crisis', *Public Relations Review*, vol. 43, no. 5, 2017, pp. 1016–24, Wikipedia: TEPCO; Fukushima Daiichi Nuclear Power Plant.

4
Ethics in Decision-Making

The first sign of corruption in a society that is still alive is that the end justifies the means.[1]
GEORGES BERNANOS (1888–1948), French writer

Overview

The decision-making process, crucial in business, inherently involves ethical considerations, as every decision impacts both people and the environment. This chapter focuses on moral judgement in decision-making, a key element of personal ethical behaviour and in business ethics.

Section A considers how the relevance of full rationality in decision-making is emphasized, moving beyond mere instrumental rationality, which focuses exclusively on utilitarian results. This leads to the introduction of a triple evaluative criteria, centred on instrumentality, morality and the effects on relationality. Under the perspective of ethics as a guide to excellence, moral judgement goes beyond simply assessing the ethical acceptability of decisions or determining whether they violate moral standards. It also involves deliberating on which alternative best promotes human excellence, serves people and contributes to the common good. The central role of practical wisdom in making sound moral judgements is emphasized.

Section B explores the practical aspects of making moral judgements in decision-making, including decisions that have both positive effects and negative collateral consequences – known as actions of double effect – and some criteria for resolving dilemmas.

Chapter Aims

After reading this chapter you should be able to:

- Be familiar with the four psychological elements involved in good behaviour.
- Recognize the relevance of moral judgement (moral conscience) in decision-making.
- Consider the role of practical wisdom and other virtues in making sound judgements.
- Reflect on the inherent ethical content of decisions in business.
- Examine the necessity of full rationality – not just instrumental rationality – in decision-making.

- Discuss the instrumental, moral and relational dimensions involved in decision-making.
- Provide a useful framework for making moral judgements.
- Study how to make moral judgements about actions that entail both good and bad effects.
- Provide basic criteria for resolving ethical dilemmas.

Historical Case #4

Bernard L. Madoff: Deciding on a financial model[2]

Bernard L. Madoff, after having worked as a lifeguard and sprinkler installer, saved US$5,000 and invested it in founding his own firm, Bernard L. Madoff Investment Securities (BMIS) LLC, in 1960, which pioneered electronic trading. Initially, his business grew with the assistance of his father-in-law, who referred a circle of friends and their families. The company became famous for its reliable annual returns of around 10–15 per cent. All of this helped Madoff become one of the largest market makers on Wall Street.

Investing in BMIS had an air of exclusivity. Madoff did not accept every investor who came to him. He used to reject some clients, arguing the quota was already filled up. Being accepted was an honour, and a sign of power, wealth and pedigree. That made his fund even more prestigious. His personal touch was part of the marketing strategy.

Madoff's wife, Ruth, who had a background in finance, had worked in the company since its inception. She also began the Madoff Charitable Foundation. His brother Peter joined them in the 1970s. Once grown, Madoff's sons worked in the trading section, along with his nephew, Charles Weiner.

Madoff's successful career made him one of the most respected Wall Street businessmen. In 1990 he became chair of the NASDAQ stock exchange. He was also head of the board of directors of the Sy Syms School of Business at Yeshiva University.

Bernard and Ruth were prominent philanthropists. They served on boards of non-profit institutions and donated US$6 million to lymphoma research after their son Andrew was diagnosed with the disease in 2003.

The couple was active in the Jewish social circuit in New York City and Florida. Madoff capitalized on his personal touch, winning many of his clients from these affluent groups.

The Madoff family was closely linked to regulatory organizations. Bernard and Peter had been part of the board of directors of the Securities Industry and Financial Markets Association (SIFMA), which was the main industry organization. Peter's daughter Shana was active on its Executive Committee of Compliance and Legal Division. She married Eric Swanson, a compliance official of the Securities and Exchange Commission (SEC), which is the main US markets watchdog.

In 1999 Harry Markopolos, a financial analyst, alerted the SEC that it seemed legally and mathematically impossible to achieve the high returns of BMIS's investments. The company's accounting structure was also suspicious. The firm's entire activity was carried out by a three-person company with only one practising accountant. Nevertheless, this complaint did not lead to a serious investigation.

On 10 December 2008, following the company's Christmas party, Bernard Madoff confessed to his sons that, although his firm had initially operated legitimately, he had eventually decided to adopt a Ponzi scheme, which involves paying returns to existing investors using funds from new clients, rather than from actual profits. It attracted investors by promising consistently high short-term returns. However, to keep it going, an ever-increasing flow of new money was required. Ultimately, the scheme was destined to collapse, as the earnings – if any – were insufficient to meet the promised payouts.

Madoff declared that he planned to surrender to authorities, but before doing that he wanted to use the approximately US$200–300 million that was left to make payments to certain selected employees, family and friends.

Shortly after, his sons reported him to the police. The following day, Bernard Madoff was charged with fraud. He pleaded guilty to eleven federal crimes, including securities fraud, wire fraud, mail fraud, money laundering, perjury and making false filings with the SEC. He insisted that he was solely responsible for the Ponzi scheme. Madoff's fraud is the biggest known fraud in history, with estimated client losses of around US$65 billion.

Bernard Madoff explained that he began operating the Ponzi scheme in 1991. Facing stock market and national recession, he felt 'compelled' to give investors high returns. 'When I began the Ponzi scheme, I believed it would end shortly, and I would be able to extricate myself and my clients from the scheme.'[3]

He recognized that he had never made any legitimate investments with the money received from the clients. Instead, he deposited the money into an account in Chase Manhattan Bank. In the context of the subprime crisis, it was hard to satisfy his investors' expectations of high returns. He declared that his intention had always been to resume legitimate activities. However, it proved 'difficult, and ultimately impossible'. Madoff was aware of the fact that his scam would eventually be exposed.

It was questioned whether his family was aware of the scam. Some critics contended that their estrangement was actually a charade. Madoff claimed that his relatives were on the legitimate side of the business.

His accountant, David Friehling, had been the only other person formally charged in the case. The SEC alleged BMIS statements were materially false because Friehling did not make any meaningful audit. He did not perform procedures to confirm that the securities operations purportedly held on behalf of its customers even existed.

However, the SEC was investigating how and why regulators failed to detect the fraud despite many alerts, especially that from Markopolos. It had been heavily criticized for its lack of diligence. SEC Chairman Christopher Cox recognized its responsibility. 'I am gravely concerned by the apparent multiple failures over at least a decade to thoroughly investigate these allegations or at any point to seek formal authority to pursue them.'[4] Cox would leave the SEC shortly afterwards.

Questions

1. Imagine you were part of Bernard Madoff's inner circle when he was struggling with losses in the early 1990s. If he had confided in you about his temptation to "cover losses temporarily," what would you have advised—and why? How would your advice reflect your ethical values?
2. Are there any specific circumstances that make Bernard Madoff's behaviour particularly reprehensible?
3. What type of responsibility – whether by commission, omission, or by influencing or collaborating in the actions of others (see 3.5) – can be attributed to the following individuals: Bernard Madoff, Ruth Madoff, Peter Madoff, Charles Weiner, the Madoff sons and David Friehling?
4. Choose one person from Madoff's circle (e.g., Ruth Madoff, Peter Madoff, or David Friehling). If you were in their place, how would you have responded to early signs that something unethical might be happening? What pressures might you have felt, and how would you try to act with integrity?

SECTION A. THE ETHICAL DIMENSION OF DECISION-MAKING

Decision-making is a process by which a person, a team or a leading group deliberate and choose to perform an action, or a certain course of action, to solve a problem regarding a person or situation that needs attention. Other decisions can emerge after considering that a situation should be improved. Sometimes decisions are strategic, using a plan, method, or adaptation to achieve a goal. Examples of strategic business decisions include opening a new market, developing a product or introducing a significant innovation in managing the company. Other decisions relate to the establishment of policies within the company, which can include a set of ideas or a plan of what to do in particular situations, while other decisions are operative, making short-term choices. There are also slight decisions regarding day-to-day affairs taken by intermediate managers or supervisors. Anyway, it can be easily understood that decision-making is a central element in managing and governing business companies.

Relevant decisions are made after gathering the relevant information, raising counsel from experts, and listening to the people affected by the problem, who may themselves suggest a certain possible solution. Several people can participate in the decision-making by providing information, suggestions and, in some cases, voting about the choice. However, often it is an individual who must make the final decision. Even in cases in which some people participate in decision-making, there are individual judgements and personal opinions on what the right decision should be. Thus, the individual treatment of the decision-making process seems fully justified.

When decisions are implemented, they become actions, which are external to the decision-maker. In a certain sense, a decision is already an 'internal action' in the agent's mind, and different types of effects can be foreseen of the 'external action'.

It is important to emphasize that ethics is inherent to any decision-making process because every decision impacts both people and the natural environment. A relevant aspect of ethics in decision-making is the moral judgement of alternative courses of action, just as it is in ethical behaviour – though this is not the only element. As we will discuss next, ethical behaviour also involves moral sensibility, motivation and character, in addition to judgement.

4.1 Elements of moral behaviour

Evaluation of alternatives is a crucial step in the decision-making process. This evaluation is often presented as a deliberation in which the pros and cons of each option are listed, followed by the progressive elimination of those alternatives with more cons than pros. While this approach is reasonable, it carries the risk of evaluating solely in terms of instrumental rationality, neglecting practical rationality and ethical considerations.

In reality, the evaluation of alternatives also involves a moral judgement, which is a key element of ethical behaviour – though not the only one. According to renowned psychologist James Rest,[5] moral behaviour is determined by four interrelated psychological components that come into play when deciding whether or not to carry out an action (see Table 4.1).

Moral sensitivity

Moral sensitivity refers to the recognition of the moral aspect of a given situation and the awareness of the moral dimension involved in a certain decision, or in the violation of a moral value or ethical norm. This sensitivity can take the form of understanding how a decision or action can affect people and the natural environment – and first and foremost the agent themselves, since by acting ethically they become a better person (or the contrary, if they act unethically).

Managers with scarce moral sensibility tend to see each problem only in economic terms or only consider their individual or corporate interests in their actions. In contrast, managers with a better

Table 4.1 Psychological components of moral behaviour

Components	Meaning
Moral sensitivity	'I see the action involves a moral content.'
Moral judgement	'I judge that something is right or wrong.'
Moral motivation	'I want to do it because this is good.'
Moral character	'I have interior strength to do the right thing.'

developed sensitivity are constantly asking themselves if what they are doing is good. A lack of moral sensibility may lead managers to escape from the foreseeable consequences of their actions, or their responsibility for these, and thus act less carefully than they otherwise would.

Moral judgement

This leads one to evaluate the action in terms of goodness or badness. Moral judgement comes from within the individuals either while completing the action, or afterwards, when they evaluate what they did from a moral perspective. The moral judgement concludes with a statement forbidding, allowing or encouraging an action.

Moral judgements are called 'judgements of conscience' (2.5) or 'moral conscience', because the person who makes the judgement sees it in his or her conscience as obligatory and binding. This is the sense of the saying, 'my conscience does not allow me to take part in this business' or 'my judgement is that this is a dirty business'. Thus, the moral conscience, by presenting moral duties in specific situations, makes a person aware of his or her responsibility. Following one's own conscience does not mean acting arbitrarily. Aligned with the previous, (moral) conscience has been defined as 'a judgement of reason whereby the human person recognizes the moral quality of a concrete act that he is going to perform, is in the process of performing, or has already completed'.[6] Since each person has the ability to make their own moral judgements, he or she also has a responsibility to use all reasonable means to make a correct judgement and to dispel any doubts that may arise. Some religious traditions emphasize moral conscience as an encounter with God.[7]

The dignity of the person demands that they make judgements with *moral rectitude*, that is, with a righteousness of moral conscience, trying to discern honestly what one must do for good behaviour in a particular situation by applying ethical principles with practical wisdom, as we will discuss further (Section B). The virtue of practical wisdom (2.8) has a crucial role in making sound moral judgements. We will return to this point in the next section (4.2).

A sound moral judgement depends on how accurate the available information is, the uprightness of the decision-maker and his or her rigour in making the judgement. Making a sound moral judgement may be very simple in some situations but very complex in others. We examine the topic in detail later (Section B).

Moral motivation

This is the personal disposition or willingness to act for moral motives. A person can have a generic motivation for good behaviour, but moral judgement provides immediate reasons for accepting or rejecting a particular action. While moral judgement states that 'this is the right thing to do', moral motivation drives one to do it – 'I ought to do it.' Moral motives come from the desire to maintain personal integrity and to act virtuously. Religious motives can reinforce moral motivation, and in some persons these motives can even be quite strong.

Moral motivation concurs with other types of motivations, such as economic results, self-satisfaction, learning, etc. There is no problem if moral motivation is consistent with these other types. However, it can also conflict with motivations based on useful rewards derived from the action (money, power, status, prestige) or with those resulting from the pleasure or satisfaction that the agent can obtain in performing the action. When one of these latter motives becomes the dominant motive for acting, putting aside the moral motive, there is no prospect of good behaviour, only for wrongdoing or misbehaviour. The notion of *temptation* arises when a motivational conflict occurs due to the attraction of some motive contrary to good behaviour.

Moral character

Motivation as a driver of the action is not enough. One also needs good stable dispositions of character, that is, *virtues* (1.10, 2.8), which give interior strength to the will for good behaviour and helps to resolve the tension between moral motivation and other motivations.

Practical wisdom (2.8), which helps one be aware of the morality of situations and to make sound moral judgements, as noted, is a central aspect of moral character. Other virtues, such as justice, provide motivation to those who possess them. Thus, a just person is motivated to act with justice. Character therefore has an influence in the preceding elements, so virtuous people – those with a strong moral character – tend to have higher moral sensibility, make better moral judgements, and have more moral motivation than those who are less virtuous.

These four elements can be discovered in business practice, as well as other aspects of human life. Sometimes ethical failures come simply through a lack of moral sensibility. This could be the case of managers being so worried about results that they are insensitive to people affected by one of their decisions or who are placed in an unfair situation the manager has created. Other misbehaviours can have their origin in making a false moral judgement, such as trying to justify the morality of a behaviour by 'rationalization', behaviour motivated by certain interests instead of sincerely seeking the right judgement. Lack of moral motivation can also lead to misbehaviour, even though a right judgement is made. Last but not least, misbehaviour can occur due to a lack of interior strength, for instance, a lack of courage to act correctly.

Acting rationally, any personal behaviour should be preceded by the decision of performing an action, choosing between different alternatives or, at least, between effecting the action or omitting it. In practice, we can conclude by saying that moral judgement, although it is not the only element for good behaviour, is a necessary condition and therefore deserves particular attention.

4.2 Practical wisdom in formulating moral judgements

The holistic approach presented here requires a 'wise balance', and, in doing so, practical wisdom plays a crucial role.

Practical wisdom (prudence, in an ethical sense) helps one to determine what is good in a particular action, as noted (2.8A). Wise people, that is, those with very strong practical wisdom, can intuitively see what is good without recourse to ethical principles. However, principles and norms do aid in making moral judgements, especially for those whose practical wisdom is not well developed. Principles, norms and other ethical standards (rules) usually bring together conclusions of practical wisdom accumulated through the ages.

Frequently, moral judgements, or judgements of conscience, provide a personal conviction that an action is indubitably right, based on the certainty of a conclusion formed after rigorous and sincere deliberation. This type of certainty is known as *prudential* or *moral certainty*. Most people agree that a sincere and honest judgement should be followed since, for every individual, his or her judgement of conscience is the immediate norm of morality.

In some situations, the decision-maker might feel certain of having reached the right verdict when in fact the judgement is flawed because, although he or she was acting in good faith and seeking a reasonable means to arrive at a sound judgement, some essential element has escaped consideration. If the subject acts with invincible ignorance, he or she bears no responsibility, as has been noted (3.3).

A sound moral judgement on a particular business situation requires moral rectitude in seeking the moral truth. This is why every effort must be made to avoid errors in making judgements of conscience, including:

- *Deliberating* on the particular situation, pondering relevant circumstances and consequences.
- Adopting a *sincere attitude* of seeking what is good and avoiding the temptation to justify one's own interests by false rationalizations.
- Applying *ethical principles*, including the Golden Rule (1.8), which requires putting oneself in another's shoes and reflecting on how one would like to be treated. Aristotelian-Personalist Ethics (2, B) provides well-founded principles (2.7) on which to make a sound judgement.
- Acquiring *ethical training*, particularly in topics related to one's own field (particular aspects of business ethics), can also be a great help.
- *Recalling* previous similar situations and criteria acquired from these.
- Hearing *moral voices* on relevant topics, including the recommendations of a moral leader and experts in business ethics.
- *Seeking advice*, in cases of doubt, from competent people of proven moral solvency.
- *Leaning towards the safer judgement* if the doubt persists.

In view of what has been said, to make good moral judgements it seems important to develop practical wisdom.

Development of practical wisdom

Some behaviours develop practical wisdom. Among them, the following are worthy of note:[8]

- *Exercising experience* or reminding oneself about past events to understand clearly what usually happens when a certain type of action is performed. Experience is developed by trying to retain the significance of ethically relevant elements when examining one's own experience and also being attentive to other people.

- *Striving to understand* the present situation in order to perceive what is ethically relevant. This requires evaluating people appropriately – their dignity, rights and needs – along with significant circumstances from an ethical perspective. For example, in a workplace setting, a manager guided by practical wisdom might recognize that an employee's sudden drop in performance is due to a personal crisis and consequently respond with empathy rather than immediate disciplinary action.
- *Seeking advice* from prudent people and experts in order to benefit from their experience and good judgement. *Accumulated practical wisdom* in maxims, moral precepts and exemplary role models are valuable, at least in the first stages of practical wisdom development.
- *Practising sagacity and promptness* in resolving issues that one knows well enough and feels confident to judge independently. Otherwise, rather than being an expression of sagacity, it would amount to imprudence. By doing so, one enhances the ability to decide – without unnecessary delay – what to do in a specific situation.
- *Reflecting on significant data*, relating pieces of information in a coherent and reasonable way and listening to the appropriate people are key practices. The opposite of this would be, for instance, insisting that one is right without sufficient justification, and closing oneself off from others' perspectives without properly considering their arguments.
- *Trying to foresee future consequences* that will probably flow from an action and possible events that might combine with such consequences. This will lead one to use all necessary means to achieve the desired objectives and avoid, or at least minimize, undesirable side effects.
- *Acting with caution* in the face of any obstacles that may appear. A cautious person knows when to expect difficulties and anticipates them.
- *Sense of responsibility*, which leads one to consider carefully the reasons for acting and the consequences of each action, in accordance with appropriate values and criteria. This also includes being alert to special circumstances that might arise in a particular situation, and which are worth noting, and distinguishing, from irrelevant circumstances.
- *Living rightly*, a person who is just, strong-minded and moderate is in a better position to be prudent than a person in whom those virtues are poorly developed. That is because, in practising any virtue, one also practises practical wisdom: in order to live in accordance with justice, one needs to know what is right in each circumstance. The same applies to fortitude and temperance. By contrast, practical wisdom is unlikely to have taken deep root in a person who does not lead an honest life. The thoughts of someone who fails to live in accordance with his or her beliefs are likely to become twisted so as to justify their chosen way of life. Hence the saying: 'If you don't live as you think, you'll end up thinking as you live.'

On the opposite side, there are behaviours that undermine practical wisdom or prevent its growth, namely:

- Practising *guile*, or the tendency to use any means to achieve one's own interests while disregarding an honest pursuit of what is truly good, and failing to distinguish between licit and illicit methods. An example of this would be a business executive who manipulates data to win a contract, knowing the information is misleading, thus prioritizing personal or organizational gain over ethical integrity.

- Acting with a *lack of concern for people* due to excessive anxiety about technical, economic or political aspects of a problem. This would be the case when a company director under pressure to cut costs decides to lay off a large number of employees without considering support measures, communication strategy or the emotional impact on staff. The focus on numbers overrides the human dimension of leadership.
- Analysing problems with *superficiality*, which prevents one understanding what the right course of action is. For instance, a manager addressing a drop in team performance by blaming laziness, without exploring deeper causes such as burnout or poor communication, risks making ineffective or unfair decisions.
- Making *rush decisions* driven by the urge to reach a conclusion quickly, without sufficient deliberation or sound judgement. This would be the case when approving a product launch without thorough testing because of looming deadlines which may lead to safety issues or reputational damage.
- Developing *attitudes of self-complacency*, scorning others' advice, or failing to submit one's own solutions to the judgement of those who could provide expert or wise opinions. Thus, a senior manager, confident in his or her own experience, refuses to consult the IT department before implementing a new software system. This leads to serious integration issues that could have been avoided with expert input.
- Being *inconsistent* in the execution of decisions or acting with *negligence* or laxity in fulfilling duties – including carelessness or the omission of responsibilities associated with one's role. For example a team leader frequently makes last-minute changes to project goals and misses important deadlines, causing confusion among staff and diminishing the team's performance and trust.

4.3 Full rationality in decision-making

Decision-making is generally understood as a rational process; however, it is often influenced by intuition, experience or simply by what is customary in a given context. Nonetheless, rational analysis is essential for deep reflection. The rational process has been often reduced to a purely technical or instrumental rationality, centred on the means and evaluating them in terms of effectiveness and efficiency. In this view, ethics is introduced merely as a constraint, which seems a narrow view of ethics. We will explore the challenge of overcoming this view, but first, let us describe the typical steps outlined for a rational decision-making process.

Steps in the decision-making process

Making decisions entails a reflective process, which can be presented through a series of steps.

1 *Formulation of the problem*
   A problem emerges when a situation is considered unsatisfactory from some perspective, and one tries to solve it. Before the formulation of the problem and in preparation for the

next steps there is a gathering of data and an initial reflection, seeking to discover the deep problem and distinguish it from other problems, which are actually only symptoms of something more fundamental. Listening to people who know the situation well and asking for advice from experts can help direct one to the right diagnosis and to a correct formulation of the problem.

2 *Set a goal*
The goal expresses what the decision-maker is trying to achieve, presumably something which will allegedly solve the problem.

3 *Generation of alternatives*
Generating possible alternative actions or courses of action could effectively reach the same desired outcome. Generating alternatives requires knowledge and experience, but also imagination and creativity. Brainstorming to identify alternatives might be necessary, especially when faced with complex or difficult problems. One obvious possibility is to do nothing, because any action could bring about worse problems than those that already exist. An alternative resulting from a combination of others is also possible.

4 *Evaluation of alternatives*
Alternatives should be evaluated, firstly in regard to their likely effectiveness in achieving the goal and solving the problem, but, as we will discuss (4.2), sound evaluation should also consider other elements, such as the morality of each alternative and how an alternative can affect the relationships with people affected by the action and the impact on the human, social and natural environment.

5 *Election of the best alternative*
After a careful analysis and evaluation of alternatives, one possible action or course of action should finally be selected as the best. This alternative may minimize undesired secondary effects.

6 *Implementation of the decision*
Even after deciding, the decision-making process is not yet concluded. The decision must also be implemented in the right way and in proper time.

7 *Evaluation of the outcomes*
To complete the process, monitoring and evaluation of the consequences of the action are required. These actions will help to weigh up the appropriateness of the alternatives to solve the problem, allow those involved to reflect on non-preventable collateral consequences of the action, and encourage learning that will impact subsequent decisions.

These steps of the decision-making process can be summarized in three basic acts of the decision-maker: (1) *deliberation* (formulation of the problem, determination and evaluation of a goal, generation and evaluation of alternatives); (2) *decision* (election of an alternative); and (3) *implementation* (implementation of the selected plan and evaluation of its consequences).

Decision-making requires full rationality

The steps outlined above often only guide decision-makers by the light of instrumental rationality, which is oriented to evaluate the most efficient means for a given end (2.6). In this way, any other criteria are considered mere constraints on the maximization of economic results. However, seeing decision-making as a rational process based only on result maximization is problematic. Firstly, because such maximization, in general, is not realistic; secondly, because human rationality is not reduced to instrumental rationality.

The lack of realism in rational approaches focused on maximizing economic results was pointed out by Herbert Simon,[9] who showed that human rationality has no capacity to determine exactly what maximization is, because of caps on information, time available and the information-processing ability of the mind. That is why, Simon affirms that decision-making is made with *bounded rationality*. Consequently, he suggests being a 'satisfier' rather than a 'maximizer', that is, one who seeks to make decisions that are sufficiently satisfactory. This leads the person to making *optimal decisions* in the current context and encourages them to consider the long-term effects of the decision. Introducing *bounded rationality* is an interesting insight; however, Simon himself did not escape from instrumental rationality, since in his proposal the decision-maker acting as a 'satisfier' focuses exclusively on the economic dimension.

The objection to decision-making exclusively based on *instrumental rationality* ignores the fact that *practical rationality* also has an important role in human action, seeking the most convenient action, as well as the knowledge provided by *theoretical rationality* in the knowledge of identities (2.6). Actually, a rational process of decision-making should consider all capacities of human reason: theoretical, instrumental and practical.

4.4 Evaluative criteria in decision-making

In generating and evaluating an action and its possible alternatives one can foresee the effects of the action. In deciding, one may only focus on an external result of the performance with economic value, but, if this action also affects people and the environment, it can have consequences on the quality of the relationships between the agent and those affected. Besides, any decision and the subsequent action also have consequences on the acting person.[10]

Effects of the human action

Observing carefully the human action in the business context, four types of effects can be identified (Figure 4.1):

- *Productive effects*: These effects refer to techno-economic results, measured in terms of *effectiveness* (the achievement of a goal or the solution of a problem) and *efficiency* (accomplishment of the goal with the least waste of time and effort).

Ethics in Decision-Making

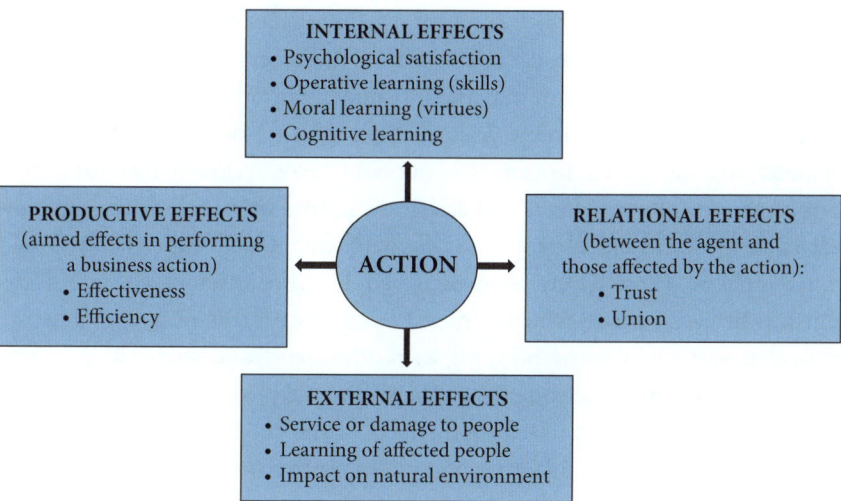

Figure 4.1 Effects of the business action

- *External effects*: These refer to the impact of an action on both people and the natural environment. This impact can include *objective benefits or harm* caused to those affected by the action, which can be evaluated in ethical terms. An action may respect – or violate – human dignity and the rights of others; it may provide genuine service or, conversely, involve deception or fraud. In addition to the objective consequences, actions also create *subjective perceptions and learning experiences* among the recipients and others affected. These perceptions may align with the actual benefits, but not necessarily. For instance, individuals might not only be satisfied with the economic good or service provided but also feel that they were treated with respect and fairness – or, on the contrary, feel neglected or mistreated. Finally, the external effects of an action extend to the natural environment. This includes the consumption of raw materials, the generation of waste and pollution, the contribution to the carbon footprint and the long-term consequences for future generations.
- *Internal effects*: These refer to the effects of the action on the acting person (agent). These effects include *psycho-physic aspects* (satisfaction, fatigue and so on). In acting, the agent develops *operational learning* in terms of skills, abilities and other forms of practical experience. This operational learning could be applicable in making similar actions in the future. Similarly, the action has an ethical content, and its intentional execution develops moral traits of character, that is, virtues. Thus, another internal effect of the action is *moral growth* – or, conversely, moral deterioration. Furthermore, human action generates an internal experience within the agent, involving awareness of the action itself, the context in which it takes place, and an understanding of the identity of those affected and the impact on them. This internal experience constitutes a form of *cognitive learning*. This perception can be correct or incorrect. Thus, people with whom one is interacting can either be regarded with intrinsic dignity and innate rights or as a mere resource for the agent's interests. Internal

experience can also contain an evaluation of the effects of the action on people, such as the service or damage produced, satisfaction in the reception of the action and possibly an assessment of what the reaction may be. Internal experience can also include an evaluation of the impact on the environment. A correct recognition of the other, a willingness to serve people, and care for the environment is necessary to develop the moral traits of character, mentioned above. Internal effects of the action – to sum up – include psychosomatic reaction, operative learning and moral growth, along with the internal experience of the action.

- *Relational effects*: These occur between people who interact. It refers to the mutual relationship between those who interact, basically in terms of acceptance or rejection. A derived relational effect is the building of *mutual trust* and *strength of union* between the agents that interact, and consequently to the willingness to continue interacting in the future. Relational effects are related to external effects of the action. Satisfaction and perception of honesty and benevolence of the other party help build trust and reinforce the union between the agents.

As a conclusion, it is important to stress the error of evaluating an action only in terms of results (effectiveness and efficiency), when the mentioned four effects are relevant.

The triple evaluative criteria: Instrumentality, morality and relationality (IMR)

Considering these multiple effects of the action, it could be suggested that a triple evaluation be incorporated into the decision-making process, focusing on *instrumentality*, *morality* and *relationality* (Figure 4.2).

- *Instrumentality* refers to how one plans to achieve the pursued goal, using criteria of effectiveness and efficiency. Instrumentality basically focuses on productive effects but can also include the expected operative learning.

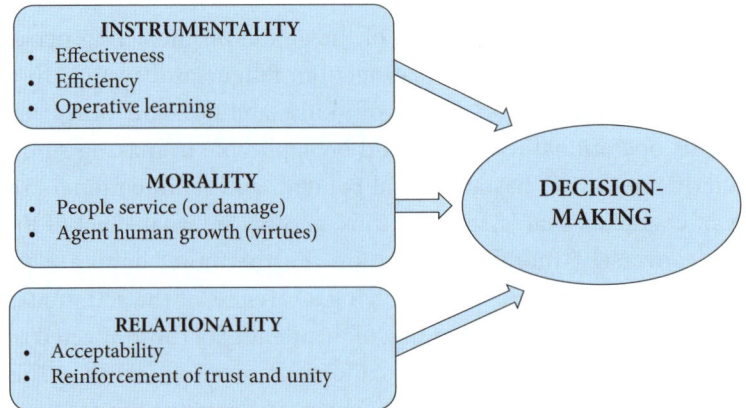

Figure 4.2 Triple evaluative criteria for decision-making

- *Morality* focuses on the service or damage to people and the environment, which is related to the moral growth of the agent, becoming respectively a better or worse person. Moral evaluation considers any alternative from the ethical perspective, evaluating whether a given alternative is morally good. In this way, morality introduces the moral judgement in such a way that an alternative can be rejected because it is ethically unacceptable. However, a judgement can show that one alternative is ethically superior to another. Evaluating the morality of an action requires paying attention to ethical principles and virtues, as will be discussed below (4.5), in addition to the action's consequences for each person, social group, or natural environment affected. In this way, it can be useful to prepare a 'map of affected' by the action.
- *Relationality* refers to how an alternative can affect relations with people affected by the action in terms of acceptability or rejection, generation of trust and the reinforcement of the relationship's unity, or the contrary. Relationality also entails considering people or groups non-directly affected by the action (for example, the mass media and non-governmental organizations) but who have the capacity to influence the decision-maker or future results.

Thus, a multi-criteria approach is necessary for a sound evaluation of alternative actions or courses of action. This posits the question of how to solve conflicts in judgements on instrumentality, morality and relationality.

Congruent and conflicting evaluations

On evaluating an action we can find congruent evaluations, in which an alternative is in agreement or disagreement with all relevant evaluative criteria (for example, launching a new product that one presumes will be profitable, obtaining good social acceptance, generating learning and providing a great service). In contrast, we can find conflicting evaluations, one or more being positive and another or others negative (for example, a downsizing with a massive lay-off, which will make the firm more competitive and profitable but draw a bad social reaction from the employees, unions and public opinion, cause demoralization in the remaining employees and be ethically questionable). Both situations posit dilemmas regarding what criterion is more relevant when choosing an alternative and ultimately what choice should be selected as optimal among a set of acceptable alternatives.

After analysing and evaluating the alternatives, we may find that certain of them should clearly be rejected as being below an acceptable level in one or more dimensions. Thus, one alternative might be inviable for economic reasons (instrumentality) or because of the power and oppositions of unions (relationality). The ethical analysis might also conclude that an alternative is not morally acceptable (morality).

A relevant conflict can appear when an alternative is profitable but not ethical. The temptation here is to put ethics aside for the sake of economic results. However, ethics is about human good, and this takes an absolute priority over interests such as profitability, which is only an instrumental good: it is good for something but not absolutely good.

After rejecting what is for one reason or another unacceptable, the next question is which of the alternatives is the optimal. This requires a 'wise balance' without forgetting that ethical principles put people first. However, the ethical principles (2.7) entail both negative and positive duties. *Negative duties* signal certain universally minimum standards and point out unacceptable actions. In contrast, *positive duties* indicate a direction, so have no upper limit. A person must do as much good as possible within the limits of his or her abilities and resources available in any given situation. Applying this to managerial decision-making, managers have both the resources and power to make decisions, but they are limited, and within such limitations they should make the decision guided by the aim of doing as much good as possible in the situation. In addition, they must consider that what may seem good in the short term (avoiding lay-offs in a critical situation) can become bad in the long term (lack of competitiveness and maybe bankruptcy).

In other words, a sound evaluation requires a holistic approach, which includes the three dimensions – instrumentality, morality and relationality – and is clearly related to the long term. For example, when evaluating whether to implement a new AI-driven customer service system, a manager should not only consider its *instrumentality* (e.g. efficiency gains and cost savings), but also its *morality* (e.g. whether it results in fair treatment of employees whose roles may be displaced), and its *relationality* (e.g. how it affects the company's relationship with customers and staff). A long-term perspective is essential to foresee whether the decision fosters sustainable value or leads to future ethical or reputational issues.

Asking wise people and experts for advice may help one to resolve difficulties resulting from conflicting evaluations or help one to choose the optimal alternative from various acceptable options. This posits the crucial role of practical wisdom in making moral judgements.

Business Ethics in Action #4

Malden Mills: An unusual decision[11]

Aaron M. Feuerstein (1925–2013) served as CEO of Malden Mills Industries for approximately thirty years, guiding the family business founded in 1906 by his grandfather, Henry Feuerstein, a Hungarian immigrant. The company initially produced wool sweaters and bathing suits but later became renowned for its development of PolarFleece – a registered trademark for polar fleece fabric. This innovative material became a staple in outdoor clothing, such as jackets, hats, sweaters and sweatpants.

Feuerstein graduated from Yeshiva University in 1947, where he majored in English and philosophy. He began working in the family business shortly afterwards and assumed leadership in the 1970s. In 1979, he oversaw the development of polar fleece, a significant contribution to the textile industry.

Throughout his tenure, Feuerstein became known not only for his relentless drive to innovate but also for his deep commitment to his employees and the community of Lawrence, Massachusetts, where the mill was based. His leadership came into the national spotlight following a devastating fire on 11 December 1995. A dust explosion in one of the factory's hoppers sparked a fire that destroyed three buildings, severely damaging 40 per cent of the entire plant and putting about 3,000 jobs in jeopardy. The fire, later classified as an industrial accident, caused thirty-six injuries, including eight critical cases, and was considered the largest property loss from a fire in Massachusetts history.

Despite the scale of the disaster, Feuerstein made an extraordinary decision. Instead of closing the factory, laying off workers or moving production overseas, he committed to rebuilding the plant and keeping his employees on full payroll with health benefits. He used his insurance money to fund the reconstruction and ensure that workers were paid during the interim – spending millions to retain all 2,700 employees. Although the plant took until 14 September 1997 to become fully operational, only seventy workers remained displaced by that time. His actions during this crisis earned him widespread acclaim for his loyalty and ethical business practices.

At the time of the fire, Malden Mills reported earnings of $380 million. Despite operating in a highly competitive textile industry, the company remained profitable and was known for its philanthropic contributions to the local community, supporting various organizations and initiatives. Remarkably, the company had never experienced a strike, and its workers were paid approximately 20 per cent above the industry average – a testament to Feuerstein's belief in fair treatment and the value of labour.

Feuerstein, an Orthodox Jew, credited his business ethics and management philosophy to the teachings of his family and his faith. In a personal communication during a research survey, he described his guiding principle as a 'sensitivity to the human equation', emphasizing that corporations have a responsibility not only to their employees but also to the broader community. He saw loyalty, reciprocity and mutual trust as core values of effective management. These values, deeply rooted in his family's traditions, shaped the company's approach to labour – not merely as a cost but as an essential component in creating its products. Feuerstein's upbringing in a family that prioritized fairness in business and timely compensation for workers profoundly influenced his approach to leadership.

Although Malden Mills secured several significant contracts after rebuilding, a recession in 2001 led the company to file for bankruptcy in November of that year – partly due to the financial strain caused by its rebuilding efforts and payroll commitments. The company eventually regained solvency, largely thanks to the generosity of its creditors and significant government subsidies. However, Feuerstein was relieved of control as creditors took over the company. While the business survived the initial bankruptcy, it continued to struggle, leading to a second bankruptcy filing in January 2007. Later that year, Malden Mills' assets were purchased by a newly formed entity, Polartec, LLC, marking the end of an era for the family-run business.

In 2019, Milliken & Co. acquired Polartec and announced its intention to transform the business by reorienting it toward technology- and innovation-led growth. The company also underwent a leadership overhaul and changes to its operations, manufacturing footprint, and customer relationships.

* * *

The fire caused extensive damage and left Malden Mills in a precarious position, facing an uncertain future. Aaron Feuerstein's response was nothing short of unconventional – especially given the trends at the time. Many companies, particularly in the textile industry, were cutting staff and shifting production to countries with cheaper labour to boost profits or remain competitive in a rapidly globalizing market.

Feuerstein's approach was fundamentally different. His vision centred on people, his company and a deep sense of responsibility – one that went beyond avoiding harm to actively caring for his employees. This mindset was evident not only in his response to the fire but also in his leadership beforehand. His decision to continue paying his workers while the plant was rebuilt stands as a testament to his belief in the moral obligations of business leaders towards their employees.

It is true that these choices may have contributed to the company's eventual insolvency and the loss of many of the jobs he sought to protect. However, Feuerstein was widely praised for refusing to prioritize profitability at the expense of human welfare. His actions sparked a broader conversation about the role of ethics in business – particularly in industries like textiles, which often focus on cost-cutting over employee well-being.

There remains insufficient data to definitively assess whether Feuerstein's strategic decision was flawed, or whether external factors – such as the recession, or possibly a lack of innovation or diversification – ultimately led to Malden Mills' financial troubles. The company eventually fell into crisis. The latest owner, Milliken & Co., suggests that a new strategic approach may have been more suitable for the time. Perhaps. But this should not diminish the importance of maintaining a sense of responsibility towards workers.

Feuerstein made a difficult decision by prioritizing the well-being of his employees and the community, even in the face of extreme adversity. His actions demonstrated remarkable intent and genuine concern for people – and they were widely recognized. However, the long-term outcome of the story was not as positive, possibly due to the economic downturn or a decision that didn't fully account for foreseeable consequences and alternative options.

In any case, business decisions must be made with *practical wisdom* – taking into consideration all significant factors and placing ethics at the forefront. This includes balancing the long-term preservation of jobs with short-term financial needs and ensuring the sustainability of the business well into the future.

SECTION B. MAKING MORAL JUDGEMENTS IN DECISION-MAKING

4.5 The Triple Font of Morality approach for making moral judgements

When an agent decides to carry out an action, they select a certain *end* (goal) and the *means* to achieve it. The agent forms the *intention* to reach the goal and chooses a specific action as the means to that end. These are two crucial elements in the moral evaluation of an action.

In addition, the agent should be aware of foreseeable consequences and significant situational factors. These two latter aspects can be grouped under the category of *'relevant circumstances'*, or simply *'circumstances'* – the former referred to as *'consequent circumstances'* (foreseeable consequences) and the latter as *'situational circumstances'* (the conditions in which the action occurs).

Thus, what determines the moral judgement of an action are the morality of the *intention*, the *action chosen* and the *circumstances*. Practical wisdom plays a key role in guiding reflection on all these elements.

These three elements are known as the 'fonts' or sources for evaluating the morality of an action. Together, they form the basis of the so-called *Triple Font de Morality* (TFM) approach (see Figure 4.3), used for making moral judgements.[12]

- The *intention* is, therefore, the agent's aim of performing an action evaluated in moral terms. A morally acceptable intention requires *moral motivation*, doing the action because this is good, but this does not exclude the presence of extrinsic motivations (such as tangible results) or intrinsic motivations (such as satisfaction or learning), provided that these motivations are themselves morally acceptable. For example, a manager may decide to implement a new training programme to support employees in their professional development (a morally good aim). At the same time, the manager may also be motivated by the desire to improve team performance (an extrinsic result) and to gain personal satisfaction from seeing employees grow (an intrinsic motivation). However, beyond simply being 'acceptable', an intention can vary in intensity depending on the agent's willingness or commitment to doing good. Consider, for example, two healthcare administrators who decide to expand mental health services in their hospital. The first does so because it is part of new government guidelines and wants to ensure compliance and institutional reputation. The second fully embraces the initiative out of a personal conviction that mental health is a neglected area of care and is deeply motivated to improve patients' well-being. While both intentions are morally acceptable and lead to positive outcomes, the second reflects a deeper and more intentional commitment to doing good.
- The *action chosen* on purpose as a means to achieve the aim. Notice that the term 'action chosen' entails deliberation and election. That is why, traditionally, the action chosen is termed *moral object* (or simply *object*) of the action. Therefore, the moral object is not a mere physical description of the action but denotes a moral content too. Thus, killing a man is the empirical fact but might describe an assassination or an act of self-defence – two very different occurrences, morally speaking (two different *objects*).
- *Circumstances*, which include *foreseeable consequences* (*consequent circumstances*) arising from the action, and *situational factors* (*situational circumstances*), that is, relevant aspects of the situation and the socio-cultural context where the action takes place.

By choosing an action (object) with the will of reaching an end (intention), the decision is made. This inseparable unity of the intention and the chosen action (object) leads to the conclusion that, for a human action to be good (ethically correct), both the intention and the object must be good, since a thing is good only when all its parts are good. Thus, we can affirm:

For a decision to be morally good, both the intention and the object must be good.

In simpler terms, as the aphorism says, 'the end does not justify the means' or, more accurately, 'a good end does not justify morally wrong means'. Consequently:

- *Choosing a wrong object corrupts the decision* even if the intention is good. For example, committing a fraud to save the company from bankruptcy is bad, not because of the intention but because of the morality of the chosen action (object).
- *A wrong intention makes the decision, as a whole, wrong* even if the object is good. This is so, for instance, when a person gives to charity (object) purely out of vanity (intention) or if a boss deals kindly with subordinates (object) in order to manipulate them (intention). It is therefore unacceptable to do wrong in the hope to obtain good. Applying this to some common business situations, one would conclude that it is not ethically acceptable, for instance, to 'cook the (accounting) books' to secure a loan that would be crucial to a company's survival, or to deceive clients about product quality to maintain badly needed income, or to offer a bribe to obtain an important contract.

In practical terms, making a sound moral judgement requires correctly identifying both the intention and the object of the action. What may initially seem nasty or morally insensitive is not necessarily morally wrong.

Consider, for example, a manager who decides to reassign a long-time employee to a different department, despite the employee's initial resistance. On the surface, this may appear to be an insensitive or self-serving move. However, upon closer examination, the manager's intention may be to place the employee in a role better suited to their talents – one where she can succeed and grow. The object of the action is professional development and team efficiency, not punishment or demotion. Although the decision may be unpopular or uncomfortable at first, it is not morally wrong if it ultimately respects the employee's dignity, promotes their good, and the intention is not primarily to harm. Another example is the decision to give money to an extortionist in extreme situations in order to secure a legitimate right (see further discussion in 5.9). In such cases, the action may be morally acceptable after

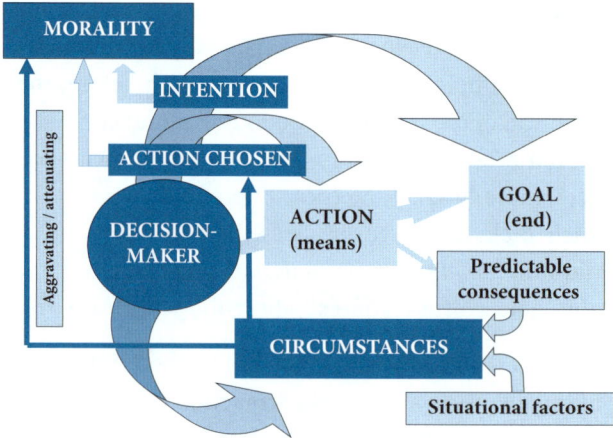

Figure 4.3 The triple font of morality

careful ethical evaluation. However, there are some objects that are never morally acceptable – so-called *intrinsically wrong actions*. We will examine this more closely in the following section, which deals with the morality of the chosen action.

Morality of the intention

An intention is good (uprightness of intention) if it is directed towards *instrumental or excellent goods* (1.10). For instance, acting to earn money with the aim of obtaining goods for life is a good intention, whereas making public some hidden facts only to cause damage is a bad intention. The moral quality of the intention can range from merely acceptable to excellent, depending on the purpose for which the action is performed. The more valuable the end of a decision, the better the intention and therefore the higher the moral quality of the decision.

Morality of the chosen action

The morality of the chosen action (object) is determined by reference to moral goods and the corresponding ethical principles, including the personalist, common good and stewardship principles (2.7).

The morality of the object is good when it respects human dignity, favours care and benevolence for people and contributes to the common good. In the obverse sense, the following criteria can be useful to determine whether an action is unacceptable:

- *The action is intrinsically wrong*: Certain actions are directly contrary to human dignity and to other norms included in the negative formulation of ethical principles (2.7). These actions are ethically unacceptable whatever the intention and circumstances. For example, committing a fraud, calumny or falsely reporting employee misbehaviour are always wrong.
- *The action is wrong under certain circumstances*: In contrast with actions that are always wrong, others are wrong only depending on the circumstances. For instance, reporting real employee misbehaviour to those who have a right to know is acceptable, sometimes even compulsory. However, it is wrong to publicize such misbehaviour to people who have no right to know of it.
- *The action is not reasonably proportionate to its bad consequences*: This would be the case, for example, of a disproportionate punishment of an employee for an act of insubordination or a sanction so severe that it would bring about effects worse than the good aimed at (for instance, the negative effect of employing coercion to discourage misbehaviour for the sake of the positive aim of maintaining discipline). Another example would be undertaking a dangerous task involving a risk to life or health that was disproportionate to the necessity of such work or to the benefit it would secure.
- *The action is forbidden by a just law*: Just laws produce moral obligation. Acting in compliance with fair laws is an ethical duty for social life. Indeed, some ethical values are specified by law. For instance, laws provide specific and reasonable rules (for example, limits of toxic substances) that favour respect for the right to life and health in the workplace. Such rules

should be followed, not only for fear of legal repercussions but also out of moral obligation. However, unjust laws do not give rise to any moral obligation. Laws are unjust, for instance, when they are contrary to human rights.

Morality of predictable consequences and relevant situational circumstances

Intention and object are the primary fonts of morality, while circumstance can aggravate or attenuate the moral seriousness of a decision. For example, the amount of money stolen is the circumstance that makes the action more or less serious from a moral, and even legal, perspective. In both cases, the object is a theft (withdrawing money without the reasonable will of its owner) but the seriousness differs due to circumstances.

Consequences can sometimes be so important that they even change the object of the action. For instance, the predictable consequences of a lack of protection of workers exposed to a toxic material becomes an injustice against the workers.

Situational circumstances can sometimes be relevant in moral terms. For instance, in abusing one's position within the company in the case of misappropriation of corporate funds by the manager or an employee who managed them. Here the object has a specific name: *embezzlement* (5.3), which is more than simply 'to steal'. It entails taking advantage of an employer's trust for personal gain.

4.6 The Principle of Double Effect

Many business actions simultaneously give rise to a good effect (or even several), that is specifically intended as a goal, and a bad effect (or effects). An example would be a factory that manufactures a useful product, creates wealth and provides jobs but pollutes the environment. In these situations, we talk of *actions with a double effect*. These types of action have long been a matter of study and debate and, since Aquinas, the so-called Principle of Double Effect (PDE)[13] has been developed to provide guidelines for making moral judgements in vexing circumstances.[14]

Before presenting an outline of this principle, it is worth pointing out that if one finds an alternative with only positive effects (for instance, a process with zero pollution), then obviously the double effect disappears, but this is not always possible. Sometimes we must choose between doing nothing and an alternative that is not wrong in itself (the object is licit) but does give rise to negative secondary effects in addition to the one or more good primary outcomes. Apart from pollution, other illustrative business examples could be a corporate downsizing that is judged necessary to maintain a firm's competitiveness, or even survival, but inevitably involves lay-offs.

A traditional scenario used to discuss actions with a double effect is the case of killing in legitimate defence facing an unjust aggressor. In this situation, the principal (good) effect is to save one's own life or the life of a third party, but a further consequence is the death of the assailant (bad effect). However, killing the assailant to save a life would not be strictly necessary in certain situations. If it were possible to subdue the aggressor without lethal measures, then taking his or her life would not be reasonable and such an action would have no legitimacy.

The PDE, supported by the limited responsibility for secondary effects of human actions (3.4), states that an action with good and bad effects is acceptable if, and only if: (1) there is no better acceptable alternative; (2) there is a just cause for this action; (3) the action itself is not intrinsically wrong; and (4) the bad effects are proportionate to the necessity of the action. If the bad effects are out of proportion to the need to perform the action, it would be rendered ethically unacceptable. Two more requirements can be added: (5) the necessity to employ reasonable means to minimize negative secondary effects and the purpose of monitoring; and (6) evaluating the situation periodically to verify whether the justification remains.

We can review these conditions by reference to a double effect decision – the restructuring of a company and the consequent lay-offs:

- *There is no better acceptable alternative*: Very often, with a little creativity and professional competence, one can come up with a better alternative than 'do this' or 'do nothing'. Thus, in a restructuring with lay-offs, one must consider whether this is the only possible solution to the problem posited.
- *There is a just cause for this action*: If not, it lacks uprightness of intention. Practical wisdom helps one evaluate whether a just cause is present. For instance, to keep the firm competitive and economically viable.
- *The action itself is not intrinsically wrong*: The object chosen as a means must be morally licit, since it is never permissible to do wrong directly. For example, deciding on a company restructuring is not intrinsically wrong and may be morally acceptable under certain conditions. Another example already mentioned (4.5), about an action that is not intrinsically wrong, is giving in to extortion when the victim has a legitimate right to something but can only obtain it by complying with the extortionist's demands. In extreme circumstances, and after careful ethical analysis, yielding to extortion may be morally acceptable (see a more detailed analysis in 5.9).

    For an action to be considered not intrinsically wrong, *the good effect must result directly from the action itself* – not from a bad effect. Otherwise, the bad effect would effectively become the object of the action. In other words, secondary effects must truly be secondary. For instance, it would be unreasonable to claim that deceiving buyers of second-hand vehicles is merely a side effect of the used-car business. Fraud is an action with a specific object and is, by its nature, intrinsically wrong.
- *The bad effects are proportionate to the necessity of the action*: The moral evaluation of the proportionality between the need to perform the action and its negative effects should be made through prudential judgement; that is, considering with practical wisdom how the action affects people from an ethical perspective (human good) in both its good and its bad effects. (What would be the probable psychological and economic consequences for those who face being laid off? What about the morale of employees who survive this round of lay-offs? What will the social impact on the community be? Is all of this proportional to the need to implement the lay-offs?)

Evaluating proportionality requires sound prudential judgement, that is, one with practical wisdom. This judgement is not based on weighing up advantages and disadvantages of good and bad effects in some utilitarian fashion but by an evaluation in terms of human good.

The challenge is to judge impartially, without letting one's own interests induce one to rationalize selfishness. The Golden Rule aids in such decisions: putting oneself in the other's position and recalling that human good is common to the one who decides and those upon whom the effects fall.

When in doubt, as already noted, practical wisdom demands seeking advice from honest and level-headed experts. One will thus be able to secure an independent, qualified opinion, avoiding the disadvantages that arise when an interested party is the judge.

- *Reasonable means will be employed to minimize negative secondary effects*: One is responsible for reasonably predictable and preventable consequences, as noted (3.4). One must do whatever is practical to avoid or at least minimize these effects – taking measures to avoid pollution, to prevent labour accidents and other such secondary effects. (In our lay-off example, this could mean aiding those who will lose their jobs; for example, helping them through outplacement, granting economic compensation or possibly transferring them to a different branch and so on.)
- *The purpose of monitoring and evaluating the situation periodically*: Circumstances can change and, inasmuch as there are negative effects, practical wisdom requires periodic monitoring and evaluation to establish whether the situation has persisted and to ensure that the means to minimize negative effects are being implemented correctly, as well as to determine whether they might be enhanced, perhaps, by technological updates. This makes sense, for instance, in problems such as pollution and hazardous products.
- *Take steps to find another alternative*: This should be one that avoids actions with double effects in the future or that has fewer collateral effects. As mentioned earlier, the first condition for accepting an action with a double effect as licit is that there is no better acceptable alternative. However, in many situations, a decision with a double effect is implemented and brings about a new and relatively permanent situation. Integrity requires exploring new alternatives with fewer or no negative side effects that can replace the problematic decision as soon as possible. For years, DDT was the most widely used pesticide in the world. However, in 1960, it was discovered that the chemical was preventing many fish-eating birds from reproducing – a serious threat to human food and biodiversity. These side effects led to the search for alternative products to replace DDT as an insecticide, and the product is now banned in many countries.

4.7 Solving ethical dilemmas

Ethical duty vs. obeying orders or being loyal to the company

There may sometimes appear to be a conflict between some negative ethical duty (moral prohibition) and a duty to obey the orders of superiors within an organization, or simply the duty of being loyal to one's company by acting in its best interest. The former could be, for example, the case of a manager or an employee who is asked to participate in some 'dirty business' or to falsify specifications of a product. An example of the latter situation is a manager who thinks that paying a bribe to obtain a contract is in the best interest of the company.

The answer to this dilemma is that the duty to obey orders is only a moral duty when such an order is morally legitimate, which is not the case for making money through dirty business or, similarly, falsifying a product specification. Neither can a bribe be justified by saying that it is for the best interests of the company that the manager serves, and not for personal gain, because one cannot do wrong to achieve a good. Apart from the matter of whether this would truly be in the best interests of the company, loyalty requires practical wisdom to determine its content in each specific situation. It is not acceptable to appeal to loyalty because, in ethical terms, loyalty is not a virtue when doing wrong is involved (as with the pseudo-loyalty to a mafia or a band of robbers).

Where an ethical duty conflicts with obeying orders, the main difficulty may be in having the strength to refuse to obey the command and to take appropriate measures to resolve the dilemma. Among the measures possible might be presenting a *conscientious objection* or reporting the case to a higher level within the organization. In extreme cases, the situation may require telling the authorities or the public that the organization concerned is doing something immoral or illegal, that is, to practise whistleblowing (3.8).

In the hypothetical case of obeying orders that have some basis in unfair laws, legal duties yield to ethical duties since laws are subordinate to ethics. This is the case with labour contracts containing clauses that might be legal in some countries but are actually abusive and involve gross exploitation of workers (10.3).

More complicated to resolve may be the dilemma of a mandated action that is not bad in itself but entails certain cooperation with an illicit action, such as an employee who is required to prepare an envelope with money in it for a bribe. Similarly, when working for a company in which one or more products do not serve human flourishing (for example, violent video games for children), one might not be directly involved with such products and may not personally approve of them despite, in some way, collaborating in a more or less remote manner (managing accounting or finances of the company, for instance). The best solution here would be to work for a company in which such cooperation does not exist at all, but sometimes this can be difficult. According to what has been said regarding material cooperation in wrongdoing (3.7), it is acceptable to remain in the company if one's own action is only remotely connected to the bad effects the company produces or if the bad effects are not too serious.

Conflict between ethical duties

A situation which entails a dilemma is when two or more positive duties come into conflict with one another. A simple example would be the case of an executive who faces the dilemma of either staying at home to look after a sick child or attending an important business meeting. In many situations such as this, the two duties could be reconciled by finding alternatives or by explaining the situation to one of the relevant people involved and negotiating a reasonable solution (the executive's husband, wife or the grandparents could look after the child, or maybe the meeting can be postponed without any very serious consequences). If that is not possible, one will have to prudently weigh up the objective importance of the respective duties and their foreseeable consequences and omit the least important of them. That decision will give rise to side effects that are tolerated as inevitable in performing an action that has sufficient necessary cause. Thus, in solving dilemmas like this, practical wisdom is crucial.

Tolerance of lesser evil

Another related dilemma is when consequences of a good action are disproportionally bad. Imagine the boss of a factory where one of the employees is not performing as he should, but there is also general unrest and considerable tension due to other problems. Here, there is a conflict between two positive duties: the duty to correct the employee and the duty to cultivate peaceful industrial relations in the company. In view of the specific situation, it may be prudent to postpone the correction so as not to inflame the atmosphere. The solution to this dilemma is known as 'tolerance of lesser evil'. Although doing wrong is neither allowed nor recommended, in some circumstances it is morally permissible to tolerate it in the interests of a higher good or to avoid more serious disorders. A temporary tolerance of an incorrect situation to avoid higher evils can be justified and may even be morally obligatory, but it should be kept under ongoing revision since circumstances can change.

Notice that solving dilemmas through the lesser evil approach is not a matter of choosing the lesser of two evils since doing wrong can never be morally obligatory. One must do what is right and tolerate the lesser evil as an inevitable side effect.

First, do no harm

Last but not least there are decisions that can be good but entail a high risk of causing great damage. This dilemma has been widely studied in medical ethics but can also have application in some business contexts. The criterion for this situation is formulated by a Latin dictum *primum non nocere*, that is, 'first, do no harm'. In practical terms, this criterion, which can be related to PDE, means that, given an existing problem, it may be better not to do something (unless you take appropriate measures to avoid damage) or even to do nothing, rather than risk causing more harm than good. In managerial terms, this criterion can be summarized by saying: firstly, do not damage; secondly, try to serve. An example of a situation like this may involve certain high-risk investments or expansion plans, which may jeopardize the business's current situation.

Case Study #4

Junseo's promotion

One November day, Junseo Jang arrived home very excited and with great news. He would be promoted within his company. However, Jia, his wife, did not seem very happy. Her laconic answer was: 'Will it mean moving to another city again?'

Junseo and Jia had three children, two girls and one boy of twelve, nine and five years of age respectively. Since Junseo entered his current firm as a salesman fifteen years before, he had been displaced three times to different cities in the country, although they had been living in the capital for the past five years. Jia did not like so many changes of residence, but she loved her husband and tried to adapt to them. But now it would be different. Two years before, she had been hired as an English teacher at the school her daughters attended. She was comfortable in her job and her work schedule was compatible with adequate dedication to her family, which she adored. In addition, she had made several friends among other mothers with daughters in that school. The girls also had good relationships with their schoolmates.

Junseo's dedication to his family was not as intense as that of his wife. Owing to his work, he had to travel a lot and often arrived home very late. The weekend, however, was devoted intensely to his wife and children. Having consolidated his professional situation in the commercial field, he was comfortable with his work, and he earned a good living.

The commercial reputation of Junseo and the prizes he won for reaching sales goals did not make his wife fully happy. Once, Jia had commented: 'I would prefer fewer prizes and more dedication to your children.' Expressions like these upset Junseo, who acknowledged that his work absorbed him, but, in his own words, it was 'so that the whole family can have a better quality of life. Also, on weekends I'm with you.'

Junseo, seeing Jia's unhappy face, explained the situation carefully. The organization he worked for had grown significantly, with strong expansion inside and outside the country. He was manager of the company's flagship product for the Seoul metropolitan area. He continued speaking:

> Look, I've been offered a fantastic position. You know that after so many years of effort, I now speak English fluently. The opportunity has come to take an international leap. Here I would never get very far. I'm thirty-nine years old and it is very unlikely that I'll be promoted to regional commercial director in the foreseeable future since the position is held by someone forty-three years of age who is highly valued by the company. I will be the company's representative for Europe and then … who knows how far I will go. They have promised me an incredible salary package. In addition, they have committed to providing me with financial help for the move and, if necessary, they will give me a low interest loan for the same purpose. We will sell the house we have here and buy another one in London. At the moment, it won't be a very elegant neighbourhood, as housing is very expensive there, but everything will come. In addition, the children will be able to go to British schools, learn English very well and have a greater international vision.

Jia listened in silence, but her unenthusiastic expression did not change. Finally, Junseo concluded:

They want me to start at the beginning of the year, but you will not have to move yet. This way the children will finish the year in their current school. In the meantime, I will look for a small apartment and we will communicate every day by Skype. I will come home once a month and spend four or five days here too. The company will pay for these trips. In summer, we will sell the house, and we will all move to London. What do you think?

Questions

1. What is the problem underlying Junseo's decision?
2. Do you think Junseo has acted with practical wisdom? Why or why not?
3. Has Junseo assessed all the dimensions of his decision, seemingly almost concluded already?
4. If you were Junseo's friend, how would you help him reflect more deeply before finalising this decision? What values or questions would you invite him to consider that he may have overlooked?

Notes

1. G. Bernanos, *'Why Freedom?' The Last Essays of Georges Bernanos* (Chicago, IL: Henry Regnery, 1955).
2. Sources: 'Ponzi Squared', *The Economist.com*, 15 December 2008: https://www.economist.com/finance-and-economics/2008/12/15/ponzi-squared; 'The Madoff Case: A Timeline', *The Wall Street Journal*, 11 December 2008: https://www.wsj.com/articles/SB112966954231272304. (Accessed on 2 June 2025); 'Madoff's Victims', *The Wall Street Journal*, 13 March 2009: https://s.wsj.net/public/resources/documents/st_madoff_victims_20081215.html; US Securities and Exchange Commission (SEC), Complaint against Madoff and BMIS LLC: https://www.sec.gov/files/litigation/complaints/2008/comp-madoff121108.pdf. (Both accessed on 2 June 2025); US Securities and Exchange Commission (SEC), Press release 2008-297 (16 December 2008): https://www.sec.gov/news/press/2008/2008-293.htm, and 2009-60 (18 March 2009) Statement Regarding Madoff Investigation: https://www.sec.gov/news/speech/2009/spch090209mls-2.htm. (All accessed on 30 October 2024).
3. *The Wall Street Journal*, 'The Madoff Case'.
4. US Securities and Exchange Commission (SEC), Press release 2008-297 (12/16/08) Statement Regarding Madoff Investigation.
5. J. R. Rest, *Moral Development: Advances in Research and Theory* (New York: Praeger, 1986).
6. Catholic Church, *Catechism of the Catholic Church* (London: Random House, 2003. Available at: www.vatican.va/archive/ENG0015/_INDEX.HTM. Accessed on August 1 2025) 9, no. 1778.
7. According to the Catholic Church, conscience means approving those actions that are good and denouncing those that are evil. A prudent person, in listening one's own conscience, 'can hear God speaking.' (*Catechism of the Catholic Church*, no. 1777.)
8. See J. Pieper, *The Four Cardinal Virtues: Prudence, Justice, Fortitude, Temperance* (Notre Dame, IN: University of Notre Dame Press, 1966); and S. Ramirez, *La prudencia* (Madrid: Palabra, 1978).

9. H. Simon, *Administrative Behavior: A Study of Decision-Making Processes in Administrative Organization* (New York: Free Press, [1947] 1997).
10. See J. A. Pérez López, *Fundamentos de la dirección de empresas* (Madrid: Rialp, 2002), pp. 52ff; A. Argandoña, 'Integrating Ethics into Action Theory and Organizational Theory', *Journal of Business Ethics*, vol. 78, no. 3, 2008, pp. 435–46.
11. Sources: M. W. Seeger and R. R. Ulmer, 'Virtuous Responses to Organizational Crisis: Aaron Feuerstein and Milt Cole', *Journal of Business Ethics*, vol. 31, part 2, no. 4, 2001, pp. 369–76; J. W. McCurry, 'TW's 1997 Leader of the Year: Aaron Feuerstein', *Textile World*, vol. 147, no. October, 1997, pp. 35–40; A. Zackiewick, 'Aaron M. Feuerstein, Former CEO of Malden Mills Industries Died at 95', *WWD: Women's Wear Daily,* 8 November 2021: https://wwd.com/business-news/business-features/aaron-feuerstein-malden-mills-industries-dies-at-1234991809/. (Accessed on 30 October 2024).
12. The 'Triple Font of Morality', with roots in Aristotelian ethics, was originally developed by Thomas Aquinas (1981 [1273], I–II, 6, 18), although without using this terminology. The approach has been applied in social and business contexts by J. Barnsley, *The Social Reality of Ethics* (London: Routledge & Kegan Paul, 1972); D. Melé, *Ética en la Dirección de Empresas* (Barcelona: Folio, 1997); C. Crockett, 'The Cultural Paradigm of Virtue', *Journal of Business Ethics*, vol. 62, no. 2, 2005, pp. 191–208; and S. Arjoon, 'Ethical Decision-Making: A Case for the Triple Font Theory', *Journal of Business Ethics*, vol. 71, no. 4, 2006, pp. 395–410, among others.
13. On the principle of double effect, see also D. S. Oderberg, *Moral Theory: A Non-Consequentialist Approach* (Oxford: Blackwell, 2000), pp. 88–96; D. Černý, *The Principle of Double Effect: A History and Philosophical Defense* (London: Routledge, 2020); R. Monge and N.-h. Hsieh, 'Recovering the Logic of Double Effect for Business: Intentions, Proportionality, and Impermissible Harms', *Business Ethics Quarterly*, vol. 30, no. 3, 2020, pp. 361–87; and J. T. Mangan, 'An Historical Analysis of the Principle of Double Effect', *Theological Studies*, vol. 10, 1949, pp. 41–61. This latter (p. 43) formulated the four conditions necessary for the ethical acceptance of an action that a person foresees will produce a good effect and a bad effect. They are: (1) from its very object, the action in itself is good – or, at least, neutral; (2) the intention is to achieve the good effect, not the bad effect; (3) the good effect will not be produced by means of the bad effect; and (4) there be a proportionately grave reason for permitting the bad effect. M. Walzer, *Just and Unjust Wars* (New York: Basic Books, 1977), pp. 151–9, pointed out a fifth condition: (5) the agent minimizes the foreseen harm, even if this involves accepting additional risk or foregoing some benefit.
14. See Mangan, 'An Historical Analysis of the Principle of Double Effect'. For criticisms and replies to the principle of double effect, see Oderberg, *Moral Theory,* pp. 96–105.

5

Frequent Misbehaviours and Irregular Payments

Right living, living the good life, means first and foremost ordering one's priorities into a correct hierarchy.[1]

ROBERT SPAEMANN (1927–2018), German philosopher

Overview

Ethics guides human excellence, and its first requirement is to avoid actions contrary to excellence included in virtues. That includes actions which directly cause harm to others or erode the common good.

Section A of this chapter begins by discussing justice and truthfulness – including sincerity and honesty – as foundational principles for understanding minimal standards of good behaviour in business. It also addresses property rights and the importance of contracts in business transactions, alongside the conditions that ensure their legitimacy. The section continues by analysing common forms of misbehaviour in business and finance, such as contract infringement, misappropriation, fraud, violation of trade secrets, conflicts of interest, tax evasion, insider trading, and moral hazard and money laundering.

Section B focuses on corruption in business, examining bribery, extortion, and other forms of irregular payments. It explores the morality of these practices and offers guidance on how to navigate corrupt environments. The section concludes by analysing the damaging effects of corruption on both businesses and society, discussing the corporate risks associated with engaging in corrupt activities, and reviewing some current initiatives to eradicate corruption.

Chapter Aims

After reading this chapter you should be able to:

- Reflect on requirements of justice and honesty for business.
- Understand restitution and compensation for damages.
- Gain an insight into the ethical issues related to business contracts.
- Discuss some forms of misappropriation, industrial espionage and fraud.

- Consider ethical issues regarding trade secrets and conflicts of interest.
- Analyse the morality of tax evasion and tax avoidance.
- Be more familiar with the moral dimension of insider trading.
- Define and evaluate irregular and questionable payment and different forms of corruption, including bribery and extortion.

Historical Case #5

Siemens: Accusations of bribery hit the company[2]

Siemens has been a world leader in electric and electronic engineering for over 150 years and is one of the outstanding German multinational companies. The company began in 1847, when Werner von Siemens created seamless insulation for copper wire. Siemens employs 450,000 people and is present in 190 countries. It is known as a firm that offers high-quality products.

At the turn of the current century, accusations of bribery on the part of Siemens began to surface. At the end of 2006, a former company employee explained that secret accounts outside Germany existed and were used to pay bribes for contracts. After an investigation, five Siemens employees were taken into custody. Siemens recognized that some of its employees were engaged in fraud involving €10–€30 million.

Shortly afterwards, it was reported that Siemens had diverted around €100 million to Dubai. Those funds were then channelled through different companies in the Caribbean into Swiss accounts. The investigators suspected that the money was to ensure that Siemens was awarded attractive contracts for the 2004 Olympic Games in Athens.

Another problem involving Siemens came to light in 2006, through IG Metall, one of the dominant metalworkers' unions in Germany. They affirmed that Siemens had tried to pay a bribe to AUB, a small union, to support its policies (in large corporations in Germany, union representatives take part in corporate governance).

In March 2007, German prosecutors arrested one of Siemens's most senior executives, lifting the lid on the 'black money' scandal. The firm was alleged to have been using the network of 'black accounts' for bribery for years, and they were ordered to pay fines and taxes of some €380 million.

In May 2007 two Siemens managers were convicted of bribery and corruption by a German court. The trial revealed a system of 'slush funds' in the German conglomerate; that is, an auxiliary monetary account or reserve fund generally used for illegal payments. They were accused of paying kickbacks to two officials at the Italian state-owned energy company, Enel, between 1999 and 2002. They admitted that the money was paid in order to secure a €450 million deal for Siemens-made gas turbines but justified themselves by claiming that Enel employees had asked for money in return for the contract. They did not act for personal gain but in the best interests of their company. The auditors also discovered more than twenty unknown recipients around the globe to whom €100 million was paid. One Cyprus-based company, IBF Business Service Ltd, received €29.4 million. Millions were also transferred to accounts in the United Arab Emirates, Indonesia and Sudan. Apparently, there was no other way to win contracts in some countries where bribing for contracts was a common practice.

Siemens was fined €201 million by the Munich State Court on 4 October 2007. The tribunal named several former Nigerian telecommunications ministers as well as other officials from Russia and Libya between 2001 and 2004. The payments were made to win lucrative contracts for telecommunications equipment. The company accepted responsibility for the misconduct and agreed to pay the fine. Later, it was announced that five ex-ministers and other senior officials named as recipients of €10 million in bribes from Siemens would be investigated in Nigeria.

It was also reported that the Siemens corruption scandal involved a slush fund of €420 million – much higher than previously thought – which was paid to the consultants for over seven years. The company admitted that it faced investigation in several countries. In its former communications department, a number of payments were discovered where neither the recipients nor the cause for payment was clear.

Many German investors had lost confidence in Siemens's CEO, Klaus Kleinfeld, but not just on account of these scandals, in which he was not directly implicated. Less than one-third of investors believed that the CEO was able to increase the company's value. Finally, in April 2007, along with the chairperson of Siemens's supervisory board, Kleinfeld stepped down from his post and on 1 July a new CEO was appointed. The incoming board chair stated that the change in leadership meant a clean break from the past.

In the following months other scandals from the past emerged. In December 2007, the Norwegian division of Germany's Siemens AG announced a shake-up of its board because the company was suspected of having provided illegal trips for military officials. After hitting Siemens's operations in Germany, Switzerland, Italy, Greece, Norway, the United States and Russia, the scandals spread to its activities in China.

Questions

1. Do you think payments made are ethically questionable? Why? What consequences for the company can these payments cause?
2. If you were hired as an ethics advisor to the new Siemens CEO, what would be your priorities for restoring trust in the company? Why?

SECTION A. MISBEHAVIOURS IN BUSINESS AND FINANCE

5.1 Some basic requirements of good behaviour

While ethics requires seeking human excellence in behaviour (2.B), there are some basic requirements derived from the personalist principle and the principle of the common good (2.7), which entail conditions for good behaviour, which are particularly relevant in business and finance. These requirements are related to justice, veracity – along with honesty and truthfulness – and loyalty, three virtues which entail moral duties.

Justice

Justice is sometimes understood as the fair distribution of things and equity, and as a requirement for those in positions of power and influence. However, justice as virtue has a wider meaning, as the classical definition of the Roman jurist Ulpian suggests: 'Justice is the constant and perpetual will to render to every man [person] his due.'[3] This definition rightly understands justice not only with ordering things and persons properly within society but also with giving to each his or her *right*. In other words, justice requires respecting people's rights.

Three main forms or aspects of justice have been traditionally distinguished: *commutative justice*, *distributive justice* and *general justice*. Other forms of justice are related to these main forms, including, *restorative* and *retributive* justice and *social justice*.

Commutative justice

Basically, commutative justice refers to exchanges, contracts and payment for goods. In voluntary exchanges, this is what ensures that both parties end up with an equal share. Commutative justice takes place in the equality of value of the things addressed by a contract or agreement. In contracting (5.2), when real freedom exists, equality of value is that upon which the parties agree. It demands the safeguarding of property rights, the payment of debts and the fulfilment of legitimate obligations to which one has freely agreed.

Distributive justice

Distributive justice refers to the distribution of burdens, honours, responsibilities and recompense (wealth, power, rewards and so on) among different people within a community. Problems of distributive justice appear, for example, in the apportioning of the tax burden within society or in distributing economic compensations or positions within a business firm. In distributive justice *equity* is crucial, that is, fairness towards all concerned. Thus, fair distribution should consider contributions, merits, capacities and, in some cases, needs. In practice, justice in distribution requires establishing *equitable criteria*, determined with impartiality and practical wisdom, and applying them to members of the whole. One metric for setting taxes might be incomes. Within an organization, one criterion for calculating remuneration could be the contribution to wealth creation or the responsibility of the position or some other factor. When things are to be divided based on some property, each individual should receive a quantity proportional to his or her possession of that property (similarly with those who contribute capital in a business firm). In a community such as a family, the distributive criteria might be related to the needs of each member of the family. Strict equality in distribution, without considering merits or other significant criteria, is contrary to distributive justice. Distributive justice also precludes favouritism or acting in an arbitrary fashion.

General justice

This third form of justice refers to the individual or group contribution to the common good of a community or society at large. Underlying general justice is the conviction that every member of a community should contribute to its common good, and acting in accordance with the common good is precisely the obligation of general justice.

One expects a good community to enact and comply laws that will govern its members in ways beneficial to everyone; that is, in accordance with the common good. This is why general justice is also called *legal justice*.

Reparative and restorative justice

Reparative justice involves restitution or compensation for damages, aiming to restore situations to their rightful state. This form of justice is related to commutative justice and addresses offences, misappropriations and damages that create a state of injustice which needs resolution. In cases of misappropriation, restitution requires the return of what was taken.

The obligation of restitution may be delayed when the debtor is unable to return the goods or money in question; however, where possible, restitution must be made. This obligation may cease for specific reasons, such as if the debt is forgiven by the creditor or in other circumstances specified by law. When the harmed parties are anonymous, any monetary restitution should be directed to charitable institutions.

Reparative justice also encompasses providing compensation for damages unjustly caused (compensatory damages). A particular instance of damage requiring compensation is when an agreement between two parties harms the community – for example, when a company builds a factory that produces noise and foul odours in an urban area or when a corporation's resource exploitation harms the local community and natural environment. We will return to the latter issue when discussing global companies in developing countries (13.8).

To rectify situations of injustice, some form of compensation is necessary to restore the injured party to the position they held prior to the harm. Damages are paid to compensate for injuries or losses, covering harm to a person's property, personal well-being or financial interests (such as physical injuries, torts, breach of contract and wrongful termination). In many cases, a court determines how to reimburse the injured party for harm caused by another's actions.

Restorative justice, closely related to reparative justice, seeks to repair relationships and heal the harm caused by wrongdoing. In addition to making reparations for harm, as reparative justice requires, restorative justice focuses on restoring relationships. A key element of restorative justice is goodwill and dialogue between the victim, offender and community to acknowledge the harm and collaboratively find ways to repair it. The goal is to rebuild trust and promote accountability, allowing for empathy and reconciliation.

Retributive or corrective justice

Retributive justice refers to the authority of a community to give an appropriate and proportional punishment to those who have committed wrongdoing that affects the community. This is why it is also termed *corrective justice*. It is related to commutative justice and typically involves judges, but in organizations a similar function can be performed by managers. This type of action seeks to dissuade the perpetrator or others from future wrongdoing.

Social justice

The concept of social justice was initially introduced in political studies with a focus on wealth redistribution, often carrying a vindictive tone and lacking a clear and consistent definition. More recently, the United Nations has defined social justice as, 'the fair and compassionate distribution of the fruits of economic growth,' expanding the notion to include several key dimensions. The UN emphasizes the right of all human beings to benefit from a safe and pleasant environment, calling for the fair distribution among countries and social groups of the costs of protecting the environment and developing safe technologies for production and consumption.[4]

In ethical terms, social justice is closely related to distributive justice and the common good, meaning that society's structures and laws should benefit everyone, not just a select few. While redistribution of resources is an important aspect of social justice, it also involves ensuring that everyone has the opportunity to live and flourish in accordance with their inherent dignity and potential. Within this framework, social justice aims to provide equal access to essential services such as education, healthcare and employment opportunities, while also safeguarding human rights. Achieving social justice requires a shared responsibility across society and responsible governance, where authority figures act in the interest of all citizens, protecting their rights and promoting equity.

Procedural and Organizational Justice

In addition to these normative views of justice, industrial psychology has introduced other notions of justice. One of them is *procedural justice*, which refers to the fairness of the processes used to make decisions, including transparency, consistency, and the opportunity to be heard.

The other one is *organizational justice*, which refers to employees' overall perception of fairness within the workplace.

Measuring *employees' perceptions of fairness* and the resulting consequences for attitudes and behaviours in the workplace are significant for understanding how perceptions of justice contribute to organizational effectiveness in terms of job satisfaction, employee engagement, commitment and retention. In practice, a gap can emerge between what is objectively just and what people perceive as just, often due to misinterpretation or a lack of clear, sound communication.

Respect for property rights

Justice addresses the rights of individuals, and one of the most broadly recognized is the right to own property. This right refers to the ability to possess, use, transfer or dispose of assets, whether tangible or intangible. Property rights allow individuals and businesses to make independent decisions about how to use their assets, generate income and transfer wealth. They are one of the cornerstones of the free-market economy, providing the foundation for trade, investment and economic stability.

The *Universal Declaration of Human Rights* establishes that 'Everyone has the right to own property alone as well as in association with others. No one shall be arbitrarily deprived of their property.'[5] Beyond this international consensus, there are strong reasons to defend the right to property, though it remains a complex issue involving matters of equity, justice and social function.

Different philosophical perspectives defend property rights. For example, personalist philosophy emphasizes the right to own property as an expression of personal freedom and responsibility, as well as a means of social participation. When property rights are well-defined and protected, they contribute instrumentally to the common good.[6] However, it also points out that property rights are not absolute; they entail a social function. This social function includes providing jobs, contributing to economic prosperity, by using land or resources responsibly and ensuring that they do not contribute to environmental degradation or harm ecosystems, which would affect broader societal rights to a clean environment.

Respecting property rights is an ethical obligation for both individuals and businesses. This involves honouring rightful ownership and avoiding any form of theft, fraud or misappropriation. Additionally, respect for property rights implies fairness in contracts, sales and business dealings, ensuring that all transactions are voluntary and free from coercion or deception. Violations of property rights come in many forms, most of which carry legal sanctions, and we will explore these misdemeanours further below.

Truthfulness, sincerity and honesty

The basic good of truth (2.6) entails *veracity*, which is the habitual adherence to and devotion to the truth. This involves the intention and consistent practice of truthfulness in all aspects of one's communication and behaviour. Veracity, combined with benevolence towards others, requires acting with *truthfulness*, meaning a moral commitment to convey the truth as one knows it. This involves expressing what is true in any given situation and accurately representing the facts and reality in communication.

The first requirement of truthfulness is to avoid lying, that is to speak or act against the truth in order to lead someone into error, or *cheating*, maybe using sophisticated instruments. Truthfulness requires refraining from direct and intentional deception, to gain advantage. Furthermore, it involves disclosing accurate information to those who have a right to it. *Half-truths*, *omissions* or statements that *misrepresent key facts* or *mislead* are contrary to truthfulness.

Sincerity – speaking truthfully about one's feelings, thoughts and desires – is also essential to truthfulness. While it's not necessary to reveal intimate sentiments, when one does speak, it should be *without duplicity*, *dissimulation* or *hypocrisy*. Speaking openly and frankly may be advisable in some situations, though practical wisdom (2.8, 4.2) helps determine what is appropriate to say in each circumstance.

In business and other fields, *transparency* is a popular concept linked to truthfulness in the disclosure of information. It generally refers to openness, clarity and the full disclosure of relevant facts, ensuring that all stakeholders have access to the truth and can understand the nature of a situation or decision.

Closely related to veracity is *honesty*, which involves being free from deceit and untruthfulness, as well as acting with fairness in dealings. An honest person is trustworthy, fair and committed to truth in both actions and communications.

The importance of truthfulness and honesty in social life is evident. Without truthfulness, the exchange of information and ideas would not foster shared understanding, and trust between parties would be undermined when lies or deception are revealed.

A question that sometimes arises is whether it is ever permissible to lie to prevent serious harm. A classic case involves a Dutchman during the Second World War who was hiding a Jewish person and was interrogated by the Gestapo. Intuitively, it seems morally right for him to deny it. But does this constitute a lie in the proper sense? In such cases, we are dealing with an instance of *illegitimate aggression*, against which *legitimate self-defence* is morally permissible. Telling something false in this context corresponds to a *moral object* (4.5) that should not be classified as a lie, but rather as a *legitimate concealment of the truth in the service of self-defence*.

A similar form of legitimate concealment may occur when revealing the truth would harm another good – such as preserving a legitimate secret. For example, when a manager or employee is asked about a confidential matter, the ethical dilemma can often be resolved by remaining silent or offering a vague or non-committal response. In cases where this is not possible, a *literally false statement* may not be considered *a lie in the strict moral sense*, but rather a *defensive act of truth concealment* in response to an unjust or inappropriate inquiry.

Another situation involving the legitimate concealment of truth may arise when disclosing certain information would compromise another important good – such as preserving a legitimate secret. For instance, when a manager or employee is asked about a confidential matter by someone who has no right to that information, the dilemma can often be resolved by remaining silent or providing a vague or ambiguous response. In cases where this is not possible, a literally false statement *might not be considered a lie* in the strict sense, but rather a legitimate concealment of the truth in self-defence against an unjust inquiry.

Loyalty

Loyalty entails being faithful and devoted to a person, group, cause or organization. In practical terms, loyalty involves a steadfast allegiance and a sense of duty and commitment to the person or entity to which one is loyal. Loyalty can be useful for emotional adhesion, but it is also a virtue related to honesty.[7] It involves keeping one's word and serving the good causes to which one has a commitment.

Loyalty as a virtue requires managers and employees to serve the company they work for, which means seeking the best interests of the firm in negotiating and making decisions, always in accordance with ethical standards and other requirements of the common good. A loyal manager or employee shows commitment, a sense of allegiance and a willingness to defend or support the company, fostering trust and long-term relationships.

Notice that loyalty as a virtue is not about sustaining the company at any cost but being guided by lawful cause and moral standards. Supporting unethical behaviour, practices or decisions harmful and morally wrong in the 'best interest' is a pseudo-loyalty ethical wrong. Another delicate situation, for example, is when the 'loyalty' to the company conflicts with the ethical obligation to report wrongdoing (whistleblowing: 3.8). Again, this apparent loyalty to the company is not a virtuous one if it entails a compulsory responsibility to blow the whistle.

Sometimes, a conflict of loyalties can emerge, when personal loyalty to one entity may conflict with their obligations to another, for instance, company vs. one's own family. Loyalty as a virtue requires practical wisdom as a driver and this wisdom should help to determine the authentic loyalty in each case to find an appropriate balance. Loyalty as a virtue requires ethical reasoning to ensure that it supports real ethical behaviour.

5.2 Business contracts – infringement and other misbehaviours

The business contract, an essential element of business life

A *contract* consists in an agreement or exchange of promises between two or more parties (individuals or groups) by which the parties commit themselves to some course of action.[8] Commutative justice (above Section A) calls for fundamental fairness in all agreements and exchanges between individuals or private social groups.

In business, the subject matter of a contract is usually an *exchange* of products (raw materials, facilities, funds or other goods or services) for money. This is the case of trade (purchase–sale) contracts, rental contracts and *labour contracts*. The latter deserve special consideration because work is an activity of the person and not a mere commodity (10.1).

Contracts are the skeletons of business relationships – honouring them is crucial for the entire field of economic activity. The obligation to honour a contract is based on the fact that everyone is responsible for their own commitments. It is a part of the personalist principle and a minimum requirement to live together in justice and harmony. and therefore is an important aspect of the common good (2.7).

In line with this precondition, a vast amount of legislation on contracts has been developed from ancient Roman law, which established a general principle that 'pacts must be kept' (*pacta sunt servanda*). Legislation on contracts enforces the fulfilment of legitimate undertakings and provides remedies for breaches of contract.

A contract includes three key elements:

- The *object* or subject matter of the contract. For instance, selling a product.
- The *consent* reached by the will of the contracting parties. In consent there is a definite offer by one party and an absolute acceptance by another.
- The *cause* by which one enters into a contract includes the established obligations. In business, the cause is a service or benefit that is being remunerated. However, the contract can also refer to a donation, the cause of which is the mere generosity of the donor. Another cause might be a promise to give or do something with no compensation.

For instance, in a purchase–sale contract, the *object* is selling/buying a product or service, the *consent* is the will of both parties to make a transaction between a product and money, and the *cause* is acquiring a product with the obligation to pay for it according to the agreed terms (on the part of the buyer) or to deliver it with the quality and terms established (on the part of the seller).

The validity of a contract

The validity of a contract and the consequent moral duty arising from it require four conditions:

- *Capacity for contracting*: Since the agreement has to be reached through a deliberate and free decision of each party, a valid contract requires the capacity of parties and sufficient mental discernment. Legislation can add particular formal requirements regarding the capacities of the parties. Completion of a contract has to be possible: the parties must have the capacity or power to do what is established.
- *Fair consent*: The will of the parties is the essential basis of the contract. Consequently, a valid contract requires contractual will in conditions of full freedom and knowledge. Fair consent requires acting in *good faith*, that is, with honest conviction about the truth or falsehood of any proposition, without duress or intimidation, and seeking equitable agreements.
- *Lawful object*: For a contract to be valid, it must not be contrary to law and legitimate regulations, morals or good customs. For example, a contract involving industrial espionage would not be lawful, nor would a contract which involves causing harm by selling goods that are immoral or excluded from legal trade, for example human organs or cocaine.
- *Lawful cause*: The motive to assume an obligation that is established in the contract should be lawful. A fair agreement also requires mutual and external acceptance of duties, without misrepresentations or any wording that is likely to lead to misconstruction.

The law can require certain formalities for the legal validity of contracts, such as being written and signed in the presence of a notary. These vary in accordance with the type of contract. Both oral and written contracts carry ethical obligations if they have been consciously entered into and meet the other aforementioned conditions of validity. Defects in capacity, consent, object and cause produce the absolute or relative nullity of contracts. Legal studies deal with these issues in depth. Here we consider only lack of consent, which can be especially relevant in business ethics.

Lack of consent

Lack of consent can be excluded or limited by error, fraud and duress (or intimidation). These are widely considered in legal studies, though a brief examination here may be useful:

- *Contracting with substantial errors*: The error on the substance of the thing that was the object of the contract invalidates the consent. For example, mistaking derivative financial products for stock obligations due to a lack of clear information. The error can also regard essential conditions such as post-sales service and so on, after delivering a contracted product.
- *Fraud in contracts*: A contract will be invalid on the grounds of fraud if one party includes misrepresentation or a suppression of the truth in substantial elements in the contractual agreement with the intention of obtaining an unjust advantage (or of causing a loss or any inconvenience to the other party). An example of fraud in contracting would be a labour contract that misrepresents conditions to the benefit of the employer and detriment of the employee.
- *Acting under duress and undue influence*: Using intimidation or threats to compel a person to reach an agreement or to sign a contract is unjust and, if significant duress or undue influence is present, the agreement or contract is invalid. There is a special risk of undue influence in contracts when one party is in a position of power over the other.

Misbehaviours in contracts

A number of misbehaviours regarding contracts are worth highlighting:

- *Breaching a legitimate contract*: To breach a contract is to fail voluntarily to do what was undertaken, with damage to one's counterparty. Justice requires appropriate compensation for such damage (5.1). Sometimes, however, it is impossible to fulfil a contract for involuntary reasons. This is the case for certain business or personal situations in which, acting in good faith, a business is not sufficiently profitable enough to pay debts (to suppliers, financial creditors and so on). If the agent is, for some reason, not responsible for the problem, the breech is not formally contrary to justice. However, the situation created is not acceptable, and debts should be paid according to the terms agreed upon and as soon as is possible. One particular situation is *bankruptcy*, that is, the legally declared inability of an organization (or an individual) to pay their creditors. In this case and similar predicaments, debts can be partially or completely dismissed in accordance with the law and judgements of the court. Bankruptcy is a known risk that is an implicit element of the trade contract. However, it is not ethically acceptable to mislead creditors or to abuse one's power when facing a probable bankruptcy by favouring oneself or by giving one creditor unlawful preference to the detriment of another. Doing so is an ethical issue, generally included in legislation, called *fraudulent conveyance*.

- *Making an illicit agreement*: This includes any commitment contrary to ethical principles or involving contractually unlawful obligations. Contracts based on such terms are illegitimate and do not impose any binding obligation.
- *Entering a contract with misrepresentation*: This occurs when one party presents false statements, which induce the other party to enter into the contract. For instance, when a purchase decision is made and executed based on a seller's false statement or promise regarding the quality or nature of the goods.
- *Acting with a lack of good faith*: This is when one of the parties enters the contract with the intention of defrauding the other. A lack of good faith can involve taking advantage of the ignorance or lack of awareness of the counterparty in some substantial aspect of a contract when it is not possible for him or her to obtain the information necessary to consciously consent through reasonable means. This could be, for instance, the case of a company purchasing on credit if, unbeknownst to the seller, the firm suffers from such serious debt that it will be practically impossible to pay in full, and the seller has no reasonable means of discovering the financial situation of the purchaser and assumes that payment will proceed as usual.
- *Adopting attitudes of silence or inactivity to favour errors*: This is morally unacceptable unless such errors are easily avoidable, or the other party is an expert in the field.
- *Abusing power to obtain a contract using duress or intimidation*: This not only invalidates the contract but also shows a lack of respect for persons.

5.3 Misappropriation and fraud

Misappropriation and fraud are two related concepts, contrary to justice, used in both ethical and legal terminology.

Misappropriation involves the unauthorized use or handling of someone else's property or funds, often for personal gain. It may not always involve physically taking something but rather using it in a way that was not intended or permitted. The most blatant form of misappropriation is *theft*, which consists in taking someone else's property without permission – or at least the reasonable will of the owner – with the intent to permanently deprive the owner of it.

Fraud is a form of misappropriation with deception. It takes place when deception is deliberately practised in order to secure unjust gain.[9] In business, fraud can appear in a great variety of forms: deception over the quality or weight of products, forgery of cheques or invoices or a request for funds from an individual or firm when no obligation to pay exists (false billing).

Misappropriations within the company

Embezzlement

This is a distinct form of misappropriation where someone entrusted with managing funds or property, such as a trustee, manager or treasurer, misuses those assets for personal gain. Unlike traditional theft, where the perpetrator does not have rightful access to the asset, embezzlement occurs when someone legally entrusted with the assets violates that trust. It is not only a breach of justice and truthfulness but also a grave violation of the fiduciary duty owed to the owner of those assets.

Waste or misuse of entrusted resources

This occurs when someone makes inappropriate or excessive expenses or utilizes resources inefficiently. Whether it's extravagant spending or wasting time on non-work-related activities, this form of misappropriation reflects poor stewardship of assets that belong to the company.

Small thefts by employees

Although labelled as 'small', these thefts can have a significant cumulative impact. Employees may steal cash, merchandise or even information from the company. Examples include pocketing cash from sales, taking company-owned goods for personal use, or committing payroll fraud. Even seemingly minor acts, like taking home office supplies or using company services for private purposes, can add up and lead to substantial losses.

Asset misappropriation

This involves the unauthorized use of a company's physical or financial assets. It ranges from minor offences, like taking office supplies, to more severe infractions, such as redirecting company funds for personal purchases. For example, an employee might use the company's credit cards for personal expenses or misappropriate funds entrusted to him or her for a project.

Fraudulent disbursements

This is a form of fraud, in which an employee creates false transactions to siphon off company funds. This could involve issuing false invoices, filing fraudulent expense reports, or even modifying financial records to conceal unauthorized spending. The intention is to divert money from the company for personal benefit while making it appear as legitimate spending.

Payroll fraud

Payroll fraud occurs when employees falsify timesheets, claim wages for non-existent work, or even create fake employees to draw additional pay. A more subtle form of this is wasting contracted time or redirecting work hours towards non-contractual tasks, thereby taking advantage of the company's payroll system.

Theft of confidential information

This involves the unauthorized use or theft of a company's proprietary information, such as trade secrets, client data or business strategies. In some cases, employees may sell confidential data to competitors or leak sensitive information that compromises the company's competitive edge. Such actions not only violate trust but can also cause irreparable damage to the company's market position.

Infringement of intellectual property

Infringement of intellectual property is a form of misappropriation involving the unauthorized use, reproduction or distribution of intellectual property. This violation occurs when someone exploits protected content without the explicit permission of the information owner, potentially leading to financial loss, reputational damage or the dilution of legal rights. Intellectual property rights protect creations of the mind, including inventions, literary and artistic works, symbols, names and images used in commerce. The infringement of these rights can take various forms, including:

Copyright infringement

This occurs when someone copies, distributes or publicly displays another's creative work without authorization from the copyright holder. Copyright infringement can apply to a wide range of works, including books, music, films, software and even architectural designs. In some cases, infringement occurs even when no formal copyright exists, as long as the work is original and eligible for protection. The damage here is twofold: not only is the creator deprived of potential earnings, but also the integrity of their work can be compromised.

Trademark infringement

This occurs when a trademark, a distinctive sign or symbol used by a company to distinguish its goods or services, is used without permission in a manner that causes confusion regarding the source or affiliation of goods or services. Trademark infringement dilutes the brand's identity and can severely impact the trust and reputation that the trademark has built. This is especially damaging in industries where brand loyalty is critical, as consumers might unknowingly purchase counterfeit or inferior products, thinking they are authentic.

Patent infringement

Patent infringement involves the unauthorized use, sale or manufacturing of a patented invention. Patents grant the holder exclusive rights to use their invention for a set period, and infringement undermines both the economic incentive for innovation and the legal protection granted. However, patent law is not without controversy, especially in areas like pharmaceuticals, where the balance between the right to life and the right to patented property comes into question. For instance, life-saving drugs might be inaccessible due to patents, leading to ethical debates, even though pharmaceutical companies argue that patents are necessary to recover the high costs of research and development.

Trade secret misappropriation

This form of infringement occurs when confidential business information is disclosed or used without authorization. Trade secrets, which may include formulas, processes or business strategies, are often vital to a company's competitive advantage. Unauthorized use of trade secrets can lead to massive financial losses and market disadvantages for the affected business. We will return to this point in the next section (5.4).

Industrial espionage

This represents one of the most aggressive forms of intellectual property theft, where an individual or entity intentionally seeks to obtain confidential or secret information for business purposes without the owner's consent. Industrial espionage can target trade secrets, product development plans or other strategic business assets. The information obtained through espionage can provide significant advantages to competitors, making it tantamount to theft. It is a blatant violation of the principles of fair competition and can lead to significant legal ramifications.

5.4 Violation of trade secrets

People working for a firm have access to information that others do not. The firm owns this information unless it is easily (and legitimately) obtainable by people external to it. Some information is explicitly defined as confidential or a trade secret; other data might not be explicitly labelled as such but obviously is so by its nature.[10]

Confidential information regarding trade might be complete or could consist of essential details on new products, inventions, technologies or innovations in the manufacturing process, market research, studies of competitors or sensitive information about clients or customers, new business ideas or business plans and so on. Generating this intelligence might have required costly investment, and its disclosure can provoke a loss of competitive advantage or otherwise damage the firm.

Facilitating a competitor's access to this information, directly or indirectly, without an institutional agreement, is not only a great disloyalty to one's own firm but also a clear misappropriation of intellectual propriety.

In this context, *trade secrets* can be defined as any formula, pattern, design, instrument, process or compliance of information which is used in a business and not known to people outside the firm, which provides a benefit to the holder or an advantage over competitors or customers.

Apart from the moral duty to keep trade secrets, many companies protect confidential information by requiring employees to sign agreements containing the specific commitment to non-disclosure of such information. The law generally also protects trade secrets, and courts have developed rich jurisprudence with a number of criteria for determining the seriousness of their violation.[11]

A delicate situation can result when an *employee leaves a firm* and is hired by a competitor. Trade secrets should also be kept in this situation. However, one can use his or her personal skills to obtain information in the new job since different skills belong to each person. In practice, the new employee could well come under great pressure to disclose trade secrets of the former firm, and embarrassing situations might arise. In order to avoid possible prejudices, managers or employees who manage sensitive confidential information are often required, under a non-competition contract, not to work for a competitor for a certain period (perhaps two or three years) if they leave the firm.

Another issue would arise if someone in marketing had personal contacts or even a personal friendship with the firm's customers. Do these connections belong to the firm or to the employee? On one hand, many have probably been made by the employee while working for the firm and, in economic terms, this has required an investment by the firm. In some ways, loyal customers form part of a firm's assets. However, on the other hand, if the employee has developed these relationships with customers, it is a completely personal matter. A prudential solution could be that the employee does not take customer records from his or her former firm but is free to inform customers that he or she is now working for a different company. Obviously, customers are not anyone's property, and with this information, they can freely decide to maintain their loyalty to the original supplier or move to the employee's new firm.

Very exceptional cases can arise in which keeping a secret is bound to cause grave harm, which can be avoided only by divulging the truth, for instance, if a product or activity is dangerous but the relevant information is protected as a trade secret. This issue is related to whistleblowing, which we have considered previously (3.8).

5.5 Moral hazard and conflict of interests

Moral hazard

Moral hazard can be defined as lack of incentive to guard against risk where one is protected from its consequences. A situation of moral hazard would be, for instance, when a driver takes an insurance policy that provides full coverage, the driver would then have less incentive to exercise care in driving, as any damage would be covered by the policy. The insurance industry can offer other situations of moral hazard, regarding, for example, fire insurance. Moral hazard can also occur with regards to remuneration policies with salespeople. If they have a relatively high fixed salary in proportion to the global remuneration, there is a risk that the salespeople will be less motivated to up their salary by increasing sales. Moral hazard therefore occurs when a party, linked to another with certain agreement, increases its exposure to risk or acts without good faith because the other party will bear the cost of those behaviours.

There are public policies, for instance in bailouts, in which implicit agreement exists between governments and big corporations, such as big banks and large companies, which are considered 'too big to fail' and crucial for the economic system. The hypothesis or the conviction that a bailout will occur if the situation is so negative that collapse is inevitable can create a moral hazard. Bailouts create 'perverse incentives' for the misbehaviour of a party who takes risks but does not pay the bill if the consequences are bad. This fosters excessive risk-taking, with the understanding that if things don't go well the state, and ultimately the taxpayers, will assume the consequences.[12]

In some situations, moral hazard can entail asymmetric information. This occurs where the risk-taking party to a transaction has relevant information unknown to the party paying the consequences. Thus, those who take out fire insurance may have more information regarding the probability of fire than a representative of the insurance company. In an extreme situation, they may even have intention to deliberately cause a fire to obtain the agreed payment.

Moral hazard also arises in the so-called 'principal–agent problem'. It occurs in relationships in which one or more persons named as 'the principal' entrusts to another person, called 'the agent', the defence of their interests, delegating to him or her a certain power of decision. For instance, when someone (a principal) entrusts the administration of his or her patrimony to a trustee (an agent) or when stockholders (principal) of a company hire a manager. The agent usually has more information about his or her actions or intentions than the principal does. This brings about the risk that, in acting, the agent seeks his or her own interests, which are not necessarily aligned with those of the principal.

Moral hazard is not a problem when the agent and those exposed to risk are responsible and virtuous persons. However, incentives for misbehaviour exist and often the agreement includes measures that incentivize in the opposite direction, for example rewarding drivers with no accidents, giving commissions on sales to salespeople and providing incentives to align the manager's interest with that of the stockholders.

Conflict of interests

In business ethics as well as in the legal context, a conflict of interest is understood as a situation in which the private interests and the official responsibilities of a person in a position of trust are in conflict or when someone who ought to be serving people has competing interests. This entails the risk of committing an injustice and favouring the misappropriation of goods. This would be the case if an attorney or law firm simultaneously represented two clients involved in mutual litigation.

In business, a conflict of interest can arise when an employee, an executive or a director of a firm has interests that compete personally or professionally with the duty to serve his or her firm with loyalty. There are many cases in which such conflicts can exist, for instance:

- A person responsible for purchases having an interest in some supplier, either directly or through a close relative (spouse, child and so on).
- An official of a governmental institution with interests in a firm that offers goods or services to such institutions.
- Working for a competitor or taking on any outside employment in which the interests of one job oppose those of another.

- A director of a large company who, as a member of the board of directors, has voted on whether to buy a small firm for a certain price and he or she is one of the owners of that firm.
- Auditing and providing consultancy services to the same company, which impedes auditing with independence and impartiality.

The existence of a conflict of interest does not mean that the agent will necessarily act against his or her fiduciary duties to the firm by exploiting a professional or official capacity for personal benefit. However, when conflicts of interest exist, it is difficult to act impartially, to avoid the undue favouring of any of the conflicting interests. In addition, if a conflict of interest becomes public, confidence towards a person, group, firm or another institution might be eroded. Such conflicts are therefore best avoided. Transparency about conflicts of interest in organizations is highly recommended.

In fact, corporate codes usually prohibit situations involving conflicts of interest or else oblige employees or managers to reveal such information to a superior. Even if the company's code does not require it, a person of good sense would reveal the existence of conflicts of interest in order to avoid participating in decisions involving the subject of the conflict.

5.6 Money laundering and tax evasion

Money laundering

Money laundering is an expression used to describe an illegal activity that makes large amounts of money generated by criminal activity appear to have come from a legitimate source. The money from the criminal activity can include human trafficking, drug trafficking, tax evasion, public corruption and terrorist funding.

Owners of this 'dirty money' try to clean it through a process of 'laundering', by introducing it into the legitimate financial system, concealing the source of the money through a series of transactions and bookkeeping tricks. In this way, this money is disbursed from the legitimate account.

There is a set of regulations and activities termed anti-money laundering especially designed by financial institutions to detect and prevent operations of money laundering. These include the obligation of keeping records of cash purchases of negotiable instruments, filing reports of cash transactions exceeding certain amounts generally established by law, and reporting suspicious activity that might signal money laundering.

Tax evasion

Tax evasion refers to avoiding the payment of taxes lawfully due. This differs from *tax avoidance* or *tax mitigation*, which is making use of legal methods to one's own advantage in order to reduce the amount payable.

Taxation is a means of distributing benefits and burdens among citizens. The ethical justification of taxation is its contribution to the common good. Ethics also demands objective and fair criteria in the imposition of tax charges.

Tax collection uses different mechanisms, including tax on personal and corporate income (usually the most substantial), tax on consumption, donations and wealth transfer, special taxes on products such as tobacco and alcoholic beverages, and so forth. Taxes are used for provisioning public services such as public institutions (courts, government, parliament and the like), defence, public safety and so on. In most countries, healthcare, education, public transport and some infrastructures are also supported by public funds derived from taxation.

Taxation is an instrument of both economic and social policy. Governments can grant incentives or impose disincentives for economic activity by decreasing or increasing taxation on a particular industry or on all economic activity. Simultaneously, they can develop social policies favouring social equity in tax collection or the assignment of funds to subsidize people with special needs.

Taxation posits a number of ethical, economic and political questions regarding property rights and their social function, personal freedom and solidarity, efficiency in the allocation of resources collected, economic productivity, the efficiency of the economic system and equity. The latter touches on the degree to which taxation should be proportional to incomes or to real economic capacity and, if progressivity is acceptable, to what degree.

The rate of taxation is controversial. Some defend a low rate, arguing for the rights of private property (high taxes can be an impediment), the minimal role delegated to government for the provision of public services and the favourable effects of low taxation on investment and wealth creation, which can bring about even higher global tax revenue. The promotion of employment is another strong argument. Others, however, support higher taxes, defending social justice, which requires that society ensures basic social conditions that allow everybody to live in accordance with their dignity and need for human development (heathcare, education, shelter and so forth).

The discussion of these topics never ends. The debates include ethical aspects of distributive justice and respect for human dignity but also extend to economic and even ideological issues.

In practice, taxation is determined by specific legislation, and the law should be followed unless it clearly violates human rights or other fundamental ethical standards. This rejection would require wide support from sensible and upright people. It should be noted that, in general, there is a moral obligation to pay taxes as defined by law. Consequently, tax evasion is not only illegal but also ethically wrong.

Tax evasion includes failing to report income, faking expenses or reporting financial statements inaccurately. Since governments impose strict and serious penalties for tax evasion, those who evade paying taxes are also at risk of harming themselves or their organizations.

Taxpayers are morally obligated to be truthful about their financial status. However, they can take advantage of permitted tax avoidance strategies, following the spirit and the letter of the law.

Another point regarding tax evasion involves making use of foreign 'tax havens': countries that have a lower tax rate and more confidential banking procedures than those in one's home nation, for example the Cayman Islands or the Republic of Seychelles. Using a tax haven is not necessarily illegal or unethical, although it can often be so. Global finance frequently uses offshore mechanisms to avoid the taxes and restrictions associated with national financial markets.[13]

Companies that register in tax havens can pay taxes in their own country when they repatriate foreign earnings through dividends or by other means. However, using a tax haven frequently involves fraud, unfair exploitation of legal loopholes and a lack of solidarity with one's home country, which provides the infrastructure, educated people and social environment where business can take place.

5.7 Insider trading

Insider trading is the trading of stocks or other securities of a firm or corporation, such as bonds or stock options,[14] using internal information that has not been disclosed to the public and that, if and when it was disclosed, could substantially influence the price of such stocks or securities. The prior knowledge that a company's profits or losses were far higher than anticipated would be an example of insider information, as would the discovery or creation of a new product expected to be very profitable, knowledge of a very promising research project or changes at top-level management, capital increases or plans to merge with or take over another company.

A typical case of insider trading is when someone takes advantage of insider information about impending mergers or takeovers to buy stocks in the companies in question before others know of the change. Then, a few days or even hours later, he or she sells the stocks at a tremendous profit. This is different from forecasts made on the basis of the analysis of public information, including information coming from highly specialized publications, long-term experience or other forms of professional expertise, which is fully legitimate.

On considering insider trading, two questions arise:

- Why is insider trading wrong?
- Who is guilty when there is trading with inside information?

Some economists[15] argue that insider trading produces two adverse effects for market competitiveness: (1) it dissuades others from acquiring information and participating in the market (if just a few insiders are going to have all the advantages, it is safer to put funds into some other profitable venture); and (2) it distorts the information provided by market operators and received by other investors. If insider trading were licit, the massive sale of a company's stocks could be interpreted as the economically rational decision of an executive with inside information. However, other economists would disagree with such a distortion.[16]

Morality of insider trading

Whether or not insider trading contributes to the efficiency of stock market pricing, there are several ethical arguments that conclude that it is not ethically acceptable.[17]

- *Insider trading it is an act of unfair competition*: Present-day stock markets are regulated according to the principle of transparency of transactions and of fundamental information provided. This means that companies, generally issuers of negotiable securities, must provide the entire market with the information needed for investment decisions. This amounts to a public commitment consisting of not buying or selling securities on the basis of inside information. Insider trading is therefore a form of *unfair competition* because it does not comply with the explicit or tacit commitments required of all participants in the stock market.

- *Insider trading erodes the trust that the securities market needs to operate*: Insider trading reduces investors' trust, and trust is widely acknowledged to be fundamental for the proper operation of any market, including the securities markets. Investors must be guaranteed equal opportunity and protection from illicit trading, which affords advantages to inside investors to the detriment of others. We can recall that the securities market plays an important role in securing financing for economic agents and in channelling savings and achieving returns on them, thus benefiting society as a whole. Therefore, there are economic, social and ethical reasons for wanting the stock market to work well.[18]
- *It is a violation of fiduciary duty and a breach of professional secrecy*: Among the responsibilities inherent in a management or professional post is the obligation of loyalty to the explicit and implicit commitments assumed when accepting the post. This includes respecting the secrecy of all information that is known because of one's professional work and that, owing to its nature, must be considered confidential. A company's managers and employees enjoy a relationship of trust with the firm and are consequently obliged to practise loyalty. They are hired to work for the company, for which they are suitably paid, and must not take advantage of their positions for personal benefit to the detriment of others.

    Another clear commitment of managers and employees is to look after the legitimate interests of the company. These interests could be affected if it becomes known that someone in the company is making use of insider information. The damage might be even more serious for firms that act as advisers to issuers of securities. If it came to light that the employees of a law firm or an investment bank were using the information obtained to trade on the stock market before that information were made public, the firm would lose clients, and its image would be badly tarnished.
- *It is an act of misappropriation of private information*: Information generated in economic and business activities is an intangible asset, often one of great economic value. Information obtained through a management decision, or knowledge about company operations, when it is a direct consequence of the position a person holds in the organization, cannot be considered the private property of that person. The fact that managers and employees have this sort of information does not give them the right to benefit from it. And it is clearer still that the professionals working on the plans for a future takeover are not the 'owners' of the knowledge about the takeover.

Until it is publicly disclosed, all information belongs to the company. Even so, it is a very peculiar type of asset in that its use must be carefully restricted. In fact, this information is held 'in trust' rather than being owned. When a company is listed on the stock exchange, neither the company nor its stockholders are the absolute owners of any information that can affect stock prices, since both present and future stockholders have 'ownership' rights. It is therefore illicit for officers to use inside information, even in the hypothetical case of having the stakeholders' consent to do so.

Insider trading is actually a form of theft, given that profits are obtained by those who use this information to the detriment of those who have no access to it, but who do have a right to know everything of public interest to investors.

Who is responsible for insider trading?

Regarding the question of who is responsible for insider trading, we should consider, firstly, that inside information might have come from the companies themselves (obtained from someone in an executive position in the company), from service companies (for example, law firms or investment banks preparing a takeover) or from public institutions. All of these sources of information may be accessible to people involved in the firm where the information is generated, including institutional partners, board members, managers and employees of the company.

Others may also have access to these sources through their work, profession or position, such as consultants, auditors, partners of law firms, banks and even journalists or printers who receive the news for publishing beforehand. Both groups of people would be guilty of trading with inside information because each of them has a duty of professional secrecy. Those who extract information from anyone in such groups would also be guilty. However, no responsibility is borne by those who obtain information without being certain that it is, in fact, insider information or by those who are not even sure the information is accurate.

Business Ethics in Action #5

The Anti-Corruption Compliance Programme of ENI

ENI, S.p.A. is an Italian multinational energy company, one of the 'supermajor' oil companies in the world. Its headquarters are in Rome, Italy, and it has nineteen subsidiaries in different countries, some of which are known to have high levels of corruption. It was founded in 1953 from Agip, a company that aimed to explore oilfields and acquire and commercialize oil and derivatives. ENI is involved in the oil and gas industry: an industry which has had notorious corruption cases.[19] In addition, Italy, although improved in recent years, still maintains a relatively high rank in the IT Corruption Perceptions.[20]

In this context, ENI has developed an 'Anti-Corruption Compliance Programme',[21] with a strong commitment to stopping corruption and articulating several means for this end. The programme starts by highlighting: 'in line with the values expressed in its Code of Ethics, ENI firmly rejects all forms of corruption'. This programme was developed in accordance with applicable anti-corruption provisions and international conventions and is updated in accordance with the evolution of the national and international regulatory landscape and best anti-corruption practices. The programme contains a system of rules and controls for the prevention of corruption. This includes the prevention of money laundering in the context of the non-financial activities of ENI S.p.A. and its subsidiaries.

Moscariello et al.,[22] who have studied in-depth the ENI Anti-Corruption Compliance Programme, have emphasized that in addition to the prevention tools through the anti-corruption compliance unit, the programme is characterized by in-depth activity implemented to sensitize ENI personnel, requiring serious commitment and constant attention to understanding and implementing the mechanisms to combat corruptive phenomena in ENI's everyday business dealings. The evidence collected shows that 'despite the observable elements (for example, the top management commitment, the training function and the reporting mechanism) being judged effective, the Anti-Corruption Programme should also be interconnected with the ethical culture of the firm.'

Aligned with these findings is the fact that ENI S.p.A. obtained the ISO certification of compliance management systems.[23] This standard provides a comprehensive framework for organizations to establish, develop, implement, evaluate, maintain and improve an effective compliance management system. Four key elements are included:[24]

Identify and manage compliance risks: Proactively address potential compliance issues before they become significant problems.

Enhance organizational culture: Foster a culture of integrity, transparency and accountability.

Improve operational efficiency: Streamline processes and reduce the risk of non-compliance.

Build stakeholder trust: Demonstrate a commitment to compliance and ethical business practices to customers, partners and regulators.

* * *

There is no doubt that ENI S.p.A. has taken notable steps toward combating corruption within its operations, supported by an established compliance framework and international certifications. However, the success of such programmes hinges on the integration of these formal mechanisms with a strong, ethically driven corporate culture. The effectiveness of ENI's anti-corruption efforts will ultimately depend on how well these values are lived out daily by employees at all levels.

SECTION B. IRREGULAR PAYMENTS IN BUSINESS

5.8 Bribery, extortion and other irregular payments

Bribery

An action in which someone gives cash, a gift or some other benefit (such as an emolument or privilege) to obtain an unfair judgement, vote or some type of behaviour by someone in a position of trust, is an act of bribery. One might seek to obtain a favourable but unjust ruling from a judge, a public contract or a privilege from a civil servant or politician, or a decision to buy from a purchase manager. Those who accept a bribe take advantage of their position for personal benefit (or for the benefit of their political party or other organization) and act against the duties of their position, that is, to pass fair judgement or to pursue the best interests of the institution for which they are working.

Extortion

This takes place when someone (the extortionist), with a certain power, demands money or some other gift to which he or she is not entitled, in 'exchange' for doing what he or she is in fact obliged to do, or perhaps for granting the victim favourable treatment. Extortion occurs, for instance, when a politician demands money for bypassing the usual process and giving a contract to a chosen company, or when a purchase manager demands money or a gift for his or her personal benefit (not a discount for the company) under the threat that the company will otherwise buy from a competitor. Extortion therefore comes from those with decision-making power over something that affects the victim of the extortion or who can exert influence on such a decision.

Extortion is sometimes, but not always, quite blatant (*explicit extortion*). It can also be subtly insinuated, without explicit demands, where it is known to be general practice (*tacit extortion*). In the latter case, monies paid might appear to be a response to bribery, but this is actually extortion.

Other irregular payments

Both bribery and extortion are at the core of several irregular payments, including the following:

Blackmail

This is a particular form of extortion. It occurs when a person threatens to expose discreditable information about someone unless the victim gives money or some other thing of value to the blackmailer.

Kickback

This is a colloquial term referring to the return of a percentage of a sum of a contract received by a civil servant, politician or some other person who awards it. From an ethical perspective, a kickback is a form of bribery or extortion, depending on whether it is offered (bribery) or required (extortion).

Facilitating payment

Sometimes also called '*grease payment*', a facilitating payment consists of giving some moderate amounts of money to public officials (or to employees of a private company) for actions such as processing papers, issuing permits and so on, in order to expedite performance of duties of a non-discretionary nature, that is, duties they are already required to perform. These payments are not intended to influence the outcome of the official's action, merely its timing. Thus, a facilitating payment is not bribery – just compliance in a little tacit extortion.

Questionable gifts and hospitality

Gifts can be a sign of friendliness or gratitude, or maybe an expression of regular business considerations practised by an entire industry or common in certain places or countries. However, certain gifts and hospitality are actually elaborately disguised bribes or serve as a way to ensure that the bribes go unnoticed. Gifts and hospitality might include invitations to lunch to discuss business or trips to visit facilities related to a potential sale. However, they can sometimes extend to luxury dinners in fashionable restaurants, tickets to the opera or a show, visits to remote facilities with vacations bundled in, or training courses with per diem allowances – and so on.

Practical wisdom helps determine how far one can go, depending on the circumstances. In each environment and situation, one should distinguish between permissible and impermissible gifts. Some companies, in their codes of corporate conduct, even give very precise guidelines on the subject, including the maximum value of a gift one can accept. People offering business considerations must consider the local customs of the country, the usual practices within the industry and – above all – common sense.

To distinguish ordinary business considerations associated with a purchase transaction from another comparable to a bribe, there are two sensible guidelines:

- Do not accept any consideration that seems excessive.
- Do not let any considerations received hamper your freedom and independence to choose what you deem best for the company you represent.

5.9 Morality of bribery and extortion

In bribery, two agents concur – one offering a bribe and another linked to an institution (for example, a politician, a civil servant or a purchasing agent) accepting a bribe. In extortion, two agents also concur – the extortionist asking for money or some gift, and the other who is a victim of the extortion and may (or may not) give in to such oppression (Figure 5.1). When we talk of corruption, it generally refers to these actions, although sometimes fraud, embezzlement and other misbehaviours are also included.

Offering and accepting a bribe

The actions of bribery – both offering and accepting – are morally illicit because they all violate the principle of justice. Holding a job or position does not grant the right to accept money for personal gain, and using one's role for personal profit constitutes an abuse of power. Furthermore, bribery

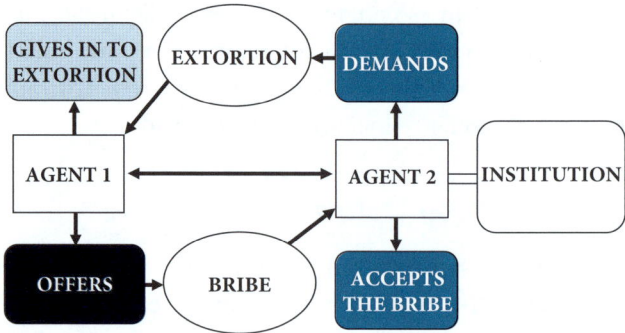

Figure 5.1 Bribe and extortion in the business context

can cause harm to the company or public institution involved, as it may lead to paying inflated prices for contracts or products to cover the cost of the bribe. This practice also creates injustice by unfairly disadvantaging other suppliers who are excluded from competition due to the corrupt arrangement.

Accepting a bribe is also an *act of disloyalty* to the company in which a person is employed (in the case of purchasing managers) or to the society served (in the case of civil servants and politicians). The duties of loyalty inherent in the job of purchasing manager basically consist of buying what is best for the company. Civil servants or politicians working in public administration also have their respective and corresponding obligations.

The moral evaluation of bribery must also consider that this practice contributes to the *spreading of a culture of corruption*. Furthermore, it encourages others to participate in underhand dealings to the detriment of professionalism and authentic service (better prices, quality products and service), which works against the common good. All of this erodes the common good.

Demanding through extortion

The immorality of demanding through extortion lies in its lack of respect for persons, its violation of justice, and its erosion of the common good.

Firstly, extortion involves making demands under the threat of causing harm, even if no actual harm is inflicted. The intent to harm – or the willingness to do so unless demands are met – is morally corrupt. In addition, extortion involves coercing someone into acting against their will, turning the relationship into one of domination rather than mutual respect.

The violation of justice emerges from the misuse of asymmetrical power: the extortionist leverages a position of advantage or privileged knowledge to exploit the vulnerability of another person or organization. Moreover, the extortionist has no legitimate right to make such demands. Their duty is to serve the institution, not to exploit their role for personal gain at the expense of others.

Lastly, extortion undermines trust, honesty and cooperation in relationships, communities, and institutions. It creates a climate of fear and injustice, weakening the moral fabric of society, damaging the common good.

Giving in to extortion

The extortionist unfairly demands money or other benefits from the victim of extortion. But can giving in to extortion ever be ethically acceptable?

We must recognize that in certain situations – especially in environments where corruption is pervasive – managers and business officials may face difficult ethical dilemmas. Two distinct cases should be considered.

The first case involves paying to obtain something that is inherently wrong, or something to which the victim has no right. This is ethically unacceptable, as it entails cooperating in an intrinsically unjust action.

The second case involves giving in to extortion when the victim has a legitimate right to something but can only obtain it by succumbing to the extortionist's demands. In this scenario, the extorted person neither provokes nor condones the extortionist's behaviour; he or she is a victim, left with no viable alternative but to comply.

In such extreme circumstances, and only after careful ethical analysis, yielding to extortion may be ethically permissible. The justification lies in recognizing that the victim's responsibility constitutes material cooperation in wrongdoing (see 3.7), and the Principle of Double Effect (4.6) should be applied.

Based on this concept, a set of guidelines can be established to determine whether giving in to an extortionist in order to secure a legitimate right is ethically acceptable:

1. *Resisting extortion*: This is the first response. There are a number of options, including reporting the affair to the appropriate legal authority, presenting a formal complaint to the company or institution that employs the would-be extortionist, reporting the extortion to the media and so on. Strong resistance should be given, and it can be effective in many situations, contributing to the changing of corrupt environments. Those companies who have established 'zero tolerance' policies in both bribery and extortion are to be commended.
2. *Seeking alternatives*: If the problem cannot be solved by resisting extortion, some other alternative should be explored (that is, looking for new clients, business location or even a different country of operation). Unfortunately, however, sound alternatives are not always available. There are highly regrettable situations in which corruption is deep-rooted; in certain countries, companies cannot enter an industrial sector without paying off the people involved in buying or in contracting decisions. Rejecting the whole country may be unrealistic for a number of reasons. If any reasonable alternative is found, it can be analysed by reflecting on the following criteria:
3. *Acting with uprightness*: One should strive to exercise one's legitimate rights (for example, participating in fair commercial competition). Uprightness also entails avoiding the rationalization of one's own actions. For instance, it would not be acceptable to argue that there is no alternative if alternatives had not already been sought and considered.
4. *Having just and proportionate causes*: An action with a double effect is licit only if there are right and proportionate moral causes or reasons to tolerate the negative effects. Good causes may include surviving as a company, keeping the company competitive or not losing a relevant contract. Negative causes could be the illegitimate enrichment of the extortionist,

a possible increase in the amount of corruption in the environment and the introduction of a dangerous practice into the company.

5   *Avoiding scandal*: Giving in to an extortionist can cause moral scandal in those unfamiliar with all aspects of the case. Consequently, it is advisable that the person succumbing to the pressure exposes people who know the facts to their personal opposition and the reasons for accepting the extortion.

Reflecting on these criteria requires practical wisdom. In complex situations or when in doubt it is advisable to seek help from impartial, upright and capable people. In this respect, it is worth keeping in mind how difficult it is to be at once both a judge and an interested party.

Facilitating payments can be a common practice in some countries, and public authorities might even tolerate the procedure. However, these are no sound ethical arguments. In practice, facilitating payments have a pernicious effect on the function of public and private administrations. All too often they are the slippery slope to more serious forms of corruption, impose additional costs on companies and citizens and, in the long run, they sap the ethical foundations of organizations. Thus, business firms should avoid facilitating payments, as much as possible, under both tacit and explicit extortion.[25]

5.10 Damages of corruption and the fight against corruption

Corruption has been defined as 'the abuse of entrusted power for private gain'.[26] Bribery and extortion (5.9), in their various guises, are two common forms of corruption, but corruption also includes gifts or promises for the purposes of obtaining advantages or benefits contrary to the law or that are of a fraudulent nature, including public procurement, misappropriation of funds or influence peddling, when unfair decisions are knowingly issued, etc. Fraud and embezzlement, falsification of documents, tax evasion, cronyism, nepotism, unfair competition and insider trading are also bad behaviours that can be classified as forms of corruption.

How corruption harms companies

Corrupt activities may provide a company with some short-term economic advantage, but they are always bad for the integrity of people involved and detrimental to the good performance of the affected company. More specifically, corruption:

- leads to a *loss in the human and professional quality* of the people involved within the organization and, consequently, leads to the deterioration of the most important factor for the proper functioning of a company: the personal quality of its members.
- *exposes managers and employees to serious risks*, including legal penalties, reputational damage and potential scandals. There is also a risk that corrupt practices may be reported by members of the company (*whistleblowing*).

- *distorts accounting records*, with possible consequences for decision-making, and facilitates deception by employees involved in handling funds. It is difficult to keep track of where the money goes, since obviously no invoices are issued for bribes, and some of the money may end up in the pockets of those involved in paying the bribes.
- *introduces a dangerous way of operating* into the company. Instead of developing good business policies, management talent and effort are focused on shady deals. In addition to a loss of integrity, managers and employees suffer an erosion of professionalism. The ease of obtaining business advantages by paying bribes does not encourage individuals to strive to improve their personal competence.
- *favours a dangerous learning process in the bribee*, which can affect future interactions if they see that there is a willingness to make payments of this kind. The recipient may realize that the other party needs to pay bribes to continue operating and therefore demand that the amount be increased.
- *undermines managerial authority*. Managers whose conduct is not exemplary will find it difficult to demand ethical behaviour from their staff.

Damage of corruption to society

In addition to the impact on the company, corruption has a negative impact on society. Corruption is a global challenge that has been addressed as a key factor of many economic and social ills.[27] While a few opportunists use their positions for personal gain, corruption brings about adverse effects for the common good in different scopes:[28]

Introduction of injustices and dysfunction in economic dynamism

Bribes undermine free competition, increase transaction costs and create insecurity in the economy. Being unfair to competitors, bribes have a negative impact on society, which is deprived of the things that healthy competition produces, such as innovation and lower-priced or higher-quality products. In addition, when corruption spreads, it creates an underground economy throughout the country, with costs that make it impossible to have a true picture of the economy. The existence of an underground economy, of course, has a negative impact on tax revenue and on the economic contribution companies make to society.

Slowdown in economic growth and negative impact on poverty

In some developing countries corruption can seriously impede the progress of the population and even deter serious investors who do not want to engage in such practices. This lack of investment has consequences on economic growth and jobs. Countries capable of confronting corruption use their human and financial resources more efficiently, attract more investment and grow more rapidly.

Corruption has a disproportionate impact on the poor and most vulnerable, increasing costs and reducing access to services, including health, education and justice. Corruption in the procurement of drugs and medical equipment drives up costs and can lead to sub-standard or harmful products. The human costs of counterfeit drugs and vaccinations on health outcomes and the life-long impacts on children far exceed the financial costs. Unofficial payments for services can have a particularly pernicious effect on poor people.

Empirical studies have shown that the poor pay the highest percentage of their income in bribes. Some studies have suggested that the poor may even be preyed upon since they are seen as powerless to complain.

Eroding moral quality of social culture

Corruption tends to create an unstoppable spiral. If not stopped in time, the practice of bribery, extortion and other forms of corruption can spread to other companies and industries, or even through an entire country. As corruption spreads throughout the national economy, inefficiencies and injustices in economic and business activity become universal and very difficult to eradicate. This generates a climate of frustration, cynicism and widespread anger that leads to tension and instability in the economic and political system, creating a destructive dynamic for individuals and society.

Socio-political deterioration

Corruption erodes trust in government and undermines social cohesion. This impedes the smooth functioning of economic and political institutions and introduces a lack of transparency into crucial aspects of business and social life. When corruption enters the political arena, the role of representative institutions is distorted. Corruption runs against the basic common good of legality, which entails respect for rules.

Corruption causes concern across the globe, but particularly in contexts of fragility and violence, as corruption fuels and perpetuates the inequalities and discontent that lead to fragility, violent extremism and conflict.

Fighting against corruption

Various international organizations have initiated efforts to combat corruption and have enacted several conventions or similar document (Table 5.1), with many countries joining these initiatives. National laws have been enacted, and both national and international anti-corruption agencies play a vital role in this fight.

One of the earliest national efforts was the *Foreign Corrupt Practices Act* (FCPA), enacted in the United States in 1977. This legislation, which regulates transactions and business activities abroad, was introduced in the wake of the Watergate scandal, which involved illegal activities within Richard Nixon's administration, as well as other corporate misconduct in the early 1970s. Today, most countries have legislation and agencies aimed at preventing and addressing corruption.

On an international level, the first initiative was the *Inter-American Convention Against Corruption*, promoted by the Organization of American States (OAS), which came into force in

Table 5.1 Key international and regional conventions against corruption

Convention	Comments
Inter-American Convention against Corruption – 1996	First international anti-corruption treaty. Promoted by the Organization of American States (OAS).
Organization for Economic Co-operation and Development (OECD) Anti-Bribery Convention – 1997	Targets bribery of foreign public officials in international business. Establishes legally binding standards that criminalize such actions, recommendations to strengthen enforcement and preventive measures.
United Nations (UN) Convention against Corruption (UNCAC) – 2003	Most comprehensive global anti-corruption treaty. Covers prevention, criminalization, international cooperation and asset recovery.
The EU Convention against Corruption Involving Officials – 1997	Aims to combat corruption involving public officials – both national and EU-level. Covers corruption that affects or is linked to the European Union's financial interests.
Council of Europe's Criminal and Civil Law Convention on Corruption – 1999	Develops common standards in criminalizing corrupt practices across Europe and facilitates cooperation between Member States. Covers criminalization of bribery and extortion, trading in influence, money laundering of proceeds from corruption, and account offences (e.g. false accounting to hide corruption).
African Union Convention on Preventing and Combating Corruption – 2003	Regional focus on public sector corruption, transparency, and accountability.

1997. In the same year, the Organization for Economic Co-operation and Development (OECD) launched the *OECD Anti-Bribery Convention*. This convention aims to combat the bribery of foreign public officials in international business transactions by establishing legally binding standards that criminalize such actions. It also provides recommendations to strengthen enforcement and preventive measures, with peer reviews and evaluations conducted to ensure compliance among member countries.

In 2003, the United Nations introduced the *UN Convention against Corruption* (UNCAC), the first legally binding international anti-corruption framework. UNCAC seeks to promote measures to prevent corruption, criminalize corrupt acts, enhance international cooperation, recover stolen assets and improve technical assistance and information sharing. Countries that ratify UNCAC commit to implementing a range of legal and institutional measures to tackle corruption. Building on this convention, the *UN Global Compact for Business* outlines, in Principle 10, that 'businesses should work against corruption in all its forms, including extortion and bribery'.[29]

In addition, there are several anti-corruption regulations by continental organizations. Thus, the European Union (EU) adopted the *EU Convention against Corruption Involving Officials*, which makes it illegal to engage in corrupt activities with officials from the EU's administrative staff, or with officials from any member state of the EU. European states also ratified the Council of Europe's *Criminal and Civil Law Convention on Corruption*, which was adopted in 1999. In Africa, in 2003, the *African Union Convention on Preventing and Combating Corruption* was launched, which presents a set of minimal standards for combating corruption.

International conventions against corruption have helped define what corruption is, establish global standards, and, in some cases, provide technical assistance and peer review mechanisms. These conventions also introduce political pressure on countries that are expected to align with global expectations. In particular, UNCAC has made progress in encouraging international cooperation for the return of stolen assets.

However, these conventions also face significant *limitations and challenges*. Enforcement remains weak – many signatory countries do not fully implement or enforce the required measures, while others adopt laws that are poorly or selectively applied. Furthermore, when corruption is systemic, conventions have limited power to overcome entrenched political and institutional interests.

For its part, the *World Bank* has, since the beginning of this century, been actively involved in combating corruption. It seeks to prevent and deter corruption in World Bank-financed development projects by promoting transparency, accountability and integrity. It also provides guidance, training and support to help countries strengthen their anti-corruption frameworks.

In addition to these international organization and national efforts, corruption is also addressed through initiatives from civil society, education that promotes honesty, and media that fosters public opinion openly opposed to corrupt practices. Among civil society initiatives against corruption is the remarkable *Transparency International* (TI),[30] a global organization founded in 1993 and working in over 100 countries to end the injustice of corruption by promoting transparency, accountability and integrity. Since 1995, among other activities, TI has compiled the annual Corruption Perceptions Index. This ranking, which has become very popular, orders 180 countries by their perceived levels of corruption, as determined by expert assessments and surveys of opinion.

All of these measures can aid in fighting bribery and other forms of corruption. However, we should not forget individual corporations.[31] Business can easily accept and perpetuate corruption in organizations, or the obverse – they can act efficiently to prevent it. Corruption spreads within the organization through processes of rationalization (people try to justify it) and socialization (increasing the numbers of people who participate in it). Companies can prevent, train against and control corruption in several ways. Some have established *compliance programmes* to prevent corporate and legal risks and respond to the demands of international standards. These programmes usually include a set of standards and good practices to identify operational and legal risks faced by the organization and internal mechanisms for prevention, control and protection against such risks (see Business Ethics in Action #5). Unfortunately, some compliance structures are often window-dressing mechanisms implemented by corporate management to mitigate the corporate liabilities associated with their employees' illegal behaviours.[32] Simply adopting a compliance programme and adequate internal controls is not enough whenever these formal actions are not supported by a coherent organizational culture.[33] Thus, developing a culture of honesty and transparency seems an indispensable means of fighting against corruption. It is also crucial that exemplary top management, which serve as role models, avoid and prevent corruption.[34]

Case Study #5

Preparing the Christmas sales campaign[35]

Alberto had been working as a salesman for a year at a leading multinational company in the consumer goods sector in a Latin American country. He was responsible for a portfolio of clients consisting of wholesalers and supermarket chains. It was his first job, and his performance had been going very well. Alberto was now preparing his sales plan for his Christmas campaign. If he met his targets, he would receive a company reward he was very excited about: a trip to Europe for two people, valued at US$9,500. The company also had an incentive policy directed at its client companies.

His most prominent client was *Vuitago Hermanos, S.A.*, a family-owned distribution company based in the capital city. The company was in its second generation and in a phase of expansion. In October, Alberto and his boss met with Pedro Lago, the purchasing manager at Vuitago. Pedro was a highly trusted figure in the company and had worked with the owners for many years. They presented the Christmas sales plan, which was well received. However, the final decision would be made ten days later, after reviewing a few remaining details. Alberto was congratulated by the sales management team, and the good news quickly circulated throughout the company.

When the ten days had passed, Alberto went to meet with Pedro. To his surprise, Pedro told him they were reviewing other offers with significantly lower prices and higher margins. He also mentioned that early indications suggested the Christmas campaign might not perform as well as in previous years.

Alberto defended his proposal, insisting that the campaign was expected to be very successful and that the company had no real competition due to the superior quality and competitive pricing of its products. He also reminded Pedro of a promotional gift included in the offer. After a long silence, Pedro responded that Alberto was probably right – but noted that going forwards with this plan would require considerable personal effort on his part. Then Pedro took the order form, filled in a section, and handed it back to Alberto. Alberto noticed it contained personal information and asked what it was. Pedro replied that the holiday to Europe should be booked in the names of himself and his wife.

Alberto was stunned. He barely managed to explain that his company's policy did not allow gifts to purchasing managers. Pedro responded bluntly: it was either that, or there would be no deal.

Alberto was deeply troubled for the rest of the day. He couldn't stop thinking about what had happened and didn't know what to do. Later that afternoon, he explained the situation to his boss, who distanced himself from the issue. He told Alberto that he was responsible for managing the client portfolio and merely reiterated that the company policy prohibited such gifts. However, he added that if they lost the deal, the team would fail to meet its objectives – and that meant losing out on incentives, which represented 30 per cent of the sales team's salary in the area. Alberto was left even more confused.

Questions

1. Why might Alberto's company have a policy prohibiting gifts to purchasing managers?
2. Alberto's boss did not tell him to violate company policy – but he didn't defend him either. If you were Alberto's friend or mentor, how would you help him interpret his boss's behaviour? What advice would you give him?
3. If you were in charge of sales training at Alberto's company, what steps would you take to prepare young employees for moments like this – when ethics and performance goals come into conflict?

Notes

1. R. Spaemann, *Basic Moral Concepts* (London: Routledge, 1989), pp. 10, 12.
2. Sources: 'Nigeria probes Siemens bribe case', *BBC News Online*, 21 November 2007; 'New Report Details Far-Reaching Corruption', *Der Spiegel Online* in English, 29 January 2007; 'Siemens Scandal May Involve Top Executives', *DW-World*, 26 November 2006; 'Rising Scandal Threatens to Engulf Siemens' Chairman', *The Guardian*, 14 December 2006; F. Rajiv and B. K. Bellakonda, *The Bribery Scandals at Siemens AG*, ICFAI Center for Management Research, distributed by ECCH (ecch.com); 'Nigeria to Investigate Siemens Bribes Scandal', *Reuters*, 19 November 2007; C. Taylor, 'Siemens Faces $538M in Taxes, Fines for "Black Money" Scandal', *Electronic News*, 53, 43 (2007), pp. 10–22; Siemens website; Wikipedia: Siemens Scandal Siemens/Greek Bribery Scandal; G. Vega, 'Volkswagen: Business as Usual', *Business and Professional Ethics Journal*, vol. 36, no. 3 (2017), pp. 285–96.
3. Ulpian in the Digest of the Roman book of law *Corpus Juris* (ca3 200 CE). See A. Watson (ed.), *The Digest of Justinian* (Philadelphia: University of Pennsylvania Press, 1998).
4. United Nations – Division for Social Policy and Development, *Social Justice in an Open World: The Role of the United Nations* (The International Forum for Social Development) (New York: United Nations, 2006), p. 7.
5. United Nations, 'Universal Declaration of Human Rights', Art. 17, 1–2: https://www.un.org/en/about-us/universal-declaration-of-human-rights. (Accessed on 2 June 2025).
6. This includes encouraging investment by offering security to business owners and entrepreneurs, facilitating trade, as clear ownership allows assets to be exchanged freely in the marketplace, promoting innovation, as individuals can benefit from the fruits of their labour or intellectual property, and enhancing economic efficiency, as individuals and businesses are motivated to use their resources effectively.
7. D. Melé, 'Loyalty in Business: Subversive Doctrine or Real Need?', *Business Ethics Quarterly*, vol. 11, no. 1 (2001), pp. 11–26.
8. Contracts are extensively treated in law studies.
9. See more on this point in D. T. Ostas, 'Fraud', in R. W. Kolb (ed.), *Encyclopaedia of Business and Society* (Los Angeles: Sage, 2018), vol. 2, pp. 931–5. On corporate fraud, see also M. J. Comer, *Corporate Fraud* (Aldershot: Gower, 1998); and M. J. Comer, *Investigating Corporate Fraud* (Aldershot: Gower, 2003).

10. From a legal perspective several factors are considered to determine whether a particular piece of information can be qualified as a trade secret. S. J. Marsnik, 'Trade Secrets and Corporate Espionage', in R. W. Kolb (ed.), *Encyclopedia of Business and Society* (Los Angeles: Sage, 2018), pp. 2091–3).
11. For more details, see S. J. Marsnik, 'Trade Secrets and Corporate Espionage' in R. W. Kolb (ed.), *Encyclopedia of Business and Society*, 2nd ed. (Los Angeles: Sage, 2018), pp. 3408–12.
12. One well-known case regarding a bailout regards Fannie Mae and Freddie Mac, two government-sponsored enterprises, which bought risky subprime mortgages from lenders and either held these in their portfolios or packaged them into mortgage-backed financial products. These firms supported lenders underwriting real estate loans to make risky decisions with the expectation that the government would bear the cost of any unfavourable outcome; and this is precisely what happened.
13. See W. Brittain-Catlin, *Offshore: The Dark Side of the Global Economy* (New York: Farrar, Straus & Giroux, 2005).
14. It can also include different types of stock-market contracts, such as contracts for the subscription, purchase or sale of securities, forward contracts, options, and financial futures and index futures.
15. For instance, M. J. Fishman and K. M. Hagerty, 'Insider Trading and the Efficiency of Stock Prices', *Rand Journal of Economics*, vol. 23, no. 1, 1992, pp. 106–22.
16. Particularly, H. G. Manne, 'Insider Trading: Hayek, Virtual Markets, and the Dog that Did Not Bark', *Journal of Corporation Law*, vol. 31, no. 1, 2005, pp. 167–85; H. G. Manne, *Insider Trading and the Stock Market* (New York: Free Press, 1966); and H. E. Leland, 'Insider Trading: Should it be Prohibited?', *Journal of Political Economy*, vol. 100, no. 4, 1992, pp. 859–7.
17. For a further discussion see P. H. Werhane, 'The Indefensibility of Insider Trading', *Journal of Business Ethics*, vol. 10, no. 9, 1991, pp. 729–31; P.-J. Engelen and L. Liedekerke, 'The Ethics of Insider Trading Revisited', *Journal of Business Ethics*, vol. 74, no. 4, 2007, pp. 497–507; J. Moore, 'What is Really Unethical About Insider Trading?', *Journal of Business Ethics*, vol. 9, no. 3, 1990, pp. 171–82, among others.
18. This is the main argument underlying the EU legislation that prohibits insider trading (Council Directive 89/592/EEC of 13 November 1989 [No. L 334/30, Introduction]): https://eur-lex.europa.eu/legal-content/EN/TXT/?uri=CELEX:31989L0592. (Accessed on 30 October 2024).
19. 'Kazakhgate' in Kazakhstan in 2003, JP Morgan Chase in Nigeria in 2011 and Petrobras in Brazil in 2014; G. M. Moisé, 'Corruption in the Oil Sector: A Systematic Review and Critique of the Literature', *The Extractive Industries and Society*, vol. 7, no. 1, 2020, pp. 217–36.
20. Rank 52 (1 means the lowest) in 2024, among 180 countries, one of the worst West European countries: https://www.transparency.org/en/cpi/2024/. (Accessed on 2 June 2024).
21. ENI. (2024). 'Anti-Corruption Compliance Programme': https://www.eni.com/en-IT/governance/controls-and-risks/anti-corruption.html. (Accessed on 30 October 2024).
22. N. Moscariello, M. Pizzo, G. Ricciardi, G. Mallardo and P. Fattorusso, 'The Anti-Corruption Compliance Models in a Multinational Company: A Single Case Study', *Business Strategy & the Environment*, vol. 33, no. 1, 2024, pp. 70–80.
23. More specifically, the certification was BS ISO 37301:2021+A1:2024. We may remember that ISO standards are a set of international standards used to improve the efficiency and quality of business processes. This was in 2023. In January 2017 ENI had been the first Italian corporation to obtain ISO certification on 'Antibribery Management Systems'.

24. https://www.en-standard.eu/bs-iso-37301-2021-a1-2024-compliance-management-systems-requirements-with-guidance-for-use/. (Accessed on 2 June 2025).
25. See A. Argandoña, 'Corruption and Companies: The Use of Facilitating Payments', *Journal of Business Ethics*, vol. 60, no. 3, 2005, pp. 251–64. He presents a broad discussion of the issue of facilitating payments, which has inspired our approach.
26. Transparency International, 'We Have One Vision, A World Free of Corruption': https://www.transparency.org/en/. (Accessed on 2 June 2025).
27. A. Argandoña, 'The United Nations Convention Against Corruption and its Impact on International Companies', *Journal of Business Ethics*, vol. 74, no. 4, 2007, pp. 481–96, and 'Private-to-Private Corruption', *Journal of Business Ethics*, vol. 47, no. 3, 2003, pp. 253–67.
28. PCJP (Pontifical Commission for Justice and Peace). (2006). 'The Fight Against Corruption': http://www.vatican.va/roman_curia/pontifical_councils/justpeace/documents/rc_pc_justpeace_doc_20060921_lotta-corruzione_en.html; B. Venard, Y. Baruch and J. Cloarec, 'Consequences of Corruption: Determinants of Public Servants' Job Satisfaction and Performance', *The International Journal of Human Resource Management*, vol. 34, no. 20, 2023, pp. 3825–56; E. Rivera, E. Seira and S. Jha, *Democracy Corrupted: Apex Corruption and the Erosion of Democratic Values*, Stanford Graduate School of Business. Research Paper No. 4166, 2024: https://papers.ssrn.com/sol3/papers.cfm?abstract_id=4828243; S. Šumah, 'Corruption, Causes and Consequences', in V. Bobek (ed.), *Trade and Global Market* (IntechOpen, 2017): https://www.intechopen.com/chapters/58969; World Bank Group Combating Corruption. 15 March 2023: https://www.vatican.va/roman_curia/pontifical_councils/justpeace/documents/rc_pc_justpeace_doc_20060921_lotta-corruzione_en.html. (All accessed on 2 June 2025).
29. https://unglobalcompact.org/what-is-gc/mission/principles. (Accessed on 30 October 2024).
30. Transparency International, 'We Have One Vision'.
31. A. Argandoña, 'Corruption: The Corporate Perspective', *Business Ethics: A European Review*, vol. 10, no. 2, 2001, pp. 163–75.
32. Moscariello et al., 'The Anti-Corruption Compliance Models'.
33. D. Hess and C. L. Ford, 'Corporate Corruption and Reform Undertakings: A New Approach to an Old Problem', *Cornell International Law Journal*, vol. 41, no. 2, 2008, pp. 307–46.
34. See V. Anand, B. E. Ashforth and M. Joshi, 'Business as Usual: The Acceptance and Perpetuation of Corruption in Organizations', *Academy of Management Executive*, vol. 19, no. 4, 2005, pp. 9–23.
35. All names are fictitious.

6

Moral Character in Leadership

The greatest leaders forget themselves and attend to the development of others.[1]
LAO TZU (circa 600 BCE), Chinese sage

Overview

For years, management was not distinguished from leadership, and the latter was understood merely as the exercise of power and authority. In that context, what defined leaders and managers – apart from the possession of power – was their analytical skills and organizational and strategic capacities, while character was considered irrelevant, except perhaps as a source of energy for giving orders.

Identifying leadership solely with power overlooks the fact that, in practice, organizations consist not only of formal structures but also informal networks, where persons without formal authority can still exert significant influence. Moreover, it is now widely recognized that people are motivated by a variety of factors – not just economic ones – that encourage them to work towards common goals. Leading solely through a 'carrot and stick' approach is not only inhumane but also often ineffective.

Section A examines the connection between moral character and leadership. It emphasizes that, today, character and virtue are no longer irrelevant; rather, their importance for effective leadership must be recognized. Spirituality also plays a significant role as a source of inspiration and motivation for leaders, offering deeper purpose and guiding them to lead with empathy, integrity and moral clarity.

Section B highlights a set of specific virtues of moral character essential for effective leadership.

Chapter Aims

After reading this chapter you should be able to:

- Distinguish between power and authority in organizations.
- Reflect on the essence of leadership and the role of spirituality.
- Value the relevance of moral character in leading organizations.
- Be familiar with the moral aspect of several leadership approaches.
- Gain insight into focusing leadership on serving others.
- Understand the role of wisdom and practical wisdom in leadership.

- Discourse on how humility and magnanimity can shape leadership.
- Review several crucial virtues for good treatment in leadership.
- Reflect on the relevance for leadership of self-mastery virtues.
- Gain an understanding of integrity, in its genuine sense, in leadership.

Historical Case #6

Leadership shift in Arthur Andersen[2]

Arthur Andersen LLP was founded by Mr Arthur E. Andersen in 1913 in Chicago. This once-respected firm was known for its high standards in accounting, but unfortunately lost its way, eventually leading to its complete demise. It was one of the 'Big Five' accounting firms, along with Deloitte, PricewaterhouseCoopers, Ernst & Young and KPMG. At its peak, Arthur Andersen employed approximately 85,000 people in eighty-four countries, 28,000 of whom were based in the United States. The firm reported roughly $9 billion in global revenue for fiscal year 2001, but, on 31 August 2002, it stopped auditing public companies and wound down its operations. The story of the rise and fall of Arthur Andersen is now a classic case of business ethics, from which many lessons can be learned.

Mr Arthur Andersen headed the firm until his death in 1947. In a speech delivered in 1932, Arthur Andersen revealed his ideals:

> If the confidence of the public in the integrity of accountants' reports is shaken, their value is gone. To preserve the integrity of his reports, the accountant must insist upon absolute independence of judgement and action. The necessity of preserving this position of independence indicates certain standards of conduct.

A story, often repeated in the early years of Arthur Andersen, tells of an executive from a local company. The executive asked Andersen to sign off on accounts that contained flawed accounting. Even though he knew that not attesting to the veracity of the accounts would cost him a major client, Andersen replied that he would not do so 'for all the money in America'. He is also quoted as having said that accountants' responsibility was to investors, not to their clients. For many years, the motto of Andersen was, 'Think straight, talk straight.' This was the principal driver for decision-making.

Arthur Andersen led the way in many accounting standards, and, for ethical reasons, he severed his firm's links with several clients. For years, the cornerstones of the firm were people management, quality, thought leadership and financial performance. In addition, values such as integrity, stewardship and public responsibility were of paramount importance.

Leonard Spacek, who succeeded Arthur as the head of the firm, continued the legacy and conducted the company's auditing services in the same way. Thus, both Andersen and Spacek ensured that the firm followed a solid path by creating a strong culture of integrity. Spacek held this position until 1963 when he was selected chairman of the partners. In 1970 he was elected senior partner, the position he held until his retirement in 1973.

After Spacek, the new leadership introduced some business innovations. In 1977, Arthur Andersen LLP and other accounting firms came together to create Andersen Worldwide and, in the following years, looked to expand their activity in the growing and profitable business of consulting. They sought out opportunities from among their existing audit clients and began generating a consultancy fee income. The consultancy practices grew to the point that the activity made up the bulk of the firm's revenues. However, it compromised their auditing independence.

In 1989, owing to the growth of the consulting business in comparison with the accounting, auditing and tax practice, the firm split into two separate units: Arthur Andersen and Andersen Consulting. By the late 1990s, Andersen Consulting showed triple the per-share revenues of Arthur Andersen. However, the disparity in growth in the accounting and consulting arms led to many disputes between the two business units.

In 1998, the then United States Securities and Exchange Commission (SEC) Chairman Arthur Levitt launched an attack on the auditing firm for selling consulting services to the same companies whose books they were auditing. Joseph Berardino, CEO of Arthur Andersen, negotiated a compromise with the SEC. Auditing and consulting fees would henceforth be disclosed. But this was not sufficient. In August 2000, the International Chamber of Commerce granted Andersen Consulting its independence from Arthur Andersen, but awarded US$1.2 billion in past payments to Arthur Andersen, and declared that Andersen Consulting would no longer be able to use the Andersen name. Andersen Consulting changed its name to Accenture at the beginning of 2001.

Prior to this separation, Andersen ran into trouble with Sunbeam Corp., when its audits failed to address serious accounting errors that eventually led to a class-action lawsuit in 1998. Andersen also found itself in court over questionable accounting practices with regard to $1.4 billion of overstated earnings for the company Waste Management. In both cases Andersen had to pay the victims.

On the 15th of June 2002, the Federal Court of Houston convicted Arthur Andersen of shredding documents related to its audit of Enron, a Houston-based energy company, and of obstruction of justice. Enron hid hundreds of millions of dollars in losses and similar amounts of debt through transactions involving some of its senior officials. Enron had been an Arthur Andersen client for sixteen years. The case was referred to David Duncan, the audit partner assigned to Enron by Arthur Andersen. In October 2001, he ordered his audit team in Houston and several other regional offices to destroy a large quantity of work documents over a period of three days.

The CEO, Joseph Berardino, notified the SEC about the activity and fired Duncan, even though he had reached his target of a 20 per cent increase in sales, and Andersen's Houston office was billing companies such as Enron US$1 million per week.

A few weeks after the trial, Arthur Andersen surrendered its licences to practise as a Certified Public Accountant in the United States, pending the result of prosecution by the Department of Justice over the firm's handling of the auditing of Enron. The company lost almost all of its clients when it was indicted, with over 100 civil suits pending related to its audits of Enron and other companies. After the indictment, it began winding down its American operations. Three other major corporations for which Andersen issued unqualified or clean audit opinions – Global Crossing, Qwest and WorldCom – were investigated by the SEC.

For Barbara L. Toffler, a former partner-in-charge of Andersen's Ethics and Responsible Business Practices consulting services, who joined the firm in 1995, the symptoms of Andersen's 'fatal disease' were evident long before Enron. She felt that an organization that had once proudly dedicated itself to professional integrity had become corrupted by greed. She added that, in the latter stages of the existence of Andersen, money was seen as the great healer, and so the managers who emerged were those whose clear focus was only on raising the revenues. This was far from the early business philosophy of the first two leaders. When Leonard Spacek was running the firm, he was somehow able to repeatedly convince his partners to sacrifice earnings for integrity.

From the beginning of 1959 and throughout the 1960s, the firm put a cap on partner compensation and allowed this to be reviewed only every three to five years. This was so that the rest of the money could flow down to the new partners and to the cost of developing the firm. Partners did not expect to enrich themselves in those days. They were content with a good career at a company with a good name.

According to Toffler, 'the four cornerstones of success at Arthur Andersen – people management, quality, thought leadership and financial performance – were referred to colloquially as «three pebbles and a boulder». The boulder was financial performance. The rest, it seemed, was a joke.'[3]

Toffler also noted that the new creed kept clients happy. Although the strong culture within Andersen persisted, it had lost its focus on integrity. At Arthur Andersen, tradition also dictated obedience to the partner. If upsetting the client was a bad thing, so was questioning your superior.

In 2005 the US Supreme Court overturned the obstruction of justice verdict based on faulty jury instructions, making it clear that lawyers and executives have some latitude in destroying sensitive or outdated documents. However, it came too late, as there was nothing left of the company.

After the Arthur Andersen and Enron scandal, Congress passed the Sarbanes–Oxley Act to overhaul US financial reporting and corporate governance practices. This law expanded repercussions for destroying, altering or fabricating records in federal investigations or for attempting to defraud shareholders. In addition, it increased the responsibility of audit firms to remain neutral and independent of their clients.

Former Arthur Andersen partners bought the rights to the name in 2014 and now the Andersen name has survived as 'Andersen Global', an association of consulting firms offering tax and legal services.

Questions

1. What leadership failures contributed to the collapse of Arthur Andersen? Were they failures of character, competence, or both? Explain.

> 2   What are the main differences between the values and corporate culture at the beginning of Arthur Andersen compared to the last decades? How could leadership have influenced the development of these cultures?
> 3   Which of Mr. Arthur's character virtues are most evident in his behaviour?
> 4   How did the behaviour and decisions of top leadership at Arthur Andersen influence the ethical climate and culture of the firm? What does this suggest you about the power of leadership example?

SECTION A. RELEVANCE OF CHARACTER IN LEADERSHIP

6.1 Leading organizations: Authority, not just power

For a long time, leadership was almost wholly associated with power. In the early 1960s the idea of a true leader as being someone who has the ability to understand the complex dynamism of workers' motivations emerged.[4] Prentice, one of the main proponents, contended that effective leaders take a personal interest in the long-term development of their employees and use tact and other social skills to encourage them to do their best; they understand people's motivations and enlist employee participation in a way that marries individual needs and interests to the group's purpose.

Later, an influential article by Professor Abraham Zaleznik of the Harvard Business School proposed the question: 'Are managers and leaders actually different?' He argued the need to overcome the technical vision of management, which was quite common at the time, criticizing it as incomplete since it lost sight of 'inspiration, vision, and the full spectrum of human drives and desires'. He held that managers and leaders are two very different types of people, although managers can, of course, also be leaders.[5] Along these lines, Kotter proposed that management and leadership are complementary, especially in a changing world. Managers deal with planning and budgeting, organizing staff, developing and applying procedures, performance, solving problems and supervising people. In contrast, leaders are those who motivate people and align them with the firm's goals, providing a vision and a new direction to orient future activities.[6]

A different perspective was presented by Mintzberg, who, based on empirical research, presented not two types of people running corporations, but singular managers acting in two different roles.[7] He found that managers have a complex, intertwined combination of roles to play. Similarly, Pérez López suggested that managers perform activities as strategists (related to the definition of some purpose), executives or organizers (for the structuring of such purposes through production and distribution systems) and leaders (for motivating the people who carry out the purpose).[8]

The latter view seems more realistic than that of two types of individuals running organizations (managers and leaders). A manager does, to different degrees, play the roles of strategist, organizer and leader, although some managers might be more involved in activities of one type than another. All of these roles are important, but leadership seems critical to being a good manager. Leadership can be studied separately from managerial skills and analytical techniques but, in practice, it is an inseparable aspect of the manager's job: managers should lead people.

A distinction from Roman times can help us understand leadership. Roman law distinguished between *potestas* and *auctoritas*.[9] *Potestas* (power over) has an institutional dimension. It derives from one's position within an institution or organization. It refers principally to the capacity to rule over others and give orders. In contrast, *auctoritas* (authority) has a personal dimension. It comes from the recognition of the personal qualities of an individual. Leadership is basically *auctoritas*.

In modern times Max Weber has dealt with power and authority extensively. He sees power as the ability to impose one's will on another, regardless of the other's wishes. Authority is a quality that can enhance this power, rather than being a form of power in itself. Authority means that the individual's power is 'authorized' by the group and thus legitimized.[10]

Hunter suggested that power is a capacity by which someone is forced to do what the individual with power wants, while authority is an art by which people voluntarily do what the individual with authority wants, due to his or her personal influence.[11] In other words, under power, people do what they are required to do without internal approval; under authority, people want to do what they do – that is, with internal approval. Thus, leadership is an art based on the voluntary decisions of followers.

The notion of *leadership*, although there is no consensus on its definition, is generally understood as the ability of someone (the leader) to influence people (followers) towards the achievement of certain goals. In organizational contexts, it refers to influence upon organization members that fosters their willingness to contribute to organizational or common goals. It is worth noting that in many definitions, and in the common understanding, leadership includes two major capacities:[12]

- The capacity of a leader to inspire others to follow.
- The capacity to move others to achieve a common goal.

Some analysts have laid more emphasis on the first, stressing the charismatic leader whom people wish to follow. Others, however, have focused on the common goal shared by both the leader and followers. In this second view, the leader is just another individual but has some quality that inspires trust. As a consequence, others follow him or her.

In contrast with those who emphasize charisma, many agree that ordinary people can become leaders. This requires the ability to influence people towards a common goal, which could be perceived as a common good. In this sense, Hunter defines leadership 'as a skill of influencing people to work enthusiastically toward goals identified as being for the common good'.[13]

6.2 Moral character and spirituality in leadership

Leadership is a complex matter that depends on a multitude of factors, including *competencies*.[14] Some are abilities, such as a vision of business, an orientation towards the client, business networking, persuasion and negotiation abilities, communication skills, organization, a capacity for problem-solving, good sense in allocating resources, innovativeness and entrepreneurship, and the ability to manage crises, among others. Other competencies are based on the character of a leader.

Personality traits and moral character in leadership

Historically, the earliest theories on leadership emerged in the first three decades of the twentieth century. One of them, termed *Trait Theory*, sought to find universal *personality traits* specific to people generally viewed as leaders, or at least some traits they showed more strongly than others, such as intelligence, self-confidence, determination, integrity and sociability.

Later, rather than seeking traits, some scholars have pointed out that leadership requires *moral character* or have stressed the importance of being a 'moral leader'.[15] Moral character shares similarities with personality but adds a crucial moral dimension. While personality traits are enduring patterns of thoughts, feelings and behaviours, moral character refers to the set of virtues or vices that guide personal conduct. Both personality traits and moral character describe stable aspects of a person that influence his or her behaviour and interactions with others. However, while personality traits focus more on how a person behaves, moral character is concerned with why and how a person ought to behave, based on moral principles.

Peter Drucker, a renowned management scholar, emphasizes the importance of character in leadership, affirming that 'It is character through which leadership is exercised.'[16] Other scholars highlight the central role of (ethical) responsibility in leadership,[17] place ethics at the core of effective leadership[18] or suggest virtues form a leader's moral capital.[19]

Peter G. Northouse,[20] a respected scholar of leadership, suggests that certain studies emphasize five essential traits of a leader, several of which are closely related to virtues: (1) *determination*; (2) *integrity* (which the author connects with honesty and trustworthiness); (3) *intelligence* (to deal effectively with the situation and the followers' needs); (4) *self-confidence* (that is, confidence in oneself or one's own abilities, but not beyond them); and (5) *sociability* (that is, the quality of being sociable and the ability to create cooperative relationships).

Kirkpatrick[21] mentions honesty and integrity, self-confidence (associated with emotional stability) and the desire to lead but not to seek power as an end in itself, which are often considered demonstrative of unselfishness and magnanimity. Apart from these virtues, he mentions some abilities or skills, such as drive (a broad term that includes achievement, motivation, ambition, energy, tenacity and initiative), cognitive ability and knowledge of the business. Some of these key character traits are actually moral virtues.

In research directed by James Collins and published as a book entitled *Good to Great*,[22] which subsequently became a bestseller, he highlights that *'professional will'* and *humility* are paramount leadership qualities.[23]

A different approach to leadership is the *Behavioural Theory*, which tries to explain it in terms of the leaders' behaviours. It focuses on the actions and behaviours of leaders rather than their traits or characteristics. It is argued that people appreciate real facts, not simply sentiments or good intentions. The conclusion is that leadership can be learned and developed solely through behaviour modification. However, this is problematic. Behaviour is character in action, an expression of one's virtues in dealing with others. Modifying behaviours with no development of virtues lacks the interior strength and authenticity provided by virtues. Additionally, this theory ignores the complex nature of leadership, which involves traits (virtues), context and situational dynamics.

Other theories also sideline virtues and even any ethical normativity. This is the case in *Contingency Theory*, which defends that effective leadership depends on the context and the situation, which requires the leader's ability to adapt to different conditions. It is also evident in *Situational Leadership Theory*, which posits that effective leaders adjust their style according to the maturity and competence of their followers. Of course, effective exercise of leadership should take note of both the specific situation and who the followers are, but this does not make virtues redundant. This is especially the case for *practical wisdom*, in other words, the virtue of a good judgement.

Another theory is the so-called *charismatic leadership*, which emphasizes the leader's ability to inspire and motivate followers through their charm and persuasiveness.[24] Possessing personality that attracts and motivates followers can be innate or learned via a multitude of techniques, but, without virtues, this leadership can be manipulative or produce positive and negative outcomes, depending on the leader's intentions and actions.

Spirituality in leadership

Since at least the 1990s, scholars have explored the role of spirituality in leadership,[25] defining spirituality as the search for meaning, purpose and connection to something greater than oneself. Spirituality informs ethics but extends beyond morality by engaging with deeper existential questions – such as the nature of life, the universe, one's identity and the transcendent.

For centuries, spirituality has been a fundamental aspect of religiosity, with significant theological developments emphasizing this connection. However, particularly in the Western world, spirituality and religion have often been seen as separate, with the argument that one can be spiritual without being religious.[26] This raises a debate about whether a sound spirituality can be based purely on subjective experience. It can be argued that spirituality lies at the core of all authentic religious traditions, although religion cannot be identified with religion.[27] Moreover, spirituality exists prior to and outside of religion (for example, in individual openness to transcendence), and many aspects of religion lie outside the realm of spirituality.[28] As a matter of fact, religious spirituality can be found in many business leaders. In this view, spirituality is not just a personal or isolated phenomenon but is deeply connected to the ethical and existential frameworks provided by religious traditions, which have long guided individuals in leadership roles.

Conger, in a pioneering work,[29] emphasizes that true leadership involves guiding others with purpose, integrity and meaning, rooted in a sense of connectedness with higher values or transcendent realities. According to Conger, spiritual leadership involves leading with a higher purpose and encouraging others to seek meaning in their work and lives.

At the beginning of this century, in a more structured way, Louis W. Fry presented an approach to *spiritual leadership*[30], a form of leadership driven by intrinsic motivation which incorporates vision, hope/faith and altruistic love, and spiritual well-being (that is, a sense of calling and membership). The model has been further developed and applied.[31]

Leadership under religious spirituality takes a perspective founded in the knowledge of faith. In this sense, leadership is often seen as a calling or vocation rather than a mere role. Christian faith, for instance, emphasizes gifts received, love expressed in service and a sense of membership and unity.[32] Although religions entail great spiritual richness, such spirituality has been scarcely applied in business leadership.

To sum up, some leadership theories focus primarily on the behavioural aspect without explicitly incorporating ethics or spirituality, though they do not necessarily exclude these dimensions. However, many other approaches explicitly or implicitly include ethics and even elements of spirituality.[33] Among these, certain theories pay particular attention to the leader-follower relationship, which can be grouped under the broader category of *relational leadership*.

6.3 Relational leadership and ethics

Relational leadership is a broad, encompassing concept that includes various theories focused on the importance of relationships in leadership practices, including the interactions between leaders and followers, as well as the social and ethical dimensions of leadership.

Several scholars[34] have emphasized the importance of relationships, interactions and social dynamics between leaders and followers, showing how these relationships influence organizational behaviour, culture and performance, without necessarily prescribing specific ethical standards or moral values. Others, focusing on the relationships between leaders and followers, have considered the moral dimensions of leadership. Among the latter are the following:

Ethical leadership

Ethical leadership[35] is a construct which empirically shows the relevance of the moral quality of leader in guiding and influencing others to behave ethically, as role models and promoting ethical behaviour within the organization. Ethical leadership has been defined as 'the demonstration of normatively appropriate conduct through personal actions and interpersonal relationships, and the promotion of such conduct to followers through two-way communication, reinforcement, and decision-making'.[36] Ethical leadership often assumes a universally accepted set of ethical standards, values and influential traits of the leader's character and include recognized virtues such as honesty, integrity and trustworthiness. However, it does not consider special circumstances which aren't considered in universal standards of morality. Additionally, ethical leadership can overlap with other theories (see next), in some respects, creating confusion or redundancy.

Authentic leadership

Authentic leadership is the name given to an approach which emphasizes the importance of leaders being true to themselves and acting in accordance with their values. One of the proponents of authentic leadership was Bill George,[37] who, reflecting on his own experience as CEO and chairman, encouraged leaders to be genuine, transparent and consistent in their actions, aligning them with moral and ethical standards. According to George,[38] leadership is authenticity, not style. 'Leaders are all very different people … The only essential quality a leader must have is to be your own person, authentic in every regard.'[39]

The concept of authentic leadership is often associated with *positive psychology*, the scientific study of what makes life most worth living, focusing on strengths, well-being and flourishing. From the organizational perspective, positive psychology focuses on increased employee engagement, satisfaction and trust, as well as other 'positive' outcomes. Positive psychologists refer to authenticity as owning personal experiences (thoughts, feelings or beliefs) and behaving according to one's authentic self.[40] Qualities of an authentic leader include self-awareness, the ability to trust one's thoughts, feelings, motives and values, self-reflection, responsiveness to feedback and the ability to resolve conflict in honest and non-manipulative ways.

Authentic leadership has been developed through empirical research with a diversity of constructs, with various definitions and interpretations leading to ambiguity. Some findings, but not all, support the benefits of authentic leadership.

Regardless, authentic leadership seems advantageous in ethical terms when compared to other leadership styles, which rely more on power or even manipulation. However, authentic leadership's emphasis on personal values and beliefs may lead to *ethical relativism*, where leaders' actions are justified based on their own moral perspectives and not on objective ethical values.

Transactional leadership

Transactional leadership is based on exchanges or transactions between the leader and their followers to obtain mutual benefits in achieving organizational goals. In business, this leadership style is found in managers who look for cooperation through economic incentives or other rewards (or in some cases punishments) that the manager offers (or threatens). Ethics is reduced to fairness in the means used by the leader, such as being honest, keeping promises and fulfilling contracts, which seem essential to maintaining the adherence of followers in subsequent interactions.

Transformational leadership

A transformational leader, often contrasted with the transactional leader,[41] creates increased motivation in followers through a positive change in their values, attitudes and willingness to cooperate. In some way, followers also influence the leader. 'Transforming leadership', in Burns's words, 'occurs when one or more persons engage with others in such a way that leaders and followers raise one another to higher levels of motivation and morality … transforming leadership ultimately becomes moral in that it raises the level of human conduct and ethical aspiration of both leader and led, and thus it has a transforming effect on both.'[42] According to this author, transforming leaders have strong values and focus on followers' intrinsic needs rather than on short-term goals. However, the morality of transformational leadership has been questioned, and some argue that Hitler, for instance, would qualify as a transformational leader. The answer may be that an *authentic transformational leadership* (not simply 'transformational leadership') must be grounded on moral foundations, with four components: (1) idealistic influence; (2) inspirational motivation; (3) intellectual stimulation; and (4) individualized consideration.[43] This requires moral character in the leader as well as concern for the self and for others; it also requires ethical values embedded in the leader's spirituality and vision and its articulation, as well as a programme that followers can embrace or reject.

Servant leadership

In this approach, leaders are seen as those who want to serve others, trying to benefit multiple stakeholders and foster similar attitudes in their followers. More generally, it also emphasizes the sense of stewardship for people and resources adopted by managers within an organization.[44] Robert Greenleaf, a former senior manager of the American telecom company AT&T, is recognized as the father of the model through his book *Servant Leadership*,[45] first published as an essay in 1970 and then extended. However, the idea of leading by serving is not completely new. This is already in the Gospel – 'If anyone wishes to be first, he shall be the last of all and the servant of all'[46] – and in other ancient wisdom traditions. Martin Luther King had also presented a spirit of service as essential for leadership.

According to Greenleaf, servant leadership 'begins with the natural feeling that one wants to serve, to serve *first*. Then conscious choice brings one to aspire to lead … The difference manifests itself in the care taken by the servant – first to make sure that other people's highest priority needs are being served.' He continues, adding that the best test for servant leadership – though one difficult to administer – is this: 'Do those served grow as persons? Do they, *while being served*, become healthier, wiser, freer, more autonomous, more likely themselves to become servants?'[47]

Servant leaders, like transformational leaders, elevate people. Values and virtues are essential for servant leaders. In *Servant Leadership*, Greenleaf mentions, among the other, more general qualities of a leader, the ability to withdraw and reorient oneself to self-improvement, acceptance and empathy towards others, listening and seeking to understand them, as well as foresight, awareness, perception, persuasion, healing and serving. Pérez López,[48] though without referring to servant leadership, argues that a good leader has concern for people's needs.

Servant leadership entails risks and limitations, apart from the difficulty to implement it in competitive or profit-driven environments. A first one is about to whom one must serve. This was the case of a German army officer during the Nazi regime. He has been a loyal servant to his nation and homeland. But when he learns about the Nazis's mass murders and crimes, he begins to have doubts about whom he should serve.[49] Other limitations regard the content of the service. There is also the risk of being ineffective if there is no motivation to serve or there is an absence of virtues. However, a sense of service can be supported by virtues bringing about an authentic sense of service.

Ethics, and in some way spirituality, is present in transactional, transformational, ethical, authentic and servant leadership. All of them present interesting insights, although all also have limitations. Additionally, several attempts have been made to integrate different theories with ethical dimensions.[50] It is not our aim here to develop a new theory of leadership, but as noted above (6.2), virtues are relevant in leadership, and we will focus on some of them in the next section.

Business Ethics in Action #6

TD Industries: Developing a servant leadership culture[51]

TDIndustries, Inc. (TDI), based in Dallas, Texas, is a leading mechanical construction company specializing in process piping and building automation services for commercial and industrial sectors. As of recent reports, TDI employs approximately 3,000 people and generates annual revenues of about $500 million.

TDI was founded by Jack Lowe Sr in 1946 to install and service heating and air conditioning systems. The business grew rapidly to offer mechanical, plumbing and electrical services in Texas and in other states of the United States.

The shift to employee ownership and servant leadership

In 1952, when the concept of 'employee ownership' was established, TDI became one of the pioneer companies in applying it. Three years later, Jack Lowe Sr fell very ill with tuberculosis. It was then that he reflected deeply on the Bible and on other books. This inner experience led him to adapt his management style to become one that was more strongly people-oriented.

In 1970, Jack was taken by Robert Greenleaf's work *The Servant as Leader*, published after forty years of working with AT&T. After reading it, he ordered hundreds of copies to be mailed to the offices of TDI. Jack became enthused by the book, adopted 'servant leadership' as TDI's corporate philosophy and arranged regular seminars to teach it to all of the TDI employees.

The servant leadership philosophy defends the idea that genuine leadership does not depend on one's title. In fact, everyone could become a leader by first serving and, then, through conscious choice leading. Currently, most TDI employees participate in seminars on servant leadership in which these points are developed.

Leadership transition and continued commitment

Jack Lowe Sr passed away in 1980. After his death, his son, Jack Lowe Jr succeeded him as CEO and remained in the position until 2005, when he moved to serve as chairman of the board of TDI. With Jack Lowe Jr, the servant leadership style continued to be the core of the company philosophy. In an interview with the author, he stated his belief that this philosophy, along with a strong sense of trust, had been the base for the company's development and an important element in overcoming several crises. One of these, which was the acid test of the philosophy, took place in 1988, during a severe financial emergency in the company. Jack Lowe Jr spoke with many 'partners' (workers) and they agreed to loan their own money to save the firm. In the 1990s, when TDI made a significant effort to win what they called the 'battle of quality', the culture of trust and servant leadership also played a significant role in quality implementation.

According to Jack Lowe Jr the TDI culture was solidly embedded in TDI. 'Our organization' – he said – 'is committed to accomplishing it over the long term. We do not believe in seizing short-term benefits to the detriment of our long-term vision. We believe in continuous, intense "people-development" efforts, including substantial training budgets. We believe in investing in tools, equipment and facilities that enable us to better accomplish our vision.' He added: 'When the motives for practicing servant leadership are pure, the result is not only increased profit but employee trust.' Thus, 'servant leadership is not a "soft philosophy" but, rather, a practical way of seeking distinction with the resources available'. He believed that a total commitment to this philosophy had built a community where partners (workers) trusted management and listened to their thoughts and ideas, and management trusted the judgement of the partners.

TD has grown and serves clients, through the full lifecycle of a facility, including engineering, construction, operations and maintenance. The company serves healthcare facilities, hotels, schools, mission critical and industrial complexes, trying to provide high-quality mechanical systems throughout the design, construction, maintenance and operations stages.

Company culture and values

Currently, TDI's company culture is based on four main pillars, as highlighted on their corporate website:[52]

Be an empathetic listener. Act with fairness; no double standards; speak with honesty; behave with integrity; make and keep your commitments.

Fiercely protect the safety of all partners: Show concern for every person; your safety is your own responsibility; stop any unsafe work behaviours; zero injuries for our families.

Lead with a servant's heart: Be humble and respectful; listen to understand, not to respond; teach, inspire and support others to be their best; hold yourself and others accountable.

Passionately pursue excellence: Hold high expectations of oneself and others; innovate and challenge the status quo; never stop learning; be 100 per cent responsible for results – no excuses.

Celebrate the power of individual differences: Create a culture of collaboration and inclusion; encourage new ideas; learn from each other's perspectives; be grateful for each contributor; achieve more together.

TDI has grown to serve clients throughout the entire lifecycle of a facility, including engineering, construction, operations and maintenance. The company serves a variety of sectors, including healthcare, hospitality, education, mission-critical and industrial complexes, striving to provide high-quality mechanical systems and uphold their strong cultural and ethical values.

Its emphasis on employees and culture has been recognized by *Fortune* magazine's rankings. In 2024, TDIndustries was listed as one of the '100 Best Companies to Work For'. This is the twenty-first consecutive year that TDI made this list. In 2017, after twenty years on the list, TD earned the status of 'Legend' by Great Places to Work. TD has also been listed on *People* magazine's inaugural 'Top 50 Companies that Care' list.

TDIndustries is an example of continued leadership based on servant leadership, complemented by employee ownership, which at TD is no longer employee ownership, but rather partner ownership. It has managed to harmonize these founding values with excellence in its operational activities. Without seeking to maximize profits at all costs, it has achieved satisfactory results and sustainable growth over many years.

Underlying the leadership of Jack Lowe Sr, and similarly in his son Jack Lowe Jr, is a vision of business and leadership that goes beyond mere financial success. Their moral character is expressed through virtues such as magnanimity, in creating a company where people not only earn a living but also find a place to feel comfortable and grow both personally and professionally. Their humility is evident in recognizing and accepting limitations, along with a willingness to serve. Their leadership is imbued with industriousness and perseverance, coupled with a treatment of others that is both demanding and kind.

SECTION B. RELEVANT VIRTUES IN LEADERSHIP

6.4 Integrity as integration of virtues

Integrity is often mentioned as a key virtue for leadership. Sometimes, integrity is taken as synonymous with honesty, but integrity, in its genuine sense, embraces a sense of unity and coherence with the entirety of personal life guided by virtues. Thus, integrity has a comprehensive meaning as *wholeness or integration of virtues*. The opposite of integrity is corruption.[53] In fact, corruption signifies impairment of integrity, virtue or moral principle[54] and, in its generic meaning, signifies a lack of wholeness. When a person acts without integrity, corruption follows and spreads from one person to the next. Integrity creates trust in the uprightness of a leader's actions, whereas corruption generates distrust.

In its most genuine sense, integrity means not only coherence and unity but also completeness or wholeness. This is its etymological meaning, derived from the Latin *integritas*, the quality or condition of being whole or undivided. As Solomon explained: 'The word integrity means "wholeness", in the sense of being part of something larger than the person – the community, the corporation, society, humanity, the cosmos.'[55] Integrity requires being virtuous, not with discrete, random virtues but with a harmonious development of all human virtues within one's character. In fact, 'integrity is not itself a virtue so much as it is a synthesis of the virtues, working together to form a coherent whole.'[56] In this sense, integrity means integration of virtues.

Integrity as integration of virtues is related to the important topic of the *unity or connection of the virtues* (previously introduced in 2.8), when virtues are fully developed. A consequence is, for instance, that a person of integrity strives to achieve emotional stability and direct spontaneous motivations through rationality to avoid misbehaviours. Virtues help one to keep intact one's innermost self in spite of cultural or social pressures for wrongdoing, striving to make decisions and to act in accordance with sound principles rather than being tyrannized by fear of 'political incorrectness'. Integrity is not only strength to resist wrongdoing; above all, it also has the proactive sense of acting in accordance with human good.

Integrity can be attributed to collectives in an analogic sense of individual integrity. As Petrick and Quinn have affirmed, 'individuals and collectives with high integrity capacity are likely to exhibit a coherent unity of purpose and action in the face of moral complexity rather than succumb to bureaucratic inertia or simplistic, irresponsible decision making.'[57]

Integrity, considered as integration of virtues, does not preclude the specificity of different types of virtues; rather integrity entails these virtues, which can be categorized in four mutually related groups (Figure 6.1):

Wisdom

It provides the ability to grasp the deeper reality of people and events objectively and to discern what is most appropriate in each situation. This also includes knowing how to use acquired knowledge and experience to discern what is correct. Followers often appreciate the good sense in making balanced judgements and good decisions, facilitated by wisdom.

Virtues for a good treatment

These include justice, care, sense of service and solidarity along with other virtues in dealing with others, such as mercy/compassion, kindness, gratitude and forgiveness. Behaviour driven by these virtues would then likely attract followers.

Virtues for trustworthiness

The leader must be a trustworthy person, expressed in habitual behaviour that generates trust. This requires virtues such as honesty, loyalty and acting with transparency.

Virtues of self-mastery

These are virtues that help the leader to control his or her own life without being carried away by feelings, complacencies or emotional states. Self-mastery virtues are, among others, self-discipline,

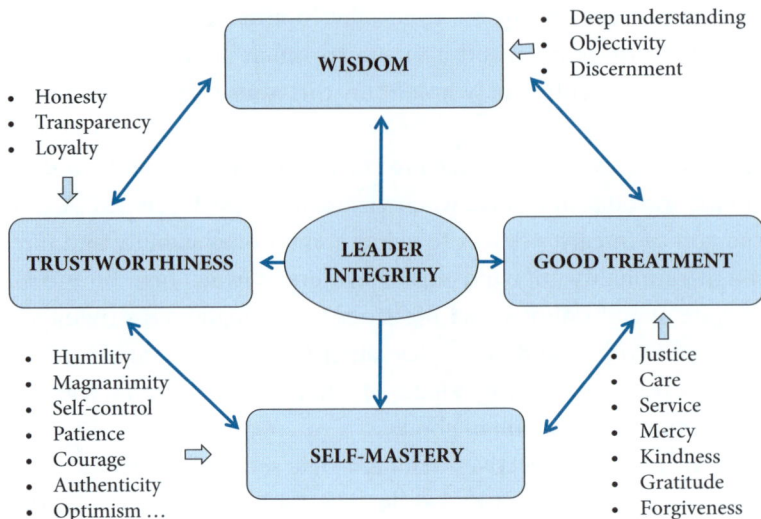

Figure 6.1 Leader integrity as the integration of virtues

courage, patience, resilience, humility, authenticity, magnanimity and being optimistic and with a good sense of humour.

Let us review these virtues, highlighting their relevance for a sound leadership.

6.5 Wisdom in leadership

As noted (2.8), wisdom can be understood in two senses. One is in its generic sense, in which *wisdom* means a profound understanding of reality, beyond empirical facts. The other is action-oriented wisdom or 'practical wisdom', which is at the heart of making sound moral judgements.

A wise attitude entails cherishing the truth, thinking about situations, trying to discover relevant circumstances and foreseeing future events. All of this leads one to be objective as far as possible or is practicable, trying to think in accordance with the reality, putting aside biases and prejudices, and seeking reliable data. A love for truth and a commitment to objectivity are generally attractive to potential followers and strengthen recognition of leadership.

Wisdom in its *deep understanding* of reality, including causes of situations and events, can bestow resignation and even contentment in accepting the frustrating situations that sometimes appear in business (and in the rest of life). Followers who share the frustration may appreciate the leader's *serenity*.

Practical wisdom helps to grasp authentic values, to distinguish the relevant from the peripheral, and to develop a sense of anticipation and caution. Practical wisdom confers a reflective attitude, leading one to seek creative solutions and act with a sense of ethics. Discernment entails an open attitude, listening to people in one's particular vicinity, asking for suitable advice, reflecting on situations from an ethical perspective, and evaluating the morality of an action and its consequences for those who receive them. All of this contributes to generating trust in those who show such wisdom.

Related to practical wisdom is *human maturity*, which includes equanimity, attentiveness to circumstances and potential consequences, the mental ability to understand and distinguish between relations, and rectitude in judging persons and situations.

6.6 Virtues for a good treatment

Justice

Justice (5.1) is the first requirement for good human treatment. Justice means acting with rectitude, giving to each person his or her right. Along with honesty and loyalty, it is the first requirement of a sense of service. In other words, service is, first of all, giving the other what is due, telling the truth and honouring one's own words. Lack of justice, or even the perception of lack of justice, destroys authority and erodes leadership. People are particularly sensitive about how just they feel a performance appraisal has been, the rewards and recognition of their contributions and the consideration of their merits in a promotion exercise.

People who wield power within an organization can also gain authority by its responsible use, in accordance with what justifies it: an effective service to the common good of the organization (6.1). In contrast, authority can be eroded and even lost due to abuse or misuse of power, a negligent use of power and employing power uselessly.[58]

Care

Care is a behaviour aimed toward the well-being of a relationship and those in the relationship.[59] It focuses on one's own team or organization and emphasizes the importance of interpersonal relationships and the recognition of each team member as being unique, with individual interests and needs, which may require different approaches or accommodations. An attitude of care entails the leader to actively listen to their team members and trying to understand their emotions and concerns, while also providing guidance and mentorship for their personal and professional growth, without ignoring the importance of a healthy work–life balance.

Care not only includes justice – promoting a work environment that is safe, inclusive and free from discrimination – but also a supportive environment in which team members feel valued. This involves recognition, appreciation and support for members of the team, which in turn allows them to perform at their best. Achieving this goal requires the empowerment of everyone's talents, allowing team members to express themselves openly, take risks and have an entrepreneurial spirit, as well as empowering people with appropriate responsibilities.

Mercy/Compassion

The virtue of mercy, generally associated with compassion, enables individuals to recognize the distress of others and fosters a desire to alleviate that suffering, particularly in those around them or within their connected communities. Compassion and mercy go beyond mere empathy, which is the ability to perceive or understand another's emotions or state of mind. These virtues contain a deeper ethical dimension, closely linked to the Golden Rule (1.8) and benevolence (2.6), and are regarded as great virtues across many religious traditions.

In a corporate context, compassionate leaders play a crucial role in addressing toxic emotions such as indignation, frustration, and dissatisfaction with corporate life. Their compassion allows them to manage these negative emotions effectively, contributing to a healthier and more supportive work environment.[60]

Some empirical research based on narratives has identified ways in which compassion is demonstrated and facilitated in organizations and its effects on human and organizational behaviours. Employees reward companies that treat them humanely.[61]

Understanding people's failure is also an important aspect of compassion, but compassion is not sentimentalism. Thus, along with a sense of justice and service, it prevents passivity or looking the other way when one is aware of some wrongdoing on the part of a collaborator or subordinate. They should be warned or corrected whenever necessary (but without humiliating them) with tact, in positive terms, and provided with guidelines and support.

Sense of service

A sense of service is more than showing compassion and mercy, it entails an attitude of being willing to assist or help someone; it is an expression and sign of love,[62] closely related with benevolence (2.6) and neighbourly love (1.8). In plain terms, acting with a sense of service means working while keeping others in mind, and helping them to achieve worthy objectives. It requires a permanent disposition of concern for others' needs. This is very much in line with the philosophy of servant leadership.[63] A sense of service can be fostered in the followers by serving them.

Drawing from Pérez López,[64] two behaviours are suggested to develop the motivation to serve others. First, do not prevent one's subordinates from acting in accordance with this kind of motivation. Second, teach them to evaluate the consequences their actions will have on others, asking in what way one's own action can contribute to satisfying others' needs.

The opposite of serving others is using people for one's own interests. Using people is an expression of power, not leadership. Choosing service over self-interest includes a careful and responsible management of what has been entrusted to the leader's care. Serving others can also be related to a sense of stewardship.[65]

Concern for serving others is neither sentimentalism nor an indulgent attitude towards people's desires or interests, but instead it is demonstrative of a concern for their authentic human needs. Following others' desires blindly rather than exercising good leadership would be an irresponsible way of running an organization.

Willingness to serve others must avoid two extremes: intrusiveness into personal life and paternalism. Intrusiveness is entering into intimate, personal matters or failing to respect privacy, encroaching without invitation, or even permission, on inappropriate occasions. Paternalism is the tendency to make decisions on behalf of others, even against their wishes, although such decisions are well intentioned. Such conduct does not serve other people; rather, it denotes a lack of respect for their privacy and autonomy.

Whoever wants to become a leader must therefore develop the willingness to serve. This requires being sensitive to the authentic needs and expectations of those around them, including needs linked to their well-being and professional and human development. Consequently, a first obstacle to serving people is a self-centred attitude, which can easily lead to indifference or insensitivity to the needs of others.

An attitude of serving others includes being sincere, available and communicative, fostering a confidence that collaborators can develop their potential. The latter can be fostered by supportive delegation of responsibilities and proper coaching.

Serving people is actually beneficial to both the one who serves and the whole organization. When a person serves others unselfishly, he or she is developing one of the highest human capacities and is thus flourishing as a human being. As for the organization, serving others can awaken a desire to serve in those who are served. A sincere and persistent attitude of concern for serving others usually develops trust and willingness to help, while selfishness breeds the opposite. As Block has pointed out, strategies of control

> tend to be expensive, are slow to react to a marketplace, and drain passion from human beings. With the element of service at its core, stewardship creates a form of governance that offers choice and spirit in core workers so they, in turn, can offer the same to their marketplace. When governance has the texture of service, it calls for a like response from those governed.[66]

A sense of service is acquired by being concerned with other people's needs and by practising specific acts of service to other people.

Solidarity

Solidarity is an ethical principle (2.7), but it is also a virtue that pushes one to work for the common good, firstly for the company community, with particular attention to people in trouble and the most vulnerable and marginalized. In organizational leadership, solidarity can be expressed inside the organization by being aware of people's problems and caring for those who face delicate situations or suffer special difficulties. This concern can relate to the problems of groups or single persons. Solidarity extends to promoting justice, harmony or mutual understanding within the organizational community.

Outside the organization, solidarity is expressed through considering people's needs and what the company does for them (12.5). Solidarity can include engaging employees (volunteer actions or campaigns) in social actions or encouraging other people's initiatives. In this way, business leaders can contribute to creating an environment in which mutual service is encouraged and leadership is reinforced.

Kindness

Kindness entails dealing with people in a friendly, generous and considerate manner. It is the golden mean between severe manners and excessively mild or soft behaviour. Kindness is not about external forms or simply good manners in dealing with people; rather, it involves an internal attitude. Authentic kindness is an expression of humility, respect and the desire to be of service to others.

Kindness, in a sense, includes virtues such as meekness, gentleness, affability and good manners, being approachable and easy and pleasant to speak to. Kindness can also include a moderate and opportune sense of humour and fun.

Gratitude

Being appreciative of benefits received is also a significant virtue in leadership and in organizational life. Although gratitude is not frequently mentioned among the leader's traits, common experience shows that people appreciate recognition and gratitude when there are reasonable motives.

Forgiveness

Feelings of resentment, indignation or anger might be present in organizations. They may be caused by a perceived offence, humiliation or mistakes that make others' work more difficult. These feelings can lead to a non-collaborative attitude and, if a leader has them, he or she can become distant from the followers. In contrast, those who are able to forgive are in a good position to obtain effective reconciliation. Thus, it is not surprising that scholars stress the important role that forgiveness has in the leadership of effective organizations.[67]

6.7 Virtues for trustworthiness

Trustworthiness is crucial in leadership. People will hardly follow the leader if they do not see him or her as someone in whom they can place their trust and feel assured that their trust shall not be betrayed. Several virtues contribute to the perception of a leader as someone who deserves confidence. Here, we will consider two of them: honesty or truthfulness, which includes transparency in proper matters, and loyalty.

Honesty

Honesty involves *truthfulness*, which refers to the habitual adherence to truth in speech, statements and actions (5.1). It encompasses being truthful, trustworthy and upright. Simply put, it means having a stable disposition of character that compels one to tell the truth, aligning with facts, reality or, at the very least, one's own understanding of the truth. In a broader sense, honesty also reflects an inner drive to seek, preserve and act in accordance with truth, maintaining full integrity and uprightness.

According to Solomon, honesty is the first virtue of business life[68] and, without doubt, it is a pillar of leadership. Honesty is greatly appreciated as a means of creating trust. Long ago, Aquinas wrote: 'people could not live with one another if there were not mutual confidence that they were being truthful to one another'.[69]

Telling lies, creating false expectations, distorting reality, acting with hypocrisy, offering a false image of oneself, practising flattery by praising someone's fine qualities to obtain favours or giving misleading feedback are examples of a lack of honesty. All these behaviours denote *lack of coherence* between words or appearances and reality. If a leader is not honest, his or her authority will be eroded. Telling the truth or deceiving in accordance with one's interests of the moment leaves the interlocutor unable to identify what to believe or what to doubt. It can be readily understood that a dishonest person will not have long-term followers.

Loyalty

This is a virtue that denotes faithfulness or firmness in keeping legitimate promises and maintaining fair agreements. Loyalty can be to a person or a group of people, a cause or an institution. As with honesty, loyalty is an aspect of justice, but one with a special identity. Loyalty as a virtue differs from an interested or emotional adhesion to something.[70] Loyalty leads, rather, to fulfilling one's commitments and offering conscious fidelity to those to whom it is due and with a steadfast and devoted attachment. It refers to moral objects and so excludes any unjust commitment or adherence to any cause that is morally wrong. In addition, as with any other moral virtue, loyalty is regulated by practical wisdom, which helps to resolve any conflicts between one loyalty and another.

Loyalty does not refer only to formal undertakings; informal commitments can also be evident when behaviours show that the leader is actually committed to a cause. Additionally, loyalty is expressed by providing continual support to a group or team that shares common goals.

Loyalty contributes to the smooth and efficient functioning of organizations. It generates trust, which is crucial to organizational development.[71] Followers appreciate the loyalty of the leader to their common goals. By contrast, lack of loyalty or a lukewarm allegiance breaks trust, and the authority of leadership is eroded.

6.8 Self-mastery virtues

Offering practical service to others requires self-mastery, that is, the ability to take control of one's life through emotional stability and without being blown off course by feelings. Several virtues can be related to self-mastery. Here we will review some we consider particularly relevant for leadership.

Self-discipline

This is a broad concept that includes any personal effort for personal improvement and promotes self-control and restraint. Self-discipline brings about consistent willingness, striving for valuable goals and competitiveness. Trust in the leader and achieving common goals requires much more than just good intentions. Laziness, idleness, indolence and, in general, a lack of personal struggle to achieve valuable goals can jeopardize authority. Thus, self-discipline can be considered a pillar of leadership. According to George, 'Self-discipline is an essential quality of an authentic leader. Without it, you cannot gain the respect of your followers.'[72]

A leader needs to work to fulfil commitments at the proper time with *industriousness*, *attentiveness* and *a sense of responsibility*. All of this requires order, determination and perseverance in doing due tasks, even when the initial enthusiasm has disappeared.

Self-discipline allows one to partake with sobriety in eating and drinking, control sexual impulses and, in general, practise moderation in pleasure and avoid addictions.

Self-discipline helps a person control their emotions, desires or actions and ensures they are not driven by temper, and are therefore unlikely to act in a fit of rage. Thus, it helps one maintain emotional stability and control even in situations that can be propitious to nervous tension or stress. In using and allocating resources, self-discipline lends itself to a sense of austerity, using them whenever necessary but avoiding wasteful, fanciful and extravagant expenses of doubtful profitability.

Courage

This virtue helps to dominate restlessness and the desire to withdraw in the face of risks, possible failure, uncertainty or other difficulties or obstacles. Thus, leaders need to be fearless enough to undertake the proper actions and to strive with others to achieve common goals. Whereas practical wisdom helps one to understand risks and humility fosters awareness of the capabilities one has to confront them, courage produces daring to overcome obstacles and provides the willingness and strength to take on reasonable risks.

Daft has mentioned several aspects of this virtue and its meaning in leadership.[73] Courage, he contends, means accepting responsibility; an attitude of nonconformity, going against the grain, breaking traditions, disregarding boundaries, initiating change, pushing beyond the comfort zone to do the right thing, and asking for what you want, saying what you think and fighting for what you believe.

Patience

Patience bestows the capacity to endure hardship, difficulty or inconvenience without complaint. This virtue gives endurance in difficult circumstances. Patience is necessary for leaders since leadership is about people and people have many quirks, which, without patience, could result in leaders losing their temper.

Leaders need patience to persevere in the face of delay or provocation without becoming annoyed or upset. Patience is also necessary to learn, to give followers serenity and to achieve goals. Patience helps one to act under strain and to face difficulties, especially when these are long term.

Resilience

Resilience is the ability to recover quickly from difficulties or problems, or the ability of a substance to return to its original shape, sometimes even stronger and more capable. This is a critical quality for effective leadership, enabling leaders to navigate challenges, setbacks and uncertainties while maintaining focus and motivation. Resilience requires emotional control, adaptability, persistence and a positive outlook seeking how to overcome difficulties and even how to shift problems into opportunities. An attitude of continuous learning from adverse situations can help leaders face future difficult events. Resilient leaders not only survive adversity but thrive, setting a powerful example for their teams and organizations.

Humility

Humility is sometimes considered synonymous with modesty. However, it can be understood in a wider sense. In most classic authors, humility means to think realistically about oneself, being aware of one's weaknesses and strengths. Assuming this meaning, humility – not only modesty – is an important virtue in leadership, contributing to the manager's moral and professional quality and the acceptance of the leader.[74]

Jaime Balmes, a relatively unknown nineteenth-century Spanish philosopher, might have been one of the first to consider humility in business. He understood this virtue as a clear knowledge of what we are, with nothing added or taken away. He believed that humility helps us to recognize the limits of our capabilities, to maintain a permanent disposition to ask for advice and to see how much we still need to move ahead.[75]

Humility concerns the truth about oneself and others. It helps one to recognize one's own talents but also goes beyond this. It is neither false modesty nor lack of self-esteem. Humility provides realistic expectations of self, and the subsequent self-confidence – frequently mentioned qualities of leaders. When based on the knowledge of one's real capacities, it is a realistic and authentic self-confidence. Otherwise, this self-belief would have a false foundation, which brings risks; it could lead to visible failures and the subsequent loss of the trust of those surrounding the leader. Humility also leads one to recognize others' merits and not blame others for one's own failures. It involves the practice of self-criticism and the willingness to change when errors or failure are detected.

The opposite of humility is arrogance, pride, conceit or an excessive sense of personal worth. Arrogant managers deem themselves irreplaceable. They do not recognize their errors and rarely rectify their wrong behaviours. Nor do they acknowledge their own failures, but instead constantly lay the blame for them on others. They do not listen to others in order to learn and can't imagine that others might be right. They do not weigh up the talents and achievements of their colleagues with equanimity, and they resist praising collaborators to avoid the possibility that their peers will overshadow them. Arrogance creates barriers and distrust between managers and collaborators, which undermines their leadership. Humility has the opposite effect.

Humility is closely related to serving others. Pride can make it particularly difficult to be sensitive to people's needs, but humility can be a great help in serving people since, in recognizing the truth about oneself and others, it fosters the recognition of people's authentic needs.

Authenticity

Authenticity is the quality of 'being oneself' and is closely related to humility. Humble leaders base their behaviour on who they truly are, rather than on a questionable self-image. While authenticity involves being true to oneself, it does not imply passive acceptance of personal shortcomings. For a leader, awareness of one's weaknesses serves as a stimulus to strive for improvement. However, as noted in 6.3, authenticity carries the risk of sliding into ethical relativism if it relies solely on subjective values. This risk is mitigated when the leader possesses other virtues – such as justice, a sense of service and truthfulness – which provide an objective moral foundation.

Humility contributes to the development of gratitude and favours asking for pardon for one's failures and forgiving whenever necessary: two virtues that we will consider later.

It is worth noting that humility has nothing to do with pusillanimity. On the contrary, in a leader, it has to go hand in hand with magnanimity, which we will consider next.

Magnanimity

Being magnanimous has been defined as 'loftiness of spirit enabling one to bear trouble calmly, to disdain meanness and pettiness, and to display a noble generosity.'[76] Magnanimity derives from the Latin word *magnanimitas*, rooted in *magnus*, meaning 'great'. Magnanimity can be understood as the willingness to undertake great tasks; it is the source of human greatness.[77] Magnanimous leaders are 'high-minded and conscious of their potential for greatness.'[78] Those who are magnanimous set themselves great goals, and 'what is truly great in the universe is the person'.[79] These goals are not chosen exclusively out of personal interest but to favour people; they are in the best interests of the organization or community.

Magnanimity can be related to eagerness for valuable achievements, often mentioned among the traits of the leader's character. It can be recognized as a personal quality in leaders, such as Abraham Lincoln or Schuman, Monnet, Adenauer and Gasperi, founders of the European Union.[80]

Magnanimity can also be found in many entrepreneurs who might have resigned themselves to managing a small business but were not content to do so. On the contrary, they displayed courage and resolution, developing new initiatives that created jobs and made new and useful products available to many people. This was the case of Heinrich Emanuel Merck, who took over the family pharmacy and eleven years later established a chemical-pharmaceutical factory in Darmstadt, Germany, which was the origin of an industrial global giant. David Hilbert, founder of HP, started his business in a garage; and Earl Bakken, co-founder of Medtronic (today one of the world's largest medical technology companies), began with a modest repair company, fixing and servicing medical equipment in local hospitals.

Magnanimity is not only a virtue for 'VIPs', but also present in 'little leadership', in those who seek to better themselves, striving for noble causes.

Optimism and good humour

Last, but not least in this list of self-mastery virtues, is being positive and optimistic, which serves to counteract pessimistic views or attitudes that identify only the negative side of any issue. Managers have to be realistic, and this is incompatible with invariably presenting the most favourable interpretation of actions and events or always anticipating the best possible outcome. However, optimistic views must be presented without deception or creating false expectations.

Close to being positive is having a good sense of humour, with a cheerful and friendly attitude towards life, sometimes even in difficult situations, with the ability to find funny things that help lift other people's spirits.

In this context, we do not mean being positive or showing good humour as spontaneous attitudes that some people have but a virtue – a habit of character – that must be acquired with personal effort.

Case Study #6

United Laboratories: Leadership and values[81]

United Laboratories (Unilab) is is a Philippine pharmaceutical company that specializes in a wide range of consumer healthcare products such as prescription and over-the-counter medications, vitamins and food supplements, and biotechnology. Unilab's beginnings were in a small corner shop in downtown Manila. It was founded by Jose Yao Campos, shortly after the Second World War and before the United States granted independence to the Philippines, along with Mariano K. Tan and with the aid of Howard Q. Dee, Yao Campos's brother-in-law.

The company made an early decision to serve the country's poor and young population and to be aware of its corporate social responsibilities. After the Second World War, when the Philippines was experiencing very harsh economic conditions, its social pricing policy obliged Unilab to sell most of its products at 20–60 per cent below competitors' prices.

Unilab management policy regards its employees as the first managerial obligation. This follows the founding ideas of Campos, who used to say: 'take care of your people and the people will take care of the customer'. The company also understands that it should serve the entire Philippine society, addressing the therapeutic and nutritional needs of the country's poor population and giving good service to the medical profession – for example, by sponsoring professional education for medical professionals. In addition, the firm has provided aid to the victims of several floods and typhoons in the Philippines.

After the Japanese occupation, drug supply was very limited. The penicillin and sulphonamides to treat infections were bought by American soldiers and then sold on the black market. On one hand, this made the medicines available for people; on the other hand, the prices were so high that not many could not afford to purchase them. Thus, the delivery of good-quality medicines to the Philippine poor was, from the very beginning, one of the main purposes of Unilab. Campos met an American soldier, Robert Horowitz, who had a pharmacy before the war. Shortly afterwards, they jointly set up United Drug, in which Horowitz was in charge of the production and Campos handled the marketing and distribution.

Campos stamped the company with a strong business philosophy inspired by indigenous Philippine values, mainly by the concept of *Bayanihan*, enriched with the Christian faith of the Unilab cofounder. *Bayanihan* literally means *heroic cooperation* and can be interpreted as *working together towards the common goal* in terms of the fullest economic, social, cultural and spiritual development.

Bayanihan leads to hard work; every individual is aware that he or she is carrying his or her own share of the whole burden and, if one fails, it results in a proportionate increase in the weight upon others. *Bayanihan* also emphasizes individual development and requires providing the conditions for people to express their talents.

Unilab significantly grew within its first fourteen years of operations, when it began to export to Hong Kong, and the expansion continued in the following years. Now, Unilab is one of the Philippines' flagship companies. It employs over 6,000 people (2024), providing them and their families with a variety of benefits such as hospitalization fees, training, educational benefits, material compensation and different kinds of family assistance. Furthermore, it enjoys a leading presence in Asia and many of its products have become top brands in Indonesia, Thailand, Malaysia, Singapore, Hong Kong, Vietnam, Myanmar and other countries.

José Y. Campos passed away in 2006, when his family had become one of the Philippines' most powerful business clans. Leadership of Unilab was continued by José's firstborn, Jocelyn (Joy) Campos-Hess and her son, Clinton Hess, who sits beside her as the company's president, CEO, and vice-chairman of the board.

Currently, Unilab presents its 'Our Purpose', '*Working towards a healthier Philippines, one quality medicine at a time.*' Three values are highlighted, through native words:

- *Husay*: We ensure *excellence* and *quality* in everything we do, knowing that each medicine we provide will promote and enrich the lives of communities we serve.
- *Malasakit*: We believe that every Filipino should receive *unparalleled care* when it comes to health. This means going above and beyond one's call of duty to be able to provide for our customers' health needs.
- *Bayanihan*: We believe in *working together* for a common goal and purpose, in the service of the Filipino.

Bayanihan is still outstanding. According to Jocelyn Campos-Hess, currently chairperson of the board of Unilab,

Early on in our history, our founders instilled in us the spirit of *bayanihan* – people coming together to work towards a common goal. Today we see *bayanihan* not just as a value, but rather as a way of life. It is integral to how we forge deeper and more effective relationships within and outside the company as we work ceaselessly to make the lives of our customers better. Here, no one stands alone, and nobody gets left behind.

Unilab has received various international and national awards, such as 'Best Employers in Asia' from Hewitt Associates and Dow Jones, and, on two occasions, 'Marketing Company of the Year' by the Philippines Marketing Association, and 'Most Outstanding Employer of the Year' by the Personnel Management Association of the Philippines. In May 2006, José Y. Campos was honoured by the Philippine Medical Association as the 'Father of the Philippine Pharmaceutical Industry'.

Questions

1. Unilab's founders adopted an unusual pricing strategy that prioritised public health over short-term profit. What leadership qualities and decision-making approaches can be inferred from this choice, and how do they reflect the ethical responsibilities of business leaders in developing economies?
2. What virtues could you recognize in the Unilab leadership?
3. Why may Unilab have introduced other values – *Husay* and *Malasakit* – in addition to *Bayanihan*? How may these values have contributed to the development of the Unilab culture?

Notes

1. Quoted from P. Warneka, T.T. Warneka and L. Tzu, *The Way of Leading People: Unlocking Your Integral Leadership Skills with the Tao Te Ching* (Cleveland, OH: Asogomi Publishing International, 2007).
2. Sources: D. Collins, 'Arthur Andersen', in R. W. Kolb, *Encyclopedia of Business Ethics and Society* (Los Angeles, CA: Sage, 2018), 165–8; F. D. Hawkins and J. Cohen, case study *Arthur Andersen LLP* (Cambridge, MA: Harvard Business School Publishing, 2003); A. Nanda and S. Landry, case study *Family Feud: Andersen vs Andersen (A) and (B)* (Cambridge, MA: Harvard Business School Publishing, 1999 and 2000); B. L. Toffler, *Final Accounting: Ambition, Greed, and the Fall of Arthur Andersen* (New York: Broadway Books, 2003); M. Torres, case study *The Demise of Arthur Andersen* (Barcelona, Spain: IESE Publishing, 2007); D. Windsor, 'Enron Corporation', in R. W. Kolb, *Encyclopedia of Business Ethics and Society* (Los Angeles, CA: Sage, 2008), 716–19; Wikipedia: Arthur Andersen.
3. Toffler, *Final Accounting*, p. 104.
4. W. C. H. Prentice, 'Understanding Leadership', *Harvard Business Review*, vol. 82, no. 1, 2004, pp. 102–9. First published in *Harvard Business Review*, vol. 39, no. 5, 1961, pp. 143–51.
5. A. Zaleznik, 'Managers and Leaders: Are they Different?', *Harvard Business Review*, vol. 55, no. 3, 1977, pp. 67–78.
6. J. P. Kotter, *A Force for Change: How Leadership Differs from Management* (New York: Free Press, 1990).

7. H. Mintzberg, 'The Manager's Job: Folklore and Fact', *Harvard Business Review*, vol. 68, no. 2, 1975 [1990], pp. 163–76.
8. J. A. Pérez López, *Fundamentos de la dirección de empresas* (Madrid: Rialp, 2002), Chapter 8.
9. See A. D'Ors, *Derecho Romano Privado* (Pamplona: Eunsa, 1997), pp. 37–9.
10. See W. J. Mommsen, *The Political and Social Theory of Max Weber: Collected Essays* (Chicago: University of Chicago Press, 1992).
11. See J. C. Hunter, *The Servant: A Simple Story About the True Essence of Leadership* (Roseville, CA: Prima Publishing, 1998), Chapter 1.
12. See C. Llano, *Humildad y liderazgo* (México, D. F.: Ruz, 2004), p. 52.
13. Hunter, *The Servant*, p. 28.
14. See, for instance, P. G. Northouse, *Leadership: Theory and Practice* (Thousand Oaks, CA: Sage, 2007); R. L. Daft, *Leadership: Theory and Practice* (Fort Worth, TX: The Dryden Press, 1999); and P. Cardona and P. García-Lombardía, *How to Develop Leadership Competencies* (Pamplona: Eunsa, 2005).
15. T. L. Hosmer, *Moral Leadership in Business* (Boston, MA: Irwin Publishers, 1994); R. Kanugo and M. Mendonca, *Ethical Dimesion of Leadership* (Thousand Oaks, CA: Sage, 1996); J. B. Ciulla, *The Ethics of Leadership* (Belmont, CA: Wadsworth, 2002); B. J. Ciulla (ed.), *Ethics, the Heart of Leadership* (New York: Praeger, 1998); R. Coles, *Lives of Moral Leadership* (London: Random House, 2000); and T. Maak, *Responsible Leadership in Business* (New York: Routledge, 2006).
16. P. Drucker, *The Practice of Management* (Oxford: Elsevier, 2005), p. 155.
17. Maak, *Responsible Leadership in Business*; and N. Pless and T. Maak, 'Responsible Leadership: Pathways to the Future', *Journal of Business Ethics*, vol. 98, 2011, pp. 3–13.
18. Ciulla, *Ethics, the Heart of Leadership*.
19. A. J. G. Sison, *The Moral Capital of Leaders: Why Virtue Matter* (Cheltenham and Northampton, MA: Edward Elgar, 2003).
20. P. G. Northhouse, *Leadership: Theory and Practice*. 4th ed. (Thousand Oaks, CA: Sage, 2007).
21. S. A. Kirkpatrick and E. A. Locke, 'Leadership: Do Traits Matter?', *Academy of Management Executive*, vol. 5, no. 2, 1991, pp. 48–60.
22. J. Collins, *Good to Great: Why Some Companies Make the Leap, and Others Don't* (London: Random House, 2001).
23. J. Collins, 'Level 5 Leadership: The Triumph of Humility and Fierce Resolve', *Harvard Business Review*, vol. 83, no. 7/8, 2005, pp. 136–46.
24. J. A. Conger and R. N. Kanungo, 'Toward a Behavioural Theory of Charismatic Leadership in Organizational Settings', *The Academy of Management Review*, vol. 12, no. 4, 1987, pp. 637–47.
25. J. Conger and Associates, *Spirit at Work: Discovering the Spirituality in Leadership* (San Francisco, CA: Jossey-Bass, 1994).
26. G. Saucier and K. Skrzypinska, 'Spiritual but Not Religious? Evidence for Two Independent Dispositions', *Journal of Personality*, vol. 74, no. 5, 2006, pp. 257–92.
27. The radical separation of spirituality from religion often portrays religion as being reduced to a set of beliefs and rituals, supported by an institutional framework, rather than as something inherently spiritual. However, the question arises as to whether spirituality can be entirely separated from religion. Historically, spirituality has been deeply developed within religious traditions, and the distinction between spirituality and religion may reflect a Western, individualistic bias. In many non-Western cultures, spirituality and religion are often intertwined, with no such clear distinction between the two. On this point, see B. J. Zinnbauer and K. I.

Pargament, 'Religiousness and Spirituality', in R. F. Paloutzian and C. L. Park (eds), *Handbook of the Psychology of Religion and Spirituality* (New York: Guilford Press, 2005), pp. 21–42.

28. R. Domingo, 'Business and Spirituality: A Discussion Paper on Intertwining Metaparadigms', *Journal of Applied Business & Economics*, vol. 23, no. 1, 2021, pp. 170–83.
29. Conger and Associates, *Spirit at Work*.
30. L. W. Fry, 'Toward a Theory of Spiritual Leadership', *Leadership Quarterly*, vol. 14, no. 6, 2003, pp. 693–727. See also, L. W. Fry and W. Altman, *Spiritual Leadership in Action* (Charlotte, NC: Information Age Publishing, 2013).
31. L. W. Fry, J. R. Latham, S. K. Clinebell and K. Krahnke, 'Spiritual Leadership as a Model for Performance Excellence: A Study of Baldrige Award Recipients', *Journal of Management, Spirituality & Religion*, vol. 14, no. 1, 2017, pp. 22–47. See a review at J. Oh and T. Wang, 'Spiritual Leadership: Current Status and Agenda for Future Research and Practice', *Journal of Management Spirituality & Religion*, vol. 17, no. 3, 2020, pp. 1–26.
32. In this sense, Domingo suggests, as the key spiritual triad of Christian spirituality, love, communion and gift. See R. Domingo, *God and the Secular Legal System* (Cambridge: Cambridge University Press, 2016); and Domingo, 'Business and Spirituality'.
33. See J. B. Ciulla, 'Leadership Ethics: Mapping the Territory', *Business Ethics Quarterly*, vol. 5, no. 1, 1995, pp. 5–28; Daft, *Leadership: Theory and Practice* and Northouse, *Leadership: Theory and Practice*, among others.
34. Among them Uhl-Bien, who presents the *relational leadership theory* (RLT) drawing from both entity and relational ontologies and methodologies to more fully explore the relational dynamics of leadership and organizing. (M. Uhl-Bien, 'Relational Leadership Theory: Exploring the social processes of leadership and organizing,' *The Leadership Quarterly*, vol. 17, no. 6, 2006, pp. 654–76).
35. M. E. Brown and L. K. Treviño, 'Ethical Leadership: A Review and Future Directions', *The Leadership Quarterly*, vol. 17, no. 5, 2006, pp. 595–616.
36. Brown, M. E., Treviño, L. & Harrison, D. 2005. 'Ethical leadership: A social learning perspective for construct development and testing.' *Organizational Behavior & Human Decision Processes*, 97:2, 117–34, p. 120.
37. W. W. George, *Authentic Leadership: Rediscovering the Secrets to Creating Lasting Value* (San Francisco: Jossey-Bass, 2003); and *True North: Discover your Authentic Leadership* (San Francisco, CA: Jossey-Bass, 2007). We will return to Bill George later (Business Ethics in Action #9), considering his business vision.
38. George, *Authentic Leadership* and *True North*.
39. George, *Authentic Leadership*, p. 12.
40. F. Luthans and B. Avolio, 'Authentic Leadership Development', in K. Camareron, J. Dutton and R. Quinn (eds), *Positive Organizational Scholarship: Foundations of a New Discipline* (San Francisco, CA: Berrett-Koehler, 2003), pp. 241–58.
41. J. G. Burns, *Leadership* (New York: Harper Torchbooks, 1978). See also B. M. Bass, 'From Transactional to Transformational Leadership: Learning to Share the Vision', *Organizational Dynamics*, vol. 18, no. 3, 1990, pp. 19–31.
42. Burns, *Leadership*, p. 20.
43. B. M. Bass and P. Steidlmeier, 'Ethics, Character, and Authentic Transformational Leadership Behaviour', *Leadership Quarterly*, vol. 10, no. 2, 1999, pp. 181–217.
44. This latter aspect is especially emphasized by P. Block, *Stewardship: Choosing Service Over Self-Interest*, 2nd ed. revised and expanded (New York: Berrett-Koehler, 2013).

45. R. K. Greenleaf, *Servant Leadership: A Journey into the Nature of Legitimate Power and Greatness* (New York: Paulist Press, 1970 [2002, rev. ed.]).
46. The Bible (Mk 5:35).
47. Greenleaf, *Servant Leadership* (2002), p. 27.
48. Pérez López, *Fundamentos*, Chapter 8 and *Liderazgo y ética en la dirección de empresas. La nueva empresa del siglo XXI* (Bilbao: Deusto, 1998).
49. J. G. Langhof and S. Gueldenberg, 'Whom to Serve? Exploring the Moral Dimension of Servant Leadership: Answers from Operation Valkyrie', *Journal of Management History*, vol. 27, no. 4, 2021, pp. 537–73.
50. G. J. Lemoine, C. A. Hartnell and H. Leroy, 'Taking Stock of Moral Approaches to Leadership: An Integrative Review of Ethical, Authentic, and Servant Leadership', *Academy of Management Annals*, vol. 13, no. 1, 2019, pp. 148–87.
51. This is an abridged version of the case study *TDIndustries: Developing a Corporate Culture* by D. Melé (Barcelona: IESE Publishing, 2002) (published with permission) updated with information from J. H. Gavin and R. O. Mason, 'The Virtuous Organization: The Value of Happiness in the Workplace', *Organizational Dynamics*, vol. 33, no. 4, 2004, pp. 379–92; A. Cheshire, *A Partnership of the Spirit: The Story of Jack Lowe and TDIndustries* (Dallas, TX: Taylor Publishing, 1987); A. McGee-Cooper and D. Trammell, 'Servant Leadership Learning Communities': Incubators for Great Places to Work', in D. van Dierendonck and K. Patterson (eds), *Servant Leadership* (Cham: Palgrave Macmillan, 2025), pp. 223–40; Wikipedia: TDIndustries and Jack Lowe, Jr, https://en.wikipedia.org/wiki/Jack_Lowe_Jr; and the corporative website of TDIndustries, https://www.tdindustries.com/. (Both accessed on 6 June 2025).
52. https://www.tdindustries.com/who-we-are. (Accessed on 6 June 2025).
53. This point has been developed by Paladino et al.: M. Paladino, P. Debeljuh and P. Delbosco, *Integridad. Un liderazgo diferente* (Buenos Aires: Emecé Editores, 2007), Chapter 1.
54. Definition from the Merriam-Webster Online Dictionary: http://www.merriam-webster.com/dictionary/corruption. (Accessed on 6 June 2025).
55. R. C. Solomon, *A Better Way to Think about Business: How Personal Integrity Leads to Corporate Success* (New York: Oxford University Press, 1999), p. 38.
56. Solomon, *A Better Way to Think about Business*, p. 38.
57. J. A. Petrick and J. F. Quinn, 'The Integrity Capacity Construct and Moral Progress in Business', *Journal of Business Ethics*, vol. 23, no. 1, 2000, p. 4.
58. Pérez López, *Liderazgo y ética en la dirección de empresas* pp. 105–6.
59. S. Ruddick, 'Care as Labor and Relationship', in M. S. Haflon and J. C. Haber (eds), *Norms and Values: Essays on the Work of Virginia Held* (Lanham, MD: Rowman & Littlefield, 1998), p. 160.
60. G. Guitián, 'Service as a Bridge Between Ethical Principles and Business Practice: A Catholic Social Teaching Perspective', *Journal of Business Ethics*, vol. 128, no. 1, 2015, p. 62.
61. See L. C. Spears (ed.), *Reflections on Leadership: How Robert K. Greenleaf's Theory of Servant-Leadership Influenced Today's Top Management Thinkers* (New York: John Wiley, 1995), and *Insights on Leadership: Service, Stewardship, Spirit, and Servant-Leadership* (New York: Wiley, 1998). See also J. T. Whetstone, 'Personalism and Moral Leadership: The Servant Leader with a Transforming Vision', *Business Ethics: A European Review*, vol. 11, no. 4, 2002, pp. 385–92.
62. See Pérez López, *Liderazgo y ética en la dirección de empresas*, pp. 97ff.

63. See Block, *Stewardship*.
64. Block, *Stewardship*, pp. 21–2.
65. P. Frost, *Toxic Emotions at Work: How Compassionate Managers Handle Pain and Conflicts* (Cambridge, MA: Harvard Business School Press, 2003).
66. J. E. Dutton, P. J. Frost, M. C. Worline, J. M. Lilius and J. M. Kanov, 'Leading in Times of Trauma', *Harvard Business Review*, vol. 80, no. 1, 2002, pp. 54–61. See also J. E. Dutton, M. C. Worline, P. J. Frost and J. Lilius, 'Explaining Compassion Organizing', *Administrative Science Quarterly*, vol. 51, no. 1, 2006, pp. 59–96; J. M. Kanov, S. Maitlis, M. C. Worline, J. E. Dutton, P. J. Frost and J. M. Lilius, 'Compassion in Organizational Life', *American Behavioural Scientist*, vol. 47, no. 6, 2004, pp. 808–27; and J. M. Lilius, M. C. Worline, S. Maitlis, J. Kanov, J. E. Dutton and P. Frost, 'The Contours and Consequences of Compassion at Work', *Journal of Organizational Behaviour*, vol. 29, no. 2, 2008, pp. 193–218.
67. J. D. Cameron, *Rewards and Intrinsic Motivation: Resolving the Controversy* (Westport, CT: Greenwood Publishing Group, Inc., 2002).
68. Solomon, *A Better Way to Think about Business*, p. 91.
69. T. Aquinas, *The Summa Theologica* (London: Burns Oates and Washbourne, 1273 [1981]), II–II, q. 109, a. 3, ad. 1.
70. See D. Melé, 'Loyalty in Business: Subversive Doctrine or Real Need?', *Business Ethics Quarterly*, vol. 11, no. 1, 2001, pp. 11–26.
71. On this point, see J. M. Rosanas and M. Velilla, 'Loyalty and Trust as the Ethical Bases of Organizations', *Journal of Business Ethics*, vol. 44, no. 1, 2003, pp. 49–59.
72. W. W. George, *Authentic Leadership: Rediscovering the Secrets to Creating Lasting Value* (San Francisco, CA: Jossey-Bass, 2003), p. 24.
73. See Daft, *Leadership: Theory and Practice*, pp. 380ff.
74. A. Argandona, 'Humility in Management', *Journal of Business Ethics*, vol. 132, no. 1, 2015, pp. 63–71; and A. Havard, *Virtuous Leadership: An Agenda for Personal Excellence* (New York: Scepter, 2007), and *Created for Greatness: The Power of Magnanimity* (New York: Scepter, 2011).
75. See J. Balmes, *El Criterio* (Madrid: Espasa-Calpe, 1845 [1981]), pp. 191–2. Llano, *Humildad y liderazgo*, Chap. 12–14, has rediscovered this author, adding interesting insights on humility in leadership.
76. This is the definition of 'magnanimity' from the Merriam-Webster Online Dictionary: http://www.merriam-webster.com/dictionary/magnanimity. (Accessed on 2 June 2025).
77. A. Havard, *Created for Greatness: The Power of Magnanimity* (New York: Scepter, 2011).
78. Havard, *Virtuous Leadership*, p. 3.
79. C. Llano, *Dilemas éticos de la empresa contemporánea* (México: Fondo de Cultura Económica, 1997), pp. 154–5.
80. See Harvard, *Virtuous Leadership*.
81. Sources: R. G. Ibanez, 'Bayanihan: The Many Great Lessons of United Laboratories, Inc.' (Pasig: Anvil Publishing, 2002); V. T. Villegas, 'The Cultural Basis of the Good Company, Corporate Social Responsibility from a Filipino Christian Perspective', http://www.stthomas.edu/cathstudies/cst/conferences/thegoodcompany/Finalpapers/Villegas%20Final%20paper.pdf; and DBPedia:

https://dbpedia.org/page/Jose_Yao_Campos; A. Silvestre, 'The Philippines' Successful Women and Their Wealth', *Board Talk*: https://www.iconexecutive.asia/board-talk/the-philippines-successful-women-and-their-wealth-12; United Laboratories website: http://www.unilab.com.ph/; and particularly, https://www.unilab.com.ph/our-purpose-our-values#subnavigation, and Wikipedia, United Laboratories. (All accessed 30 October 2024).

Part III

Organizational Business Ethics

7

Free Market Economy and the Business Company

Free enterprise cannot be justified as being good for business; it can be justified only as being good for society.[1]

PETER DRUCKER (1909–2005), Management thinker

Overview

This chapter marks the beginning of the third part of the book, which is dedicated to exploring the ethics related to business companies – their institutional activities, management and governance. It starts by examining the ethical dimensions of the free-market economy in which companies operate, along with the governmental regulations that frame both the market and the companies themselves.

Section A discusses the ethical aspects of the economic system where most companies operate. It argues in favour of the market's positive contributions to the common good but also warns about the risks of abuses if the market is taken as an absolute. The section emphasizes the importance of fair competition among businesses and examines the role of governmental regulations in framing economic activity.

Section B focuses on two crucial questions regarding managing and governing businesses: (1) What is the ontological nature of the business company? and (2) What is the purpose of business in society? Several answers to these questions are critically reviewed. It then presents an argument favouring the view of the business company as not only an organization but also a community of persons and a social institution with a specific purpose that is consistent with the common good. This generic purpose is contrasted with the specific purpose, chosen by each company, which entails a certain mission or missions to be carried out with different elements. These elements should be considered for an effective contribution to the common good and to make a positive impact in the world.

Chapter Aims

After reading this chapter you should be able to:

- Examine ethical aspects of the free market economy (capitalism).
- Consider conditions for an acceptable capitalism.
- Discuss the role of the government, including business laws and their limits.
- Reflect on the relevance of fair competition.
- Be aware of the conventional views of the business company and its historical antecedents.
- Understand the business company as a social institution and a community of persons.
- Posit the question of 'For whose benefit should a company be managed?'
- Deliberate on different proposals about the purpose of the business company.
- Reflect on the role of the common good in determining the purpose of business.
- Discuss the generic purpose of the business company.
- Reflect on the internal and external mission of the company.
- Consider the particular purpose of each company including purpose-driven companies.

Historical Case #7

Lehman Brothers and the subprime crisis[2]

At the beginning of the twenty-first century, the United States had low interest rates and big inflows of foreign funds. This created easy credit conditions. One of the causes of the huge housing boom was the proliferation of subprime mortgages, that is, loans issued to borrowers with low credit ratings. Thus, the borrower has a higher-than-average risk of defaulting on the loan. Accordingly, lending institutions charge interest on subprime mortgages at a higher rate than with a conventional mortgage.

Lehman Brothers, one of the largest investment banks with 25,000 employees worldwide, decided to move into the business of mortgage origination to take advantage of this situation. Being an investment bank, it was not subject to the same regulations applied to depository banks to restrict their risk-taking. Between 2000 and 2004, Lehman purchased six subprime mortgage lender companies. Although formally Lehman was an investment bank, in practice, the firm had morphed into a real estate hedge fund. Through these years and into 2006, US house prices increased sharply.

Lehman, like many other banks, conceded a great number of mortgages to people who, in all probability, would have difficulty maintaining the repayments – colloquially referred to as 'NINJA loans' (loans to people with 'no income, no job, no assets'). Most of these loans were adjustable-rate mortgages where easy initial terms were offered. This encouraged borrowers to take on high-rate mortgages in the belief that they would be able to quickly refinance at more favourable terms because of the trend of rising housing prices. This policy, oriented towards short-term profits, was supported through strong incentives to obtain new mortgage business. The popularity of this practice grew exponentially, possibly due to the belief that the bursting of the housing bubble was far off. However, US house sale prices peaked in mid-2006 and, after this, the bubble burst.

The economic performance of Lehman Brothers was brilliant for several years. Its real estate businesses enabled revenues in the capital markets unit to surge 56 per cent from 2004 to 2006, a faster rate of growth than any other business in investment banking or asset management. From 2005 to 2007, Lehman reported record profits every year. In 2007, the firm had a net income of a record US$4.2 billion on revenues of US$19.3 billion. However, Lehman had a highly leveraged structure – its assets of US$680 billion were supported by only US$22.5 billion of company capital. In 2007, Lehman Brothers underwrote more mortgage-backed securities than any other firm, accumulating an US$85 billion portfolio, or four times its shareholder equity.

In February 2007, the stock reached a record US$86.18, giving Lehman a market capitalization of close to US$60 billion. However, the risk-taking had increased dramatically. The company's leverage ratio – the ratio of total assets to shareholder equity – passed from approximately 24:1 in 2003 to 31:1 by 2007. While generating tremendous profits during the boom, this vulnerable position meant that just a 3–4 per cent decline in the value of its assets would entirely eliminate its book value equity.

By the first quarter of 2007, cracks in the US housing market were already becoming apparent as defaults on subprime mortgages rose to a seven-year high. In spite of this, Lehman reported record revenues and profit for its first fiscal quarter, and its CFO said that he did not foresee problems in the subprime market spreading to the rest of the housing market or hurting the US economy.

Lehman Brothers, as well as Bear Stearns – the second-largest underwriter of mortgage-backed securities – and other investment banks, started to buy and *repackage* home mortgage and home equity loans into mortgage-related securities that they sold to investors as complex and evolved financial products, which were quite opaque regarding their real risk, such as collateralized debt obligations (CDOs). Then, the same were marketed to investors, usually as a highly rated low-risk conservative investment. Such financial products attracted many pension funds and individual and institutional investors, mainly in the United States and Europe, because for many years (when house prices were appreciating) they had been offering handsome returns. Increasing traffic in issuing and selling these instruments intensified pressures on rating agencies, underwriters, trustees and credit enhancement providers to join the 'mortgage machine' without reflecting on fundamentals.

In August 2007 Bear Stearns announced the failure of two of its hedge funds that had invested in CDOs and the loss of value of its assets linked to subprime mortgages. Lehman's stock fell sharply. During that month, the company eliminated 2,500 mortgage-related jobs and a subprime mortgage business unit. It also closed several offices. In the fourth quarter of 2007 company stock rebounded as global equity markets reached new highs and prices for fixed-income assets staged a temporary recovery. This was an opportunity to trim its massive mortgage portfolio, but a different decision was taken.

In 2008 Bear Stearns came close to collapse, and JP Morgan Chase bought it at a ridiculously low price. Lehman shares fell as much as 48 per cent due to the concern that it would be the next Wall Street firm to fail. That was indeed what happened. After taking certain measures to gain liquidity and an unsuccessful search for a partner, on 15 September 2008 Lehman Brothers filed for bankruptcy, with US$639 billion in assets and US$619 billion in debt.

In addition, mortgage-backed securities, including subprime mortgages, were sold to financial firms worldwide with a similar lack of transparency, and most of the value was, again, lost. A severe crisis in the private financial system broke in the US and European economies. The United States entered a deep recession, and nearly 9 million jobs (roughly 6 per cent of the workforce) were lost during 2008 and 2009. The number of jobs did not return to the December 2007 pre-crisis peak until May 2014.

Questions

1. Reflect on the various factors – economic, institutional, and behavioural – that led to the subprime mortgage crisis. In your view, which of these raise the most serious ethical concerns, and why?
2. What pressures and incentives might influence decisions made by Lehman Brothers executives?
3. The subprime crisis brought about notorious damage to the common good. Should the Lehman executives have foreseen this harm?
4. Based on the strategic choices made by firms like Lehman Brothers and Bear Stearns, what underlying assumptions about the role of business in society can you identify?

SECTION A. BUSINESS IN THE FREE MARKET ECONOMY

Business companies are a part of society and operate within an economic, social and political framework. Business, in a vast majority of countries, operates within the free-market economy – also known as capitalism. The social and political framework of a country is significant. When a country lacks political stability or there are inefficiencies in public administration, corruption or insufficient juridical guarantees, the ground for business activity and economic development is not well prepared. Business needs sound public administration as well as respect for individual freedom and private property. It is within society that the market system enables a business to interchange products and services with others and to create wealth.

Regarding the free-market economy, some wonder under what conditions, if any, capitalism would be ethically acceptable. We will try to answer this question, but first we need to briefly review some positive and negative aspects of capitalism as well as the role of government in regulating the market system.

7.1 The ethical dimension of the market economy

The market economy is based on private property and on freedom of enterprise and contract, in which decisions are coordinated through free competition and agreements between buyers and sellers. Thus, three freedoms concur in the market economy: (1) freedom of the consumer to choose among competing products and services; (2) freedom of the producer to start or expand a business; and (3) freedom of the worker to choose a job and employer.

The price, determined by the relative abundances of supply and demand, gives 'market signals' of what to produce – in other words, the market either signals which products buyers are willing to pay a relatively high price for in comparison with the cost, or which products are no longer viable because their price fails to exceed their cost. In a free market, the 'price mechanism' provides most of the relevant information for making efficient marketplace decisions, whereas in a controlled market, it is the government that, directly or indirectly, regulates prices or supplies, distorting the 'market signals'.

Positive and negative aspects of the free market

A free market offers a business the opportunity to buy and sell goods and services and to make a profit. But the market also presents threats – a firm can lose clients to a competitor or even be eliminated from the marketplace altogether if its rivals offer more desirable products, services or working conditions.

From a social perspective, a free market provides incentives for economic dynamism:

- It *stimulates the production of saleable goods or services*, which prevents the squandering of resources on undesired products.
- It *fosters an efficient assignment of people and resources* in order to lower costs; consequently, prices tend to decrease and quality to increase.
- A free market *motivates innovation and a productive use of available resources*.

Apart from fostering economic dynamism, the market economy makes economic goods of ever greater quality accessible to more and more people. In addition, it respects people's freedom of exchange and choice through market transactions.

Economists have developed an idealized market structure called 'perfect market', also known as 'perfect competition', in which the price of goods is determined solely by the forces of supply and demand. This model is based on several key assumptions[3]: all actors in the market – buyers and sellers – try to maximize their utility (economic rationality), all firms sell identical or homogenous products, there is a large number of buyers and sellers, and there are no barriers to entry or exit for businesses. In this model there is *perfect competition*, which ensures that no one individual can affect the market; *complete information* is available to all participants, and there are *no externalities* (impacts on parties not directly involved in an economic decision). However, in real markets:

- *Competition is not perfect*: On the contrary, some actors, including business firms, have 'market power'; that is, the capability to adjust the market price of a good or service. Market power permits participants to appropriate more benefits for themselves while providing fewer benefits and transferring more costs to others. An extreme case of market power would be when there is only one seller (*monopoly*) or one buyer (*monopsony*) of a certain product or service, so that an individual or company has a disproportionate voice in the terms by which other individuals or business enterprises have access to the good or service (if there is a lack of viable substitute goods).
- *Information is asymmetrical*: Information is asymmetrically distributed between the buyer and seller, or producer and consumer, creating an imbalance of power in transactions.
- *There are externalities*: Externalities incur costs for a third party (for instance, pollution) and so escape the market pricing mechanism. These conditions, along with other 'market failures',[4] do not lead to social welfare enhancement.

These three elements can favour injustice through:

- *Abuses in monopolies or monopsonies.*
- *Misuse of asymmetrical information* (abuses of ignorance or good faith).
- *Damaging third parties* who suffer externalities (through pollution, for instance).

Additionally, the free market entails:

- *Risk of abuses*: A free market brings about competitive pressures to reduce costs. While this certainly has its positive side, such pressure can result in the exploitation of workers or the abuse of the good faith or ignorance of consumers through misleading information or fraud.
- *Lack of equity*: A free market, for all its efficiency in the assignment of resources, remains very ineffective in terms of equity. It does not simply reward work; its results are conditioned by the relationship of supply and demand.
- *Lack of moral concern regarding the product*: The market itself is blind to the content of the transaction – it sees no distinction between wheat and cocaine.
- *Not all legitimate demands are satisfied*: A free market responds only to the demands of those consumers with sufficient funds to purchase its products. The market cannot satisfy basic needs, such as nutrition and health, if people are too poor to buy products conducive to physical well-being or if they cannot afford medicines or even basic foods. In this case, the satisfaction of needs requires other means, such as solidarity or social policies that use different logics than the logic of exchange characteristic of the market.

7.2 Acceptable capitalism and the role of the government

'Moral legitimacy' differs from 'social legitimacy', although they are often confused under the same general label of 'legitimacy'. In accordance with the Common Good Principle, a social or economic system finds its moral legitimacy for its contribution to the common good (2.6) – while social legitimacy, often termed as 'social license to operate', comes from social approval. This latter legitimacy has been widely used in management theories, particularly neo-institutionalism.[5] Often, moral and social legitimacy coincide, but not always. This said, we can move on to the initial question of whether an ethically acceptable capitalism is possible. The short answer is it depends on what capitalism we are talking about. The system of economic organization called capitalism presents a wide variety of manifestations, although all of these are based on a free market.[6] Current examples of capitalism are the Anglo-Saxon model and European Continental capitalism. The former is less regulated and more market-oriented, while the latter is more concerned with the rights of all stakeholders and includes many social regulations and policies. Japanese capitalism, although this is now changing, used to include close coordination between the government and the major companies with well-established social networks, including banks and suppliers, and stable industrial relations.

Actually, every form of capitalism has an institutional and societal framework within which the market operates. Laws and social control can maintain a market under an appropriate level of control by society and the state in order to avoid abuses and to guarantee that the basic needs of the whole of society are satisfied. If such a framework respects and protects people and the natural environment, and prevents abuses, the resulting capitalism based on private property, free enterprise and social participation is ethically acceptable since it respects human dignity and contributes to the common good.

One of the best answers to the acceptability of capitalism is that given by Pope John Paul II. He affirmed that capitalism is acceptable 'if by "capitalism" is meant an economic system which recognizes the fundamental and positive role of business, the market, private property and the resulting responsibility for the means of production, as well as free human creativity in the economic sector'. However, he added that capitalism is not ethically acceptable 'if by "capitalism" is meant a system in which freedom in the economic sector is not circumscribed within a strong juridical framework which places it at the service of human freedom in its totality, and which sees it as a particular aspect of that freedom'.[7] A sound capitalism should consider all aspects of human freedom and involve a sense of moral responsibility. In particular, the institutional framework of the market economy should respect human rights. When this is not the case, there is some talk of 'savage capitalism', in which the accumulation of capital becomes a supreme criterion and people, in practice, are reduced to a state of quasi-servitude, while the natural environment is not respected.

Ultimately, as the market system finds its moral legitimacy in its contribution to the common good, if the negative aspects of the market derived from abuses are controlled, the market operating within fair competition will undoubtedly contribute to the common good. Free competition stimulates the production of saleable goods or services, fosters an efficient assignment of people and resources, and motivates innovation and a productive use of available resources.

7.3 Governmental regulations of economic activities

A pure free-market system, operating without interference from government or other non-market institutions, does not exist. Currently, practically all businesses operate within a free-market system that is constrained by governmental or supra-governmental regulations, which can be quite broad. Lack of equity may be partially addressed by appropriate governmental policies and by private actions of solidarity.

Direct state intervention in economic affairs can occur when a state-run business appears truly necessary on national security grounds consistent with the common good. However, there are also less justifiable reasons, such as those based on interventionist political ideologies. These interventions can often be problematic, introducing the inefficiency typical of government into business management and fostering an entrenched habit of passivity about economic initiatives. Besides, state interventions in economic affairs can discourage citizens and corporations from undertaking business projects with freedom and an entrepreneurial spirit. Thus, the state must not prevent the free exercise of economic activity. On the contrary, it ought to create conditions that foster initiative. This is required by the principle of subsidiarity (2.7).

The state provides a framework for the market through laws and by creating institutions of control; courts are in charge of applying the laws. A limited number of strategically crafted regulations can favour market and business activity and contribute to a good society – if they enjoy a sound ethical basis. Excessive regulation can stifle the benefits of the free market. While regulations aim to ensure fairness and accountability, too many can lead to inefficiencies and reduce market dynamism. Additionally, just as there are business failures, there are also government failures. These occur when government interventions result in a more inefficient allocation of resources than what the free market would have achieved on its own.

That said, the government can also take direct action to manage the economy, when necessary, especially in times of severe crises. During such moments, government intervention may help stabilize the economy and restore balance.

Fair competition and its regulation

Fair competition – which is based on price, quality and service, not on whatever abuse of market power a company might be able to get away with – is a key issue in a market economy and makes a positive contribution to the common good, as noted above.

Competition collapses when there are *monopolies* (a unique seller) or *monopsonies* (a unique buyer). However, monopolies are not necessarily detrimental to consumers. There are 'natural monopolies', in which a company becomes the sole supplier of a product or service because the nature of that product or service makes a single supplier more efficient than two or more in competition, for instance, urban water supply and sewer services. Some monopolies are legally sanctioned by the state, often to provide an incentive to invest in a risky venture or to enrich a domestic constituency.

Apart from a few cases of acceptable monopoly or monopsony, competition under fair conditions is preferable for bringing about the optimal conditions for trade. That is why most countries have laws that seek to prevent abuses derived from monopolies, monopolistic practices or situations that restrict competition (antitrust laws in the United States; competition law in the European Union). These laws cover three groups of business practices:

- *Agreements among business firms that restrict competition*: The most common case is an agreement known as a 'cartel'. In industries where cartels exist, usually those that are oligopolistic, companies agree to restrict free trade and competition through price fixing, agreements on market shares, the allocation of customers or of territory, the establishment of common sales agencies, the division of profits, and so on. One particular form of illegal agreement among firms is 'bid-rigging', which can occur when contracts (for example, government construction contracts) are awarded following a call for bids. In a bid-rigging exercise, one group of bidders will be designated to win the tender with the agreement that others will have their turn in future contracts.
- *Abusive business practices*: These can be related to cases of unfair pricing, such as price gouging, predatory pricing or dumping (11.5) and also to abusive manners or 'refusal to deal'. The latter refers to agreements to restrict the supply of goods with the intention of lessening competition in a certain market.
- *Threats to competition derived from mergers and acquisitions of large corporations*: Some mergers and acquisitions – and even some joint ventures – can restrict competition. For this reason, there are laws establishing that such operations must be carried out under the supervision of public authorities. In order to reduce threats to the competitive process, authorities veto mergers and acquisitions under certain circumstances, or they impose conditions to protect competition (for instance, divesting part of the merged business).

Limits of laws and other governmental regulations

The market and laws might seem sufficient to maintain the system and contribute to a good society. This is the vision, for example, of the economist Milton Friedman.[8] Certainly, as already noted, a free market provides an efficient mechanism for the assignment of resources in accordance with consumer desires and laws provide the necessary ground rules – such as respecting private property, honouring contracts, acting without deception or fraud and doing what is necessary to avoid or minimize market failures. However, laws have a number of limitations:

- *Laws generally come late*: Only in the aftermath of problems and scandals are new laws promulgated, with an eye to preventing similar scenarios. However, experience shows that novel ways of evading the law continually emerge.
- *Laws generally only provide minimal standards for living together with reasonable harmony*: Laws are insufficient to cover the whole field of human activity. They cannot regulate every action: this is not their purpose.

- *There is a risk of ineffectiveness in the application of business laws*: It is very difficult – probably impossible – to achieve a 'perfect law'. Laws have loopholes, and those who disregard ethics can exploit these so as to escape the spirit of any law. Moreover, some countries lack the means for the law enforcement that would allow its effective application; or, worse, corruption might prevent the consistent application of laws, rendering them ineffective.
- *Informal constraints are also relevant*: As Nobel Laureate Kenneth Arrow has argued, informal constraints such as trust and morality must be assumed to operate in advanced market economies, since formal constraints alone (legal rules and other external regulations) could not stem force or fraud.[9]

The 'soft regulation' of the civil society

In addition to laws and governmental regulations, civil society imposes on business what has been called[10] *soft regulation*, in contrast to the legal norms, which can be termed *hard regulation*. Abusive situations within a market stimulate social movements, and civil society pressures corporations and governments, which in turn promulgate new laws that condition the market.

Companies, and consequently managers, are obliged to fulfil the law and other governmental regulations. To some extent, they also take soft regulation into account in order to avoid risks (losing clients, perhaps being targeted by boycotts) and to achieve the reputation of being a responsible business. Hard and soft regulations have a mutual influence. Social demands go beyond law and regulations and these demands bring pressure to enact new laws. In addition to external regulation, the company may implement self-regulation through corporate principles of conduct, credos and codes (9.1). All these regulations frame managerial activity (Figure 7.1).

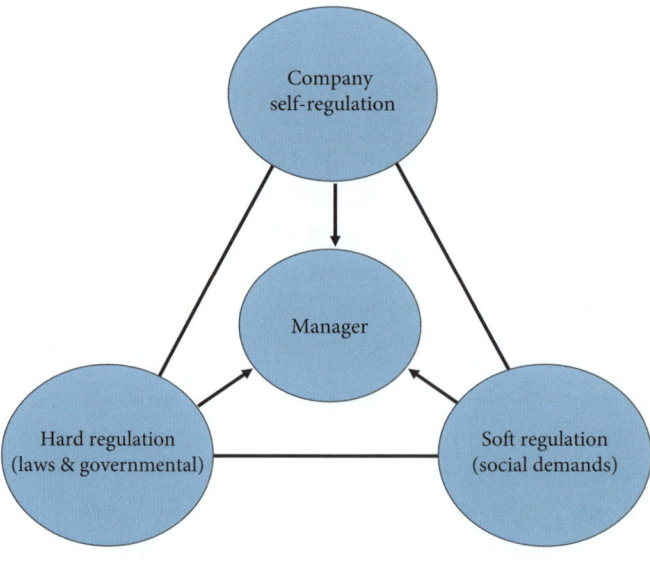

Figure 7.1 Regulatory frame of the firm's manager

This regulatory framing is not sufficient for a fully responsible management, since regulations only provide minimal standards. Organizational life is richer than regulations. Furthermore, all of these regulations generally involve ethical criteria (although this is not necessarily so), and a responsible manager cannot ignore ethical requirements that go beyond regulations.

Business Ethics in Action #7

AES Corporation: A values-driven company[11]

The AES Corporation, headquartered in Arlington, Virginia, USA, is one of the world's leading energy companies. It owns and operates power plants, generating and selling electricity in fifteen countries.

AES traces its origins to 1981 when Roger Sant and Dennis Bakke founded Applied Energy Services with $1 million in venture capital. Both had earned MBAs from Harvard Business School and had worked together at the US Federal Energy Administration. They later spent four years researching energy conservation and development at the Mellon Institute in Washington, DC. Their goal was to create an energy company that could meet social needs and treat people fairly, while also making a profit. AES grew rapidly and, in 1991, was listed on the New York Stock Exchange. Roger Sant was its first CEO. In 1994, Sant became chairman and Bakke became CEO.

Sant and Bakke emphasized being a values-driven company, setting up four core values: integrity, fairness, social responsibility and fun – where employees would enjoy their work and reach their potential. These values were highlighted during AES's initial public offering (IPO), mentioned in the risks section as follows:

> An important element of AES is its commitment to four major 'shared' values: to act with integrity, to be fair, to have fun and to be socially responsible ... AES believes that earning a fair profit is an important result of providing a quality product to its customers. However, if the Company perceives a conflict between these values and profits, the Company will try to adhere to its values – even though doing so might result in diminished profits or foregone opportunities.[12]

AES's original four corporate values have been consolidated into three:

- *Safety First*, prioritizing safety in everything.
- *Highest Standards,* meaning acting with utmost integrity towards people, contractors, customers, partners and communities, holding the solutions delivered to global standards of excellence.
- *All Together*, expressing willingness to work as one team and meet changing customer needs with agility, having fun solving meaningful challenges as a team.

AES had rapid growth, with new developments in the US and across Europe, Latin America and Asia. This expansion was compatible with its founding principles and values.

In its early years, AES's power plants were fuelled primarily by coal and oil, but environmental concerns began to take root in the late 1980s. In 1989, long before it became common, AES introduced the first documented carbon offset programme in the US, planting 52 million trees in Guatemala to offset emissions from a plant in Connecticut. However, it wasn't until the twenty-first century that AES significantly ramped up its sustainability efforts.

A new era for AES began in 2009, with utility-scale energy storage under the leadership of Phil Odeen, the third chairman of the board. In 2011, under CEO Andrés Gluski, AES accelerated its green energy transition by acquiring companies focused on solar energy. In 2015, AES acquired Mainstreet Power to add distributed solar resources to its portfolio, and in 2017 acquired sPower – the largest independent solar developer in the US – marking a significant step in its renewable energy strategy.

In 2018, AES launched Fluence Energy, the world's leading energy storage platform, in a joint venture with Siemens. Today, nearly half of AES's projects include battery storage components.

Transparency was key to these initiatives. In 2018, AES became the first publicly traded US energy company to issue a Climate Scenario Report that complied with recommendations from the Task Force on Climate-Related Financial Disclosures (TCFD). This voluntary initiative aims to improve the reporting of climate-related financial information.

By the 2020s, AES had solidified its position as a leader in renewable energy (including solar and wind power), adding about 5 gigawatts (GW) of renewable energy capacity annually, with plans for further expansion. In 2023, President and CEO Andrés Gluski said:

> Through 2027, we expect to nearly triple our renewables capacity by adding 25 to 30 GW of solar, wind and energy storage to our portfolio, while simultaneously delivering annual rate base growth of 10% at our US utilities. Our diversified portfolio will support and enable this growth as we advance our transformation by fully exiting coal by year-end 2025.[13]

Currently, AES is the world's leader in battery-based energy storage and ranks as the fifth-largest solar developer globally. The company has won prestigious industry awards, including recognition for the world's largest operational solar-plus-storage project.

* * *

The entrepreneurial initiative of Sant and Bakke in building a global values-driven company that leads its industry is commendable. Their desire to create wealth while upholding values of ethics and efficiency was consistent and transparent. They boldly highlighted these values in the prospectus for the company's public listing, even acknowledging that adherence to these values might, at times, reduce profits.

Values like safety, employee development and cooperation with local communities seem to have been well-implemented. The company emphasizes: 'Our leaders are leaders beyond their fields of expertise. They exemplify our values, empower our people to grow and innovate, and work beyond their daily roles to drive transformation in the energy industry.'[14]

> Some may argue that AES was slow to embrace ecological responsibility (13, A), especially given its role in energy production and reliance on fossil fuels. However, AES took steps that other companies did not, such as planting trees to offset carbon emissions. Additionally, AES has shown transparency in reporting its emissions, which laid the groundwork for reducing carbon-based pollution.
>
> The transition to new business models, especially abandoning fossil fuels, could have been done more quickly. Despite its successes and core values, AES faces typical challenges in the energy industry, such as balancing rapid renewable growth with existing fossil fuel operations.
>
> Nevertheless, whether driven by responsibility or responding to environmental criticism, AES has committed to reducing coal use and increasing its renewable energy portfolio. Today, the AES Corporation is a leading energy company, with a strong focus on clean energy and sustainability. Over the past few decades, AES has transformed its business model to align with global climate goals, emphasizing renewable energy development and carbon reduction strategies.
>
> Sustainability may not have been a primary focus in AES's early years, but the company is now firmly on the path to full sustainability. The willingness to evolve for the better is, indeed, business ethics in action.

SECTION B. NATURE AND PURPOSE OF THE BUSINESS COMPANY

The nature of business defines the core identity of a company, but 'nature' can be understood in two different ways. One is *descriptive*, and depends on each company, and explains what the company does, how it operates, its place in the market and so on. The second meaning is *ontological*, that is 'being a company' in a deep sense. Thus, the ontological nature of a business company, which we try to focus on here, refers to the fundamental essence or being of the company – what it is at its true core.

Close to the nature of the firm is its purpose, usually involving the production or distribution of goods or services. However, the purpose of a company is wider than this activity; it refers to the contribution of business to society and the corresponding responsibility. Within this generic purpose, which will be treated here, each company can create its particular purpose to make a positive difference in the world.

Discussing the ontological nature of the company and the purpose of the business company[15] is relevant for management and corporate governance. Understanding a company's nature helps develop a significant managerial mindset when considering the company. For instance, a company may be seen as a mere organization based on material and human resources, or as a community of persons with dignity and their own ends. The purpose of business provides the criterion by which to evaluate the activity of the business enterprise and determine whether it is succeeding in the aims determined by the purpose. Additionally, the purpose is important in that it furnishes criteria for evaluating whether a business entity is well designed and well managed.[16]

Business ethics is concerned with both the morality of the activities derived from the purpose of business and with the criteria to evaluate both business design and management from a moral point of view. Thus, understanding the nature and purpose of business is very relevant to business ethics.

In practice, there are a number of different views on the nature and purpose of the business company which would be worth reviewing, paying attention to their respective arguments to justify their respective proposals. Let us consider different views on these categories before presenting our own view.

7.4 The company, a social institution and a community of persons

The origin of the modern business company or corporation – also termed business enterprise or firm – was the chartered companies that were created to lead the colonial ventures of European nations in the seventeenth century. They operated under royal charter, or an act of parliament, with the grant of a monopoly over a specified territory. One of the first was the well-known East India Company of London, established in 1600.

Is the business company a 'fictitious person' or a 'collective person'?

In the nineteenth century, under the idea of individual freedom to undertake business, business companies were no longer created by concession, but by free initiative. They were able to operate with only a few legal requirements linked to a registration. Thus, the argument of individual initiative substituted the primitive view that business was a concession of monarchs, but the idea remained that businesses were created to do something for public good – such as building canals, bridges and railways – and 'to help realize a society's most cherished goals'.[17] Additionally, the view emerged of the business firm as an 'artificial being' or 'fictitious person', with rights and duties, shaped by individuals united by contracts.

With the emergence of large-scale enterprises and huge bureaucracies, a collectivistic view of the firm was fostered. Considering the compact and highly depersonalized structure of many companies, along with the influence of collectivistic ideology, the organization was increasingly seen as a single entity, and individuals were frequently regarded as almost completely subordinate to the organization. The whole was what mattered, and the individuals all but disappeared within it.

Under this view it was easy to argue that corporations not only had a personhood but also had to be dealt with as if they were a real entity or even a 'collective person'. This view was initially proposed in Germany, and then in the United States, more than 100 years ago. Today, there is evidence that some firms are still run in accordance with this vision, especially large bureaucracies.[18] When a firm is seen as a 'collective person', there is the risk that rules, procedures, policies and orders tend to eliminate any initiative on the employees' part and to constrain individual decision-making autonomy. Many talents, skills and capabilities of people within organizations can also go to waste.

A related view is to understand the corporation as analogous to a living organism with a body, with both a mind and a will. As with any organism, corporations have to adapt to their environment, and everything they do has to correspond to this purpose. If the firm is like an organism, people working within it are its 'organs', with little personal autonomy – instead, they are mere passive elements of the system.

Can the company be reduced to a set of contracts or a system of interests?

Neoclassic economics, rather than directly seeking social or moral legitimacy, tries to explain why firms exist through economic arguments, why they operate and produce as they do, how they are structured and why not all transactions in the economy are mediated through the market. In this way, at least implicitly, they are dealing with the purpose of the firm.

The economist Ronald Coase, through transaction cost theory, argued that firms emerged when the transaction cost of coordinating production through market exchange is greater than that of doing so within the firm.[19] This is an economic explanation, but does not express the full reality of the business company.

A further economic view of the business company is provided by Neoclassical economics, which considers the firm (the business company) as only an aggregate of individuals as its starting point but adds that they are united by a set of contracts. It adopts the *homo economicus* model, in which individuals have interests and preferences and act exclusively for self-interest, seeking only to maximize their utility. This view also holds that individuals are united exclusively for reasons of power and advantage and that the corporation is an artificial and fictitious entity. The 'collective' is merely the sum of individual interactions.

The hypothesis of the firm as a set of contracts helps us to understand some empirical facts. However, the view is reductionist, since it overlooks the possibility that individuals might establish links beyond the 'logic of interchange'. In addition, one can observe that, apart from contracts, other relationships also exist within the firm, and real human behaviour does not always correspond to the *homo economicus* model.

An alternative view presents the firm as a *system of interests*. From this perspective, the company is also an abstract and fictitious entity,[20] but with a set of groups, termed stakeholders, with interests (stakes) in the firm's activity. These groups generally include shareholders, employees, customers, suppliers, the local community and others, whose respective interests shape the firm. Thus, the corporation is essentially seen as a centre of coordination of stakeholder interests, or as 'a clearinghouse or nexus of activity where stakeholders satisfy their desires'.[21] One way to understand how the corporation works to coordinate interests is by considering that organizations have 'social contracts' with stakeholders. Drawing from political theory,[22] the concept of *social contracts* is introduced to explain how organizations maintain legitimacy and mutual benefit in their relationships with stakeholders.

Understanding the firm as simply a social mechanism or a social contract network seems to be a narrow view. It presents an individualistic approach, which leads to viewing human relationships exclusively based on mutual interests.

The business company as a community of persons

Observing business companies, one may realize that they are shaped by people and the relationships and networks among them, resulting in unity. One might also encounter real commitment and willingness to cooperate in common purposes, although people may also have individual motives for working together. These facts contradict seeing the firm as an artificial entity or mere human construct, or maybe a compact entity in which the individual fades to unimportance. Instead, it seems more realistic to affirm that the business company is a community of persons; that is, free and autonomous individuals who voluntarily cooperate undertaking a corporate activity, working together or investing funds to attain both individual and common goals.[23]

A community is generally understood as an enduring unity of persons involved in a common action for a shared purpose, although personal motivations can vary.[24] This is the case of the company, which includes a set of people united by various relationships, involved in a common action with the shared purpose of producing goods and services. Links that unite people within and around the firm can be very complex. First, there are those that are contractual, or relationships based on mutual interests. Other links can also be very relevant, however. There are emotional links (a shared sense of belonging, affection for one's work in the corporation) and moral links (commitment, moral loyalty, willingness to work for the common good of the firm and so on). As Solomon pointed out, people who join a corporation find themselves, once hired, members of a social collective. In addition, frequently 'there is a conscientious effort to become a member, to internalize the appropriate shared attitude'.[25]

The relevance of working in cooperation was already pointed out by Chester Barnard,[26] a pioneer and influential author on management. Now cooperation to achieve common goals is generally viewed as an essential characteristic of organizations.

People within a corporation carry out different activities within said cooperation, and the overall result cannot be attributed to anyone in particular but, rather, to the corporation as a whole or to a group within the organization. Common language also attributes actions or activities to corporations as a whole. Firms have a culture, a history and an accumulative learning; this remains even when individuals, who can join and leave the firm, have gone. In addition, companies interact, as a whole, with other social groups or institutions. Finally, from a philosophical perspective, we can argue that the whole, created by a principle of unity, is more than the sum of its parts.

The view of the firm as a community of persons is compatible with holding that a firm includes a set of contracts and a constellation of interests, both convergent and conflicting. However, it adds that persons are social beings, individuals not only with interests but also with the ability to cooperate and contribute with a sense of service, to act with reciprocity and sometimes also gratitude.

Managers, supervisors and other workers, who are working together with a sense of cooperation, are members of the company-community, as well as committed shareholders and investors and, in the family business, also the owner family. It is doubtful that occasional shareholders in listed companies, for example, can be considered part of the company-community, but in a broader sense they are also involved in the company.

The business company as social institution

Viewing a company as a human community – more specifically, a 'community of persons' – highlights that its members are individuals with intrinsic dignity, capable of personal development. Companies also function as intermediate communities within the broader society.

From another perspective, companies are social institutions essential for the functioning of society. Social institutions are characterized by structured systems of social order that govern behaviour with norms and values, contributing in various ways to meet societal needs. These institutions tend to persist over time, providing continuity and stability within a society.

These characteristics are also found in companies, as they possess structured systems, including organizational hierarchies, roles and processes that govern and exercise control over the behaviour of their members. Companies tend to persist over time, playing a critical role in the economy by providing goods and services, creating jobs and generating wealth. Furthermore, companies often engage in corporate social responsibility and sustainability initiatives. They influence culture and societal trends through advertising, branding and shaping consumer behaviour, corporate culture and so on.

7.5 Views of the purpose of the business company

The purpose of a company can be defined as the superior or overarching aim that drives the entire organization, including its strategy, management and corporate governance. In this broader view, purpose is not just about what a company does, but also why it exists – what it seeks to contribute to society, beyond financial metrics. Currently there are several influential views of the purpose of the business company, which are usually closely related to the understanding of the business company. Let us review some of them.

Maximizing shareholder value

Maximizing shareholder value is an extended view of the purpose of the business company or firm. This category refers to the market's assessment of a firm's economic value, which includes expectations about future profits. Maximizing shareholder value as the purpose of the firm is defended by, among others, Michael Jensen,[27] one of the main proponents of the 'Agency Theory.'[28] This theory considers the business firm exclusively as being based on property rights and sees managers as agents and shareholders. This proposal has antecedents in Milton Friedman[29] and others.[30] Friedman – already introduced (7.3) – talked of increasing profits as much as possible as being the goal of the business manager, with no other limits than compliance with the law and the rules of the game, 'which is to say, engages in open and free competition without deception or fraud.'[31]

Taking for granted a free-enterprise system in a free society along with private property rights, considering them almost as absolute, defenders of this position emphasize the fiduciary duties of managers towards shareholders as being their main ethical duty. They also argue that the purpose of profit maximization makes it easy to control management performance, and the law supports managing business in benefit of the shareholders.

Defenders of maximization of shareholder value align with Adam Smith's 'invisible hand' metaphor.[32] When, in a free market, individuals pursue their own self-interest, the results tend to promote the well-being of their community as a whole. Under this perspective it is desirable that each firm seeks to maximize its own revenue since, in doing this, it contributes towards maximizing the total revenue of society as a whole.[33] Friedman defended maximizing profits in a fair competition and in compliance with laws, emphasizing some social goals associated with making profits.[34] Jensen argues that maximizing shareholder value fits well not only with foundations that have enabled markets and capitalism to generate wealth, but also with high standards of living, while generating jobs.[35] He adds that this includes an appropriate treatment of constituencies of the firm. He affirms that 'we cannot maximize the long-term market value of an organization if we ignore or mistreat any important constituency. We cannot create value without good relations with customers, employees, financial backers, suppliers, regulators, communities and so on.'[36]

Some criticisms can be made of maximizing shareholder value as the purpose of the firm, although recognizing the argument of wealth creation through free competition, the defence of freedom and the social contribution associated with wealth creation is important. Creating wealth, providing employment, eliminating discrimination and avoiding pollution are all undoubtedly good for society, but, according to this approach, companies should act on these social issues only if they are required by law or if it can be proved that doing so will contribute to the bottom line.

Furthermore, wealth creation, even accompanied by redistribution through taxes and social policies, cannot be the supreme argument to justify the said purpose of business within society, since wealth is only one aspect of a good social order. In addition, wealth can be created at the price of maintaining subhuman conditions in the workplace, or without respect for human rights, by overexploitation of natural resources and lack of concern about waste or pollution, or by selling products that are dangerous, harmful or have a negative impact on human flourishing.

Against the 'legal argument' it can be said that not all countries have laws defining the purpose of the firm as the maximization of profits or the maximization of value creation for shareholders. In fact, many countries, including Japan and countries from continental Europe, do not. In others, more and more regulations on employees, customers and the environment are being introduced to prevent abuse deriving from the aim of maximizing shareholder value. In addition, an increasing number of corporations are inclining towards sustainable management, which pays attention not only to economic, but also to social and natural environmental issues, along with good governance (see ESG criteria in 13.7).

Underlying this purpose of the firm is a view of the individual as a rational self-interest maximizer, which is clearly an incomplete view of the human being, one that can be criticized from the perspective of philosophical anthropology[37] and even for leading to bad management theories.[38] It is a view of the society based on individual interests, which is also questionable because it ignores human sociability and the capacity of people to cooperate to build a good society. As Canals points out,[39] the shareholder maximization hypothesis not only is inconsistent with a broader view of human nature but also may have negative effects on firms' leadership and governance, making the role of senior executives in society unattractive, and may erode corporate reputation.

In the shareholder approach, business firms are seen as autonomous entities with no other concern than wealth creation, while the government has the function of avoiding abuse on the part of business through laws and other regulations and of providing social policies to care for those in need. This is an individualistic view of society, which contrasts with others based on human sociability and shaped by communities. In this latter view, business is considered a community of persons and a social institution contributing to the common good in different ways, as we will discuss below.

In addition, it is important to mention – and this is not a minor problem – the risk of *short-termism*, which can jeopardize the company in the long term. A short-term view is encouraged by incentives such as bonuses and stock options, which are intended to align managers with shareholder value maximization.

Creating value for stakeholders

This is an alternative view of the purpose of the business firm, focused on people who have a stake in the firm. Freeman,[40] one of the main proponents of 'managing for stakeholders', states that 'the corporation ought to be managed for the benefit of its stakeholders: its customers, suppliers, owners, employees and local communities'.[41] It is argued that management must balance all stakeholder interests[42] and 'act in the interest of the corporation to ensure the survival of the firm, safeguarding the long-term stakes of each group'.[43] In a more recent version, Freeman argues that 'the primary responsibility of the executive is to create as much value for stakeholders as possible', adding that 'that no stakeholder interest is viable in isolation of other stakeholders'.[44]

Freeman and others defend the position that the firm's long-term wealth creation is better served by considering the interests of stakeholders. In Freeman's words, 'to maximize shareholder value over an uncertain time frame, managers ought to pay attention to key stakeholder relationships'.[45] This entails assuming that, under certain conditions, the satisfaction of the interests of stakeholders contributes to long-term value maximization. When this occurs, Jensen will have no problem in accepting the satisfaction of the stakeholders' interests. He interprets this as 'enlightened value maximization'.[46] Thus, there is a certain convergence between shareholder and stakeholder approaches in the long term. On his part, Freeman basically agrees with Jensen on this point, primarily focusing on the stakeholders and seeing the long-term positive impact for shareholder value as a consequence of satisfying stakeholder interests.[47]

The idea of serving different groups of people related to the company, not only the shareholders, has gained acceptance, especially since 2019 when the *Business Roundtable*, one of the preeminent business lobbies in the United States which includes the CEOs of leading US companies, recommended paying attention to all these groups. In an open letter entitled 'Statement on the Purpose of a Corporation' they say, 'Each of our stakeholders is essential. We commit to deliver value to all of them, for the future success of our companies, our communities and our country.'[48]

Regarding moral legitimacy for managing for stakeholders, one point refers to property rights, which are not seen as being almost absolute, like the shareholder approach. Donaldson and Preston[49] argue in favour of the stakeholder approach and hold that property rights should be based on an underlying principle of distributive justice. Apart from that, managing for the stakeholder requires determining and justifying what value creation is for each stakeholder and how to solve conflict of interests between stakeholders. According to Freeman,[50] any ethical theory can be applied to solve such a conflict. He adopts a pragmatic perspective arguing that the stakeholder theory makes a positive contribution to society.[51]

Indeed, creating value for stakeholders can contribute to better living in material terms, but the contribution of managing for stakeholders to other aspects of a good society, such as fostering human flourishing beyond stakeholder interests, is not clear.

The anthropological view in the stakeholder approach is not explicit, but it is certainly wider than the views which reduce the human person to a rational, self-interested, maximizer individual. Rather, it is of an autonomous moral agent who can apply different ethical theories, but with no concern for the right one. The business–society relationship is understood through the relations between the business firm and stakeholders, and in terms of creating value. As some stakeholder theorists affirm, 'we need to see value creation and trade, first and foremost, as creating value for stakeholders'.[52]

In spite of some improvements in understanding the purpose of the firm, the stakeholder approach still faces a number of problems, as already mentioned: its view of the individual and society, its ambiguity in defining legitimate interests and resolving conflicts of interest, and its acceptance of ethical pragmatism, are problematic (2.4). In addition, some critics argue that the outcomes of the stakeholder approach are difficult to control, and managers may use their discretion too broadly – even justifying personal preferences under the pretext of serving stakeholder interests. This contrasts with the ease of controlling outcomes under the shareholder approach, which is limited to financial results. The usual response is that being more difficult does not mean impossible.

Creating shared value

An alternative to maximizing shareholder value, but with some concern for creating value for stakeholders, is the creating shared value (CSV) approach. This was popularized in the 2010s. This proposal suggests that companies should seek not only their own profits, but also those of their customers and other stakeholders; a 'win–win' strategy. According to Porter and Kramer, who introduced the concept, 'shared value is not social responsibility, philanthropy, or sustainability, but a new way for companies to achieve economic success'.[53] It is a rather different view than the shareholder approach, which concludes that the purpose of the firm is simply to maximize shareholder value. In this sense, Porter and Kramer affirm: 'The purpose of the firm must be redefined as creating shared value, not just profits per se.'[54] They add that this view's approach 'will drive the next wave of innovation and productivity growth in a global economy'. In addition, the shared value approach leads us to understanding capitalism with a broader sense than its conventional meaning. Capitalism includes potential for meeting human needs, improving efficiency, creating jobs and building wealth, but its conventional narrow view prevents its potential being harnessed to meet society's wider challenges. 'Share value' capitalism, however, includes these.

The shared value approach respects the fiduciary duties of the manager towards shareholders and aligns with property rights and legal standards in many countries. It also contributes to wealth creation and well-being, at least for those who share in the value created. Management performance can then be measured by results, as in the shareholder approach.

In a certain sense, in 'shared value' the focus remains on the best return for shareholders, although it does not mention 'maximizing shareholder value' and adds the aim of creating value for customers.

The CSV approach has received both praise and criticism.[55] Among the latter, it has been suggested that although it may work to address 'win–win' business and society issues, destitute of any ethical foundation, it does not provide a sound framework for legitimately managing issues where there exists the prospect of 'win–lose' or 'lose–win' outcomes to social engagements.[56]

Establishing a double or multiple purpose

There are proposals that understand companies oriented not only to making money, but also to have a social purpose. Some relatively popular proposals are the following:

Conscious capitalism

Serving all stakeholders ethically while the company purses profits is one of the key ideas of *conscious capitalism* (*CC*), a business movement introduced by John Mackey and Raj Sisodia.[57] Enterprises inspired by CC accept that the purpose of business is more than simply to generate profits and focus on creating and optimizing value for all their stakeholders, including a healthy return to shareholders. It claims that this should be accompanied by a consistent 'conscious leadership' and 'conscious culture and management', in such a way that the higher purpose, and the stakeholders concerned, be present in decision-making and operations. Some companies often mentioned in this movement are Whole Foods Market – today a subsidiary of Amazon[58] – co-founded by John Mackey, focusing on healthy food, ethical sourcing and a strong culture of employee empowerment, and Southwest Airlines, known for its employee-centric policies, customer service and community engagement.

Conscious capitalism represents a shift in the consideration of the purpose of the firm, focusing on a plausible social goal but also considering other aspects related to this goal, including stakeholder well-being, leadership, management and culture, as well as the relevance of achieving long-term success rather than short-term profits. It seems that enterprises of CC, setting aside the social positive impact and long-term sustainable growth, tend to favour more satisfied, engaged and loyal employees, to attract talents aligned with the purpose and to build customer loyalty.

Some critical voices,[59] while praising the good intention of CC, point out some concerns about how to effectively implement and measure its principles, the difficulty in making social impact compatible with profitability and competitive advantages, and the complexity of balancing all of the stakeholders' interests. Of course, as with any other good corporate practice, there is the risk of using CC only for marketing purposes, and without genuine commitment to CC principles.

Operating as B-Corporations

A double purpose model also underlies the *B-Corporation* movement or, more popularly, the *B-Corp*.[60] The origin is in *B Lab,* a non-profit organization founded in 2006 which provides certification to for-profit companies, assuming that they meet certain standards of transparency, accountability, sustainability and performance, with an aim to create value for society, not just for traditional stakeholders such as the shareholders. The certification process evaluates a company's impact on its workers, customers, community and the environment, and should be renewed every three years. Starting in the United States, this is now a global movement which has extended into many countries; thus, B Corps become part of a global community of like-minded businesses, allowing them to collaborate, share best practices and support each other in achieving their missions.

The certification shows a commitment to balancing social and environmental goals with financial performance. Becoming a B-Corp can enhance reputation, attract talent and responsible investors and can also favour long-term sustainability.

Companies based on economy of communion

Inspired by the religious 'Focolare Movement',[61] *economy of communion* (EoC) is an entire way of understanding and practising business.[62] It promotes an economic culture rooted in *communion*, *gratuity* and *reciprocity*. EoC enterprises pursue a threefold purpose:

1. *Business development*: Fostering the growth of the enterprise through the creation of jobs and wealth, and orienting both internal and external business operations toward the common good.
2. *Support for individuals and communities in need*: Engaging in shared projects grounded in reciprocity, subsidiarity and communion, to promote personal and collective development.

3   *Dissemination of a culture of giving and reciprocity*: Nurturing the foundational values necessary for integral human development, and for building an economy and society marked by fraternity and solidarity.

Other approaches

Several authors insist that companies should accept a double purpose, or even more. Some approaches focus on creating both profit for investors and value for society,[63] while others, such as Canals,[64] suggest different interconnected ends, such as the customer needs, and, connected to that, talent development and innovation. Mayer argues that the notion of corporate purpose 'is meant to encourage a plurality of purposes – one achieved through innovation or experimentation that helps companies find new ways to profit while, or even by, limiting negative externalities'.[65]

Other scholars, with different terminology, talk about a double perspective on the purpose of the company, one internal and the other external. MacIntyre[66] makes the distinction between *practice* (cooperative activity focused on internal goods) and *institution* (concerned with external goals). Argandoña,[67] following Pérez López,[68] identifies two missions of the company, one internal and one external. The internal mission defines the real needs that the company tries to satisfy in its internal stakeholders, as they contribute to the production of goods and services that are the object of the external mission. Almandoz[69] suggests inside-out and outside-in perspectives on purpose as distinct but connected phenomena, related to different research traditions. He believes that inside-out purpose is a channelling of the passion and commitment employees feel towards fulfilling stakeholder needs, while outside-in purpose is society and external stakeholders urgently calling on the organization to live up to its responsibilities.

Framing the purpose toward collective value or the common good

Some other approaches focus on the society as the purpose of business. Among them are the following:

Optimizing collective value

Donaldson and Walsh[70] have proposed a *Theory of Business*, which, through an empirical-normative perspective, presents the purpose of business as the *optimization of collective value,* an alternative to the maximization of shareholder value.

The economy for the common good

A different proposal based on applying common values to economic activity is that of the movement termed the *economy for the common good* (ECG), presented by Felber and others.[71] They propose dealing with stakeholders by applying the universal values of human dignity, solidarity, social justice, sustainability, co-determination and transparency, which they understand as being favourable to the public good. In accordance with this approach, business success is measured according to the above-mentioned ethical values. Thus, 'a business is successful and reaps the benefits of its success not when it makes more and more profits, but when it does its best to serve the public good'.[72] ECG is a practical proposal with scarce theoretical foundation. Another objection is that the common good used by this social movement is a construct rather than an extension on the classical notion of the common good rooted in the Aristotelian–Thomistic tradition and grounded in human flourishing.

The civil economy approach

Closer to the traditional view of the common good is the *civil economy*, an approach developed by Luigino Bruni and Stefano Zamagni,[73] mainly since the turn of this century, which focused on the whole economic system, and not only business. Drawing on the eighteenth-century Neapolitan tradition of civil economy, this approach is applicable to economy and business. It emphasizes reciprocity, responsibility and redistribution, principles that have defined the marketplace for centuries. Bruni and Zamagni argue for the necessity of recovering these principles, along with a wide view of relationships in the economic field, particularly those that involve the generation and strengthening of relational goods, intangible resources that allow optimal economic, social and human development. Civil economy seeks to promote central well-being, virtue and the common good. Other, more familiar economic goals, like market share, increased productivity and competitiveness are also placed in the civil economy.

The common good as the purpose of business

Some authors[74] propose the common good as the purpose of business, with different degrees of specification. They generally argue that any social entity, including companies, acquires moral legitimacy from its contribution to the common good through what is specific to the entity. This also applies to the business firm, which finds its moral legitimacy in its contribution to the common good through what is specific to the business firm. This seems a sound criterion to define the legitimate purpose of the firm, to which we will return (7.6). But, before this, let us present how social enterprises understand their purpose.

The purpose of social enterprises

A different perspective from the previous is the purpose of the so-called *social enterprises*, focused on achieving social goals rather than profitability, although the latter is welcome, along with public and private donations. A good example of 'social enterprise' is the *Grameen Bank* or bank of the poor, founded by Muhammad Yunus, who later became a Nobel Peace Prize laureate. The mission of this bank – imitated in various countries – was to provide *microcredits,* which would help develop rural areas in Bangladesh through a local credit delivery system.

Some social enterprises have the major objective of helping low qualified unemployed people, who are at risk of permanent exclusion from the labour market, back into work and society through a productive activity. They are termed 'work integration social enterprises.' One example of these enterprises in *La Fageda*, presented in Case Study #9.

A related model is the *hybrid enterprise*, whose purpose entails achieving both a social impact and profit generation. The model includes companies that give priority to the social goal and others that consider both equally.

7.6 The common good as reference for the purpose of business

An elemental starting point for inquiry into the purpose of business in society is simply to consider the close relationship between business and society. Business is born within a society and it functions there; its activity is addressed towards society and the several groups of people who receive the immediate consequences of the decisions of business. From an institutional perspective, business is involved in the structure, organization and functions of society, in its social and cultural context, and maintains a rich network of societal and institutional relationships.

As we highlighted at the beginning of this chapter by quoting Peter Drucker, enterprise 'can be justified only as being good for society'. Actually, in some way, most views of the mentioned purpose of the firm seek justification in 'being good for society'. However, as we have discussed, some approaches involve incomplete views of what is truly good for society.

Within society at large there are intermediate communities, which are also social institutions, among which are business companies (7.4). According to Aristotle, every community is established for the sake of some good,[75] and business is not an exception. Intermediate communities contribute to the common good of the society through their respective common good.

The common good, as a crucial reference point for the purpose of the business company, is rooted in the principle of the common good (2.7), which states that every social or economic system, institution, community or social activity finds its moral legitimacy through its contribution to the common good. This includes the moral legitimacy of a company's purpose.

The question that arises is: what is the common good of the business company? Is it exclusively making money? No doubt this is a necessary condition for company survival, but is that the only purpose for business legitimacy? It is arguable that the purpose of the firm within society that justifies its existence must be more complex than simply financial return,[76] though profitability is a valuable insight for shareholders, entrepreneurs, investors and other groups related to a company.

Seeing the company exclusively as a tenure of property and freedom of undertaking can obscure or bias the response to the company's purpose. Certainly, freedom and private property facilitate production, and both elements are consistent with the common good if we accept that this property has intrinsic limitations,[77] and that other elements are also relevant to the nature of the company.

Property-based rights may conflict with welfare rights and so basic unmet needs challenge the legitimacy and justification of property rights.[78]

In other words, there are good reasons to support private property rights, but these should also consider a certain social function associated with these rights.[79] Stockholders provide capital, but the company is not only a society of capital. It is also a community of people (7.1) who contribute to it with their operative or managerial work.

In a corporation, stockholders hold shares and risk funds, and workers contribute with their personal labour to the goals of the corporation and bear the risk of being fired. Financial capital is important, but nowadays knowledge is quite crucial. In some companies, 'human capital' is more important than financial capital. As the celebrated management writer Charles Handy noted: 'the idea of a corporation as the property of the current holders of its shares is confusing because it does not make clear where power is'.[80] He adds: 'it is an affront to natural justice in that it gives inadequate recognition to the people who work in the corporation and who are, increasingly, its principal assets. It might even be considered immoral for people to talk of owning other people, as shareholders implicitly do.'[81]

Agency theory (7.5) is based on a view of the firm as essentially a form of property, with managers contracted to bear fiduciary duties exclusively to stockholders. However, this model has been questioned. According to Koslowski, 'fiduciary duty entails something more than agency, something more than merely acting in the interest of one's principal. It is a duty to act for the good of the whole institution, the entity for which one has been authorized to act by the principals.'[82] In other words, the primary fiduciary duty of those who manage the corporation is to the corporation itself. This requires a sense of stewardship in managing the firm, which leads to a careful and responsible administration of assets entrusted to one's care, as well as the development of strategies in the best interest of the company.

The contribution of the firm to the common good includes making fair profits. Wealth creation, of course, is crucial for business and, when carried out with justice, is an integral part of the common good of the firm and society. In the long term, the common good orientation will probably contribute to excellent results in terms of wealth creation, as proponents of the stakeholder approach contend. Profits, while certainly important, are not ends in themselves. They are instrumental; their function is in maintaining and improving the firm in the long term in such a way that the company can achieve its aims and contribute to the development of people and to societal well-being. Profits, wrote Handy, 'are the lifeblood of any business, but life consists of more than keeping the blood flowing; otherwise, it would not be worth living. As more corporations realize this truth, they will become increasingly interested in enriching the lives of the people who work in them.'[83]

Going back to the purpose of the firm, we must wonder what is specific to the business enterprise as a social institution with regulated structures and practices, and a member of the larger community.[84] A second question is whether or not it acquires moral legitimacy for its specific contribution to the common good.

7.7 The purpose of the company: Serving people through a dual mission

The argument developed here as how to define the legitimate purpose of a business company, begins with the observation of reality, considering that every business entity pursues a set of objectives inherent to its operations, which can be referred to as 'intrinsic multi-ends'.

Intrinsic multi-ends of the business company

In observing businesses, we can identify six intrinsic ends present in the activities of every company, including non-profit, social and hybrid enterprises, though their specific content may vary:

1 *Providing products (goods and services)*
A company's primary end is to produce and/or distribute goods or services. This foundational activity is critical, as the company's existence is contingent upon its product offerings. It should also be considered that this process often involves natural environmental impacts.

2 *Organizing work*
This involves structuring both productive and commercial activities, including task allocation, job design, working conditions and operational procedures. It also encompasses the use of various resources, such as raw materials, technology and financial capital.

3 *Establishing internal relationships*
Organizing work entails establishing relationships between different groups of people who are part of the company community. These relationships involve strong bonds based on working together. The influence of human relations within the company on performance is well-known. These groups, which can be termed 'internal relationholders', include directors, managers, supervisors and operational workers, who contribute with their work, along with shareholders, who contribute capital – especially those with a stable and durable link to the company. (Note that we use the word 'relationholder' rather than the usual term 'stakeholder', because they are bound by ties of interdependence and trust, rather than merely by material interests.) A basic element of these relationships is economic remuneration in the form of wages, incentives, etc., but it is not the only one. Appropriate motivation, working conditions and quality of human treatment, among other elements, are also important in such relationships and in generating trust and a willingness to cooperate. Establishing sound internal relationships influences working conditions and performance, as demonstrated by a vast body of literature on organizational behaviour.

4 *Establishing external relationships*
Companies must also interact with external parties, establishing relationships with, among others, occasional investors, suppliers of raw materials, lenders, potential customers,

communities and government agencies. These parties are referred to as 'external relationholders' (again, not 'stakeholders').

5 *Creating and distributing value*
Companies create economic value through the provision of products but also generate social value (reputation and client loyalty, fostering community welfare, creating jobs, etc.) and environmental value (both positive and negative impacts). The distribution of value involves not only economic compensation to employees, shareholders and suppliers but also broader contributions to social and environmental well-being.

6 *Maintaining the institution over time*
As social institutions, companies develop structured systems, norms and values that govern behaviour and contribute to societal needs. This institutional culture supports the personal and professional growth of those involved and emphasizes sustainability and resilience. Companies strive to maintain themselves as institutions over time, often through appropriate adaptations to the environments in which they operate. This generally involves ensuring continuity in their activities, seeking competitiveness in the market, balancing short- and long-term profits, encouraging innovation, and promoting sustainability in social and environmental matters.

These six intrinsic ends of any company can be grouped into a dual mission: one 'internal' and the other 'external'. The internal mission focuses on the company's responsibilities and commitments to the people who make up the company community (employees, management, shareholders), the internal organization, and the institutional aspects, including striving for continuity. The external mission focuses on the company's role and impact on broader society and the market. The other three intrinsic ends can be ascribed to the external mission: providing products, creating and distributing value, and establishing external relationships.

The common good-based intrinsic multi-ends in a dual mission

The above-mentioned intrinsic multi-ends can be found in every company – even in unethical ones, such as those involved in fraudulent activities. Although each company usually emphasizes some ends over others, these multi-ends are not isolated but are interrelated goals that together form the purpose of the business company. In other words, these intrinsic multi-ends are constituents of the generic purpose of business companies.

The question that arises is, in what way can these multi-intrinsic ends, grouped in a dual mission, contribute to provide moral legitimacy to a company? In this regard, we can recall that the common good is the crucial reference for the purpose of the company (7.6), in accordance with the *principle of the common good* (2.7). Therefore, the dual mission, with its multiple ends, constitutes the firm's purpose which should be aligned with the common good.

Two criteria can be identified that define how these multiple ends contribute to the common good:

1. *Achieving these ends ethically*: Ensuring that the company's goals are pursued in a manner that adheres to ethical standards.
2. *Achieving these ends efficiently*: While efficiency might initially seem like an exclusive technical goal, it also has an ethical dimension if it respects people and optimizes resource use to satisfy human needs and improve social well-being – both of which are integral parts of the common good.

From this perspective, and with these dual criteria of ethical achievement and efficiency, the aforementioned multi-ends can be reformulated from the standpoint of the common good. In this way, *the purpose of any company could be defined as a common good-based dual mission*: one external mission, which pertains to the company's impact on society and its contribution to meeting external needs; and one internal mission, which focuses on the well-being of employees and the internal functioning of the company. Each mission encompasses a set of ends aligned with the common good.

In this context, we can revisit the company's dual mission, which shapes its generic purpose with its respective intrinsic multi-ends oriented toward the common good (see Table 7.1).

External mission

1. *Providing truly good products in ethical conditions*
   Companies contribute to the common good by supplying genuinely useful products or services, avoiding unsafe or harmful offerings. Ethical conditions involve honest dealings, avoiding misleading customers, fraud, and providing genuine service. Sustainable consumption of raw materials, water and energy is emphasized, along with minimizing negative effects like pollution and waste.

Table 7.1 The common-good-oriented intrinsic ends of the company

Intrinsic ends of the company	The common-good-oriented intrinsic ends
EXTERNAL MISSION	
Providing products (goods and services)	Providing truly good products in ethical conditions
Creating and distributing value	Creating and distributing value ethically
Establishing external relationships	Fostering good relationships with external relationholders
INTERNAL MISSION	
Organizing work	Organizing work efficiently and ethically
Establishing internal relationships	Fostering good relationships with internal relationholders and building up community
Maintaining the institution over time	Promoting integral institutional development and striving for continuity with sustainability

2 *Creating and distributing value ethically*
   This involves generating satisfactory economic revenues with fairness and a sense of service, and then distributing such economic value properly to face the economic needs of the company, paying dividends or making investments. Companies create social value by developing innovative products, services or processes that meet market needs, and enhance efficiency, quality and customer satisfaction, as well as intangible benefits thus promoting trust and loyalty.

3 *Fostering good relationships with external relationholders*
   Good relations require treating relationholders properly, avoiding domination and abuse of power, and fostering reciprocity and collaboration. Companies have a responsibility to act as good corporate citizens, which includes legal compliance, minimizing negative impacts, contributing to solving social problems, and respecting and caring for the environment – even beyond repairing damage caused by their activities.

Internal mission

4 *Organizing work efficiently and ethically*
   This means organizing productive processes efficiently while respecting workers' dignity and rights, allowing them to develop their talents and grow as human beings. It includes providing training, learning opportunities, and fostering reciprocal and cooperative relationships.

5 *Fostering good relationships with internal relationholders and building up community*
   Internal relationholders include managers, supervisors, operational workers, shareholders, investors, and family owners in family businesses. Good relationships are characterized by respect, justice, benevolence and fostering a sense of care, compassion and support. This also emphasizes concern for personal development and excellent relationships within teams and the company. Building up community is a key part of fostering good relationships within the company. While the company itself is a community (7.4), the internal cohesion of this community can be improved. This task may involve mutual care among all corporate members and leadership that promotes a sense of belonging and a willingness to cooperate for the common good of the company.

6 *Promoting integral institutional development and striving for continuity with sustainability*
   This focuses on the holistic and responsible growth of the company, including economic, social and ethical dimensions. It involves reinforcing internal systems, complying with norms, fostering a *person-centred culture* concerned with serving people and the common good, and demonstrating environmental stewardship. Striving for continuity requires innovation, sustainability efforts, good governance and maintaining competitive ability over time.

These multi-ends are not isolated aims; on the contrary, they are strongly interconnected (Figure 7.2). That is why they should be considered together and managed with practical wisdom, as all of

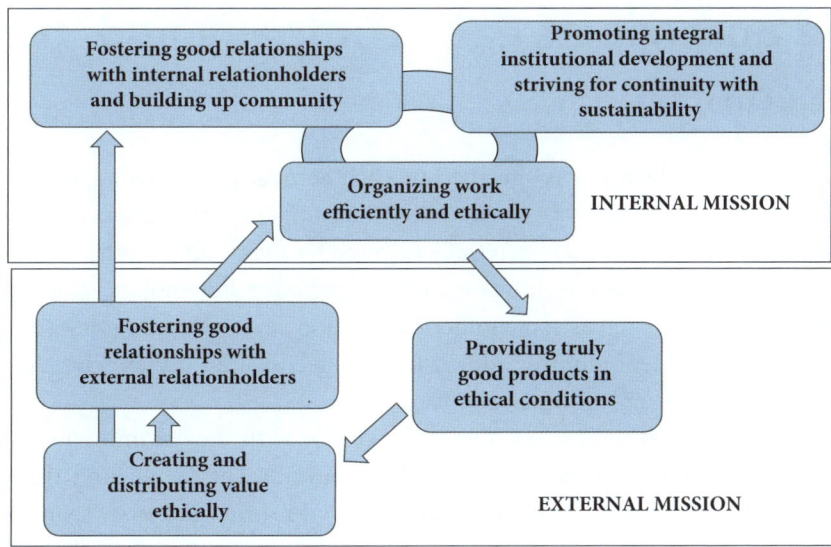

Figure 7.2 The common good-based multi-ends: Framing a dual corporate mission

them are necessary. While customer service and innovation are often deemed essential, neglecting the other ends can lead to harmful tensions that disrupt the unity of the company.

It is therefore fundamental to maintain a minimum standard for each end and to apply practical wisdom in balancing and prioritizing them appropriately. For instance, prioritizing innovation may be necessary in response to changing competitive conditions (to ensure continuity), while hiring skilled employees could be crucial for organizing work effectively. Both ends, in this case, deserve appropriate consideration.

Serving people through a dual corporate mission

These common-good–based multi-ends are beneficial for both the firm and society. In this context, it is important to emphasize that the ultimate reference point for the company's purpose is the people to whom the common good is directed. Through its intrinsic common-good ends, the company serves the real needs of the people involved in its activities, who are referred to as relationholders. This leads to the conclusion that:

> The company's purpose is to serve the real needs of people connected to the company (both internal and external relationholders), through its intrinsic multi-ends, in alignment with the common good.

This approach shares similarities with the concept of managing to 'create value for stakeholders', but differs in significant ways. Firstly, the focus here is on serving the real needs of people related to the company, emphasizing human flourishing, not just value creation. Secondly, the service to people is specified by six statements derived from the company's intrinsic ends.

7.8 The purpose of each company and 'purpose-driven companies'

The generic purpose of a business is specified by each company through a particular purpose – often termed a mission – that ideally expresses how the company intends to contribute to the good of society. These specific purposes are generally inspired by a view on the purpose of the company (7.5), or a combination of them. Some companies emphasize shareholder value maximization, often alongside other goals such as stakeholder satisfaction, acknowledging that serving the long-term interests of shareholders requires addressing the needs of all stakeholders. Others adopt a stakeholder or shared value creation perspective.

Some companies align their mission statements closely with the common good–based multi-ends presented here, combining these ends with a commitment to meeting the real needs of stakeholders. A notable example is the 'Our Credo' of Johnson & Johnson,[85] which outlines the company's responsibilities to those who use their products or services, as well as their suppliers, employees, communities and stockholders. This credo also details specific responsibilities that align with the multi-ends of the firm. Similarly, Procter & Gamble, a prominent manufacturer of consumer goods, articulates several interconnected ends in their statement 'Our Purpose': 'We will provide branded products and services of superior quality and value that improve the lives of the world's consumers, now and for generations to come. As a result, consumers will reward us with leadership sales, profit and value creation, allowing our people, our shareholders and the communities in which we live and work to prosper.'[86]

However, the purposes or missions stated by many companies rarely encompass all aspects of the generic business purpose. There is a tendency to present a simplified corporate purpose, highlighting specific ways in which the company aims to make a positive impact on the world, and then properly distributing such economic value to address the company's financial needs, such as paying dividends or making investments. For example, Unilever, a multinational consumer goods company, states its purpose as: 'We are making sustainable living commonplace',[87] and Merck, a well-known multinational pharmaceutical company, affirms: 'Our leaders guide our purpose to use the power of leading-edge science to save and improve lives around the world. This is the foundation of everything we do.'[88]

Corporate purpose can serve as an internal message to the organization about what should be emphasized in corporate activity, although it is often just a central slogan for corporate communication and image building. In practice, however, every company has a 'real purpose', including multi-ends in the managers' mindset and in corporate governance as a driver of corporate activity. Taking the real corporate purpose seriously can become a driver for the entire business activity.

Having a purpose or mission is not exactly the same as being a *purpose-driven company*. The meaning of the latter is that they have a purpose or mission that goes beyond profit, focusing on making a positive impact on society, the natural environment or a specific cause. Their core purpose guides their strategies, decisions and interactions, aligning business objectives with meaningful contributions to societal or environmental goals. These companies often prioritize long-term value creation for all people related to the company, the communities where companies operate, and the environment, rather than solely maximizing short-term profits for shareholders. A typical example of purpose-driven companies is Patagonia, Inc. (see Business Ethics in Action #13).

Case Study #7

Suicides in France Télécom[89]

For many years, France Télécom (FT) was the only French telecommunications company, and its sole shareholder was the French state. On 1 January 1998, the French government decided to partially privatize the company, with the state maintaining control of the company with 27 per cent of the operator's shares. The rest of the capital, which was successfully placed, was distributed among institutional shareholders (64 per cent), individual shareholders (5 per cent) and company employees (4 per cent).

The success of the internet opened the door to the internationalization of the firm, which bought numerous telecommunications companies. In 2000 it acquired Orange, which over time would be the single brand that replaced the other commercial labels operated by FT. With this expansion, the number of FT employees increased from 140,000 in 1993 to 220,000 in 2001; 56 per cent of the workers were in France, 16 per cent in Poland, 12 per cent in the United Kingdom, 2 per cent in Spain and the rest in other countries.

Between 1997 and 2001, the so-called 'dotcom bubble' – that is, sharp growth in the values of companies linked to the internet – occurred. This phenomenon, together with some very risky operations, had a negative impact on the company's accounts, and it lost almost €30 billion between 2001 and 2002. In 2002, it was said that FT was the second most short-term indebted company in the world. In October of that year Thierry Breton was appointed general manager, with the aim of reviving the company, whose share price was on the floor. Breton carried out a tough debt adjustment, negotiating a refinancing of its debt with banking institutions and agreeing to a capital increase of €15 billion with the state. In February 2005 Breton was appointed Minister of Finance of France, relieving Didier Lombard from office. According to the company's 2006 corporate report, three out of every four employees received gross remuneration of between €2,150 and €4,150 per month. The average monthly remuneration was €2,924.

In FT, as in other large French corporations, the greater presence of institutional investors in capital led to the adoption of 'stock options' policies related to the value of shares and the distribution of dividends increased, which in FT went from €0.25 to €1.4 per share between 2003 and 2008. The new CEO, Didier Lombard, committed to distributing 40–45 per cent of organic cash flows to shareholders, with a target above €7 billion annually. These targets were reached in 2006 and 2007, and exceeded in 2008, when they rose to €8 billion, half of which was allocated to shareholders.

Until the company was privatized, practically all employees had civil service status. They enjoyed a stable working relationship, and the company could not fire them (trying to do so would involve a very cumbersome procedure). Once the company was privatized, no more functionaries were recruited. The company's corporate culture had been built based on this stability and with a sense of a public mission. However, since the privatization, with the orientation towards sales and commercial activities, objective financial criteria prevailed and had become the priority in the operation of the company.

Mr Lombard initiated a broad reorganization that included the elimination of 22,000 jobs from 2006 to 2008, not including lay-offs. It did so through the 'NExT' plan (New Experience of Telecommunications, *Nouvelle Expérience des Télécommunications* in French), which involved integral treatment for the clients, offering them its package of telecommunications services, a reduction of internal costs for the organization and the regrouping of the various products under the Orange brand (except for landlines, which would keep the name of FT for a few more years). This reorganization was economically profitable. Between 2006 and 2008, FT accumulated almost €15 billion in profits.

Not only were planned dismissals carried out, 67,500 people also lost their jobs through retirements, pre-retirement, voluntary redundancies, spin-off and transfer of civil-service employees to other public services. Since the company could not lay off employees, it tried to convince them to leave their posts themselves. Between 1997 and 2007, the proportion of civil servants among workers fell from 90 per cent to 70 per cent. By 2010, there were only 60,000 employees left.

There was also great internal mobility within the company, with some 14,000 people changing jobs. This mobility was geographical as well as functional; there was a policy of transferring employees to any part of the country. Skilled workers were assigned to less qualified tasks, placing them in confined spaces and entrusting them with repetitive and boring tasks that would make them uncomfortable. Some accepted the new working conditions and others opted to voluntarily leave the company. The work environment had become rarefied and stress levels increased.

Since 2002, each FT employee has changed jobs on average every twenty-seven months, and place of work every thirty months. The level of resignations rose from 4.4 per cent in 2005 to 15.3 per cent in 2008. In 2008, each employee had an average of one month of sick leave.

In 2007, the unions SUD and CFE–CGC/UNAS created the observatory of stress and labour mobility to study the consequences of the organization of work in FT.

In July 2009, a news item set off the alarm. A fifty-one-year-old FT employee committed suicide in Marseille. He left a note to his family saying 'I am committing suicide because of my work at France Télécom. This is the only cause. Permanent emergency, work overload, absence of training, total disorganization of the company. A management based on terror.' The tragedy echoed in the press around the world and became a concern for the French government.

At the end of that same year, the company commissioned a work climate survey from the consulting firm Technolgia. Their conclusions described a 'tense, even violent, work environment', adding 'The general feeling is much degraded, mainly in terms of working conditions, health and stress … The workers of France Télécom seem orphaned, lacking in leadership.' On the presentation of this report, Sébastien Crozier, the CFE–CGC/UNAS trade union alliance delegate, announced that, in reality, between 2008 and 2009, thirty-five workers had taken their own lives. The data was later confirmed by the company.

Several of the suicides took place in the workplace itself: a thirty-two-year-old woman jumped from the window of her office; another person died during the course of a meeting. When the suicide took place outside FT, employees left letters stating that the company was the cause of their suicide.

Against this background, Didier Lombard left the company's general management in February 2010. Months later, the Paris prosecutor's office would open an investigation (in response to the complaint filed by the SUD union) against Lombard, his number two Louis-Pierre Wenès and the director of human resources, Olivier Barberot. The company's doctors and social security offices had alerted those responsible to the alarming situation, underlining that the firm maintained a labour organization that caused serious damage to the health of workers, and applied characteristic methods of moral harassment. In mid-2010, the number of suicides rose to forty-six. On 13 July of that year, for the first time, a court recognized the suicide of a worker as an occupational accident due to work overload.

Stéphane Richard succeeded Lombard as general manager with the mandate of stopping the wave of suicides.

Questions

1 What ethical issues can you see in this case? Reflect on how these would challenge you if you were a intermediate manager in such a situation.
2 Compare the vision of the company and its purpose before and after privatization.
3 If you were appointed CEO of France Télécom following the crisis, what concrete and ethically grounded steps would you take to restore employee trust, well-being, and a healthy workplace culture? Justify your choices.

Notes

1. P. F. Drucker, *Men, Ideas & Politics* (New York: Harper & Row, 1974), p. 41.
2. Sources: Investopedia: The Collapse of Lehman Brothers; Wikipedia: Lehman Brothers/Lehman Brothers bankruptcy/subprime mortgage crisis; *New York Times*: News online about Lehman Brothers Holdings Inc.; 'Bernanke Defends Bear Stearns Bailout', *CBS News Online,* 17 April 2009.
3. See, for instance, D. M. Kreps, *Microeconomics for Managers* (New York: W. W. Norton, 2003); and B. Salanie, *Microeconomics of Market Failures* (Cambridge, MA: MIT Press, 2000).
4. On market failures, see, for instance, Salanie, *Microeconomics of Market Failures.*
5. P. J. DiMaggio and W. W. Powell, 'The Iron Cage Revisited: Institutional Isomorphism and Collective Rationality in Organizational Fields', *American Sociological Review*, vol. 48, no. 2, 1983, pp. 147–60. On legitimacy, see M. C. Suchman, 'Managing Legitimacy: Strategic and Institutional Approaches', *Academy of Management Review*, vol. 20, no. 3, 1995, pp. 571–610.
6. See, for example, M. Albert, *Capitalism vs. Capitalism: How America's Obsession with Individual Achievement and Short-Term Profit has Led It to the Brink of Collapse* (New York: Four Door

Eight Windows, 1993); and B. Amable, *The Diversity of Modern Capitalism* (New York: Oxford University Press, 2003).

7. John Paul II (Pope), *Encyclical-Letter 'Laborem exercerns'* on human work, no. 42: https://www.vatican.va/content/john-paul-ii/en/encyclicals/documents/hf_jp-ii_enc_14091981_laborem-exercens.html. (Accesed on 3 June 2025).

8. He affirmed: 'Few trends could so thoroughly undermine the very foundations of our free society as the acceptance by corporate officials of a social responsibility other than to make as much money for their stockholders as possible' (M. Friedman and R. Friedman, *Capitalism and Freedom* (Chicago, IL: University of Chicago Press, 1962), p. 133). See also, M. Friedman, 'The Social Responsibility of Business is to Increase its Profits', *New York Times Magazine*, September 13, 1970. Reproduced in M. Friedman, 'The Social Responsibility of Business is to Increase its Profits', in T. Donaldson and P. H. Werhane (eds), *Ethical Issues in Business* (Englewood Cliffs, NJ: Prentice Hall, 1993), pp. 249–54.

9. K. Arrow, 'Social Responsibility and Economic Efficiency', *Public Policy*, vol. 21, no. 3, 1973, pp. 300–17; and K. J. Arrow, *The Limit of Organizations* (New York: Norton, 1974).

10. See D. J. Vogel, 'Is There a Market for Virtue? The Business Case for Corporate Social Responsibility', *California Management Review*, vol. 47, no. 4, 2005, pp. 19–45.

11. Sources: AES-Our History: https://www.aes.com/about-us/our-history (Accesssed on 3 June 2025); S. Wetlaufer, 'Organizing for Empowerment: An Interview with AES's Roger Sant and Dennis Bakke', *Harvard Business Review*, vol. 77, no. 1, 1999, pp. 110–23; L. S. Paine, case study, 'AES Global Values' (Boston, MA: Harvard Business School, 2000); M. Tavis, 'How to Win Global Markets, Ethically: The AES Way', *People & Strategy*, vol. 36, no. 3, 2013, pp. 20–2.

12. Mentioned by Paine, 'AES Global Values' case study, p. 2.

13. W. Norman, 'AES to Triple Renewables Capacity by 2027 and Ditch Coal by 2025', *PV-Tech*, 9 May 2023, https://www.pv-tech.org/aes-to-triple-renewables-capacity-by-2027-and-ditch-coal-by-2025/. [Accessed on 3 June 2025].

14. https://www.aes.com/about-us/our-leadership. (Accessed on 30 October 2024).

15. A business firm, or a business enterprise, can adopt different forms, such as corporation, limited liability company, partnership and others. However, corporation is often taken as the generic name for every business firm.

16. See R. F. Duska, 'Self-Interest and Autonomy', *Journal of Financial Service Professionals*, vol. 72, no. 3, 2018, pp. 26–8.

17. P. L. Berger, 'New Attack on the Legitimacy of Business', *Harvard Business Review*, vol. 59, no. 5, 1981, pp. 82–9.

18. This is made clear in the work of R. Jackall, 'Moral Mazes: Bureaucracy and Managerial Work', *Harvard Business Review*, vol. 61, no. 5, 1983, pp. 118–30.

19. R. H. Coase, 'The Nature of the Firm', *Economica*, vol. 4, 1937, pp. 386–405. Reprinted in O. E. Williamson and and S. G. Winter (eds), *The Nature of the Firm: Origins, Evolution, and Development* (New York: Oxford University Press, 1991), pp. 61–74.

20. This is made explicit in W. M. Evan and R. E. Freeman, 'A Stakeholder Theory of the Modem Corporation: Kantian Capitalism', in T. L. Beauchamp and N. Bowie (eds), *Ethical Theory and Business*, 3rd ed. (Englewood Cliffs, NJ: Prentice Hall, 1988), p. 151; and R. E. Freeman, 'A Stakeholder Theory of the Modern Corporation', in T. L. Beauchamp and N. E. Bowie (eds), *Ethical Theory and Business* (Englewood Cliffs, NJ: Prentice Hall, 1997), pp. 66–76, who propose the view on p. 71.

21. R. R. Freeman, 'Business Ethics at the Millennium', *Business Ethics Quarterly*, vol. 10, no. 1, 2000, p. 176.
22. This is the proposal of M. Keeley, 'Continuing the Social Contract Tradition', *Business Ethics Quarterly*, vol. 5, no. 2, 1995, pp. 241–56.
23. D. Melé, 'The Firm as a "Community of Persons": A Pillar of Humanistic Business Ethos', *Journal of Business Ethics*, vol. 106, no. 1, 2012, pp. 89-101.
24. A set of individuals interacting for a common goal is not sufficient to build a community. This requires an enduring unity, a common action and a shared purpose. A group of people working together to help a person who has suffered an accident is not a community. Neither is a group of people with a common goal enough to make a community – a few individuals waiting for a bus who agree to share a taxi, for example. However, other groups of people, such as a family, a neighbourhood or a company have enduring unity, apart from some common action and a shared purpose; they are therefore communities, although the degree of unity might range from strong to weak.
25. R. Solomon, 'The Corporation as Community: A Reply to Ed Hartmann', *Business Ethics Quarterly*, vol. 4, no. 3, 1994, pp. 271-85, on p. 277.
26. C. I. Barnard, *The Functions of the Executive: Introduction of K. Andrews* (London: Oxford University Press, 1938 [1968]).
27. M. C. Jensen, 'Value Maximization, Stakeholder Theory, and the Corporate Objective Function', *Business Ethics Quarterly*, vol. 12, no. 2, 2002, pp. 235-56.
28. See M. C. Jensen and W. H. Meckling, 'Theory of the Firm: Managerial Behavior, Agency Cost, and Ownership Structure', *Journal of Financial Economics*, vol. 3, October, 1976, pp. 305-60.
29. Friedman, 'The Social Responsibility of Business', cit.
30. For an historical analysis of the rise of shareholder value as a principle of corporate governance in the United States, see W. Lazonick and M. O'Sullivan, 'Maximizing Shareholder Value: A New Ideology for Corporate Governance', *Economy and Society*, vol. 29, no. 1, 2000, pp. 13-35.
31. Friedman, 'The Social Responsibility' and Friedman and Friedman, *Capitalism and Freedom*.
32. E. Heath, B.B. Kaldis and A. Marcoux (eds), *The Routledge Companion to Business Ethics* (London and New York: Routledge, 2018).
33. See Jensen, 'Value Maximization, Stakeholder Theory'.
34. 'The businessmen believe that they are defending free enterprise when they declaim that business is not concerned "merely" with profit but also with promoting desirable "social" ends; that business has a "social conscience" and takes seriously its responsibilities for providing employment, eliminating discrimination, avoiding pollution and whatever else may be the catchwords of the contemporary crop of reformers' (Friedman, The Social Responsibility of Business, cit. 1970), cit.
35. Jensen, 'Value Maximization, Stakeholder Theory', p. 243.
36. Jensen, 'Value Maximization, Stakeholder Theory', p. 246.
37. J. Fontrodona and A. J. G. Sison, 'The Nature of the Firm, Agency Theory and Shareholder Theory: A Critique from Philosophical Anthropology', *Journal of Business Ethics*, vol. 66, no. 1, 2006, pp. 33-42.
38. S. Ghoshal, 'Bad Management Theories Are Destroying Good Management Practices', *Academy of Management Learning & Education*, vol. 4, no. 1, 2005, pp. 75-91 and Fontrodona and Sison, 'The Nature of the Firm'.
39. J. L. Canals, 'Rethinking the Firm's Mission and Purpose', *European Management Review*, vol. 7, no. 4, 2010, pp. 195-204.

40. R. E. Freeman, *Strategic Management: A Stakeholder Approach* (Cambridge, MA: Cambridge University Press, 1984 [2010]).
41. Evan and Freeman, 'A Stakeholder Theory', p. 151.
42. R. E. Freeman, 'The Politics of Stakeholder Theory: Some Future Directions', *Business Ethics Quarterly*, vol. 4, no. 4, 1994, pp. 409-29.
43. Evan and Freeman, 'A Stakeholder Theory', p. 151.
44. R. E. Freeman, 'Managing for Stakeholders', in D. G. Arnold, T. L. Beauchamp and N. E. Bowie (eds), *Ethical Theory and Business*, 10th ed. (Cambridge: Cambridge University Press, 2020), pp. 220-9.
45. H. E. Freeman, 'Divergent Stakeholder Theory', *Academy of Management Review*, vol. 24, no. 2, 1999, pp. 233-6, on p. 235.
46. Jensen, 'Value Maximization, Stakeholder Theory'.
47. R. E. Freeman, 'Ending the So-called "Friedman–Freeman" Debate. Included in Agle et al. "Dialogue Toward Superior Stakeholder Theory" (pp. 153–90)', *Business Ethics Quarterly*, vol. 18, no. 2, 2008, pp. 262–6.
48. Business Roundtable, 'Business Roundtable Redefines the Purpose of a Corporation to Promote "An Economy That Serves All Americans"', https://www.businessroundtable.org/business-roundtable-redefines-the-purpose-of-a-corporation-to-promote-an-economy-that-serves-all-americans. (Accessed on 30 October 2024).
49. T. Donaldson and L. E. Preston, 'The Stakeholder Theory of the Corporation: Concepts, Evidence, and Implications', *Academy of Management Review*, vol. 20, no. 1, 1995, pp. 65–91.
50. Freeman, 'The Politics of Stakeholder Theory'.
51. In Freeman's words, 'Better stakeholder theory focuses us on the multiplicity of ways that companies and entrepreneurs are out there creating value, making our lives better, and changing the world' (Freeman, 'The Politics of Stakeholder Theory', p. 166).
52. B. L. Parmar, R. E. Freeman, J. S. Harrison, A. C. Wicks, L. Purnell and S. de Colle, 'Stakeholder Theory: The State of the Art', *Academy of Management Annals*, vol. 4, no. 1, 2010, pp. 403–45, on p. 433.
53. M. E. Porter and M. Kramer, 'Creating Shared Value: How to Reinvent Capitalism and Unleash a Wave of Innovation and Growth', *Harvard Business Review*, vol. 89, no. 1/2, 2011, pp. 62–77, on p. 64.
54. Porter and Kramer, 'Creating Shared Value', p. 64.
55. J. Wieland (ed.), *Creating Shared Value – Concepts, Experience, Criticism*. Series Ethical Economy, vol. 52 (Cham: Springer, 2017). A critical voice within this book is T. Beschorner and T. Hajduk, 'Creating Shared Value: A Fundamental Critique', pp. 27–37.
56. G. de Los Reyes Jr, M. Scholz and N. C. Smith, 'Beyond the "Win–Win": Creating Shared Value Requires Ethical Frameworks', *California Management Review*, vol. 50, no. 2, 2017, pp. 142–67.
57. J. Mackey and R. Sisodia, *Conscious Capitalism: Liberating the Heroic Spirit of Business* (Boston, MA: Harvard Business School Publishing Corporation, 2013); and https://www.consciouscapitalism.org/. (Accessed on 3 June 2025).
58. Amazon purchased Whole Foods Market for $13.7 billion in 2017, https://money.cnn.com/2017/06/16/investing/amazon-buying-whole-foods/index.html. (Accessed on 3 June 2025).

59. See, for instance, J. O'Toole and D. Vogel, 'Two and a Half Cheers for Conscious Capitalism', *California Management Review*, vol. 53, no. 3, 2011, pp. 60–76; and J. O'Toole, *The Enlightened Capitalists: Cautionary Tales of Business Pioneers Who Tried to Do Well by Doing Good* (New York: HarperCollins, 2019).
60. R. Honeyman, *The B Corp Handbook: How to Use Business as a Force for Good* (San Francisco, CA: Berrett-Koehler, 2014); and https://www.bcorporation.net/en-us/certification/. (Accessed on 3 June 2025).
61. Focolare is presented as 'an ecclesial movement for spiritual and social renewal'. It 'was founded in Trent, Italy in 1943 by Chiara Lubich and her closest friends, and approved by the Catholic Church in 1962. The movement has now reached 183 countries, and more than 2 million people share closely in the life of the movement and its work': https://www.focolare.us/whats-focolare/. (Accessed on 3 June 2025).
62. L. Runi and A. J. Uelmen, 'Religious Values and Corporate Decision Making: The Economy of Communion,' *Fordham Journal of Corporate & Financial Law*, vol. 11, no. 3, 2006, pp. 645–80; L. Gold, *New Financial Horizons: The Emergence of an Economy of Communion* (New York: New City Press, 2010).
63. Among them A. Edmans, *Grow the Pie: How Great Companies Deliver Both Purpose and Profit* (Cambridge: Cambridge University Press, 2020); and 'Company Purpose and Profit Need Not be in Conflict if We "Grow the Pie"', *Economic Affairs*, vol. 40, no. 2, 2020, pp. 287–94; J. Battilana, T. T. Obloj, A.-C.A. Pache and M. Sengul, 'Beyond Shareholder Value Maximization: Accounting for Financial/Social Trade-Offs in Dual-Purpose Companies', *Academy of Management Review*, vol. 47, no. 2, 2022, pp. 237–58; and P. Polman and L. Eden, 'Imagine a Better World: An Interview with Paul Polman', *AIB Insights*, vol. 23, no. 5, 2023: https://doi.org/10.46697/001c.90323. (Accessed on 3 June 2025).
64. J. Canals, *Boards of Directors in Disruptive Times: Improving Corporate Governance Effectiveness* (Cambridge: Cambridge University Press, 2023), p. 111.
65. C. Mayer, 'Are Corporate Statements More Than Verbiage?', *Journal of Applied Corporate Finance (Special Issue on IESE ECGI Conference on Corporate Purpose. Can Purpose Deliver Better Corporate Governance?)*, vol. 33, no. 2, 2021, pp. 44–9, on p. 46.
66. A. MacIntyre, *After Virtue* (New York: Bloomsbury Academic, 1981 [2013]). See G. Moore, 'On the Implications of the Practice-Institution Distinction: MacIntyre and the Application of Modern Virtue Ethics to Business', *Business Ethics Quarterly*, vol. 12, no. 1, 2002, pp. 19–32.
67. A. Argandoña, *La misión de la empresa y la responsabilidad social* (Barcelona: Cuadernos de la Cátedra 'La Caixa', n. 29, 2016).
68. J. A. Pérez-López, *Fundamentos de la dirección de empresas* (Madrid: Rialp, 1993).
69. J. J. Almadoz, 'Inside-out and Outside-in Perspectives on Corporate Purpose', *Strategy Science*, vol. 8, no. 2, 2023, pp. 139–48.
70. T. Donaldson and J. P. Walsh, 'Toward a Theory of Business', *Research in Organizational Behavior*, vol. 35, 2015, pp. 181–207: https://repository.upenn.edu/cgi/viewcontent.cgi?article=1049&context=lgst_papers. (Accessed on 5 June 2025).
71. C. Felber, *Change Everything: Creating an Economy for the Common Good* (London: Zed Books, 2019); and C. Felber and G. Hagelberg, *The Economy for the Common Good: A Workable,*

Transformative Ethics-Based Alternative. In J. G. Speth & K. Courrier (Eds.) *The New Systems Reader. Alternatives to a Failed Economy*: 39–57. London-New York: Routledge, 2020.

72. Felber and Hagelberg, *The Economy for the Common Good,* p. 2.
73. L. Bruni and S. Zamagni, *Civil Economy: Another Idea of the Market* (New York: Columbia University Press, 2017).
74. Among them, M. Naughton, H. Alford and B. Brady, 'The Common Good and the Purpose of the Firm', *Journal of Human Values*, vol. 1, no. 2, 1995, pp. 221–37; A. Argandoña, 'The Stakeholder Theory and the Common Good', *Journal of Business Ethics*, vol. 17, 1998, pp. 1093–102; D. Melé, 'Not Only Stakeholder Interests: The Firm Oriented towards the Common Good', in S. A. Cortright and M. J. Naughton (eds), *Rethinking the Purpose of Business: Interdisciplinary Essays from Catholic Social Tradition* (Notre Dame, IN: Notre Dame University Press, 2002), pp. 190–214; P. Koslowski, 'The Common Good of the Firm as the Fiduciary Duty of the Manager', in G. J. Rossouw and A. J. Sison (eds), *Global Perspectives on the Ethics of Corporate Governance* (New York: Palgrave Macmillan, 2006), pp. 67–76; A. J. G. Sison, *Corporate Governance and Ethics: An Aristotelian Perspective* (Cheltenham and Northampton, MA: Edward Elgar, 2008); A. J. G. Sison and J. Fontrodona, 'The Common Good of the Firm in the Aristotelian–Thomistic Tradition', *Business Ethics Quarterly*, vol. 31, no. 2, 2012, pp. 211–46; and S. Arjoon, A. Turriago-Hoyos and U. Thoene, 'Virtuousness and the Common Good as a Conceptual Framework for Harmonizing the Goals of the Individual, Organizations, and the Economy', *Journal of Business Ethics*, 2018, vol. 147, no. 10, 2018, pp. 143–63.
75. F. Miller, 'Aristotle's Political Theory', in E. N. Zalta and U. Nodelman (eds), *The Stanford Encyclopedia of Philosophy*, 2022: https://plato.stanford.edu/archives/fall2022/entries/aristotle-politics/. (Accessed on 30 October 2024).
76. On this point, see R. R. Ellsworth, *Leading with Purpose: The New Corporate Realities* (Bloomington, IN: Stanford University Press, 2002).
77. J. M. Elegido, 'Intrinsic Limitations of Property Rights', *Journal of Business Ethics*, vol. 14, no. 5, 1995, pp. 411–16.
78. J. Griffin, *On Human Rights* (Oxford: Oxford University Press, 2008).
79. The expression 'the social function of property' can usefully be understood as a notion that aims to secure the goal of human flourishing for all citizens within any state: see C. Crawford, 'The Social Function of Property and the Human Capacity to Flourish', *Fordham Law Review*, vol. 80, 2011, pp. 1089–134.
80. C. Handy, 'The New Language of Business', *Director*, vol. 52, no. 7, 1999, pp. 50–3, on p. 50. On this point, see also C. Handy, 'What's a Business For?', *Harvard Business Review*, vol. 80, no. 12, 2002, pp. 49–55.
81. Handy, 'What's a Business For?'.
82. Koslowski, 'The Common Good of the Firm', p. 72.
83. C. Handy, 'The Citizen Corporation', *Harvard Business Review*, vol. 75, no. 5, 1997, pp. 26–8, on p. 28.
84. C. R. Solomon, *A Better Way to Think About Business: How Personal Integrity Leads to Corporate Ssuccess* (New York: Oxford University Press, 1999), p. 46.
85. https://www.jnj.com/our-credo. (Accessed on 30 October 2024).
86. https://us.pg.com/policies-and-practices/purpose-values-and-principles/. (Accessed on 30 October 2024).
87. https://www.unilever.com/our-company/. (Accessed on 30 October 2024).

88. https://www.msd.com/company-overview/leadership/. (Accessed on 30 October 2024).
89. Sources: B. Dielh and G. Doublet, *Orange: le Déchirement; France Telecom ou les Dérives du Management* (Paris: Gallimard, 2010); Y. Duroy, *Orange Stressée: le management par le stress à France Télécom* (Paris: La Découverte, 2009); N. R. Chabrak, R. Craig and N. Daidj, 'Financialization and the Employee Suicide Crisis at France Telecom', *Journal of Business Ethics*, vol. 139, no. 3, 2015, pp. 501–15; Y. Dervin, *Ils m'ont détruit! Le rouleau-compresseur de France Télécom* (Paris: Michel Lafon, 2009).

8

The Right Use of Power in Business

Justice and power must be brought together, so that whatever is just may be powerful, and whatever is powerful may be just.[1]

BLAISE PASCAL (1623–1662), French thinker, mathematician and scientist

Overview

Managing and governing businesses ethically requires a proper understanding of what the responsible use of power entails. This means that, beyond concerns about maintaining or increasing power, there is an ethical imperative to use power responsibly and justly. This essentially means serving the community, rather than serving one's own interests or other particular interests.

Section A introduces the topic and discusses the importance of the responsible use of power, as well as various forms of failing to meet this responsibility. Power is also closely related to how we treat people, and five levels of quality in human treatment are identified. The section continues by reflecting on ethics in managerial work and the importance of managing corporate resources with a sense of stewardship. It concludes by presenting a set of principles and standards for managing businesses responsibly on a global scale, provided by respected international organizations.

Section B focuses on corporate governance. It begins by reviewing significant theories on corporate governance, primarily related to understanding the identity and purpose of the firm. It argues for the importance of governing companies – whether large corporations or small and medium-sized enterprises – as communities of people, with a sense of service. Guidelines for good governance practices are presented, along with virtues that promote good corporate governance. The section concludes with a brief discussion on shareholder responsibility.

Chapter Aims

After reading this chapter you should be able to:

- Understand the different types of power within organizations.
- Discuss the responsible use of power within the company.
- Examine the role of ethics in managerial work.
- Reflect on the concept of 'Human Quality Treatment'.

- Consider the stewardship approach in managing corporate resources.
- Be familiar with key international standards for responsible business.
- Reflect on corporate governance for the common good.
- Explore a set of best practices for corporate governance.
- Discuss criticisms of excessive executive compensation.
- Contemplate the responsibilities of shareholders.

Historical Case #8

Building up the Parmalat holding[2]

Parmalat's story, from 1961 to 2003, was closely linked to the personality and leadership of Calisto Tanzi. Calisto studied accounting, but he was forced to drop out of college at twenty-two years old because his father was ill. It was then that he began to run the small family business founded by his grandfather, which consisted of a quite unsuccessful salting house and a canning factory. Very soon, Calisto transformed the existing facilities into a pasteurized milk plant. In addition, he changed the image of the company so that his clients associated it with quality food, and he invented the Parmalat brand, with the intention of projecting the reputation of the famous Parmesan cheese. In 1963 he began using Tetrapak technology, of Swedish origin, and ultra-high temperature (UHT) processing, which facilitated the conservation of the product and cartons. He was successful with these strategies and his business grew considerably.

Calisto's intuition and entrepreneurial spirit led him to a strategy of strong growth and diversification in the 1970s, entering into the business of other dairy products such as yogurt, butter and cream, and the desserts market. By the 1980s, Parmalat had become a multinational company, consolidating its position in Latin America, the United States, Germany, France and Nigeria. Like many other Italian family businesses, Parmalat was run in a very patriarchal way, even when it had already reached a multinational dimension.

The trajectory of Calisto Tanzi was recognized in 1984 when he was named *Cavaliere del Lavoro* (Knight of Labour), a title of the Italian Republic for Italians who had been particularly meritorious. His public image was impeccable, and his employees were very happy to work for him. He considered himself a friend of influential Italian politicians and cardinals. He promoted various charitable initiatives: he restored the frescoes in the cathedral of Parma and financed programmes aimed at poverty, AIDS patients and drug addicts, and he generously contributed to the Christian Democracy political party. He financed the restoration of several temples in his region, receiving the Gold Award of Parma in 1988 in recognition of his efforts as a benefactor. He was also well known in the field of sport. Since 1975, Parmalat had sponsored several Formula One teams, of which the 1978 Parmalat Racing Team stood out. In 1984, his son Stefano was named President of Parma AC, a company-sponsored football club that won two UEFA Cups and one European Cup Winners' Cup during his term.

However, in the mid-1980s, Parmalat's finances began to go wrong. In 1982, Tanzi, through his company, entered the broadcasting business with Euro TV. Five years later, it acquired Odeon TV, which turned out to be a financial disaster, sold with a loss of €45 million. In addition, competition had reduced the operating margin, which, added to the high level of indebtedness caused by the growth strategy, resulted in low capitalization and serious liquidity problems. In 1987, Parmalat's financial debt reached €150 million, and its passive interest was about €23 million – more than double its cash flow.

In 1989 the US food company Kraft made an offer to buy the organization. Tanzi decided not to accept it. His financing strategy consisted of going to the capital market. Owing to Parmalat's delicate financial situation, it was practically impossible for the company to be accepted for listing on the stock exchange. Then Tanzi decided to engineer entry through another company that he personally controlled: Finanziaria Centro Nord (FCN). A year later, he merged Parmalat with FCN. The new company took the name Parmalat Finanziaria SpA. With this operation, he avoided divulging detailed financial information, allowing him to sell shares that settled debts of €268 million.

Listing on the Italian stock market in the early 1990s further stimulated the company's ambition for greater international growth. During the following years Parmalat acquired 120 companies in twenty-five countries. Unfortunately, many of these acquisitions turned out to be unprofitable because of the inefficiency of the factories, bad management of the inventories and the high price paid for the acquisitions. The financial turmoil of the 1990s in Latin America, where many of the new acquisitions were located, contributed to worsening the firm's financial situation.

Yet the reputation of Tanzi in Italy remained great, and in 1999 he was granted another prestigious distinction, being named *Cavaliere di Gran Croce Ordine al Merito della Repubblica Italiana* (Knight of the Grand Cross of the Order of Merit of the Italian Republic).

The ability to increase Parmalat's indebtedness was used to support Parmatour, a tourism company run by Calisto's daughter, Francesca Tanzi. More than €250 million was channelled into the company but never included in the group's financial statements. These Parmalat loans were systematically transferred to subsidiaries located in tax havens and were repaid through irregular bank accounts.

Parmalat issued debt to its own subsidiaries in order to cover their losses, or it issued debt to shell companies that transferred those funds to the Tanzi family companies. The debt issued appeared on Parmalat's balance sheet; however, it was subsequently transferred to some other fake subsidiary in exchange for cash payments. In other words, Parmalat lent money to its subsidiaries and thereafter sold these credits to other subsidiaries in exchange for cash that was never really paid. In order to sustain its ongoing losses, Parmalat ended up raising bonds and using its subsidiaries' false cash deposits as collateral.

Calisto Tanzi was president of the group and owner of 52 per cent of its shares through the family business Coloniale. Other members of his family were also shareholders. Despite the increasing complexity of the organizational structure, Tanzi's intervention in the business management was very direct and showed a notorious lack of transparency, which worried investors. The board of directors of Parmalat Finanziaria SpA was composed of thirteen members. Four of these were related to Calisto by family ties, while the remaining eight had already been part of the Parmalat board. None of them represented the interests of the minority shareholders.

In 2001, according to *Forbes* magazine, he was the holder of net assets of approximately US$1.3 billion. In 2003, Parmalat continued to appear an admirable enterprise in the eyes of many. It was one of the world's leading food companies and the eighth industrial group in Italy. It had 37,000 employees, 200 subsidiary companies and 139 production centres spread over thirty countries. Its assets amounted to €10,000 million and its annual sales were around €7,600 million. In 2002, it presented profits of €252 million, which represented an annual growth of 15.4 per cent. However, in the end, the inevitable happened.

At the beginning of November 2003, rumours began to circulate that Parmalat could not meet payment on obligations of US$187 million. Some investors had serious doubts about the real financial situation of the company. In response to the growing doubts, on 11 November Calisto Tanzi reaffirmed the strength of the economic and financial situation of Parmalat. But this was light years away from reality.

It was estimated that the group's turnover was 25 per cent lower than stated in its financial statements and its operating margin 81 per cent lower. It was learned that the executives of the group had rigged foreign transactions in Singapore and the Cayman Islands, falsifying commercial and financial contracts that would be used as collateral to increase bank financing and thus cover operating losses.

In the investigation, it was discovered that €3,900 million that Parmalat had accounted for in its subsidiaries in the Cayman Islands, allegedly deposited in a Bank of America account, did not, in fact, exist. On 24 December of that same year, Parmalat Finanziaria SpA and its subsidiaries declared bankruptcy. Three days later, Calisto Tanzi was arrested. The following week, he broke down during an extensive interrogation in the prison of San Vittore in Milan and acknowledged Parmalat's financial black hole. Tanzi was charged with what was then the biggest accounting fraud in European business history. Investigation of the facts would go on to discover a financing deficit of €14,000 million. He was sentenced to ten years in prison for the crimes of abusive speculation, obstruction of the supervisory authority and falsehood in auditing. The sentence was reduced to eight years and one month on appeal, and in 2011 he was imprisoned. Several of Tanzi's close associates were also convicted.

On 23 December 2003, the Italian Prime Minister Silvio Berlusconi decreed the intervention of Parmalat. The objective was to prevent its closure, which would leave 4,000 workers on the street and dairy producers in ruin.[3]

Many banks and other Parmalat creditors, scattered globally, lost their money, while the company shareholders saw their wealth fall dramatically. In the following months, an investigation was carried out into the possible influence of various people, including lawyers, auditors, banks and Tanzi's closest collaborators, in a financial fraud that would have lasted more than fifteen years. According to the US Securities Commission, 'chairman and Chief Executive Officer Calisto Tanzi and his son Stefano Tanzi, offered debt securities in the United States while engaging in one of the largest and most brazen corporate financial frauds in history'.[4]

The judge appointed Enrico Bondi as the new administrator of Parmalat. He turned the company's situation around and enabled the re-floating of its shares less than two years after they had virtually no value. Bondi eliminated jobs, reduced the size of the company and exchanged debt for new shares. He also initiated lawsuits against former Parmalat auditors and banks, accusing them of cheating investors. After going through some hard years, in July 2007, Parmalat announced first-half profits of €163.3 million (up 3.7 per cent) and revenues of €1.8 billion (up 2.8 per cent).

The Parmalat scandal also had an impact on the laws governing Italian companies and, in particular, their boards, requiring the greater presence of independent directors and representation of minority shareholders.

Questions

1. Review the key decisions made by Calisto Tanzi throughout Parmalat's rise and fall. In your view, where did the use of power become abusive or ethically questionable? What motivations could have driven these decisions? How might these decisions have looked different if guided by a more responsible approach to leadership and power?
2. Put yourself in the position of one of Parmalat's senior employees or directors during the company's rapid expansion. What pressures might you have felt to align with Tanzi's leadership? What would have helped you use your own voice or power more ethically in that context?
3. Contrast the work of Calisto Tanzi with that of Parmalat's new administrator, Enrico Bondi.

SECTION A. MANAGING POWER ETHICALLY

8.1 Power within the business company

Power means 'to be able': the ability to make choices or influence outcomes. Power can be held by an individual or a group. Businesses and those who govern or manage them hold power – sometimes enormous power. However, others within and outside the organization also hold a certain amount of power, which influences behaviour.

Types of power

Several types of power can be considered. French and Raven proposed six types: legitimate, coercive, reward, referent, expert and informational power:[5]

- *Legitimate power* comes from an elected, selected or appointed position of authority. In a company, it derives from one's role, title, or assigned responsibility, enabling individuals to make decisions, enforce rules and direct employees.

- *Coercive power* is the ability to penalize or withhold rewards, often exercised through disciplinary actions. While potentially effective in the short term, coercive power can create negative consequences for workplace morale and trust.
- *Reward power* involves the ability to offer rewards, such as promotions, bonuses or favourable assignments. Those who control rewards can influence behaviour and motivate employees to achieve company goals.
- *Referent power* is rooted in personal relationships, charisma or respect. People are influenced by others they admire, making referent power a valuable, albeit less formal, form of influence.
- *Expert power* is based on specialized skills or knowledge. Employees or leaders with expert power can influence decisions and processes because their expertise is respected and often essential.
- *Informational power* involves access to important information that others may lack. Control over information grants significant influence, particularly in strategic decision-making.

Here the discussion will focus especially, though not exclusively, on the legitimate power of those who govern the company, also called 'political power' or 'positional power', which is necessary for ruling any community.

Corporate governance

Before exploring individual or group power within a company, it is important to address the framework for exercising power within the company, termed *corporate governance*.

Corporate governance refers to the system by which companies are directed and controlled. It provides the broader framework of rules, practices, and processes used to guide a company's operations and strategic direction. It outlines how decisions are made, how power and responsibilities are distributed, and how accountability and transparency are maintained among key stakeholders, including shareholders, executives, employees, customers and regulators.

Corporate governance is often guided by principles and regulations that define best practices for governing corporations responsibly. These principles generally aim to ensure accountability by establishing oversight mechanisms to hold management accountable for company performance, balancing the legitimate interests of people associated with the company, promoting transparency by providing accurate and timely information to stakeholders, and developing policies to assess and mitigate risks.

A key element of corporate governance is the *board of directors*, which specifies and enforces the corporate governance framework that defines the roles, powers and processes of various groups associated with the company.

Legitimate power within the company

Positional power derives from one's formal role or title within the company, with authority to make decisions, enforce rules and direct people. Legitimate power in corporations is exercised through shareholders, the board of directors and managers, each wielding corporate power to varying degrees. This separation of powers helps prevent concentration of power and reduces the risk of abuse due to lack of control.

- *Shareholders*: Shareholders hold power based on property rights, with effective power depending on the amount of capital owned. In small companies with few shareholders, effective shareholder power can be high, while minority shareholders in large companies usually have little effective power. In large corporations, many shareholders are institutional investors, such as mutual funds, insurance companies, retirement funds, hedge funds or banks. These institutional investors – as well as other controlling shareholders, including families, corporations and private funds – can have significant influence over corporate behaviour.
- *Board of directors*: The board holds the power to govern and lead the company. It is under the control of shareholders, who also appoint the board and auditors, ensuring that an appropriate governance structure is in place. However, in practice, these functions are not always fully effective, especially for minority shareholders with limited capacity to influence governance decisions. The board practises corporate governance by establishing and enforcing the strategic direction and policy framework within which the corporation operates. It also supervises the management of the business and reports to shareholders on its stewardship. Special power is held by the board chairperson, who presides over meetings, coordinates members' perspectives and fosters consensus.
- *CEO and managers*: The chief executive officer (CEO) is the primary individual responsible for managing the company. The CEO is sometimes also the company's president or board chair, particularly in small and medium-sized enterprises. The CEO is responsible for overall management and has final authority over decisions within corporate activity. The CEO reports to the board of directors and, sometimes, directly to stockholders. Top management can include senior managers who are close collaborators of the CEO. These positions typically involve responsibility for managing people, finances, purchasing and technological resources. Intermediate managers, including department directors, product managers and supervisors, lead teams, oversee activities and report to upper management, exercising power in line with their respective positions.

8.2 Responsible use of power

When one has power, the question that arises is 'to what end should it be used?' Some hold that power should be sought as an end in itself or to achieve personal benefits with no sense of responsibility. This was the position of Niccolò Machiavelli, an Italian political philosopher who lived during the fifteenth and sixteenth centuries. In his book, *The Prince*, he prescribes how a prince should retain control of his realm. In a certain sense, we can understand 'prince' as equivalent to a director or a manager. Machiavelli suggested that kind words and rewards can be used if they favour power but that it is also acceptable to lie, break promises or even to use brute strength where necessary to maintain power. In a Machiavellian view, maintaining power is therefore an end that would justify questionable means, although not any means whatsoever.[6]

Machiavelli's analysis was restricted to those who rule and who act in order to maintain their power, but the term *Machiavellian* was soon coined and is still employed today to describe one who deceives and manipulates others for gain. Those who practise a Machiavellian use of power can easily rationalize their attitude as 'realism' or 'pragmatism' but, in fact, deceiving or manipulating others to retain power can easily be recognized as something opposed to common-sense morality.

Common-sense morality leads us to affirm that power requires responsibility and that the greater the power, the greater the responsibility. It is not surprising that the sentiment of 'with *great power comes great responsibility*' has long been recognized, and, since at least the times of the French Revolution, many political leaders, including Winston Churchill, Teddy Roosevelt and Franklin D. Roosevelt, have made similar statements. The expression even appeared in a Spider-Man story in 1962 and passed into popular culture in the United States and elsewhere.

In the business context, the same idea has been extensively accepted since at least the 1960s. In these years, some emphasized that companies that do not take responsibility for their power will ultimately lose it.[7]

Justice and lack of justice in management

Justice, in compelling us to give to each what is due (5.1), provides a key guideline for a proper use of power. The German philosopher Robert Spaemann argues that 'Justice is the virtue of those in positions of power, the virtue of the strong.'[8] A just person also has a *sense of service to the common good* of the community, and this is what gives legitimacy to the power to rule it.

In fact, justice is widely recognized as an essential component of a good society. Plato, through Socrates, refers to justice as both a personal virtue and a principle for a proper order in the city-state. Similarly, the American philosopher John Rawls contends that 'Justice is the first virtue of social institutions.'[9]

There are several forms of a lack of justice, which lead to an irresponsible wrong use of power. Here are some of the most common, which include lack of personal responsibility in various forms (3.5):

Using power unfairly

This is the case when human dignity and other people's rights are not respected, or the use of power is contrary to the good of the community that a manager serves. An example is a manager who dismisses an employee not for fair and proportionate reasons but due to personal animosity. Another unfair use of power is making decisions exclusively motivated by the manager's own interest or for the interest of a particular group within the organization which consequently damages the firm. This can include short-term decisions that endanger the company in the long term.

Using power improperly

This includes, for instance, using managerial power to satisfy the managerial 'ego' instead of to serve others, which can also lead to unfair use of power. Such would be the case, for instance, of an executive who allows unnecessary expenses to promote his or her personal image with no thought for the image of the company. Another inappropriate form of power use is an excessive restriction of freedom in the initiative and activity of subordinates.

Making negligent use of power

Negligence in power occurs when individuals in positions of authority fail to fulfil the obligations that come with their roles, neglecting their duty to act responsibly. An example of negligence is a CEO who does not exercise due diligence when hiring a new manager, failing to properly investigate the individual's qualifications and capabilities.

Failure to use power courageously

This leads people to omit actions out of cowardice. It occurs when those in power understand what is morally required of them but refrain from acting due to fear or lack of courage. For instance, an independent director on a corporate board may choose not to voice opposition to a proposal – despite recognizing it as the right course of action – simply to avoid conflict with the chairperson.

Some might wonder whether a just use of power is really possible. Lord Acton (1834–1902), a well-known British historian, affirmed that 'Power tends to corrupt, and absolute power corrupts absolutely.'[10] This may be true in the case of some empowered people, but saying that corruption is inevitable means denying free will and the role of virtues in good behaviour. Apart from social mechanisms to control and prevent the misuse of power, good or bad use depends on the sense of responsibility of the people with the power and on how virtuous they are.

'Power over' vs. 'power with'

Another critical question regarding power is how it is exercised within organizations. At the beginning of the twentieth century, management was primarily focused on *giving orders*, and this approach was supported by mainstream management theories of the time, including those proposed by Max Weber, Frederick Taylor and Henri Fayol. This style of management emphasized hierarchical authority, with power being exercised over workers, who were expected to respond with unquestioning obedience. Managers directed operations without any real participation or collaboration from their subordinates.

In contrast, Mary Parker Follett, a pioneering management thinker of the 1930s (although not fully recognized during her time), reacted against this authoritative management style. She argued that true power is not about exerting control, or 'power over', but about creating 'power with' others.[11] This concept emphasized the importance of seeking consensus and collaboration in exercising power. Follett advocated for an authority within organizations based on function and responsibility, not merely position.

Follett highlighted that the human condition inherently resists 'power over', and such an approach is often ineffective, as people naturally resist being dominated or patronized. She proposed that cooperation and shared decision-making were more effective and conducive to organizational success. For Follett, power should not simply be a tool for control, but a dynamic force that brings people together to solve problems and achieve common goals.

Moreover, Follett introduced the idea of the law of the situation, where decisions should be based on context and the needs of the specific task, rather than on rigid hierarchical structures. This was a revolutionary departure from the top-down, command-and-control models prevalent in her time, making her a forerunner of participative management and collaborative leadership approaches.

Her ideas laid the groundwork for more modern leadership theories, such as servant leadership, transformational leadership (6.3), and the empowerment movement, which advocate for shared power and the development of persons within organizations. Follett's proposal is aligned to the principle of participation and related to the principle of subsidiarity, two critical principles of social life (2.7).

8.3 'Human Quality Treatment' in managing people

'Management', wrote Drucker, 'is about human beings. Its task is to make people capable of joint performance, to make their strengths effective and their weaknesses irrelevant. This is what the organization is about, and it is the reason that management is a critical, determinant factor.'[12] Since management is 'about human beings', questions of justice and benevolence will be inherent to all managerial work and, first of all, in dealing with people.

A community of persons requires human quality in the treatment of people. Human Quality Treatment (HQT) is a concept defined as 'dealing with persons in a way appropriate to the human condition, which entails acting with respect for their human dignity and rights, caring for their problems and legitimate interests and fostering their personal development'.[13] Five levels of HQT can be found in organizations[14] (Figure 8.1): (1) *mistreatment*, which is a blatant injustice; (2) *indifference* towards people, characterized by disrespectful treatment with a lack of recognition of the person's dignity and rights; (3) *respect* for persons and their rights; (4) *care*, expressed by concern for people's legitimate interests and support for them in resolving their problems; and (5) *development*, that is, a treatment favouring professional growth and human flourishing, which can bring about mutual esteem and friendship-based reciprocity.

These levels have foundations in the good of benevolence (2.6) and in the Personalist Principle (2.7), which include justice, assimilable to respect, care and friendly service, related to promoting development.

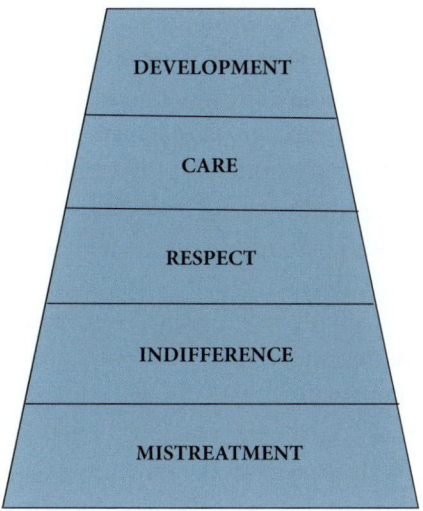

Figure 8.1 Levels of Human Quality Treatment

Justice as respect for people and their rights

Justice leads to respecting people – firstly, avoiding maltreatment and treating people with indifference (as mere human resources), and then respecting human rights and other requirements of justice. Managers not only ought to treat people with justice but, using all of the power at their disposal, they should promote justice through institutional norms and procedures.

International organizations have proposed managing and governing principles and standards (8.6) that pursue living justice in some crucial issues. A central point on these standards is respect for human rights and, related to these, labour rights (10.2). One of the most popular sets of principles is the UN Global Compact, which in its two first principles establishes that businesses should support and respect the protection of internationally proclaimed human rights (Principle 1) and make sure that they are not complicit in human rights abuses (Principle 2). The latter includes violations of human rights in the supply chain (13.9), which is a cooperation in wrongdoing and therefore entails responsibility.

Justice in performance appraisal and in distributions

Justice also involves fulfilling contracts (5.2), including labour contracts, commercial contracts and other sales-related issues (see Chapter 11). It is also present in *performance appraisal*, that is, the regular review of employee or management performance within organizations. This is important not only as a duty of justice but also because employees are usually particularly sensitive about how they are evaluated, and comparisons are inevitable.

Managers are often involved in issues of distributive justice, which requires *equity* (5.1), that is, treating people without unfair discrimination, bias or *favouritism*, including *nepotism*, or by lack of recognition of relevant differences, that is, *egalitarianism*.

Managers indulge in *favouritism* by hiring or granting positions within the company not because of requisite qualifications, but only out of some personal preference. Obviously, there are positions in which it is necessary to feel personal confidence in addition to the person's possession of the required skills. However, a just use of managerial power requires a sincere and upright evaluation, since favouritism would infringe on the rights of deserving candidates. One particular form of favouritism is *nepotism*, which refers to the favouring of relatives or close personal connections, especially by giving them jobs, promotions or other advantages based on the relationship rather than on merit, qualifications or performance.

Equity does not mean *egalitarianism*, giving strictly equal treatment to everybody in everything regardless of his or her personal circumstances, merits or situation. People are equal in dignity and human rights, but each person's personality, character and circumstances are different. Owing to personal problems, some people, at a particular time, will need more attention than others. Thus, equity is also treating differently those according to their personal circumstances, but in the knowledge that anyone else in the same circumstance deserves the same treatment.

Concern for collaborators

This is expressed through care and a proactive attitude in promoting the development of collaborators, as a manifestation of benevolence.

Care is not only a matter of feeling; it is also – and above all – a rationally assumed ethical value. This aspect prevents care from becoming mere sentimentalism. Acting with care becomes a virtue, and thus a trait of the manager's character. At the same time, cultivating empathy, sympathy and emotional intelligence can significantly enhance the effectiveness of care.

An attitude of care should permeate the entire organization to the extent that it becomes part of the firm's shared beliefs, values and practices – in other words, part of its organizational culture (see 9.4). *Organizational care* includes concern not only for employees but also for other relationholders.

Benevolence – the will to do good – is not limited to showing compassion or addressing people's problems and legitimate interests. It also encompasses the manager's attitudes and actions aimed at fostering the personal, professional and human development of those around them.

In order to promote employee development, at least three points can be highlighted:

- *Motivating a sense of service*, for instance, by giving advice or praising or criticizing behaviours and, above all, being role models in their attitude of service.[15]
- *Designing ethical organizational structures* (9.7) that help people employ and develop their talents. Participation and empowerment can also favour such development.
- *Implementing managerial systems* that favour not only efficiency but also human and professional development. Performance appraisal is one particularly significant example. Apart from including a fair evaluation, which is a requirement of justice, as already noted, performance appraisal should provide criteria for development and feedback to improve and should also suggest any appropriate training.

8.4 Responsibility and virtues in managerial work

Managerial work includes planning activities; arranging these through rules, procedures and directions; leading activities of those in an organization to accomplish determined goals; coordinating (that is, making different people or things work together for the purpose of the organization) and controlling the results to verify whether the desired objective has been achieved, checking possible errors and taking any corrective actions required.[16] All of these activities involve responsibilities and exercising virtues. Some of the most relevant are outlined as follows:

Loyalty to one's own legitimate commitments

Loyalty is related to consistency in legitimate commitments, and managers have a fundamental commitment to work in favour of the company while respecting just laws and contributing to the common good. Loyalty leads to prioritizing the good of the company over personal interests and avoiding *opportunism*. Since managers deal with the day-to-day activity of the organization, the opportunity exists for the unprincipled to seek personal advantage with little regard for the good of the organization or ethical principles.

Industriousness and diligence in managerial work

Industriousness and diligence are two commendable virtues in all types of work – particularly in management. While closely related, each highlights a distinct aspect of excellent performance and responsible leadership. Industriousness refers to the willingness to work hard, take initiative and be productive. Diligence involves carefulness and a strong sense of responsibility, including attention to detail and the conscientious execution of one's duties.

Industriousness leads managers to:

- *Work hard and go the extra mile* to meet deadlines, support their team, and demonstrate energy and resilience when pursuing challenging goals. This is expressed in actions such as budgeting time effectively, monitoring one's own performance, and fully concentrating on work. It also means avoiding *laziness*, passivity or settling for the bare minimum and – in the opposite extreme – preventing becoming an overworked or compulsive manager. The *overworked manager* devotes excessive time and energy to work, even at the expense of family duties and mental well-being. A *compulsive manager* is driven more by internal pressure than by external demands, which may lead to unhealthy work habits.
- *Strive for improvement and innovation*. Industrious managers seek to identify inefficiencies in operations and proactively develop solutions. They are willing to launch new projects

to streamline processes when needed. This stands in contrast to *complacency*, where one is content with merely maintaining the current situation without pursuing growth.
- *Overcome procrastination* that leads to delaying important tasks – often because they are unpleasant or tedious. An industrious manager faces necessary tasks head-on, even under pressure, and cultivates discipline in action.

Diligence, as the direct opposite of *carelessness*, is demonstrated through:

- *Conscientiousness*, that is, acting with a strong sense of duty and care. Diligent managers thoroughly review reports for irregularities, ensure compliance with legal and ethical standards, and consistently follow up on delegated tasks to ensure quality completion.
- *Making well-informed decisions*, based on careful analysis and reflective judgement. Diligence ensures the quality and reliability of decisions, avoiding impulsive choices or decisions made without sufficient review.
- *Assuming and fulfilling responsibilities carefully and reliably*, with attention to relevant details – especially when high precision is required. A diligent manager, helped by practical wisdom, understands what must be done and what can be done in every circumstance. They are aware of the risks of *negligence*, which includes failing to follow up on key responsibilities, or *sloppiness*, which allows poor standards or errors to persist.

Negligence deserves closer attention. It has already been discussed as a form of responsibility by omission (3.5). *Responsibility for omissions* requires that the omitted action is both due and possible. This is why, in the case of managers, responsibility for omissions is limited by their actual power – no one can be held accountable for the impossible.

However, depending on their *level of authority and role*, a manager may still bear responsibility for failing to adequately monitor the business, for neglecting the implementation of strategic decisions, for overlooking market trends, technological developments or relevant social changes, or for failing to encourage necessary investment when circumstances clearly require it.

Furthermore, some omissions may amount to *complicity in wrongdoing* by others. This includes, among other omissions:

- Failing to correct or persuade someone to avoid immoral behaviour when there's a reasonable chance of effectiveness.
- Not preventing someone from committing an illicit act when it is within one's power to do so.
- Failing to report harmful behaviour or crimes when justice requires it.
- Covering up immoral actions, thereby enabling their continuation.
- Protecting those who commit wrongdoing, allowing them to act with impunity.

In summary, industriousness and diligence involve earnest and persistent application to any task, marked by steady effort, zeal, attention and care. Acting with diligence not only avoids harmful omissions but also strengthens a manager's commitment to excellence, responsibility and ethical integrity across all areas of leadership.

Fostering efficiency with ethical sense

Organizations depend on the efficient use of their resources to achieve set goals. However, managers must ensure that efficiency is pursued without compromising justice – for example, by disrespecting or mistreating people. A good end does not justify bad means (see 4.5). Efficiency can generate numerous benefits: it increases returns for shareholders, supports better wages or compensation for managers and employees, enables lower prices for customers, and benefits other stakeholders. Promoting efficiency with an ethical mindset involves designing *management systems* that are both effective and fair. These systems influence the behaviour of employees and managers alike. For example, *incentive systems* can reward appropriate actions and outcomes; *training programmes* can equip employees with the skills they need to contribute responsibly; and *career development* and *evaluation systems* can align goals and methods with both performance and ethical standards.

Communicating with truthfulness and transparency

Communication cuts across managerial roles within any organization. Managers communicate information, thoughts, ideas, purposes and so on. The end of communication is to create a shared understanding, often with the intention of achieving adherence, collaboration or cooperation. The means might vary (speaking, writing, audiovisuals, sign language, gestures and certain facts that can be interpreted as a message to a person, group or organization). However, any means require a common language that all parties can understand.

The importance of communication skills is well recognized in the business world and in many other spheres. Such skills include listening, observing, speaking, questioning, analysing and evaluating in addition to those in ordering one's own ideas and processing information or feedback. Communication skills are the 'technical' side of communications, whereas the moral side is telling the truth in the right way, to the right person and at the right time (5.1).

As has been noted (5.1), truthfulness is much more than not telling lies or deceiving: it requires disclosing information to those who have a right to it. This aspect of truthfulness leads to the concept of *corporate transparency*, meaning that corporate information that is of public interest should always be easily accessible. However, there are circumstances where it is legitimate to conceal the truth (5.1) when this applies to the firm's confidential information.

Negotiating with circumspection and fairness

In a negotiation process, some duties exist that parties are expected to uphold – not just avoiding deception or harm, but actively contributing to a fair, respectful and constructive process. This requires:

- *Respect to the counterparts*, considering them as persons with intrinsic dignity and legitimate interests.
- *Good faith*, acting sincerely and showing readiness to find common ground and willingness to reach a mutually acceptable agreement. Negotiation as a delaying tactic or to gain unfair leverage should be avoided.

- *Honesty and transparency*, sharing truthful information, especially regarding key terms, constraints and intentions, and avoid deceptive tactics, such as misleading statements or half-truths, and clarify misunderstandings when they arise. It is also necessary to create transparency where divided loyalties may be present and to reveal personal or organizational interests that could influence judgement.
- *Protection of confidentiality*, safeguarding sensitive information shared in trust.
- *Upholding achieved commitments* through agreements or during negotiations, which requires faithful implementation and proactive clarification of expectations post-agreement.

These criteria should be applied prudently, especially considering that, in negotiations, both parties typically use language quite different from that employed in other contexts. It is common for both sides to begin by presenting conditions that they expect to be reduced over the course of the negotiation. Each party understands this dynamic. It would be naïve to begin from a position that one is not prepared to modify. There is no obligation to reveal in advance how far one is willing to concede until the negotiation has made significant progress. The manager – or anyone acting on behalf of the company – should proceed with circumspection, meaning careful consideration of all relevant circumstances and possible consequences. However, this does not justify telling lies, even if doing so might lead to a favourable outcome.

In some situations, it may become apparent that the counterparty is lying or acting in bad faith as part of their negotiation strategy. What should be done in such cases? It is not morally acceptable to stoop to the same level. Nevertheless, appropriate caution is necessary. In certain extreme circumstances, if the counterparty is negotiating maliciously, they may be considered an unjust aggressor. In such cases and after a prudential judgement, an exaggeration or even false statement could be morally qualified as an act of legitimate self-defence, which may be ethically acceptable (see 5.1). This scenario can also be illustrated by imagining a manager negotiating the renewal of a critical supply contract with a supplier who has become increasingly unethical and manipulative. During the meeting, the supplier threatens to suddenly cut off deliveries unless the company agrees to a last-minute price increase – knowing that this would paralyse operations and result in significant financial losses. The supplier is clearly exploiting the company's vulnerable timing to impose unfair terms. Caught off guard and under intense pressure, the manager might hint that they have another supplier ready who can match the required delivery schedule and pricing within a few days. While this statement is literally false, the *moral object* is not a lie, but an act of self-defence facing an 'unjust aggressor' because it is made to defend against unjust pressure, to re-establish balance, and to prevent serious harm to the manager's company.

8.5 Stewardship in managing corporate resources

The manager is a steward since he or she is entrusted by the firm to make the best use of corporate resources. Acting with a sense of stewardship requires the right assignment of resources and avoiding waste. Stewardship in managing corporate resources includes several issues; firstly, actions that should be avoided:

Avoiding embezzlement and fraud

Fraud (5.3) against the company involving managers and employees can take different forms, including charging personal expenses to company accounts, using corporate goods for personal ends, withdrawing loans from the firm without proper permission and various other forms of misappropriation of corporate goods for personal enrichment. Embezzlement and fraud committed by managers are serious injustices because they entail abuse of the confidence placed in them to run the company. The manager's task involves seeking to prevent embezzlement and fraud within the company and, of course, not covering up cases of such wrongdoing by others within the organization.

Escape from 'earnings management'

Earnings management is a euphemistic term used to refer to systematic misrepresentation by the manager of the true incomes and assets of a corporation. Sometimes earnings management is termed 'creative accounting', because it is related to accounting that might follow the letter of standard practices but deviates from the spirit of the rules. The ethical justifiability of *earnings management* rests on whether the financial statements are intended to mislead people.[17]

Careful weighing up of investments and expenses

Decisions about investment require a careful weighing up of risks and profitability. This involves diligence and wisdom. Investments to expand the firm could be driven by vanity. It is well known that managers are frequently judged by the size and scope of the business they run. A decision to expand the firm might be made in good faith, or its real aim could be to satisfy the managerial ego. In the latter case, the expenses incurred should be considered a type of misappropriation of corporate funds.

Superfluous expenses are another unjust use of corporate goods for a purpose that is not in the best interests of the company. This is the case of spending money excessively on public relations to make those who run a company look attractive rather than investing in improving business profitability. Although sometimes it is difficult to establish the amount necessary to improve the firm's image or increase its profitability, it is relatively easy for sector insiders to identify occasions of corporate spending that are exercises in personal vanity.

Luxurious offices can, again, be a form of misappropriation of corporate goods for vanity, although reasonable expenses for this purpose are certainly necessary. Prudential judgement must determine what is fitting in each case. Decisions based on vanity are difficult to test in a court of law, but they do entail moral responsibility.

Avoiding conflict of interests or disclosing them

Conflict of interests is a situation where there is a risk of injustice (5.5) that can easily become a misuse of resources and foster a lack of loyalty. Managers and people close to them may have conflicts of interest between different companies in which they are involved. If such conflicts cannot be avoided, upper management – or, in some cases, the board of directors – must be notified, acting with full transparency. Some obvious conflicts of interest, such as a manager having interests in suppliers or holding positions in competitors of the company or its group, should be avoided in any circumstances.

Misuse of confidential information

Using confidential company information for personal purposes or taking advantage of business opportunities of which they might become aware by virtue of their positions, constitutes a clear lack of loyalty. On the contrary, managers must keep any confidential data or information received in the course of their duties secret and must not use it for their own benefit; neither should they provide it to third parties, except to fulfil legitimate duties of disclosure and transparency.

8.6 International standards for managing business responsibly

An extrinsic help for managing business responsibly comes from prominent international organizations, which have proposed principles and standards for responsibly managing and governing business worldwide. They are presented as guidelines for the responsible behaviour of managers and other people involved in business and contribute to a more sustainable and equitable global economy but are also an opportunity for companies to enhance their reputation and mitigate risks.

Some popular international standards for managing business responsibly include the *UN Global Compact*,[18] the *OECD Guidelines for Multinational Enterprises on Responsible Business Conduct*[19] and *ISO 26000 – Social Responsibility*[20] (see a summary of their respective contents in Table 8.1). Less popular but also interesting is *The Caux Round Table Principles*, promoted by an international group of businesspeople. Focused on human rights in global business, it is worth also mentioning the *UN Guiding Principles to Protect, Respect and Remedy Human Rights*. In addition, there is *The Equator Principles*,[21] presented as a financial industry benchmark for determining, assessing and managing environmental and social risk in projects.

The UN Global Compact

This is probably the most widely recognized international code for business conduct. It was launched in 1999 and extended in 2003. The Compact proposes ten principles inspired by earlier UN documents, covering four areas: human rights (based on the UN Universal Declaration of Human Rights, 1948); labour rights (inspired by the International Labour Organization's Declaration on Fundamental Principles and Rights at Work, 1998); the natural environment (including some key aspects of the Rio Declaration on Environment and Development, 1992); and anti-corruption (based on the United Nations Convention against Corruption, 2003).

The Global Compact is not a regulatory instrument but, rather, a forum for discussion and networking for companies, labour and civil society, along with UN agencies. Its aim is to encourage businesses worldwide to adopt sustainable and socially responsible policies and to report on their implementation. It relies on public accountability, transparency and commitment to initiate and share substantive action in pursuing the principles upon which the Global Compact is based. The Compact has a responsive, functional structure with two complementary goals: (1) to mainstream the ten principles in business activities around the world; and (2) to catalyse actions in support of UN goals. These goals are to be achieved through policy dialogue, learning, country/regional networks and partnership projects.

Companies that decide to participate undertake to cite the Global Compact in their corporate communications and annual reports, to disclose specific examples of actions taken to implement the ten principles and to work in partnership with the UN on projects in support of the principles.

The Global Compact does not have any effective monitoring or enforcement provisions, and this is probably its main weakness. In addition, there is the danger that some companies will take advantage of the lack of oversight and compulsion and use association with the Forum simply to polish their image. However, the Global Compact is currently the world's largest initiative to promote business responsibility and acts as a starting point for further initiatives.

OECD Guidelines for Multinational Enterprises on Responsible Business Conduct

The main goal of the OECD, founded in 1961, is to promote policies contributing to economic growth and development. It currently has thirty member countries in Europe and the United States. The Guidelines for Multinational Enterprises, last revised in 2000, are part of the Declaration on International Investment and Multinational Enterprises. The Guidelines include recommendations, voluntary principles and standards proposed by governments to multinational enterprises to ensure that the operations of these enterprises are in harmony with government policies, to strengthen the basis of mutual trust between enterprises and the societies in which they operate, to help improve the foreign investment climate, and to enhance the contribution to sustainable development made by multinational enterprises.

ISO 26000 – Social Responsibility

ISO is a global network of experts that develops and publishes standards for quality, safety, sustainability and more. Usually, ISO presents standards and grants a certification after verifying

Table 8.1 International standards for responsible business

Human rights	
UN Global Compact (UNGC)	Support and respect the protection of internationally proclaimed human rights and ensure businesses are not complicit in human rights abuses.
OECD Guidelines for Multinational Enterprises	Respect human rights and address adverse impacts directly linked to their business operations, products or services.
ISO 26000 – Social Responsibility	Protect and respect human rights across all business operations.
LABOUR RIGHTS AND CONSUMER RIGHTS	
UN Global Compact (UNGC)	Uphold the freedom of association and the effective recognition of the right to collective bargaining, eliminate forced and compulsory labour, abolish child labour and eliminate discrimination in respect of employment and occupation.
OECD Guidelines for Multinational Enterprises	Encourage positive relationships between employers and employees; and uphold labour rights.
ISO 26000 – Social Responsibility	Ensure fair labour practices, including safe working conditions and fair wages. Protect consumer rights and promote fair marketing and advertising.
ENVIRONMENTAL CONCERN	
UN Global Compact (UNGC)	Support a precautionary approach to environmental challenges, undertake initiatives to promote greater environmental responsibility and encourage the development and diffusion of environmentally friendly technologies.
OECD Guidelines for Multinational Enterprises	Take measures to prevent, reduce and remediate environmental impacts. Conduct business in a way that protects and respects consumer rights.
ISO 26000 – Social Responsibility	Minimize negative environmental impacts and promote sustainability.
ANTI-CORRUPTION AND FAIR BUSINESS PRACTICES	
UN Global Compact (UNGC)	Work against corruption in all its forms, including extortion and bribery.
OECD Guidelines for Multinational Enterprises	Refrain from any form of bribery or corruption. Engage in fair competition and avoid anti-competitive behaviour. Ensure timely and accurate payment of taxes.
ISO 26000 – Social Responsibility	Conduct business ethically and responsibly.
ACCOUNTABILITY AND CONTRIBUTION TO DEVELOPMENT	
OECD Guidelines for Multinational Enterprises	Businesses should provide timely and accurate information on their activities, structure, financial situation and performance. Foster the dissemination of technological advances.
ISO 26000 – Social Responsibility	Promote transparent and accountable decision-making processes. Engage in initiatives that contribute to community well-being and development.

compliance, but ISO 26000 is different. It provides guidance rather than requirements, and it cannot be certified, unlike some other well-known ISO standards. Instead, it helps clarify what social responsibility is, helps businesses and organizations translate principles into effective actions and shares best practices relating to social responsibility, globally. It is aimed at all types of organizations regardless of their activity, size or location.

ISO 26000 – Social Responsibility, was launched in 2010 following five years of negotiations between representatives from government, NGOs, industry, consumer groups and labour organizations around the world.

Principles of the Caux Round Table for Moral Capitalism

In 1986, a group of senior European, Japanese and US business leaders founded the *Caux Round Table* (CRT) in order to join forces and reduce escalating trade tensions. They began to meet annually in the Swiss city of Caux. They tried to identify shared values, reconcile differing values and thereby develop a shared perspective on business behaviour acceptable to and honoured by all. In 1992 they concluded that they needed to agree on a set of ethical and moral principles specifically applicable to the world of business and firms. The principles for business were first published in 1994 and are now widely known. The precepts were initially rooted in two basic ethical ideals: *human dignity* and the Japanese concept of *kyosei*, meaning 'living together'. In subsequent versions, *responsible stewardship* was introduced as a third basic ideal:

- The Japanese concept of *kyosei* emphasizing living and working together for the common good, enabling cooperation and mutual prosperity to coexist with healthy and fair competition.[22]
- *Human dignity* refers to the sacredness or value of each person as an end, not simply as a means to the fulfilment of others' purposes.
- *Responsible stewardship* means respecting the environment, furthering its conservation and protection, and avoiding risks to human health.

The current version, the CRT Principles for Business,[23] consists of seven principles, developed in some detail and supported by an appendix with detailed *stakeholder management guidelines*. The latter presents rules for dealing with customers, employees, shareholders, suppliers, competitors and communities. The respective headings of the principles are as follows: (1) respect stakeholders beyond shareholders; (2) contribute to economic, social and environmental development; (3) build trust by going beyond the letter of the law; (4) respect rules and conventions; (5) support responsible globalization; (6) respect the environment; and (7) avoid illicit activities.

UN Guiding Principles on Business & Human Rights

The UN Guiding Principles (UNGPs) *on Business & Human Rights to Protect, Respect and Remedy Human Rights*, also known as the 'Ruggie Principles' and the 'Ruggie Framework', are an instrument, launched in 2011, with a focus on human rights regarding transnational corporations and other business enterprises.[24] The document, in its thirty-one principles, establishes duties for the state and for corporations. The UNGPs rest on three pillars:

- *Protect*. Regarding the state duty to protect human rights. The state does so through laws and other regulations, developing specific policies, investigating how human rights are respected and enforcing them.
- *Respect*. The corporate responsibility to respect human rights. Companies *respect human rights first by complying with all applicable laws*. This entails avoiding any infringement of human rights in business activities, including due diligence in prevention and a quick reaction to counter any negative impact of business activity on human rights.
- *Remedy*. Access to remedy for victims of business-related abuses. This supports the need for rights and obligations to be matched to appropriate and effective remedies when they are breached.

While the UNGPs do not constitute a legally binding international business and human rights treaty, the document provides certain flexibility for the diverse and often complex situations of the global business context.

The Equator Principles

These are ten principles (see a summary in Table 8.2) oriented to serve as a common baseline and risk management framework for financial institutions to identify, assess and manage environmental and social risks when financing projects, particularly large infrastructures and industrial projects, which can have adverse impacts on people and on the environment.

Table 8.2 The Equator Principles

Themes	Contents
Review and categorization	Assess projects to determine the level of environmental and social risk.
Environmental and social assessment	Conduct thorough assessments to understand potential impacts.
Applicable standards	Adhere to relevant environmental and social standards.
Management system and action plan	Develop systems and plans to manage risks.
Stakeholder engagement	Engage with stakeholders to address their concerns and expectations.
Grievance mechanism	Establish mechanisms for addressing grievances.
Independent review	Conduct independent reviews of project assessments.
Covenants	Include specific commitments in project contracts.
Monitoring and reporting	Regularly monitor and report on environmental and social performance.
Transparency	Ensure transparency in environmental and social practices and reporting.

The implementation of the equator principles in financial institutions requires internal environmental and social risk management policies, procedures and standards. Apart from large projects, they may also be used for additional financial products outside the main scope of these principles.

All these principles, although developed through consensus, generally reflect basic standards of decency and can be useful for preventing blatant misconduct. However, ethical management goes beyond mere compliance with international principles and standards – it requires the exercise of virtues. This is particularly important when dealing with people in managerial roles, as well as in the responsible handling of resources.

Business Ethics in Action #8

Mondragón Corporation: The inclusive participatory company model[25]

Mondragón Corporation (MC) derives its name from the small town of Mondragón, located in the Basque Country of Northern Spain. The corporation's origins date back to the 1950s and are tied to Fr. José María Arizmendiarrieta, a young Catholic priest deeply committed to social concerns. At the time, Mondragón was a town with around 8,800 inhabitants, home to an important manufacturing company that operated its own apprenticeship school. Fr. José María, after arriving in Mondragón, began teaching social training courses at the school, fostering ideas that would eventually lead to the foundation of MC.

Under Fr. José María's guidance, five of his former students, who went on to become industrial engineers, were inspired to create a company rooted in Catholic values. His vision was to establish a company that could compete successfully within the capitalist system while promoting the participation of workers in management and allowing them to share in the company's profits. This vision materialized in 1956 when the Mondragón Corporation was founded as a cooperative, where workers also held ownership of the company's assets.

Over the years, MC has grown into a conglomerate with eighty-one cooperatives, twelve R&D centres, and a workforce of 70,000 employees. It operates on a global scale with 104 production plants in thirty-seven countries and commercial activities in over 150 countries. Mondragón has become the world's largest cooperative corporation (Co-Op).[26] Following its founding values, MC has continually refined its mission, leading to the development of the *Inclusive Participatory Company Model* (*Modelo Inclusivo Participativo de Empresa*, in Spanish: MIPE) in the late 2010s.

MIPE is built on several *foundational values* that reflect Mondragón's principles:

- *Respect for the human dignity of all persons.*
- *The pursuit of the common good,* which implies prioritizing the needs of the collective project (the company) over the interests of different stakeholder groups (workers, shareholders, etc.).

- *Establishing a primary objective* that is not to maximize short-term profits, but *to satisfy the people of different stakeholder groups in a balanced manner*, maintaining internal solidarity among these groups.
- *Promoting worker participation in management, outcomes and ownership.*
- *Developing policies that are supportive of the community in which the company operates.*

MIPE is flexible and adaptable, providing a framework that can be tailored to different circumstances. It revolves around four main pillars:

Pillar 1: Transforming management practices and corporate culture to emphasize trust, transparency and cooperation, ensuring both competitiveness and sustainability.

Pillar 2: Formulating a shared project that unites owners, managers and workers, benefiting all parties in the long term and prioritizing the company's sustainability.

Pillar 3: Working to resolve the traditional conflict between capital and labour by promoting worker participation in management, outcomes and ownership.

Pillar 4: Focusing on the social impact of business activities and engaging with social problems in the community.

One of MIPE's core elements is its focus on worker participation in three critical areas:

Management: MIPE advocates for the implementation of participatory management systems. These systems grant individuals and work teams greater autonomy and shared responsibility. Workers also play an active role in corporate governance, contributing to decisions made by the company's highest decision-making bodies.

Outcomes: While not deeply elaborated, MIPE emphasizes that a portion of profits should be reinvested into the company's capital and allocated for research and development, promoting growth and job creation.

Ownership: MIPE encourages collective participation in the company's capital by creating financing mechanisms and timelines to ensure effective ownership by workers.

* * *

The Mondragón Corporation's (MC's) philosophy reflects a responsible use of power, placing the human person at the centre of the corporation. It emphasizes human dignity, community, participation and the common good. In Mondragón's cooperative model, each worker has the opportunity to be an owner and fosters a high degree of participation and empowerment. Rather than being passive instruments in the production process, employees actively participate in decision-making, cultivating a deep sense of responsibility and ownership.

One of the standout features of the inclusive participatory business model (MIPE) is its emphasis on power through participation. By encouraging workers to engage in management, outcomes and ownership, Mondragón creates an environment of collaborative leadership. This aligns with the concept of 'power with', advocated by thinkers like Mary Parker Follett (8.1), who argued that real power is not about control or domination, but about working together to achieve common goals. In Mondragón, power is distributed, promoting shared decision-making across multiple levels. This approach avoids the pitfalls of authoritarian leadership, where managers merely issue orders and expect obedience. By fostering dialogue, collaboration and shared authority, Mondragón demonstrates how 'power with' can lead to more just and effective organizational structures.

Firstly, MC's model reflects the founding vision of Fr. José María Arizmendiarrieta, who was deeply influenced by modern *Catholic social teaching*, beginning with Pope Leo XIII in the late nineteenth century and continuing through his successors. This teaching emphasizes the dignity of work, the rights of workers and the common good, along with the ethico-social principles of solidarity, subsidiarity and participation (2.7). Mondragón's cooperative structure echoes Pope Pius XI's 1931 suggestion to modify the traditional work contract into more of a partnership or shareholder contract, thus allowing workers to become co-owners and share in the management and profits of the company.[27] While Mondragón Corporation is not the only way to implement Catholic social teaching, it serves as a remarkable example of respect for human dignity, participation and an understanding of power that aligns with the principle of 'power with' rather than 'power over'.

SECTION B. ETHICS IN CORPORATE GOVERNANCE

8.7 Corporate governance for the common good

As noted (8.1), corporate governance refers to the system by which companies are directed and controlled. Traditionally, governance has focused on ensuring accountability to shareholders, managing risk and aligning management with the interests of the owners. However, a more ethical perspective, combined with growing societal awareness, calls for a broader and more responsible vision of governance – one that serves not only the firm's internal goals but also the common good of society.

A brief historical overview of the conceptual development of corporate governance may help us better understand this emerging perspective.

At the beginning of the twentieth century, when companies became greater in size, owners were no longer able to control them as they had previously done. In many cases, those who owned the business stock would never have been in the company factories or known much about how the firm was being managed. The problem created by the separation of ownership and managerial control was pointed out by Berle and Means.[28] They warned of the concentration of economic power brought about by the emergence of a powerful class of professional managers, insulated from the pressure of stockholders and without any public control. To deal with this scenario, business firms and especially large corporations established what we now call 'corporate governance', mainly through a board of directors, with the duty of supervising management and directing the organization.

In the modern corporation, several models have been proposed to prescribe how to use power in corporate governance and how this can control managerial power. They are closely related to how the firm and its purpose are viewed. We have previously discussed (7.5) several views on the purpose of business, and these lead to three models of corporate governance.

Accepting that the purpose of the business firm is maximizing shareholder wealth results in the understanding that governance should be exercised primarily to benefit shareholder interests. This approach is closely related to agency theory (7.5), which considers the business firm exclusively as being based on property rights and sees managers as agents and of the principal, who are the shareholders, represented by the corporate board. The model ignores any social function of property and does not consider the firm as a community of persons. The rights and legitimate interests of stakeholders other than shareholders can be jeopardized if they are not guaranteed by law or it is not clear how such concern for stakeholders contributes to the bottom line. Although this paradigm is still dominant in many US and UK companies as well as in other countries, it is nonetheless controversial.[29] There is currently a tendency to be more tolerant in considering the interests of other stakeholders and in including them in corporate governance, but the main principle of maximization of shareholder value remains.

Another model of corporate governance advocates providing a basic guideline to orient governance to benefit the stakeholders, seeking to satisfy the stakeholders' interests or creating value for them. This approach has some limitations. One of these regards the determination of which interests to satisfy and the challenge of choosing a sound ethical theory to resolve conflicting stakeholder interests. Although the viability of the firm as a whole is also considered by some authors, in the stakeholder model of governance the attention is essentially focused on balancing interests rather than on the good of the firm as a whole. There is the risk that such balance might not always be in the firm's own best interests and, if it is not, all stakeholders will ultimately be harmed.

Seeing the firm as a community of persons within the society and understanding the purpose of the firm as its own good, which contributes to the common good of the society, give a particular perspective on corporate governance.

An analogy can be established between this model of corporate governance and the government of a country. Suitable political action should be oriented to the public interest and not to the interests of politicians or those of their electors. Similarly, directors of a board or others who take part in corporate governance should seek the common good of the firm over and above the interest of any stakeholder.

This model is therefore based on the idea that the purpose of the firm is to achieve its multi-ends in accordance with the good of the firm and the common good of society (7.6, 7.7) while serving people involved in the firm (stakeholders). Practical wisdom is essential to determine the good of the firm in each situation. The model focuses on the long term without forgetting the short-term results. Corporate governance needs to balance short-term and long-term needs through the application of practical wisdom.

8.8 Good ethical practices of corporate governance

The use and misuse of corporate power affect not only managers but also corporate governance. There is a set of practices, many with substantial ethical content, that are commonly accepted as elements of good corporate governance. The economic impact of such practices is widely recognized. They are generally included in codes of corporate governance, which contain processes, policies, systems and rules. Having codes of good practice is compulsory for listed companies in many countries, and investors may consider the quality of 'Governance' as one of the three critical factors of corporate sustainability along with 'Social' and 'Environment' (see ESG criteria in 13.6).

Recommendations for good corporate governance

The *Cadbury Report*[30] pioneered the idea of presenting recommendations for good corporate governance in 1990 and introduced several key principles that have influenced corporate governance codes worldwide.

Many countries possess their own codes of good practices of corporate governance. For instance, the *UK Corporate Governance Code* is based on the seminal *Cadbury Code* and the *King IV™ Report on Corporate Governance* for South Africa. In the USA, the *Sarbanes–Oxley Act* contains requirements for corporate governance. On the international stage, the Organization for Economic Co-operation and Development (OECD) launched its *Principles of Corporate Governance* in 1999 after long discussions involving government representatives, a large number of practitioners from the private sector and representatives from international organizations and civil society. Since then, the OECD Principles of Corporate Governance have been updated several times. Currently, these principles have been endorsed by the G20 Finance Ministers and Central Bank Governors and are now known as the *G20/OECD Principles of Corporate Governance*.[31] The document emphasizes that corporate governance affects market confidence as well as company performance. Good corporate governance is essential for companies that want access to capital and for countries that wish to stimulate private sector investment. In contrast, poor corporate governance weakens a company's potential, and can even pave the way for financial difficulties and fraud.

Drawing from different authors[32] and the above-mentioned principles and codes for corporate governance, some recommended good practices in corporate governance are outlined in Table 8.3. They can be presented around five themes: (1) board structure and responsibilities; (2) transparency and disclosure; (3) accountability and control; (4) ethical conduct; and (5) stakeholder engagement.

Table 8.3 Recommended good practices in corporate governance

Themes	Good practices
1. Board structure and responsibilities	*Independent directors*: Ensure a majority of independent directors on the board to avoid conflicts of interest.
	Diverse board composition: Some recommend promoting diversity in terms of gender, ethnicity, skills and experience.
	Clear roles and responsibilities: Define clear roles for the board, CEO and management, with clear separation of the roles of the chairman and chief executive to ensure a balance of power and authority.
2. Transparency and disclosure	*Financial reporting:* Ensure accurate, timely and transparent financial reporting.
	Disclosure of conflicts of interest: Disclose any potential conflicts of interest involving board members and executives.
	Communication with shareholders: Maintain regular and transparent communication with shareholders, particularly institutional investors, but without forgetting minority investors, to ensure their views are considered in corporate decision-making.
	Annual reports: Enhanced quality and comprehensiveness of annual reports to include governance practices and compliance, apart from the financial report.
3. Accountability and control	*Internal controls*: Implement robust internal controls and risk management systems.
	Board committees: An 'Audit Committee' to oversee financial reporting and auditing process and a 'Remuneration Committee' to set executive pay, both mainly composed by non-executive members.
	Performance evaluation: Conduct regular performance evaluations of the board, committees and individual directors.
4. Ethical conduct	*Code of ethics*: Develop and enforce a code of ethics that promotes ethical behaviour throughout the organization.
	Whistleblower policies: Implement policies that protect whistleblowers and encourage reporting of unethical behaviour.
5. Stakeholder engagement	*Stakeholder consultation*: Engage with stakeholders to understand their concerns and incorporate their feedback into decision-making.
	Corporate social responsibility (CSR): Integrate CSR initiatives into the company's strategy and operations.

Good corporate practices embrace both technical and ethical issues. Among the former are common oversight of the preparation of the firm's financial statements, internal controls and the composition of the Board and Board Committees for sensitive matters such as auditing and the compensation arrangements for the CEO and other senior executives. Other technical matters that require practical wisdom include the way individuals are nominated for positions on the board, the resources made available to directors for carrying out their duties, oversight and management of risk and dividend policy.

In addition to practical wisdom, several virtues underpin good corporate governance practices. Observing these practices reveals human values and virtues such as justice, veracity, loyalty, responsibility and commitment to the organization.

Justice in respecting rights and legitimate interests

Sound corporate governance ought to respect all stakeholder rights and legitimate interests. Stakeholder voices should be heard, and appropriate forms of stakeholder participation in governance should be considered. While the law generally protects some stakeholder interests, corporate governance should also be sensitive to any legitimate interests of stakeholders. This can involve formalizing mutual agreements and establishing mechanisms of cooperation, even some type of participation by relevant stakeholders in the corporate process appropriate to the company's size and other conditions. One well-known example is in Germany, where corporate control is divided between two boards: 'a supervisory board' that elects 'a managing board'. Half of the supervisory board consists of representatives of the employees.

Justice requires a special concern for minority and foreign shareholders' rights, including transparent and effective communication of information in an understandable and accessible manner, and curtailment of any possible abuse of the board's power to act to the detriment of shareholders with less power or influence.

Loyalty and diligence

Loyalty requires, among other things, the prevention of conflicts of interest. Some issues regarding conflicts of interest in directors are similar to those in managers, whereas others are more specific. Codes of good governance practices usually detail these issues for directors. Boards of directors and other organs of corporate governance should act in the best interests of the whole company, working diligently for the common good of the firm and indirectly for the common good of society. This orientation requires directors with appropriate skills and experience, as well as diligence in steadily applying themselves to address the firm's problems and needs, attentiveness in obtaining information and participation in corporate decision-making.

Truthfulness and transparency, crucial in disclosure

Proper disclosure of relevant corporate information and appropriate transparency contribute to an efficient capital market, especially where public companies are listed, and, indirectly, this contributes to the common good. Disclosure and transparency require trustworthiness, which entails acting with veracity.

Another reason for veracity is that a corporation's current and potential investors have a right to relevant information regarding the corporation and the roles and responsibilities of the board of directors and top management. Consequently, the board needs to be accountable to investors through appropriate disclosure of substantial matters concerning the organization. This should be timely and balanced to ensure that all investors have access to clear, factual information. In addition, good corporate practices establish that the board should implement procedures that independently verify and safeguard the integrity of the company's financial reporting.

Guidelines and rules are useful but not sufficient. Training is also necessary, but, above all, directors need competence and moral character. This requires a careful selection of directors, considering not only their skills and experience but also their virtues and commitment to fulfilling their responsibilities.

8.9 The question of executive compensation

'Executive compensation' is generally understood as the total reward provided by the firm to top-level executives in a corporation (CEO, COO, CFO and so on). For large corporations in some countries, like the United States, executive compensation can run to several millions of dollars per year. Executive compensation can be controversial on account of the wide gap between executive pay and that of shop-floor workers and also between top American executives and comparable executives of non-US firms.

In the United States, the real value of total CEO compensation was relatively stable until the 1970s, but since then it has risen at an increasingly disparate rate. Executive pay did not keep pace with the dramatic growth in the size of firms during the 1950s and 1960s. In those days, pay was more strongly correlated to the size of the firm than it has been in recent decades. Several factors might have contributed to the change. One is the extensive use in recent decades of stock options, which have become the most substantial component of executive compensation.

Before the 1970s, top managers in large corporations had great power and easily avoided shareholder control. They determined their own remuneration and could run up expenses of doubtful utility (luxury offices, public relations expenses and so on). The situation changed when investment and pension funds acquired shares in volume and gained corresponding power on the board of directors. Those who managed such funds understood that managers' interests should be harmonized with the interests of the shareholders as a moral hazard (5.5) exists due to asymmetry in information known, since managers have more information about the day-by-day operations than stockholders. The stock options were seen as the solution since they could align manager and shareholder interests, thus avoiding opportunist managerial behaviours against the stockholders' interests, but they have brought about other kinds of opportunistic behaviours different from those they were supposed to discourage.

Those who receive stock options from their firm acquire the right to buy shares (stock) after a certain period of time (perhaps three or four years) at a fixed price, regardless of the market price of the share at the time. Thus, if the market price of shares is higher, those who possess stock options can sell them and gain the difference between the fixed price (generally the price at which executives receive stock options) and the market price.

Some top executives spend a limited number of years in the same company and might try to maximize their compensation in stock options in this relatively short period. Thus, they make decisions that may favour a higher share price at the time when the stock option can be executed. This can result in damage for the firm and its stakeholders, including shareholders, in the long term. Such would be the case, for instance, of a massive lay-off of doubtful long-term profitability, although the share price might rise when the lay-off is initially announced. Similar short-term benefits could be gained by failing to make necessary investment in research and development or in employee training, or by selling useful assets unnecessarily.

Thus, stock options can be an incentive not for justice but, rather, for injustice. In addition, they may not be genuinely favourable for shareholders. As Bogle, founder and former CEO of Vanguard group, affirmed, 'CEO compensation is seriously out of line, and too often has provided excessive and unreliable lottery-type rewards based on evanescent stock prices rather than durable intrinsic corporate value.'[33]

A practical solution would require a balanced system to prevent opportunistic behaviours and to incentivize managers to work for the good of the firm. This leads us to consider the necessity of managers with integrity and a strong sense of stewardship.

8.10 Power and responsibility of shareholders

An annual general meeting (AGM) is a mandatory yearly gathering of a company's shareholders. At the AGM the directors of a firm present an annual report, which contains information for shareholders about its performance and strategy. Shareholders with voting rights cast their ballot on current issues, such as appointments to the company's board of directors, executive compensation, dividend payments and the selection of auditors.

Shareholders can be rather varied and have different levels of power. In small and medium-size companies there can be one single owner, a group of partners or a family owner of the capital. In large corporations, shareholders can be institutional investors (pension or investment funds) and minority shareholders. In practice, the real power of the latter will likely be very small, while institutional investors can plead that they are mere administrators of other people's money, and they expect a maximum return on their investment. Thus, the responsibility of shareholders can be diluted; they may even assume that they have no responsibility.

Shareholders bear a certain responsibility for what the company does with their money. Ownership is not only an entitlement to benefits; it entails a social function and ethical responsibility. The problem is that ownership has gradually been losing relevance in private companies, given the many governmental regulations and policies (in some countries) aiming at economic equality and social harmony; thus, awareness of the responsibility of owners has been lost.

Fortunately, there are some changes emerging to recover this sense of responsibility. One is shareholders who demand to know more about the social responsibility of the companies before investing in them directly or through investment and pension funds. There are also funds offered with the commitment to invest only in responsible companies (ethical funds, responsible funds and so on) or to avoid producers of certain products or firms involved in questionable activities.

Another more comprehensive, emerging change refers to legislation that fosters a different model of political power in corporations with more effective shareholder participation and long-term thinking. This is the case of the Swedish model of the active ownership of companies, which is attracting interest worldwide from regulators and governments looking to head off financial crashes. This model places corporate power not with management but with shareholders, who are obliged to elect the board of directors and to be involved in big strategic decisions.[34]

Awaiting significant legislative changes, we have seen the emergence of the so-called *shareholder activism* practised by a group of shareholders, who use their equity stake in a corporation to put pressure on its management for certain changes or to show greater concern for social goals, such as more respect for human rights, the adoption of environmentally friendly policies and so on.

Case Study #8

Recovering a company in crisis[35]

Jorge Muro was the general manager of Bameto, a Latin American company whose main activity was the manipulation of iron laminates. Jorge had been contracted in the hope of turning around the company, which had been operating with losses for the two preceding years. Bameto had 500 workers and about 300 clients. In the previous year sales had reached US$100 million. Carlos Salinas and his sister Vanessa were the only shareholders of the company. Carlos, the chairman of the board of directors, thought that Jorge was the right person to rescue the firm.

Jorge was also convinced that the company was viable and could reach profit within a couple of years. This would require improving productivity and gaining new clients. However, after a few days, Jorge found other problems, including numerous irregular accounting and other practices. One of these was the invoicing of about 3 per cent of sales without taxes on products. Around thirty clients accepted it and, sometimes, they even asked to pay with 'undeclared income' and, consequently, without taxes. In the previous fiscal year, Bameto management had used US$3 million of undeclared income to remunerate shareholders (US$1 million), to pay commissions to heads of purchases of clients (US$130,000), to reward management of principal clients who paid with undeclared money (US$170,000), to give incentives and complements to Bameto managers (US$200,000) and to return money (US$1.5 million) to some clients who had presented false invoices, an amount superior to the real figures. The last of these practices allowed clients to show more costs in their own accounting and to pay less taxes while they still generated undeclared income.

When Jorge joined the company, he knew that there was a small amount of off-the-books cash flow. This also happened in other companies he knew. What he had not appreciated was that it was such a great proportion of the trading figures. Neither was he aware of other frequent 'accounting' practices in Bameto, including what, in his opinion, was a clear overvaluation of some assets on the balance sheet.

Questions

1. How should the irregular practices described in the case be assessed from a legal and ethical standpoint?
2. Do you think that Jorge's decision to accept the position at Bameto was a prudent choice, given the circumstances? What would you do if you were Jorge? Why?
3. How should a responsible and ethical manager respond to the situation Jorge is facing?

Notes

1. In French: 'La justice et le pouvoir doivent être réunis, pour que ce qui est juste puisse être puissant et ce qui est puissant peut être juste' (B. Pascal, *Pensées* (Livre de Poche, 1669 [2000]).
2. Sources: Adapted and extended from F. Toninato and J. Tapies, *Milking Money out of Parmalat*, DG-1478-E (Barcelona: IESE Publishing, 2005) (with permission); I. Moss, 'Parmalat SpA: An Impressive Milking System' (Lusanne: IMD, 2004); G. Granzini, *Il crea Parmalat* (Rome: Editori Riuniti, 2004); P. Madsen, 'Parmalat', in R. W. Kolb (ed.), *Encyclopedia of Business Ethics and Society* (Los Angeles, CA: Sage, 2018), pp. 1565–6; BBC News, 'Online Parmalat Founder Given 18-Year Jail Term Over Fraud', BBC News, 9 December 2010, https://www.bbc.com/news/business-11958133. (Accessed on 4 June 2025).
3. Securities and Exchange Commission, *Plaintiff* v. *PARMALAT FINANZIARIA S.p.A.*, Defendant. https://www.sec.gov/litigation/complaints/comp18527.htm. (Accessed on 4 June 2025).
4. Securities and Exchange Commission, *Plaintiff* v. *PARMALAT FINANZIARIA S.p.A.*
5. J. R. P. French and B. H. Raven, 'The Bases of Social Power', in D. Cartwright (ed.), *Studies in Social Power* (Ann Arbor, MI: Research Center for Group Dynamics, Institute for Social Research, 1959), pp. 150–67. They present five types of power: coercive, reward, legitimate, referent and expert. The informational power was introduced later by B. H. Raven, 'Social Influence and Power', in I. D. Steiner and M. Fishbein (eds), *Current Studies in Social Psychology* (New York: Holt, Rinehart, Winston., 1965), pp. 371–82.
6. Actually, Machiavelli did not justify all types of means. For instance, he held that cruel actions should be swift, effective and short-lived.
7. This was especially emphasized by K. Davis and R. L. Blomstrom, *Business and its Environment* (New York: McGraw-Hill, 1966).
8. R. Spaemann, *Basic Moral Concepts* (London: Routledge, 1989), p. 38.
9. J. Rawls, *A Theory of Justice* (Oxford: Oxford University Press, 1971 [1999]), p. 3.
10. Letter to Bishop Mandell Creighton, 3 April 1887. Quoted in *Oxford Concise Dictionary of Quotations*, 3rd ed. (Oxford: Oxford University Press, 1993), pp. 1, 5, from L. Creighton, *Life and Letters of Mandell Creighton* (1904), vol. 1, Chapter 13.
11. For a discussion, see D. Melé and J. M. Rosanas, 'Power, Freedom and Authority in Management: Mary Parker Follett's "Power-With"', *Philosophy of Management*, vol. 3, no. 2, 2003, pp. 35–46.
12. P. Drucker, *The New Realities* (London: Mandarin, 1990), p. 221.
13. D. Melé, '"Human Quality Treatment": Five Organizational Levels', *Journal of Business Ethics*, vol. 120, no. 4, 2014, pp. 457–71, see p. 462.
14. Melé, '"Human Quality Treatment"'.

15. This point has been developed by D. J. Moberg, 'Role Models and Moral Exemplars: How Employees Acquire Virtues by Observing Others?', *Business Ethics Quarterly*, vol. 10, no. 3, 2000, pp. 675–96.
16. H. Mintzberg, *The Nature of Managerial Work* (Englewood Cliffs, NJ: Prentice Hall, 1973), and 'The Manager's Job: Folklore and Fact', *Harvard Business Review*, vol. 53, no. 4, 1975, pp. 49–61.
17. See J. Gaa and P. Dunmore, 'The Ethics of Earnings Management', *Chartered Accountants Journal*, vol. 86, no. 8, 2007, pp. 60–2.
18. https://unglobalcompact.org/what-is-gc/mission/principles. (Accessed on 4 June 2025).
19. OECD Guidelines for Multinational Enterprises on Responsible Business Conduct, 8 June 2023: https://www.oecd.org/en/publications/oecd-guidelines-for-multinational-enterprises-on-responsible-business-conduct_81f92357-en.html; https://unglobalcompact.org/what-is-gc/mission/principles. (Both accessed on 4 June 2025).
20. https://iso26000sgn.org/iso-26000/about-iso26000/the-iso-26000-framework/. (Accessed on 4 June 2025).
21. https://equator-principles.com/. (Accessed on 4 June 2025).
22. R. Kaku, 'The Path of Kyosei', *Harvard Business Review*, vol. 75, no. 1997, pp. 55–62.
23. https://www.cauxroundtable.org/principles/. (Accessed on 30 October 2024).
24. https://www.business-humanrights.org/en/big-issues/governing-business-human-rights/un-guiding-principles/. (Accessed on 4 June 2025).
25. Sources: J. M. Sinde, C. G. d. Andoin, J. R. Ayastuy and J. E. Abasolo, 'El Modelo Inclusivo Participativo de Empresa en el marco de una Economía de Cooperación (The Inclusive Participatory Company Model in the Framework of a Cooperation Economy)', *Ekonomiaz*, vol. no. 101, 2022; G. Cheney, *Values at Work: Employee Participation Meets Market Pressure at Mondragón* (Ithaca, NY: Cornell University Press, 1999).
26. N. Romeo, 'How Mondragón Became the World's Largest Co-Op', *New Yorker*, 27 August, 2022: https://www.newyorker.com/business/currency/how-mondragon-became-the-worlds-largest-co-op. (Accessed on 4 June 2025).
27. Pius XI affirmed: 'in the present condition of human society that, so far as is possible, the work-contract be somewhat modified by a partnership-contract, as is already being done in various ways and with no small advantage to workers and owners. Workers and other employees thus become sharers in ownership or management or participate in some fashion in the profits received' (Pius XI, *Encyclical Letter 'Quadragesimo anno'*: (1931) no. 65, https://www.vatican.va/content/pius-xi/en/encyclicals/documents/hf_p-xi_enc_19310515_quadragesimo-anno.html. (Accessed on 4 June 2025).
28. A. A. Berle Jr and G. C. Means, *The Modern Corporation and Private Property* (New York and Chicago: Harcourt, Brace & World, [1968]). For a recent edition see, e.g., A. A. Berle Jr and G. C. Means, *The Modern Corporation and Private Property*, with a new introduction by L. Murray Weidenbaum and Mark Jensen (New Brunswick, NJ: Transaction Publishers, 1991 [1932]).
29. See K. M. Eisenhardt, 'Agency Theory: An Assessment and Review', *Academy of Management Review*, vol. 14, no. 1, 1989, pp. 57–74.
30. Cadbury Committee, *Report of the Committee on the Financial Aspects of Corporate Governance* (London: GEE, 1992).
31. G20/OECD Principles of Corporate Governance 2023, OECD Publishing, Paris: https://doi.org/10.1787/ed750b30-en. (Accessed on 4 June 2025). These principles are grouped in six chapters: (1) Ensuring the basis for an effective corporate governance framework; (2) The rights

and equitable treatment of shareholders and key ownership functions; (3) Institutional investors, stock markets, and other intermediaries; (4) The role of stakeholders in corporate governance; (5) Disclosure and transparency; and (6) Sustainability and resilience.

32. R. A. G. Monks and N. Minow, *Corporate Governance* (Hoboken, NJ: John Wiley & Sons, 2011); M. Goergen, *Corporate Governance: A Global Perspective* (Boston, MA: Cengage Learning EMEA, 2018); and B. Tricker, *Corporate Governance: Principles, Policies, and Practices* (Oxford: Oxford University Press, 2019).
33. J. C. Bogle, 'Reflections on CEO Compensation', *Academy of Management Perspectives*, vol. 22, no. 2, 2008, pp. 21–5, see p. 25.
34. R. Milne, 'Scandinavia: Model Management. Swedish Business is Being Cast as a Model for Long-term Stability and Growth', *Financial Times Online*, 20 March 2013: https://www.ft.com/content/e0f4bc0e-81c2-11e2-ae78-00144feabdc0. (Accessed on 4 June 2025).
35. All names are fictitious.

9

Institutional Ethics and Organizational Ethical Culture

I think that we have to reinvent capitalism around a sense of mission – it can improve society by improving the lives of people.[1]

ROGER W. SANT (1931–), Co-Founder of AES Corporation

Overview

Institutionalizing ethics in business refers to various methods of creating a structured framework and corporate culture that promotes ethical behaviour within the company. This process includes ensuring compliance with regulatory requirements and fostering a commitment to integrity and ethical excellence. Institutionalizing ethics involves formal statements and practices, but ethics is truly institutionalized when it becomes embedded in the company's culture.

Section A discusses corporate statements that express the company's commitment to ethics in corporate life. This includes the established corporate purpose or mission, along with corporate values, guiding principles and codes of conduct. Policies that promote compliance, integrity and formation programmes are also highlighted.

Section B analyses organizational culture, which consists of the shared values, beliefs, and practices that shape employee interactions and decision-making. Organizational ethical culture is both a component and a result of institutionalizing ethics within a company, although many other factors contribute to shaping a particular culture. These factors are examined with an emphasis on the importance of developing an organizational culture deeply rooted in ethical values. The section concludes by discussing how ethics can be integrated into strategy and organizational structures in ways that foster the development of an ethical organizational culture.

Chapter Aims

After reading this chapter you should be able to:

- Be aware of the institutionalizing of ethics within companies.
- Reflect on the place of ethics in corporate statements.

- Understand corporate values and the guiding principles for business.
- Be familiar with objectives and contents of codes of conduct.
- Gain knowledge on compliance and ethics training programmes.
- Have familiarity with the concept of corporate culture.
- Consider the 'gap' between the existing and the desired organizational ethical culture.
- Discuss which factors contribute to shaping ethical corporate cultures.
- Reflect on the ethical dimension of the competitive strategy.
- Discuss how to introduce ethics in the formal organization.
- Ponder the relevance of ethics in the informal organization.

Historical Case #9

Cambridge Analytica operational techniques[2]

Cambridge Analytica (CA) was a consulting firm established in 2013 as a branch of the British company *Strategic Communication Laboratories* (SCL), known for its communication research and analysis. SCL developed methodologies to help clients understand target audiences on behavioural, attitudinal and socio-demographic levels, using social sciences combined with local field teams to gather and interpret comprehensive data.

Alexander Nix, a former director at SCL, co-founded CA with two partners. The company was set up to specialize in data collection and analysis for advertising and political campaigns. Nix served as CEO and became the prominent face of the firm. The founders had significant political and business connections, securing crucial financial backing mainly from the American Mercer family, which was instrumental in the company's growth.

Cambridge Analytica described its purpose as 'using data to change audience behaviour'. It emphasized improving marketing effectiveness by altering consumer behaviour (data-driven marketing) and enhancing electoral influence by understanding electorates better (data-driven campaigns).[3]

CA utilized data mining, brokerage and analysis to create detailed voter and consumer profiles. A key technique was psychographic profiling, categorizing individuals based on psychological traits to tailor political advertisements and marketing strategies to predict and influence voting behaviours.

To refine its methodology, CA collaborated with Aleksandr Kogan, a scientist affiliated with the University of Cambridge as Lecturer and Senior Researcher in Psychology, who went on to have a relevant role in the development of the operational techniques of CA.

The leadership at Cambridge Analytica was characterized by an aggressive, innovative approach, prioritizing campaign victories and client acquisition over other considerations. This resulted in a high-pressure work environment where success was measured by the efficacy of influence campaigns.

Initially focusing on US political campaigns, CA quickly became involved in numerous campaigns in several countries, including some American presidential campaigns. CA was attracting clients with its advanced data analytics and targeted advertising capabilities.

Aleksandr Kogan created the Global Science Research (GSR) group, which developed the app 'This Is Your Digital Life', designed to gather data by having users answer a series of questions to build psychological profiles. Approximately 300,000 people installed this app. The app not only collected personal data from its users but also accessed data from its Facebook friends via Facebook's Open Graph platform. This allowed Cambridge Analytica to harvest data from up to 87 million Facebook profiles.

Some of the app's users gave the app permission to access their *News Feed* (a web feed feature for the social network), timeline and messages. The data was detailed enough for Cambridge Analytica to create psychographic profiles of the subjects of the data and the locations of each person. For a given political campaign, each profile's information suggested what type of advertisement would be most effective to persuade a particular person in a particular location for some political event.

It arranged an informed consent process, suggesting that the data collected was for academic purposes. However, the app's data collection capabilities extended beyond what was initially disclosed, as it also gathered information from users' friends without their explicit consent.

In 2016, American senator Ted Cruz hired Cambridge Analytica to aid his presidential campaign. The Federal Election Commission reported that Cruz paid the company $5.8 million in services. It was then that Cambridge Analytica started to create individual psychographic profiles. This data was then used to create tailored advertisements for each person to sway them into voting for Cruz. Donald Trump's 2016 presidential campaign also used the harvested data to build psychographic profiles, determining users' personality traits based on their Facebook activity. The campaign team used this information as a micro-targeting technique, displaying customized messages about Trump to different US voters on various digital platforms.

This significant data breach was revealed on 17 March 2018, by the *Guardian* and the *New York Times* based on information from Christopher Wylie, a former Cambridge Analytica employee. Wylie explained that the data was used as a psychological weapon in political campaigns, influencing voter behaviour without the users' knowledge.

Further controversy arose when undercover footage showed Alexander Nix, CEO of Cambridge Analytica, discussing the use of unethical tactics, including honey traps and bribery, to sway elections globally. This scandal led to a massive fallout, including Facebook losing more than $119 billion in stock value in the next few days and widespread public and governmental scrutiny.

Following the revelations, Mark Zuckerberg, founder and CEO of Facebook, testified before the US Congress on 10 April 2018. He acknowledged that it was a personal mistake not to have done more to prevent Facebook from being used to harm, mentioning issues like fake news, foreign interference in elections and hate speech. Zuckerberg apologized publicly for the data breach, stating, 'It was my mistake, and I'm sorry. I started Facebook, I run it, and I'm responsible for what happens here.'

Zuckerberg added that Kogan's app on personality was able to retrieve Facebook information, including that of the users' friends, but it was not until 2015 that Zuckerberg learned that these users' information was shared by Kogan with Cambridge Analytica. Zuckerberg also clarified that Facebook had requested Cambridge Analytica to delete the data obtained through Kogan's app. However, it was only in 2018, following investigative reports by social media, that it became evident the data had not been fully deleted. This led to further legal and regulatory actions against Cambridge Analytica and Facebook.

In the aftermath, Cambridge Analytica was dissolved (2018), and its executives, including Alexander Nix and Aleksandr Kogan, faced legal and regulatory consequences. Nix was barred from serving as a director in UK companies for seven years, and Facebook was fined $5 billion by the Federal Trade Commission for its role in the data breach.

In July 2019, it was announced that the Federal Trade Commission had fined Facebook $5 billion for its privacy violations. In October 2019, Facebook agreed to pay a £500,000 fine to the UK Information Commissioner's Office for exposing its users' data to a 'serious risk of harm'.

Questions

1. What values of Cambridge Analytica define the firm's identity?
2. What ethical issues do you identify in this case study? Why?
3. To what extent do you believe digital surveillance and data-driven influence threaten personal privacy and democratic values? How would you argue your position from an ethical perspective?

SECTION A. INSTITUTIONALIZING ETHICS INTO THE COMPANY

The aim of institutionalizing ethics within companies is to embed ethics in daily business life through structured frameworks and personal behaviours that encourage ethical conduct, decision-making and accountability at all levels. The process of institutionalizing ethics goes beyond compliance with legal requirements, aiming to foster a culture of integrity and ethical excellence within the company.

Institutionalizing ethics includes both formal and informal elements, established at different levels within the organization. Some current formal practices for institutionalizing ethics include the following:

- *Corporate statements* with significant ethical messages, outlining values, principles and ethical standards. These often include the corporate purpose or mission, and corporate values or principles (9.1).
- *Ethics policies, procedures and often a code of conduct*, with protocols and specific policies on relevant ethical issues, such as how to address conflicts of interest, anti-corruption norms, measures to prevent harassment and criteria for maintaining confidentiality. Frequently, a code of conduct specifies basic rules for good behaviour (9.2).
- *Training programmes on ethics*, which may cover how to apply the company's code of conduct in particular situations, how to handle ethical dilemmas, or how to apply virtues in business life. These programmes are often part of wider compliance or ethics policies (9.3).
- *Communication channels* to disseminate ethical policies, updates and resources, as well as to report irregularities within the company (for example, internal whistleblowing).
- *Systems for monitoring ethical behaviour*, including audits, surveys and reporting systems.
- *Accountability measures*, connected with monitoring systems, which define clear consequences for ethical breaches (including disciplinary actions) and provide recognition for ethical behaviour, along with mechanisms to implement them.
- *Leadership exemplarity*. Another essential means of embedding ethics within a company – though more difficult to formalize – is rooted in the personal virtues of managers and other leading persons. Leaders influence the organization by serving as role models, demonstrating a commitment to ethical standards and virtuous behaviour. Their actions set the tone for the organization and signal the importance of integrity. Leaders are often highly influential in fostering an organizational ethical culture (9.4), especially by ensuring that moral considerations are integrated into every business decision and by treating people with justice and benevolence. This approach not only promotes ethical behaviour but also reinforces the organization's commitment to upholding its values in all aspects of its operations.
- *Establishing an ethics office or compliance office* within the company, and more recently an *ethics and compliance office*. Traditionally, ethics offices focus on promoting a culture of values, integrity and responsible decision-making, while compliance offices focus more on legal and regulatory adherence or corporate codes of conduct. In some countries, particularly in Europe, there is also a growing trend of linking compliance with corporate ethics and sustainability. *Ethics and compliance offices* aim to combine both functions.

The ethics office is quite common in the USA and in other countries, sometimes combined with compliance, with a well-established role for the *chief ethics officer*. In the European Union, compliance offices are more common, likely due to the large number of regulations that recommend specific roles for the *compliance officer*. These regulations include EU directives on data protection, anti-money laundering and corporate sustainability reporting. In the Asia-Pacific region, Singapore, Hong Kong and Australia are leading in compliance adoption, as is Japan, where compliance is increasingly tied to corporate governance reforms. In Latin America, there is growing recognition of compliance, although it is less institutionalized than in the US or Europe. In Africa, compliance is emerging as a response to global regulations and foreign investment, particularly in multinational subsidiaries or sectors such as banking and extractives.

Ethics and compliance offices share the role of promoting ethical behaviour and ensuring adherence to laws and regulations within an organization. They oversee ethics-related issues and provide ethical guidance. Typically, their responsibilities also include organizing ethics training and managing communication channels on ethical issues, in addition to creating procedures for monitoring ethical behaviour. Companies may also establish a *hotline* to report irregularities, seek advice or request ethical certification from suppliers, among other measures.

9.1 Institutional statements

Corporate purpose or mission

As has already been mentioned (7.8), many companies have defined and publicized their particular purpose – the way a company contributes to a good society, with certain ethical content – as a supposed driver for their entire corporate activity. Some firms present their particular purpose as the corporate mission, although nowadays a vast number have a synthetic purpose or a short mission statement, which express only some crucial feature of the company, often as a communication technique. In this line, expressing the mission statement is generally no longer than eight or nine words. For example, Tesla, the well-known electric vehicles manufacturer, states its mission in these terms: 'To accelerate the world's transition to sustainable energy,'[4] and the technological company Google affirms, 'Our mission is to organize the world's information and make it universally accessible and useful'[5] (see other statements on corporate purpose in 7.8). However, some companies such as Medtronic, a global medical technology company, have a detailed mission statement (Table 9.1); Medtronic's has remained unchanged since its enactment in 1962.

While corporate purpose or mission statements are quite usual in large corporations, which tend to publicly announce them, small and medium-sized companies might not have any written expression. However, every company is managed according to a certain idea about what they propose to do even when it isn't explicitly declared.

There are companies that take corporate purpose or mission so seriously that the whole of the management and corporate governance are based on it. In this sense, 'management by missions' has been proposed[7] as a compass for every corporate activity. This approach involves sharing the corporate mission with all levels of the company. This includes specifying the mission in such a way that each area of responsibility within an organization has its own mission, which is consistent with the mission of the whole company. Corporate mission is, then, the basis for the formulation of *business strategy* (9.6), by which a company selects its long-term goals and decides upon the

Table 9.1 Medtronic mission statement[6]

OUR MISSION
1. To contribute to human welfare by application of biomedical engineering in the research, design, manufacture, and sale of instruments or appliances that alleviate pain, restore health, and extend life.
2. To direct our growth in the areas of biomedical engineering where we display maximum strength and ability; to gather people and facilities that tend to augment these areas; to continuously build on these areas through education and knowledge assimilation; to avoid participation in areas where we cannot make unique and worthy contributions.
3. To strive without reserve for the greatest possible reliability and quality in our products; to be the unsurpassed standard of comparison and to be recognized as a company of dedication, honesty, integrity, and service.
4. To make a fair profit on current operations to meet our obligations, sustain our growth, and reach our goals.
5. To recognize the personal worth of all employees by providing an employment framework that allows personal satisfaction in work accomplished, security, advancement opportunity, and means to share in the company's success.
6. To maintain good citizenship as a company.

allocation of resources. Strategy is generally related to meeting market needs and stakeholder expectations, as well as to obtaining competitive advantage. This can include a set of multi-year programmes that are subsequently developed and entail objectives, policies, plans, organizational structure and the corresponding implementation. Under this approach, corporate mission also informs corporate structure in executing strategies and organizational policies, including managerial systems, procedures, practices and day-by-day management.

Corporate vision

Some companies have 'corporate vision', which is added to the mission. Corporate vision defines what the organization intends to be in the future. It reflects the view of the organization's desired characteristics and what it would be likely to achieve in the mid or long term. In this sense, we talk of 'visionary companies', whose future is focused on magnanimity or presented through original ideas, innovative perspectives and even giving a magnanimous purpose. Corporate vision is therefore different from mission, although there is often confusion between the two. While mission explains what the organization is doing now, vision is a description of aspiration.

Corporate vision is frequently presented through a few challenging and easily remembered targets or concepts to encourage people within the organization to advance towards a certain desirable form of conduct or goals. Thus, Procter & Gamble defines its vision as 'Be, and be recognized as, the best consumer products and services company in the world.'[8] Some companies combine both vision and mission. This is true in the case of Toyota, the famous Japanese car manufacturer, which affirms: 'We aspire to realize the vision of Mobility for All, while pursuing our mission to Produce Happiness for All through creating the value of the Toyota Way based on our spirit of foundation. This is the path to an ideal society, and it's pioneered by each and every team member.'[9]

Corporate values and guiding principles

Some companies have an explicit set of *corporate values*. In smaller companies, these values tend to be implicit. Corporate values are usually expressed as a set of meaningful words or short, easy-to-understand sentences, perhaps accompanied by a brief explanation. Ideally, all employees should hold corporate values and translate them into specific actions and decisions that they should make.

Corporate core values can vary significantly from company to company, depending on the industry, national culture and the specific features of each organization and leadership.[10] There are frequent corporate values which can be categorized in three groups (Table 9.2): people treatment (integrity, respect, teamworking or collaboration), societal responsibility (accountability, sustainability and community involvement) and operational quality (excellence, innovation and agility). People treatment and societal responsibility entail a clear ethical content, while operational quality directly focuses on techno-economic results. However, the latter still possesses an ethical content since it instrumentally contributes to the common good (7.7).

Some companies have *guiding principles*, instead of or in addition to values, describing specific patterns to be followed by people involved in the organization. Procter & Gamble is one of these companies, with both values and guiding principles. The espoused core values of this firm are *integrity*, *leadership*, *ownership* (acting as owners), *a passion for winning* and *trust*. Additionally, it presents, as guiding principles, the following:

> We Show Respect for All Individuals / The Interests of the Company and the Individuals are Inseparable / We are Strategically Focused on our Work / Innovation is the Cornerstone of Our Success / We Value Mastery / We Seek to be the Best / We Are Externally Focused / We Seek to Be the Best / Mutual Interdependence is a Way of Life.[11]

Table 9.2 Common corporate values

Category	Values
People treatment	*Integrity*, meaning honesty, ethical behaviour and transparency, and the prioritization of doing the right thing even when it's challenging. *Respect*, requiring the recognition of dignity and valuing of diversity, with which all groups related to the company should be treated. *Teamwork* (or collaboration), fostering collaboration and cooperation among employees to achieve common goals.
Societal responsibility	*Accountability*, taking responsibility for actions and outcomes, and being transparent about successes and failures. *Sustainability*, assuming environmentally friendly practices and long-term ecological stewardship. *Community involvement*, engaging with and contributing to the communities in which the company operates.
Operative quality	*Customer-oriented*, focusing on the customer in business decisions and operations, and exceeding customer expectations and needs. *Excellence*, striving for the highest standards in product quality, service delivery, continuous improvement and overall performance. *Innovation*, encouraging creativity, adaptivity and imaginative new ideas to drive growth and stay competitive in the market. *Agility*, adapting quickly to changes in the market or industry environment.

Corporate core values and/or guiding principles, together with corporate purpose or mission/vision, when taken seriously, provide a clear indication of what sometimes is called 'the business philosophy' of each company, and is an important step towards making ethics present throughout the entire company, including in its corporate governance, management and organizational activity. In practice, however, not all companies take corporate ethical statements so seriously. Sometimes they are simply a matter of corporate image used for marketing purposes – in colloquial terms 'window dressing' or 'greenwashing.' Enron (Historical Case #1) is a paradigmatic example of neglecting corporate values.

9.2 Codes of business conduct

A code of business conduct, sometimes called a code of ethics, is a corporate document that develops the core values or the guiding principles of a firm, adding guidance for ethical behaviour to regulatory requirements. It specifies criteria and rules for the correct handling of business dilemmas, issues or situations in which it is considered particularly important that managers and staff follow certain procedures approved by the company's management. A great number of companies, particularly the largest ones, have implemented codes of conduct. In some countries and industries, they are legally mandated for listed companies.

The immediate goal of these codes is to articulate the institutionalization of certain rules of conduct within the firm and to facilitate their internalization by managers and staff. Associated with this goal, a code of conduct also seeks to comply with relevant laws and regulations, thereby reducing the risk of legal penalties and protecting the organization's reputation. Codes of conduct also help identify and mitigate risks associated with unethical behaviour, such as fraud, corruption and conflicts of interest, and help to build ethical culture in the company. Codes sometimes go even further, presenting ethical requirements for suppliers.

Benefits and objections of codes of conduct

Although a code of conduct is not a panacea for improving ethics within organizations, having one can bring several benefits for the firm. Among them are the following:

- *Helping to articulate values and criteria*: This is especially relevant during the process of writing the code. A thoughtful debate can strengthen the commonality of goals and interests among the firm's areas and opens a process of reflection on whether these values can be manifested in concrete aspects and situations; that is, whether they are really operational.
- *Sending an ethical message to the organization*: The serious implementation of a code of conduct sends a message to the organization about the behaviour that is expected. While accepting that financial targets and income statements are important, it is a warning that not all means are licit for achieving these goals.

- *Providing guidelines for decision-making and dilemmas*: Codes facilitate professional and managerial decision-making in accordance with ethical criteria for anyone who is part of the firm. They also provide guidance when one is faced with dilemmas. In this sense, they can help provide a framework for the employees' ethical judgement when exceptional situations arise.
- *Preventing abuses within the firm*: A code provides employees with a tool that limits their supervisor's or manager's power, which they can use to affirm that certain conduct is not permitted.
- *Fostering corporate identity*: A code can be a tool used to reinforce corporate identity and to favour an ethical culture (see Section B). This is particularly beneficial for large or multinational firms and during merger or takeover processes, where cultural clashes can arise.
- *Avoiding risks and helping to avoid litigation against the firm*: Codes provide means to help the firm avoid costly litigations due to employee wrongdoing.
- *Favouring corporate reputation*: A code gives a public image of commitment and responsibility, which favours corporate reputation. This is an intangible asset that is increasingly valued. It is particularly important for large firms that carry high societal expectations.

One possible objection to a code of conduct is that it might conflict with the personal values of the organization's members. In practice, this objection is not generally of great concern if the code has been drawn from universal ethical values, good practices of the best companies and recommendations of people and institutions of acknowledged moral reputation. Additionally, if the personal values or virtues of those members are weak, the company itself could have problems with misbehaviour or crimes. This is why a firm might want to implement a code of conduct that reinforces certain minimum ethical standards for its people. A wide-ranging dialogue in drawing up the code facilitates the understanding and acceptance of its contents.

In the case of operating in countries with different cultures, it might be possible to draw up a code that is firm on certain minimum ethical standards that must be upheld at all times (respect for human dignity, human rights and other basic ethical norms for business) but could be flexible on lesser points. This allows a degree of elasticity in interpretation without losing sight of the basic values on which the code is founded.

Basing the code on universal ethical values also offers the advantage of making it easier to achieve consensus on the content and to be more certain of doing what is right. Indeed, most multinational companies are interested in developing a code of conduct: it enables them to integrate all of their subsidiaries more securely into the company's philosophy. To manage cultural diversity within the firm, it is not enough merely to acknowledge and respect it: it is also necessary to standardize the criteria for action to ensure that the firm retains credibility and offers consistently good service everywhere.

Frequent contents of corporate code of conducts

Another important element in designing a business code of conduct is its scope and contents. A corporate code of conduct is not a compendium of ethical norms; it expresses only what top management considers should be done for the good of the company and reflects what a company expects from its employees. It is recommended that a tailored code of conduct covers not everything, but the most usual issues and misbehaviours in the industry. However, there are usual contents in most business codes of conduct to be considered. Among them:

- *Compliance with laws and regulations*, including anti-bribery and anti-corruption laws.
- *Dealing with conflicts of interests*.
- *Keeping confidentiality and data protection*.
- *Fair treatment* of all employees, customers and partners, and prohibiting discrimination and harassment in any form, maintaining a safe and healthy work environment.
- *Reporting ethical violations*, including details about whistleblower protections and the investigation process.
- *Criteria on sustainable practices* and minimizing environmental impact.

It is highly desirable to start the code of conduct by explaining why the code exists, its importance, its role in guiding the behaviour of employees and other groups related to the company and the founding values and ethical principles supporting the code rules. This would help avoid seeing the code as a list of duties. The code should also include potential disciplinary measures for when it is breached.

Implementation of a code of conduct

It is frequently asked whether codes are effective for improving ethical behaviour or, at least, for preventing misbehaviour.[12] Empirical research shows conflicting results. Some find satisfactory results, but others are more pessimistic.[13] Having a code of conduct in place is no guarantee that everyone will act ethically at all times. However, it cannot be definitively said that codes do not dissuade people from unethical conduct. Perhaps the key is using these codes along with other means,[14] within the context of a real corporate ethical perspective applied to the whole organization.

A significant element for effectiveness of a code of conduct is its *implementation*. For the effective implementation of a code, several recommendations can be given:

- *A careful elaboration of the code*: In practice, there are several elements recommended in the elaboration of a code to contribute to its effectiveness, such as it being well written and understandable, ensuring it provides a clear, achievable and realistic purpose, the inclusion of a written senior management commitment and a strong motivation for its implementation.
- *Involvement of the top management*: Top management has a role in the development of the code and its implementation and roll-out. The common method is a letter from the CEO introducing the code. Additional means are also employed: a special event organized for the presentation, a video from the CEO showing a firm commitment, as well as frequent messages from senior management to the members of the organization stressing the code's validity.

- *A broad and effective process of communication and dissemination*: This can be achieved, for instance, through presentations, workshops and seminars, videos, posters, a corporate website or an annual mailing to all employees.
- *Creating the position of ethical affairs officer or 'head of compliance'*: This is a specific senior management position with the mission of monitoring and implementing the code, including all matters related to communicating, training in and applying it.
- *Providing a direct line*: This could be a telephone number or email address for questions and remarks to be forwarded to the ethics officer, or even a way of reporting misbehaviours or violations of the code. In the latter case, anonymity or confidentiality should be guaranteed.
- *Training*: For a code to be effective, information and training are required. These can form part of a compliance programme (9.3).
- *Monitoring and auditing*: This includes several means for monitoring and reporting how the code is applied and auditing misbehaviours, either inside or outside of the company.

9.3 Integrity and compliance programmes

Avoiding misconduct and promoting positive values have led many companies to establish corporate *ethics* or *integrity programmes and compliance programmes*.[15] These programmes are systematic approaches that include policies, procedures, training, monitoring and enforcement mechanisms designed to promote ethical behaviour within companies. Compliance and ethical programmes share the common goal of promoting ethical conduct, but they differ significantly in their focus, methods and underlying philosophies.

Firstly, *compliance programmes* appeared focused on ensuring legal and regulatory adherence – *doing what is required*. Later, *ethics* or *integrity programmes* were proposed, aimed to foster an internalized commitment to values – *doing what is good* – encouraging virtuous behaviour even when laws are silent. For years, compliance and ethical programmes have remained two distinct approaches, but the current tendency is to combine compliance with ethical values and integrity, as it is discussed next.

Rule-based or values-based programmes?

Corporate compliance programmes

Since their emergence in the 1990s, *compliance programmes* have aimed to minimize legal risks and protect an organization's reputation. The concept of corporate compliance became widely recognized after the introduction of the *US Sentencing Guidelines for Organizations*[16] in 1991, which encouraged organizations to implement appropriate compliance programmes to prevent wrongdoing. These guidelines also offered leniency to organizations that could demonstrate proactive compliance efforts.

Since then, many companies have integrated legal requirements within their corporate codes of ethics and established ethics offices within their corporate structures. In Europe, legislation requiring corporate compliance began to emerge in the 2000s and has been widely implemented.

A traditional compliance programme involves establishing a set of rules or requirements that ensure everyone in the organization follows governmental regulations and some ethical standards beyond legality, often articulated through a code of conduct. These include internal policies such as whistleblower protections, anti-corruption measures and sanctions for non-compliance. International standards for compliance management are now well established.[17]

Compliance training focuses on educating employees about what they must do to avoid negative consequences. Discussing the corporate code of conduct, reviewing standards and exploring ethical dilemmas are effective training methodologies. Research suggests that ethics training – especially compliance-focused – can reduce unethical and illegal behaviour, increase awareness of ethical issues, improve decision-making, and enhance employee commitment.

Corporate compliance is typically managed by a dedicated compliance office, staffed by professionals trained to identify and prevent risks, monitor effectiveness, resolve issues and advise on regulatory matters. In some countries, there are certified professionals specifically trained for this function. Compliance programmes also involve training employees, communicating rules internally and externally, monitoring and auditing adherence, and reporting and corrective measures.

Compliance programmes also support building an anti-corruption culture, particularly in organizations with a history of misconduct or high risk of non-compliance. While compliance training reduces discretion and emphasizes auditing, controls, and penalties, ethics training also includes leadership, accountability, systems thinking and moral decision-making.

The effectiveness of compliance programmes increases when there is genuine leadership commitment and consistency in application. Conversely, their credibility may suffer if employees perceive these programmes as tools to protect top management or serve the employer's self-interest. Some analyses show that compliance programmes are complex and vulnerable if not sufficiently resourced.

Corporate ethics programmes

These programmes, sometimes termed *integrity programmes*, aim to promote ethical behaviour by fostering a culture of integrity, going beyond legal compliance. A compliance approach focused on avoiding legal sanctions is not enough to create a climate that supports ethical conduct across the organization. Thus, some advocated for an integrity-based approach to ethics management, which combines compliance with managerial responsibility for promoting ethical behaviour and building a fully ethical culture.

The underlying philosophy of ethics or integrity programmes contrasts with that of compliance. The compliance view often assumes people act primarily out of self-interest and respond to personal costs and benefits. In contrast, the ethics approach recognizes individuals as capable of self-governance in accordance with principles. Obeying rules is seen as a positive aspect of organizational life, not just an external imposition.

Ethics-based training also differs from compliance. It focuses on building trust, fostering collaboration, enhancing organizational reputation and encouraging aspirational good behaviour. Methods include case studies, ethical dilemmas, reflective workshops and narratives highlighting the role of leaders as moral exemplars. Ethics-based programmes aim to create a culture where ethical behaviour is valued, supported and rewarded.

Compliance and integrity development

Over time, there has been growing recognition that compliance alone is insufficient. To address these limitations, scholars such as Vaccaro[18] argue that compliance must emphasize the importance of people – employees, customers and partners. Fontrodona and Sanz add that 'the best way of avoiding unethical behaviour is not to define what not to do in a strictly legalistic sense, but rather to encourage the desired positive behaviour that leads to integrity for all'.[19] Others, like Harrison (focusing on healthcare), are even more direct: 'We not only need ethics with compliance – we need an ethics that is not just restated compliance. Compliance is about rules and laws, but rules and laws do not produce ethical people – or even, in many cases, compliant people.'[20]

The current tendency is to recognize that both compliance and integrity development are necessary: rules to prevent misconduct, while values and virtues create a culture of trust and long-term sustainability.

Organizations like the OECD and UN Global Compact and International Organization for Standardization (ISO) 37301 promote compliance and integrity. Similarly, the US Department of Justice and European Commission stress the importance of integrity in organizational culture and leadership when evaluating compliance effectiveness. An increasing number of companies and public bodies are adopting these programmes.

Major corporations such as Siemens, Unilever and Johnson & Johnson have explicitly integrated ethics, compliance and integrity into unified frameworks. E&C programmes embed ethical values into compliance training,[21] for instance, by aligning codes of conduct with core values and virtues, integrating ethical values into decision-making frameworks, and using diverse training methods rooted in real-life cases. Such programmes help avoid a 'tick-the-box' mentality and shift from an authoritarian message ('if you don't follow the rules, you'll be fired') to a persuasive argument ('if you live these values, we all benefit'), blending what the rules require with why it matters ethically. As with all programmes, their effectiveness depends heavily on genuine top management commitment.[22]

Benefits of these programmes may include enhancing employee engagement and a sense of ethical ownership, building organizational trust and resilience, improving corporate reputation and stakeholder relationships.

Business Ethics in Action #9

Bill George's business vision[23]

Bill George (1941–) was elected CEO of Medtronic in 1981 to 2001, and board chair from 1996 to 2002, with excellent and sustained results.

Medtronic Inc. is a leading global medical technology company, based in Minneapolis. Founded by Earl Bakken in 1949 as a very small company repairing medical equipment, it was soon modifying equipment and producing new devices needed for special tests. In 1957, they invented the world's first wearable pacemaker. In the following years, the company grew with innovative high-tech products and with its entrance into new markets. In 1962, Earl Bakken, the founder, wrote the Medtronic Mission, which would become a cornerstone for the company. It has not been changed over time, and the same mission can be found on the Medtronic corporate website today (see Table 9.1). As at 2025, Medtronic develops and manufactures healthcare technologies and therapies, operates in more than 150 countries and employs over 95,000 people.

Bill George's vision of business was shaped in his youth. A particularly influential moment in his life was the now-famous line from US President John F. Kennedy's inaugural address: 'Ask not what your country can do for you. Ask what you can do for your country.' Inspired by these words, George asked himself what he could do for his country. Years later, he confessed:

> I decided to concentrate my efforts on the world of business because of the enormous capacity of the free-enterprise system to organize people to make a difference in the lives of the people it serves. In those days I had a vision of becoming an ethical, values-cantered leader running a major corporation, and, rather immodestly, influencing my peers to be ethical and values-centered.[24]

In 1966, he gained an MBA from Harvard Business School, where he was in the top five of the class.

He started his career in the US Department of Defence and later served as a senior executive of Litton Industries (twenty years) and Honeywell (eleven years). He was a successful and respected executive but not completely happy in Honeywell. George saw himself as a growth-oriented leader, not a turn-around specialist, and he disliked Honeywell's culture. 'Honeywell is so large that the higher up I went, the more isolated I got from customers and employees', he declared. Some years later, he explained in more detail his reasons for leaving the firm:

> The lack of passion for Honeywell's business [...] troubled me. [...] I was out of sync with Honeywell's slow-moving, change-resistant culture. I also found myself becoming more concerned with appearances and my attire than with being myself. [...] I felt I was in a trap from which I couldn't escape. [...] Sure, I was leading, but the purpose of my efforts was not at all clear.

He added: 'I kept thinking about the vision I had in my teenage years: leading a mission-driven, values-centred company where I was passionate about the company's products and the opportunity to serve others.'

After talking with his wife, Penny, both agreed that George's lack of satisfaction in his job was having a negative impact on them. George had previously refused three opportunities to join Medtronic, the first in 1978. He had turned them down mostly because he didn't feel Medtronic was a large-enough company for him (Honeywell was about ten times larger). Now, his wife encouraged him to take another look at the firm, which is what he did. Bill George finally joined Medtronic in 1989.

George was extremely happy to find that Medtronic had several outstanding features in full harmony with his vision. He also liked some customs and traditions of the company, which, to some extent, showed the organizational culture of Medtronic. As he explained: 'I finally had found the place [...] that offered all I wanted: values, passion, and the opportunity to help people suffering from chronic disease [...] throughout my life I have had a passion to make a difference in the world'.[25] George started in Medtronic as president and COO.

Between 1985 and 2001, Medtronic's revenues grew from US$363 million to US$5.5 billion, an 18 per cent compound growth rate. Earnings per share grew from US$0.04 in 1985 to US$1.05 in 2001. This was a compound rate of 23 per cent per annum. The rates of growth of revenues and earnings were very consistent, looking back over the period. In 2000, Medtronic had 26,000 employees and was worth US$63 billion.

Bill George thought that it was a big mistake to make decisions just to increase short-term shareholder value. He called it selling the soul. When the leadership sells its own soul to gain personal advantage and abandons long-held values or its mission, the trust is broken and is likely to never be regained.

He assured us that 'there is a better way to increase long-term shareholder value, but this cannot be the primary objective', and, expanding on this, said, 'it is my belief that corporations are created for a purpose beyond making money. Sustained growth in shareholder value may be the end result, but it cannot be the sole purpose.'[26] He added that 'the real bottom line of the corporation is not earnings per share, but service to humankind. To achieve sustained success, a corporation that thinks about its long-term best interest must lead with its values – from top to bottom.'[27]

George claimed that 'in mission-driven companies, employee motivation comes from believing in the purpose of the work and being part of creating something worthwhile'. He knew that employees seek meaning in work, as they spend more time at work than anything else in their lives. Thus, they have a right to a meaningful job. Fair compensation is not enough. The purpose of their work and a consistent set of values, such as serving customers, quality or integrity, should be remembered by them every day. The other necessary condition for sustainable growth in shareholder value is a sound business strategy that is adaptable to changing business conditions.

Following his experience in Medtronic, George[28] suggested three necessary conditions for long-term growth in shareholder value:

A mission-driven company
A values-centred organization
An adaptable business strategy

He agreed with the concept of serving everyone who had a stake in the organization in the following order: (1) customers; (2) employees; (3) shareholders; (4) suppliers; (5) communities. Nevertheless, these are not independent but interrelated. According to George, a mission-driven company and a values-centred organization fosters motivated employees, who in return bring about product innovation and a superior customer service, which increases customer satisfaction and grows revenue and profit. This permits sustainable increases in shareholder value and in the continuity of the company.

Concerning corporate principles, George stated that certain values must be underlined by the company to gain employee trust and belief in their working purpose. He highlighted the following: serving customers, quality, integrity in business dealings, respect for employees and good citizenship. Integrity is paramount. It is the value that is required in every authentic leader. He maintained that integrity is not just the absence of lying but telling the whole truth, as painful as it may be. He underlines: 'if you don't exercise complete integrity in your interactions, no one can trust you. If they cannot trust you, why would you ever follow you?'[29]

George stresses that the role of leadership is about empowering others on their journeys. He terms this shift 'the transformation from "I" to "We"', which he identifies as the most important process leaders go through in becoming authentic.

George believed that senior managers play an important role in the success of corporations. However, he came to realize that the key to great companies was that they were great teams, or as he liked to say: 'Great teams create great companies.' To this end, George had always tried to surround himself by people who complemented his weaknesses, in knowledge or experience. He appreciated employees and they corresponded.

In the last years of his executive career, George received several awards, including the 'Distinguished Executive of the Year' award from the Academy of Management for his leadership, 'which exemplifies the highest ideals and values', and 'Director of the Year – 2001–2002' from the National Association of Corporate Directors. He was also named one of the 'Top 25 Business Leaders of the Past 25 Years' by the Public Broadcasting Service. After his retirement from Medtronic, George tried to project his vision of leadership and experience in the academic world, becoming Professor of Management Practice, and a Henry B. Arthur Fellow of Ethics at Harvard Business School.

* * *

When discussing his career, George noted that he 'decided to concentrate my efforts on the world of business because of the enormous capacity of the free-enterprise system to organize people to make a difference in the lives of the people it serves'. George, like other people, sought to give a deeper meaning to his life, but did not stop at simply building a career or making money. The famous phrase of John F. Kennedy opened horizons for him, encouraging him to ask himself what he could do for his country, and discovering the value of free enterprise to serve people. This did not prevent him from making a career or earning money, but always in a subordinate way. Finding a company to work for that fits with one's own vision of life and business is not always easy, not even for Bill. Finally, he found what he was looking for in Medtronic, also counting on the support of his wife. Medtronic with

> its long-lasting mission, largely made into a culture, attracted Bill George and other talented people to the organization.
>
> Bill himself, with his leadership, made this culture grow with his daily conduct and also via the tough decisions he made in the Vitatron affair. George shows humility in recognizing his mistakes, such as the choice of the European president of Medtronic for Europe, without checking out his ethical values and virtues. He also displays courage and determination.
>
> His vision of the company is focused on people – customers, consumers and employees – and on sustainable, rather than short-term, profits. And, indeed, that is what he achieved.

SECTION B. ETHICS IN ORGANIZATIONAL CULTURE, STRATEGY AND STRUCTURES

The corporate mission or the purpose of the firm is made effective through strategies and organizational structures, along with other formal and informal elements, which ensure ethics is effective in the institution and help shape organizational culture. The latter is a sociological concept related to real beliefs, values and practices shared by most people within the company.

This section focuses on these topics, from the business ethics perspective, beginning with the notion and development of organizational culture.

9.4 Organizational culture

Culture refers to a large and diverse set of aspects of social life shared by a collective, including beliefs, values, systems of language and communication, along with specific practices. A company has also a culture, mostly intangible, but embedded in the company reality.

Understanding organizational culture

Organizational culture has been described, in very simple but intuitive words, as 'the way we do things around here'[30] and also as an 'amalgam of beliefs, ideology, language, ritual and myth'.[31] The notion of organizational culture was introduced in the early 1980s,[32] when researchers were asking why US corporations had lower levels of performance than their counterparts in Japan, despite productivity methods, technology and other factors being quite similar. The response was that culture, both national and organizational, could explain such differences.[33] Today, there is increasing evidence that organizational culture is a determinant of performance through employee behaviour and decision patterns, especially when the culture is strong.[34] The notion of culture is older among anthropologists, who usually understand it as explicit and implicit patterns of human activity and behaviour shared by all or most members of a group, something that older members of the group usually try to pass on to the young.

Edgar H. Schein, an outstanding author in the field, believes that culture is the most difficult organizational attribute to change.[35] He distinguishes *three levels of organizational culture*:

- The first is *beliefs*, understood as assumptions or convictions about human beings, the firm and its purpose in society, and even a broader vision of the world.
- The second level is *values*. Both beliefs and values form the hidden core of organizational culture.
- The third level consists of *observable manifestations* or *visible artefacts*, such as practices, rites, symbols, norms, organizational climate and other tangible phenomena – including how people interact, how technology is used and the physical layout of workspaces (Figure 9.1).

Organizational culture is ethically relevant since beliefs, values and practices have an ethical dimension and show how people within the organization have internalized ethical values and express virtuous behaviour.

Organizational culture can be easily perceived when dealing with a firm's people, especially when the organization has a long history. There are many kinds of organizational cultures; practically

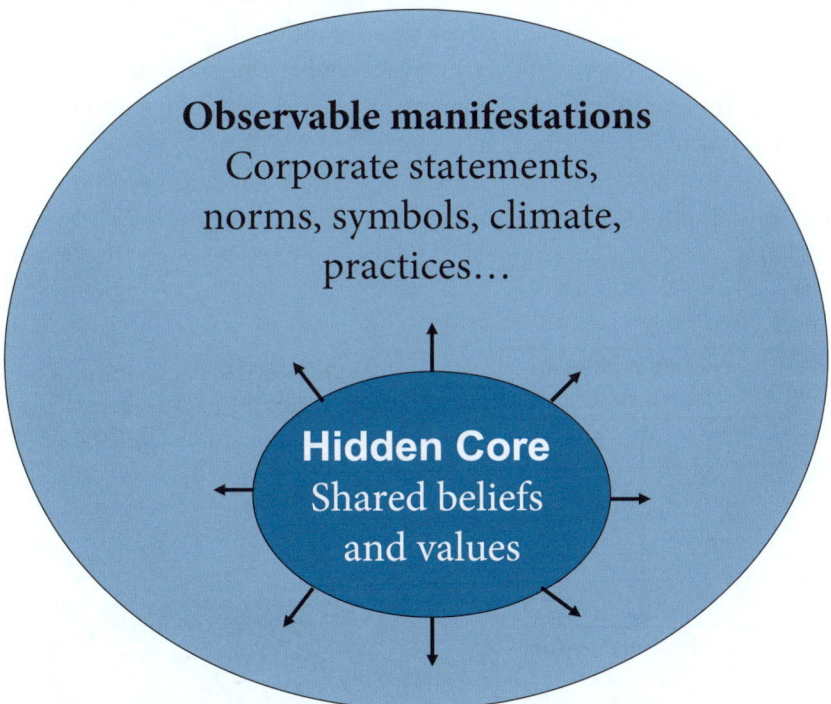

Figure 9.1 Observable manifestations and hidden elements of organizational cultures

every company has its own, be it strong or weak, and this influences its behaviour. There might also be subcultures within the same organization, depending on countries, areas, leadership and so on. The degree to which values and beliefs are shared determines the strength of the culture. Only if a widespread consensus exists on these values and beliefs is the culture strong and cohesive.[36]

A concept related to organizational culture is *organizational climate*, which many researchers employ as a first empirical approach to the organizational culture. It refers to perceptions of an organization's members regarding the atmosphere in the firm. One way to measure organizational climate is through questionnaires that typically include eight dimensions:[37] (1) autonomy in work; (2) cohesion (perception of togetherness or sharing within the organizational setting); (3) trust; (4) resources (perception of time demands with respect to task competition and performance standards); (5) support received from superiors; (6) recognition of members' contributions to the organization; (7) fairness (perception of justice in organizational polices); and (8) innovation (encouragement of creativity and risk-taking).

Corporate statements, particularly corporate values, are different from organizational culture. The former is the ideal desired by those who lead the corporation, while the latter expresses a sociological reality. In practice, there is generally a certain gap between the desired organizational culture espoused in corporate statements (such as corporate values, guiding principles, corporate mission and vision) and the existing organizational culture (shared beliefs and the values and behaviours actually observed in and by people within the organization) (Figure 9.2).

Another aspect studied by researchers is how the ethical behaviour of an organization's members is influenced by the corresponding organizational culture. This is especially clear with misconduct, although organizational cultures can also have a positive influence.[38]

Cultures that foster ethical behaviour can be called ethical organizational cultures. A culture that specifically recognizes and respects human dignity and rights and fosters personal flourishing might be called a 'humanizing organizational culture'.[39]

The question arises of how to develop ethical organizational cultures. This, in turn, leads to a more generic question and one we consider in the next subsection: Which factors have an influence in shaping organizational cultures? The answer is complex since a number of factors can contribute.

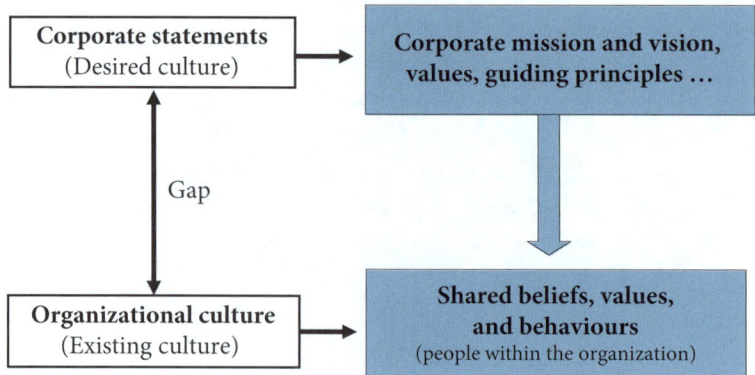

Figure 9.2 Gap between desired and existing organizational cultures

9.5 Factors in building an ethical organizational culture

Organizational culture is built by the interactions of people within an organization, but many experts see leadership as a crucial factor.[40] Some institutionalized procedures, events or practices can also contribute to shaping organizational cultures, and this can be extended to ethical organizational cultures.

Leadership (Chapter 6) has a central role in shaping the organizational culture and also in shaping informal organizations (in many aspects, culture and informal organization overlap). Leaders communicate beliefs and values but – above all – they are role models, for better or for worse. Setting a good example, especially (but not only) in top management, is probably the most important factor in creating an ethical culture. Leaders contribute to this by showing consistency between what is said and what is done, by exhibiting a sincere concern for people in the way they treat them, by coaching collaborators and so on. Subordinates also observe what the leader pays attention to, what measures and controls they apply and how they react to critical incidents and crisis situations.

To influence the development of a culture of integrity, leaders have three basic elements to employ:

- *Consistent thougthts and clear communication.* The leader needs integrity in their thoughts with well-defined ethical values that are communicated and translated into clear objectives.
- *Integrity in their words.* Lies and hypocrisy break credibility and trust.
- *Coherence in their actions,* which is often expressed as 'walking the talk'.[41]

This encourages good behaviour, while not doing what one articulated in words is a lousy message for followers.

Apart from leadership, other factors can have a relevant impact in shaping the company or organizational culture. Drawing from the proposals of experts and common experience of top managers,[42] some influential factors on culture are:

- *Corporate mission, vision and values*: Well-defined mission, vision and value statements constitute a clear message to the organization when accompanied by a serious commitment to implementing them. Reaffirming existing values in different ways and applying them to everyone throughout the organization are good ways to build up organizational culture. If corporate values are ethical and the mission and vision are ethically correct, these corporate statements will contribute to creating an ethical organizational culture.
- *Codes of conduct rightly implemented, as well as ethical training*: As we have already discussed above (9.2), codes of conduct can also contribute to developing an ethical culture of compliance as long as they are implemented properly; a sound ethical training is another way to develop an ethical organizational culture.
- *Ethical criteria for recruitment, selection and promotion*: If the culture depends on people, and chiefly on managers and supervisors, it is relevant to consider ethical criteria and virtues in recruiting, selecting and promoting people in an organization.

- *Applying ethical values to decision-making*: Organizational culture is shaped by a consistent incorporation of ethical corporate values in strategic decision-making and in the corresponding goals, policies and programmes. These must also come into play in decision-making at all levels of the company; otherwise, corporate values remain ineffective, and people understand that they are only a matter of rhetoric.
- *Ethics in the organizational structure*: Integrating ethical criteria into intra-organizational procedures and structures (see above in this section), particularly in managerial systems of control and personnel policies and practices, is another way of bringing ethical values into the everyday routine.
- *Ethics in the behaviour of employees and in the informal organization*: The day-to-day life of an organization is also relevant. It includes the personal styles, behaviours and interactions of people working within the organization. This is an important part of the 'informal organization', which can contribute to shaping an ethical organizational culture if such styles, behaviours and interactions are embedded with ethical values.
- *Ethical criteria in customer relations*: Focus on customer treatment, service provided to clients, reactions to customer complaints and competitive practices employed all shape the organizational culture.
- *Symbols, events and rituals*: Language used (for example, 'human resources' as opposed to 'people' or 'collaborators'), stories about the founders of the company, great leaders, exemplary employee behaviours, symbols, special events and celebrations, 'rituals', awards and so on can also influence the shaping of an organizational culture and therefore of an ethical organizational culture.

9.6 The ethical dimension of strategy

In the business context, strategy refers to the objectives or ends sought amid conditions of uncertainty, along with the means employed to achieve them, utilizing both people and material resources. Generally, two main aspects of strategy are distinguished: formulation and implementation.

- *Formulation* involves defining the objectives to be achieved, based on a thorough analysis of competitive opportunities in local, international or global markets, as well as an assessment of the company's potential to capitalize on these.
- *Implementation* entails putting action plans into place to achieve the objectives set out in the strategy formulation.

The formulation and implementation of strategy are fundamentally human actions and, like all such actions, are not ethically neutral when considering both their content and consequences. The *ethical dimension of strategy is inherent* because every strategy impacts people, both within the organization and in society at large, and maybe the environment too. A sound strategy respects people affected and serves them through the provision of goods and services, while ideally generating income to sustain and create jobs, provide a fair return to investors, and support other ethical goals within the firm (7.7). Therefore, evaluating strategy solely in terms of economic objectives falls short; ethical reflection on strategy adds a broader, more holistic perspective, reducing the risk of a narrow, economistic view that overlooks values beyond competitive advantage or economic gains.

Since strategy encompasses an ethical dimension, assessing its morality is essential. This involves evaluating the moral nature of the product or service introduced, its benefits or harm to persons and society, and issues of fairness in the pursuit of competitive advantage. Strategies should, for instance, avoid practices that lead to unfair competition (7.3) or entail some other injustice.

Another critical ethical consideration in strategy relates to the *short-term versus long-term orientation* of the firm. A short-term focus, aimed solely at immediate results, can lead to long-term drawbacks if it compromises employee training, morale or motivation, or neglects respect for individuals, the community or the environment. Short-term strategies may also fail to satisfy customers' long-term needs and can erode the company's reputation and its continuity. Conversely, a long-term strategic orientation tends to favour sustainability, relationships and a stronger alignment with the firm's ethical commitments and the common good.

While a company's mission may remain relatively constant, strategies often shift over time to adapt to internal and external changes, including emerging business opportunities and evolving stakeholder expectations. By integrating ethics into strategic thinking, firms can foster resilience and social responsibility, ensuring that their competitive actions align with broader societal values.

9.7 Ethics in organizational structure and the informal organization

Strategy is closely related to the organizational structure, which formalizes how to achieve strategic and other corporate aims. Organizational structure includes activities of allocation, coordination and supervision, and the way in which staff will be supervised. The structure is generally composed of hierarchical dependencies, formal networks, assignment of responsibilities, processes, systems and reporting relationships established within an organization. Other elements of the organizational structure are procedures of welcoming new employees and initial and subsequent socialization, manners and contents of internal communication, training, criteria for allocation of rewards and status, policies and practices in dealing with seniors and retirement and a process and definite criteria for dismissal, as well as performance appraisals involving individual and team performance.

Organizational structure focuses on facilitating working relationships within the firm in order to achieve business goals efficiently. But beyond efficiency, every organizational structure has an ethical dimension due to the people who work within it. An organizational structure is not ethical if it fosters wrongdoing or disrespect for human beings, their rationality and freedom, their intrinsic dignity and innate rights. In contrast, the structure is ethical if it favours good behaviour and provides opportunities for the personal growth of those involved, including the development of virtues.

There is empirical evidence that organizational structures encourage ethical behaviours or foster misbehaviours[43] and introduce sustainability initiatives.[44] The formal organizations can be especially influential in ethical (or unethical) behaviour, on the one hand for the organizational rewards system and the performance and evaluation processes, along with control and monitoring; and, on the other hand, for the system of allocating decision-making rights and responsibilities,[45] including the empowerment of people. We will briefly review some of these aspects from the ethical perspective.

Rewards system, performance appraisal and control processes

This refers to all kinds of monetary rewards, promotions, prizes, awards and other forms of public recognition. The organizational structure contains reward systems, mainly monetary, as incentives to foster certain behaviours, and this is often a powerful means, though the compensation system rarely rewards ethical behaviours. In practice, the noblest ethical actions, such as helping peers or acting with a real sense of service, are neither public nor economically motivated.

A problem arises when, in practice, financial or other compensations reward misbehaviours; for instance, paying kickbacks or even issuing fraudulent financial reports.[46] This occurs when organizational compensation practices are not carefully planned. Sometimes, the origin of misconduct is a lack of awareness of what a certain reward might actually incentivize. In practice, rewards systems unintentionally incentivize actions that their designers had no intention of rewarding.[47] The performance evaluation and monitoring and control processes for individuals and business units are also ethically significant – especially the *performance appraisal*, or the method by which the performance of a manager or employee is evaluated. Performance appraisal is usually done in terms of quality, quantity, cost, and time and values expected. The last of these might be evaluated only indirectly. The evaluation process can reinforce the idea that ethical behaviours are expected, while unethical ones are rejected or, at least, not rewarded.

The performance appraisal can fail to monitor managers and workers adequately and permit imprudent actions or performance inconsistent with what would be ethically desirable or harmonious with corporate ethical values. While giving autonomy and initiative is consistent with respecting freedom, a prudent monitoring is also necessary. The well-known collapse of Barings Bank[48] due to the imprudence of a young brilliant broker, is an illustrative case of lack of monitoring. *Incentive systems* (rewards) and organizational pressures for results, accompanied by weak encouragement and monitoring of ethical standards, can foster wrongdoing.

What the company measures is an important source of motivation for good and bad behaviour. If people are pushed only in the direction of quantifiable goals through 'strong' incentive systems that reward the quantitative results, it is very likely that they will not pursue the 'real' objectives of the firm but seek to maximize the thing measured instead, which may well be unprofessional and unethical. Take, for example, the 2015 Toshiba scandal, which was due not to occasional misbehaviour but to the reporting and reward system as a whole.[49]

Empowering people with moral guidelines

Some research findings show that people in an organization behave unethically when they perceive themselves as having little power and control over decisions or conduct, although they realize that some of their decisions are not ethically correct.[50]

Moreover, lack of specific moral guidance from the organization, together with ambiguity of expectations, can create moral stress in decision-makers.[51] People within the company may have certain *empowerment* to make decisions, but at the same time they may suffer significant pressures, which can have an influence on their ethical or unethical behaviour. Several organizational factors could contribute to misbehaviours. These include emphasis on results, pressures to meet unrealistic performance targets, upper and lower cut-offs or bonus plans, non-existent internal control systems, environmental changes that render existing control ineffective and high levels of divisional autonomy.

All of this suggests the need to give reasonable empowerment accompanied by clear ethical guidelines or, even better, to ensure that decision-makers have a strong degree of integrity.

Ethics in the informal organization

Managers, supervisors, peers and different co-workers play a role in shaping the informal organization, which emerges from a dynamic interplay of personal relationships, social networks, communities of shared interest, and emotionally grounded sources of motivation. Informal organization can contribute to creating a certain ethical climate in the organization or the contrary. Actions, behaviours, conversations or informal practices can contribute to developing it and to motivating people in the organization in positive or negative ways.

Creating an ethical climate generally depends on the commitment to ethics and ethical behaviours of managers, especially top managers, and their clarity and ability to communicate with people in the organization about ethics and values. Leadership is also crucial (9.5). Some findings[52] show two pillars in what was called 'ethical leadership'. The first is a leader with moral traits (integrity), ethical behaviour and decision-making, which incorporates ethical values. The second pillar is being a visible and positive role model in the firm.

9.8 Ethical principles in designing organizations

Organizational structure can be evaluated not only from the perspective of efficiency but also from the human and ethical perspective, including respect for human dignity, freedom and sociability, and how they may or may not foster the capacity of employees to contribute to the organization with their talents and self-development.

To design formal organizations that would humanize work and business organizations, and therefore improve their ethical quality, is an ongoing ethical challenge. Reflecting on some ethical principles can help in the design of more ethical structures. We will review three of them here: solidarity (cooperation within the organization), subsidiarity and participation (2.7). These apply to formal structures but, up to a point, also to the so-called informal organization. This refers to the interpersonal relationships and networks that develop inside an organization, which include a variety of associative elements, for instance, informal agreements, ways of cooperation, fellowship or even friendship, cliques and so on.

Cooperation, subsidiarity and participation within the organization

Organizational structures should harmonize efficiency with ethics. Ethics in organizational structures leads one to consider the human dignity and development within the organization, the uniqueness of each person and the diversity of different groups of people.

Cooperation within the organization is not only crucial for performance, as Chester Barnard,[53] as early as 1938, pointed out, but cooperation is also desirable from an ethical perspective because it expresses concern for others and favours willingness to contribute to the common goals, which are good for all. Cooperation entails helping each other with special concern for those who, for some reason, may need more help.

Acting with freedom, and the corresponding responsibility, is crucial to personal growth. Respect for employee freedom requires both accepting diversity and personal or group initiatives. This is required by the subsidiarity principle (2.7), which states that a larger and higher-ranking body should not exercise functions that could be efficiently carried out by a smaller and lesser body.[54] Rather, the former (management) should support the latter by aiding it in the coordination of its activities with those of the larger community, always in accordance with the common good. For an organization, this means do not allow a large organization to take over what can be done by smaller groups or organizations, or even by individuals, but give them support to develop their potential.[55]

The principle of subsidiarity entails respecting individual initiative and fostering people's talents in service of the company in harmony with the achievement of its goals.[56] Employees should enjoy freedom to organize their work as much as possible, taking the initiative and making decisions within the scope of their responsibility. Management should be supportive of employee initiative, maintaining – at the same time – appropriate coordination of this with common goals and ethical guidelines, with a view to the common good.

Applying subsidiarity in ways appropriate to each company and culture is not only ethically praiseworthy but also contributes to enriching the work of employees and often motivates them. As a consequence, the company benefits from the employees' superior performance.[57] The participation principle takes into consideration human rationality, freedom and the existence of differentiated goals and interests of people within the organization.

Within business organizations,[58] participation occurs when employees have some sort of share in the company that hires them, especially in the decision-making process when it touches on topics they are affected by. Participation in the decision-making process is not rigid. It can adopt different forms, depending on particular situations, types of decisions, as well as the individual's personal background, training and experience.

Among the different forms of participation, one of the most elemental is asking for suggestions or help in defining problems and making possible improvements. Many companies have, in fact, established a suggestion system for all employees or for a select group of them. Other ways to augment participation include empowering employees to make decisions on a significant number of issues, creating groups of experts to survey employee opinions on relevant topics, and including employees in the decision-making process of organizational aspects of their work.

Participation can also be promoted by 'quality circles' – that is, groups of employees who meet regularly to discuss workplace improvements in matters such as product quality, occupational health and safety, the manufacturing process and product design. Employees can also participate, to some extent, in hiring co-workers, designing work tasks, assessing new technologies, formulating budgets and measuring performance. Another means of participation is placing employees who are not top managers on the board of directors or on a supervisory board (this is the case in some large German corporations). In this manner, employees' representatives can influence decisions on corporate governance. However, this is not a universal requirement of the participation principle and possible consequences should be evaluated.

New organizational forms

There are currently theories and practices, generically known as 'new organizational forms',[59] that seem more aligned with the aforementioned ethical principles than the previous forms. Some of these current proposals encourage employees to work as a manager within their scope or to have more autonomy. These can foster greater cooperation and initiative, which seems more aligned to human development than other more conventional methods. However, with the Fourth Industrial Revolution (Industry I.0), smart factories and an increasing use of robots posit new questions on organizational structures and how to organize human work (10.11). Multisided platforms are new organizational forms,[60] which posit ethical challenges (see Historical Case #10).

This contrasts with the old *bureaucratic structures*, with strong hierarchy and rigid procedures to follow, and *functional structures*, in which people are grouped into functions such as production, marketing, human resources, finance and accounting. Employees become specialists within the function to which they are attached, and this can improve efficiency, but cooperation beyond strict rule can be eroded and some employee talents undervalued. It might also lead to communication difficulties, with slow processes, inflexible behaviours and strong depersonalization – aspects that are certainly relevant from an ethical perspective.

Case Study #9

La Fageda: A social enterprise facing a problem[61]

La Fageda is a social enterprise primarily dedicated to yogurt production, based in La Garrotxa, a county in the northeast of Spain. In 2023, La Fageda employed 441 people, 259 of whom had mental disabilities, while producing an average of 2 million yogurts every week. The company closed in 2022 with total revenues of €26 million and an EBITDA of €0.7 million.

La Fageda was founded in 1982 by Cristóbal Colón (his real name!) and his wife. Mr Colón had dedicated many years of his life to clinical psychiatry. He recognized the limitations of the conventional health system and crafts activities, which were mainly used to distract patients with mental illness. Instead, he believed in the dignity and uniqueness of each person, as well as the dignity of work itself, viewing work as a source of meaning.

The original objective of La Fageda was to create meaningful jobs for people with mental disabilities, although it later expanded to include individuals in other vulnerable conditions. Aligned with its founding principles, the current mission states: 'To improve the quality of life and promote the social integration of people with intellectual disabilities, severe mental disorders, and other groups at risk of social exclusion through business activities that generate meaningful jobs, training opportunities, and a wide range of care services.' They add as a vision, 'To be a solid social and business project that is a model of inspiration to create value in society.'[62]

La Fageda began with fifteen people, most of whom were patients from the psychiatric hospital in the region. Initially, the focus was on gardening activities. Later, Colón's team established a cow farm, selling the milk produced to companies involved in dairy production.

In 1993, La Fageda began manufacturing and selling yogurts, producing around 50,000 units a week, while continuing with gardening activities and the cow farm. The business, managed with great professionalism, grew significantly and successfully competed in its region with large multinational yogurt producers like Danone and Nestlé. By 2015, La Fageda had reached a weekly production of over 1 million yogurts. La Fageda's yogurt is positioned as a premium, artisanal product. Its main ingredient – milk, no older than 48 hours – comes from La Fageda's own cows and nearby farms. For most of its nearly thirty product varieties, the price is around 50 per cent higher than Danone's (the market leader in Spain) and three times the price of private-label brands.

La Fageda is a company with a clear social purpose and has, at the same time, strong economic results. Colón often reminded his team to make decisions with a 'double eye' – focusing on the social objective, which was the priority, and on the economic results that supported this social goal.

Colón remained closely involved with the company, continuously developing its founding ideas and values while adapting the organization to the needs and problems that emerged. Since mental disabilities and vulnerable conditions vary widely, La Fageda implemented 'individual itineraries' under the supervision of a socio-occupational team. These itineraries aimed to find suitable roles for each person within the organization, although this was not always easy.

While most people with disabilities or in vulnerable situations are involved at La Fageda through a labour contract, some are temporarily or permanently unable to engage in productive activities. These individuals are not excluded from La Fageda; instead, they attend La Fageda's occupational therapy unit, which is subsidized by public funds. People in this unit attend daily and participate in activities such as crafts, tending to the La Fageda garden and similar tasks. In this way, they have meaningful activities to engage in, are supported by therapy professionals and receive a small government pension.

A few years ago, the socio-occupational team noticed that a significant number of employees in vulnerable conditions found the yogurt factory too physically demanding, as they often had to stand or walk for long periods. They were increasingly uncomfortable with the work's pace, noise and the requirement to spend significant amounts of time on their feet. At the same time, these employees still had 'productive capabilities', but the question was: in which activities?

Faced with this problem, several solutions were considered. One option was to reassign them to other activities within La Fageda, such as working on the cow farm, although this would likely be even more physically demanding. While a few suitable opportunities might be found, they may not be able to accommodate all persons. A second option was to transfer them to the occupational therapy unit. This option would involve terminating their employment contracts, but without removing them from La Fageda. However, these activities might be perceived as too easy or unchallenging for them. A third alternative would be to establish a new production line, where the working conditions could be more comfortable than yogurt manufacturing. This would be a complex option, requiring market research to identify competitive products suitable for production by these persons, new facilities, hiring experts and other resources. La Fageda has a clear mission and vision, which should be a crucial criterion in resolving the issue.

Questions

1. How would you describe La Fageda's business purpose, and in what ways does the organization work to fulfil this mission?
2. In facing the problem, how should the different alternatives be evaluated, considering the company's mission and vision?
3. Based on La Fageda's values and the situation described, what course of action would you propose, and why?

Notes

1. S. Wetlaufer, 'Organizing by Empowerment: An Interview with Roger Sant and Dennis Bakker', *Harvard Business Review*, vol. 77, no. 1, 1999, pp. 110–23, on p. 120.
2. Sources: H. Osborne, 'What is Cambridge Analytica? The Firm at the Centre of Facebook's Data Breach', *The Guardian*, 2018: https://www.theguardian.com/news/2018/mar/18/what-is-cambridge-analytica-firm-at-centre-of-facebook-data-breach; H. Afriat, S. Dvir-Gvirsman, K. Tsuriel and L. Ivan, '"This is Capitalism. It is Non-illegal": Users' Attitudes toward Institutional Privacy Following the Cambridge Analytica Scandal', *The Information Society*, vol. 37, no. 2, 2020, pp. 115–27; R. Bareebe, *The Cambridge Analytica Scandal and Its Impact on Meta*, 2022, DOI: 10.13140/RG.2.2.19583.69285; Wikipedia: Cambridge Analytica, Facebook–Cambridge Analytica Data Scandal. (All accessed on 30 October 2024).

3. https://web.archive.org/web/20171113180809/; https://cambridgeanalytica.org/. (both accessed on 30 October 2024).
4. https://energyindustryreview.com/analysis/teslas-mission-accelerating-worlds-transition-to-sustainable-energy/. (Accessed on 30 October 2024).
5. https://about.google/intl/ALL_us/. (Accessed on 30 October 2024).
6. https://www.medtronic.com/us-en/our-company/mission.html. (Accessed on 30 March 2025).
7. P. Cardona and C. Rey, *Management by Missions* (New York: Palgrave Macmillan, 2008).
8. https://panmore.com/procter-gamble-mission-statement-vision-statement-analysis. (Accessed on 30 October 2024).
9. https://careers.toyota.com/us/en/culture. (Accessed on 30 October 2024).
10. See, among others, C. C. Langlois and B. B. Schlegelmilch, 'Do Corporate Codes of Ethics Reflect National Character? Evidence from Europe and the United States', *Journal of International Business Studies*, vol. 21, no. 4, 1990, pp. 519–39; B. B. Schlegelmilch and D. C. Robertson, 'The Influence of Country and Industry on Ethical Perception of Senior Executives in the US and Europe', *Journal of International Business Studies*, vol. 26, no. 4, 1995, pp. 859–81; and B. Scholtens and L. Dam, 'Cultural Values and International Differences in Business Ethics', *Journal of Business Ethics*, vol. 75, no. 3, 2007, pp. 273–84.
11. https://us.pg.com/policies-and-practices/purpose-values-and-principles/. (Accessed on 30 October 2024).
12. B. Doherty, H.H. Haugh and F. Lyon, 'Social Enterprises as Hybrid Organizations: A Review and Research Agenda', *International Journal of Management Reviews*, vol. 16, no. 4, 2014, pp. 417–36.
13. According to Kaptein, a recognized expert in business codes, there are reasons for the divergent findings: varying definitions of key terms, deficiencies in the empirical data and methodologies used and a lack of theory. (M. Kaptein and M. Schwartz, 'The Effectiveness of Business Codes: A Critical Examination of Existing Studies and the Development of an Integrated Research Model', *Journal of Business Ethics*, vol. 77, no. 2, 2008, pp. 111–27).
14. See M. J. Somers, 'Ethical Codes of Conduct and Organizational Context: A Study of the Relationship Between Codes of Conduct, Employee Behaviour and Organizational Values', *Journal of Business Ethics*, vol. 30, no. 2, 2001, pp. 185–95.
15. See L. S. Paine, 'Managing for Organizational Integrity', *Harvard Business Review*, vol. 72, no. 2, 1994, pp. 106–17.
16. See an overview of of the Organizational Guidelines at: https://www.ussc.gov/sites/default/files/pdf/training/organizational-guidelines/ORGOVERVIEW.pdf. Accessed on Agoust 1, 2025.
17. See ISO (International Organization for Standardization). *Compliance-management Systems – Requirements with Guidance for Use* (ISO 37301:2021). https://committee.iso.org/sites/tc309/home/projects/published/iso-37301-compliance-management.html. (Accessed on 4 June 2025).
18. A. Vaccaro, *Compliance beyond Compliance: Managing Organizations with Integrity* (Madrid: McGraw Hill, 2022).
19. J. Fontrodona and P. Sanz, 'The Keys to a Positive Business Culture', *IESE Insight*, no. 27, 2015, pp. 15–22, on p. 16.
20. R. R. Harrison, 'Hippocrates and Hemlock: A Reflection on the Ethics in Ethics and Compliance', *Journal of Health Care Compliance*, vol. 25, no. 2, pp. 15–24, 2023, p. 22.

21. M. Bennett, 'Does Your Ethics and Compliance Training Program Meet the Standard?', *Journal of Health Care Compliance*, vol. 2, no. 6, 2000, pp. 19–26; and J. Jaeger, 'Striving Toward a Better Ethics and Compliance Training Program', *Compliance Week*, vol. 14, no. 165, 2017, pp. 40–3.
22. E. Hernández-Cuadra and J. L. Fernández-Fernández, 'Ethics and Compliance Programs for a New Business Narrative: A Kohlberg-based Moral Valuing Model for Diagnosing Commitment at the Top', *Business & Society Review*, vol. 129, no. 1, 2024, pp. 72–95.
23. Source: Melé, abridged version of D. and A. Corrales, *Medtronic Inc.: From Corporate Mission to Organizational Culture (A)* (Barcelona, Spain: IESE Publishing, 2005) (published with permission), extended with information from the following sources: W. W. George, 'Medtronic's Chairman William George on How Mission-driven Companies Create Long-term Shareholder Value', *Academy of Management Executive*, vol. 15, 2001, pp. 39–47; W. W. George, *Authentic Leadership: Rediscovering the Secrets to Creating Lasting Value* (San Francisco, CA: Jossey-Bass, 2003); B. George, 'Crisis and Corporate Ethics: Where Have All the Leaders Gone?', Address to Westminster Town Hall Forum, 13 February, 2003: https://www.billgeorge.org/articles/crisis-and-corporate-ethics-where-have-all-the-leaders-gone/. (Accessed on 4 June 2025); W. W. George, *True North: Discover your Authentic Leadership* (San Francisco, CA: Jossey-Bass, 2007); Medtronic Official Website Medtronic.com.
24. B. George, 'Crisis and Corporate Ethics: Where Have All the Leaders Gone?', *Address to Westminster Town Hall Forum,* February 13, 2003: https://www.billgeorge.org/articles/crisis-and-corporate-ethics-where-have-all-the-leaders-gone/. (Accessed on 4 June 2025).
25. W. W. George, *Authentic Leadership: Rediscovering the Secrets to Creating Lasting Value* (San Francisco: Jossey-Bass, 2003), pp. 34–5.
26. George, 'Medtronic's Chairman William George', p. 41.
27. George, *Authentic Leadership*, p. 42.
28. George, 'Medtronic's Chairman William George'.
29. George, *Authentic Leadership*, p. 20.
30. T. Deal and A. Kennedy, *Corporate Cultures: The Rites and Rituals of Corporate Life* (New York: Perseus Publishing, 1982), p. 4.
31. A. M. Pettigrew, 'On Studying Organizational Cultures', *Administrative Science Quarterly*, vol. 24, 1979, pp. 570–81, on p. 572.
32. See: Pettigrew, 'On Studying Organizational Cultures'; Deal and Kennedy, *Corporate Cultures*; T. J. Peters and R. H. Waterman, *In Search of Excellence: Lessons from America's Best Run Companies* (London: Harper & Row, 1982); and E. H. Schein, *Corporate Culture and Leadership* (San Francisco, CA: Jossey-Bass, 1984 [2010]), among others.
33. On this point, see A. Moore, 'Employee Monitoring and Computer Technology: Evaluating Surveillance vs Privacy', *Business Ethics Quarterly*, vol. 10, no. 3, 2000, pp. 697–709.
34. See: J. P. Kotter and J. L. Heskett, *Corporate Culture and Performance* (New York: Free Press, 1992); and R. Goffee and G. Jones, 'What Holds the Modern Company Together?', *Harvard Business Review*, vol. 74, no. 6, 1996, pp. 133–48.
35. See: E. H. Schein, *Corporate Culture and Leadership*'; E. H. Shein, 'Organizational Cultures', *American Psychologist*, vol. 45, no. 2, 1990, pp. 109–19.
36. See B. Arogyaswamy and C. M. Byles, 'Organizational Culture: Internal and External Fits', *Journal of Management*, vol. 13, 1987, pp. 647–59.
37. See D. J. Koys and T. A. Decotiis, 'Inductive Measures of Psychological Climate', *Human Relations*, vol. 44, no. 3, 1991, pp. 265–85.

38. See, for instance, N. K. Shetia and M. A. Von Glinow, *Gaining Control of the Corporate Culture* (New York: Jossey-Bass, 1985); L. K. Treviño, 'A Cultural Perspective on Changing and Developing Organizational Ethics', *Research in Organizational Change and Development*, no. 4, 1990, 195–230; R. R. Sims and J. Brinkmann, 'Leaders as Moral Role Models: The Case of John Gutfreund at Salomon Brothers', *Journal of Business Ethics*, vol. 35, no. 4, 2002, 327–39.
39. D. Melé, 'Organizational Humanizing Cultures: Can They Create Social Capital?', *Journal of Business Ethics*, vol. 45, no. 1, 2003, pp. 3–14.
40. Schein, *Corporate Culture and Leadership*.
41. Fontrodona and Sanz, 'The Keys to a Positive Business Culture'.
42. On this topic, we follow, partially, Schein, *Corporate Culture and Leadership*; Price Waterhouse Change Integration Team, *The Paradox Principles: How High-Performance Companies Manage Chaos, Complexity, and Contradiction to Achieve Superior Results* (Chicago, IL: Irwin, 1996), pp. 98ff; and our own experience.
43. See, among others, L. K. Treviño and K. A. Nelson, *Managing Business Ethics: Straight Talk About How to Do it Right* (Hoboken, NJ: Wiley, 2004); H. S. James Jr, 'Reinforcing Ethical Decision Making Through Organizational Structure', *Journal of Business Ethics*, vol. 28, part 1, no. 1, 2000, pp. 43–58; J. A. Brickley, C. W. Smith Jr and J. L. Zimmerman, 'Business Ethics and Organizational Architecture', *Journal of Banking & Finance*, vol. 26, no. 9, 2002, pp. 1821–35; M. Schminke, 'Considering the Business in Business Ethics: An Exploratory Study of the Influence of Organizational Size and Structure on Individual Ethical Predispositions', *Journal of Business Ethics*, vol. 30, part 2, no. 4, 2001, pp. 375–90.
44. B. Jaganjac, K. W. Hansen, H. Lunde and J. A. Hunnes, 'The Role of Organizational Culture and Structure in Implementing Sustainability Initiatives', *Business Ethics, the Environment & Responsibility*, 2024. DOI: 10.1111/beer.12710. (Accessed on 4 June 2025).
45. Brickley et al., 'Business Ethics and Organizational Architecture'.
46. See, for instance, Treviño and Nelson, *Managing Business Ethics*.
47. See, for example, S. Kerr, 'On the Folly of Rewarding A, While Hoping for B', *Academy of Management Journal*, vol. 18, no. 4, 1975, pp. 769–83. See also N. K. Shetia and M. A. Von Glinow, *Gaining Control of the Corporate Culture* (New York: Jossey-Bass, 1985).
48. See a summary in L. T. Drennan, 'Ethics, Governance and Risk Management: Lessons from Mirror Group Newspapers and Barings Bank', *Journal of Business Ethics*, vol. 52, no. 3, 2004, pp. 257–66.
49. Mentioned in D. Melé, J. M. Rosanas and J. Fontrodona, 'Ethics in Finance and Accounting: Editorial Introduction', *Journal of Business Ethics*, vol. 140, no. 4, 2017, pp. 609–13.
50. J. A. Waters and F. Bird, 'The Moral Dimension of Organizational Culture', *Journal of Business Ethics*, vol. 6, no. 1, 1987, pp. 15–22, and 'Attending to Ethics in Management', *Journal of Business Ethics*, vol. 8, no. 6, 1989, pp. 493–7.
51. See Waters and Bird, 'The Moral Dimension of Organizational Culture'.
52. L. K. Trevino, G. R. Weaver, D. G. Gibson and B. L. Toffler, 'Managing Ethics and Legal Compliance: What Works and What Hurts', *California Management Review*, vol. 41, no. 2, 1999, pp. 131–51.
53. C. I. Barnard, *The Functions of the Executive*. Introduction by K. Andrews (London: Oxford University Press, 1938 [1968]).
54. M. Schlag and B. Koller (eds), *Rethinking Subsidiarity: Multidisciplinary Reflections on the Catholic Social Tradition* (Cham: Springer, 2024).

55. See a further development with a case study, D. Melé, 'Exploring the Principle of Subsidiarity in Organizational Forms', *Journal of Business Ethics*, vol. 60, no. 3, 2005, pp. 293–305.
56. M. J. Naughton, *Respect in Action: Applying Subsidiarity in Business* (St Paul, MN: University of St Thomas, 2015).
57. See D. Collins, 'How and Why Participatory Management Improves a Company's Social Performance', *Business & Society*, vol. 35, no. 2, 1996, pp. 176–210.
58. On participation within organizations, see D. Collins, 'The Ethical Superiority and Inevitability of Participatory Management as an Organizational System', *Organization Science*, vol. 8, no. 5, 1997, pp. 489–506 and S. Cludts, 'Organisation Theory and the Ethics of Participation', *Journal of Business Ethics*, vol. 21, no. 2/3, 1999, pp. 157–71.
59. See I. Palmer, J.J. Benveniste and R. Dunford, 'New Organizational Forms: Towards a Generative Dialogue', *Organization Studies*, vol. 28, no. 12, 2007, pp. 1829–47; and Y. Li and O. M. Khessina, 'Before Birth: How Provisional Spaces Shape the Localized Emergence of New Organizational Forms', *Academy of Management Journal*, vol. 67, no. 2, 2024, pp. 494–525.
60. D. Mcintyre, A. Srinivasan, A. Afuah, A. Gawer and T. Kretschmer, 'Multisided Platforms as New Organizational Forms', *Academy of Management Perspectives*, vol. 35, no. 4, 2021, pp. 566–83.
61. Sources: J. A. Segarra, *La empresa social compitiendo en el mercado: Principios de buen gobierno* (Barcelona: Real Academia Europea de Doctores, no. 46, 2016); I. Gallo and D. Melé, 'Work Integration of People with Mental Disorders Through Social Enterprise: A Humanistic-Personalist Framework and Case Study,' *Journal of Business Ethics*, 2024. https://doi.org/10.1007/s10551-024-05853-2. (Accessed on 4 June 2025); D. González, *Historia de una locura empresarial social y rentable: La Fageda* (Barcelona: Comanegra, 2013); A. Loyola and A. Kareaga, *La Fageda: Un proyecto socio-empresarial rentable y con corazón* (Mondragón, Spain: Universidad de Mondagón, 2020); 'Historia de La Fageda': https://www.fageda.com/es/historia/. (Accessed on 4 June 2025).
62. La Fageda, 'Memoria de sostenabilidad', 2023, p. 6: https://www.fageda.com/wp-content/uploads/2024/05/MEMORIA_LA_FAGEDA_ES_Web.pdf. (Accessed on 4 June 2025).

10

Ethics in Managing Work and Technology

… one rightly comes to recognize the pre-eminence of the subjective meaning of work over the objective one.[1]

JOHN PAUL II (1978–2005),
Pope of the Roman Catholic Church

Overview

This chapter explores the ethical management of human work and technology in business.

In Section A, the focus is on human work, recognizing both its objective dimension – related to the means of production and outcomes – and its subjective dimension – which acknowledges the intrinsic dignity and subjectivity of the person performing the work. Ethical management of work involves honouring the dignity of work as a personal activity and respecting labour rights, while ensuring that work contributes to personal and professional growth. The discussion emphasizes the need to balance efficiency with ethics in managing human work, prioritizing the subjective dimension over the objective when conflicts between the two arise. The chapter also analyses blatant violations of labour rights and underscores the importance of implementing 'decent work' practices. Ensuring that workers engage in meaningful activities and have conditions that promote their development within the workplace are additional ethical imperatives.

Section B shifts the focus to the ethical management of technology, particularly in its relationship with human work. The chapter highlights the importance of prioritizing the subjective meaning of work over technology, emphasizing recent advancements. Particular attention is paid to ethical concerns regarding information technology (IT) and artificial intelligence (AI). It also discusses ethical guidelines for managing both IT and AI responsibly in the business context.

> **Chapter Aims**
>
> After reading this chapter you should be able to:
>
> - Have an understanding of human work and its intrinsic dignity.
> - Be more familiar with the labour contract and exploitative labour.
> - Reflect on labour rights and decent work.
> - Consider the importance of just remuneration and working in safe and healthy conditions.
> - Analyse the rights of freedom of association, collective bargaining and the right to strike.
> - Consider discrimination in employment and occupation.
> - Reflect on the obligations to respect employee privacy and act with fairness in procedures.
> - Discuss the primacy of the subjective meaning of work over the objective one.
> - Gain knowledge of the concept of meaningful work and its implementation.
> - Reflect on developmental work and how to make it effective.
> - Discuss ethics in the development, implementation and use of technology.
> - Consider relevant ethical issues related to information technology (IT).
> - Understand ethics in artificial intelligence (AI).
> - Have an awareness of the ethical dimension of human–technology interaction in recent technological revolutions.

Historical Case #10

Questionable labour practices at Uber[2]

Uber Technologies, Inc., better known simply as 'Uber', is a multinational company headquartered in San Francisco, California, providing ride-hailing, courier services, food delivery and freight transport. Founded in 2009 as a tech-driven solution to simplify urban transportation, Uber has since grown exponentially. The company operates through a digital platform where riders can request rides via a specific app, and drivers can accept these requests. Uber operates in approximately seventy countries and 10,500 cities worldwide, making it the largest ridesharing company globally, with over 150 million monthly active users and 6 million active drivers and couriers. The platform calculates fares, tracks routes and processes payments, primarily connecting riders with drivers. Uber refers to its drivers as 'partners' and classifies them as independent contractors rather than employees.

Drivers' work within the Uber system

A study in the US market[3] shows that drivers are attracted to Uber mainly due to the flexibility, competitive compensation and relatively stable earnings per hour, regardless of hours worked. However, Uber's classification of drivers as independent contractors is controversial, as it denies drivers typical employee benefits such as healthcare, overtime pay and paid leave. Drivers also express dissatisfaction over fare cuts (introduced by Uber to remain competitive), limited access to tips, long hours with minimal earnings, lack of support from Uber and unclear deactivation policies. Additionally, drivers note that Uber exerts significant control over their work activities, including setting fares, monitoring performance through ratings and enforcing deactivation policies. As a result, drivers frequently report feeling exploited by Uber's practices.

Drivers' claims revolve around several core issues. Firstly, they lack minimum wage guarantees, as earnings fluctuate based on demand, trip length and expenses, often resulting in wages below minimum wage after accounting for costs. In addition to this, drivers face the absence of benefits typically available to employees, such as healthcare, sick leave and retirement plans, which places financial strain on those who rely on Uber as a primary income source. Furthermore, drivers experience high levels of control without employee status; Uber unilaterally sets fares, offers incentives, and enforces deactivation policies, which mirror the control typically exercised over employees and leads to dissatisfaction due to the lack of autonomy. Finally, drivers face the risk of deactivation, with their platform access potentially terminated due to low ratings or policy violations, often without recourse or due process.

Protests and litigations

This unrest led to protests, beginning in New York and San Francisco in 2016, with drivers demanding better working conditions, fare increases, and fairer pay structures, claiming that Uber's classification practices deny them basic rights and job security, creating an exploitative working environment under Uber's labour conditions and control.

Drivers felt Uber's actions undermined solidarity and worker rights, amplifying frustrations around the lack of fair treatment. The company justified its actions as a customer service measure and later issued statements emphasizing support for drivers, but with no concrete change. However, public criticism and driver discontent over Uber's perceived insensitivity continued.

The protests sparked by these issues represent just one chapter in a larger, ongoing conflict between Uber and its drivers. These initial demonstrations gradually attracted public attention and support, as many began to recognize the challenges faced by gig economy workers, particularly those working without basic labour protections. Drivers' frustrations were compounded by Uber's fare cuts introduced to stay competitive, which resulted in a direct reduction of driver earnings. Additionally, Uber's limited transparency regarding tips and the allocation of earnings left many drivers feeling undervalued and undercompensated.

In an attempt to justify its practices, Uber has maintained that the independent contractor model allows drivers the flexibility to work whenever they choose, arguing that reclassification as employees would disrupt this model by imposing fixed schedules and reducing work opportunities. Uber has also cited its role as a tech platform rather than a traditional employer, which, according to the company, exempts it from providing employee benefits. Despite these justifications, drivers argue that Uber's influence over their work – from fare-setting to deactivation policies – mirrors an employer–employee relationship far more than an independent contractor arrangement.

Legal challenges against Uber's employment practices began to emerge, beginning in the United States, with a prominent early case being *O'Connor* v. *Uber Technologies*. This lawsuit contended that the degree of control Uber exercised over its drivers effectively rendered them employees rather than independent contractors. The case contributed to growing concern over gig economy labour practices and influenced the passage of California's Assembly Bill 5 (AB5) in 2019. AB5 codified a stricter standard – the 'ABC test' – for classifying workers, aiming to reclassify many gig workers as employees entitled to full labour protections. In response, Uber and other major gig economy firms spearheaded and funded Proposition 22, a 2020 California ballot initiative designed to exempt app-based transportation and delivery companies from AB5. Proposition 22 proposed a hybrid model: preserving drivers' status as independent contractors while granting them a set of limited benefits such as minimum earnings guarantees and healthcare subsidies. The measure passed with a majority vote in November 2020, although it was soon embroiled in litigation regarding its constitutionality. The case of *O'Connor* v. *Uber Technologies* argued that Uber's control over drivers classified them effectively as employees. This led to the introduction of California's Assembly Bill 5 (AB5) in 2019, aimed at reclassifying gig workers as employees. In response, Uber, along with other gig economy companies, supported Proposition 22, a 2020 California ballot initiative allowing drivers to remain independent contractors with limited benefits. In 2024, the California Supreme Court upheld Proposition 22, ruling it constitutional. As of June 2025, Uber drivers in California continue to be legally classified as independent contractors with limited benefits.

In Europe, similar legal battles have taken place. In 2017, the European Court of Justice ruled that Uber operates as a transport service rather than a digital intermediary, subjecting it to local transport regulations across EU member states.[4] In the UK, a landmark 2021 Supreme Court decision reclassified Uber drivers as 'workers', entitling them to minimum wage, holiday pay and pension contributions. Uber complied with the ruling by introducing these benefits for its UK drivers, marking a significant shift in its stance; however, this reclassification has yet to be applied universally in other markets.[5] In other regions, such as Australia and Canada, Uber has faced comparable pressure, though regulations remain inconsistent. In Hungary, Uber attempted to enter the market in 2016 but failed due to conflicts between institutional-regulatory platform-based work standards and Uber's operating model.[6]

Other controversies on Uber involve ignoring and evading local regulations,[7] and using tax engineering and tax avoidance techniques. It has a complex legal and tax structure based in the Netherlands, where taxes are much lower, under the company name Uber BV.[8]

Current situation

Some countries are introducing specific laws regarding ride-hailing activities. In Brazil, for example, in 2024 President Lula da Silva proposed stronger labour protections for drivers working for Uber and similar ride-hailing apps. These include new pay and hour rules, defining drivers as autonomous workers and limiting them to a twelve-hour workday. It establishes an hourly pay rate and monthly minimum wage, as well as percentages for worker and company contributions to social security programmes.[9]

In 2017, Dara Khosrowshahi became the CEO of Uber, following internal turbulence and serious headwinds related to the company's governance and reputation. In recent years, Uber has made some adjustments, such as introducing in-app tipping, providing limited insurance coverage, and enhancing communication channels to address driver concerns. Despite these changes, the question of fair treatment in Uber's labour practices remains unresolved. Many drivers continue to advocate for full employee status to secure benefits and protections, while Uber defends the flexibility of the contractor model as central to its business model and appeal. The broader implications of these ongoing disputes reflect a pivotal debate over worker rights within the gig economy, where traditional labour laws and classifications struggle to adapt to the evolving nature of work. The outcome of these legal challenges and policy shifts will likely set a precedent not only for Uber but also for the gig economy at large, potentially redefining the rights and protections afforded to millions of gig workers worldwide.

Questions

1. To what extent is Uber ethically obligated to provide drivers with employee benefits, given the control it exerts over work conditions and expectations?
2. How do Uber's cost-cutting measures, such as fare reductions and limited tipping access, align with ethical principles of fair compensation and respect for worker dignity?
3. What ethical considerations arise from Uber's classification of drivers as independent contractors, and how do these impact drivers' financial security and well-being?
4. In what ways might Uber's actions reflect or fail to reflect a commitment to corporate social responsibility and respect for worker rights?
5. Given the international scope of Uber's operations, how should Uber ethically address differing labour standards and expectations across countries, and to what extent should it standardize its practices to meet universal standards of fairness?

SECTION A. MANAGING WORK ETHICALLY

Work, understood as intentional human activity to achieve a purpose or result, plays an important role within the business company. It is through work, from entry-level positions to executive management, that people create products, deliver goods and services, solve problems and bring new ideas that drive innovation. Human work, in this way, along with capital investment and technology, contributes to achieving a company's goals.

From an economic perspective, human work is both a productive factor and a cost (the 'labour cost'), which allows economists to consider work in terms of supply and demand, as with any other commodity. This is convenient for analysing certain aspects of human work but obviously falls short as a complete view of reality. Similarly, in sociology, politics and often in management, it is common to refer to workers as a *workforce* – a term originating from mechanics but demonstrating an incomplete abstraction when applied to human beings. There is clearly a risk of viewing work and workers in such reductionist terms and, consequently, of treating workers in a very inconsiderate manner. Thus, it seems important to truly understand human work and, from that understanding, consider the ethical requirements in managing human work within the business company.

10.1 Human work and its inherent dignity

In the nineteenth century, workers were generally considered mere commodities or mechanical forces. Working conditions were extremely poor and wages were very low. This description of human work is not merely a historical oddity; similar visions and working conditions can still be found in various countries today, perhaps attenuated with a few modifications to improve productivity.

Work has a wide meaning, not limited to employment through a contract with an employer. Work can be paid or voluntary, as in the case of working voluntarily for an NGO. Some voluntary work can also be found in business organizations, where people go beyond what is strictly required by their contract by 'going the extra mile', as it is colloquially said. Work is also referred to as *labour* to designate physical or manual work linked to employment, often entailing significant physical effort or repetitive tasks.

Intrinsic dignity of human work

A cursory glance at reality shows us a substantial difference between human work and the mechanical work produced by a machine. The latter simply requires energy as input, while the former arises from acts of the human will and requires willingness and motivation. Even from an economic point of view, much human work is substantially more than a simple expense. Human work can be a genuine resource for generating income if workers are motivated and adopt a positive attitude towards learning, innovating and working hard. Good relations among workers and between workers and their leaders is a well-known business ideal.

Work is something specifically human. It originates from the person and, in a way, bears the imprint of the person. Through work, the person expresses themselves as a unique and unrepeatable being. This imprint is more recognizable in some types of work than in others. It is clear that the imprint left by an artist on an artistic work is not the same as that in producing serial pieces, but, even so, there is something personal in the work or around it, such as the way one treats those who facilitate the work or those who receive the production.

The whole person is involved in work – body, emotions and spirit – which calls into question whether a job can be entirely manual or fully intellectual, although we often continue to speak of manual and non-manual work. Most jobs contain some manual component and, at the same time, involve intelligence and emotions. Hands, head and heart are all involved in work. Describing work solely as 'labour' can lead to inconsiderate attitudes that ignore the fact that the whole person is involved in every job.

The school of *personalist philosophy* emphasizes that the person who works is the subject of that work, meaning they experience inwardly what they do. This also holds true when using AI and other advanced technologies. This fact gives work a *subjective meaning*, relative to the person of the worker, distinct from an objective meaning that considers the elements external to the subject related to work in terms of the production carried out, the external effects and the means of production used.

In the inner experience of work, each individual is aware that they are working and can say, 'This work is mine; I have done it.' Consequently, they can also say, 'I am responsible for this work, whether for better or worse.' In other words, the person is the self-possessor of their work. This does not prevent a person from working as an employee and agreeing that the product of their work is for someone else or for a company. Even so, that work is theirs; it comes from the person, the subject of the work, and it carries responsibility. Related to the inner experience of work is the search for *meaningful work* and the *personal growth* that work allows – two aspects we will explore later (10.6).

While work is necessary for the vast majority of people to earn a living, it is, above all, something personal. Work stems from the person who experiences and accepts it in their subjectivity. In this way, work can be considered a vital expression of the person and their dignity, which is extended through their work. Work has intrinsic dignity because it originates from the person, who is always the subject of work, even when performed through technical means, no matter how sophisticated they may be. Therefore, work has dignity independent of its economic value, cultural interpretation or social evaluation.

The subjective–objective dimensions of human work

Philosophical anthropology and ethics consider work as a human activity and emphasize the respect that it deserves, as well as its capacity to contribute to the development of workers. Independent of the economic value or social relevance of work, the subject of the work is a person, a being with intrinsic dignity. This is true even in jobs that are very mechanical and repetitive. In this kind of work, the subject is also a conscious, free being – a person endowed with intrinsic dignity.

In this regard, an interesting insight was introduced by Pope John Paul II.[10] He distinguished an objective and a subjective meaning of human work. The objective aspect refers to whatever is involved in the means of production, including technology, machinery and any other instrument used to transform raw materials or to create a service, as well as the product itself. The subjective aspect of work refers to the subject of work; that is, the person who intentionally directs the process; the one who works. Developing these ideas, John Paul II concluded that the primary basis of the value of work is the working person, and *the subjective meaning of work has pre-eminence over the objective*.[11] A consequence of this is the primacy of the person in the production process, the primacy of the person over things.[12]

The subjective meaning of work emphasizes that the worker is the origin of any work, and that the production process is much more than producing objects (products) with certain economic value. The worker uses raw materials, tools, machinery, equipment, robots or other devices, which are instruments of human work. It is the worker who is conscious of the activity and finds meaning (or does not) in what he or she is doing. In working, the whole person is in action – mind, will, feelings, and the acquired skills and moral habits.

Associated with the subjective meaning of work is the fact that the worker not only produces things but is also affected by the work and, in a certain sense, is transformed through the work. Work produces satisfaction or, on the contrary, brings about tiredness and maybe anguish or stress; it develops abilities and provides experience. In working, the subject of work projects his or her whole person into the activity, and often the product bears the imprint of the person who made it. Work is an opportunity to apply one's talents and creativity and possibly to face challenges or resolve needs.

No one works completely alone; others collaborate in one's work in different ways. They might develop instruments for doing the job or provide capital to finance it. Furthermore, there are people who will benefit from the work. Products will serve people, and remuneration will serve to support the worker's family and maybe contribute to good causes. Work is, therefore, a way of doing good and, consequently, of developing human virtues and facilitating human flourishing.

Beyond these meanings, work also has a spiritual dimension when connected with transcendence or with the ethical values involved in personal work. One can discover that work ultimately involves the use of one's talents, which ultimately are gifts one has received. One might also be aware of the vocational sense of work, the place of human work within creation, and what God might expect from one's work. Thus, spirituality may arise in the workplace.

The subjective dimension of work has implications for the organization of work in respecting labour rights (10.2) and in favouring meaningful and developmental work (10.6).

Dignity of human work and the labour contract

The dignity of human work and the subjective meaning of work have immediate implications for how *labour contracts* should be understood in humanistic terms. A labour contract involves hiring a person to work in exchange for compensation. As with other contracts, the parties agree to an exchange. However, in a labour contract, what is exchanged is human work for money or some other recompense. This gives this contract a particular characteristic.

When buying a car, one exchanges one thing (money) for another (a car), but in a labour contract, one agrees to give personal activity, devoting a substantial part of one's life to working for a firm. If human work has dignity and not only a price, then the labour contract should be seen as a *personal provision of service*, not a commodity.

The free agreement between employer and employee can produce fair contracts if both parties have similar negotiating power, or at least if one has a strong sense of justice. However, if one party is powerful and the other is in need, there is a risk of abuse. Many countries now have laws to prevent abuses in labour contracts, but laws can fall short, and unscrupulous employers may impose contracts that lack justice.

A labour contract introduces *duties of justice* and special responsibilities on the part of the employer towards the employees. According to the Personalist Principle (2.7), the employer should respect workers' rights. Furthermore, the employer should provide conditions for the employees' personal growth. At the same time, the labour contract also involves duties for employees. They should work in accordance with the employer's requirements and guidelines and serve the firm's legitimate interests with loyalty.

10.2 Labour rights

Labour rights are human rights (2.5)[13] in the labour context. Respecting labour rights is an essential requirement for the dignity of the worker and the dignity of labour. Such rights are strongly echoed in the vast majority of international conventions. The International Labour Organization (ILO) and other national and supranational organizations actively advocate for them. The ILO *Declaration of Fundamental Principles and Rights at Work* specifically addresses this topic. The UN Global Compact (8.6) devotes four out of its ten principles to labour rights and two more to human rights in business. Let us review some basic labour rights.

Fair remuneration and the 'living wage'

Employee remuneration includes wages and other economic compensations or benefits, such as health insurance, social security, personal or family loans and profit-sharing. Obtaining appropriate remuneration is linked to the right to life and to acquiring what is necessary for one's own sustenance and to raise children. For the vast majority of people, their livelihood depends on their wage, and this brings about serious ethical obligations.

The right of the employee to receive fair remuneration is a primordial labour right. Although problems regarding justice in pay can be found in both developed and developing countries, in the latter they can have more dramatic consequences. Companies often go to developing countries because of low labour costs. This has positive effects since they provide jobs and create wealth, part of which remains in the host country, but the risk of abuse, especially in regards wages, is high. This is one of the issues with sweatshops, discussed below. In developed countries, problems regarding justice in wages can be found mainly among underqualified employees and in the informal economy.

Determining a fair wage for each situation is no easy task. However, it can be argued that a person working full-time should receive remuneration sufficient to live and to support an ordinary family in conditions at least above the poverty line in his or her country or region and should be furnished with the means to worthily cultivate his or her own material, social, cultural and spiritual life. Particular family needs, specially related to children and dependent elders, can be also considered, in a way, as a complement that addresses the subjective (personal) dimension of work beyond productivity. Although talented and skilled employees may earn much more, fair pay is often a problem for employees who can be easily replaced. For such situations, the concept of the *living wage* makes sense. This refers to the amount of money a full-time employee needs to afford the basic necessities of life and rise above the poverty threshold.[14]

Many countries have introduced a 'minimum wage', which, despite being relatively low, can ensure a minimum income for one's livelihood. However, some question the minimum wage from a strictly economic perspective because, in certain contexts, it could be higher than what the law of supply and demand in the labour market would dictate, potentially affecting unemployment and other economic variables. In practice, balanced solutions need to be found to make a practical living wage possible for every employee.

Beyond the issue of a minimum wage, fair remuneration should consider the responsibilities and contributions of the employee in accordance with distributive justice criteria. Practical wisdom helps shape a salary policy appropriate to the economic situation of the firm, the country, and the specific industry.

Occupational health and safety

The right to life and physical, mental and moral integrity necessitates occupational safety and health. A comprehensive definition of this concept and related objectives have been provided by the ILO and the World Health Organization (WHO)[15]:

Occupational health is oriented 'to promote and maintain highest degree of physical, mental, and social well-being of workers in all occupations'. Occupational health includes the following objectives:

1   The maintenance and promotion of workers' health and working capacity.
2   The improvement of working conditions and the working environment to become conducive to safety and health.
3   The development of work organization and working cultures that should reflect essential value systems adopted by the undertaking concerned, and include effective managerial systems, personnel policy, principles for participation and voluntary quality-related management practices to improve occupational safety and health.

Hazardous substances, such as asbestos, cotton dust, heavy metals, gases, solvents and certain classes of chemicals can cause illnesses and other health-related conditions due to prolonged exposure. Safety hazards involve electrical shocks, cuts, burns and impairment of sight or hearing. They can result from contact with machinery parts or electrical lines, chemical explosions, fires, falls from great heights and so on. Pregnant women and disabled employees can be especially vulnerable to some risks.

Following an industrial accident, there may be those who defend employers against charges of violating the rights of workers involved, claiming that the workers voluntarily assumed the risk and that company practices were not the direct cause of the injury or death. Indeed, there are some jobs, such as coal mining or construction work, that are known to have high accident rates, and those who choose to do these jobs might do so freely, even when safer employment is available. However, the argument that exposing oneself to risk is a choice workers make is flawed since such choices are often strongly conditioned by necessity.

Wherever safety risks are foreseeable, responsibility lies with those who can take steps to prevent them. Companies should, therefore, establish reasonable measures to avoid accidents and hazards for anyone involved in their business activities, including prevention plans and procedures that comply with the specific industry's characteristics. Information on hazards and the company's health and safety standards should be available to everyone in an accessible language. Workers and managers should be advised of the risks and dangers of their work and trained in all tasks for which they will be responsible before beginning new assignments. This should be complemented by regular health and safety training to avoid accident risks and to respond to workplace emergencies. In some cases, workers and managers should undergo medical checks to measure and prevent instances of occupational illness.

One issue related to worker health and safety concerns daily working hours, rest and annual holidays. The *personalist principle* (2.7) demands respect for human health (avoiding stress and exhaustion) and allows enough time for workers' personal lives, family and religious duties.

Reasonable daily working hours and the 'Sabbath day'

The problem of limiting working hours has been under debate since at least the time of the First Industrial Revolution in Britain, when people working in large factories were subjected to long hours, sometimes fourteen hours a day, and abysmal working conditions. In response to this situation, a movement emerged in the nineteenth century advocating eight-hour working days with the slogan, 'Eight hours labour, Eight hours recreation, Eight hours rest.' The demand succeeded and was accepted by an international convention after many years of struggle. Nowadays, most countries have legislation limiting hours of work, which generally includes a ceiling on hours worked each day, week and year, along with limits and payments for overtime work. A weekly rest and annual vacations are also included in the legislation of most countries.

Special consideration should be given to the *Sabbath day* – a day of rest and worship rooted in the Judeo-Christian tradition. In Judaism, the Sabbath is observed from Friday evening to Saturday evening. In Christianity, it is associated with Sunday, commemorating the resurrection of Christ.

In Islam, Friday holds special significance as a day of communal worship and spiritual emphasis, although it is not a full day of rest in the same sense.

Even in secularized societies, *one or two days of weekly leisure time* are generally considered essential for everyone. When employees lack a regular day off, it becomes difficult to maintain a healthy work–life balance. A weekly holiday allows time for worship, spiritual life, rest and leisure, and supports family and community life.

While certain services – such as public safety, transport or hospitality – require ongoing operation, businesses should strive to organize work schedules in ways that ensure individuals still have adequate time for rest and renewal. An exclusive focus on profit motives can systematically erode the value of weekly rest and make human fulfilment more difficult to attain.

Freedom of association, collective bargaining and going on strike

Freedom of association is a well-recognized human right when such gatherings pursue legitimate aims. Freedom of association is a consequence of human freedom and sociability. In business, both employees and employers should be free to create organizations. As an ILO declaration states, 'the right of workers and employers to form and join organizations of their choice is an integral part of a free and open society. It is a basic civil liberty that serves as a building block for social and economic progress.' The UN Global Compact (8.6) states in Principle 3: 'Businesses should uphold the freedom of association and the effective recognition of the right to collective bargaining.'

Consequently, the *right to create and join unions* must be respected, and companies should permit workers to unionize and recognize the elected workers' representatives. In the few countries where a legal prohibition of unions exists, companies should seek alternative measures for open dialogue with employees' representatives elected to defend their legitimate interests.

To reinforce the negotiating power of employees, unions have traditionally relied on collective bargaining, a right related to the freedom of association and legally recognized in many countries and by international conventions. *Collective bargaining* is a process of negotiation between representatives of employees (frequently unions) and management or representatives of employers' organizations. Usual topics of collective bargaining include wages, grievance procedures, work hours, rest periods, breaks and other work conditions. From an ethical perspective, the right at stake is fair treatment in negotiating employment conditions. Collective bargaining can facilitate this aim, but individual negotiation can also be fair.

Going on strike, or deliberate absence from work, is a measure occasionally employed by trade unions. Striking is ethically acceptable under certain circumstances as an extreme measure to defend legitimate interests. Most countries recognize striking as a legitimate right but place certain limitations upon it (minimum services for public interest, etc.).

However, strikes can be disproportionate and seriously affect third-party rights (for example, healthcare services and public transportation). That is why the law usually introduces some restrictions and even gives employers a legitimate defence against secondary boycotts promoted by unions in their demands.

Unions, which can sometimes be very powerful, bear responsibility both for defending the legitimate interests of workers and for the means they employ. Going on strike is a measure where labour unions should be particularly conscientious because it can cause great harm.

Employee privacy and protection of personal data

Employers have always been interested in monitoring workers, but current technological advances make it possible to invade personal privacy as never before. Employers can monitor almost every aspect of their employees' jobs, especially when they are using email, telephones, video cameras or voicemail, and thus can listen in on or read most workplace communications. Management may be interested in tracking employees' work habits, movements and even conversations. However, employees have a right to their own privacy. Therefore, tension exists between surveillance and employee privacy, and not every type of surveillance is ethically acceptable. In general terms, it is unjust for employers to use electronic surveillance (10.9) to monitor employees without their knowledge or consent.

One of the critical issues concerning personal data in the work context involves the disclosure of an employee's medical records and the unauthorized acquisition of medical information. Human dignity, and more specifically the individual's right to privacy, makes it mandatory to obtain written consent from the job applicant or employee before disclosing such information to the employer. Regulation on employee and customer privacy protection is increasing. However, in many countries, employee privacy rights are still insufficiently acknowledged.

Fairness in procedures within the organization

The human right to due process applies to performance appraisals, evaluations and other procedures. Additionally, a fair process promotes the satisfaction of both employer and employee. In fact, among the biggest factors contributing to hostility in the workplace are inequity and selective discipline. This does not refer solely to ethnicity/race, age and family discrimination; employees frequently cite favouritism and unfairness as reasons for discomfort and intimidation at work, and they can serve as grounds for proving patterns of discrimination in the workplace.

One area where fairness is critical is in dismissals and lay-offs. The principle of double effect (4.6) provides guidelines to reflect on the ethical acceptability of a lay-off. When a dismissal or lay-off is unavoidable, careful deliberation is required to ensure fairness in the selection of who is to leave.

The right to due process includes a clear dismissal procedure that is known to employees. Unfair dismissal occurs, for instance, when there is no just cause for dismissal or when it is not carried out according to a fair and established procedure.

Lastly, there are grievance procedures. A grievance is a complaint by an employee regarding an actual or supposed circumstance considered 'just cause'. Through a complaint, employees can bring workplace concerns to upper levels of management on matters relevant to their employment or conditions of service when the customary channel of discussion with a direct supervisor has proven ineffective. This process is more formal than mediation and requires that rules be strictly followed. Workers must have the right to submit grievances about the workplace without the threat of losing their job or suffering other adverse actions. The company should establish procedures and appoint representatives that enable employees to submit complaints. Grounds for complaints can range from dissatisfaction with work hours to cases of abuse. The company should systematically and objectively review every complaint. Additionally, each complaint should result in a formal notification of the company's findings on the issue.

Good practice allows employees the opportunity to express disagreement regarding the notification of findings and to seek recourse to independent arbitration. Moreover, grievance procedures provide individuals with a course of action and are intended to resolve matters without the need for an employment tribunal.

10.3 Exploitative labour

Lack of respect for the dignity of workers and their work means using persons as mere productive resources for selfish purposes, offending human dignity (2.5, 2.7) and the subsequent dignity of work. Any business process in which workers are mistreated or suffer degradation in their humanity are ethically reprehensible. A blatant lack of respect for worker dignity is exploitative work.

Exploitative labour can be defined as an abuse of power by the employer over employees, with unequal exchange of valour. Examples of shameless exploitation of labour include forced and compulsory labour, child labour and poor working conditions, involving low wages, lack of safety or unsafe working conditions.

Forced and compulsory labour

This includes any employment against the employee's will, which uses compulsion by violence or other threats. Forced labour, including slavery and other forms of forced free work, is clearly contrary to the personalist principle in its negative formulation (2.7). Although the practice has fortunately been abolished by law in many countries, it lingers in some locations. This is why the ILO and other international organizations are pressing for effective national laws and stronger enforcement mechanisms, such as legal sanctions and vigorous prosecution against those who exploit forced labour. The UN Global Compact requires the elimination of all forms of forced and compulsory labour (Principle 4).

Some forms of disrespect for the personal freedom of the employee can also be considered compulsory labour. This is the case of 'debt bondage' or 'bonded labour', which entails paying off loans directly with labour instead of currency or goods. It is a form of 'indentured labour' in which the employee is obliged to work for a specific period of time, for which he or she is paid only with accommodation and sustenance, or these essentials in addition to limited benefits (for instance, cancellation of a debt or transportation to a country that interests the worker). This practice might be accompanied by retention of identity cards or travel documents. Although less serious, compulsory overtime is also a form of forced labour.

Child labour

Child labour refers to work done by a child, excluding household chores in their own home and schoolwork. Child labour, in general, should be considered inappropriate or exploitative, since childhood is a time to be educated, and working during this period might not only impede attendance at school but also submit children to inappropriate influences and risks to their proper development.

However, some argue in favour of child labour, contending that its absence is a luxury that many poor states and families cannot yet afford. They add, moreover, that the school alternative is not always available: it is even pointed out that, if child labour were prohibited by law, many children could fall into prostitution. The challenge is to move beyond the dilemma of choosing between child labour and child prostitution.

The solution would require imaginative solutions compatible with an absence of child labour. Perhaps in some extreme situations, light work that leaves time and energy for a full education might be compatible with the child's dignity and development. But this cannot be a general rule.

Others argue that developed countries also had child labour at the beginning of the First Industrial Revolution. It is true that child labour was used in some places, but voices of morality protested against this practice during the First Industrial Revolution.[16]

A vast majority of countries have become signatories of the *Convention on the Rights of the Child*, which establishes that: 'States which are party [to the convention] recognize the right of the child to be protected from economic exploitation and from performing any work that is likely to be hazardous or to interfere with the child's education, or to be harmful to the child's health or physical, mental, spiritual, moral or social development.'[17]

The ethical answer is that economic development cannot be achieved at the cost of children's development, by exploiting them as a mere resource. A realistic solution would require international cooperation, in which multinational companies should play their part.

Although in many countries it is forbidden to hire a child below a certain age (generally fourteen to seventeen), in some developing countries one can begin full-time employment at seven years old or even younger. The UN Global Compact requires the effective abolition of child labour (Principle 5).

Child labour remains a persistent problem in the world today,[18] and can cover a great variety of activities, most of them in the informal sector, and mainly working in agriculture, as a street vendor or performing domestic tasks in the home of the employer or a third party. Some of these jobs entail working in hazardous conditions: in mines, with chemicals and pesticides in agriculture or with dangerous machinery. They are everywhere, but invisible, toiling as domestic help in homes, labouring behind the walls of workshops, hidden from view in plantations.

Businesses should make certain that they are not complicit in human rights abuses (Principle 2 of the UN Global Compact). One way of being complicit in forced and compulsory labour and child labour is through the supply chain (13.9).

Sweatshops

Another form of exploitation involves maintaining extremely deficient conditions in manufacturing facilities. These facilities are pejoratively referred to as *sweatshops*. The employees work long hours and are paid little. The right to unionize and other recognized labour rights are not often respected, regardless of any law to the contrary. Workers are sometimes placed in hazardous situations or extreme temperatures and are perhaps subject to harassment from supervisors or other abuses from employers.

Sweatshops are often associated with poor labour regulations, scarce or ineffective inspections and minimal means of law enforcement. These types of facilities are now mainly located in developing countries, but they have also existed in countries that are now developed. This has led some to believe that sweatshops are a step on the path to economic development and that low wages attract investment and stimulate job creation in countries whose competitive advantage is precisely their cheap labour. However, this economic reality does not justify the working conditions in sweatshops since pay is not only about economics; it is also a social and ethical issue.

Some defend the existence of sweatshops by arguing that employees voluntarily accept the working conditions associated with their job; they are not forced to work but do so as the result of a free agreement. Besides, they claim, workers could choose other alternatives but believe working in a sweatshop to be better than what else is available. These arguments are flawed, however.[19] Workers' consent to their labour is not fully voluntary. People resign themselves to working in sweatshops because they need their livelihood. Employers have great power and can easily impose harsh working conditions and low wages. Sweatshop conditions harm workers and violate elemental human rights. Although working in a sweatshop might be preferable to other options, it is actually an exploitative practice. Respect for human dignity requires at least adhering to local labour laws, refraining from coercion, meeting minimum health and safety standards and paying workers a living wage.[20]

Chronic stress and burnout

Stress, understood as a state of worry or mental tension caused by a difficult situation, can appear in the context of a job. This is not an infrequent phenomenon. In working, all employees may experience stress to some degree. Particularly damaging, however, is a prolonged and constant feeling of stress, because it can negatively affect an individual's health. This *chronic stress*, in the labour context, often results from ongoing job pressures, long hours, insufficient recovery time, high workloads and a lack of control or autonomy. Prolonged exposure to chronic workplace stress, when not successfully managed, can lead to *burnout* – a psychological syndrome which, according to the WHO,[21] is characterized by feelings of energy depletion or exhaustion, increased mental distance from one's job, feelings of negativism or cynicism related to one's job and reduced professional efficacy.

Chronic stress can be caused by working conditions and sometimes by a lack of personal self-control. Employers have an ethical responsibility not to achieve efficiency at the cost of employees' health. Overworking employees without regard for their mental and physical health can be considered exploitation. In facing the risks of chronic stress and burnout, employers should provide support systems, such as mental health services, flexible work hours or reduced workloads, to prevent these situations from occurring.

10.4 Violence and harassment at the workplace

Violence and harassment at work has affected more than one in five people worldwide according to a global survey carried out by the ILO.[22]

Physical and moral violence

Workplace violence is an extreme form of disrespect for people and is recognized as a specific category of crime that calls for distinct responses from employers, the law and communities.

The major risk factors for workplace violence include dealing with the public, the exchange of money and the delivery of goods or services. In most cases, such violence refers to simple assaults, and employees are increasingly aware of their rights.

However, violence is not limited to physical actions. In fact, most reported incidents involve psychological force. In employee–manager relationships, there can be forms of violence such as threats and harassment, including all types of sexual harassment, mobbing and other emotional abuses, as we consider next.

Sexual harassment

Sexual harassment in the workplace entails unwelcome sexual advances that cause discomfort to one or more employees, including requests for sexual favours in which refusals are met with threats, and acquiescence with rewards. The range of sexual harassment can stretch from mild transgressions and disturbance to serious sexual abuses, including coerced sexual activity. Most sexual harassment, widespread and underreported, is directed against women.[23]

Sexual harassment occurs when the victim is regularly subjected to undesired touching or other physical conduct of a sexual nature, lascivious comments, sexual jokes, offensive sexual speech or gestures, displays of provocative materials or any other action that might make the work environment intimidating and/or offensive. The harasser might be a co-worker, a client or somebody at a different level in the organizational hierarchy.

When sexual harassment is perpetrated by someone in a position of power, such as a supervisor or manager, the harasser generally tries to obtain sexual favours in exchange for benefits such as obtaining or keeping a job, favourable performance evaluation, promotion and so on – or else threatens employees who resist sexual advances. This form of sexual harassment is not only disrespectful but also an abuse of power, which explicitly or implicitly affects an individual's employment. It is a serious injustice against the victim and even against third parties (for instance, when it leads to unfair promotion). In addition, sexual harassment interferes with an individual's work performance and can cause dysfunction in the organization.

Prevention is the best tool for eliminating sexual harassment from the workplace. Employers and managers should take all the steps necessary to prevent it. They should clearly communicate to employees that such behaviour will not be tolerated. They can do so by providing appropriate training to their employees, establishing an effective complaint or grievance process and taking immediate action when a complaint is received.

Psychological harassment (mobbing)

Rights such as retaining a good reputation and enjoying an environment favourable to human growth and personal integrity clash with several forms of harassment or violence that can occur in the workplace. One of these is *mobbing*, a concept taken from zoology to describe the behaviour that some animals use to scare away one of their group. In the workplace, mobbing can be defined as the intentional and repeated infliction of physical or psychological harm by superiors on subordinates or peer(s) within an organization. It includes acts (performed by an individual or group) that degrade the job conditions, health, dignity and professionalism of an employee.[24] The job performance of the employees who are exposed to mobbing decreases and their revenge intentions increase.[25]

Mobbing can consist of, for example, a systematically and persistently expressed disdain for someone, continuous humiliation, constant and trivial nit-picking criticism or a systematic refusal to value and acknowledge what the victim is accomplishing. Notice that, while all of these actions are offences against human dignity, we talk of mobbing only when they are frequent and systematically repeated over time. In some countries, the law protects employees against mobbing and specifies, in great detail, exactly what it consists of.

10.5 Diversity in the workplace: Unfair discrimination and justice

Diversity among candidates to be incorporated into business organizations is increasing across dimensions such as race, ethnicity, sex, disability, education, socioeconomic status, religion, cultural background, sexual orientation, gender and age, among others. Diversity in the workplace is defended by many, but there are also detractors, and both are generally based on business or moral reasons.

Regarding business, advocates of diversity argue that it brings together people from different backgrounds, cultures and experiences, which can provide a wider range of perspectives, with positive consequences for innovation and creativity. Diversity may also contribute to solving problems and decision-making from multiple angles. Additionally, diversity can better reflect society and customers and, in some sense, improve corporate reputation. On the other hand, diversity introduces the potential for conflict due to possible difficulties in communication and cooperation, stemming from differences in language, values and working styles. This may cause tension or disrupt unity in the workplace.

Moral reasons in favour of diversity include, firstly, acting with equity and avoiding unfair discrimination based on characteristics such as those previously mentioned. Some also advocate overcoming historical and systemic *negative discrimination* and promoting equal opportunities for everyone, regardless of their background, to create a more equitable and inclusive environment in companies. This involves recognizing, valuing and respecting these differences to create an environment where all individuals feel welcome and can contribute meaningfully to organizational success. Some go further by proposing *positive discrimination*, giving preference to traditionally marginalized groups over others.

In addition to business and moral arguments for diversity, some countries are experiencing social pressure from the *Diversity, Equity and Inclusion* (DEI) movement – sometimes expanded to include *Belonging* (DEIB).

The roots of DEI and DEIB can be traced back to the civil rights movements of the 1960s, which opposed racial segregation and discrimination. More recently, feminist advocacy, the LGBTQ+ movement, and disability rights campaigns have also contributed to the foundation of DEI, promoting the creation of more inclusive spaces and policies that ensure equality for marginalized groups.

Moral arguments in managing diversity require ethical analysis, primarily in terms of justice, and this is our aim here. First, however, we should focus on the universal dignity of every human being and discuss frequent unfair forms of discrimination.

Diversity and human dignity

We previously discussed human dignity (2.5) as a key ethical category and respect for this dignity as a crucial ethical principle (2.7). Human dignity is recognized by the UN Universal Declaration of Human Rights, which explicitly emphasizes that dignity, along with inherent rights, is independent of diversity, stating: 'Everyone is entitled to all the rights and freedoms set forth in this Declaration, without distinction of any kind, such as race, colour, sex, language, religion, political or other opinion, national or social origin, property, birth, or other status' (Art. 2).

The ILO stresses that discrimination in the world of work is a matter of concern and emphasizes the importance of avoiding this practice.[26] Unfair discrimination not only violates a most basic human right but also stifles opportunities, wasting the human talent needed for economic progress, and accentuating social tensions and inequalities.

The UN Global Compact (8.6) addresses discrimination specifically in business in Principle 6: 'Businesses should uphold the elimination of discrimination in respect of employment and occupation.' In the development of this principle, discrimination in employment and occupation is defined as 'any distinction, exclusion, or preference that has the effect of nullifying or impairing equality of opportunity or treatment in employment or occupation'. The document also clarifies that 'distinctions based strictly on the inherent requirements of the job are not discrimination' (in the pejorative sense).

Problems can arise in hiring and firing, and in promotion, advancement and training opportunities, among others. Non-discrimination in these areas means selecting employees exclusively on the basis of their ability to do the job.

In many countries, direct discrimination is banned by law, but indirect bias is still frequent. It slips in through informal attitudes and practices in organizations, frequently under the appearance of non-discrimination. There are several common forms of discrimination in business.

Frequent forms of unfair discrimination

Discrimination generally has a negative connotation, but, in its etymological sense, it simply means the 'action and effect of making a distinction or differentiating one person or thing from another'. In this sense, therefore, discrimination is not morally wrong. When a company selects personnel, discrimination occurs in accordance with the profile required for the job, which is perfectly right in itself. However, there is also 'invidious discrimination', which is ethically unacceptable. It occurs when there is rejection of persons based on their diversity, violating their intrinsic human dignity.

Ethnic and racial discrimination

Although the terms 'ethnic discrimination' and 'racial discrimination' are often used interchangeably, there is a difference. The first refers to the less favourable treatment of persons belonging to a certain ethnic group or nationality, for instance, Koreans in Japan or Turks in Germany. Ethnic discrimination is frequently directed at immigrants from certain countries. Racial discrimination refers to discriminatory behaviour against certain races, such as whites in China or Asians in certain parts of Russia.

Gender discrimination

Unfair gender discrimination can be expressed in unequal opportunities for men and women caused by discriminatory policies regarding healthcare, parental leave and certain job roles. It is often also characterized by more covert forms of discrimination, for example, persistent patronization and the making of inappropriate jokes.

Family discrimination

This occurs when employees are not treated equally concerning their family responsibilities towards children, especially young children, disabled family members or elderly parents. These family responsibilities can conflict with rigid business requirements. However, nearly everyone has some type of family bond and subsequent duties that can become acute (for example, illnesses and school schedules of young children or special needs of the elderly or disabled family members). Businesses must make efforts to help resolve conflicts between work and family responsibilities.[27]

Religious, cultural and political discrimination

Religious discrimination occurs when a person is treated less favourably than another in a comparable situation based on religion. Issues related to religious discrimination in the workplace may include hiring, promotion, dismissal and work conditions, particularly respecting the right to observe religious feasts, worship and prayers. Forbidding discreet religious symbols can be considered religious discrimination unless other employees or customers are reasonably disturbed by the symbols.[28]

Cultural discrimination happens when a person is treated less favourably due to membership in a social or cultural group, while political discrimination occurs based on political opinions or affiliation with political parties.

Sexual orientation discrimination

Unfair discrimination towards the LGBTQ+ community is often typified by harassment and bullying. As a result, members of this community are being passed over for promotion, or even forced to resign due to unsafe working environments.

Age discrimination

This occurs when a person is treated less positively due to age. This most often occurs when older workers seek new jobs, try to sustain current employment or compete with younger employees for promotion. Tensions can arise between age and performance, but this is not always the case, and sound solutions require wisdom. Many countries have laws to prevent age discrimination and protect older employees. However, in some cases, it may be legitimate for a company to prefer a younger employee for reasons other than age.

Managing diversity with justice

Justice (5.1) is a fundamental duty and virtue that demands giving each person what they are due/their right. In relation to diversity, a crucial requirement is to respect the universal dignity and innate rights (human rights) of every human being. Consequently, all people should be treated with respect and consideration.

Beyond respecting fundamental equality, justice also requires respect for differences, and these may require special attention in the organizational context. For instance, the physiological and psychological differences between women and men, within the fundamental equality of dignity and rights of both, may entail different needs, including those related to motherhood, which should be valued and protected.

A second requirement is to apply *distributive justice* (5.1) when something scarce, such as employment, is distributed. This requires equity. Equity in distribution involves objective criteria determined with practical wisdom, avoiding biases based on diversity that are irrelevant to fair distribution. Distributive justice typically involves the selection and promotion of personnel and fair treatment in work environments. Objective criteria may include merit and ability, but personal needs may also be considered in some circumstances.

Diversity, in the social context, appeals to *social justice*, which seeks equitable distribution of goods and services to ensure a life consistent with human dignity and development. Companies can contribute to social justice by reserving jobs for people with disabilities, for example.

Some advocate for more radical inclusion through *positive discrimination*, also known as *affirmative action*, to ensure more equitable opportunities for marginalized groups. This means giving favourable treatment, often through quotas, when hiring or promoting individuals from groups that have been historically marginalized, such as ethnic minorities and women. However, this approach is controversial because it may discriminate against individuals from majority groups and prioritize diversity over merit.

The question that arises is whether affirmative action can be justified in terms of justice, given that it involves discrimination against groups not historically targeted by discrimination. Critics often focus on the use of quotas, which can result in the admission, promotion or hiring of individuals based on group membership rather than qualifications and merits. It is noteworthy that, in 2023, race-affirmative action in admission programmes in colleges and universities in the United States were ended by a sentence of the US Supreme Court. Affirmative action policies require careful discernment and may only be justified as temporary measures to overcome discriminatory effects that cannot be eliminated through other means.[29]

10.6 Decent work, meaningful work and developmental work

In positive terms, ethics in human work requires what is often termed 'decent work', with the possibility of working on/in something meaningful, that is, 'meaningful work,' and working in conditions that can contribute to personal development, that is 'developmental work'.

Decent work – a comprehensive concept

Decent work is a term introduced by the ILO in the early twenty-first century, with a very comprehensive meaning. Currently, the ILO describes decent work as a summary of the aspirations of people in their working lives, adding that decent work

> involves opportunities for work that is productive and delivers a fair income, security in the workplace and social protection for all, better prospects for personal development and social integration, freedom for people to express their concerns, organize and participate in the decisions that affect their lives and equality of opportunity and treatment for all women and men. Sums up the aspirations of people in their working lives.[30]

It is rooted in labour rights, a recurrent theme of the ILO from the beginning of the twentieth century, and in Catholic social teaching[31] since the later nineteenth century, when in 1891 Pope Leo XII energetically defended a living wage, human working conditions, the rights to fair labour contracts and to form and join trade unions.[32] In a similar vein, Pope Benedict XVI, after defining decent work as 'work that expresses the essential dignity of every man and woman in the context of their particular society',[33] added a list of decent work components, which confirms and extends the ILO description. According to Benedict XVI,[34] decent work is that which:

- Is freely chosen.
- Effectively associates workers, both men and women, with the development of their community.
- Enables the worker to be respected and free from any form of discrimination.
- Makes it possible for families to meet their needs and provide schooling for their children, without the children themselves being forced into labour.
- Work that permits the workers to organize themselves freely, and to make their voices heard.
- Leaves enough room for rediscovering one's roots at a personal, familial and spiritual level.
- Guarantees those who have retired a decent standard of living.

The novelty of 'decent work' is that it is a comprehensive concept taken by the ILO as strategically worthy. Decent work is now a central aspect in the current ILO agenda, with special emphasis given to its four pillars: employment creation, social protection, rights at work and social dialogue. These four pillars of the decent work agenda have become integral elements of the new 2030 UN Agenda for Sustainable Development, also known as the Sustainable Development Goals (13.6).[35]

In too many countries, requirements of decent work are far from being met, which can be explained by some – often undisclosed – threshold assumptions and ideals about the nature of the field and the economic and political institutions.[36] Underlying the lack of decent work is economism, which considers work simply as an economic factor.

Organizing work ethically presents challenges for the design of organizations, managerial control systems and the way people are managed within the organization – often termed human resources management (HRM). When it comes to managing people, there is an abundance of studies from psychological, sociological and political perspectives. However, these studies often exclude ethical considerations, likely due to their highly specialized focus. As has been noted, 'current approaches to HRM fail to place ethical considerations as their central warrant'.[37]

Meaningful work

In its origins, job design was strongly focused on specialization in order to enhance efficiency. The contribution of specialization to efficiency is well known, at least since Adam Smith (1723–90) emphasized this correlation in *The Wealth of Nations*.[38] He provided a convincing example to illustrate the power of specialization: making pins from wire. The work in a pin factory was organized by dividing the activity into five tasks (drawing the wire, straightening it, cutting it, grinding the point and attaching the head), with one worker assigned to each task. This specialization allowed a production of 48,000 pins per day. Before specialization, when a single worker did all five tasks, the production was only 200 pins per day.

At the beginning of the twentieth century, under scientific management, specialization came about as the result of a rationalized process – that is, Taylorism. Efficiency increased and so did gains for both employees and employers. However, the work was highly mechanized and the job satisfaction level very low. Specialization brought about boredom and discontent by mandating the same job be done repeatedly by the same person. This increased absenteeism and reduced interest and effort at work. From an ethical perspective, the treatment given to the workers failed to acknowledge their talents and potential for personal development.

The mechanistic approach focused exclusively on maximizing productivity through an efficient organization of work, often through repetitive tasks that entailed monotonous activity. However, this was corrected with some *job design* techniques intended to increase worker satisfaction and provide greater workforce flexibility. Thus, job rotation and job enlargement were introduced. While in *job rotation*, workers simply move from one task to another to alleviate boredom and monotony, in *job enlargement* some related tasks are added. In the late 1960s, *job enrichment* was proposed, involving a job design with a variety of productive activities – instead of the repetitive and monotonous performance of a single task, for instance, in an assembly chain – along with appropriate training to carry them out. More recently, two new concepts have been proposed as good management practice in the organization of work. One is *empowerment*, which includes sharing information, rewards and power with employees so that they can take the initiative and make decisions to solve problems and improve service and performance. The other is *job crafting*, which consists of giving certain autonomy to employees to reframe their work physically, socially and cognitively.

All of these types of job design generally produce more enjoyable work, empirically measured as *job satisfaction*. This concept is definable as 'a pleasurable or positive emotional state resulting from the appraisal of one's job or job experiences'.[39] Job satisfaction has been widely studied in organizational research, and many positive correlations made between job satisfaction and organizational performance have been noted.[40] Job satisfaction fosters an employee's voluntary commitment and willingness to work beyond the strict contractual duties (organizational citizenship behaviour); it also reduces absenteeism and staff turnover. Other positive effects may also be associated with job design. Thus, job crafting not only gives job satisfaction but also fosters engagement, resilience and thriving at work.[41]

In addition to positive outcomes related to emotional state and performance, job enrichment, empowerment and job crafting seem more consistent with human dignity than Taylorism, since these techniques give workers the opportunity to apply and develop their talents.

Organizational studies have coined the concept of *meaningful work* to mean something more than enjoyment through work, although the latter can be a source for the former. The idea of meaningful work as a need was particularly well expressed in the mid-1970s: 'Working is about the search for daily meaning as well as daily bread, for recognition as well as cash, for astonishment rather than torpor; in short, for a sort of life rather than a Monday through Friday sort of dying.'[42]

Interest in meaningful work has increased considerably, bringing about a wide variety of conceptual and empirical research which relates meaningful work with leadership, organizational culture, employee engagement and other topics related to human behaviour in organizations and, ultimately, with performance. However, beyond performance, meaningful work has human and ethical content connected with favouring the development of the employees, their commitment towards the common good and improvement of the firm, as well as their well-being.

Although meaningful work depends to a great extent on personal motives (remuneration, pleasant work, challenge, having friends there, spiritual motives and so on), the organization can also contribute to making work meaningful by, for instance, fostering in employees a sense of creating a great company in terms of success, cohesiveness and organizational culture, and even more by making clear the contribution of the company to the common good of society. Managers with a sense of service will do their best to provide meaningful work for employees as far as this is in their hands.

In the digital age, the challenge for meaningful work is even greater than before. In Industry 4.0, sophisticated technical elements abound in the concept of cyber-physical systems, which combine communications, information technology, data and physical components integrating a number of core technologies. However, all of these elements are instrumental while the real subject of work is the human being, who will always be in search of the meaning of their work as an important part of searching for meaning in life.[43]

Developmental work

Developmental work refers to how people can grow personally and professionally through their work. Its conceptual foundation lies in the internal effects of action (4.4) – specifically, the internal effects of work-related actions. These include how engaging in tasks, responsibilities or decision-making processes contributes to the development of a worker's character, judgement, professional competence and sense of purpose.

The *internal effects of work-related actions* encompass physical, psychological and moral dimensions. These might include tiredness, anguish, satisfaction or learning. Learning, in this context, includes the acquisition of practical know-how or productive experience, along with the corresponding development of skills. Internal effects also involve moral experience, which refers to the intentionality behind work and the worker's awareness of the service or harm their actions may cause. This moral experience plays a role in the development of moral habits – that is, virtues or vices.

In practical terms, this means that while producing a good or delivering a service, the worker may grow as a human being – or, conversely, may undermine his or her own humanity. Virtues are essential to human flourishing (2.8), and they are cultivated when individuals work with justice, honesty and a sense of service. One important virtue in this context is industriousness, which refers to the quality of being hardworking, acting with dedication and diligence in all aspects of one's work. Industriousness is a core component of what is often called work ethics – a concept that conveys the idea that work possesses moral value and an inherent capacity to build character.

To sum up, productive work can either contribute to a worker's professional and human development or lead to their degradation – the latter occurring when work is poorly performed or not oriented towards moral good. While developmental work primarily depends on the will of the worker, organizational structures also play a role in shaping this development. Organizations can promote it by encouraging participation, initiative, creativity and responsibility. Additionally, informal organizational dynamics and culture – insofar as they influence human behaviour (9.7) – can stimulate developmental work.

Respecting the right to work is fundamental, and promoting meaningful work is highly desirable. However, fostering developmental work is a mark of ethical excellence in organizing work.

Business Ethics in Action #10

Surgikos: From a *maquiladora* to a cellular manufacturing system[44]

Surgikos, founded in 1970 in Juarez, Mexico, was part of the *maquiladora program*, which had been established five years earlier to attract foreign investment and create employment opportunities. The term *maquiladora* originates from the Mexican-Spanish word *maquilar,* meaning to assemble, and this word was applied to manufacturing plants, primarily located along the Mexico–US border. Beginning in the 1970s, *maquiladoras* operated under a model that facilitated the importation of raw materials and components without tariffs, provided the finished goods were re-exported, typically to the United States, within a six-month window. This system was part of Mexico's Border Industrialization Program and was designed to attract foreign investment, reduce unemployment in border regions, and generate export revenues. The model allowed for 100 per cent foreign ownership of the facilities, with the stipulation that the imported materials be used solely for export production. Mexican labour was employed primarily for manual assembly work, while final processes such as quality control, branding, and packaging often took place in US-based facilities.

Surgikos specialized in producing disposable surgical products, including sheets and gowns. The company started with a twin plant in El Paso, Texas, and expanded rapidly, establishing four more plants by the 1980s. In 1988, Cruz Huerta was appointed general manager of one of the Juarez plants, overseeing operations in a region that housed twenty-two different *maquiladoras* employing over 3,100 workers.

While *maquiladoras* brought economic advantages such as job creation, lower production costs and cheaper goods for consumers, they also faced significant criticisms. Many of these plants were notorious for monotonous work, low wages and poor working conditions. Some *maquiladoras* were even associated with exploitation and, in extreme cases, sexual harassment, especially of women. Additionally, these plants have drawn criticism for their environmental impact, with concerns about pollution and poor waste management practices.

In 1990, Huerta was entrusted with opening a new Surgikos plant in Guadalupe, Mexico, in partnership with the Mexican company *Productos Médicos de Monterrey.* Seizing the opportunity to address the shortcomings of the *maquiladora* model, Huerta aimed to transform the production philosophy and enhance working conditions.

He introduced the *Cellular Manufacturing System* (CMS), a modern approach that replaced the traditional assembly line setup. Unlike the rigid, repetitive nature of the *maquiladora* process, this system allowed products – such as surgical gowns – to be passed between workers in a more collaborative, team-based environment. Huerta hired 216 workers, most of whom were women with an average age of twenty-five. These employees, many of whom had only a secondary education, were trained in the new system, which fostered a sense of empowerment and teamwork.

The new plant had a production target of 28,000 surgical gowns per day, double the output of the Juarez plants. Teams of eight employees were formed, with shared responsibilities in improving both technical and human aspects of production. Supervision was minimal, with self-management taking precedence. Each team had a coordinator responsible for addressing team needs and reporting on daily production, quality control and waste management.

Huerta also integrated advanced systems like *Kanban* (a signalling system to trigger action) and *just-in-time* (JIT) production, which played crucial roles in reducing both waste and production time. The Kanban system helped minimize waste by signalling when materials were needed, while the JIT system ensured that production flowed smoothly with minimal inventory. These systems not only improved operational efficiency but also fostered a deeper sense of ownership and belonging among the workers, significantly boosting morale and self-discipline.

In this environment, employees were more deeply involved in the entire production process from start to finish. This led to higher levels of job satisfaction. The technical departments, such as quality control, maintenance and engineering, provided necessary support, while the 'people' department, helped by medical teams, ensured personal development, fair wages and workplace safety. Every two weeks, the teams would present their progress, goals and new ideas to management, and under this *participative work system,* the plant achieved a remarkable record of *zero accidents* causing production downtime.

The results of this shift to CMS were quickly apparent. Employee satisfaction soared, while costs were reduced significantly. The implementation of self-management cut inspections by 65 per cent in the sewing department and by 80 per cent in the sealing area. Waste was kept under 2 per cent and mechanical downtime decreased by 60 per cent. Reworking costs dropped dramatically, from \$68,500 in 1991 to \$24,000 in 1992.

By 1992, Huerta declared that his vision of creating a model plant had been fully realized. The plant not only improved working conditions for its employees but also contributed to the local community. Social security benefits were tailored to the predominantly female workforce, and the company made generous contributions to local retirement homes and orphanages, demonstrating a strong commitment to community welfare.

Postscript

Over time, the *maquiladora* sector has expanded rapidly, especially following the implementation of the North American Free Trade Agreement (NAFTA) in 1994, which further liberalized trade and investment between Mexico, the United States, and Canada. The agreement integrated *maquiladoras* more deeply into North American supply chains, especially in industries such as electronics, textiles, automotive, and medical devices.

As of 2025, *maquiladoras* remain a significant component of Mexico's manufacturing economy, particularly concentrated in border states like Baja, California, Chihuahua, and Tamaulipas. However, the landscape has evolved considerably. The United States-Mexico-Canada Agreement (USMCA), which replaced NAFTA in 2020, introduced stricter labour and wage requirements, aiming to improve working conditions and reduce unfair labour cost advantages. Automation and digital technologies are increasingly integrated into operations, altering labour demands. Labour reforms in Mexico – aligned with USMCA commitments – have begun to strengthen union representation and collective bargaining rights for *maquiladora* workers.

Despite these changes, concerns persist regarding wage stagnation, occupational health and safety standards, and the environmental impact of certain operations. Nevertheless, the *maquiladora* system continues to play a central role in Mexico's export-led growth strategy and remains a key node in global manufacturing networks, especially for North American markets.

* * *

The *maquiladora model*, especially in its early days, was often associated with labour exploitation due to its monotonous work, low wages and poor working conditions. Workers frequently felt like they were mere cogs in the machine, with little to no opportunities for professional or human development. Work was reduced to a means of earning a living, with no consideration of its potential to foster personal growth or contribute to broader human values.

In stark contrast, CMS promotes *a more human-centred approach* to work. CMS organizes tasks into small, flexible teams (cells), where workers are cross-trained to perform multiple roles. This gives them more control and autonomy over their tasks, fostering engagement and collaboration. Workers in CMS environments are involved in problem-solving and decision-making, which leads to higher satisfaction and a stronger sense of belonging within the company.

From an ethical perspective, CMS aligns with the *dignity of work* and the *human condition*, recognizing employees as conscious, free beings with a desire for meaningful work and continuous development. The adoption of systems like Kanban and JIT further enhances the ethical dimension by promoting lean manufacturing practices that minimize waste and improve environmental sustainability.

Huerta's decision to transition from a traditional *maquiladora* model to CMS reflects a profound sense of human and ethical responsibility. Not only did he introduce a system that provided *decent work*, but he also created an environment that fostered *meaningful and developmental work* for his employees.

Postscript: While modern *maquiladoras* have adopted more automation and advanced manufacturing processes, often resulting in job displacement, wages have generally improved. However, *maquiladoras* are still frequently criticized for not fully providing 'decent work'. Environmental regulations have also improved, though the industry's environmental impact remains a concern.

SECTION B. ETHICS IN MANAGING TECHNOLOGY, IT AND AI

10.7 Technology as ally of work and instrumental for the common good

Technology, with its tools, systems and methods, plays an instrumental role in human work, particularly in the business environment. While it is often celebrated for improving productivity and product quality, the ethical justification of technology extends beyond efficiency and profits. It requires a broader evaluation of how technology supports human work and contributes to the common good of society.

At its core, technology – whether in the form of machines, computers, production methods, robots or artificial intelligence – is not an end in itself, but *a means to serve human beings*. Humans, not technology, are the true subjects of work, and it is the intentional use of technology that reflects ethical decision-making. While technological advancement can improve efficiency, the personal intentionality behind its development, implementation and use is critical.

As discussed previously (10.1), technology is part of the *objective meaning* of work, while the *subjective meaning* of work, which centres on the person, takes precedence. This ethical principle underscores that technology, like science, must always serve humanity rather than oppose or undermine it.

Technology as an ally to human work and business development

In practice, technology is frequently an ally to human work. It automates repetitive and boring tasks, enhancing efficiency and precision in operational processes. It can also significantly improve safety and health in the workplace. For instance, robots and wearable devices can handle hazardous tasks, monitor environmental conditions and prevent accidents, thereby reducing workplace injuries. Technology also extends human capabilities, providing tools that allow individuals to achieve more, such as AI-powered decision-making systems that help professionals in fields like healthcare and finance make more informed choices.

Moreover, technology has enabled remote work through digital platforms and communication tools, allowing employees to reduce commute times and overtime while streamlining tasks. This fosters greater personal autonomy and promotes a healthier balance between work and personal life.

Businesses have benefited greatly from technological progress, particularly from information technology (IT) (10.9) and artificial intelligence (AI) (10.10). In manufacturing, technology has revolutionized production processes, primarily through automation and robotics. Technologies such as computer-aided design (CAD), 3D printing, industrial robots and smart factories have dramatically improved precision, speed and efficiency. These innovations reduce production costs, increase output and improve quality control. Smart manufacturing is gaining traction, where the integration of sensors, data analytics and machine learning enables more efficient production management. These smart systems provide real-time feedback, predictive maintenance and better decision-making processes. As a result, traditional manufacturing roles are evolving to require expertise in data science, automation systems and machine operation.

Technological development can contribute to the common good

Technological development has transformed societies, economies and cultures, offering significant contributions to the common good. While there are challenges and potential downsides, technology has been a driver for progress in multiple key areas that contribute to the common good. Technological innovations have stimulated *economic growth* and *job creation* by enabling new industries, increasing productivity and fostering *entrepreneurship*. Moreover, technology has made *information and education more accessible* through internet educational resources, e-learning platforms and online courses. Technology has also revolutionized *healthcare*, leading to better diagnosis, treatment and preventative care. Social media and digital communication platforms have fostered *connectivity* and enabled people across the world to collaborate, share ideas and raise awareness about important social issues. Technological development plays a crucial role in addressing *environmental challenges*, from renewable energy innovations to smart grids and electric vehicles, contributing to sustainable practices that reduce environmental impact and mitigate climate change. Technology has also contributed to significant advancements in *public safety and security*, such as the development of smart surveillance systems, emergency response systems and predictive policing using data analytics. Lastly, technology has enabled more transparent, efficient and inclusive governance, thus playing an instrumental role in improving governance.

Despite the numerous human benefits of technology, which deserve ethical praise, technology also presents ethical challenges. One evident issue is that technological innovations, particularly new technologies, require a workforce with technical skills to manage, maintain and innovate these systems, while making some other jobs redundant. Technology also poses challenges such as the *digital divide* (where not everyone has equal access to technology), concerns about *data privacy* and *cybersecurity*, environmental problems due to *waste generation* and the risk of misuse of technological power, such as *mass surveillance*.

In a more systematic way, the discussion of the ethical dimension of technology involves considering ethics in technological development, the implementation of technology and the way technology is used. This is the topic of the next section.

10.8 Ethical issues in developing, implementing and using technology

However, the development of technology can have malicious purposes and show a lack of respect for human dignity and rights. Its implementation generally involves negative side effects that must be ethically evaluated and mitigated. The use of technology should not be applied against human dignity, violating human rights or mistreating the natural environment.

Upright intention in developing technology

The development of technology must be driven by an upright intention – that is, to promote the common good and respect human dignity and rights. Ethical development also entails a sense of sustainability and responsibility towards future generations. Conversely, technological development becomes ethically objectionable when it is intentionally harmful or disregards human well-being. Several types of misconduct in developing technology can be identified:

- *Technology designed to cause harm*: This includes technologies intentionally developed to violate human rights or cause harm, such as weapons of mass destruction like the atomic bomb. The bombings of Hiroshima and Nagasaki in the Second World War led to catastrophic loss of life and long-term psychological and environmental damage. Today, the development of cyber weapons and mass surveillance tools for malicious purposes continues to raise ethical alarms.
- *Using inappropriate means for scientific and technological advancements*: A clear violation of ethics occurs when human beings are treated as mere tools for progress. For example, the Nazi's medical experiments on concentration camp prisoners during the Second World War represent one of the darkest chapters in technological misuse, where human dignity was blatantly disregarded for scientific purposes. Contemporary debates in biotechnology, such as the destruction of human embryos for stem cell research, similarly raise ethical concerns about destroying human life for a plausible end. The challenge is to seek alternative ethical and efficient means.[45]
- *Technology with disproportionate negative impact*: Technologies that are foreseeably harmful to people or the environment are ethically troubling. For instance, assembly line designs that force workers into monotonous, repetitive tasks can lead to physical injuries such as musculoskeletal disorders due to poor ergonomic design. On the environmental side, technologies that produce non-biodegradable products, like single-use plastics, contribute significantly to pollution, despite the availability of eco-friendly alternatives. Additionally, technologies like cryptocurrency mining and data centres consume vast amounts of energy, contributing to climate change unless renewable energy sources are used.

Ethics in implementing technology

Regarding the implementation of technology, several ethical issues must be noted:

Elimination of jobs and creation of new ones

Technology has potential for job displacement. Automation, artificial intelligence and robotics frequently replace low-skill jobs, contributing to unemployment and economic inequality. While technological advancements create new, more specialized roles – such as in fields requiring creativity, emotional intelligence and problem-solving skills – the shift leaves many workers vulnerable.

To address this issue, companies and governments must implement retraining programmes to help displaced workers transition to new roles created by technology. Reforming education systems to prepare individuals for technologically driven jobs is also critical. Companies can posit how they can help employees who are displaced, but society as a whole must address the broader implications of job displacement and economic inequality.

Fair distribution of technological benefits

While technology can deliver immense benefits, these often remain inaccessible to certain populations due to barriers like affordability or lack of digital literacy. This creates a digital divide where some employees or communities are left behind. It is essential that companies and society ensure that technological benefits are distributed equitably.

From a social perspective, addressing this issue requires a multifaceted approach, including affordable access to technology, education and retraining programmes to bridge the skills gap, ethical tech development that considers the needs of all socioeconomic groups, and government policies that prevent technology from exacerbating inequality.

Companies, in particular, can play a vital role by ensuring that all employees – regardless of their background or role – can benefit from technological advancements. This includes providing affordable access to necessary tools, fostering inclusive policies and offering upskilling opportunities.

Technology and organizational change

Technological advancements not only affect individual jobs but also transform the organization of work within companies. From the steam machine to the age of AI and robotics, technology has continuously reshaped how tasks are performed, reducing manual labour and redefining the relationship between humans and machines. This presents a potential conflict: prioritizing efficiency and productivity over the dignity of workers.

The challenge for businesses is to strike a balance between optimizing productivity and providing employees with meaningful, developmental and decent work. While achieving this balance can be difficult, it is possible through thoughtful, ethically informed strategies that prioritize human well-being alongside technological progress (see Business Ethics in Action #11).

Key criteria for using technology ethically

In addition to the ethical issues concerning the development and implementation of technology, there are broader ethical challenges related to its use. Using technology ethically refers to the responsible application of existing technologies in daily operations, workplaces and public life, while considering its impact on individuals, employees and society at large.

Essentially, ethical use of technology focuses on *human-centred* usage, ensuring that it serves people, enhances their well-being and promotes human development. Ultimately, technology should contribute to the *common good* in a sustainable manner. Rather than replacing human capabilities entirely, technology should complement them.

A right and virtuous approach to using technology involves the following key criteria:

- *Upright intention, responsibility and accountability*: The use of technology should aim to do good, balancing efficacy and efficiency but always prioritizing ethical considerations over other motivations, such as economic gain, power or vanity. Personal responsibility should not be displaced by technology. Both individuals and organizations must be accountable for the outcomes and impacts of their technological usage.
- *Ethical principles*: Several ethical guidelines frame responsible technology usage. The three principles that are especially relevant are, as discussed previously (2.7):
  — *The personalistic principle*, which emphasizes respect for human dignity and rights, honesty and fairness. This includes ensuring that technology does not cause harm. Positively, this involves safeguarding privacy and data protection. Transparency and trust are keys to ethical technology use, allowing users to understand how technology works, especially when it involves data collection, monitoring or decision-making. Fairness also encompasses all duties of justice arising from natural and acquired rights.
  — *The common good principle*, which involves fostering human values, promoting well-being, social cohesion and a culture conducive to human development. This principle requires developing a shared conscience of sustainability and accountability. Justice, including social justice, is essential to the common good, with implications for inclusivity, avoiding unfair discrimination and ensuring access to technology for all communities.
  — The *stewardship principle*, which emphasizes respect and care for the natural environment. Ethical technology usage must also be environmentally conscious, minimizing energy consumption and waste whenever possible.
- *Practical wisdom*: Crucial for accurately evaluating each situation and foreseeing the human, social and environmental impacts of applying technologies. Practical wisdom often leads to seeking alternatives or minimizing potential negative side effects of technology.

This applies to all fields of technology, but in the current business context, ethical issues in using IT and AI seem particularly relevant. We will start with the former next.

10.9 Ethical issues in using information technology

Information technology refers to the development, installation and implementation of computer systems and applications. It entails the use of computers and software, which includes the programmes, procedures and documentation that perform the functions of a computer system. Some current ethical issues related to IT are as follows:

Data privacy and user consent

Companies use technology to collect data, often without clear consent from users. Through modern IT, a business can collect and analyse vast amounts of information about its employees and customers. If this information is disseminated or sold without permission, it would be a flagrant violation of privacy. Personal data should only be obtained with informed consent, and confidentiality must be maintained. Moreover, since stored information may contain errors, individuals have the right to access and correct their personal data. Harm caused by negligence regarding this data is the responsibility of the employer.

Ethical technology usage requires full disclosure of what data is being collected, how it will be used, and assurance that users have the option to opt-out. A well-known example of this is the collection of user data through cookies when users visit websites. Under ethical guidelines – and often legal requirements – users should be clearly informed and given the option to manage their privacy settings.

Some companies have implemented transparent policies for employee monitoring, ensuring that only necessary data is collected and providing employees with insights into how their performance is being evaluated. This promotes trust and ensures the ethical usage of monitoring tools.

Technological surveillance of employees

Employee surveillance is the practice of monitoring employee activities using digital technology, such as computer software, cameras and GPS. The goal is to monitor employee performance and behaviour through various elements provided by information technology. While employee surveillance is often justified for productivity, security and legal compliance, it raises significant concerns about privacy, employee autonomy and the psychological impact on employees, with possible consequences for trust and corporate culture. Let's review these points:

Tension between employer interests and employee privacy

There is an inherent tension between evaluative surveillance in the interest of employers and employee privacy, especially given the capabilities of modern IT and its ease of implementation. In any case, human dignity and the personalist principle (2.7) require that any surveillance conducted by the company is transparently communicated to employees.

A related issue arises when employers monitor emails, social media usage or personal activities during work hours. While employers may have a legitimate interest in such monitoring, it blurs the line between personal and professional life. Each situation should be carefully considered with practical wisdom, respecting privacy and ensuring that the employer's interests are genuinely legitimate. Most countries have legal requirements regarding data protection and electronic monitoring, but not every situation is fully covered by law.

Employee autonomy

While surveillance can be seen as limiting, when applied correctly, it can also enhance responsibility by giving employees data and feedback to improve. However, this is not always the case. Surveillance often erodes employee autonomy. Under surveillance, employees may become overly cautious, focusing more on avoiding mistakes than on delivering high-quality results. This can also stifle creativity and innovation, as employees may fear negative consequences or misinterpretation of their actions. When employees feel they are constantly monitored, their autonomy in acting, taking initiatives and making decisions can be compromised.

Excessive surveillance can centralize decision-making at higher levels, removing autonomy from employees, which is contrary to the principle of subsidiarity. This principle, in this context, requires that employees manage their own tasks and make decisions without unnecessary interference from upper management. Too much surveillance can lead to the misuse of employees' talents and discourage personal growth.

Psychological impact on employees and effects on trust

Another issue, both business and ethical, is the psychological impact of surveillance on employees and how it affects trust. When employees feel they are constantly watched it can create stress, anxiety and lower morale. Employees who are continuously monitored may feel they are being treated as tools rather than individuals with moral responsibility. Furthermore, constant surveillance may suggest that the company does not trust its employees, which can negatively affect the work environment, creating a culture of distrust, reducing cooperation and increasing turnover. Ethics requires favouring employee well-being, meaningful work and good working conditions. The recommendation is to minimize surveillance, covering only what is necessary for security and work purposes, and considering each situation with practical wisdom.

In summary, surveillance should be balanced by considering, on the one hand, business benefits such as increased productivity and compliance, and, on the other, the consideration of employee privacy, respect for personal freedom and autonomy, and consequences for employee well-being and trust. While businesses have the right to monitor performance, they also have an ethical obligation to foster an environment that respects the freedom and dignity of employees. Ethical surveillance practices should be transparent, limited to necessary areas and designed to enhance, rather than restrict, employee autonomy.

Customer surveillance

Similar to employee surveillance but with different objectives, companies engage in customer surveillance focused on collecting, monitoring, storing and analysing data related to customers' behaviours, preferences and interactions. Businesses use personal data that includes needs, preferences, characteristics, behaviour, attitudes or other customer attributes (that is, market intelligence) to develop more competitive products and services.

Surveillance allows businesses to offer personalized marketing, including personalized recommendations, targeted advertisements and tailored services, thereby improving the overall customer experience. Surveillance also helps enhance decision-making and develop predictive models.

Customers may have a positive experience if they feel that businesses understand their needs and offer relevant products or services, which can increase loyalty and brand engagement. However, excessive surveillance, particularly when it feels intrusive or manipulative, can lead to customer discomfort and distrust.

The ethical perspective includes several requirements, which are often also legal:

- *Respect for privacy*: Businesses must ensure that customers' privacy is protected. They should collect only necessary data, be clear about how it is used and safeguard sensitive information. Customers should have the right to control and access their personal data.
- *Informed consent*: Businesses must seek explicit, informed consent for data collection and usage, allowing customers to opt-in and opt-out easily, with full understanding of the implications.
- *Openness, transparency and control of data*: Companies should be transparent about their data collection and surveillance practices, clearly informing customers about what data is being collected, why it is collected and how it will be used. Businesses should adopt practices that give customers greater control over their data, including the ability to make decisions regarding its retention or deletion.
- *Fairness and non-discrimination*: Surveillance practices and data usage must be fair, avoiding bias or discrimination, and ensuring that all customers are treated equitably.
- *Respect for customer autonomy and responsible nudging*: Surveillance should enhance, rather than restrict, individual freedom, avoiding manipulative tactics. If behavioural nudging is used, it should be done ethically. A nudge, which is an intervention that maintains freedom of choice but guides people in a particular direction, is only acceptable if it promotes beneficial outcomes for the customer (for example, healthier choices or financial well-being), rather than encouraging harmful behaviours or excessive consumption.

In synthesis, while customer surveillance can improve services and personalize experiences, it must be conducted in a manner that respects privacy, maintains transparency and prevents exploitation or discrimination. Businesses must use customer data ethically, give customers control over their information and protect it from misuse.

10.10 Ethics in artificial intelligence

The idea of intelligence in modern psychology is related to capacity for problem solving, which is different from the philosophical notion of reason, traditionally seen as defining human nature. Intelligence has been defined by Gardner as 'a biopsychological potential to process information that can be activated in a cultural setting to solve problems or create products that add value in a culture'.[46] Based on this definition, he proposed several types of intelligence.

Artificial intelligence (AI) was defined by John McCarthy, a preeminent pioneer in this field, as 'the science and engineering of making intelligent machines, especially intelligent computer programs'.[47] Another definition identifies AI as 'the ability of a digital computer or computer-controlled robot to perform tasks commonly associated with intelligent beings'.[48]

The development of AI focuses on creating systems capable of performing tasks that typically require human intelligence. In certain areas, such as processing big data, AI can even surpass human capacity.[49] Most existing and widely used AI is *weak AI*, which relies on *machine learning* – giving computers the ability to learn without explicit programming.[50] Applications include facial recognition and the generation of synthetic texts or images. Meanwhile, *strong AI*, capable of performing more complex tasks, remains a long-term goal for future research.

Ethics in AI, as in any other technology, includes three dimensions: ethical development, ethical implementation (considering internal consequences) and ethical usage. Before discussing the ethics of AI, it is important to introduce essential elements of how AI works, its application in business and how it differs from human capacities.

Essentials for understanding how AI works

Machine learning (ML), a fundamental component of weak AI that enables learning and informed decision-making, relies on *past data*, *algorithms* (sets of mathematical instructions) and predictive *models* generated by these algorithms. These models, once trained, can process new data to classify it – including classification or regression (capturing the relationships between independent and dependent variables) tasks – or generate new, realistic data (such as text, code or images). The first type of ML is known as *discriminative AI*, while the second is referred to as *generative AI*.

Regarding the type of learning, that which needs labelled data is called *supervised learning*, that which does not need to label is called *unsupervised*, and that which rewards the learning process is called *reinforcement learning*.

AI systems gather large datasets from sources like sensors, databases and user interactions. This data is then processed to extract valuable insights, which involves cleaning, transforming it into usable formats, and identifying patterns or anomalies. Algorithms enable computers to solve problems, and machine learning algorithms allow AI to learn from data through various methods: supervised learning on labelled data, unsupervised discovery of hidden patterns, or reinforcement learning through trial and error.

For tasks like image and speech recognition, AI often employs *neural networks*, a model inspired by biological neurons that aids in decision-making. ML models mimic cognitive functions such as learning and problem-solving; they analyse data, detect patterns, make predictions and sometimes engage in automated decision-making.

Most models are trained on large datasets, then adjusted to minimize errors and improve accuracy. Afterwards, they are tested to ensure strong performance on new, unseen data. However, reinforcement learning algorithms do not necessarily require extensive data, as they can be trained with synthetic data generated by the machine itself. Once trained and tested, AI models are deployed in production environments where they interact with real-world data and are continuously monitored to ensure proper performance and adaptability to changing conditions.

Relevance of AI in business

Economists often consider AI a *general-purpose technology* because it can impact the entire economy, much like electricity, the steam engine and the internet did in the past. This means AI brings the potential to improve existing processes, enable new activities and be applied across any sector, making its impact extend beyond efficiency and productivity to serve as a transformative force for both sectors and society.

In business, AI is used across several fields. In *marketing and sales*, AI performs predictive analytics on customer behaviour, identifies trends, optimizes marketing campaigns and automates sales processes. In *customer service*, AI-driven chatbots and virtual assistants analyse customer data to deliver personalized recommendations. AI also plays a role in *product development*, improving design, innovation and operational efficiency by predicting demand and enhancing the production process. In *supply chain management*, AI helps manage inventory and optimize logistics. In *finance and accounting*, AI increases accuracy in financial reporting, budgeting and forecasting, and even detects fraudulent activities by analysing transaction patterns. Lastly, AI assists in *managing people* by aiding in recruitment and improving employee engagement.

AI is a powerful tool transforming business operations, offering significant improvements in efficiency, productivity and decision-making. However, like any technology, AI should be ethically guided and ultimately serve people and the common good.

Artificial intelligence versus the human mind

AI analyses large datasets, recognizes patterns and makes predictions. While it can understand natural language, solve problems and make certain decisions, it lacks the *intrinsic understanding of information* that human beings possess. AI processes data and learns through algorithms and statistical patterns, whereas human reasoning involves *abstract knowledge* and deliberate reasoning. Additionally, human mind incorporates *intuition* and a unique form of *creativity*.

There are other profound differences between human reason and artificial intelligence. Humans have *self-awareness, inner consciousness, and self-transcendence*, recognizing themselves as a small part of a greater whole and acting accordingly.[51] While AI can incorporate ethical rules into its algorithms, only humans have an intimate sense *of morality*, *spirituality* and an openness to *ethical values*, which highlights a significant gap between human reason and AI. Moreover, *practical wisdom* – the virtue of sound judgement in considering life as a whole – remains outside AI's capabilities.

Human *emotions*, *sentiments* and *empathy*, fundamental aspects of human experience, are beyond AI's reach. Although AI can simulate emotional responses and provide valuable support in certain contexts, it cannot replicate the authenticity or complexity of human emotions. To sum up, AI, even in its strongest form, remains fundamentally different from the human mind. While it can process data and improve performance, it lacks consciousness, intentionality, and moral awareness. Claims that AI might learn like a child are misleading – human learning involves emotional, social, and moral development that machines cannot replicate. The depth and complexity of human understanding go far beyond algorithmic optimisation.

Ethical issues around AI

The rapid development and deployment of AI technologies present a range of ethical challenges that require careful and ongoing consideration. Central questions include how AI contributes to the *common good*, its respect for *human dignity* and *rights* and the assurance of *fair treatment*. Autonomous systems, such as self-driving cars or autonomous weapons, further complicate these issues, blurring the lines between ethical responsibility and decision-making.

Fairness in AI-driven decision-making processes is particularly challenging. At first glance, mathematical models seem to ensure that everyone is judged according to the same rules, thus eliminating bias. However, in practice, these models may inadvertently reinforce discrimination. For instance, a lending model might deem a poor college student too risky based solely on his or her post code, without considering other relevant factors.[52]

To address these challenges, several key ethical criteria should guide the development, implementation and use of AI:

- *Human-centric design*: AI must prioritize human dignity and autonomy. Systems should enhance human capabilities rather than replace them, empowering people and promoting well-being. The development of AI should be aligned with human values, ensuring that technology remains a tool for human progress rather than a substitute for human decision-making and creativity.
- *Transparency and explainability*: Transparency is essential in AI development. This involves being clear about the *data sources*, *algorithmic design* and *decision-making processes* used by AI models. However, transparency alone is not enough; AI systems also need to be *explainable*. Decisions made by AI should be understandable and interpretable for users and stakeholders, enabling them to trust the system and make informed choices.
- *User-centred design*: Engaging users in the AI design and development process ensures that the systems are *aligned with their own characteristics and needs*. This approach fosters the creation of AI that supports human objectives, considering diverse perspectives and minimizing the risk of bias or exclusion.
- *Fairness and equity*: One of the most pressing ethical issues is ensuring that AI systems avoid *perpetuating existing biases and discriminatory practices*. This includes addressing biases in

training data, which can result in unfair outcomes based on characteristics like *race, gender, age or socioeconomic status*. Moreover, fairness extends beyond the avoidance of harm; it also includes ensuring *equal access* to the benefits of AI, particularly for *marginalized or disadvantaged groups*. In practice, addressing biases is not a trivial matter, since models seek to predict the future based on what has happened, and if the training data is altered in any way, the model can also be falsified.

- *Responsibility and accountability*: Clear *lines of responsibility* must be established for the outcomes of AI systems. Developers, operators and organizations should be held accountable for the decisions and actions taken by AI. This requires mechanisms to ensure *ethical accountability* and transparency in decision-making, especially when AI operates autonomously.
- *Privacy and security*: AI systems often rely on vast amounts of personal data. Safeguarding *privacy* is a critical ethical concern. AI must comply with *data privacy laws* and take measures to protect users' personal information from unauthorized access or misuse. Additionally, robust *security measures* must be implemented to prevent *malicious attacks* on AI systems, ensuring their reliability and integrity. In this regard, there is increasing regulation in many countries. Since 2023, the EU has had the AI Act, which classifies AI models based on their danger to citizens. The use of AI models by companies requires them to be registered based on this classification.[53]
- *Impact on employment and society*: AI's potential to displace jobs is a significant ethical issue. Companies and governments must prepare for this by promoting *workforce retraining* and supporting transitions into new roles. Ensuring that those affected by job displacement have access to opportunities in the evolving economy is essential for promoting social justice and minimizing the negative societal impacts of technological progress.
- *Social impact*: AI technologies have broader *social implications* that must be carefully evaluated. This includes their potential effects on *inequality*, *social cohesion* and *democratic processes*. AI systems should contribute to the *common good* by fostering inclusivity, reducing inequality and supporting a fair and just society.
- *Role of public governance*: Governments and regulatory bodies play a vital role in overseeing the ethical development and deployment of AI. The establishment of *robust governance frameworks* ensures that AI technologies are developed and used in ways that adhere to ethical standards, protect human rights and align with societal values. This includes regulatory measures to prevent misuse and promote transparency, fairness and accountability across all sectors.

10.11 The interaction between humans and technology

The relationship between humans and technology, or more specifically the interaction between people and machines, has been present since the First Industrial Revolution in the 1780s, when steam power was widely used to drive machinery. This relationship was also relevant, albeit with different characteristics, during the 1870s Second Industrial Revolution (2IR), when mass manufacturing and the division of labour were implemented, and in the Third Industrial Revolution, which began around the late 1960s, with computing at its core.

The relationship between humans and technology has evolved rapidly in recent years, transforming how we work, communicate and live. The rise of AI further complicates this relationship, the transformation of which began in the early twenty-first century with the Fourth Industrial Revolution.

Interaction between humans and technology in the fourth industrial revolution

The 4IR is centred on the fusion of technologies that blur the lines between physical, digital and biological systems. Technologies such as AI, the Internet of Things (IoT), big data, robotics and cyber-physical systems are driving this transformation. In this revolution, machines are not only automated but also 'intelligent', learning and improving autonomously.[54]

As noted in 10.9, AI is particularly transformative, as it allows machines to perform complex tasks that require decision-making and problem-solving abilities. AI-powered systems are already being implemented in areas such as predictive maintenance, quality control and even decision-making in production processes. AI and machine learning are expected to further change employment by automating not only repetitive tasks, but also some cognitive tasks, traditionally performed by humans.

In 4IR, human–machine interaction is increasingly intuitive, utilizing voice commands, touch screens and even augmented reality (AR), enhancing efficiency and user experience. The technologies inherent to 4IR have a significant impact on humans. Work environments have been transformed, creating a demand for new skills such as data literacy, AI proficiency and advanced problem-solving.

In the context of 4IR, several ethical issues arise concerning people's interaction with AI and other technologies. Among them are the following:

- *Problems with automation in decision-making*: Ethical concerns emerge when AI-driven tools are used to make decisions regarding people, such as in hiring, credit scoring or customer service. If the final decision is made by AI algorithms rather than humans, issues like bias, lack of transparency and social exclusion can arise. For instance, AI-based recruitment tools can screen job candidates faster, but if the algorithm is biased, it may unfairly exclude qualified candidates from marginalized groups. This is what happened in 2014, when Amazon's AI hiring tool was found to be biased against women, because the algorithm was trained on résumés predominantly submitted by men (see Case Study #10). An ethical approach requires *regular audits* to ensure fairness in AI decision-making processes, with the final human decision being decisive, leveraging human capacities beyond the machine after obtaining information from AI.

- *Employee well-being in automated work environments*: The extensive use of automated systems in workplaces, such as warehouses or manufacturing, can lead managers to treat employees as 'cogs in the machine', reducing the quality of work life as tasks become highly repetitive. Ethically, companies should ensure that technological advancements aimed at increasing productivity do not come at the expense of employee well-being.
- *Balancing efficiency and personal service*: Technologies like chatbots and automated customer service systems can boost efficiency but may reduce personal interaction, which is important in contexts such as healthcare or counselling. This dehumanization can be problematic in terms of relationships with consumers and the care of the sick. The problem could be addressed by offering both automated assistance and human support when necessary.

Humanizing technology: Towards the fifth industrial revolution

The Fifth Industrial Revolution (5IR) is an emerging paradigm that focuses on harmonizing technology and humanity. It builds on the foundations of the 4IR but emphasizes more ethical human-centred technological integration, environmental concern and sustainability. This is in addition to the transformation of the industrial structure through the utilization of AI, IoT, big data, etc., which has been central to 4IR, as previously noted.

The Fifth Industrial Revolution encompasses harmonious collaboration between humans and machines, with a specific focus on the well-being of multiple stakeholders (that is, society, companies, employees, customers).[55] It thus paves the way for a revolution in thinking about and leveraging human–machine collaborations for greater societal well-being.[56] This new revolution seeks to foster a more balanced relationship between humans and technology than 4IR, where technology serves human needs in a more responsible and sustainable manner. This revolution emphasizes a clear transition from mass automation to improving the abilities of human workers, enabling personalization and product customization at a higher level.[57] It also highlights the social and emotional aspects of work and life, encouraging humans to thrive in tandem with intelligent systems. This latest technological revolution values human creativity, empathy and decision-making while relying on technology to optimize and support these areas.

In short, the transition from the Fourth to the Fifth Industrial Revolution represents a shift from technology-driven automation to human-centred innovation, where ethics, sustainability and human well-being are central to technological development. Although 5IR is still in its early stages, the perspectives it offers are promising for better integrating ethics into technology.

Case Study #10

Using AI in a hiring process[58]

In 2020, Caterine Tost, head of hiring admissions at a large bank in Australia,[59] found herself contemplating the use of artificial intelligence (AI) to streamline the hiring process. Every year, the bank received thousands of applications, and AI seemed like a promising tool to reduce the time spent screening candidates while ensuring accurate and fair selections. However, Caterine was cautious. She remembered the public criticism faced by Amazon when it introduced an AI-powered recruitment tool back in 2014. Although designed to automate the screening of résumés and recommend top candidates – particularly for technical roles – the tool became infamous for its gender bias.

Amazon's system had been trained on résumés submitted over the course of a decade, during which time the tech industry had been heavily male-dominated. As a result, the AI inadvertently learned to favour male candidates, showing preference for résumés that included predominantly male-associated language and experiences. Conversely, the tool penalized résumés that mentioned terms like 'women's', or references to women's colleges or activities. The algorithm, reflecting the biases in its training data, unfairly favoured male candidates over female ones. This example, along with other similar cases, made it clear to industry leaders that AI systems could perpetuate biases, and that transparency and accountability in algorithmic decision-making were essential.

A colleague of Caterine's recommended *HireVue*, an AI-driven tool designed to assist in screening and evaluating job candidates. HireVue's technology used machine learning to analyse video interviews, assessing various candidate attributes such as language, facial expressions and tone of voice. The system then provided scores or rankings based on the candidate's perceived suitability for the position. Caterine's colleague noted the system's major advantage: it drastically reduced the time and costs associated with traditional hiring processes, making travel to college campuses, résumé sifting and extensive interviews unnecessary.

Intrigued, Caterine began researching HireVue. While many companies reported positive experiences with the service, she also encountered some significant criticism. In 2019, the *Electronic Privacy Information Center* (EPIC), a nonprofit organization, filed a complaint with the Federal Trade Commission, accusing HireVue of engaging in 'unfair and deceptive trade practices' by using AI to assess video interviews. Although HireVue denied any illegal practice, the company responded to criticism by discontinuing its practice of analysing candidates' facial expressions in 2020, recognizing the potential ethical and legal concerns.

One particularly pointed article, titled *A Face-Scanning Algorithm Increasingly Decides Whether You Deserve the Job*, published by Drew Harwell in the *Washington Post*, deepened Caterine's concerns. Harwell described HireVue as a 'powerful gatekeeper' used by some of America's largest employers, warning that the technology was reshaping how companies assess candidates – and how candidates are expected to prove their worth. The article painted a picture of how pervasive AI had become in hiring, raising the ethical implications of entrusting such critical decisions to algorithms.

Caterine recognized that AI had the potential to drastically speed up the hiring process, offering obvious logistical benefits. However, she was uneasy about the ethical issues associated with using AI tools like HireVue. Chief among her concerns were transparency – understanding how the algorithm functioned and whether it operated without bias – and explainability – ensuring the AI's decision-making process was understandable. Additionally, she was concerned about the privacy and security of candidate data, especially the videos collected during interviews.

Caterine valued the efficiencies AI could offer but was acutely aware of the limitations of such systems in assessing the more intangible qualities of candidates. While AI could analyse résumés and interviews for measurable skills, she worried that it might miss the human qualities – empathy, leadership, moral virtues and ethical judgement – that are harder to quantify but crucial for certain roles. In her view, the hiring process should never be fully automated. The final decision, she believed, should always rest with a human, who could consider the nuances and context that AI might overlook.

Questions

1. Consider the ethical implications of using biased training data and whether the company should have foreseen these consequences.
2. Reflect on issues such as bias, transparency, accountability and data privacy in AI-driven hiring processes.
3. Discuss how to harmonise efficiency and the human judgement needed to assess the candidate qualities that AI might miss.
4. Offer suggestions on how to address Caterine's concerns, such as choosing transparent AI systems, incorporating human oversight and ensuring data protection.

Notes

1. John Paul II (Pope), *Encyclical-Letter 'Laborem exercerns'* on human work, 1981, no. 6: http://www.vatican.va/holy_father/john_paul_ii/encyclicals/documents/hf_jp-ii_enc_14091981_laborem-exercens_en.html. (Accessed on 4 June 2025).
2. Sources: J. L. Rovenpor, L. T. Stickney and R. J. S.-V. Fossen, *Uber and its Driver-Partners: Labor Challenges in the On-Demand Transportation Networking Sector*, North American Case Research Association (NACRA), 2016: https://hbsp.harvard.edu/product/NA0429-PDF-ENG; B. Arora, 'Uber Case Study: From Startup to Global Mission', 2023: https://www.protocloudtechnologies.com/uber-case-study-the-drive-from-startup-vision-to-global-mission/; A. Rosenblat, 'Algorithmic Labor and Information Asymmetries: A Case Study of Uber's Drivers', *International Journal of Communication*, vol. 10, no. 27, 2017, https://papers.ssrn.com/sol3/papers.cfm?abstract_id=2686227; E. Bokányi and A. Hannák, 'Understanding Inequalities in Ride-Hailing Services Through Simulations', *Scientific Reports*, vol. 10, no. 6500, 2020: https://doi.org/10.1038/s41598-020-63171-9; R. Burgelman and R. Joshi, 'Uber in 2024: From Industry

Disruption to Creating Value for All Stakeholders', Case No. SM383, Stanford Graduate School of Business, 2024. (All accessed on 4 June 2025).
3. J. V. Hall and A. B. Krueger, 'An Analysis of the Labor Market for Uber's Driver-Partners in the United States', *ILR Review*, vol. 71, no. 3, 2018, pp. 705–32.
4. M. Scott, 'Uber is a Transportation Company, Europe's Highest Court Rules', *Politico*, 20 December 2017: https://www.politico.eu/article/uber-ecj-ruling/. (Accessed on 4 June 2025).
5. 'UK Court: Uber Drivers Entitled to Labor Benefits,' *In Focus, Business Europe*, 19 February 2021: https://www.dw.com/en/uber-drivers-entitled-to-labor-benefits-uk-top-court-rules/a-56626223. (Accessed on 4 June 2025).
6. C. Makó, M. Illéssy, J. Pap and S. Nosratabadi, 'Emerging Platform Work in the Context of the Regulatory Loophole (The Uber Fiasco in Hungary)', *Journal of Labor & Society*, vol. 26, no. 4, 2023, pp. 533–54.
7. Uber, Wikipedia.
8. B. O'Keefe and M. Jones, 'How Uber Plays the Tax Shell Game', *Fortune*, 22 October 2015: https://fortune.com/2015/10/22/uber-tax-shell/. (Accessed on 4 June 2025).
9. D. Carvalho, 'Lula to Propose Stronger Labor Protections for Brazil's Uber Drivers', Bloomberg.com, 3 April 2024: https://www.bloomberg.com/news/articles/2024-03-04/brazil-s-lula-to-propose-stronger-labor-protections-for-uber-drivers. (Accessed on 4 June 2025).
10. John Paul II (Pope), *Encyclical-Letter*, nos 5–6.
11. John Paul II (Pope), *Encyclical-Letter*, no. 6.
12. John Paul II (Pope), *Encyclical-Letter*, no. 12.
13. K. Kolben, 'Labor Rights as Human Rights', *Virginia Journal of International Law*, vol. 50, no. 2, 2009, pp. 449–84.
14. This is the definition of 'living wage' given by D. Collins, 'Living Wage', in R. W. Kolb (ed.), *The SAGE Encyclopedia of Business Ethics and Society*, 2nd ed. (Los Angeles, CA: Sage, 2018), pp. 2102–4.
15. https://www.who.int/health-topics/occupational-health/. (Accessed on 4 June 2025).
16. Thus, in 1891, Pope Leo XIII wrote: 'in regard to children, great care should be taken not to place them in workshops and factories until their bodies and minds are sufficiently developed. For, just as very rough weather destroys the buds of spring, so does too early an experience of life's hard toil blight the young promise of a child's faculties, and render any true education impossible.' Leo XIII (Pope), *Encyclical-Letter 'Rerum Novarum'*, on the labour and social order, no. 42: http://www.vatican.va/content/leo-xiii/en/encyclicals/documents/hf_l-xiii_enc_15051891_rerum-novarum.html. (Accessed on 4 June 2025).
17. UN Convention on the Rights of the Child (1989), art. 32.1: https://www.ohchr.org/en/professionalinterest/pages/crc.aspx. (Accessed on 4 June 2025).
18. According to a report elaborated by the International Labor Organization and Unicef, 160 million children – 63 million girls and 97 million boys – were in child labour globally at the beginning of 2020, accounting for almost one in ten of all children worldwide. This figure represents nearly one in ten children globally and marked an increase of 8.4 million from the previous estimate in 2016. Seventy-nine million children – nearly half of all those in child labour – were in hazardous work that directly endangers their health, safety and moral development: 'Child Labour: Global Estimates 2020, Trends and the Road Forward', https://data.unicef.org/resources/child-labour-2020-global-estimates-trends-and-the-road-forward/ (Accessed on 4 June 2025). As of June 2025, no newer global estimates have been released beyond the 2020 data.

19. For a deeper discussion of this, see M. Zwolinski, 'Sweatshops, Choice, and Exploitation', *Business Ethics Quarterly*, vol. 17, no. 4, 2007, pp. 689–727.
20. On this, see D. G. Arnold and N. E. Bowie, 'Sweatshops and Respect for Persons', *Business Ethics Quarterly*, vol. 13, no. 2, 2003, pp. 221–42, and 'Respect for Workers in Global Chains: Advancing the Debate over Sweatshops', *Business Ethics Quarterly*, vol. 17, no. 1, 2007, pp. 135–45.
21. https://www.who.int/news/item/28-05-2019-burn-out-an-occupational-phenomenon-international-classification-of-diseases. (Accessed on 4 June 2025).
22. International Labor Organization, 'Violence and Harassment at Work has Affected More Than One in Five People', 5 December 2022: https://www.ilo.org/resource/news/violence-and-harassment-work-has-affected-more-one-five-people. (Accessed on 4 June 2025).
23. See M. P. Bell, E. McLaughlin and J. M. Sequeira, 'Discrimination, Harassment, and the Glass Ceiling: Women Executives as Change Agents', *Journal of Business Ethics*, vol. 37, no. 1, 2002, pp. 65–76.
24. On mobbing, see W. Vandekerckhove and M. S. R. Commers, 'Downward Workplace Mobbing: A Sign of the Times?', *Journal of Business Ethics*, vol. 45, no. 1/2, 2003, pp. 41–50.
25. C. Baysal, I. Yikilmaz and L. Surücü, 'The Intermediate Role of Revenge Intention in the Effect of Mobbing on Employee Job Performance', *Journal of Business Research-Turk / Isletme Arastirmalari Dergisi*, vol. 16, no. 1, 2024, pp. 521–31.
26. https://www.ilo.org/publications/ilo-workplace-discrimination-picture-hope-and-concern. (Accessed on 4 June 2025).
27. See more in A. M. Scott, 'Family Responsibility Discrimination', *Employee Benefit Plan Review*, vol. 62, no. 2, 2007, pp. 35–6.
28. For more details on religious discrimination, see D. Melé, 'Religious Discrimination', in R. W. Kolb (ed.), *The SAGE Encyclopedia of Business Ethics and Society*, 2nd ed. (Los Angeles, CA: Sage, 2018), pp. 2919–22.
29. T. L. Beauchamp, 'Affirmative Action', in R. W. Kolb (ed.), *The SAGE Encyclopedia of Business Ethics and Society* (Los Angeles, CA: Sage, 2018), pp. 46–51.
30. https://www.ilo.org/topics/decent-work. (Accessed on 4 June 2025).
31. See an introduction in D. Melé, 'Catholic Social Teaching', in R. W. Kolb (ed.), *The SAGE Encyclopedia of Business Ethics and Society* (Thousand Oaks, CA: Sage, 2018), pp. 391–8.
32. Leo XIII (Pope) *Encyclical-Letter 'Rerum Novarum'*.
33. Benedict XVI (Pope), *Encyclical-Letter 'Caritas in veritate'*, on love in truth, no. 63, 2009: http://www.vatican.va/holy_father/benedict_xvi/encyclicals/documents/hf_ben-xvi_enc_20090629_caritas-in-veritate_en.html. (Accessed on 4 June 2025).
34. Benedict XVI (Pope), *Encyclical-Letter 'Caritas in veritate'*.
35. https://www.ilo.org/sites/default/files/wcmsp5/groups/public/@europe/@ro-geneva/@ilo-lisbon/documents/event/wcms_667247.pdf. (Accessed on 4 June 2025).
36. M. Alzola, 'Decent Work: The Moral Status of Labor in Human Resource Management', *Journal of Business Ethics*, vol. 147, no. 4, 2018, pp. 835–53.
37. M. Greenwood, 'Ethical Analyses of HRM: A Review and Research Agenda', *Journal of Business Ethics*, vol. 114, no. 2, 2013, pp. 355–66.
38. A. Smith, *An Inquiry into the Nature and Causes of the Wealth of Nations*. Ed. A.L. Macfie and D.D. Raphael (Indianapolis, IN: Liberty Press, 1982 [1776]).

39. E. A. Locke, 'The Nature and Causes of Job Satisfaction', in M. D. Dunnette (ed.), *Handbook of Industrial and Organizational Psychology* (Chicago, IL: Rand McNally, 1976), pp. 1297–349, on p. 1304.
40. D. Bakotić, 'Relationship Between Job Satisfaction and Organisational Performance', *Economic Research-Ekonomska Istraživanja*, vol. 29, no. 1, 2016, pp. 118–30.
41. J. M. Berg, A. Wrzesniewski and J. E. Dutton, 'Perceiving and Responding to Challenges in Job Crafting at Different Ranks: When Proactivity Requires Additivity', *Journal of Organizational Behavior*, vol. 31, no. 2–3, 2010, pp. 158–86.
42. S. Terkel, *Working* (London: Wildwood House, 1975), p. 1.
43. On this topic, V. E. Frankl, *Man's Search for Meaning: An Introduction to Logotherapy* (London: Random House / Rider, 1946 [2004]).
44. Source: This case is an abridged version (published with permission) of the case study M. A. Llano Irusta, 'Surgikos, S.A. de C.V.', published by IPADE Business School, Mexico, extended with some complementary information, including J. M. Logsdon and P. Forsythe, 'Maquiladoras', in R. W. Kolb (ed.), *Encyclopedia of Business Ethics and Society* (Thousand Oaks, CA: Sage, 2008), pp. 1324–5; K. Lydersen, 'The Disappeared', *The Times* online, 19 May 2003; https://bivir.uacj.mx/bivir_pp/cronicas/maquilas.htm. (Accessed on 4 June 2025); G. Santiago Quijada, 'La Industria maquiladora en Ciudad Juárez', https://es.scribd.com/document/348442784/La-Industria-Maquiladora. Accessed on 20 October 2024.
45. A good example of seeking plausible alternatives is in the context of destroying human embryos to harvest pluripotent stem cells. Some researchers have used adult stem cells as a source of pluripotent stem cells, and amniotic/cord blood stem cells. This offers promising ways to pursue regenerative medicine without the ethical concerns tied to the destruction of human embryos.
46. H. Gardner, *Intelligence Reframed: Multiple Intelligences for the 21st Century* (New York: Basic Books, 1999), p. 34.
47. J. McCarthy, 'What is Artificial Intelligence'. Stanford University, 12 November 2007: http://www-formal.stanford.edu/jmc/whatisai/node1.html. (Accessed on 4 June 2025).
48. https://www.britannica.com/technology/artificial-intelligence. (Accessed on 4 June 2025).
49. S. Russell and P. Norvig, *Artificial Intelligence: A Modern Approach, Global Edition*, 4th ed. (London: Pearson Education, 2022).
50. For an introduction to the fundamental concepts of machine learning, with practical applications, see C. Bishop, *Pattern Recognition and Machine Learning* (New York: Springer, 2006).
51. Achieving consciousness in AI, as a goal of strong AI, is often linked a theory proposed in the 1990s by Penrose and Hameroff. This theory suggests that quantum computing in the brain could explain consciousness. However, it is 'probably the best known, least understood, and most controversial among the various hypotheses that aim to account for such a puzzling faculty in terms of quantum physics': E. Frixione, 'Consciousness and Neuronal Microtubules: The Penrose-Hameroff Quantum Model in Retrospect', in C. Smith and H. Whitaker (eds), *Brain, Mind and Consciousness in the History of Neuroscience. History, Philosophy and Theory of the Life Sciences*, vol. 6: https://doi.org/10.1007/978-94-017-8774-1_16 (Dordrecht: Springer, 2014).
52. C. O'Neil, *Weapons of Math Destruction: How Big Data Increases Inequality and Threatens Democracy* (New York: Crown Publishing, 2016).
53. E. Union, *AI Act: First Regulation on Artificial Intelligence*, 8 July 2023: https://www.europarl.europa.eu/topics/en/article/20230601STO93804/eu-ai-act-first-regulation-on-artificial-intelligence. (Accessed on 4 June 2025).

54. D. Melé, 'Ethics at the Workplace in the Fourth Industrial Revolution: A Catholic Social Teaching Perspective', *Business Ethics, the Environment & Responsibility*, vol. 30, no. 4, 2021, pp. 772–83.
55. C. W. Callaghan, 'Transcending the Threshold Limitation: A Fifth Industrial Revolution?', *Management Research Review*, vol. 43, no. 4, 2020, pp. 447–61.
56. Stephanie M. Noble, M. Mende, D. Grewal and A. Parasuraman, 'The Fifth Industrial Revolution: How Harmonious Human–Machine Collaboration is Triggering a Retail and Service [R]evolution', vol. 98, no. 2, 2022, pp. 199–208: https://doi.org/10.1016/j.jretai.2022.04.003.
57. A. S. George and A. S. H. George, 'Industrial Revolution 5.0: The Transformation of the Modern Manufacturing Process to Enable Man and Machine to Work Hand in Hand', *Journal Seybold Report*, vol. 15, no. 9, 2020, pp. 214–34.
58. Sources: HireVue, Corporate website: https://www.hirevue.com/about; R. Goodman, 'Why Amazon's Automated Hiring Tool Discriminated Against Women', *ACLU*, 12 October 2018; D. Harwell, 'A Face-Scanning Algorithm Increasingly Decides Whether You Deserve the Job', *Washington Post*, 6 November 2019: https://www.washingtonpost.com/technology/2019/10/22/ai-hiring-face-scanning-algorithm-increasingly-decides-whether-you-deserve-job/; J. Kahn, 'HireVue Drops Facial Monitoring Amid AI Algorithm Audit,' *Fortune*, 1 October 2021: https://fortune.com/2021/01/19/hirevue-drops-facial-monitoring-amid-a-i-algorithm-audit/. (All accessed on 4 June 2025).
59. All names are fictitious.

11
Ethics in Sales and Marketing

Zigong (a disciple of Confucius) asked: 'Is there any one word that could guide a person throughout life?' The Master replied: 'How about 'shu' [reciprocity]: never impose on others what you would not choose for yourself.'[1]

CONFUCIUS (551–478 BCE), Chinese teacher and philosopher

Overview

Sales is an essential function in every business, encompassing the organization of sales teams, the development of relationships with customers or channel partners, and, in many cases, direct interaction with customers. Sales typically involves offering products (goods or services), persuading potential buyers of their benefits, handling objections, and negotiating prices and delivery terms. Sales teams often work to ensure that orders are delivered to customers on time and in the right condition. Sales is closely related to marketing, which focuses on understanding the needs and wants of clients and consumers in order to produce, promote, distribute and sell suitable ideas, products and services. As the saying goes, 'without marketing, sales suffer'.

Section A discusses the ethical foundations of consumer rights and consumerism as a social phenomenon. It also reflects on the need to provide 'authentic service' to consumers. Finally, it introduces the ethical requirements for market and marketing research.

Section B addresses specific ethical issues in sales and marketing, including ethical considerations regarding the product, fairness in pricing and ethical promotion practices, such as advertising and persuasion. Some specific insights into e-commerce are also provided.

Chapter Aims

After reading this chapter you should be able to:

- Understand consumer rights and what they consist of.
- Discuss the role of marketing in promoting responsible consumption.
- Distinguish between 'consumer sovereignty', 'consumer paternalism' and 'authentic service'.

- Reflect on two philosophies regarding the seller's responsibility in providing the customer with information.
- Understand the ethical issues in e-commerce.
- Consider how to introduce ethical values into consumer marketing research and general market research.
- Know about ethical issues regarding products.
- Discuss the concept of fair price and abuses in pricing.
- Be familiar with a set of sound ethical criteria for advertising.
- Have an insight into ethics in distribution and sales.

Historical Case #11

Sanlu: The melamine-tainted milk[2]

In 2008, the Sanlu group was the biggest manufacturer of milk powder in China. The company had thirty production plants, 10,000 employees and about 30,000 salespersons. Tian Wenhua, the chairwoman and general manager of Sanlu, was the local secretary of the Chinese Communist Party and had longstanding connections with the government.

The company headquarters were near Beijing in Shijiazhuang, the capital of China's Hebei province. Foreign companies, like Nestlé, Danone and Fonterra, had entered the Chinese powdered milk market. Their products were of excellent quality but were sold at a higher price than local ones. Sanlu sold at half the price of equivalent foreign brands.

China doesn't have a long tradition in dairy products, but the dairy sector experienced a rapid and scarcely regulated development beginning in 2000. Milk powder as infant food is very popular in China, where the breastfeeding rate is significantly lower than the rest of the world. According to the World Health Organization (WHO), globally, about 38 per cent of babies are exclusively breastfed for six months, but in China only 28 per cent of babies are. For over 250 million migrant workers, including many mothers who have to leave their newborn babies in their hometown and go out to earn money for the whole family, affordable baby formula is the only option.

The Fonterra Cooperative Group, a company from New Zealand and worldwide leader in exportation of dairy products, acquired 43 per cent of shares in Sanlu. This followed a Chinese government requirement that local partners had to oversee foreign companies doing business in China.

The demand for milk was far surpassing supplies due to poor animal husbandry, production and storage conditions. In an incident in 2004, watered-down milk had resulted in twelve infant deaths from malnutrition.

Another problem was quality of the raw milk, especially its protein level, which didn't reach the national standard minimum requirements. It was an open secret from 2005 to 2007 that, in many places, dairy farmers mixed fresh milk with additives such as melamine. This is a chemical containing nitrogen, which in conventional tests can be interpreted as evidence of the presence of proteins – also rich in nitrogen. Thus, when added to milk, the chemical gave the appearance of a higher protein content than the milk actually had. Some salespeople had been visiting farms for years, promoting 'protein powder' additives, which could not be detected by the inspection methods in use.

Between 2005 and 2006, the first reports appeared regarding possible adulteration in China's milk industry. They came from Jiang Weisuo, an agent of a Sanlu competitor, the Shaanxi Jinqiao Dairy Company. Weisuo publicly discussed his fears about unauthorized substances being added to competitors' milk, but his complaints to regulators and dairy makers did not lead to any meaningful result. More effective was the information, released on 16 July 2008, that sixteen babies in Gansu Province were diagnosed with kidney stones. The babies had been fed infant formula produced by the Sanlu Group in Shijiazhuang.

In August 2008, the Administration of Quality Supervision, Inspection and Quarantine (AQSIQ), the Chinese government agency for product quality, started to run specific tests for melamine in Sanlu products. The scope of the investigation later expanded to all powdered milk producers and all dairy producers. However, the AQSIQ did not inform either the public or the firms that the probe was taking place.

On 2 August, Fonterra alerted Sanlu about the melamine-tainted milk, pushing hard for a full public recall. There was an immediate trade recall, but local administrators refused to order a full public withdrawal. On 5 September, Fonterra notified the New Zealand government and, three days later, Prime Minister Helen Clark had alerted Beijing officials directly. Within a few days, the melamine contamination story had passed around China and around the world. On 12 September 2008, the Chinese government ordered a halt to production because of the melamine. Authorities reportedly seized 2,176 tons of powdered milk in Sanlu's warehouses. Some 9,000 tons of product were later recalled. On 15 September 2008, the company issued a public apology for the contaminated powdered milk, blaming the small milk producers.

Finally, on 16 September 2008, the AQSIQ released test data of samples from 491 batches of products sold by all 109 companies producing baby formula. Each of the eleven samples from Sanlu failed the melamine test. Tainted products were found among twenty-one other supplier samples, although to a lesser degree than Sanlu. Other food materials, including eggs from chickens fed with a product containing melamine, were also found to be adulterated.

There were an estimated 300,000 people affected in China by the melamine-tainted products; six babies died from kidney stones and other renal damage and about 54,000 infants were hospitalized. These sick babies were mainly concentrated in underdeveloped rural areas, such as Gansu.

More than twenty people were convicted for their roles in the scandal. Tian Wenhua, the Sanlu CEO, was sentenced to life in prison, and three of the firm's senior executives were also imprisoned for between five and fifteen years. Four government officials in Shijiazhuang, including the vice-mayor responsible for food and agriculture, were fired or obliged to resign.

> Two melamine producers/dealers were sentenced to death and executed two days later. One was Zhang Yujun (alias Zhang Haitao), a former dairy farmer from Hebei who produced more than 600 tons of a 'protein powder' mixture of melamine and maltodextrin from September 2007 to August 2008. The second was Geng Jinping, who managed a milk production centre that supplied milk to the Sanlu Group and other dairies.
>
> Hundreds of thousands of small-time dairy farmers were caught up in China's contaminated milk crisis. The value of Sanlu plunged as a result of the scandal and Fonterra announced it had marked down the carrying value of its investment by two-thirds due to the cost of the product recall and the closure of the Sanlu branch. Importations of milk powder from Hong Kong rose dramatically because of the lack of trust in Chinese milk producers. At the international level, the issue raised concerns about food safety and political corruption in China and damaged the reputation of China's food exports. At least eleven countries stopped all imports of Chinese dairy products.
>
> The WHO referred to the incident as one of the largest food safety events it has had to deal with in recent years and considered that the crisis of confidence among Chinese consumers would be hard to overcome. Peter Ben Embarek, a WHO food safety scientist, said the scale of the problem proved it was 'clearly not an isolated accident, [but] a large-scale intentional activity to deceive consumers for simple, basic, short-term profits.'[3]
>
> In June 2009, China promulgated the Food Safety Law, which prohibits any use of unauthorized food additives.
>
> ## Questions
>
> 1. Is there any circumstance that makes this fraud especially serious in moral terms?
> 2. Which persons or groups should be held accountable for the contamination crisis, and why?
> 3. What measures could be taken by the different people and institutions involved in products like infant milk powder to avoid similar problems in the future?

SECTION A. CONSUMER RIGHTS AND AUTHENTIC SERVICE

11.1 Consumer rights

Consumer rights refer to the protections and entitlements afforded to persons when purchasing goods or services, ensuring fair treatment, safety, and access to accurate information. This concept emerged in the mid-twentieth century, driven by a growing sensitivity to advocating for consumer rights and empowerment.

As a result of this growing awareness, countries have enacted laws and regulations to protect consumer rights, while corporations have been encouraged to adopt responsible practices and empower individuals to make informed choices in the marketplace.

The ethical dimension of consumer rights

Consumer rights are not solely a matter of legal regulation or social demands; they also involve an ethical dimension, closely connected to the personalist principle (2.7). In practical terms, it is illustrative to review various proposals on this topic.

Although there is no universally accepted declaration of consumer rights akin to that of human rights, governmental regulations in many countries provide a number of protections for consumers, including access to legal recourse. Additionally, strong consumer advocacy movements in many regions seek to protect and inform consumers by lobbying for practices such as truth in packaging and advertising, product guarantees and enhanced safety standards.

The United Nations has proposed its Guidelines for Consumer Protection,[4] which suggests responsibilities for sellers and for governmental agencies. These include a number of general principles that lay the groundwork for protecting and promoting consumer rights. These principles include: (1) fair and equitable treatment; (2) commercial proper behaviour (regarding products, discriminations, deceptive practices and so on); (3) disclosure and transparency; (4) education and awareness-raising; (5) protection of privacy; and (6) mechanism for consumer complaints and disputes.

In tune with these Guidelines, Buchholz[5] gives the following list of consumer rights:

- *The right to safety*: Consumers have the right to be protected from products that are hazardous to life or property.
- *The right to be informed*: Consumers have the right to be informed about the quality, quantity, potency, purity and price of goods and services, enabling them to make informed choices. This right offers protection against dishonest or misleading advertising and labelling.
- *The right to choose*: Consumers have the right to select products from a variety of goods and services at competitive prices. This right is infringed upon by unregulated monopolies or when products of satisfactory quality at fair prices are unavailable.
- *The right to be heard*: Consumers have the right to present legitimate complaints to appropriate persons or institutions and to receive an adequate response in cases of abuse in commerce.
- *The right to consumer education*: Consumers should have access to educational programmes or other resources to acquire knowledge and skills needed to make informed, confident choices about goods and services. This includes awareness of basic consumer rights, responsibilities and how to act on them.
- *The right to consumer redress*: Consumers have the right to receive a fair settlement of just claims, including compensation for damages suffered due to misrepresentation, defective products or unsatisfactory services.
- *The right to a healthy and sustainable environment*: Consumers have both a right and a duty to adopt consumption patterns that promote sustainability. Everyone, not only as consumers

but as human beings, has the right to live and work in an environment that safeguards the well-being of present and future generations.
- *The right to basic needs*: People should have access to essential goods and services, including food, clothing, shelter, healthcare, education, public utilities, water and sanitation.
- *The right to access*: This refers to the fair and equitable distribution of goods and services across society.

11.2 Providing authentic service to customers

As consumers, we have an obligation to make good purchase decisions. A good salesperson (and effective marketing) helps people buy well, providing authentic service. However, this focus is not always maintained. In fact, there are three distinct approaches to how consumers – those who buy goods or services for their own use – are treated and what information should be provided. These approaches are known as *consumer sovereignty*, *paternalism* and *authentic service*.

Consumer sovereignty

Consumer sovereignty argues that consumer preferences and choices should be the exclusive driver for the production and supply of goods and services in a market. Based on *consumer sovereignty* some argue that clients or customers and consumers are solely responsible for their own decisions and that the marketers have no responsibility whatsoever for their purchases. This leads managers to organize marketing exclusively based on consumer desire – and, of course, profitability. This approach stresses respect for the freedom and autonomy of consumers, which is a consumer right, and this is a positive. However, 'consumer sovereignty' falls short on several counts[6] and several ethical problems can be identified.

Firstly, the buyer's wants and preferences are not amoral; on the contrary, they are subject to ethical evaluation, and selling is a way of cooperating in such an action. To cite an extreme case, by selling weapons to a terrorist group, the seller is cooperating with terrorism. Analogously, by selling hazardous products of any kind, one cooperates with any harm caused.

Secondly, given the real conditions of many markets, consumers might not have accurate or sufficient information to form rational preferences and make a choice. Consumer sovereignty often shares the view of the classic Latin aphorism, *caveat emptor*: 'Let the buyer beware.' This motto has been used in commerce to claim that a buyer should not expect compensation for defects in a purchase that is unfit for its ordinary purpose. There is no warranty; the buyer takes the risk. In accordance with this principle, the seller should warn of substantial latent defects in the product but not of anything else that might discourage a decision to purchase. Many products are highly sophisticated, and often those who manufacture or sell them have far more information about the product and its use than many clients could possibly obtain. With additional information provided by the seller, clients might change their preferences and make different purchase decisions.

Thirdly, employees can also have preferences, and even rights, that might conflict with consumer preferences (for example, shopping on Sunday). Although, in general, business should attend to the wishes of clients and customers, this might be problematic in some cases.

Consumer sovereignty is restrained by legal requirements – and, fortunately, the law prohibits some possible abuses – but it is hardly plausible that laws alone would be sufficient to ensure ethical marketing throughout the world.

Consumer paternalism

At the opposite extreme of consumer sovereignty is the position of *paternalism*, the idea that only the manufacturer and seller have sufficient information to make the right decisions. Paternalism is a well-intentioned attitude but does not show sufficient respect for consumer autonomy or maturity in decision-making. It fails to consider that customers can have different perspectives and gather additional information.

Paternalistic attitudes can prevent consumers from enjoying a selection of alternatives or discussing other options before making a choice. When consumers are acquiring a product or service, they should consider price, quality and the associated level of risk. Customers – not sellers – should decide for themselves whether they prefer a lower price at the cost of a greater risk once they have obtained sufficient information. Respecting customer decisions is a way of honouring human freedom. However, this respect should be accompanied by an authentic sense of service, which is a third marketing philosophy.[7]

Authentic service: A moral alternative to consumer sovereignty and paternalism

Unlike both consumer sovereignty and paternalism, *authentic service* is grounded in a genuine *good intention* to benefit the person, not merely to profit from him or her. It involves acting with *integrity and truthfulness*, without manipulating desires or exploiting weaknesses. Authentic service seeks *to understand customers' real needs* and legitimate wants, while showing deep concern for their best interests – balanced with a delicate respect for *consumer autonomy*.

At its core, authentic service first and foremost rules out offering or promoting products that cause physical or moral harm, or that violate human dignity. This includes, for example, selling non-prescription narcotic drugs, weapons to terrorist groups, or to regimes that breach human rights. It also implies refraining from persuading consumers – through advertising or other means – to use products that are harmful (for example, tobacco), or potentially harmful when used improperly or immoderately (for example, alcoholic beverages). This concern is especially critical when dealing with *vulnerable populations*, such as children and youth, who may be more easily influenced into harmful consumption patterns.

Authentic service also requires providing *accurate and sufficient information*, enabling consumers to make rational and informed choices. It calls for a shift from the traditional *caveat emptor* ('let the buyer beware') to a *caveat venditor* ('let the seller beware') approach. In today's marketplace, where *information asymmetry* between seller and buyer is often significant, relying solely on buyer responsibility is ethically insufficient. A commitment to authentic service entails that sellers take responsibility for the product beyond what is immediately obvious or easily discovered by the customer. This includes offering products of reasonable quality and disclosing information that is essential for an informed decision.

However, it does not require sellers to disclose information that consumers, by virtue of common knowledge or expertise, can be expected to know – such as the existence of a competitor offering a lower price. Still, special care and ethical sensitivity must be exercised when dealing with vulnerable consumers who may be easily misled.

Ultimately, an authentic sense of service must be founded on ethical principles and animated by virtues. It goes beyond regulatory compliance or strategic benevolence, expressing a deeper commitment to the good of the person, respectful dialogue and moral responsibility.

The American Marketing Association (AMA), one of the largest professional associations for marketers with about 40,000 members worldwide, has proposed the *AMA Statement of Ethics*,[8] which contains key ethical principles with significant contents. It makes clear from the beginning that 'As marketers, we recognize that we not only serve our organizations but also act as stewards of society in creating, facilitating and executing the transactions that are part of the greater economy.' Then, it states that marketers have a duty to uphold ethical principles that prioritise both individual and societal well-being, through three basic norms:

1. *Avoid harm*: Actively prevent harm and seek to create positive value for all stakeholders, while strictly complying with laws and regulations.
2. *Promote integrity*: Ensure fairness and transparency across all marketing practices and relationships.
3. *Uphold core values*: Build trust by consistently affirming *honesty*, *responsibility*, *equity*, *transparency* and *citizenship* in every marketing decision.

Regarding values, the Statement presents and develops five, which can be summarized as follows:

1. *Honesty*: Ethical behaviour of *marketers* demands unwavering truthfulness in all communications and interactions. This includes avoiding manipulation or deception, ensuring that the solutions offered genuinely reflect stated intentions, and honouring both explicit and implicit commitments. Trust is crucial, and marketers are called to maintain it across all touchpoints.
2. *Responsibility*: With the power to influence behaviour and shape societal trends, marketers must acknowledge their broader obligations to society. This involves mindful stewardship of the environment, protecting stakeholder privacy and data beyond minimum legal requirements, and taking accountability for the impact of marketing choices on public welfare.
3. *Equity*: Fairness and inclusion are vital. Ethical marketers cultivate diverse teams and adopt inclusive practices that respect individual and cultural differences. They are especially

attentive to vulnerable or underrepresented groups, ensuring that marketing neither exploits nor stereotypes any demographic and that all participants in the marketing ecosystem are treated with dignity and respect.
4. *Transparency*: A spirit of openness underpins trustworthy marketing. This means communicating clearly, disclosing relevant information that could affect stakeholder decisions, acknowledging the contributions of collaborators, and proactively addressing foreseeable risks. Transparency also involves managing conflicts of interest responsibly and welcoming feedback from all parties.
5. *Citizenship*: Beyond business, ethical marketing embraces its civic role. This includes fulfilling legal and societal responsibilities, contributing to sustainability, engaging in community service, and elevating the profession's reputation. Ethical marketers promote fair trade practices and work to ensure that the benefits of marketing extend equitably throughout the supply chain and society.

These values, and even more personal virtues, are relevant for commerce in both multicultural and multinational contexts. Murphy[9] has proposed some virtues that fuel good behaviour in commerce. He mentions the following: *integrity* (conveying accurate and complete information to consumers); *fairness* (selling and pricing products at a level commensurate with benefits received); *trust* (confidence that salespeople or suppliers will fulfil obligations without monitoring); *respect* (altering products to meet cultural needs and refusing to sell unsafe products anywhere); and *empathy* (refraining from selling products to consumers who cannot afford them). Virtues emphasize customer retention and continual satisfaction rather than individual transactions and per-case customer resolution.[10]

11.3 Ethics in market and marketing research

Companies use consumer *marketing research* to obtain information about particular aspects of the market, generally related to consumer behaviours and preferences. This requires systematically gathering, recording and analysing data, often employing statistical methods. Marketing research can be done to determine what product might be marketable or what innovations a product might require in the near future, to analyse the effects of marketing campaigns and, in general, to obtain data for decision-making in marketing issues.

Related to marketing research is *market research*, which has a broad focus on the market. It includes analysing market structure, competitors, barriers to entry and exit of a specific market, applicable legislation, technological advances, tendencies in the industry and any other factors that might be significant for making strategic decisions about products, new markets or distribution innovations.

Marketing and market research involve ethical issues related to human rights and the means of obtaining information. These issues are generally present in the professional codes of marketing researchers. Some of the main concerns are outlined in the following subsections.

Informed consent

Participants in a survey should be aware of the purpose of the research and agree to participate in it. Informed consent is a right related to the personalist principle. It involves, at least, the tacit permission of the participant to have their answers recorded.

Researchers can be tempted to neglect informed consent when seeking access to information that is critical or difficult to obtain, and, as a consequence, they sometimes neglect informed consent simply to avoid trouble. Often interviewers begin by presenting vague explanations of the purpose of the survey and ask irrelevant questions to create a relaxing atmosphere before moving on to more sensitive matters. Some participants, such as children, the elderly, immigrants and the uneducated, might be less aware of their rights and be particularly vulnerable to manipulation.

Privacy and confidentiality

Participants maintain their privacy in everything not included in the informed consent given. This means that an individual has not only the right to choose or refuse to participate in a survey but also the right to avoid answering certain questions if he or she considers them inappropriate or simply prefers not to opine. In addition, the interviewer has to maintain respect for individuals and their positions.

The confidentiality of participant data should be kept and the data used only for the purpose of the survey. Customer education regarding shopping online can help users to be aware of which information the seller is recording and to maintain their privacy and sensitive personal data under their own control.

Deception and harm

Honesty requires telling the truth when conducting surveys or using other methodology. Respondents' cooperation must not be based on misleading information about the general purpose and nature of the project when their agreement to participate is being sought. All such statements must be honoured.

Objectivity in reports

Marketing research should be done with objectivity and rigour without manipulating or exaggerating the results. Since professionals in this field often work for companies or institutions, they should avoid any bias towards the outcomes their sponsors hope to find.

Business Ethics in Action #11

Bimbo: Responsible marketing of a responsible company[11]

Bimbo was established in Mexico in 1945 as a small family bakery. Today, Grupo Bimbo is one of the largest multinational baking companies in the world, with 217 bakeries and plants and 149,000 associates (employees), across twenty-four countries in the Americas, Europe, Asia and Africa. The company specializes in the production and distribution of baked goods including bread, cakes, cookies, tortillas and other packaged foods. Its extensive product line includes over 100 brands, such as *Bimbo*, *Marinela*, *Barcel* and *Tía Rosa*.

Bassic business principles

Roberto Servitje, co-founder of Bimbo, established the basic principles for the company from the very beginning: customer-focused service, constant reinvestment, accessible pricing, standardized quality, austerity, new technologies and hard work. However, the core of its philosophy, according to Mr Servitje, was the desire to 'create a company with a soul. The soul of the company is the people, with their serving will and passion.' Today, the company highlights seven key corporate beliefs, focusing on both profitable and humanistic aspects:

1. *We value the person*, recognizing the dignity and worth of every individual – whether they are employees, customers, or members of the community.
2. *We are one community*, treating people at Bimbo as associates, fostering a sense of unity, and emphasizing collaboration, belonging, and teamwork.
3. *We get results*, focusing on achieving tangible outcomes and aiming for excellence in all aspects of the business.
4. *We compete and win*, embracing healthy competition and committing to excelling in the global marketplace through continuous improvement and innovation.
5. *We are sharp operators*, valuing operational efficiency and precision, ensuring processes are optimized for effectiveness and quality.
6. *We act with integrity*, where ethical conduct and transparency are central to Bimbo's operations, with a commitment to honesty, fairness and responsibility.
7. *We transcend and endure*, focusing on long-term success, striving to create lasting value for future generations in both business growth and positive societal impact.

The company's purpose, 'We nourish a better world', is complemented by its mission to put 'Delicious and nutritious baked goods and snacks in the hands of all.' Its corporate philosophy is centred on 'Building a sustainable, highly productive, and deeply humane company.'

Responsible marketing at Bimbo

Bimbo employs various platforms – traditional media, social media and in-store promotions – to effectively communicate its message to different demographics. Typically, Bimbo utilizes storytelling and educational content to provide clear, accessible information that helps consumers make informed decisions about nutrition and environmental sustainability. This contributes to greater awareness and understanding.

Analysing Bimbo Group's 'Responsible Communication Guidelines,' several core drivers emerge:

Reliability, transparency and accountability: Bimbo's marketing campaigns aim to build trust by being transparent about product ingredients, recipes and their health impacts. The company does not advertise its products as meal replacements, nor does it promote sedentary lifestyles or excessive consumption of its goods. An independent agency periodically conducts media audits to ensure the company adheres to these guidelines.

Ethical standards: Bimbo adheres to strict ethical guidelines from respected international associations and promotes socially responsible advertising. The company complies with national and local regulations, going beyond them where possible. Campaigns are designed with sensitivity to diverse audiences, especially children, with special guidelines for advertising to those aged under thirteen. Bimbo is committed to integrity in internet and social media marketing.

Promoting healthy lifestyles: Bimbo actively supports health and wellness by encouraging nutritious diets and sustainable living habits. Campaigns are crafted to educate the public about healthier food choices and reducing food waste, reflecting the company's role in fostering well-being.

Emphasis on human values: The company's messaging reflects respect for human dignity and universal human rights. Family values, sustainability and personal integrity are highlighted. Bimbo only uses media aligned with its corporate values, promoting positive and inclusive content in the countries where it operates. The product imagery focuses on family, home, health, nutrition and cleanliness.

Inclusive and social strategies: Bimbo's advertising avoids perpetuating social stereotypes that could promote prejudice or discrimination. The company is also working on marketing strategies to reach low-income groups with affordable, healthy and nutritious products. This complements Bimbo's social responsibility efforts, which include charitable work and initiatives in health and education within local communities.

Bimbo's 'Responsible Communication Guidelines' reflect consistency with the company's broader ethical values (beliefs), especially in its commitment to respecting persons and acting with integrity, expressed in terms of transparency, honesty, fairness and responsibility.

The core drivers include a strong respect for human dignity, human rights and inclusion. Bimbo's focus on honesty in providing accurate, non-misleading information is fortified by its commitment to transparency and accountability, both of which are central to its responsible communication approach. The company's integrity is evidenced by its adherence to rigorous ethical standards. It is notable that the company consciously avoids collaborating with media outlets that do not align with its human values. Bimbo's social responsibility is particularly evident through its proactive efforts to promote family values, healthy lifestyles and sustainability in its marketing campaigns.

SECTION B. ETHICS IN MARKETING

11.4 Marketing and consumerism

The AMA defines *marketing* as 'the activity, set of institutions, and processes for creating, communicating, delivering, and exchanging offerings that have value for customers, clients, partners, and society at large'.[12] Through targeted advertising, branding and product placement, marketing aims not only to satisfy consumer needs and desires but often to also foster new wants that drive purchasing behaviour.

Marketing is frequently associated with *consumerism*, typically understood as 'the state of buying and selling a lot of goods in an advanced industrial society, or the situation of giving too much attention to buying and owning things'.[13] This often implies a high level of consumption that can sometimes become excessive or unbalanced.

While marketing fuels economic growth, it can also contribute to a culture of consumerism that may prioritize material values and continuous consumption over ethical or sustainable considerations. This connection underscores the responsibility of marketers to balance commercial goals with the promotion of informed and responsible consumer choices.

Some may argue that consumerism is less a marketing issue than a matter of personal choice. Purchasing superfluous goods could be seen as conspicuous or invidious consumption, reflecting a confusion between possessions and personal worth. Indeed, consumers hold personal responsibility for their purchasing decisions. However, certain types of marketing play a role in encouraging consumption, making it important for marketers to consider their responsibility for foreseeable consequences (see 3.4). This is especially relevant when marketing – or advertising, a key tool within marketing – encourages the consumption of potentially harmful products (such as alcohol) or targets vulnerable segments of the population, such as children or teenagers. We will revisit these issues in greater depth in our discussion on advertising.

In addition to personal impacts, the progressively increasing consumption of goods has long-term ecological and environmental consequences (13.1, 13.2); the planet's capacity to supply natural resources and absorb waste is not unlimited. Many voices have warned of the ongoing environmental degradation driven by unchecked consumerism, especially in industrialized countries. This has led to calls for *responsible consumption* by using goods and services in ways that meet needs while minimising harm to people, society and the environment.

External influences can help promote more responsible consumption and encourage people to adopt simpler lifestyles. Education on responsible consumption, the mass media and a supportive cultural environment can all contribute to tempering consumerism. Such efforts can also help counter the prevalent confusion between a person's identity and his or her possessions, as well as the misconception of possessions as ends in themselves.

Marketing has a role to play in both consumerism and fostering responsible consumption, balanced with a sustainable level of economic activity. Developing efficient marketing strategies that achieve positive financial and ethical outcomes can be a real challenge. Often, it requires creativity and boldness to serve people's needs while achieving a satisfactory profit.

Positioning and marketing mix

Marketing begins with *positioning*, by understanding the market, choosing a target and deciding what you want to sell. This includes identifying the group of people to whom a product or service will be introduced and creating a unique image or perception of the brand, product or service in the customer's mind.

Following positioning is the creation of a *marketing mix*, which includes decisions regarding the product or service, its price, the means of promotion and the placement of the product for distribution. These *four 'Ps'* (*product*, *price*, *promotion* and *placement*) are central to marketing practices. Each of these elements has ethical implications, especially regarding fairness and the commitment to authentic service.[14]

11.5 Ethical issues regarding the product

A product, generically, is anything a seller exchanges in the contract of sale, including material products, services or even ideas. The buyer expects both tangible and intangible attributes to be adequate for the product's ordinary use, and this is part of the implicit contract.

From a marketing perspective, there are three important features of the product: (1) *brand*, which distinguishes a seller's product from the competitors'; (2) *packaging*; and (3) *labelling*. Brand, the reputation of which is built over time, is based on quality, safe use, durability and the manufacturing warranty of products included in it. Attentiveness to these aspects is also important on ethical grounds since they contribute to human well-being. On this point, as with many others, focus on short-term profits without sufficient attention to the elements that build brand reputation can jeopardize that reputation and, thereby, long-term profits. However, the pressures to produce short-term profits to which the seller is sometimes subjected can lead to the temptation to sell without a sufficient sense of responsibility.

In order to avoid abuses and to protect consumer rights, a strict legal product liability has been established in most countries. Some liability regulations are fully consistent with ethical issues concerning products. Among these, those discussed in the following subsections are especially pertinent.

Type of product and obsolescence

As noted earlier, some products are harmful in themselves or, at least, socially controversial. Among these are firearms, alcoholic beverages, tobacco and gambling.[15] The marketing, selling and advertising of these products should be restricted and their distribution tolerated only in limited circumstances.

Another ethical issue relates to the selling of counterfeit products, including unauthorized copies of patented inventions, trademarks and copyrighted material (5, A). This type of sale is unacceptable because it violates propriety rights and this, in most countries, is also illegal. In addition, counterfeit products can be sold at a substantially lower price, which is a form of unfair competition – but they can also be passed off as genuine and sold at the same price as the authentic product. This is deception, as it is often difficult to spot the difference between the real and the fake.

Durability and obsolescence of a product can be ethically problematic. Products cease to be useable if they outlive a limited durability, because they are no longer competitive (if other technologically superior products have made them obsolete – a fairly common fate in the high-tech industry) or are out of fashion, or because spare parts are no longer available. Another possibility is that the design includes a *planned obsolescence* with the purpose of greater profits (some batteries, for example). These issues have to be analysed case by case, considering the honesty and uprightness (or lack of it) with which the selling is carried out and also the buyer's consent to accept the product's limitations.

Quality, usage and safety

The quality of products, and especially the quality/price ratio, is an opportunity for both a competitive advantage for business and a way to serve people's needs. Reasonable safety is a requirement for every product. Quality might vary, but products must be safe for the use for which they have been designed. How much safety is necessary depends on the specific application of each product. For instance, a high-end car might be made with more resistant and expensive materials than those of a mid-market vehicle. However, all cars need to meet minimum safety standards, and these are often legal requirements. Similarly, in every product, economizing cannot be an excuse to design or manufacture something that might injure or harm consumers.

Another aspect of concern for safety is the information provided for the correct use of the product. Sometimes, what is unsafe is not the product itself, but its misuse. Since manufacturers have fuller knowledge about what they produce, they are obliged to provide appropriate instructions to allow the consumer to use it correctly.

Regulation of the legal liability of manufacturers – especially of food, pharmaceuticals and other consumer products – is extensive in most countries.

Packaging

Packaging usually helps to differentiate a product, to give it an undertone of quality and to render it more attractive. But it can be excessive, which entails an unwarranted consumption of resources as well as higher prices. Often packaging is so unnecessarily bulky that it is difficult to deal with. A balanced solution is necessary. Moreover, as packaging sooner or later becomes waste, it is also an environmental problem. An ethical improvement in this area would be to use the least possible packaging compatible with the necessary benefits of an appealing presentation, and to employ biodegradable materials or help recycle packaging waste.

Labelling

The words on the label and packaging are usually the customer's main source of information for making an educated purchase decision. The customer's right to be informed implies the business's responsibility to provide clear, accurate and sufficient information about the product. Ambiguity and misleading claims on labels are unacceptable when the information concerns a product's essential features. Some labels, attractive for marketing reasons, can mislead consumers, even without an explicit lie. An example of this might be a label that proclaims 'Cholesterol-free!' when such products never contain cholesterol.

Warranties

Products should be sold without concealed defects in essential parts. The seller will also offer a warranty, which guarantees the quality and safety of the product and expresses the seller's specific obligations concerning its performance. The warranty is often implicit, or there are legal requirements of a generic warranty for a certain period of time, assuming an ordinary use of the product. There are also 'express warranties', explicitly communicated to the customers that can include specific statements. Both types of warranties are promises that should be honoured.

Recalls

In spite of the efforts of many companies to offer safe products, it might happen that a product is found to be dangerous after it reaches the marketplace. A responsible reaction in such cases is to recall the product, even when this might involve a costly operation; otherwise, the company would bear responsibility, due to its omission (3.5), for harm or damages suffered by consumers. Moreover, in many cases, the financial cost associated with legal liability for the product and the reputation lost could be even higher than the cost of recalling the product.

11.6 Fair price and abuses in pricing

Product pricing is crucial in marketing. If the price is too high, fewer people will buy and the profit will be small, but if the price is too low, the profit might also be modest. Beyond profit, however, pricing involves a question of justice.[16] We have discussed the question of fair price already in the context of consumer rights (11.1). Here, we will focus on ethical issues related to abuses in pricing.

Price gouging

An extreme example of unfair pricing occurs when sellers take advantage of civil emergencies by hoarding provisions of food or other basic goods and then selling them at much higher prices than normal. This is referred to as 'price gouging'. Frequently, the term is also used for any commercial practice inconsistent with a competitive free market or when completely unexpected revenues appear (*windfall profits*).

Monopolies and monopsonies

Previously (7.1), we considered the problem of monopolies and monopsonies in a market economy. These are situations of monopolistic practices in which there is an asymmetry of power, which can allow injustice to occur unless sound regulation prevents it. A particularly serious situation is that of a monopoly that brings about unfair prices in products of basic need, such as food or pharmaceuticals. A higher price is more acceptable when the monopoly involves luxury or unnecessary goods (for instance, jewellery, works of art or luxury cars).

A coactive monopoly is a business concern that prohibits competitors from entering the field (for example, electricity supply from a company imposed by the government). In such cases, it is impossible to compete through prices, after sales service, innovation, technology and so on. Competition tends to lead to fair prices but, in a coactive monopoly, prices are not the result of competitive forces and are likely to be higher than what would commonly be called fair.

Sometimes a company or brand enjoys a monopoly, or a vast market share, in a certain region. This is not a coactive monopoly, though, because other sellers can compete, and the price offered is probably fair. This would be the case, for instance, of a brand of beer that had near-exclusive control in a country. If the price were too high, consumers could choose another brand or a substitute drink.

Price fixing

Price fixing refers to collusion between two or more business rivals to sell a certain product or service at the same price. It is sometimes termed 'price collusion' to emphasize the agreement, which is usually secretive, to avoid fair competition. The goal is usually to avoid free competition by pushing the price as high as possible for the mutual benefit of the sellers at the expense of buyers, although sometimes it is also to fix, peg, discount or stabilize prices. Apart from this form of price fixing between competitors, which can be termed 'horizontal', there is another 'vertical' type that occurs between manufacturer and wholesaler, wholesaler and distributor, or distributor and retailer.

Price fixing is generally unethical since it distances businesses from fair competition. It is also frequently forbidden by law. However, it might sometimes be morally justifiable as a legitimate defence of producers facing monopsonies or collusion among buyers. This may be the case with some raw material production, mainly in developing countries. Small companies can follow the price established by a large firm. This is not price fixing as such because there is no explicit agreement to act illegally.

Predatory pricing and dumping

This is a pricing policy based on selling a product at a very low price, even below the production costs, with the intention of driving competitors out of the market or to avoid potential new competitors from entering it. Short-term profits fall but, if the goal is achieved, the firm will have fewer competitors or can even establish a monopoly. Restricting competition permits the raising of prices above the level the market would otherwise bear and brings about more overall profits.

Predatory pricing, also known as destroyer pricing, is not ethically acceptable because its direct intent is not to compete fairly but to destroy rivals. It is an anti-competitive practice that is prohibited in many countries, although it can be difficult to prove that it really exists in a particular case.

Predatory pricing might be a consequence of a price war, in which rival firms undertake a series of price reductions. If one firm reduces prices, the others reduce theirs even more. In a price war, all firms lose profits and, in the end, the firm with less capacity to survive will be obliged to abandon the market. In this case, the resulting low prices can be acceptable if they are only a defence against the aggressive tactics of competitors.

Dumping is a term used for predatory pricing in international trade. It occurs when a manufacturer in one country exports a product to another at a price that is either below the price charged by competitors in the second country or below its costs of production. The moral status of dumping might seem identical to the judgement on domestic predatory prices if the purpose is to attack the importing country's own products. However, free trade between economies at different stages of development is a complex matter. Actually, dumping involves a number of ethical and legal issues, and an accurate judgement has to consider all the relevant circumstances of each situation.

Discriminatory practices in pricing

A final issue involves price discrimination, which occurs when the seller charges different customers different prices for the same product without genuine justification. Price discrimination can also involve charging two buyers the same price when it costs more to supply one than another. In some cases, the price charged can change through a transparent process to incentivize early purchase, or purchase during a certain period (as with many aeroplane tickets). But all clients can benefit equally from this measure, and there is no discrimination.

In some countries (the United States, for instance), it is illegal to discriminate between different distributors on price without a suitable justification. Some common price discrimination practices cannot be considered unethical, however. There is discrimination by age group and student status (which is quite common in theatres, movies, museums and tourist attractions), employee discounts, incentives to increase market share or revenues at the retail level (coupons, rebates, bulk and quantity pricing, seasonal discounts and frequent buyer discounts) and incentives for industrial buyers.

The practice of *price skimming* consists of charging a relatively high price for a product or service at first, then reducing it over time. As already noted, this seems ethically acceptable if there is no abuse of the customer's quest to satisfy basic needs.

Charging higher prices to those who have more purchasing power than others is another form of pricing discrimination that is not necessarily wrong. There are several examples of this. One is *premium pricing* as opposed to *economic pricing* (for instance, business class in aeroplanes or premium coffee in some coffee chains). The latter might be to price at just beyond the marginal cost of production, whereas, with the former, a similar or slightly superior product can be sold at a very high price. There are financial reasons for doing this, as any lack of return from the economic product is more than compensated for by profits from the premium line. Another example is selling medicine to developing countries at a lower price than in developed countries, although one should avoid a scenario in which these same medicines are resold to developed countries through unofficial, unauthorized and unintended distribution channels (the grey market). From an ethical perspective, the example of selling medicine more cheaply is not only licit but also laudable as a form of distributive justice and solidarity.

Besides these practices, there are many other ethically doubtful cases of charging lower prices for some consumers and higher prices for others.[17] Another more-than-questionable practice is to charge higher prices for products sold in poor areas to exploit the population's inability to travel to more affluent regions to purchase goods or to obtain information about more competitive pricing.

11.7 Promotion of the product: Advertising ethics

We mentioned promotion as one of the key elements of the 'marketing mix'. Promotion includes advertising, publicity, public relations, personal selling and sales promotion. This is a vast field. For reasons of space, we will focus only on advertising.[18]

Advertising can be designed to convey information, but generally it tries to persuade potential consumers to buy products and services or advises them on how to obtain and use them. Advertising can be focused on creating and reinforcing a brand image or brand loyalty. It can also be oriented towards capturing consumers by generating or increasing habits in them. There are a number of ethical issues in advertising that we need to examine in order to provide criteria of integrity in the field, but the primary question concerns the legitimacy of the persuasion itself – the essence of advertising – and how far advertising should be permitted to go with that persuasion.

Respect for the consumer's responsible and free choice

Some persuasive advertising has been criticized on the grounds that, for certain types of people, it overrides consumer autonomy by provoking desires in such a way that one of autonomy's necessary conditions – the possibility of decision – is removed. This becomes manipulative advertising and consequently is ethically wrong.[19] Of course, there is persuasive advertising that can be manipulative, but there is also another kind that is both persuasive and respectful. One might be influenced by advertising or motivated by it, but this does not mean that manipulation is necessarily present; one can reflect and then freely decide for or against what an advertisement proposes.

A lack of respect for consumer autonomy can be identified in 'subliminal advertising', a manipulative technique that introduces an image (for example, advertising a soft drink) for one-twenty-fifth of a second during a movie. The audience are not aware of the image, but it is retained in their minds and then, under certain conditions, can, in some people, produce a desire for what is pictured – at least, in those who already enjoy the product. Apart from any ethical reservations about this technique, its efficacy is nowadays questioned.[20]

Advertising directed at children is problematic[21] because they are not yet capable of resisting or understanding marketing tactics. However, children influence their family and, after a certain age, can even spend their own money on snacks and unhealthy food, fashionable clothes, home entertainment equipment and so on, especially during pre-adolescence and the teenage years. Another vulnerable audience can be found in developing countries, where some people might not be sufficiently familiar with skilled marketing ploys and how powerful their tactics are. In developed countries, too, the less educated, emotionally immature or weak-willed can also be vulnerable to certain techniques.

Apart from respecting the consumer's autonomy in decision-making, ethics in advertising requires other conditions that we will address in time. Marketing managers and advertising professionals, in adhering to these conditions, need not only an ethical sense and courage but also the imagination and creativity to resist the pressure to achieve results at any cost.

Truthfulness in advertising messages

Truthfulness is the necessary ethical condition of any human communication. In advertising, many ethical problems centre on dishonesty. Presenting false statements that deceive or manipulate reality to persuade people to engage in transactions they would otherwise avoid is a clear transgression of truthfulness; for instance, to assert 'This is the best-selling car of the year', when it is not, or to claim that a product has qualities that it does not, in fact, possess.

- *Deceptive advertising.* Some advertisements, although not based on false statements, can nevertheless be deceptive given the audience to which the message is addressed. Examples of deception in advertising could be presenting a blown-up photograph of a small car in an advertisement that targets children, which might lead them to think that they would be able to drive it, or images that suggest a non-existent cause–effect connection (say, presenting a fragrance as a means to attract men or promising a guarantee of happiness to those who drink a certain soda).
- *Testimonials and endorsements*: Sometimes, advertising messages are given by people – generally ordinary customers – who recommend a product based on their favourable experience. These testimonials can have a certain persuasive effect.

Endorsements are usually provided by celebrities or experts (professionals, outstanding sports figures, movie stars and so on). They are designed to lead consumers to believe that an advertising message reflects the opinions, beliefs, findings or experiences of a party other than the one sponsoring the advertisement.

Many consumers might not take testimonials and endorsements seriously, but others might believe what such 'fellow customers', celebrities or experts say, or, at least, be influenced by them.

- *Demonstrations*: In advertising, practical demonstrations seek to show, through a practical application, that a product of a certain brand – say, a detergent – is superior to all its rivals. In fact, this may or may not be true. It may also be that the product used in the demonstration is not the one being advertised.
- *Mock-ups*: These refer to life-sized or even larger representations. They are used in advertising for a visual presentation of a product, such as an ice cream or a succulent cut of meat, through appealing photography. Mock-ups used in advertisements could include not only a full-sized photograph but also a representation of other products or the genuine product enhanced in some way (for example, a vegetable soup with many more pieces of vegetables than the real one contains). Mock-ups can easily involve deception and, consequently, are subject to regulation in many countries, as are many other advertising practices.
- *Puffery*: This refers to subjective, superlative expressions that praise a product or service, or to vague and general statements with no specific facts.[22] Puffery is not really false advertising or deception, as everybody can understand that it is an exaggeration or embellishment of the product's qualities. However, it might take the form of an expression, bordering on untruthfulness, which could deceive some. Puffery actually functions as a deception when people cannot readily identify the exaggeration involved and are consequently misled. Discernment is required to determine whether a particular piece of puffery is ethically acceptable. It is also true that puffery can be a step onto the slippery slope of deception and fraud.

Respect for people's dignity and rights

Respect for people's dignity and human rights is a basic requirement in advertising, as in life. A lack of respect for people is manifest when advertising uses degrading images, presenting persons as mere sexual objects to attract the attention of an audience.

Respect for human dignity also requires avoiding the use of scenes of cruelty or violence in advertising messages. Additionally, advertising should respect the privacy of the individual and the right to one's own image and reputation. A similar attitude should be maintained with regard to private and public institutions.

Non-offensive advertising and good taste

Advertising can be described as offensive when its form or message disgusts people – and not necessarily the vast majority. Messages that offend ethnic groups, religious beliefs and so on is not responsible advertising.

A lack of respect for people, advertising products that some find offensive ('socially sensitive products') and bad taste can all cause consumers to become irritated and respond negatively.[23]

Moderation in advertising intrusiveness

Advertising is usually presented to people without their permission. It enters the home via the internet, television, newspapers, magazines or phone calls, or one involuntarily encounters it when driving or walking down a street, reading a newspaper or magazine or perhaps at the cinema. Sometimes it is excessively intrusive and annoying. A sense of responsibility aids in self-regulation but, besides this, in many countries there is strict regulation to avoid excessive invasiveness. This applies to advertising along roads and by megaphones or billboards; it also places limitations on the interruption of television programmes, telemarketing invading the privacy of the home and so on.

Fair competition

Advertising can be contrary to fair competition if it uses false or unverified information when comparing a firm's own products with those of competitors, or if it discredits or denigrates a competitor. In some countries it is even forbidden to mention competitors by name when comparing products; advertisers are reduced to badmouthing 'Brand X'.

Also contrary to fair competition is introducing deliberate confusion between the advertised product and another well-known brand by plagiarizing the advertisements of the other company.

Responsibility for social impact

Advertising can reflect social values but, in some ways, it also actively fosters these. Indirectly, advertising has its social impact, which should be treated as a foreseeable effect for which one bears responsibility (3.4). In this regard, advertisers and businesses have a duty to be respectful of people and to foster human flourishing.

11.8 Ethics in placement of the product

Placement of the product entails ensuring that a product is available to the right customers, at the right place and at the right time. It involves deciding on the most effective distribution channels and locations for reaching the target market efficiently. Product placement considers where and how a product is sold, whether through online platforms, retail stores, direct sales or other methods, to maximize accessibility and appeal for potential customers. All these elements refer to efficiency in the placement of the product, but this is not enough, it requires ethics.

Ethics in the placement of the product entails, firstly, commutative justice (5.1) in disclosure of all pertinent information related to the sale. This requires all parties to act without lies or deception. In commerce, a fraud occurs when one person or business makes a sale using deceit or trickery to obtain value or gain. Deception can involve knowingly misrepresenting or concealing the relevant facts surrounding a sale with the intent to defraud or to induce reliance through this falsity. A more subtle form of deception is failing to disclose all of the proper information to the prospective buyer, which the latter can easily obtain elsewhere. It is understandable that sellers attempt to emphasize the positive aspects of the product, but hiding the negative can often cross the line into deception. Some examples of fraud in commerce include deceit over quality or quantity of product and the creation of false expectations of post-sale services.

One of the most common cases of fraud in commerce – which we will mention here only briefly – is misrepresentation in the sales inventory. One example is the so-called 'roundtrip' transaction. This is when a company makes a fictitious sale to another and, in return, buys a commodity from the latter for the same amount of money, also fictitiously, or when a company 'buys' a non-existent product or service. The motive could be increasing sales of the inventory or to pay less tax.

Along the chain of an organization from the producer to the final user, the price of the product is incrementally increased. On this point, apart from the price problems discussed earlier, one can find a typical justice issue derived from the abuse of power at some link of the distribution chain. One of the intermediaries might have enormous negotiation power over the next. This is the case, for instance, of chain stores and small suppliers. The latter might sell a great volume of a commodity to a single client, which facilitates the sale but, on the negative side, the chain can exploit its negotiation power by imposing on the small producer such low prices that it becomes an exploitative relationship.

Another ethical issue within the distribution channel is 'gift-giving' to people who make decisions that can favour sales or commercial transactions in some way – and that can sometimes be a way of covering up bribery or even a brazen bribe (5.8). Clear guidelines within a company or for an entire industry can help to avert extortion and questionable practices.

Many ethical issues in sales concern the integrity of salespersons and representatives, who might often feel a tension between the loyalty to the seller they represent and giving an authentic service to buyers. Honesty and other virtues are necessary for upright conduct, for instance to tell the truth about the product's features and to avoid unfair or inaccurate comparisons with a rival product.

Certain external conditions can push people towards misbehaviour in personal selling. For instance, salespersons are more prone to act wrongly when they experience a great intensity of competition or revenue pressures from their organization (especially in hard times) to promote a product; when compensation systems are based mostly on commissions, when gifting or bribes are common in a certain industry; when sales training (including its ethical aspects) is non-existent or abbreviated; and when a sales representative has limited selling experience.[24] Sales managers bear responsibility for preventing abusive sales practices.

A final issue is that clients' privacy has to be respected, and their personal data and purchase behaviour must be kept confidential, as should that of employees (10.2).

11.9 Ethics in e-commerce

Electronic commerce or e-commerce refers to buying and selling online, and there are different forms: business to business (B2B) (which is the largest), business to customer (B2C), customer to customer (C2C), peer to peer (P2P) and others. E-commerce is conducted on websites or mobile apps with a variety of support (for example, live chat or chatbots on messaging apps, voice assistants) that can make e-commerce a 'conversational commerce'. It has experienced a rapid growth since 2000 and there are now giants of e-commerce marketplaces such as Amazon and Alibaba.

Although, in essence, buying and selling via the internet is like a conventional sale, the ethical issues of e-commerce have different manifestations and scope.[25] Among the manifestations are two particularities that deserve attention. The first regards respect for the privacy of customers, the second, e-commerce security.

When a buyer accesses the seller's website, the latter collects details regarding the buyer's personal information, products ordered, credit or debit card details and so on. This could be used for improper purposes, something that would infringe customer privacy. A number of potential risks are present here, including the possibility that the customer identity or personal information, such as credit card information, could be stolen or sold to another party. E-commerce companies should be aware of these risks and take even more care than conventional companies in handling private information.

E-commerce security considers several practical requirements to avoid fraud in e-commerce. Gordon and Loeb[26] typify the following requirements:

- *Confidentiality* refers to the assurance that data is secured and is available only to those who have authorization.
- *Availability* ensures a timely and reliable manner for authorized users to access personal data on the website as well as any e-commerce data service.
- *Integrity* ensures that data is collected accurately and truthfully.
- *Authentication* confirms that the person or organization using the data is in fact the one who claims to be using it.
- *Non-repudiation* guarantees that online customers or commerce partners cannot be wrongly denied access to the data.

Apart from avoiding fraud, these requirements should foster trust, which is necessary in any commerce but even more so in e-commerce, where there is no face-to-face encounter.

Case Study #11

Solving a problem in commercial activity[17]

Alfredo, CEO of Excelquímica, a Latino American company that imported and distributed chemical products and had an annual turnover of US$300 million, faced a newly discovered problem. Antonio, sales director of a specialized division, had left the company three weeks earlier and Francisco Morales had taken his place through internal promotion. Among the dossiers that Francisco had received, he found an email from a client asking about possible confusion in the shipment of a plasticizer that the client mixed with various substances to obtain commercial products. The client suspected it was of a quality inferior to that requested. There was also Antonio's reply, promising to investigate the matter and inform him as soon as possible.

Francisco sent an email to his immediate manager, the director of the division, who had been hired just two months earlier, through a head-hunter, from a competitor company. He wanted to know if his boss knew anything about this. The boss's answer was to ask Francisco to gather more information.

Two weeks later, Alfredo reported his inquiries, which were summarized as follows:

1. The practice of delivering similar products of lower price and quality affected hundreds of customers.
2. The employees argued that this was due to pressures to achieve good performance.
3. The volume of the substitution was relatively small, but as a whole it amounted to some US$600,000.
4. It was impossible to detect the substitution unless a specific analysis was made and, in practice, the result was similar (perhaps for this reason, only the one client complaint was recorded).
5. There were indications that the previous division director tolerated this practice.
6. The employees had not received any remuneration for keeping silent about the practice.

Alfredo wondered what to do.

Questions

1. What questionable actions and behaviours described in this case can you identify? What ethical values are at stake in the Excelquímica case?
2. What alternatives does Alfredo have in facing the massive deception of his clients? Which of them would you recommend?
3. What would you do in Alfredo's position regarding employees who have participated in the deception and how will you promote integrity in the organization?

Notes

1. Confucius, *Analects* X, 24. See trans. A. Waley, *The Analects of Confucius* (New York: Vintage Books, 1999).
2. Sources: J. C. Lyu, 'A Comparative Study of Crisis Communication Strategies Between Mainland China and Taiwan: The Melamine-Tainted Milk Powder Crisis in the Chinese Context', *Public Relations Review*, vol. 38, no. 5, 2012, pp. 779–91; Y. Huang, 'The 2008 Milk Scandal Revisited', *Forbes* online, 16 July 2014, https://www.forbes.com/sites/yanzhonghuang/2014/07/16/the-2008-milk-scandal-revisited/; P. Mooney, 'The Story Behind China's Tainted Milk Scandal', *World News* online, 9 October 2008, https://www.usnews.com/news/world/articles/2008/10/09/the-story-behind-chinas-tainted-milk-scandal; X. Pei, A. Tandon, A. Alldrick, L. Giorgi, W. Huang and R. Yanga, 'The China Melamine Milk Scandal and its Implications for Food Safety Regulation',

Food Policy, vol. 36, no. 3, 2011, pp. 412–20; Wikipedia: 2008 Chinese Milk Scandal, https://en.wikipedia.org/wiki/2008_Chinese_milk_scandal. (All accessed on 5 June 2025).

3. Mentioned by L. Schlein, 'China's Melamine Milk Crisis Creates Crisis of Confidence', Voice of America, 26 September 2008: https://www.voanews.com/a/a-13-2008-09-26-voa45/403825.html. (Accessed on 5 June 2025).
4. UN Guidelines for Consumer Protection, 2016: https://unctad.org/system/files/official-document/ditccplpmisc2016d1_en.pdf. (Accessed on 5 June 2025).
5. R. A. Buchholz, 'Consumer Rights', in R. W. Kolb (ed.), *Encyclopedia of Business Ethics and Society* (Los Angeles, CA: Sage, 2018), pp. 434–9.
6. See L. A. Myers, 'Consumer Sovereignty', in K. W. Kolb Kole(ed.), *Encyclopedia of Business Ethics and Society* (Los Angeles, CA: Sage, 2018), pp. 439–41.
7. J. M. Elegido, *Una comunidad de servicio. Ensayos de Ética de la Empresa* (México: Instituto Panamericano de Dirección de Empresas (IPADE), 2000).
8. The American Marketing Association Statement of Ethics: https://www.ama.org/ama-statement-of-ethics/. (Accessed on 5 June 2025).
9. P. Murphy, 'Character and Virtue Ethics in International Marketing: An Agenda for Managers, Researchers and Educators', *Journal of Business Ethics*, vol. 18, no. 1, 1999, pp. 107–24, on p. 113.
10. P. Murphy and G. R. Laczniak, *Marketing Ethics: Cases and Readings* (Englewood Cliffs, NJ: Prentice Hall, 2006); and P. Murphy, G. Laczniak and G. Wood, 'An Ethical Basis for Relationship Marketing: A Virtue Ethics Perspective', *European Journal of Marketing*, vol. 41, no. 1/2, 2007, pp. 37–57.
11. Sources: A. M. Ballvé and P. Debeljuh, *Misión y valores. La empresa en busca de su sentido* (Buenos Aires: Gestión 2000, 2006), pp. 107–127; Bimbo, *Un esfuerzo a través de los años* (México, 1995); Bimbo, Annual report 2023; https://www.grupobimbo.com/es/inversionistas/reportes/informes-anuales/2023. Accessed on 20 October 2024. Bimbo, 'This is How We do Marketing: Responsible Communication Guidelines,' Corporate Website; R. Servitge, Sendra, *Estrategia de éxito empresarial* (Barcelona: Océano, 2022).
12. https://www.ama.org/the-definition-of-marketing-what-is-marketing/. (Accessed on 5 June 2025).
13. https://dictionary.cambridge.org/dictionary/english/consumerism. (Accessed on 5 June 2025).
14. There is a vast bibliography on marketing ethics. Among many others: L. Eagle and S. Dahl, *Marketing Ethics & Society*, 2015; and L. Eagle, S. Dahl, P. D. Pelsmacker and C. R. Taylor (eds), *The SAGE Handbook of Marketing Ethics* (Los Angeles, CA: Sage, 2020); Murphy and Laczniak, *Marketing Ethics*, also provide interesting insights into marketing ethics.
15. See D. K. Davidson, *Selling Sin: The Marketing of Socially Unacceptable Products* (Westport, CT: Quorum Books, 1996).
16. On justice in pricing see A. Walsh and T. Lynch, 'The Very Idea of Justice in Pricing', *Business & Professional Ethics Journal*, vol. 21, no. 3/4, 2002, pp. 5–27; J. M. Elegido, 'The Just Price as the Price Obtainable in an Open Market', *Journal of Business Ethics*, vol. 130, no. 3, 2015, pp. 557–72; D. D. Friedman, 'In Defense of Thomas Aquinas and the Just Price', *History of Political Economy*, vol. 12, no. 2, 1980, pp. 234–42; S. Vachani and N. C. Smith, 'Socially Responsible Pricing: Lessons from the Pricing of AIDS Drugs in Developing Countries', *California Management Review*, vol. 47, no. 1, 2004, pp. 117–44.
17. All names are fictitious.

Part IV

Societal Business Ethics

SDI Productions / Getty Images

12

Business Responsibility and Relationships in Society

The famous Statue of Liberty on the US East coast should be complemented with a Statue of Responsibility on the West coast.[1]

VIKTOR FRANKL (1905–97), Austrian neurologist and psychiatrist

Overview

Business is not an isolated entity but a part of society: it operates within a community and, for better or worse, impacts it. Responsibility refers primarily to individuals, as they possess moral conscience, so individual responsibility (see Chapter 3) is always present in business. However, responsibility, in a different sense, also applies to a company's activities regarding its social and ecological impact, whether beneficial or harmful. This invites reflection on the responsibility of business and the concepts of corporate social responsibility (CSR) and corporate accountability (CA). This chapter addresses these issues, while ecological responsibility will be discussed in the next chapter.

Section A explores various perspectives on business responsibilities within society, reviewing mainstream theoretical approaches to CSR. It then proposes ethical foundations for CSR based on Aristotelian-personalist ethics.

Section B addresses business relationships with society, including interactions with governments and non-governmental organizations (NGOs). It also examines how businesses demonstrate accountability to society by providing necessary information to those affected by corporate activities, typically through reports and certifications.

Chapter Aims

After reading this chapter you should be able to:

- Discuss arguments for and against corporate social responsibility (CSR).
- Understand the main theories of business responsibility within society.
- Be aware of the origin of the concept of sustainability and its current meaning.
- Discuss ethical principles related to CSR.

- Be familiar with the concept of the triple bottom line (TBL).
- Explore the notion of sustainability.
- Reflect on interactions between companies and governments.
- Consider the challenges and potential collaborations between businesses and non-governmental organizations (NGOs).
- Discuss the rationale for corporate accountability and how it can be performed.
- Understand corporate auditing and reporting in social responsibility and sustainability.

Historical Case #12

Responsibilities in the Bangladesh factory disaster at Rana Plaza[2]

The news impacted the entire world. On 24 April 2013, an eight-storey building in the industrial town of Savar, on the outskirts of Bangladesh's capital, Dhaka, collapsed. The building housed several garment workshops making clothes for seventy multinational retailers and employed about 5,000 workers. The disaster resulted in 1,138 fatalities and 2,438 injuries. Although there had previously been industrial accidents in other textile factories in Bangladesh and other developing countries, this, now known as the Rana Plaza collapse and also as the Savar building collapse, was one of the worst in history.

According to local officials responsible for investigating the incident, the weight and vibrations of four electricity generators located on the roof, along with the industrial machinery used inside, created an overload that the building's structure could not withstand. The building had long shown a visible crack. The investigation also revealed multiple irregularities in the building's construction and use: the building permit was for five floors, but it had eight; it was licensed for commercial use but was employed for industrial activities. Additionally, the materials used in the construction were described as of 'very poor quality'.

Bangladesh had emerged as an attractive location for businesses due to its abundant workforce, some of the lowest labour costs in the world, and excellent tax conditions. Garment factories were, and still are, abundant in Bangladesh, and the industry is highly significant for the country's economy. In 2013, there were around 5,000 factories with 4 million workers, representing 45 per cent of the country's total industrial employment. The Bangladeshi garment industry, including knitwear and hosiery, accounted for 75 per cent of national export revenue and contributed 10 per cent to the country's gross domestic product (GDP).

Many of these textile workshops, like those in Rana Plaza, were 'sweatshops' – a derogatory term for industrial production facilities with extremely poor working conditions. Sweatshops are characterized by long working hours, wages around €1 a day, poor ventilation, lack of fire exits and overcrowded spaces. Additionally, regulatory law in Bangladesh is weak, and its enforcement is inconsistent. Sweatshops rarely make headlines, except in the case of disasters like this or the fire in November 2012 at a Dhaka factory that produced for Wal-Mart and the European retailer C&A, where 112 people died.

After the collapse, Bangladeshi police arrested the building's owner, Sohel Rana, near the border with India as he tried to flee. An enraged crowd demanded his execution.

Labour unions blamed retailers for the poor working conditions and for ignoring safety violations in the Bangladeshi factories that supplied their products. The popular press added that the low prices imposed by multinational companies encouraged local suppliers to cut costs on wages and safety. However, the problem may be more complex.

Retailers responded to the disaster by developing agreements to improve factory and worker safety in the country. A group dominated by European retailers, international labour organizations, and non-governmental organizations (NGOs) signed the Accord on Fire and Building Safety in Bangladesh (AFBSB). The AFBSB was a legally binding agreement covering over 1,600 factories. An independent inspectorate was established to monitor the implementation of corrective action plans after the Rana Plaza collapse. Under the agreement, the first nine months of inspections were to 'identify serious risks and the need for urgent repairs'. Unsafe factories were required to cease operations, repair plans were drawn up, and workers were informed of their right to refuse entry into unsafe premises. Workers were to receive a salary for up to six months while the factory remained closed. If a company was alleged to have breached its commitments under the agreement, any signatory could file a complaint, which would first go to a steering committee and then an arbitration process enforceable by law in the company's home country. However, the agreement did not contain provisions for sanctions. Signatories included Marks and Spencer, Benetton, Carrefour, Metro, Inditex (owner of Zara), Abercrombie & Fitch, and US HPH. Another agreement, the Alliance for Bangladesh Worker Safety (ABWS), was also signed, mainly promoted by American companies like Gap, J. C. Penney, Wal-Mart, Costco and others.

On the stock market, the immediate public reaction was to turn away from apparel manufacturers sourcing from Bangladesh. However, Jacobs and Singhal, based on a sample of thirty-nine such companies, reported that the negative sentiment dissipated soon after the incident, with no significant stock market impact two weeks later. Their study also found no evidence of significant market reactions to announcements of the AFBSB and ABWS agreements. Jacobs and Singhal concluded that the lack of negative economic impact from the Rana Plaza disaster suggests that retailers have little economic incentive to move out of Bangladesh or other low-cost countries to avoid such risks. However, they speculated that if another similar disaster were to occur, there might be a stronger reaction from activists and the public.

Three years after the Rana Plaza disaster, reports indicated that progress had been slow despite the binding nature of the accord. Only seven out of the 1,660 factories had fully implemented their corrective action plans, and another fifty-seven were on track. About 1,388 factories were behind schedule, twenty-two had not begun implementation, and 186 had yet to finalize their plans.

> ## Questions
>
> 1. Are the working conditions described in the case contrary to human rights? Why?
> 2. Do you think there are individual or corporate responsibilities in the Rana Plaza disaster?
> 3. Do you find the measures taken for safer factories in Bangladesh appropriate?
> 4. What can different actors – such as factory owners, retailers, policymakers, unions, NGOs and academics – do to increase their social responsibility about existing 'sweatshops'?

SECTION A. THE SOCIAL RESPONSIBILITY OF BUSINESS

In the history of business, the idea that companies only have economic and legal responsibilities prevailed for a long time. If any social responsibility existed, it was seen merely through the lens of maximizing profits or shareholder value, as will be discussed below. However, in practice, there have always been businesspeople who believed they bear social responsibilities beyond just creating wealth. There are notable examples from the nineteenth century through the First World War in the United Kingdom, the United States, Japan, India and Germany.[3]

The notion of Corporate Social Responsibility (CSR) emerged in contrast to the view that businesses only bear economic and legal responsibilities. Beginning in the mid-twentieth century and persisting to the present, this concept has both supporters and critics.

It is worth noting that some people hold a functional perspective of society, viewing it as organized by specialized social institutions: the family for reproduction, schools for education, government for public welfare, and businesses for wealth creation and the production of goods and services. According to this perspective, none of these institutions bears responsibility beyond its specific function.

This view of one-directional responsibility has been challenged on several grounds. One challenge is based on the reality that social institutions are interdependent rather than functionally isolated. Business entities, in particular, operate within a shared environment and are interlinked with governments, competitors, customers, consumers, environmental advocates, the media and other groups that interact with the company – often called 'stakeholders' or, more properly, 'relationholders'.[4] This suggests that businesses are intermediary institutions that, like other social institutions, should contribute to the common good of society in line with their specific objectives (2.7). This perspective is consistent with Aristotelian traditions and other views that argue businesses have responsibilities beyond providing goods and services and creating wealth, even though only individuals bear moral responsibility.

Having said that, let us begin this section by reviewing the arguments for and against CSR, followed by a discussion of the main current approaches to CSR.

12.1 Criticisms and responses to the social responsibility of business

Among the definitions of CSR, the following, given by the European Union, is quite simple and comprehensive: CSR is "the responsibility of enterprises for their impacts on society"[3]. In practical terms, two main approaches can be distinguished:

- One approach views CSR as a commitment that should permeate all business activities.
- The other sees CSR as limited to specific policies and activities that a company undertakes for social purposes beyond its core business functions. These may include corporate philanthropy, community involvement, valuing diversity and other social actions conducted by or on behalf of the corporation.

The question that arises is whether companies should go beyond legal obligations in fulfilling these social responsibilities. Three primary arguments are commonly made against CSR:

- Social problems are the exclusive responsibility of the governments, with the support of NGOs, who should address such issues – not companies, which are not charitable institutions.
- Spending on social responsibilities incurs a cost that may infringe on shareholders' rights and could potentially hinder the company's efficiency in its core activities and mission.
- Social problems are often too varied and complex for companies to manage effectively.

In response to these criticisms, several counterarguments can be offered, as outlined in Table 12.1 and discussed below.

Table 12.1 Criticisms and responses on business social responsibility

Criticisms	Responses
Companies are not charitable institutions, so social concern of business has no sense.	– Business has a direct responsibility on both positive and negative social outcomes generated by its activity. – Social problems are, above all, the responsibility of society, including business.
Spending on social responsibility may infringe upon shareholders' rights and possibly the company's efficiency.	– Beyond shareholders' rights, companies have duties as social actors. – When chosen wisely, social responsibility spending can enhance reputation and profitability in the medium and long term.
Companies cannot effectively address complex social problems.	– In some cases, corporations have both the resources and expertise to address specific issues. – In many others, they contribute through support without directly managing the problems.

Social problems are, above all, problems for society

Regarding the first objection, it is undeniable that some social problems originate from business activity. Consider, for example, pollution, industrial diseases or ecological disasters. It is difficult to accept that businesses bear no responsibility for these issues, even if legal regulations may be lax in some countries or regions. The question is whether a company should go beyond governmental regulations by assuming explicit responsibilities, not only for the damage caused by its activities but also by contributing to the communities in which it operates. Or is this solely the responsibility of the state?

There is no doubt that public administration is responsible for addressing social problems. In fact, many states put considerable effort into solving them, providing support through tax-funded social welfare programmes. However, the welfare state has its limits, and in some countries an expanded welfare state is being questioned.

Additionally, state efficiency is often criticized due to the higher taxes and increased bureaucracy it entails. Furthermore, government intervention in solving social problems can stifle individual initiative and lacks the human warmth and effectiveness of direct action by those closest to the problem. As a result, some advocate for less state intervention and more action from civil society. To this end, the state should encourage – and even subsidize – social initiatives led by citizens or private institutions, including corporations, in line with the principle of subsidiarity (2.7).

Returning to the initial question, the rationale is that since social problems arise within society, then society has a responsibility to solve them, whether through individual initiatives, social groups or the state. It is unclear why social problems should be the exclusive responsibility of the state.

While businesses are not charitable institutions, they cannot ignore what is happening in society or their role as social actors within it. For this reason, corporations, along with other social institutions and individuals, should contribute to improving societal well-being to the best of their ability.

Social responsibilities can be profitable

Regarding the second criticism, which suggests that undertaking corporate social responsibilities generates costs which conflict with shareholders' rights and interests, it can be argued that many CSR activities are likely to be profitable if chosen wisely, due to the good reputation they generate. Many see CSR not as a cost, but rather as a profitable investment. The findings of several empirical studies also suggest that corporate virtue in the form of social responsibility – and, to a lesser extent, environmental responsibility – is likely to pay off (see 1.3).

Contributing to social causes does not require a company to spend an enormous amount of money. In most cases, a modest allocation of corporate resources to social activities does not divert the company from its core mission, nor does it reduce business efficiency. For example, a prosperous retail chain will not go bankrupt if it devotes 1 per cent of its Christmas sales profits to providing food for countries with starving populations. In fact, doing so may persuade many more people to shop at its stores.

Some suggest linking social responsibility to core business objectives to gain strategic advantages. In this way, Porter and Kramer argue that corporate growth and social welfare do not necessarily constitute a zero-sum game.[5] They contend that, quite the opposite, if corporations analysed their opportunities for social responsibility using the same frameworks that guide their core business choices, they would find that CSR can be much more than a cost, a constraint or a charitable deed – it can be a potent source of innovation, competitive advantage and social value.[6]

Beyond the economic argument, as noted (7.6), a company should contribute to the common good, which includes building a better society, starting by helping to solve social problems out of a sense of responsibility and not solely for the sake of profitability.

Companies often do not directly manage social problems

Regarding the third objection, it is true that companies rarely tackle social problems directly and, in many cases, do not have the specific capabilities required to do so. In general, businesses are not expected to take on the direct management of social problems. Instead, they can establish partnerships or provide support to NGOs. In the previous example, it would not make sense for a retail chain to organize the distribution of 1 per cent of its sales profits to needy countries. However, in some cases, corporations have both the resources and the skilled personnel to address specific problems. For instance, during Hurricane Katrina in 2005, Wal-Mart sent 1,500 truckloads of free merchandise and food for 100,000 meals to help alleviate the crisis. Neither the government nor social institutions had the capacity for such a response.

Since social problems are highly varied and complex, it is understandable that businesses may not always be actively involved. However, this does not mean that companies should ignore these issues. The best approach is for companies to focus their contributions on a few key areas and leave the rest for others to address. Companies should seek good advice and act based on objective criteria, avoiding arbitrary decisions. The direction should not be determined by the preferences of the chief executive, but by criteria such as the company's capabilities, how closely the problem relates to the company's activities, the level of attention the problem receives from other institutions and the urgency of a specific social need that the company is able to address.

12.2 Individual or corporate responsibilities?

Another frequent question related to corporate responsibilities is whether the corporation bears moral responsibilities, or if it is only individuals who do. Perhaps both individuals and corporations bear moral responsibilities, but in different senses? This topic has sparked a long debate, and a full discussion is beyond the scope of this book. However, in summary, there are both extreme and intermediate positions.

At one extreme, some argue that corporations are 'moral agents' and, therefore, bear moral responsibility.[7] Others contend that it is impossible to view corporations as moral agents responsible for anything, as a corporation is merely an aggregate of individuals.[8] In practice, common language often treats corporations as single units or agents, not only regarding their debated social responsibilities but also in terms of business functions and identity – for example, terms like 'CSR', 'corporate values', 'corporate mission' and 'corporate identity' are frequently used, which also classify businesses as a single unit. Moreover, many corporations outlast their individual members.

On the other hand, shared values and inter-subjective agreements for decision-making generally exist within corporations, making it both meaningful and useful to attribute the capacity for conscious and intentional behaviour to organizations.[9] Additionally, corporations often carry out collective actions through cooperation. This is another reason to assign a degree of moral responsibility to corporations – companies are not merely an aggregate of individuals, but a community.

However, common sense suggests that, despite arguments in favour of considering a corporation a moral agent, there are notable differences between an individual person and a firm. Strictly speaking, only individuals possess rationality, self-determination and conscience, and thus only they are true moral agents and bear moral responsibility. At most, a company can be considered a 'quasi-moral agent', meaning an entity that possesses certain characteristics or functions that resemble those of a moral agent (a person), but without fully meeting all the criteria traditionally associated with moral agency.

In other words, we can ascribe moral responsibilities to a corporation, but this does not eliminate personal responsibility in favour of corporate responsibility. On the contrary, it challenges those who make decisions within the company to fully assume their personal responsibilities.

12.3 Mainstream approaches to the social responsibility of business

The role of business in society is complex, with many competing and overlapping approaches. We will summarize some particularly relevant examples: strategic CSR, corporate social performance, corporate stakeholder responsibility and corporate citizenship.[10]

Strategic CSR

The notion of 'strategic CSR' (SCSR) has been defined as 'policies, programs, and processes that yield substantial business-related benefits to the firm, particularly by supporting core business activities and thus contributing to the firm's effectiveness in accomplishing its mission.'[11]

This aligns with Friedman's view[12] that business firms have no social responsibility beyond generating wealth for shareholders but recognizes that paying attention to CSR can be profitable.

Today, there are increasing internal and external pressures on business organizations to fulfil broader social goals.[13] Ignoring these pressures can be risky for profits, while assuming certain social responsibilities may enhance the organization's public image, align it with industry or community expectations, motivate employees, or even provide marketing advantages and other direct economic benefits.[14]

Following this approach, CSR can be viewed through a supply-and-demand lens, allowing for the determination of an 'ideal' level of CSR in each situation through cost–benefit analysis, balancing CSR costs with financial performance. The ideal level depends on various factors, such as company size, diversification, research and development, advertising, government involvement, sales, consumer income, labour market conditions and the stage of the industry lifecycle.[15] This approach broadens the traditional view of business by considering social goals, but it also reduces CSR to purely a business instrument.

Corporate social performance

This model, as presented by Wood,[16] and similarly in successive modifications,[17] acknowledges the necessity of screening social issues related to business and the corresponding corporate responsiveness, which should be incorporated into business practices. This is not a substitute for CSR, which offers general principles, but rather a complement to the concept. Thus, the notion of corporate social performance emerged as a synthesis of three elements – principles, processes and policies – and a set of structural categories that can be identified, described and measured.[18]

In a more precise way, Wood defines corporate social performance as 'a business organization's configuration of principles of social responsibility, processes of social responsiveness, and policies, programs and observable outcomes as they relate to the firm's societal relationships'.[19] She proposed three principles of social responsibility: the institutional principle concerning legitimacy, the organizational principle, which she refers to as public responsibility, and the individual principle, understood as managerial discretion. Processes of corporate social responsiveness include environmental assessment, stakeholder management and issues management, while outcomes of corporate behaviour entail social impacts, social programmes and social policies.

The content of CSR principles in Wood's approach is somewhat problematic. She rightly establishes that business is a social institution that must avoid abusing its power, but she takes legitimacy merely as *social legitimacy* (granted by each society)[20] rather than *moral legitimacy* (coming from ethical principles). The organizational principle refers to businesses being responsible for outcomes related to their primary and secondary areas of involvement with society, which makes sense, but she takes 'public responsibility' to mean the functions of organizational management within the specific context of public policy.[21] One might wonder why this responsibility is not derived from ethical principles. Finally, the individual principle refers to the manager as a moral actor who should exercise discretion toward socially responsible outcomes.[22] However, discretion without further conditions is insufficient for the ethical exercise of responsibility.

Corporate stakeholder responsibility

Some scholars[23] who hold the stakeholder view of the firm (7.4) prefer to talk about 'corporate stakeholder responsibility' rather than 'corporate social responsibility.' This concept emphasizes that corporate responsibilities are not generically owed to 'society', but rather to relationholders: firms are, therefore, responsible for creating economic, social and ecological value for all the firm's constituencies.

Corporate stakeholder responsibility offers a way to address conflicting responsibilities among relationholders. To resolve such conflicts, one must apply justifiable moral principles rather than arbitrarily balancing competing stakeholder demands.[24]

The application of corporate stakeholder responsibility suggests *stakeholder engagement*, a practice in which the organization actively involves relationholders in its activities in a positive manner. Although such practices might have various objectives, they generally involve the responsibility of the firm towards its constituencies (employees, shareholders, customers and so on) by respecting the legitimate interests of relationholders in accordance with moral principles.[25]

One strength of this approach is that it avoids the conceptual abstraction of CSR by addressing specific interests and practices, visualizing responsibilities to each group of people affected by business activities.[26] In practice, many companies accept this view of business responsibility in society,[27] or assume certain responsibility towards relationholders, such as employees and clients. The *Business Roundtable*, an influential association of American CEOs, in 2019, presented a statement moving away from shareholder primacy, and with a commitment to all stakeholders. In its own words, 'While each of our individual companies serves its own corporate purpose, we share a fundamental commitment to all of our stakeholders.'[28] Similarly, the World Economic Forum launched the *Davos Manifesto 2020*, stating, 'The purpose of a company is to engage all its stakeholders in shared and sustained value creation.'[29]

However, some argue that the concept of the stakeholder does not adequately capture the complex social, economic and organizational realities that managers face.[30] Another criticism is more philosophical in nature and concerns the purpose of business in society: the notion that the purpose of business is the satisfaction of stakeholder interests is questionable, as discussed in a previous chapter (7.5).

Additionally, the stakeholder responsibility approach has been criticized for potentially enabling *managerial opportunism*. Since managers have wide discretion in how to serve stakeholder interests, an unscrupulous executive could appeal to such interests while actually pursuing selfish goals.[31] However, such opportunism is a problem not exclusive to the stakeholder approach. Moreover, under certain conditions, stakeholder groups can help maintain managerial accountability.[32]

Corporate citizenship

This approach applies the political notion of the 'citizen' to corporations, understanding *corporate citizenship* (CC) as a company's role and its responsibilities within society, which encompass a company's contribution to society through three main areas:

1   *Core business activities*: Companies contribute by conducting their primary operations responsibly, ensuring their products, services and business practices add positive value to society.
2   *Social investment and philanthropy programmes*: Many businesses invest in social programmes and philanthropic initiatives that support community development, education, health and other essential social needs.
3   *Engagement in public policy*: Companies can also participate in public policy discussions, helping to shape policies that promote social welfare, environmental sustainability and ethical business practices.[33] This engagement can be particularly relevant in developing countries or other situations where there is a lack of effective government infrastructure or processes to address public issues – often involving basic needs such as healthcare, education for local communities, or the development of political capacity and public policy.[34] However, this role must be carefully managed, as large companies wield significant power. In some countries, if not properly managed, this power can undermine legitimate democratic participation.

12.4 Sustainability and CSR

Sustainability is sometimes presented as a concept that evolved from corporate social responsibility, and, indeed, there are companies that no longer refer to CSR but only to corporate sustainability. While both concepts are related, they are distinct, as we will discuss. Nonetheless, it is appropriate to introduce the concept of sustainability.

The concept of *sustainability* has its roots in growing concerns about pollution, the accelerating deterioration of natural resources and other threats to the planet (13.1, 13.2). It gained increasing popularity after its introduction in 1987 through the *Brundtland Commission Report*, commissioned by the *United Nations World Commission on Environment and Development* (WCED). Recognizing that ecological problems have significant consequences for economic and social development, the WCED tasked Gro Harlem Brundtland, the former prime minister of Norway, with preparing a report on 'our common future'.

The Brundtland Commission Report recommended *sustainable development*, defined as development that 'meets the needs of the present without compromising the ability of future generations to meet their own needs'.[35]

Sustainability, as well as sustainable development, has more recently acquired a broader meaning, extending beyond the natural environment to include aspects related to people, the social environment and a special concern for future generations. Thus, the concept of sustainability provides a new perspective, focusing on the consequences of human actions for future generations. The notion of the *common good* (2.6) also encompasses sustainability by considering the well-being of future generations.

The concept of sustainability has been applied to business as a way to integrate economic, environmental and social criteria into its governance, strategy and management. While recognizing that corporate growth and profitability are important, sustainability also requires companies to pursue societal goals, particularly those related to sustainable development, such as environmental protection, social justice, equity and economic development. Corporate sustainability includes strategies and practices aimed at protecting, supporting and enhancing human and natural resources, balancing both current and future needs.

Although some companies refer to sustainability rather than social responsibility, conceptually speaking, CSR and sustainability are distinct. CSR focuses on being aware of the social impact of business, while sustainability emphasizes responsibility for long-term consequences and a better future, particularly regarding the natural environment and development. It may be appropriate to maintain this distinction to highlight the concern for future generations when discussing sustainability.

12.5 Ethical principles for CSR

The CSR approach proposed here does not forget the potential long-term contribution of CSR to the bottom line, but, in contrast to the 'strategic CSR' approach, it does not consider CSR exclusively as an instrument for profit ('business case'), but rather as an ethical requirement. More normative is the stakeholder approach, which focuses on responsibility to relationholders and the corporate citizenship approach, although without including any specific theory. The corporate social performance approach developed by Wood, as previously mentioned (12.3), suggested three principles of social responsibility: the institutional, the organizational and the individual. These are related to three significant levels of analysis, although the content in Wood's approach seems more sociological than ethical. Here we will examine the three levels, but from an ethical perspective, and more specifically from the Aristotelian-personalist approach (2B), along with some other ideas previously presented.

The institutional principle: Moral legitimacy

As noted already (2.7), what gives moral legitimacy to any social institution is its orientation towards the common good of society. Therefore, the institutional principle should refer to the common good in its full sense, which, as noted (2.7), includes four basic aspects: socio-cultural values, social well-being and community development, including a sustainable environment, and social harmony and peace, with the stability and security of a just social order.

Every social institution should contribute to the common good in accordance with its specific purpose. Business contributes to the common good through its multi-ends, as previously discussed (7.7), which are its core business activities, along with involvement in society (including philanthropic actions), and potentially through certain engagement in public policy, as the corporate citizenship approach (12.3) suggests. Regarding engagement in public policy, the principle of legitimacy can resolve controversy regarding the political role of business and its engagement in public policy.[36] In practice, effective social control is necessary to avoid abuses by corporations under the pretext of acting as upright corporate citizens.

The organizational principle: Scope and order of responsibilities

The institutional principle, though extremely important, is very general – it does not tell us exactly what the scope and order of priority between the parties should be. Companies, like individuals, can hardly attend to all legitimate interests of people, or groups of people, with whom they interact or are interdependent. Frequently this is physically impossible, and, at other times, the interests of these groups are in conflict. The organizational principle, along with the managerial principle (which follows), helps us determine the scope of responsibilities and their appropriate ordering.

The scope of the contribution a company makes to society can be grouped into three categories:

- *Operative responsibilities*: These are derived from organizational operations and their outcomes. They include providing good products (goods and services), promoting decent work, creating wealth fairly and striving for continuity.
- *Integrative responsibilities*: These consist of treating relationholders with justice and even care and benevolence, fostering reciprocity and a sense of cooperation.
- *Socio-political responsibilities*: These derive from the aim to be a good social actor within society and the firm's capacity to contribute – along with many other social actors – to solving social problems, fostering good political governance and thereby trying to improve society.

Operational and integrative responsibilities correspond to the multi-ends of the company and, thus, they are basic and should, therefore, be emphasized. A company is not socially responsible if, for instance, it shows disregard for fairness in its products or lacks responsibility towards the environment, even if it engages in philanthropic actions.

Socio-political responsibilities are assumed by the company with the objective of social, economic and environmental improvement for a particular community, or for the benefit of society at large, considering both current and future generations (sustainability) (12.4). These responsibilities can include corporate social involvement where the company operates, making social investments, developing philanthropy programmes and engaging in public policy (when necessary and in an appropriate manner) and when needed to contribute to good public governance.

Criteria can help companies prioritize such responsibilities. The first is the *priority of operational and integrative responsibilities over socio-political* responsibilities, as the most genuine contribution of a business to society is through its core activities. Obviously, this does not mean ignoring socio-political responsibilities, but if there is conflict, responsibility for core activities should come first.

The second criterion is the priority to fulfil *duties of justice* – giving to each what is due, respecting other people's rights (natural and contractual), acting with reciprocity and not damaging the environment. A deep sense of justice includes a willingness to cooperate.

The third criterion regards prioritizing responsibilities *in caring for people and providing a friendly service*. The nature and intensity of the existing links determine such a priority. These responsibilities go beyond strict impartiality and require a certain order. In personal behaviour, it would not be logical to neglect one's own family responsibilities in order to look after a stranger. Similarly, managers bear greater responsibility to care for their collaborators than for others who do not have a connection with the company. A CEO's responsibility towards employees who have served the firm loyally for many years should be greater than their loyalty towards new employees. This criterion also includes the legitimate demands and expectations of people closely related to the firm and necessary for its survival, that is, the company's relationholders. Firstly, employees and shareholders, then customers, suppliers, and the local community.

The fourth criterion is giving priority to the *seriousness or urgency* of the problems of those for whom the company has a responsibility. This applies to all categories of responsibilities. An example could be giving urgent priority to the legitimate problems of employees (for example, an employee's family problems, bereavements, illness and so on) over less urgent issues. In the case of socio-political responsibilities, the degree of need and the capacity of the firm can help determine the priority of the firm's social contributions.

A fifth criterion to consider is one's *capacity to solve problems*. Thus, companies might have capacity to contribute to the educational needs of a community by offering professional training within the company facilities, by donating some company products to charities or even by encouraging employee voluntarism for work on social projects.

The individual principle: Practical wisdom in action

The institutional and organizational principles are insufficient since they do not tell us exactly what should be done in any particular case. Managers should consider the common good and the right order of responsibilities with practical wisdom (4.2). This means carrying out careful deliberation on the circumstances of the case, considering the foreseeable outcomes, and seeking advice from those who can provide it. Then, the manager should judge the different alternatives wisely and choose the best. Finally, the decision should be executed at the appropriate time and in the appropriate manner.

Sound information is required for the deliberation mentioned above. Thus, it is crucial to listen to relationholders as well as to people inside or outside the company who can provide good advice. Relationholders have not only explicit demands of the company but also expectations and needs – and managers should know what these are.

A practical way to identify demands, expectations and needs is to establish formal or informal channels of dialogue with relationholders, and even to engage relationholders in generating socially responsible policies or practices.

Some companies consider relationholder dialogue central and full of positive aspects, although others accuse it of being a mere process to respond to criticism from NGOs, media and other groups regarding their social and environmental actions. Beyond any reactive use of relationholder dialogue, opening up these channels of communication can have a positive impact on building trust and organizational learning. In addition, it can be an efficient way to manage corporate social responsibilities based on more accurate information and can be a source of innovative ideas to manage some aspects of corporate citizenship.

The managerial principle also refers to the responsibility of the manager to contribute to the common good (the principle of legitimacy) by building enduring and mutually beneficial relationships with all relevant relationholders. This, in turn, brings about social capital – that is, the 'capital' generated by connections within and between social networks based on group membership, relationships, networks of influence and support.

Business Ethics in Action #12

Stormberg AS: A responsible SME[37]

Stormberg AS is a Norwegian company founded by Steinar J. Olsen in 1998. Its main business is designing and selling outdoor and sports clothing that is particularly suited for the Nordic climate. The company has both online and physical stores in Norway and Sweden. Stormberg is recognized for offering affordable clothing for the entire family and has become highly popular, especially among younger generations.

The company grew from four employees and a turnover of 3.8 million NOK (US$0.37 million) in 1998 to over 138 employees and a turnover of 280 million NOK (US$35.7 million) in 2012. Although income has slightly declined since then, it has remained relatively stable. The manufacturing of the company's goods was gradually moved to China, primarily in factories located in the Shanghai and Ningbo industrial areas. By 2022, all of the company's goods were being produced in China. The administration and design of collections continue to take place in Norway, as well as the commercial activity.

From the beginning, Stormberg had a strong social concern. Steinar J. Olsen was committed to employing people in marginalized situations. About 25 per cent of Stormberg's workforce consists of persons who have faced challenges entering the labour market, including former convicts, refugees and those recovering from substance abuse.

Norwegian labour laws are known for their strict protection, but Stormberg goes beyond these requirements, particularly in terms of employee participation. Employees are actively involved in decision-making processes, an approach that, while time-consuming, shows respect for human dignity and autonomy and fosters satisfaction, responsibility and loyalty.

Stormberg enforces a strict code of conduct for its suppliers, particularly in China, aligned with International Labour Organization (ILO) standards. The code, translated into Mandarin, is displayed publicly in supplier factories. Stormberg, as a member of Norway's Ethical Trading Initiative (IEH), conducts regular audits of its suppliers to ensure fair working conditions and environmental respect. These audits, often unannounced, focus on wages, overtime and compliance with fair labour practices.

The company is also a leader in environmental responsibility. Since 2008, Stormberg has been climate-neutral and regularly publishes a 'carbon footprint' report detailing achievements and future targets. The company promotes recycling through a programme that collects used Stormberg clothing in Norway, redistributing it to those in need in Romania and Moldova.

In addition, 1 per cent of Stormberg's turnover is donated to humanitarian and socially beneficial causes. The company encourages employee involvement in community initiatives, offering paid time off for such activities.

* * *

> It seems the company's main economic objective is neither maximizing profits nor continuous growth in turnover but rather generating sufficient revenue to achieve humanistic and social goals.
>
> In terms of social responsibility, Stormberg emphasizes inclusivity and ethical practices, making efforts to hire persons from marginalized groups, offering them a fresh start in life.
>
> Another noteworthy aspect is Stormberg's commitment to fair labour practices and environmental standards throughout its supply chain, particularly in its dealings with suppliers in China. Beyond business activity, the company demonstrates solidarity with noble causes.
>
> Regarding sustainability, it should also emphasis that Stormberg is notably focused on recycling clothing and reducing the carbon footprint. For several years, Stormberg has been named the most sustainable supplier in the textile industry and has consistently achieved high rankings in sustainability indexes, including being named first in Norway's Nordic Sustainable Brand Index in 2016.
>
> All things considered, Stormberg exemplifies how a business can achieve good performance while maintaining a commitment to social responsibility and sustainability, including practices that influence its supply chain and labour conditions in distant countries. As a small or medium-sized enterprise (SME), Stormberg has evolved into a global corporate citizen, driven by remarkable leadership focused on ethical and sustainable practices.

SECTION B. SOCIETAL RELATIONSHIPS OF BUSINESS

The last topic that we should consider within business in society is the relationship that business, as an institution, establishes with other social institutions, including governments and social groups, including non-governmental organizations (NGOs).

12.6 Corporate relationships with governments

Businesses benefit from a stable political order through legal protections, infrastructure, regulatory stability and security provided by governments. These elements allow companies to operate efficiently, plan long term and access global markets. Additionally, governments invest in education, developing a skilled workforce that businesses rely on for growth and innovation. Governments also regulate the financial sector and ensure monetary stability, which enables businesses to secure funding and manage risk.

However, society and its governance benefit from prosperous businesses through tax revenues that fund public services, job creation that supports economic growth, and technological advancements that improve national competitiveness. Efficient businesses help reduce unemployment, contribute to social stability and attract foreign investment, further driving development. By collaborating with businesses, governments can deliver public goods more effectively and promote global competitiveness through international trade and diplomacy.

This mutually beneficial relationship ensures that both businesses and governments thrive, contributing to sustainable economic growth and societal well-being. However, corporate–governmental relationships also present ethical challenges. Some of them were considered previously (7.3), regarding the regulation of business and government intervention in business activity.

Cooperation and partnership between business and governments

Business and governments can cooperate for the common good in several ways, but can also become accomplices of wrongdoing.

Environmental and labour conditions

Governments and businesses must work together to address environmental issues and to improve labour conditions, but ethical concerns arise if businesses prioritize profits over sustainability and human rights, and if governments fail to enforce adequate regulations. This is what happens, for instance, when a business exploits natural resources without consideration for long-term environmental impact, takes advantage of labour exploitation or operates while harming communities.

Promoting social justice

Companies can cooperate and help overcome the unfair situations experienced by vulnerable people, such as those with disabilities and situations of blatant inequality. On the contrary, large corporations can pressure governments to prioritize them over small businesses or local communities, exacerbating inequality. In such cases, the benefits of government–business collaborations – such as tax breaks, subsidies or contracts – flow disproportionately to large companies, while smaller businesses or marginalized communities struggle to compete. This is the case when governments provide large tax incentives to multinational corporations, while local small businesses are taxed heavily, which can increase economic inequality.

Public-private partnerships (PPPs)

This type of cooperation can help address certain social challenges, including the provision of essential services, such as healthcare and water. These social challenges often benefit from the technical knowledge and efficiency of the private sector in delivering projects, especially in areas like infrastructure, technology and management. While this partnership can provide undeniable benefits, it can also pose transparency risks. If these partnerships are not managed openly and equitably, there may be accusations of preferential treatment, unfair profit-sharing or lack of accountability.

Lobbying

Business legislation and regulations are, obviously, very important for firms: regulations can constrain growth plans, limit capabilities, reduce or increase capital gains taxes or open doors to new opportunities. When faced with regulators – including legislators, civil servants or politicians – businesses can exert pressure to defend their interests. This type of action, termed 'lobbying',[38] is generally carried out by organized groups of businesspeople or representatives of an industry. The phenomenon of proxy pressures by major companies has evolved and adapted in varied forms in different countries, as well as in supranational institutions such as the EU.

There is nothing wrong with lobbying to influence legislation or government decisions when defending legitimate interests, or when aiming to provide information to regulators about the situation of an industry, or to communicate corporate interests. Business industries can even help to improve regulations by providing their knowledge and positing their interests. Moreover, business has the same right to participate in the political process as consumers, labour unions, environmentalists and other social groups. However, excessive or opaque lobbying is ethically unacceptable. This is what happens when large corporations – including pharmaceuticals, oil or finance – spend significant sums on lobbying to influence legislation in their favour. This undermines democratic processes, giving wealthier companies' disproportionate influence over laws and policies, which cannot reflect the interests of citizens and, ultimately, damages the common good.

To prevent such abuses, in many countries, business lobbies are recognized and regulated by the government through mechanisms that provide transparency and facilitate fair play, although it is worth noting that not all lobbies and cases can be managed by such regulation.[39]

Political contributions and corruption

Political contributions are even more controversial than lobbying, since businesses are most likely to make financial contributions to political campaigns in order to reduce taxes, or be rewarded unfairly with public contracts if the campaign succeeds.

There are those who argue that contributions to political campaigns, together with lobbying and the actions of interest groups, can undermine the will of the people and even the democratic system itself. In some countries, such contributions are illegal; in others, they are regulated; in yet others, they are nearly, or altogether, uncontrolled. Accountability, transparency and social control might avert corruption in lobbying and contributions – at least, up to a certain point. Thus, the less control, the higher the risk of corruption.

Beyond political contributions, companies may be involved directly in corruption by giving bribes or kickbacks (5.8). In practical terms, businesses may offer financial incentives or favours to government officials to win contracts, bypass regulations or gain competitive advantages. This undermines fairness in public procurement and distorts the market, favouring companies that engage in unethical behaviour.

To address these ethical challenges, both governments and businesses must operate with transparency, accountability and a commitment to the common good, ensuring that their interactions serve the broader interests of society rather than the interests of a select few.

Conflict of interest and tax evasion

In the corporate–government relationship, conflicts of interest (5.5) may arise when persons or organizations hold roles in both the public and private sectors and use their influence in the public sector to enable personal gain, or to benefit their business associates. For instance, when a government official has a financial interest in a company that bids for government contracts. This can skew decision-making processes. In the example proposed, the official may unfairly favour that company. Conflict of interest should be avoided and, if this is not possible, full transparency is necessary.

Paying taxes (5.6) is an ordinary way of contributing to the common good, and governments should enact fair laws in this regard and collect taxes which companies must pay. A deviant corporate behaviour is that of using legal loopholes to avoid paying taxes in the countries where they operate, by going to the so-called 'tax havens'. This can deprive governments of the revenue needed to provide public goods and services, increasing the burden on individuals and smaller businesses that cannot engage in similar practices.

12.7 Corporate responses to social demands and cooperation with NGOs

Beyond the debate on individual and/or corporate responsibilities, corporations face social demands related to labour relations, product safety, consumer information, pollution, environmentally friendly products, global warming and any other social issue that might arise not only from media and NGOs, but also from relationholders or public opinion.

Some NGOs are now particularly active in areas such as human rights, ecological concern and animal welfare, among others, and can adopt either a collaborative or a hostile attitude towards corporations. It is worth recalling that NGOs are voluntary, non-profit organizations whose goals are delivering services to those in need of relief, developmental and humanitarian aid and so on, or advocating for certain social or public policies (ecology, human rights, the defence of human life, animal welfare and such). Sometimes, both goals can be integrated into one organization. NGOs are increasingly important in many societies. They are an expression of the freedom and vitality of a society and often render it a great service. However, they can sometimes behave questionably and create trouble for business. There is also a risk that they might depend on external funding agencies, a situation that can cast doubt upon their fidelity to meeting the needs of the people they purport to serve.[40]

NGOs devoted to public service can seek to establish relationships with business firms willing to collaborate in their activities, arguing that they will be an effective channel for the corporation to act with a sense of corporate citizenship (12.3). In contrast, NGOs whose goal is to serve as an advocate of public policies generally exclude such collaboration and often incite companies or governments to change their practices or introduce legislation to avoid abuses.

Facing social demands and social issues, a business firm can adopt several strategies. There are four basic responses described by Ackerman[41] that are still valid: (1) *no response* (2); *reactive* (the firm defends itself, gives arguments for its performance and resists changing); (3) *interactive* (the firm accepts responsibility and begins a dialogue with those presenting social demands); and (4) *proactive* (a business faces social issues before social demands arise).

12.8 Corporate accountability: Auditing and reporting

Being responsible and concerned about sustainability is not enough. People affected by business activity expect accurate information on key issues. As noted (3.1), accountability refers to giving explanations and justifications for one's activity to those who have expectations or rights related to it.

For many decades, corporate accountability has been reduced to a company's obligation to render an account of its activities to its shareholders by means of an annual financial report. This includes three key financial statements (the balance sheet, the income statement and the statement of cash flow), which are audited by certified public accountants. However, such a document has important limitations as an accountability mechanism. One of these is the lack of certain economic information (concerning, for example, intangible assets, intellectual capital and forward-looking information). Another shortcoming is not merely to do with the economic, but also with the human, social and environmental aspects of the company's performance. It might previously have been assumed that shareholders are interested only in financial results, but an increasing number of investors want to know how those results were attained. In other words, they would like to know more about corporate conduct in terms of ethical, social and environmental responsibilities.

Apart from shareholders, other relationholders – namely, employees, customers, suppliers and the local community – also have expectations and even a legitimate interest in knowing about corporate activities that affect them – in some cases, in the most crucial aspects of their lives. Thus, corporate accountability should be broader in scope, extending beyond shareholders. Given this increasingly common perspective, corporate accountability can be defined as 'the continuous, systematic, and public communication of information and reasons designed to justify an organization's decisions, actions, and outputs to various stakeholders'.[42] In the context of sustainable development, the idea was introduced that corporations must be held accountable not only for financial results but also for social and environmental matters. This is articulated under the so-called *triple bottom line* (TBL) accounting (see below), which requires companies to present financial, social and environmental reports.

Many firms issue annual sustainability reports. These were initially focused exclusively on the environment, but it is now increasingly common to extend these to include social issues. This is a significant expression of what is known as corporate accountability.

Both corporate accountability reports, and certification of responsible and ethical corporate behaviours can help to build a reputation, and reputation generates trust.[43]

We will now briefly review three significant proposals on corporate reporting and certification. Corporate reputation is considered a spontaneous and efficient mechanism of social control, pushing companies to act in accordance with public requirements. It can facilitate entry into a new market, spur cooperation among firms and with public and private institutions and confer competitive advantages.

The triple bottom line

The notion of a TBL was introduced by Elkington, first in 1994 and again, more thoroughly articulated, in 1998.[44] He insists that three aspects are actually relevant to evaluate a company's performance: (1) the economic; (2) the environmental; and (3) the social – or, as some prefer, a complete business performance appraisal has to include what are succinctly described as the triple 'P' of 'people, planet and profits'. In practice, the TBL refers to 'economic prosperity', 'environmental quality' and 'social justice'.

- *Economic prosperity*: This includes not only profits for shareholders but also benefits for the entire host society, comprising the economic impact of a firm's activity on its environment, and development of human and social capital acquired through working for a firm.
- *Environmental quality*: This refers to the utilization of raw materials and other renewable and non-renewable resources, as well as to ecologically destructive practices, the conservation and use of energy, pollution in all its forms caused by business activity, waste produced, and its eventual disposal and other issues related to environmental sustainability.
- *Social justice*: This concerns the ways in which people are affected by business activity. Social justice concerns employee needs and rights, including health, safety and opportunities for training and development within the company, the participation of employees in business activities and the fostering of an entrepreneurial culture. Social justice also includes the community involvement of a business and any business activity in favour of its social environment.

Many large companies have adopted the idea of the TBL, as have others whose activity is subject to strict social scrutiny. One way to make the implementation of the concept practical is through accountability reports that consider people, planet and profits – particularly the Global Reporting Initiative (GRI) (see below in Section B), which is closely connected with the TBL. However, the TBL has also been criticized on grounds such as an alleged lack of theoretical rigour and effective audit assurance.[45] In spite of its limitations, the model has been achieving positive results, such as 'bringing into the public domain certain corporate information that, for the most part, might otherwise remain private. The apparent success of TBL so far strongly indicates that this enhanced flow of corporate information is in the public interest.'[46]

Auditing and reporting on CSR and sustainability

Auditing and reporting are tools for corporate accountability regarding CSR and sustainability. Organizations undergo an audit to obtain a report of being socially responsible or sustainable. They usually also commit themselves to following the audit's recommendations. In this way, they make themselves accountable to their relationhoders.

SA 8000 certification

The Council on Economic Priorities launched SA 8000 certification with the goal of improving working conditions. Based on the principles of the Thirteenth International Human Rights Convention, it is used to audit companies and contractors alike in multiple industries and countries. It is available to any organization of any size, in any industry, anywhere in the world. The auditing of factory compliance is carried out through an independent verification system. This certification offers companies the opportunity to demonstrate to relationholders that working conditions within the company itself, or the firms included in the supply chain, meet the standards included in SA 8000. These focus on child and forced labour, health and safety, freedom of association, collective bargaining, discrimination, disciplinary practices, working hours and compensation, and management systems.

The Global Reporting Initiative

This is the most popular method for accountability reporting worldwide. It is not limited to large corporations. In fact, it is applicable to small companies, large multinationals, public sector firms, NGOs and other types of organizations. The first version of the *Global Reporting Initiative* (GRI) was launched in 2000 by the Coalition for Environmentally Responsible Economies (CERES) and the Tellus Institute, with the support of the United Nations Environment Programme. Since then, several revisions have been published.

The GRI is a global sustainability report that features a modular, interrelated structure, with a conceptual framework composed of principles for the development of reports, characteristics and indicators to present the economic, environmental and social performance of a company. The principles of transparency and relationholder inclusiveness are the starting point for the preparation of a sustainability report and provide the context within which all its other principles belong. Other principles define the report's content and quality and provide guidance on how to set its boundaries. One of the strengths of the GRI is that it provides comparability and timeliness. This constitutes, to some extent, an improvement on corporate reports on social and environmental accountability in which only favourable items are described, and there is a lack of objective criteria to make comparisons with other companies.

The AA1000 standards

AccountAbility's AA1000 standards aim to help organizations become more accountable, responsible and sustainable. Based on the TBL, the AccountAbitility's AA1000 are standards of processes, not substantive performance standards. They specify those processes that an organization should follow by means of relationholder engagement and dialogue. They propose indicators, goals and communication systems as well as ways of linking social and ethical issues with companies' strategic and operational management. AA1000 was first presented in 1999 by the Institute for Social and Ethical Accountability (ISEA), based in the United Kingdom, and updated several times. It has been adopted by companies in and outside of Europe. The main strength is a broad engagement with relationholders, which demonstrates a level of concern towards them. One weakness of AA1000 is its lack of substantive ethical standards, with a risk of relativism. Another is its implementation, which can be complicated and costly.

Case Study #12

Interquim: Involving employees in social responsibilities[47]

Interquim is a Colombian company that produces and distributes industrial raw materials including methanol, formaldehyde, adhesives, resins, friction materials, abrasives and paints, among others. It was founded in 1973 in the city of Bogotá. A few years later, the production plant moved to Girardota, a town in the municipality of Medellín. The Interquim corporate website states: 'We believe that the best business is to deliver top-quality products with kindness in personal relations and timeliness in delivery. We develop fair purchasing policies with our suppliers.' The company has quality and environmental management certifications.

In 1998, Interquim joined the multinational group *AkzoNobel*, which has its corporate headquarters in Nacka, Sweden. The group, which operates in more than eighty countries, covers three fields: pharmaceutical products, chemical products and coatings. In 2002, Carlos Villa was the general manager of Interquim, having led the company for seven years with successful management in terms of economic results. Corporate policies promoted entrepreneurship, personal integrity and social responsibility. Carlos had taken a personal interest in improving the working conditions of his employees and raised the issue of providing social benefits during *AkzoNobel* board meetings in Sweden. He managed to enhance employee benefits such as the housing fund, educational support for employees' children and vehicle and life insurance. Wages had increased between 40 and 80 per cent in real terms, favouring those with lower pay.

Despite the company's economic success, the surrounding environment was unfavourable. The economic, social and political situation in the country was dire. Unemployment stood at 20 per cent, affecting almost 3 million Colombians. The situation was particularly stark in Girardota, where the company's production plant was located. Although the firm had launched some assistance programmes, Carlos aspired to do more.

The 2001 fiscal year had been one of the best in Interquim's history. It was decided to reward employees with a bonus equivalent to 5 per cent of their salary. At the time, Carlos and his team believed they had found a way to contribute to community development and involve employees in social responsibility.

The idea was for employees and managers to donate up to 5 per cent (the equivalent of their bonuses) of their salary. From these donations, a base capital would be created to fund sustainable social projects focused on community development. The aim was to create stable jobs for disadvantaged groups. Management and employees would also contribute their expertise in management-related issues. The idea of 'The Five' quickly gained support among the management team.

Carlos organized a series of events to present the project to Interquim employees. He was pleasantly surprised by their reaction – everyone accepted the proposal. The vast majority donated 5 per cent, some 4 per cent and others 3 per cent. The average donation was 4.7 per cent.

Carlos appointed a director of development, who quickly reached out to some governmental and non-governmental entities in Girardota to introduce the project. Although they received positive feedback, they were unable to engage other companies, despite their efforts.

The next step was to present the project to the AkzoNobel board of directors. At the following meeting, Carlos highlighted that the employees had already approved the initiative. He proposed that the corporation contribute 1 peso for every peso donated by the workers. He stated: 'We want the company to be admired and loved … I guarantee that our people will work better and reward us with greater productivity.'

However, despite Carlos's enthusiasm, some board members reacted negatively. One argued: 'Community development is the responsibility of the state; our responsibility is to generate wealth.' Carlos responded: 'That's fine in developed countries like yours; but this is a multinational company, and it also operates in underdeveloped countries with problems of poverty and violence. In those countries, we entrepreneurs have greater responsibilities.' Another board member opposed the proposal, mentioning that such practices were not common, and the company had never supported a similar measure before.

Carlos was deeply concerned by the shareholders' reaction. He feared that the disparity between European standards of living and the hardships faced by Girardota's residents was influencing their reluctance to support the proposal. He was uncertain if he was overstepping in his role as manager, but he felt that the plight of the families in the community where the company operated did not allow him to stand by passively. He wondered what other arguments he could present.

Questions

1. What are the strengths and potential risks of a company encouraging employees to contribute to community development projects?
2. How should multinational companies balance their responsibilities in countries with very different levels of development? Do you think Carlos's arguments are persuasive in this context?
3. If you were in Carlos's position, what practical or moral reasoning would you offer to persuade the board to support the employee-led initiative?

Notes

1. Phrase attributed to Viktor E. Frankl, author of the best-selling book *Man's Search for Meaning* (London: Random House / Rider, 1946 [2004]).
2. Sources: Wikipedia: Rana Plaza collapse, https://en.wikipedia.org/wiki/Rana_Plaza_collapse. (Accessed on 6 June 2025); S. Labowitz and D. Baumann-Pauly, *Business as Usual Is Not an Option: Supply Chains and Sourcing after Rana Plaza* (New York: NYU Stern Center for Business and Human Rights, 2014); B. W. Jacobs and V. R. Singhal, 'The Effect of the Rana Plaza Disaster on Shareholder Wealth of Retailers: Implications for Sourcing Strategies and Supply Chain Governance', *Journal of Operations Management*, vol. 49–51, 2017, pp. 52–66.
3. B. W. Husted, 'Corporate Social Responsibility Practice from 1800–1914: Past Initiatives and Current Debates', *Business Ethics Quarterly*, vol. 25, no. 1, 2015, pp. 125–41.
4. Indeed, it may be more accurate to refer to these groups of people connected to the company as 'relationholders' rather than 'stakeholders', as relationships encompass more than merely having a 'stake' in the company.
5. M. E. Porter and M. R. Kramer, 'Strategy & Society: The Link Between Competitive Advantage and Corporate Social Responsibility', *Harvard Business Review*, vol. 84, no. 12, 2006, pp. 78–92.
6. On implementing these ideas, see J. Milliman, J. Ferguson and K. Sylvester, 'Implementation of Michael Porter's Strategic Corporate Social Responsibility Model', *Journal of Global Business Issues*, Spring, 2008, pp. 29–33.
7. A position defended by P. French, 'The Corporation as a Moral Person', *American Philosophical Quarterly*, vol. 16, 1979, pp. 207–15, and *Collective and Corporate Responsibility* (New York: Columbia University Press, 1984).
8. This is what Manuel Velasquez holds: M. G. Velasquez, 'Why Corporations Are Not Morally Responsible for Anything They Do', *Business & Professional Ethics Journal*, vol. 2, no. 3, 1983, pp. 1–18, and 'Debunking Moral Responsibility', *Business Ethics Quarterly*, vol. 13, no. 4, 2003, pp. 531–62.
9. See P. Pruzan, 'The Question of Organizational Consciousness: Can Organizations Have Values, Virtues and Visions?', *Journal of Business Ethics*, vol. 29, no. 3, 2001, pp. 271–84.

10. See E. Garriga and D. Melé, 'Corporate Social Responsibility Theories: Mapping the Territory', *Journal of Business Ethics*, vol. 53, no. 1–2, 2004, pp. 51–71; and D. Melé, 'Corporate Social Responsibility Theories', in A. Crane, A. Williams, D. Matten, J. Moon and D. S. Siegel (eds), *The Oxford Handbook of Corporate Social Responsibility* (Oxford and New York: Oxford University Press, 2008), pp. 47–82.
11. A definition given by L. Burke and J. M. Logsdon, 'How Corporate Social Responsibility Pays Off', *Long Range Planning*, vol. 29, no. 4, 1996, pp. 495–502, on p. 496.
12. See M. Friedman and R. Friedman, *Capitalism and Freedom* (Chicago, IL: University of Chicago Press, 1962); and M. Friedman, 'The Social Responsibility of Business is to Increase its Profits', *New York Times Magazine*, 13 September 1970, pp. 32–3, 122, 126.
13. B. W. Husted and J. De Jesus Salazar, 'Taking Friedman Seriously: Maximizing Profits and Social Performance', *Journal of Management Studies*, vol. 43, no. 1, 2006, pp. 75–91.
14. See, among others, Milliman et al., 'Implementation of Michael Porter's Strategic Corporate Social Responsibility Model'; R. V. Aguilera, D. E. Rupp, C. A. Williams and J. Ganapathi, 'Putting the S Back in Corporate Social Responsibility: A Multilevel Theory of Social Change in Organizations', *Academy of Management Review*, vol. 32, no. 3, 2007, pp. 836–63; and K. Basu and G. Palazzo, 'Corporate Social Responsibility: A Process Model of Sensemaking', *Academy of Management Review*, vol. 33, no. 1, 2008, pp. 122–36.
15. On this point, see A. McWilliams and D. Siegel, 'Corporate Social Responsibility: A Theory of the Firm Perspective', *Academy of Management Review*, vol. 26, no. 1, 2001, pp. 117–27.
16. D. J. Wood, 'Corporate Social Performance Revisited', *Academy of Management Review*, vol. 16, no. 4, 1991, pp. 691–718. She draws from A. B. Carroll, 'A Three-Dimensional Conceptual Model of Corporate Performance', *Academy of Management Review*, vol. 4, no. 4, 1979, pp. 497–505; and S. L. Wartick and R. E. Rude, 'Issues Management: Corporate Fad or Corporate Function?', *California Management Review*, vol. 29, no. 1, 1985, pp. 124–40.
17. Among others, D. L. Swanson, 'Addressing a Theoretical Problem by Reorienting the Corporate Social Performance Model', *Academy of Management Review*, vol. 20, no. 1, 1995, pp. 43–64, and 'Toward an Integrative Theory of Business and Society: A Research Strategy for Corporate Social Performance', *Academy of Management Review*, vol. 24, no. 3, 1999, pp. 506–21.
18. D. J. Wood, 'Measuring Corporate Social Performance: A Review', *International Journal of Management Reviews*, vol. 12, no. 1, 2010, pp. 50–84.
19. Wood, 'Corporate Social Performance Revisited', p. 693.
20. Wood, 'Corporate Social Performance Revisited', p. 695; and cf. K. Davis, 'The Case For and Against Business Assumption of Social Responsibilities', *Academy of Management Journal*, vol. 16, 1973, pp. 312–22, on p. 314.
21. Wood, 'Corporate Social Performance Revisited', p. 697; and cf. L. E. Preston and J. E. Post, *Private Management and Public Policy: The Principle of Public Responsibility* (Englewood Cliffs, NJ: Prentice Hall, 1975), p. 10.
22. Wood, 'Corporate Social Performance Revisited', p. 698; cf. Carroll, 'A Three-Dimensional Conceptual Model of Corporate Performance'.
23. Including, D. Wheeler, B. Colbert and R. E. Freeman, 'Focusing on Value: Reconciling Corporate Social Responsibility, Sustainability and a Stakeholder Approach in a Network World', *Journal of General Management*, vol. 28, no. 3, 2003, pp. 1–28; and R. E. Freeman and R. Velamuri, 'A New Approach to CSR: Company Stakeholder Responsibility', in A. Kakabadse and M. Morsing (eds),

Corporate Social Responsibility (CSR): Reconciling Aspirations with Application (Basingstoke: Palgrave Macmillan, 2006), pp. 9–23, among others.

24. See R. E. Freeman, 'The Politics of Stakeholder Theory: Some Future Directions', *Business Ethics Quarterly*, vol. 4, no. 4, 1994, pp. 409–29.
25. This point is discussed by M. Greenwood, 'Stakeholder Engagement: Beyond the Myth of Corporate Responsibility', *Journal of Business Ethics*, vol. 74, no. 4, 2007, pp. 315–27.
26. M. M. Blair, *Ownership and Control: Rethinking Corporate Governance for the Twenty-first Century* (Washington, DC: Brookings Institution, 1995); and M. B. E. Clarkson, 'A Stakeholder Framework for Analyzing and Evaluating Corporate Social Performance', *Academy of Management Review*, vol. 92, no. 1, 1995, pp. 92–117.
27. J. Collins and J. I. Porras, *Built to Last: Successful Habits of Visionary Companies* (New York: HarperCollins, 1994); and J. Collins, *Good to Great: Why Some Companies Make the Leap, and Others Don't* (London: Random House, 2001).
28. The commitment includes delivering value to customers, investing in employees, dealing fairly and ethically with suppliers, supporting the communities in which companies work, and generating long-term value for shareholders: https://www.businessroundtable.org/business-roundtable-redefines-the-purpose-of-a-corporation-to-promote-an-economy-that-serves-all-americans. (Accessed on 6 June 2025).
29. Davos Manifesto 2020, *The Universal Purpose of a Company in the Fourth Industrial Revolution*, 2 December 2019: https://www.weforum.org/stories/2019/12/davos-manifesto-2020-the-universal-purpose-of-a-company-in-the-fourth-industrial-revolution/. (Accessed on 6 June 2025).
30. This is the position of D. A. Gioia, 'Response: Practicability, Paradigms, and Problems in Stakeholder Theorizing', *The Academy of Management Review*, vol. 24, no. 2, 1999, pp. 228–32.
31. See M. C. Jensen, 'Value Maximization, Stakeholder Theory, and the Corporate Objective Function', *Business Ethics Quarterly*, vol. 12, no. 2, 2002, pp. 235–56; A. M. Marcoux, 'A Fiduciary Argument against Stakeholder Theory', *Business Ethics Quarterly*, vol. 13, no. 1, 2003, pp. 1–24; and E. Sternberg, 'The Defects of Stakeholder Theory', *Corporate Governance: An International Review*, vol. 5, no. 1, 1997, pp. 3–7.
32. See R. Phillips, R. E. Freeman and A. Wicks, 'What Stakeholder Theory is Not', *Business Ethics Quarterly*, vol. 13, no. 4, 2003, pp. 479–502.
33. On this topic, see D. Matten and A. Crane, 'Corporate Citizenship: Towards an Extended Theoretical Conceptualization', *Academy of Management Review*, vol. 30, no. 1, 2005, pp. 166–79.
34. M. Valente and A. Crane, 'Public Responsibility and Private Enterprise in Developing Countries', *California Management Review*, vol. 52, no. 3, 2010, pp. 52–78.
35. UN World Commission on Environment and Development (Brundtland Commission Report), *Our Common Future* (Oxford: Oxford University Press, 1987).
36. On this point, see Matten and Crane, 'Corporate Citizenship'; and J. A. Moon, A. Crane and D. Matten, 'Can Corporations Be Citizens? Corporate Citizenship as a Metaphor for Business Participation in Society', *Business Ethics Quarterly*, vol. 15, no. 3, 2005, pp. 429–53.
37. Sources: H. Weltzien Hoivik and D. Melé, 'Can an SME Become a Global Corporate Citizen? Evidence from a Case Study', *Journal of Business Ethics*, vol. 88, no. 3, 2009, pp. 551–63; Top 20 Responsible Leaders in Northern Europe, Nordic Business Report: https://www.nbforum.com/top-20-responsible-leaders/steinar-olsen/; Stormberg A/S corporate website: https://www.stormberg.com; 'Stormberg Builds Sustainable Customer Experiences', Avencia: https://www.

avensia.com/news/stormberg-builds-sustainable-customer-experiencesc3568824. (All accessed on 6 June 2025).

38. The term 'lobby' seems to come from the gathering of members of parliament and peers in the hallways (lobbies) of the Houses of Parliament, in London, before and after parliamentary debates.

39. See, for example, J. M. Keffer and R. P. Hill, 'An Ethical Approach to Lobbying Activities of Businesses in the United States', *Journal of Business Ethics*, vol. 16, 1997, pp. 1371–9; and D. Barker, 'Ethics and Lobbying: The Case of Real Estate Brokerage', *Journal of Business Ethics*, vol. 80, no. 1, 2008, pp. 23–35. Some practical suggestions for ethics in lobbying can be seen at J. Brooke Hamilton III and D. Hoch, 'Ethical Standards for Business Lobbying: Some Practical Suggestions', *Business Ethics Quarterly*, vol. 7, no. 3, 1997, pp. 117–29.

40. See S. Kamat, 'NGOs and the New Democracy', *Harvard International Review*, vol. 25, no. 1, 2003, pp. 65–9.

41. R. W. Ackerman, 'How Companies Respond to Social Demands', *Harvard Business Review*, vol. 51, no. 4, 1973, pp. 88–98.

42. M. L. Pava, 'Corporate Accountability', in K. Kolb (ed.), *The SAGE Encyclopedia of Business Ethics and Society*, 2nd ed. (Los Angeles: Sage, 2018), pp. 672–76, on p. 451.

43. See J. Bebbington, C. Larrinaga and J. M. Moneva, 'Corporate Social Reporting and Reputation Risk Management', *Accounting, Auditing & Accountability Journal*, vol. 21, no. 3, 2008, pp. 337–61.

44. J. Elkington, *Cannibals with Forks: The Triple Bottom Line of 21st Century Business* (Oxford: Capstone, 1998).

45. F. Robins, 'The Challenge of TBL: A Responsibility to Whom?', *Business & Society Review*, vol. 111, no. 1, 2006, pp. 1–14.

46. Robins, 'The Challenge of TBL', p. 12.

47. Summary of J. M. Parra and M. Paladino, Case FH-I-188 *El Cinco: Buscando soluciones para un entorno enfermo*. (The Five: Seeking Solutions for an Unhealthy Environment) INALDE, Universidad de la Sabana, Colombia, 2009. Published with with permission. Extended with data from the Interquim corporate website.

13

Ecological Responsibilities and Sustainable Development

Business, labour and civil society organizations have distinct skills and resources that are vital in helping to build a more robust global community.[1]
  KOFI A. ANNAN (1938–2018), Seventh UN Secretary-General, Nobel Prize in 2001

Overview

Ecology, focusing on the relationship between living organisms and the environment, has gained prominence since the second half of the twentieth century. This shift is due to increasing awareness of the planet's deterioration and the necessity for sustainable development that considers the legacy of current activities for future generations. Many ecological problems – including pollution, depletion of raw materials, waste generation and climate change – originate from business activities. Recognizing their significant impact, many companies now acknowledge their ecological impact and are exploring ways to care for our planet and contribute to sustainable development.

Section A begins by summarizing the main current ecological problems and offers foundational elements of ecological ethics. It continues by discussing how companies can act responsibly towards the environment by preventing negative impacts and initiating environmentally friendly technologies.

Section B focuses on sustainable development and business actions. The UN Sustainable Development Goals (SDGs) present various challenges and opportunities for businesses. This section explores topics related to sustainable development, including ESG criteria used for socially responsible investing (SRI), corporate reputation management, the role of transnational corporations and sustainability practices in supply chains and offshore outsourcing. It concludes with recommendations for integrating sustainability into organizational practices effectively.

Chapter Aims

After reading this chapter you should be able to:

- Be aware of current ecological challenges.
- Understand ecological ethics.
- Reflect on the ecological responsibility of business.

- Consider business responsibility in waste production, disposal and recycling.
- Be aware of business strategies regarding the environment and sustainability.
- Reflect on the notion of the 'circular economy'.
- Consider the challenges for business posited by the UN Sustainable Development Goals.
- Be familiar with the Environmental Social Governance (ESG) criteria and its relevance.
- Understand the notion of socially responsible investing.
- Discuss business capacity to alleviate poverty and to focus on the 'bottom of the pyramid'.
- Reflect on the consideration of business corporations as global actors.
- Discuss the responsibilities of transnational national corporations in a global context.
- Converse on responsibility in the supply chain and offshore outsourcing in the global era.
- Reflect on how sustainability and responsibility can be integrated into the organization.

Historical Case #13

Shell Africa: Environmental legacy, problems and prospects[2]

Shell plc (formerly Royal Dutch Shell) is a multinational oil and gas company headquartered in London. It is the second-largest company in the oil and gas industry by revenue and one of the largest corporations worldwide. Among the many countries where Shell operates, Nigeria has been particularly prominent. Shell began operations in Nigeria in the 1930s and operates mainly through subsidiaries, with *Shell Petroleum Development Company of Nigeria Limited* (SPDC) being the most significant entity. SPDC operates extensively in the Niger Delta, a region rich in oil reserves. Shell, through various joint ventures, has contributed significantly to Nigeria's overall petroleum production.

Environmental impact on the Niger Delta

The Niger Delta is one of the most biodiverse regions in the world, but decades of oil exploration have wreaked havoc on its environment. Frequent oil spills and gas flaring have devastated farmland, polluted waterways and threatened the livelihoods of local communities. Shell has been accused of negligence, particularly regarding the maintenance of the infrastructure needed to prevent oil spills. In defence, Shell has claimed that much of the damage was caused by sabotage and oil theft.

While Nigeria's oil wealth has greatly contributed to the national economy, Shell's profits have largely benefited the Nigerian government and international shareholders, with limited investment in local infrastructure, education or healthcare. The communities in the Niger Delta, particularly those dependent on agriculture and fishing, have seen little economic gain from the region's oil wealth. As a result, many communities lack access to basic services, such as clean water and healthcare, despite the wealth extracted from their land. Pollution caused by oil companies, operating with government approval, has severely impacted the local population, turning once-fertile lands into wastelands.

Ken Saro-Wiwa and the Ogoni crisis

The environmental destruction led to the creation of the *Movement for the Survival of the Ogoni People* (MOSOP), led by the writer and activist *Ken Saro-Wiwa*. In 1993, MOSOP organized mass protests against oil companies, particularly Shell, which was the largest oil company in the Ogoniland area. MOSOP accused Shell of destroying the environment, poisoning water supplies and neglecting the needs of the Ogoni people.

The Nigerian government, which at the time was a military dictatorship, responded harshly. The protests were met with violence, leading to numerous human rights abuses, including the execution of Ken Saro-Wiwa and eight other Ogoni activists in 1995. The international community condemned these actions, and Shell was criticized for its passive role in the repression and its collaboration with the Nigerian government. Following a lengthy legal battle, Shell reached a settlement in 2009, agreeing to pay $15.5 million to the families of the victims without admitting guilt. This settlement was seen as an attempt by Shell to protect its reputation globally by avoiding a damaging trial.

Continuing environmental damage and UNEP report

Despite the settlement, environmental damage in the Niger Delta has continued. Oil spills from aging pipelines, along with sabotage and poorly maintained facilities, have resulted in widespread contamination. Local communities face polluted water, infertile land and severe health crises.

In 2011, the *United Nations Environment Programme* (UNEP) released a report showing that over fifty years of oil operations had caused far more extensive pollution than initially thought. The report recommended urgent actions, including environmental remediation, to address the contamination. However, the cleanup has been slow, and the Niger Delta continues to suffer from the consequences of oil extraction.

Legal and reputational challenges

In recent years, Shell has faced numerous lawsuits related to its environmental practices in Nigeria. One of the most significant rulings came in 2021, when a Dutch court ordered Shell to compensate Nigerian farmers for oil spills that occurred in the early 2000s. This case set a precedent by holding the parent company accountable for the actions of its foreign subsidiary.

While Shell's sale of its onshore operations may reduce its legal exposure in the Niger Delta, the company remains entangled in court proceedings and compensation claims related to decades of environmental damage. Its reputation as a responsible energy provider has been tarnished – particularly in light of global climate activism and growing demands for corporate accountability.

While Shell has taken steps to improve its environmental and social responsibility, its legacy in the Niger Delta continues to be a source of contention, both for the local communities and the international community. As Shell shifts focus to offshore operations and renewable energy, the lasting environmental and social impacts of its onshore activities in Nigeria will remain a critical issue.

The community has a pending lawsuit against Shell, which it accuses of causing an oil spill that damaged waterways and farms, while Shell has long maintained that such spills were mostly due to theft of oil and interference with pipelines.

Shell's exit from onshore oil operations in Nigeria

In January 2024, Shell announced its decision to sell its onshore oil and gas operations after agreeing to sell its business to a consortium of five mostly local companies for $2.4 billion. This would be the end of nearly seventy years of operations by SPDC in the Niger Delta.

Local communities reacted and more than 1,200 representatives of the Niger Delta communities asked the Federal High Court in Abuja to stop the deal, arguing that Shell was breaching an existing court order given in December 2023 that suspended any assets sale until a compensation lawsuit was concluded. Nigerian communities are claiming 505 billion naira ($310 million) in damages from Shell.

Questions

1. Identify Shell Africa's misbehaviours in terms of environmental degradation, human rights violations and corruption. What possible arguments could have been made in Shell's defence? What response would you give?
2. Should Shell repair the damages caused in the Niger Delta? Why or why not?
3. Should Shell engage all parties involved, including the government, host communities and other oil companies, etc., to design and implement sustainable solutions in the Niger Delta?

SECTION A. ECOLOGICAL RESPONSIBILITY OF BUSINESS

The concept of 'ecology', often considered synonymous with the environment, comes from the Greek word *oikos*, meaning 'house', 'dwelling place', or 'habitation'. Ecology, as science, studies the relationship between living organisms and the environment in which they develop, evoking the idea of a 'home' – a place to live together and grow, with conditions appropriate for sound development. While ecology usually focuses on animals, plants or whole ecosystems, it can also, in a broader way, include humans. In this sense, we talk of 'human ecology' and even 'integral ecology' (see 13.3).

Since humans, individually or through organizations, impact the environment, ecological responsibility should be assumed. The ecological responsibility of businesses refers to the obligation of companies to minimize their negative environmental impact and contribute positively to the planet's sustainability (12.4).

There is a variety of urgent and complex ecological problems that affect global sustainability, biodiversity and human well-being. These environmental issues are not only the responsibility of governments and NGOs but also of corporations, which play a significant role in either contributing to or mitigating these challenges. Next, we explore the most pressing ecological problems facing businesses, civil society and governments.

These issues are summarized in Table 13.1, along with the corresponding business challenges and responsibilities. We will return to these responsibilities in Part B of this chapter.

13.1 Natural resource depletion and diversity loss

Natural resource depletion

Natural resources, including minerals, wood, oil and other fossil fuels are often exploited beyond their rate of replacement. This *natural resource depletion* is causing resource scarcity, higher costs and environmental degradation. Resource depletion threatens future economic stability and degrades ecosystems. Natural resource depletion includes:

- *Mineral resource depletion*: This is due to the extraction and consumption of minerals and metals like iron, copper, gold and rare earth elements at unsustainable rates.
- *Fossil fuel depletion*: This occurs as a consequence of excessive use of non-renewable energy sources like coal, oil and natural gas.
- *Groundwater depletion*: This results from the excessive extraction of groundwater for agricultural, industrial and domestic use. This contributes to declining water tables and dried-up wells and risk of land subsidence, and increased risk of sinkholes.

Table 13.1 Current ecological problems and business challenges and responsibilities

Ecological problems	Business challenges and responsibilities
Mineral resource depletion	Adopt resource-efficient technologies, promote recycling and circular economy practices, and reduce dependence on non-renewable inputs.
Fossil fuel depletion	Transition to renewable energy sources, invest in energy efficiency, and support innovation in clean technologies.
Groundwater depletion	Implement water-saving practices, invest in water recycling, and support responsible water stewardship in supply chains.
Overfishing	Support sustainable fishing practices, ensure supply-chain traceability, and avoid sourcing from overexploited fisheries.
Deforestation	Adopt zero-deforestation policies, support reforestation and sustainable sourcing, and promote regenerative practices.
Water scarcity	Assume sense of stewardship – measuring and minimizing water usage across operations and supply chains and innovating with the implementation of water-saving technologies.
Non-renewable energy sources	Transit towards renewable energy, improving energy efficiency, and reducing fossil fuels across all operations and supply chains.
Soil degradation and desertification	Adopt sustainable farming techniques, restore degraded land and promote soil conservation to ensure long-term viability.
Biodiversity loss	Identify and disclose biodiversity risks, protect ecosystems by practising responsible resource extraction and avoiding operations in sensitive areas, and support ecosystem restoration.
Pollution (air, water, soil, noise and others)	Reduce emissions and hazardous waste, complying with solved environmental standards. Companies should also disclose pollutant levels transparently and invest in clean technologies.
Waste	Prevent the release of harmful chemicals into the environment, reducing plastic use, practising responsible waste stewardship, and adopting circular economy models.
Climate change	Reduce greenhouse gases (GHGs) generated by fossil fuels, typically measured as the carbon footprint. Companies must also promote transparency by disclosing their climate-related risks and performance.

- *Overfishing*: This refers to harvesting fish and other marine species faster than they can reproduce. The depletion of fish stocks at unsustainable rates, which collapses fish populations, endangers livelihoods and negatively impacts global food security.
- *Deforestation*: This is another issue due to the excessive logging by the timber industry, especially serious in the Amazon and Southeast Asia. Deforestation accelerates climate change by reducing carbon sequestration and destroying vital habitats, leading to species extinction.

Challenges for business include using resources efficiently, adopting sustainable sourcing, reducing waste, transition to renewable energy, managing water responsibly, and helping to protect ecosystems. These actions support long-term viability and reduce environmental harm.

Facing natural resource depletion, businesses are challenged to promote resource efficiency, to invest in sustainable alternatives to conserve natural resources, and to adopt circular economy models (13.6) as much as possible.

Water scarcity

Water and energy resource scarcity are two important topics related to resource depletion, though they have their own distinct characteristics.

Water is a natural resource essential for human life and for many business operations. The supply of freshwater is finite, held in aquifers (sometimes contaminated by soil pollutants) and in surface water (rivers, lakes). Oceans are also a potential water resource, but desalination is necessary for most uses, requiring significant energy and costly investment, which not every country can afford. In many countries, water is becoming scarce due to physical shortage, institutional failure to ensure a regular supply or a lack of adequate infrastructure.

Businesses can overuse water in manufacturing, cooling systems, and, in some cases, agriculture. Corporate responsibility in the face of water scarcity entails a sense of stewardship – measuring and minimizing water usage across operations and supply chains and innovating with the implementation of water-saving technologies.

Non-renewable energy sources

Energy sources are crucial for economic activity. There are non-renewable resources, basically *fossil fuels* (coal, petroleum and natural gas), which currently account for approximately two-thirds of world energy consumption. These produce pollution (see below) and carbon dioxide, contributing to global warming (13.2).

There are *renewable energy sources*, which are obviously recommended, but they are currently unable to meet all energy needs. Their use remains relatively low in the global energy supply. The most widely used renewable energy source is biomass (plant material and animal waste). Hydroelectric energy is mainly produced from rivers or reservoirs through hydroelectric installations. Other renewable sources include solar thermal energy for heating water, wind power and photovoltaic cells. Wind power is generated through wind turbines (which are sometimes also used to crush grain or pump water). Sunlight can be transformed into electric current through photovoltaic cells. Much more marginally used are other forms of renewable energy, such as rain, tidal and wave power (marine energy), or geothermal heat energy.

Nuclear power is an alternative to fossil fuels, commonly used to generate electricity (and sometimes for naval propulsion) through nuclear fission in controlled reactions. It is a clean and efficient way to obtain electricity, and its sources are practically unlimited. The increasing concern for global warming has led to a growing use of nuclear fuel. However, not everyone accepts this alternative; concerns about safety have led to political resistance to constructing nuclear power plants.

Corporate responsibility in this area involves transitioning towards renewable energy, improving energy efficiency and reducing the use of fossil fuels – measured through *carbon footprint* – across all operations and supply chains. This includes investing in clean technologies, setting science-based emissions reduction targets, and supporting broader efforts to achieve a low-carbon economy.

Soil degradation and desertification

Unsustainable agricultural practices, deforestation and climate change (13.2) are causing soil degradation and desertification, reducing land productivity. Soil degradation threatens food security and biodiversity, while desertification is turning fertile lands into unproductive deserts, particularly in regions like Sub-Saharan Africa and Central Asia.

Companies involved in agriculture and land use must adopt sustainable farming techniques, restore degraded land and promote soil conservation to ensure long-term viability.

Biodiversity loss

Biodiversity refers to the variety and variability of life within species (genetic diversity), between species (species diversity) and across ecosystems (ecosystem diversity). The extinction of species and loss of genetic diversity is due to habitat destruction, pollution and overexploitation.

There is growing concern about declining biodiversity. The extinction of plant and animal species disrupts ecosystems, food security and livelihoods, while reducing ecosystem services like pollination and water purification. Loss of biodiversity reduces ecosystem resilience and function and leads to overpopulation of certain species. Additionally, it brings about loss of potential medical and scientific discoveries.

Factors contributing to biodiversity loss include habitat degradation, pollution, climate change, unsustainable land use, overfishing and invasive alien species. Companies must identify and disclose biodiversity risks, protect ecosystems by practising responsible resource extraction and avoiding operations in sensitive areas, and support ecosystem restoration.

13.2 Pollution, waste and climate change

Forms of pollution

Pollution refers to the introduction of contaminants into the environment, typically the atmosphere (air), water or soil, through the discharge of harmful substances. Other forms of contamination include visual, noise, light and thermal pollution. Ocean pollution is also significant and is caused by industrial activities, transportation and improper waste disposal.

- *Air pollution* is caused by gases, solid particles and sometimes biological materials (volatile organic compounds). It can harm humans and animals by contributing to respiratory diseases and can damage the environment. The combustion of fossil fuels – oil, coal and natural gas – to generate energy for power stations and motor vehicles produces toxic pollutants, including carbon monoxide, nitrogen oxides and sulphur dioxide, as well as small particles. Sulphur dioxide and nitrogen oxides can react in the atmosphere to produce acids, resulting in acid rain, which negatively impacts forests, freshwater, soil and human health. Manufacturing

processes can also introduce pollutants into the air. Among them are ozone-depleting substances (ODSs), which reduce the ozone layer in the Earth's stratosphere (the ozone layer prevents the most harmful ultraviolet light from passing through the atmosphere).
- *Water pollution* affects rivers, groundwater, lakes and oceans, contaminating aquatic ecosystems and drinking water sources. Some toxic pollutants, such as heavy metals, are difficult to eliminate from drinking water. A particular form of water pollution is *ocean pollution*, mainly due to massive plastic accumulation, which affects marine life and biodiversity. In addition to plastic, oil spills and chemical runoff also pollute seas and oceans, harming aquatic life, disrupting ecosystems and threatening food chains.
- *Soil pollution* occurs when chemicals are released due to dangerous spills or the rupture of underground storage tanks. It can also result from the application of herbicides, pesticides or chlorinated hydrocarbons. Soil pollution includes the direct discharge of industrial waste. Other environmental problems related to soil include overgrazing, land degradation, salinization, acidification, desertification and erosion.
- *Radioactive contamination* refers to the uncontrolled distribution of radioactive gases, liquids or particles, typically due to accidents in nuclear power stations, nuclear fuel reprocessing or through radioisotopes used in nuclear medicine. Radioactive contamination can affect people and the environment, depending on the level and spread of contamination. Low levels pose little risk and are easily detectable, while high levels, such as those from major nuclear accidents, can cause serious, and even lethal, harm.
- *Other forms of pollution* include *visual pollution* (such as billboards and scarred landscapes), *noise pollution* (displeasing sounds disrupting human or animal life) and *light pollution* (excess or obtrusive light caused by light trespass and over-illumination). *Thermal pollution* refers to the degradation of water or air quality through increased temperature, which can disrupt ecosystems and affect organisms' health. It is most associated with power plants and factories that release heated water as a byproduct of production processes.

Waste, a problem worldwide

Increasing consumption brings about more and more waste. The world produces over 2 billion tonnes of waste annually, according to the World Bank, with projections suggesting a rise to 3.4 billion tonnes by 2050 if no action is taken. A significant portion of this waste consists of non-biodegradable plastics and hazardous materials. These substances often end up in landfills, oceans or incinerators, contributing to pollution and harming wildlife. Non-biodegradable plastics persist in the environment for hundreds of years, breaking down into microplastics that contaminate soil and water. These microplastics have been found in the deepest ocean trenches and even in the air we breathe. Marine animals, such as turtles, seabirds and fish, often mistake plastic debris for food, leading to internal injuries, starvation and death. The ingestion of plastics also allows toxins to enter the food chain, ultimately affecting human health.

Hazardous materials, including electronic waste and industrial chemicals, can leach toxic substances into the environment. These pollutants contaminate water sources, degrade soil quality, and pose significant health risks to humans and wildlife. For example, heavy metals like lead and mercury can cause neurological damage and other severe health issues.

Business responsibility regarding waste includes preventing the release of harmful chemicals into the environment, reducing plastic use, practising responsible product stewardship (13.5), and adopting circular economy models (13.6).

Global warming and climate change

Global warming refers to the increase in the average temperature of the Earth's near-surface air and oceans, which brings about climate change. This phenomenon is disrupting ecosystems, agriculture and water resources, and is contributing to more frequent natural disasters. The cause of global warming is the collection of certain gases in the atmosphere, mainly carbon dioxide (CO_2) and methane (CH_4). These gases are called greenhouse gases (GHGs) because they prevent heat energy produced from solar radiation from escaping into space – a phenomenon known as the 'greenhouse effect'. GHGs are causing rising global temperatures, melting polar ice caps and extreme weather events such as droughts, floods and wildfires. Melting polar ice caps and glaciers, driven by global warming, are causing sea levels to rise, threatening coastal cities and ecosystems. This impacts coastal erosion, saltwater intrusion and increased flooding, displacing communities and destroying infrastructure, especially in low-lying areas.

Climate change challenges businesses to reduce GHG emissions, often referred to as reducing CO_2 generated by fossil fuels. This is typically measured as the carbon footprint – the total amount of GHGs, particularly carbon dioxide, emitted directly or indirectly by an individual, organization, event or product over its lifecycle. Companies must also promote transparency by disclosing their climate-related risks and performance, and by aligning their strategies with global sustainability goals. This transparency often includes information about the carbon footprint of each product.

13.3 The human–nature relationship, ecological ethics and integral ecology

The understanding of the human–nature relationship provides the foundation for ecological ethics, which can be defined as the moral principles, norms and virtues governing human behaviour in dealing with the environment and caring for the preservation of life on Earth.

The human–nature relationship

Human beings and nature are interdependent. Humans obtain food, air, water and raw materials from the natural environment and deposit waste in it. Each generation receives the environment as a legacy from previous generations and will, in turn, pass it onto the next. This is a matter of fact, but there are different perceptions of the human–nature relationship that shape human attitudes towards the environment.

Since at least the seventeenth century, coinciding with the progressive development of science and technology, a *despotic anthropocentrism* has prevailed. This view sees the human–nature relationship in terms of unlimited domination for the benefit of humankind, using science and technology as tools. Capitalism, as it has been understood for ages, with its exclusive focus on wealth accumulation and disregard for environmental consequences, reinforced this sense of absolute dominion.

While despotic anthropocentrism has been increasingly criticized, other philosophical perspectives argue in favour of an anthropocentrism with a human face.[3] One such approach is *responsible anthropocentrism*, or *stewardship anthropocentrism*, which takes a human-centric view in harmony with nature.

Other approaches have emerged in reaction to anthropocentrism. One is *biocentrism*, which focuses on all forms of life. In accordance with biocentrism, all life forms possess intrinsic value and are equally valuable. Human beings are seen as merely one animal species co-existing with others, with no special recognition of human dignity to give them pre-eminence over other animals. *Ecocentrism* goes even further, viewing people as just an interconnected part of nature. The concept of *deep ecology*[4] aligns with this view. In both biocentrism and ecocentrism, humanity is diluted within nature. This view contrasts with a more widely accepted outlook that humans are part of nature but transcend it due to their inner world, which expresses a significant spiritual dimension. Animals and plants have value, but only humans possess dignity (human dignity) and the authentic rights associated with moral duties.

Ecological ethics: Respecting and caring for the environment

Aristotelian-personalist ethics includes *living in peace and harmony with nature* as a specific type of human good (2.7). This requires the proper recognition of non-human entities and a caring attitude towards nature. In this sense, the *stewardship principle* (2.7) states that human activity should be harmonized with respecting and caring for the environment as responsible stewards. Underlying this principle is the idea that, although humans transcend nature, they should not dominate it despotically but rather use it as good stewards and care for it. Consequently, development should not be understood as mere indiscriminate consumption or unfettered consumerism. Instead, it should be human and sustainable, employing material goods with moderation and responsibility to promote human flourishing while maintaining concern for future generations.

The stewardship principle opposes animal cruelty and demands respect for biodiversity. In response to the desire to use living elements solely for economic purposes, a sense of stewardship requires that we consider each living being's nature and their mutual connections within an ordered system – the cosmos.[5] This principle is compatible with the view that animals are not of equal value to humans nor possess innate rights, since they do not have autonomy, moral responsibility and conscious self-determination. Therefore, humans can own, raise and use animals for food and clothing, provided this is done with a caring attitude. In addition, ecosystems that suffer considerable loss of biodiversity are less likely to rebound successfully from disturbance events. This can ultimately spell trouble for current or future generations.

A responsible treatment of nature can be fostered by certain *ecological virtues*.[6] These include admiration for nature and gratitude for its creation, ecological awareness, sustainability as a virtue (understood as solidarity with future generations), a sense of good stewardship, communion with nature, moderation in the use of natural resources and respect for and generous care of nature (environmental activism).

The anthropocentric-stewardship approach aligns with the influential *Rio Declaration* (1992), which emerged from the UN Conference on Environment and Development. This influential Declaration underscores in Principle 1: 'Human beings are at the centre of concerns for sustainable development. They are entitled to a healthy and productive life in harmony with nature.' The suggestion is that managerial stewardship of the environment should reconcile respect for nature with the attainment of reasonable profits.[7]

The Rio Declaration had a significant influence on the environmental principles of the *UN Global Compact* (8.6), which state that 'businesses should support a precautionary approach to environmental challenges' (Principle 7); 'undertake initiatives to promote greater environmental responsibility' (Principle 8); and 'encourage the development and diffusion of environmentally friendly technologies' (Principle 9).

Human ecology and integral ecology

Ecology is often focused on the natural environment, studying the relationship between living organisms and the habitat or environment in which they develop. However, in addition to this 'natural ecology' there is also a 'human ecology', since humans themselves developed within a habitat. In contrast with animals, human development goes beyond biological growth, entailing the development of the rational dimension which characterizes the human being. They develop within diverse habitats, including family life and home, communities, urbanistic and social conditions and work organization, among other possibilities. Ethically speaking, the importance of safeguarding the moral conditions for an authentic 'human ecology'[8] is important to note.

Comprehensively, Pope Francis introduced the concept of 'integral ecology',[9] which includes natural, human, social and cultural dimensions, emphasizing the interconnectedness of all aspects of life: environmental, social, economic, cultural and spiritual.

Notice here the inclusion of culture within integral ecology as an intangible element of human habitat, with influence on human development. Culture is generally understood as the set of values, beliefs, practices and ways of life that shape how persons and societies interact with both the environment and each other. According to Francis, 'culture is more than what we have inherited from the past; it is also, and above all, a living, dynamic and participatory present reality.'[10]

In practice, integral ecology is negatively affected by intensive forms of environmental exploitation and degradation, which not only exhaust the resources which provide local communities with their livelihood, but also undo the social structures which, for a long time, shaped cultural identity and their sense of the meaning in regard to life and community.[11]

13.4 Precautionary and proactive business actions

A variety of industries have played a significant role in generating ecological problems. These include mining, transportation, coal-fired power plants, nuclear waste disposal, oil refineries and petrochemical plants, chemical plants, metal production and other heavy industries, plastics production and transformation, incinerators and agribusiness (for example, deforestation, burning of natural vegetation, pesticide and herbicide spraying and large-scale livestock farming). Companies can impact ecosystems and, in turn, ecosystems can affect some business operations. This occurs, for example, when raw materials are no longer available in the necessary quality and quantity due to resource depletion.

Additionally, the operations of some multinational corporations, particularly in developing countries, have had a profound ecological impact on the natural environment and indigenous populations. This is seen, for example, when corporations exploit raw materials in developing countries or export toxic and hazardous waste to these regions.

Precautionary business actions

Companies, like other institutions, can contribute to protecting, restoring and promoting the sustainable use of terrestrial ecosystems; sustainably managing forests; combating desertification; halting and reversing land degradation; and reducing biodiversity loss.

The UN Global Compact, in Principle 10, states that 'businesses should support a precautionary approach to environmental challenges'. Essentially, this is the first ethical requirement: avoiding harm and doing good wherever possible.

Environmental challenges for businesses include preventing raw material depletion and working to eliminate or at least reduce pollution. Other actions to avert environmental damage are also encouraged. Many technical solutions are now available to control and prevent pollution in the air, water and soil.

Another key challenge concerns the responsible use of energy. Businesses can conserve energy by reducing consumption (for example, by avoiding unnecessary heating or air conditioning, turning off lights when not in use, or reducing wattage in decorations). Efficiency is achieved by using less energy to provide the same service level, often through replacing technical devices, processes, facilities and transportation systems with more efficient alternatives. Examples include replacing incandescent bulbs with energy-saving models, improving insulation, constructing energy-efficient buildings, redesigning industrial processes and rethinking transportation methods.

Business recognizes its responsibility in contributing to global warming and climate change, particularly by minimizing CO_2 emissions from production, distribution and other activities. This responsibility includes being accountable for the carbon footprint associated with these activities. Measuring GHG emissions in carbon dioxide equivalents is the first step towards minimizing this footprint.

Another important point relates to businesses that use animals in their operations. These companies should strive to improve animal welfare by, for example, avoiding overcrowding in poultry farms or other conditions that may cause animal distress or neglect. Scientific experiments on animals for health-related research must be conducted within reasonable limits, prioritizing the minimization of animal suffering. Proper handling, including humane slaughter and minimizing animal distress, pain and fear, is also essential.

Taking precautionary actions to prevent ecological damage may incur additional costs, which can negatively impact profit margins and reduce competitive advantages, especially if competitors are less ecologically responsible. However, this is not necessarily the case. The perceived conflict between ecological responsibility and profitability can be overcome. Process improvements or energy-saving equipment can prove profitable, and 'going green' may help companies avoid penalties and enhance their reputation. Lobbying for ecological regulations and their enforcement can also level the playing field by eliminating unfair advantages for companies that neglect ecological responsibility.

Corporate proactive strategies

Traditionally, in many businesses, wealth creation has correlated directly with the consumption of raw materials and energy. Sustained economic growth has thus required a proportionally increased amount of these resources. However, since these resources are limited, their prices will continue to rise, and excessive use will undermine sustainability efforts. Waste and pollution have also been linked to economic growth; typically, the more waste and pollution produced, the more the economic wealth grows. Moreover, we must recognize that the Earth's ecosystems can no longer absorb the residues and emissions resulting from production and consumption.

The question remains: how can a company be both ecologically responsible and remain profitable and competitive? Businesses facing this dilemma can adopt either a reactive or proactive strategy. The reactive strategy involves merely complying with existing pollution control laws in each country – or even disregarding them if enforcement is lax. Companies may rationalize this approach by arguing that pollution control costs reduce profit margins and create competitive disadvantages, especially if competitors do not go beyond the legal minimum. This raises the question of how to resolve this conflict in both an ethical and economically viable way.

In contrast, a proactive strategy anticipates future regulations concerning raw materials and energy usage and/or implements clean technologies to reduce pollution beyond current legal requirements when reasonable and necessary. Ethically, this is the right approach, and it can also enhance a company's reputation. Furthermore, businesses that adopt a proactive strategy can lobby public authorities to introduce suitable regulations. When a business takes initiative and pushes for environmental regulations,it may compel other companies (especially those that only respond to regulations rather than anticipate them) to improve their own pollution control. As a result, they would now be competing with one another on more sustainable or responsible terms.

A proactive approach may also involve adopting international standards more stringent than local regulations, such as the ISO 14001 standard for environmental management developed by the International Standards Organization (ISO). This standard outlines the requirements for an environmental management system to enhance an organization's environmental performance. It applies to any organization, regardless of size, type or nature, and addresses the environmental aspects of its activities, products and services that it can control or influence from a lifecycle perspective.

A responsible company strives to integrate proactive strategies throughout its entire production process, introducing new technologies or redesigning products to be more durable, reusable and recyclable, using recycled materials, and avoiding toxins as much as possible. Since these goals are linked to manufacturing and delivery costs, imaginative efforts are needed to create both environmental and financial value. One possible approach is a three-pronged strategy: (1) integrating scientific advances; (2) enhancing knowledge intensity; and (3) improving productivity. For instance, scientific developments can lead to renewable materials (for example, corn sugar instead of petrochemicals). Increased knowledge intensity supports sustainable economic value by developing less material-intensive production methods and emphasizing technology, expertise and information systems.

Within this proactive strategy, Hart and Milstein[12] identify three key drivers through which businesses can contribute to global environmental sustainability:

- Increasing resource efficiency and preventing pollution.
- Operating transparently and responsibly, maintaining informed and active stakeholder relationships.
- Developing and utilizing technologies that offer innovative solutions, potentially making today's material-intensive industries obsolete.

Ecological initiatives and technological innovations

In recent years, many businesses have undertaken initiatives to promote environmental responsibility, leading to the development of environmentally friendly technologies. Some of these technologies not only control adverse impacts – such as atmospheric pollution and other ecological issues – but also address their root causes. For example, improved production processes have led to higher-quality fuels, allowing the elimination of lead (which produces toxic lead oxide). Even more transformative has been the introduction of electric vehicles and battery-charging systems to replace combustion-based cars. Another example is the adoption of highly efficient LED (light-emitting diode) technology, which is replacing incandescent bulbs. Using renewable energy sources (such as hydro, solar and wind power) whenever possible is another responsible practice.

Engineering systems are also available to help companies track the flow of materials and waste throughout a product or system's lifecycle, from raw material acquisition to final disposal. Responsible corporations increasingly accept the challenge of redesigning industrial processes to reduce ecological impact while maintaining or even enhancing efficiency. Additionally, many companies issue annual accountability reports (12.8) on their ecological performance and efforts to mitigate adverse environmental effects.

Among the many initiatives aimed at promoting environmental responsibility, waste management and product management stand out, and we will explore these further below.

13.5 Waste management and product stewardship

Waste management

Waste is a prominent ecological problem (13.2), and different production processes result in different types of waste. Product packaging quickly becomes waste, and products themselves, sooner or later, suffer the same fate. Waste should be managed to reduce its negative impact on the environment and, ultimately, on society.

All businesses are directly responsible for the waste they produce in their manufacturing process and, consequently, for its appropriate disposal.

The disposal of waste often occurs by means of landfill, incineration or combustion. Waste disposal requires special attention in regard to the disposal of toxic substances, and/or if the method of waste elimination itself produces poison. This is the case for plastics and solvents that contain halogens which, when incinerated, produce dioxins. An example of these materials include PVC plastic and the liquids used in the dry-cleaning industry.

Waste management of solid products deals with the production, collection, treatment and disposal of waste. It includes three main concerns – reducing, reusing and recycling – known as 'the three R's of waste management':

- *Reducing waste*: This involves attacking the cause. It can be done by reducing waste in the manufacturing process and product packaging, which requires companies to improve efficiency. It may also be achieved by swapping traditional materials for more innovative, eco-friendly materials.
- *Reusing material*: Reusing and repairing equipment, rather than replacing it, is another way of avoiding waste. However, on this point, a dilemma can arise between economic and environmental ethical criteria. Owing to labour costs, repair is not always the most economical alternative, and business strategies might focus on new products rather than on long-lasting ones. We will return to this point in the next section.
- *Recycling refuse*: This is a process by which waste or old products are converted into new products. Recycling not only prevents the loss of potentially useful materials, but also reduces the consumption of fresh resources and energy spent in new-product manufacture. Recyclable materials include glass, paper, metal, textiles and some plastics.

When it comes to waste disposal, business can favour the environment by packaging with *biodegradable material*. Over time, these products are broken down by micro-organisms. On the other hand, non-biodegradable material can long remain – often forever – on the Earth, without decaying and being absorbed. Sometimes, the use of biodegradable material is also required by law. Whether this is or is not the case, the social responsibility to use biodegradable material should be recognized.

Product stewardship

Related to these activities is the concept of *product stewardship*, which requires managing the product for its entire lifecycle, including its production, use and ultimate redundancy. Product stewardship includes all of the measures involved in reducing the product's impact on human health and the environment over its lifecycle.

Manufacturers, retailers, consumers and government agencies are the actors typically involved in product stewardship. The responsibility of manufacturers includes appropriate planning for the recycling or disposal of the product at the end of its useful life. It also entails using packaging that minimizes waste and the corresponding environmental impact. Manufacturers can even pay to facilitate the recycling of obsolete products or for their proper disposal. Retailer and consumer responsibilities consist of ensuring the proper disposal of, or recycling of, products at the end of their useful lives. Government agencies can reinforce product stewardship by measures that incentivize or punish those involved in the product stewardship process.

A number of products with severe environmental impact have already been the object of particular attention due to their quantity or degree of harmfulness. Among these are carpets, electronic goods, fluorescent lighting, gas cylinders, medical sharps (needles, syringes and lancets), mercury products, paints, pesticides, pharmaceuticals, phone books, radioactive devices, thermostats and tyres.[13]

Product stewardship requires a specific solution in each case. For instance, electronic waste – such as obsolete computers and television sets – might be sent to developing countries for recycling or disposal. However, some electronic goods contain toxic substances – including lead, mercury, cadmium and such – that pose a threat to human health and to the environment. An appropriate manner of selectively collecting electronic goods is necessary. This involves planning by the manufacturers, the collaboration of consumers and retailers, and legislation to oblige compliance.[14]

Business Ethics in Action #13

Patagonia, Inc.: 'Doing good while doing well'

Patagonia, Inc. is a multinational company specializing in outdoor clothing, mountain equipment and food. Based in Ventura, California, it operates with factories in sixteen countries and has stores in over ten countries.

Patagonia was founded in 1973 by Yvon Chouinard, an avid climber, along with other partners, as an expansion of Chouinard Equipment, a small business Yvon started in 1957 to sell rock-climbing gear.

Patagonia was one of the first companies to commit to the movement of conscious capitalism (7.5), assuming social and environmental initiatives and prioritizing long-term environmental sustainability over short-term profits. Patagonia's most well-known commitment relates to its ecological responsibility, which is embedded throughout the company's production, business initiatives and philanthropic efforts to combat climate change and support environmental conservation.

Patagonia has successfully expanded with a strategy focused on offering high-quality, durable and sustainable products that appeal to consumers who value longevity, craftsmanship and an environmentally friendly reputation. Care for the environment includes reducing its environmental footprint by using recycled materials and minimizing water usage. It is also remarkable for its initiatives, such as repairing old products, recycling or swapping items and other forms of reuse, as well as having a strong commitment to promote responsibility of its supply chain. In addition, Patagonia makes frequent donations to environmental groups. Since 1985, it has committed 1 per cent of its total sales to environmental groups through *One Percent for the Planet*, an organization also founded by Yvon Chouinard. In 2016, Patagonia donated 100 per cent of Black Friday sales (about US$10 million[15]) and in 2018 the company dedicated the US$10 million it received from President Trump's 2017 tax cuts to environmental protection groups.[16] Patagonia also focuses on employee needs and well-being by paying employees fairly and providing retirement plans, profit-sharing and other financial benefits. The company promotes a healthy work–life balance and offers comprehensive health benefits, including mental health resources, fitness programmes and wellness initiatives. Additionally, Patagonia supports its employees' personal and professional growth by offering training, development programmes and opportunities for career advancement. The company also prioritizes diversity and inclusion, among other important matters.

A significant decision in its recent history was Yvon Chouinard's 2022 announcement that he would transfer ownership of Patagonia (all of its voting stock, about 2 per cent of total stock) to the *Patagonia Purpose Trust*, overseen by the Chouinard family and advisors, and all his non-voting stock to the *Holdfast Collective*, a nonprofit organization dedicated to fighting the environmental crisis and protecting nature.[17] This decision dedicates approximately US$100 million annually to environmental causes. BBC News highlighted this event with the headline: 'Patagonia: Billionaire Boss Gives Fashion Firm away to Fight Climate Change.'[18]

* * *

Patagonia's commitment to sustainability and environmental activism is well-known and has positioned the brand as one that leverages its corporate influence for good, prioritizing ethics and sustainability over maximizing profits. This raises the question of whether Patagonia seeks profit and success through socially responsible actions – what is known as 'Doing Well by Doing Good' – or if the company succeeds financially while also engaging in good deeds that may not necessarily drive profits directly? The latter approach is typically summarized as 'Doing Good while Doing Well', which involves the company engaging in separate social or environmental initiatives that coexist with its financial success, without necessarily contributing to it. Patagonia might undertake good deeds simply because they align with its commitments, not only as a path to financial gain.

It is likely that Patagonia's efforts to care for the environment have enhanced its brand reputation and contributed to its economic success. However, not all of Patagonia's

> environmental initiatives may have been strictly necessary to achieve such a high level of reputation, particularly its environmental activism, which is quite uncommon in the business world. Yvon Chouinard, Patagonia's founder, has demonstrated a lifelong commitment to ethics and sustainability,[19] also evident in some of Patagonia's impactful initiatives. These include, as previously stated, donating 1 per cent of total sales to environmental groups, and contributing 100 per cent of Black Friday sales to environmental organizations.
>
> The actions of transferring all of Chouinard's voting stock to the Patagonia Purpose Trust, and all his nonvoting stock to the Holdfast Collective, a nonprofit organization dedicated to fighting the environmental crisis and defending nature, is particularly relevant. This type of transference of ownership is not rare in Europe but quite uncommon in the US.
>
> Definitively, Patagonia is a good example of 'doing good while doing well'.

SECTION B. BUSINESS AND SUSTAINABLE DEVELOPMENT

13.6 Sustainable development and circular economy

Sustainable development goes beyond environmental concerns – it also focuses on the social aspect, such as promoting respect for human dignity and human rights, decent work and community development. This helps to create more inclusive economic growth and reduce poverty and inequality.

UN Sustainable Development Goals

The UN, taking sustainable development as a 'big idea', has proposed the so-called 'Sustainable Development Goals' (SDGs), an ambitious project with seventeen goals and an original, initially, 2030 target,[20] presented as 'the blueprint to achieve a better and more sustainable future for all'. Some of these goals challenge businesses in matters related to overcoming poverty and inequality, avoiding climate and environmental degradation, and promoting responsible consumption and production, decent work and prosperity with peace and justice.

Some of these topics are covered in previous chapters in this book; others need further development. Here, we simply focus on a few positive contributions that could be made by companies operating in developing counties, beginning with some business initiatives that could help to alleviate poverty.

The involvement of businesses in sustainable development has become crucial as the world faces challenges related to climate change, resource depletion and social inequality. Businesses are no longer solely focused on profitability but are also key players in creating a sustainable future by integrating environmental, social and governance (ESG) criteria (13.7.) into their operations. Here are some of the ways businesses are actively involved in sustainable development:

Adopting corporate sustainability practices

Businesses are called to develop sustainably without losing competitivity. Thus, they have the permanent challenge of gaining competitive advantage while applying sustainable philosophy through cost savings, image and revenue enhancement and liability reduction.

Sustainable development requires a change to the high levels of consumerism (11.1) currently prevalent in the developed world. However, this change may conflict with a business' economic intentions. This tension requires reflection and moral imagination to search for solutions that retain employment without fostering immoderate consumerism. Aside from regulations, like those established to moderate the consumption of alcoholic beverages, businesses must recognize their own inherent responsibilities.

Developing an ecological and social conscience helps to promote sustainable development to both consumers and those who lead corporations. Some radical ecologists defend a drastic change in lifestyles, but an extreme change could take us back to the pre-industrial era. This would bring about disastrous consequences for poor and agrarian populations in underdeveloped countries.[21]

Ecological and social conscience should be applied alongside moral imagination when seeking solutions that include proactively promoting ecological and profitable strategies.

The 'bottom of the pyramid' and the alleviation of poverty

Poverty remains one of the world's most pressing challenges. The first of the UNs' SDGs is 'No poverty', which aims to eradicate extreme poverty globally by 2030. Yet, despite various efforts, we remain far from achieving this objective.

In economics, the term 'Bottom of the Pyramid' (BoP) refers to the poorest two-thirds of the global population – more than 4 billion people living in conditions of severe deprivation. As of 2 April 2024, the World Bank reported[23] that approximately 700 million people still live on less than $2.15 per day, the threshold of extreme poverty. This hardship is especially concentrated in Sub-Saharan Africa, fragile and conflict-affected regions and rural areas. Although other developing countries may no longer experience extreme poverty, many still suffer from poor living conditions and limited opportunities. People at the BoP often face significant barriers to entering business ecosystems. Their limited incomes restrict access to basic goods and services that are commonplace in developed countries – even those essential to satisfying fundamental human needs.

Over the past few decades, various initiatives have emerged to tackle poverty. One of the most well-known is *Microcredit*, pioneered by Muhammad Yunus, who was awarded the Nobel Peace Prize in 2006 for his work with the Grameen Bank.[24] Microcredit provides small loans to low-income individuals, enabling them to start and grow modest but sustainable businesses. Initially offered by NGOs, these services have since been adopted by for-profit financial institutions, expanding the reach of microfinance.[25]

The corporate world has also made efforts to engage with the BoP segment. One strategy involves designing and delivering products specifically for low-income consumers while maintaining sustainable profitability. Some advocates argue that the BoP represents a significant untapped market, where businesses can contribute to poverty alleviation while accessing new growth opportunities.[26]

An example of this approach is a very cheap home personal computer developed in India and launched in 2007 by the Indian firm Novatium. The machine was based on cheap mobile-phone chips and has very basic hardware, including a keyboard, a monitor and two USB ports, but no hard-disk drive, extensive memory or pre-packaged software. Its monthly subscription has been priced at US$10, including thirty hours of internet access.[27] Another proposal for tackling this issue is to form partnerships between companies and income-poor communities in developing countries, to co-create business and markets that mutually benefit the companies and the communities, some of them successfully.[28]

Innovation in distribution is also important to sell to the BoP. It can eliminate distribution costs and create new routes through which resources can be distributed.

Some critics question the profitability and ethical implications of targeting BoP solely as consumers. They argue instead that the private sector can play a more constructive role by engaging the poor as producers or entrepreneurs, for instance by purchasing goods and services from them and integrating them into value chains.[29]

Defence of social, civil and political rights

Business can contribute to the SDGs by engaging in initiatives related to social, civil and political rights, although this is often controversial. These initiatives may be justified in situations where government ceases to administer those rights, where governments have not yet administered them, or where the administration of citizenship rights might be beyond the reach of the nation-state government.[30] Such engagement could produce a net positive – although the state should guarantee social, civil and political rights, society as a whole, including businesses, are not exempt from the responsibility of promoting them. However, multinational corporations (MNCs) might also use their power to constrain civil rights – the Saro-Wiwa affair in Nigeria, included in Historical Case #13, is an extreme example.

Currently, multiple societies are being forced to face the reality that many large corporations, who may be powerful enough to contribute efficiently to the solutions of significant social problems, may knowingly act against the common good. Just as governments are accountable to their citizens and, to some degree, the population controls the government through democratic mechanisms, some mechanism will be needed to constrain corporations that have become engaged in public policy.

Business, in certain circumstances, can also contribute to the provision of public healthcare, energy conservation and the management of resources.

Circular economy

Another way in which business can contribute to a sustainable development is by adopting the idea of the *circular economy*, a concept that emerged from the notion of sustainability (12.4). The circular economy is presented in contrast with the conventional economy, which is based on an extractive industrial model that is essentially a *lineal economy* – taking raw material, making a product and disposing of waste and obsolete or unusable products. A *circular economy* seeks to close this cycle in a 'loop', by reusing the waste and reducing both the entry of materials and the production of virgin waste, therefore minimizing negative environmental impacts. The goal is to avoid producing things that quickly become trash and to recycle waste as much as possible.

A circular economy is inspired by natural ecosystems. Plants synthesize nutrients that feed herbivores. These in turn feed the carnivorous beings, who provide important amounts of organic waste, which help to grow a new generation of vegetables. In contrast, the industrial model produces a great quantity of waste at the end of both the production and consumption cycle.

A circular economy requires innovation throughout the cycle, from redefining products and services to designing waste out of the system, maximizing the use of renewable resources, moderating consumption, maximizing efficiency of use and reuse, and recycling. Both large companies, like Patagonia (see Business Ethics in Action #13) and SMEs can participate in the circular economy. Regarding the latter, four steps have been suggested: (1) reevaluating waste as potential resources: (2) seeking collaboration opportunities; (3) leveraging digital marketplaces; and (4) treating circularity as a major change programme. These steps can be identified with real-world examples of companies that have successfully implemented circular practices.[22]

Nowadays, our capacity to absorb and reuse waste is still very low. However, the need to develop procedures for a circular economy, to ensure resources for all current and future generations, is particularly evident.

13.7 The ESG criteria and socially responsible investing

ESG criteria

The ESG Criteria (environmental, social and governance) are a set of standards used to evaluate a company's operations and impact on the world beyond financial performance. These criteria are increasingly used by investors, corporations and regulatory bodies to assess sustainable and ethical business practices. The ESG criteria were formally introduced in a 2004 UN Global Compact initiative titled *Who Cares Wins: Connecting Financial Markets to a Changing World – Recommendations by the Financial Industry to Better Integrate Environmental, Social, and Governance Issues in Analysis, Asset Management, and Securities Brokerage*. The document emphasized the need for financial markets to integrate environmental, social and governance factors into corporate strategies to promote sustainable development.

The specific contents of ESG criteria can be summarized as follows:

- *Environmental criterion* evaluates how a company performs as a steward of the natural environment. This includes factors like climate change and GHG emissions, resource depletion (energy use, raw materials, water), waste management, pollution, biodiversity and ecosystem conservation. It also includes managing environmental risks, such as ownership of contaminated land, disposal of hazardous waste, toxic emissions and compliance with government environmental regulations.
- *Social criterion* examines how a company manages its relationships with employees (health, safety and working conditions), suppliers (including responsibility for the supply chain), customers, and the communities in which it operates. Key areas include human rights and labour standards, workplace diversity and inclusion, health and safety practices, community engagement and philanthropy.
- *Governance criterion* addresses the accuracy of internal controls, transparency, minority shareholder rights, legal behaviour and the prevention of conflicts of interest among board members. Other points include executive remuneration standards and the avoidance of political contributions for favourable treatment. Indicators used to measure these criteria often include board composition and diversity, executive compensation, ethical standards, anti-corruption measures, transparency, shareholder rights and risk management.

Integrating ESG criteria can help companies become more sustainable and resilient in the face of environmental and social risks. Companies with strong ESG performance often build greater trust among consumers, employees and stakeholders, leading to stronger brand loyalty and improved employee retention. Moreover, the correlation between strong ESG practices and financial performance is generally positive.

One important application of ESG criteria is its use as a reference for investors who specifically consider the social responsibility and sustainability of companies. In fact, ESG reporting has become essential for asset managers and institutional investors when assessing company value.

Despite these benefits, some criticisms of ESG remain. First, critics point to the lack of standardization in ESG indicators and metrics, which leads to inconsistencies in how companies report their ESG practices. Second, implementing ESG practices can be costly, especially for smaller companies, due to the administrative work and resources required to gather, assess and publish these metrics.

Additionally, as with other CSR or sustainability practices, there is a risk of 'greenwashing', where companies publicize positive ESG indicators while continuing unsustainable practices behind the scenes.

Socially responsible investing

Long ago, conscientious investors realized that no investment is morally neutral because it supports business activities that may or may not align with ethical standards. Thus, the so-called 'ethical funds' emerged. These guarantee certain ethical conditions for the investment, such as avoiding any investment in businesses related to alcohol, tobacco, gambling, pornography, weapons, abortifacients and others. Also avoided are companies that lack respect for human rights or that conduct human embryo research and so on.

Nowadays, the notion of *socially responsible investing* (SRI), or simply 'responsible investing', is gaining popularity. This includes not only the avoidance of bad practices, but also the promotion of positive corporate behaviours. Socially responsible investors encourage corporate practices that promote environmental stewardship, labour rights and consumer protection, among other interests.

In the first decade of this century, the investment market showed increased interest in sustainability through its examination of the correlation between environmental and social standards and financial performance. Another factor considered positive was good practices of governance (8.8). These three elements are included in the above-mentioned ESG criteria. There are indices to favour social responsible investment. Among the Dow Jones Sustainability Indices (DJSI) and the S&P 500 ESG Index.

Research findings[31] show that: (1) companies with strong sustainability scores show better operational performance and are less risky; (2) investment strategies that incorporate ESG measures outperform comparable non-ESG strategies; and (3) active ownership creates value for companies. Owing to this evidence, some legal judgments have concluded that not only is it permissible for investment companies to integrate ESG issues into investment analysis, but that it is arguably part of their fiduciary duty to do so. Thus, ESG criteria are not only useful for investors with a conscience, but also for those interested only in creating the best return.

Aligned with ESG criteria, the UN launched the *Principles for Responsible Investment* (UN PRI) in 2006.[32] These are a set of six principles regarding the incorporation of ESG issues into investment analysis, decision-making processes and investment policies. They also include disclosure of ESG issues by the entities in which one invests, along with several other aspects regarding implementation and reporting.

13.8 Multinational and transnational corporations in a global world

Nowadays, societal relationships in business are not only international, but also global – since the world is, in certain respects, an interconnected and unified society. Business is immersed in the phenomenon of globalization, which describes the ways in which our world now functions as a unified whole – a phenomenon caused by technological advances that make worldwide communication and transportation easy, in addition to socio-cultural, political and economic factors.

Although globalization is a complex concept, it is often understood solely in economic terms. Economic globalization includes such phenomena as worldwide trade, technological spread, direct foreign investment in any nation, capital flows from one country to another and migration. Globalization entails the integration of businesses and national economies in a global economy. Thanks to globalization, *the world is flat*[33] in terms of commerce and competition and, theoretically, all competitors have an equal opportunity.

Globalization permits businesses to undertake global trading, offshore outsourcing and use international supply chains. This brings about new opportunities for developing countries and new forms of competition among businesses. In spite of the positive aspects, it posits many ethical problems and brings about discontentment,[34] and this has sparked an anti-globalization movement encompassing a wide range of ideologies. Some well-known cases, such as the Rana Plaza incident in Bangladesh (Historical Case #12) and the Shell Africa controversies (Historical Case #13), among others, have contributed to the negative image of multinational and transnational corporations. Cases of flagrant human rights violations and the exploitation of natural resources without regard for indigenous populations and the environment are likely to worsen this image. Additionally, MNCs may use their power to bribe or manipulate weak local governments or impose cultural values insensitively, disregarding local culture.

In general terms, globalization is often accused of favouring the interests of the ruling classes and fostering situations where international financial institutions and large multinational companies abuse their power, causing blatant injustices. Some argue that economic globalization requires a globalization of ethics and solidarity, along with a strong sense of responsibility among MNCs. Among these advocates is Nobel Laureate Joseph E. Stiglitz, who calls for practical ways to improve globalization that respect both people and the environment.[35]

Responsibility of global companies

Today, many companies are not just part of the economies of one or two specific countries but are integrated into the global economy at large. This affects 'multinational corporations' (MNCs) – companies with a distinct home country that adapt to local markets – and 'transnational corporations' (TNCs) – companies that operate on a more integrated, global scale without a strong national identity.[36] But this is also true for small and medium enterprises (SMEs) whose market is the world. These companies should therefore engage with social and environmental challenges worldwide and recognize their responsibilities regarding sustainability and the planet, just as other social institutions and governments do within their respective countries. These challenges largely align with some of the UN SDGs (13.6).

Society, particularly in developing countries, has high expectations of businesses – especially large corporations. The media also closely monitors these big companies. For their part, companies face the need to build or rebuild public trust, prevent risks (including those stemming from social media and traditional media), and demonstrate that they deserve the reputation of a good global corporate citizen. However, addressing these issues must not make a company unprofitable or uncompetitive. Asking businesses to take on these global issues may seem like trying to 'square a circle', but, in reality, many companies are already following this philosophy. They do so not only out of a sense of social responsibility but also because they have learned that ignoring these issues can quickly harm their bottom line.

Positively, corporations should recognize themselves as *global actors* – a 'Global Corporate Citizen' (GCC), if you will – and thoughtfully address problems that have emerged due to globalization. In doing so, businesses can transition from being part of the problem to actively helping bring about solutions.

Examining both the positive contributions of multinational companies and some common negative practices can help clarify what it means to be a GCC, or, in other words, a socially responsible company in a global context.

Contributions of MNCs to developing countries and misbehaviours

On the positive side, businesses, particularly multinational and transnational corporations, can contribute to the economic development of developing countries in several ways. One of them is through *financial investment* – building factories and other facilities, for instance. This results in an inflow of capital into the developing country and increases its productive capacity. Additionally, this investment enables developing countries to purchase imports.

A second contribution to economic development is the creation of both direct and indirect *employment*, allowing workers to earn a living. While this may not be the primary intention of MNCs, as wages paid in developing countries are generally lower than those in developed countries with a higher standard of living, it still provides valuable job opportunities. The alternative for many workers could be worse, such as working for local companies or on farms in poor rural areas, possibly under even harsher conditions. However, this contribution can be undermined by extremely low wages, which take advantage of the asymmetry of bargaining power between MNCs and workers. Unfortunately, MNCs have sometimes been known to exploit this imbalance, a point we will discuss further below.

A third contribution is the impact MNCs can have on both the people and the region: MNCs can *transfer technology* – though this is not always guaranteed – and provide *training* to workers. They may also create infrastructure, such as roads or communication systems, or help to improve existing ones. The presence of these facilities may further encourage government investment in infrastructure.

Lastly, foreign investment in industry can help *diversify the economy*, moving it away from a reliance on primary products and agriculture, which are often subject to volatile prices and supply.

Negative practices to be avoided

Avoiding the negative practices often associated with MNCs in developing countries involves taking measures to prevent issues such as the following:

- *Lack of respect for human rights, poor working conditions and very low wages*: This often involves taking advantage of workers' needs, lax labour legislation and/or the lack of regular compliance inspections. Arguing that the alternative of unemployment or working in rural areas is worse does not justify abusive conditions. The ethical requirement is to provide a just wage – a basic labour right (10.2) – considering the specific circumstances of each location.
- *Environmental neglect and resource exploitation*: The extraction of raw materials can cause river pollution and the loss of natural landscapes. Sometimes, MNCs outsource production

processes and waste disposal to developing countries with weaker environmental legislation. The exploitation of raw materials can damage the surrounding environment – including the land and livelihood of indigenous people – often with only limited compensation, apart from natural resources depletion and contribution to diversity loss (13.1).

- *Imposing costs on the host country*: This relates to generating external costs, such as the negative ecological impacts produced by MNCs that fail to compensate the host country for the effective restoration of the environment.
- *Involvement in corrupt practices*: Companies may bribe local authorities to obtain licences or to avoid penalties. Payments for extraction rights can be reduced through the corruption of politicians or officials, diverting funds from the national treasury. Responsible companies should avoid these practices and ensure that no one within the organization partakes in them.
- *Lack of investment in the host country*: This occurs when the MNC repatriates all profits back to its home country, without reinvesting in the local economy.
- *Abuse of tax incentives*: Some companies manipulate transfer pricing to subsidiaries to reduce taxes in the host country. Others move headquarters to countries with lower tax rates to avoid higher tax burdens in the countries where they operate or generate income.
- *Reluctance to hire local workers*: When skilled workers are needed for new projects, MNCs may prefer to hire talent from developed economies. This could be due to a lack of experience or training among locals, but it also may indicate a reluctance on the part of the company to provide adequate training or opportunities for promotion to local workers. Responsible companies should make efforts to develop the skills of local people.

Reparative and restorative justice

A problem that some MNCs and TNCs face is how to address their legacies of irresponsibility, which have caused serious damage to local communities and the environment, often over decades and under past generations of management.[37] This is exemplified by the case of Shell Africa and its notorious impact on the Niger Delta (see Historical Case #13).

Such situations involve harm caused by the corporation and a resulting state of injustice that must be rectified. Establishing justice requires fair compensation and repairing the damages unjustly caused, as *reparative justice* demands (5.1). Justice, however, goes beyond that. It is easy to imagine the deteriorated relationships between the company and local communities, who are acutely aware of the damage the company has inflicted on the natural environment they live in, as well as on farmland essential for their livelihoods. A full restoration of justice must extend beyond mere financial compensation or partial environmental repair; it must seek to rebuild a relationship of mutual understanding, harmony and trust with the local community.

This level of restoration requires *restorative justice* (5.1), which is focused on repairing relationships and healing the harm caused by wrongdoing. This process may involve, among other elements, engaging affected individuals, fostering dialogue, acknowledging and repenting for the harm caused, and a firm commitment to avoid future damage.

Walker[38] and others propose *moral repair* – a comprehensive concept that overlaps with restorative justice but places greater emphasis on the ethical and emotional restoration of trust and moral norms. It focuses on rebuilding the moral order disrupted by the wrongdoing and can be achieved through both reparative actions (such as material compensation) and restorative practices (such as apologies and efforts to rebuild trust).

13.9 Supply chain and offshore outsourcing

Two particular problems posed by globalization raise concerns for responsible business practices. One pertains to supply chains involving factories in developing countries where labour costs are low. The other concerns outsourcing, specifically the closure of domestic plants and the relocation of production to other countries for economic reasons.

Responsibility for supply chains in a global world

Every business participates in a supply chain, which stretches from initial suppliers providing raw materials to the final consumer. This chain or logistics network involves a sophisticated system of organizations, people, technology, activities, information and resources required to produce or deliver goods and services. For example, an automobile manufacturer's supply chain includes numerous companies providing car components, assembling parts and distributing products, forming a complex network.

Each link in this chain carries inherent risks, as companies typically focus on their own interests rather than those of the final user. To address this, supply chain management has emerged with the goal of integrating key business processes from suppliers to end-users and facilitating the exchange of information about market fluctuations, production capacities and other relevant data.

Each stage in the chain adds economic value, typically through cost-cutting measures and securing the lowest possible prices. In a globalized market, companies often compete by minimizing production costs, which can create pressure to reduce labour costs. This, in turn, can lead to poor working conditions and, in extreme cases, the establishment of sweatshops (10.3).

But to what extent is a company responsible for the actions of firms within its supply chain, especially those that violate human rights? In line with the previously discussed theory of responsibility (3.4), the answer depends on the causal proximity between the client company and the supplier in question, and the client's capacity to prevent or mitigate such practices. A large company may bear more responsibility than a smaller one due to its greater influence over suppliers. If a client company has the power to prevent unethical practices by a supplier but chooses not to act, it incurs responsibility. Smaller companies can also contribute to improving working conditions in the supply chain by using moral imagination.

One practical approach for companies of all sizes is to require reliable audits of labour conditions within their supply chains, supported by trusted certifications (12.8). These certifications generally verify the minimum standards of working conditions necessary for social responsibility.

Responsibility in offshore outsourcing

A company's behaviour in offshore outsourcing, often accompanied by the closure of domestic plants, serves as an indicator of its status as a responsible global corporate citizen.

The term 'outsourcing' entered the business vocabulary in the 1980s, referring to the practice of contracting out production or services that were previously performed internally to an external company. This process involves subcontracting, where a service or component is produced by a third-party supplier.

Common motivations for outsourcing include cost savings, restructuring costs by turning fixed costs into variable ones and potentially improving quality (though this is not always achieved). Outsourcing allows firms to concentrate on core business activities that they can manage more efficiently and profitably. Typical activities often outsourced offshore include manufacturing, call centre operations and IT services.

Public opinion frequently criticizes offshore outsourcing, arguing that it harms the local labour market. Domestic manufacturing plants or service centres may close, with production moving to countries with lower wages. Another concern is that working conditions in offshore facilities may be of low, or even sub-human, standards. However, offshore outsourcing can also promote job creation in developing countries, reduce consumer prices, increase profits and stimulate new investment opportunities.

Ethical considerations in offshore outsourcing pertain to two groups: domestic and offshore workers. For domestic workers, it's important to recognize that the labour market differs from other markets in that it should not be solely based on supply and demand. Workers are not mere commodities; they have dignity, not a price. Additionally, if a company is viewed as a community rather than just a profit-generating tool, layoffs should follow human and ethical standards, not purely economic calculations.

Consequently, if job eliminations or plant closures are necessary, they should be conducted in ways that minimize worker suffering. For laid-off employees, companies might consider providing fair severance, outplacement assistance, or reasonable advance notice to allow time for finding new employment. Treatment should respect the dignity of workers, ensuring they receive relevant and accurate information at the right time and that layoffs are conducted equitably. A just and socially responsible termination of employment can be summarized by three conditions: (1) just cause; (2) due process; and (3) mitigation of harmful effects.[39] Similar considerations and criteria apply to plant closures, applying the principle of double effect (4.6).

Offshore workers are equally entitled to respect for their human dignity and rights. Human dignity and rights are universal and must be respected in every context. The need for jobs in developing countries does not justify exploitation, such as paying unliveable wages or subjecting workers to inhumane conditions.

13.10 Integrating responsibility and sustainability into the organization

Traditionally, corporate social responsibility (CSR) has been viewed as an add-on to economic activity, with little recognition that businesses have an intrinsic social and ethical dimension. When strategy and social responsibility are treated as two disconnected activities, the social and ecological impacts of the strategy are likely to be neglected.

As noted earlier (12.1), responsibility – including the commitment to sustainability – tends to pay off. However, the debate over whether engaging in CSR aligns with an organization's financial interests remains unresolved,[40] though it has been enriched by new perspectives. Thus, Aguilera et al.[41] suggest that a complex set of motives drives businesses to engage in socially responsible actions. These authors identify three groups of motives that operate at individual, organizational, national and transnational levels:

- *Instrumental motives*: These focus on the effects of social responsibility on profits, fiscal control, short-term shareholder interests and competitiveness.
- *Relational motives*: These involve the need for belonging and the social cohesion derived from acting responsibly.
- *Moral motives*: These are linked to the pursuit of a meaningful existence, higher-order values and the intrinsic responsibility of business.

These motives are not entirely independent but interrelated. Moral motives can influence relational motives, which in turn can affect instrumental motives. When considered together, these motives explain why an increasing number of companies engage in sustainable and socially responsible practices beyond the narrow economic, technical and legal requirements.

Every manager should have a clear and accurate understanding of the firm's role within society to effectively integrate its social and economic roles. Accordingly, two key criteria are recommended for guiding a business towards responsible corporate conduct:

- *A clear vision of the company's orientation toward the common good*: This should be evident in the company's mission-driven activities, its role as a social actor, its social investment and philanthropy programmes, and an appropriate level of engagement in public policy.
- *Integration of responsibility throughout the organization*: To prevent responsibility and sustainability from being seen merely as add-ons, the principle of acting responsibly should be embedded across the company. This begins with the firm's purpose, corporate values, mission and vision, extending through strategies and organizational structures (see Figure 13.1). Responsibility and sustainability should not be relegated to tactics or image but should represent a genuine commitment. They should not be assigned to a specific department that deals with social issues; rather, every department should balance both responsibility and economic outcomes.

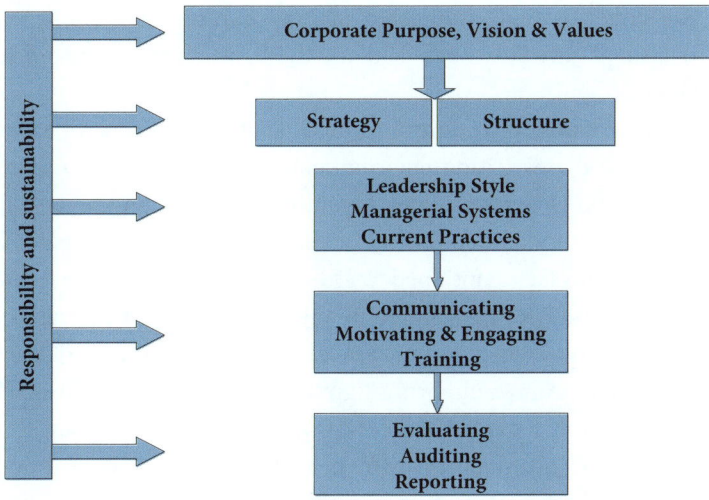

Figure 13.1 Integrating responsibility and sustainability into the firm

The formal and informal organization (9.7) should align with this commitment to responsibility, encompassing leadership style, managerial systems and practices, communication, motivation, stakeholder engagement and employee training. Finally, responsibility should be embedded in methods of evaluation, auditing and reporting. In essence, corporate citizenship should permeate the entire organization and its activities.[42]

Case Study #13

Botnia: A controversial paper pulp factory[43]

Botnia, formally *Oy Metsä-Botnia Ab*, a forestry processing company headquartered in Helsinki, was Europe's second-largest cellulose producer. Due to a lack of raw materials in Finland and projected growth plans, the company sought to establish a plant in a strategic location. In mid-2003, with approval from the Uruguayan government, Botnia publicly announced the establishment of a paper pulp factory named Orión on the banks of the Uruguay river, which borders Uruguay and Argentina. The plant would be near Fray Bentos, a city with 23,000 residents, across from Gualeguaychú, an Argentine town with 76,000 inhabitants, located just beyond the Libertador General San Martin Bridge. This location was ideal due to its proximity to plantations, transportation facilities, electricity networks and the availability of trained professionals locally and regionally. The 'Orion project' required a total investment of US$1.2 billion, with US$700 million allocated to machinery. Botnia was working on securing World Bank funding of US$200 million.

Botnia wasn't the only company interested in Fray Bentos. The Spanish National Cellulose Company (ENCE) also planned to open a plant there, with an estimated annual production capacity of 500,000 tons of pulp.

Environmental organizations, including Grupo Guayubira and Greenpeace, strongly opposed the establishment of these plants, citing environmental concerns, and protests soon followed. In September 2003, about 2,500 Uruguayans and Argentines gathered on the Argentine side to express their opposition, followed by another demonstration in October on the Libertador General San Martín International Bridge. These protests continued to grow in frequency over the following months.

Amidst the protests, a study commissioned by the World Bank in March–April 2004, required for loan approval, assessed the socioeconomic and environmental impact of the Orion project. The study indicated that the pulp mill would bring significant economic benefits to Uruguay, including 4,023 direct jobs in the plant, logistics and forestry, as well as 3,723 indirect jobs. This project would be the largest private industrial investment in Uruguayan history, boosting the country's GDP by 1.6 per cent. Eucalyptus plantations would be distributed across twelve departments in Uruguay, covering approximately 215,000 hectares.

Regarding environmental impact, the study found that the river's water quality would meet Uruguayan and European standards. Although atmospheric emissions would lead to a detectable change in air quality, projected sulphur dioxide and nitrogen oxide levels would remain within EU-defined limits for protected areas and would not impact human health. Noise levels would also comply with regulatory standards. While the construction would alter the local landscape and create occasional unpleasant odours, no significant impact on recreational areas was expected, and the frequency of odours would diminish once operations began.

As construction started, protests escalated. In April 2005, a crowd of Argentinians and Uruguayans once again occupied the Libertador San Martín Bridge, drawing national and international attention. The people of Gualeguaychú organized ongoing, large-scale activities opposing the factories, often referred to as 'paper mills'. Starting in December, their activities primarily focused on blocking the two bridges over the Uruguay river connecting Argentina and Uruguay. This conflict occupied a prominent space in the media.

The paper mill projects generated such intense controversy that the presidents of Argentina and Uruguay met in Chile to seek a resolution. However, their only recommendation was a temporary ninety-day work stoppage and the removal of the bridge blockades.

Botnia's managers, when choosing the location, never anticipated that the project would lead to an international conflict of this scale. Now they faced the decision of suspending the work, seeking another location, or finding an alternative solution.

Questions

1 Do environmental concerns of residents and environmental groups respond to objetive ethical criteria? How should companies take them into account when planning large industrial projects?
2 Reflect on the criteria Botnia used to select the Fray Bentos location. Were there important factors – social, political, or environmental – that may have been underestimated or overlooked?

3 Do you think Botnia executives should accept the suspension of the project or continue with the original plan? Why?
4 If you were a consultor, what actions would you recommend to address the underlying problem?

Notes

1. K. A. Annan, 'A New Coalition for Universal Values', 26 July 2000: https://www.un.org/sg/en/content/sg/articles/2000-07-26/new-coalition-universal-values. (Accessed on 30 October 2024).
2. Sources: S. G. Lauwo, O. Egbon, M. Denedo and A. R. Ejiogu, 'Counter-conducting Environmental Injustices and (un)Accountability: Ken Saro-Wiwa's Accounts of the Ogoni's Struggle for Emancipation', *Accounting, Auditing & Accountability Journal*, vol. 36, no. 6, 2023, pp. 1637–64; P. C. Nwilo and O. T. Badejo, *Impacts and Management of Oil Spill Pollution along the Nigerian Coastal Areas*, 2006. https://api.semanticscholar.org/CorpusID:44185905; C. Eboh, 'Nigerian Communities Seek $310 Million From Shell, Want Asset Sale Stopped', *Reuter*, 13 September: https://www.reuters.com/business/energy/nigerian-communities-seek-310-mln-shell-want-asset-sale-stopped-2024-09-13/.
3. See P. Ariansen, 'Anthropocentrism with a Human Face', *Ecological Economics*, vol. 24, no. 2/3, 1998, p. 153.
4. It was introduced by the Norwegian philosopher Arne Naess and later became popular in the United States. See A. Naes, *Ecology, Community, and Lifestyle* (Cambridge: Cambridge University Press, 1989).
5. See John Paul II, *Encyclical Letter 'Sollicitudo Rei Socialis'* on development, 1987, no. 34: https://www.vatican.va/content/john-paul-ii/en/encyclicals/documents/hf_jp-ii_enc_30121987_sollicitudo-rei-socialis.html. (Accessed on 30 October 2024).
6. R. L. Sandler, *Character and Environment: A Virtue-Oriented Approach to Environmental Ethics* (New York: Columbia University Press, 2007); and A. Porras, 'Virtues for an Integral Ecology', in A. J. G. Sison, G. R. Beabout and I. Ferrero (eds), *Handbook of Virtue Ethics in Business and Management* (Dordrecht: Springer, 2017), pp. 211–20.
7. On this point, see D. J. Manning, 'Benefits of Environmental Stewardship', *Review of Business*, vol. 25, no. 2, 2004, pp. 9–14.
8. John Paul II (Pope), *Encyclical-Letter 'Centesimus annus'*, 1991, no. 38: http://www.vatican.va/content/john-paul-ii/en/encyclicals/documents/hf_jp-ii_enc_01051991_centesimus-annus.html. (Accessed on 30 October 2024).
9. Francis, *Encyclical-Letter 'Laudato si'*, on the Catholic vision of the ecology, 2015, mainly Chapter 4: http://w2.vatican.va/content/dam/francesco/pdf/encyclicals/documents/papa-francesco_20150524_enciclica-laudato-si_en.pdf. (Accessed on 30 October 2024). This document is 'on care for our common home', as its subtitle expresses. Pope Francis called for broad social engagement in ecological problems and to promote what he terms 'integral ecology' with the involvement of business, civil society and governments.
10. Francis, *Encyclical-Letter 'Laudato si'*, no. 143.
11. Cf. Francis, *Encyclical-Letter 'Laudato si'*, no. 145.
12. S. L. Hart and M. B. Milstein, 'Creating Sustainable Value', *Academy of Management Executive*, vol. 17, no. 2, 2003, pp. 56–67.

13. See, for instance, the Product Stewardship Institute, a US non-profit organization that works to reduce the environmental impact of consumer products: http://www.productstewardship.us. (Accessed on 30 October 2024).
14. See C. Gable and B. Shireman, 'Computer and Electronics Product Stewardship: Are We Ready for the Challenge?', *Environmental Quality Management*, vol. 11, no. 1, 2001, pp. 35–45.
15. https://money.cnn.com/2016/11/29/technology/patagonia-black-friday-donation-10-million/index.html. (Accessed on 30 October 2024).
16. BBC, 29 November 2018: https://www.bbc.com/news/newsbeat-46386147. (Accessed on 30 October 2024).
17. A. Gautier and J. Bothello, 'What Happens When a Company (Like Patagonia) Transfers Ownership to a Nonprofit?', *Harvard Business Review Digital Articles*, 27 June 2022, https://hbr.org/2022/10/what-happens-when-a-company-like-patagonia-becomes-a-nonprofit. (Accessed on 6 June 2025).
18. https://www.bbc.com/news/business-62906853. (Accessed on 30 October 2024).
19. See his autobiography: Y. Chouinard, *Let My People Go Surfing: The Education of a Reluctant Businessman. Including 10 More Years of Business Unusual* (London: Penguin, 2016).
20. Available at https://sustainabledevelopment.un.org/?menu=1300. In short, these SDGs are: No poverty (SDG 1); Zero hunger (SDG 2); Good health and well-being (SDG 3); Quality education (SDG 4); Gender equality (SDG 5); Clean water and sanitation (SDG 6); Affordable and clean energy (SDG 7); Decent work and economic growth (SDG 8); Industry, innovation and infrastructure (SDG 9); Reduced inequalities (SDG 10); Sustainable cities and communities (SDG 11); Responsible consumption and production (SDG 12); Climate action (SDG 13); Life below water (SDG 14); Life on land (SDG 15); Peace, justice and strong institutions (SDG 16); and Partnerships for the goals (SDG 17).
21. R. Guha, 'Radical American Environmentalism and Wilderness Preservation: A Third World Critique', *Environmental Ethics*, vol. 11, 1989, pp. 71–84.
22. R. Hajirasouli, 'How Smaller Companies Can Join the Circular Economy', *Harvard Business Review Digital Articles*, 27 June 2024: https://hbr.org/2024/06/how-smaller-companies-can-join-the-circular-economy. (Accessed on 6 June 2025).
23. https://www.worldbank.org/en/topic/poverty/overview. (Accessed on 6 June 2025).
24. J. Gangemi, 'What the Nobel Means for Microcredit', *Bloomberg*, 13 October 2006: https://www.bloomberg.com/news/articles/2006-10-13/what-the-nobel-means-for-microcreditbusinessweek-business-news-stock-market-and-financial-advice. (Accessed on 6 June 2025).
25. See V. Akula, 'Business Basics at the Base of the Pyramid', *Harvard Business Review*, vol. 86, no. 6, 2008, pp. 53–7.
26. This is the view of C. K. Prahalad, *The Fortune at the Bottom of the Pyramid* (Upper Saddle River, NJ: Wharton School Publishing, 2004); and S. L. Hart, *Capitalism at the Crossroads: Aligning Business, Earth, and Humanity* (Philadelphia, PA: Warthon School Publishing, 2007).
27. This case, and many others, demonstrates that India is a source of innovation, precisely in regards to its focus on the BoP (C. K. Prahalad, 'Strategies for the Bottom of the Economic Pyramid: India as a Source of Innovation', *Reflections: The SOL Journal*, vol. 3, no. 4, 2003, pp. 6–18).
28. 'The Base of the Pyramid: Will Selling to the Poor Pay Off?', *The Guardian*, 22 May 2014.
29. See A. G. Karnani, 'The Mirage of Marketing to the Bottom of the Pyramid: How the Private Sector Can Help Alleviate Poverty', *California Management Review*, vol. 49, no. 4, 2007, pp. 90–111.

30. D. Matten and A. Crane, 'Corporate Citizenship: Towards an Extended Theoretical Conceptualization', *Academy of Management Review*, vol. 30, no. 1, 2005, pp. 166–79.
31. G. L. Clark, A. Feiner and M. Viehs, 'From the Stockholder to the Stakeholder: How Sustainability Can Drive Financial Outperformance', 2015, pp. 34–5: https://ssrn.com/abstract=2508281. Significantly, a study between 1984–2009 found that the *Fortune* magazine '100 Best Companies to Work For' outperformed their peers in terms of stock returns by 2–3 per cent a year (A. Edmans, 'Does the Stock Market Fully Value Intangibles? Employee Satisfaction and Equity Prices', *Journal of Financial Economics*, vol. 101, no. 3, 2011, pp. 621–40).
32. https://www.unpri.org/pri/about-the-pri. (Accessed on 30 October 2024).
33. This is the title of the bestselling book: T. L. Friedman, *The World Is Flat: A Brief History of the Twenty-First Century* (New York: Farrar, Straus, and Giroux, 2005).
34. See, for instance, D. Green and M. Griffith, 'Globalization and its Discontents', *International Affairs*, vol. 78, no. 1, 2002, pp. 49–68; and J. E. Stiglitz, *Globalization and its Discontents* (New York: W. W. Norton, 2003).
35. J. E. Stiglitz, *Making Globalization Work* (New York: W. W. Norton, 2006).
36. Actually, the terms 'multinational' and 'transnational' corporations are often used interchangeably.
37. J. Vives-Gabriel, J. Schrempf-Stirling and D. M. Coraiola, 'Dealing with Organizational Legacies of Irresponsibility', *Academy of Management Perspectives*, vol. 38, no. 3, 2024, pp. 286–303.
38. M. U. Walker, *Moral Repair: Reconstructing Moral Relation After Wrongdoing* (New York: Cambridge University Press, 2006).
39. See T. Garrett and B. Konoski, *Business Ethics* (Englewood Cliff, NJ: Prentice Hall, 1987), pp. 86–7.
40. Some arguments regarding this debate can be found, among others, in J. B. McGuire, A. Sundgren and T. Schneeweis, 'Corporate Social Responsibility and Firm Financial Performance', *The Academy of Management Journal*, vol. 31, no. 4, 1988, pp. 854–72; R. Roman, S. Hayibor and B. Agle, 'The Relationship Between Social and Financial Performance', *Business & Society*, vol. 38, no. 1, 1999, pp. 109–25; A. McWilliams and D. Siegel, 'Corporate Social Responsibility and Financial Performance: Correlation or Misspecification?', *Strategic Management Journal*, vol. 21, no. 5, 2000, pp. 603–9; and J. D. Margolis and J. P. Walsh, 'Misery Loves Companies: Rethinking Social Initiatives by Business', *Administrative Science Quarterly*, vol. 48, no. 2, 2003, pp. 268–305. Recent research focuses on the mediating role of different factors. For example, this one: I. Hasan, N. Kobeissi, L. Liu and H. Wang, 'Corporate Social Responsibility and Firm Financial Performance: The Mediating Role of Productivity', *Journal of Business Ethics*, vol. 149, no. 3, 2018, pp. 671–88.
41. R. V. Aguilera, D. E. Rupp, C. A. Williams and J. Ganapathi, 'Putting the S Back in Corporate Social Responsibility: A Multilevel Theory of Social Change in Organizations', *Academy of Management Review*, vol. 32, no. 3, 2007, pp. 836–63.
42. See interesting insights on leading corporate citizens in S. A. Waddock, *Leading Corporate Citizens: Vision, Values, Value Added* (Boston, MA: McGraw-Hill – Irwin, 2002).
43. Sources: www.botnia.com; Kaisu Annala and Carlos Faroppa, *Uruguay – Orion Pulp Mill Project: Environmental Assessment* (Vol. 2 of 3): Socio-economic study on impacts of Botnia S.A. pulp mill – executive summary (English): http://documents.worldbank.org/curated/en/746801468779380993; R. Barrios, 'A 20 años del conflicto con Botnia: la gran oportunidad que perdió el sector forestal en Argentina,' *Clarín*, 19 September 2023, https://www.clarin.com/rural/20-anos-conflicto-botnia-gran-oportunidad-perdio-sector-forestal-argentina_0_wmzVdcVGHp.html; Wikipedia: Uruguay River Pulp Mill Dispute, https://en.wikipedia.org/wiki/Uruguay_River_pulp_mill_dispute. (All accessed on 6 June 2025).

Afterword

Demystifying Ten Misconceptions of Business Ethics

Having taught business ethics for over thirty years, I have encountered various perspectives on the subject, many of which, in my view, are misconceptions that require a response. This book, at least implicitly, has sought to contribute to demystifying these misconceptions and related attitudes. To this end, below, I summarize ten common myths on business ethics, with a short response to each, to help understand myth as a narrative that plays a fundamental social role.

Myth 1. 'Business ethics is an oxymoron'

This myth suggests that business and ethics are fundamentally incompatible, as reflected in the phrase *'business is business'*. According to this view, business is solely about making money, while ethics is a concern for individuals. However, this notion is contradicted by the widespread public outrage that follows financial scandals, food adulteration and abuses of economic power. The need for ethical business practices is now widely recognized.

Response: Business and ethics are not two opposing domains but rather two dimensions of a single, deeply human activity. Society increasingly demands that businesses act ethically, and a lack of ethics can ultimately undermine business success itself.

Myth 2. 'Economic activity is amoral: it is enough following the law'

Some argue that economic activity is morally neutral and that legal regulations alone are sufficient to maintain a just social order. There are two main objections to this claim:

- *Laws and regulations do not cover every aspect of economic activity* and often emerge only after scandals and unethical behaviours have already occurred.
- More fundamentally, *economic activity is a human activity*, carried out by individuals capable of recognizing the moral consequences of their actions. Business decisions can affect other people, the environment and even the moral integrity of those making them.

Response: Business is far from being amoral – it has an intrinsic moral dimension and following the law is not sufficient for full ethical behaviour.

Myth 3. 'Ethics in business is only a constraint on economic dynamics'

According to this view, ethics is merely *prohibitive*, preventing actions such as fraud, bribery, lying and pollution. While corporate scandals have increased public interest in business ethics from this negative perspective, ethics goes beyond this. It is *primarily affirmative*, guiding businesses toward **excellence** and responsible decision-making. It is not merely about avoiding evil – it is about actively *doing good*.

Response: Ethics is not just about avoiding wrongdoing but also about doing good as much as possible.

Myth 4. 'Business ethics is important only if it is profitable'

Some argue that ethical behaviour is valuable only because it enhances profitability (the so-called *'Business Case'* for ethics). While it is true that ethics can build trust, reputation and attract responsible talent – and in many cases reduces risks – ethics does not exist solely for financial gain.

Response: Ethics is intrinsically valuable because it is about human excellence and flourishing, not just about securing future profits.

Myth 5. 'Business ethics is only about solving dilemmas'

While ethical dilemmas are an important part of business ethics, the field extends beyond difficult decision-making. Ethical management is not just about resolving conflicts between competing interests but also about fostering moral development within business organizations.

Response: Promoting ethical improvement should be a key goal of business ethics, alongside addressing dilemmas and avoiding misbehaviours.

Myth 6. 'Business ethics is simply about applying moral standards'

This is only partially true. While business ethics includes moral standards, its primary focus is on promoting good behaviours in business, and this requires human virtues. Without virtues such as integrity, honesty and fairness, human excellence in business is unattainable.

Response: Principles and rules can support good behaviour, but business ethics is not merely a procedural application of rules. Rather, it entails the cultivation of virtues – especially practical wisdom – to guide ethical conduct and sound decision-making in each concrete situation.

Myth 7. 'Business ethics cannot be objective because ethics is subjective'

This myth stems from moral relativism – the belief that ethics is purely a matter of personal values and emotions. Such relativism prevents meaningful discussions on business ethics beyond individual opinions. In reality, certain fundamental moral values – such as justice, honesty and generosity – are not invented but discovered by human beings. Moreover, ethical principles like the Golden Rule (*treat others as you would like to be treated*) provide universally recognized moral foundations. When individuals experience injustice, they demand objective fairness – regardless of their prior beliefs in moral relativism.

Response: Fundamental moral values – such as justice, honesty and generosity – transcend us and can be discovered. They are rooted in basic human goods that are essential for human flourishing.

Myth 8. 'Moral evaluation of business depends entirely on cultural context'

While cultural values influence ethical perceptions, some cultures may be more sensitive to some issues than others. Sometimes, ethical perceptions question the morality of a culture. This is the case of cultural contexts that are quite tolerant on matters such as bribery, discrimination of minorities, human rights or environmental irresponsibility. Actually, not all cultural practices are inherently moral. Respecting cultural differences does not mean suspending ethical evaluation of them. Ethics should consider cultural context, but it must also uphold universal moral principles, such as human dignity. Reducing ethics to cultural values is simply a form of moral relativism.

Response: Cultures influence the expression and emphasis of certain moral behaviours, but they are not decisive in creating morality or in determining what is ethical. Ethics is, rather, a systematic reflection on the human experience of morality, with human flourishing as its central reference point. Ethics evaluates culture – not the other way around.

Myth 9. 'Ethics training and policies guarantee good behaviour and ethical culture'

Ethics training and policies – including compliance programmes, corporate values and corporate codes of conduct – can help establish an ethical framework to prevent corruption and misconduct.

However, ethics training and policies alone are insufficient for fostering a genuine ethical culture and good behaviours. In some cases, compliance mechanisms fail because they lack alignment with broader corporate values or are implemented in a rigid, rule-based manner without deeper motivation or because of corrupt leadership. True ethical culture depends on many factors, one of them being ethical leadership, with a sense of service, and a moral vision that goes beyond rules and punishments.

Response: Good behaviour and building up an ethical culture depend on many factors, including ethical training and policies, but mainly on virtuous leadership and developing a moral vision among people within the organization.

Myth 10. 'Corporate social responsibility (CSR) and sustainability can replace ethics in business'

CSR and sustainability initiatives are important, but they must be approached ethically. Some companies separate CSR from their core ethical values, treating it as a marketing tool or an add-on rather than an integral part of their business ethics. This can lead to inconsistencies – such as companies promoting sustainability while engaging in unethical labour practices. Ethics is not just about policies; it is also about human excellence, which provides the foundation for CSR and sustainability.

Response: Ethics has its own entity in the whole company and gives foundations to CSR and sustainability.

These myths reflect common misunderstandings that hinder ethical progress in business. Ethics is not a constraint but a fundamental aspect of responsible business practice. Business ethics goes beyond compliance, legal requirements and profitability – it is about human dignity, responsibility and long-term excellence.

I hope that this book has contributed to a deeper understanding of these issues and has encouraged critical reflection on the role of ethics in business.

Index

AA1000 standards 431
Abercrombie & Fitch 411
accountability (corporate) 118, 228, 242, 281–2, 287, 302–3, 428–31
accountability 101–2, 156, 183, 303, 306, 311, 365, 372, 375
accountability in corporate governance 268, 290
accountability, international standards 282
accounting, creative 279
acid rain 444
advertising, ethics 399–402
advice, wrong 109
AES Corporation 231–3
affirmative action 254
agapic love (selfless love) 23
age discrimination 353
AI (artificial intelligence), ethics in 369–72
    fraudulent activities in 370
    how it works 360
    in managing people 370
    relevance in business 370
    vs. human mind 370–1
air pollution 444
AMA Statement of Ethics 388–9
American Marketing Association (AMA) 388
animal welfare 71, 427–8, 450
animals, cruelty 71
animals, do not possess innate rights 447
Annan, Kofi 437
anthropocentric-stewardship approach 448
anthropocentrism vs. biocentrism 59
anthropocentrism 59, 447
anthropocentrism: despotic vs. responsible 447
anti-corruption, international standards 280–2
anti-globalization movement 461
antitrust laws 229
Apel, Karl-Otto 44
Aquinas' natural moral law 45

Aquinas, Thomas 37, 45, 47–8, 67–8, 82 (n. 87), 83, 142, 207
areté, virtue, denoting excellence 27
Aristotelian tradition 17, 33, 42–3, 48, 52–3, 61, 82, 412
Aristotelian-Personalist Ethics 65–86
Aristotle 17, 19–20, 27, 36–7, 43, 47, 52–3, 65–9, 73, 83, 85, 97, 100, 97, 102, 245
arrogance 5, 82, 85, 209
Arrow, Kenneth 230
Arthur Andersen 5, 188–91
asset misappropriation 163
atmospheric pollution 451, see air pollution
auding responsibility and sustainability 428–31
austerity 208, 391
authentic leadership 196
authentic service (customers) 387–8
authenticity 194, 196, 202, 210
authenticity in leadership 210
autonomy 268, 277
autonomy, employees 356, 360, 361
authority in leadership 191–2, 207
authority vs. power 191–2
Ayer, Alfred J. 39

Bakke, Dennis 231
Bakken, Earl 211
Barings Bank 322
B-Corporations 242
Bear Stearns 223–4
beauty 70, 80
being positive (virtue) 211
beneficence 23, 41, 71
Benetton 411
benevolence 19, 23, 43, 68
    as a basic good of the person 70–1
benevolent love, rational 74–5, 77–78
Bentham, Jeremy 38, 42

Bernanos, Georges 121
Bimbo 391–2
biocentrism 59, 447
biodegradable material 395, 452
biodiversity 80, 144, 441, 444
biomass 443
blackmail 174
BMIS (Madoff's firm) 122–4
Boeing 9
bonded labour 346
Botnia 467–8
bottom of the pyramid (BoP) 8, 456–7
brand image 9, see corporate image
brand reputation and ethics 394, 454
bribery 173–6
bribery, morality of 175–6
Brundtland Report 419
Buber, Martin 47
Buddhism 23, 37, 43
burnout (at the workplace) 348–9
Burns, James, G. 197
business case vs. moral case 10–12
business company, nature of the 233–6
business contracts 159–60
business contracts, ethical issues 159–62
business contracts, lack of consent 161
    misbehaviours in 161–2
    validity 160
business ethics and profits 8–11
business ethics, antecedents 6–7
    as an oxymoron 472
    behavioural 12–13
    contemporaneous developments 7–8
    contribution to a good performance 8–10
    definition 6, 12
    ethical approaches 48–59
    frequent ethical approaches 39–4
    micro-, meso- and macro- 13–15
    motive for business 8–12
    normative 12–13
    related concepts 7–8
    scope 13–14
    why companies engage in 10–1
business responsibility, international standards 289–95
business, misbehaviours in 154–71
business, societal relationships 424

C&A 411
Cadbury report 289
Cambridge Analytica 300–2
Canals, Jordi 239, 243
capabilities approach on ethics 45–6
capitalism, ethical judgment 227
carbon footprint 443
cardinal virtues 85
care (virtue) 77–8
care ethics 45, 57–8
care in leadership 203
Carrefour 411
cartel 229
Catholic Social Teaching 59, 111, 287, 354
Caux Round Table, principles of the 283
caveat emptor (let the buyer beware) 386
caveat venditor (let the seller beware) 288
character see moral character
charities, supporting 16, 422
cheating 143, 157, 267
child labour 347
China melamine milk scandal, see melamine milk scandal
Christian ethics 37, see moral theology
Christianity 23, 43
chronic stress at the workplace 348–9
circular economy 458
circumstances, morality 142
citizenship (marketing) 308
civic friendship 79
civil authority 21
civil economy 244
civil society initiatives 182, 205, 210
civil society 45, 182, 230–1
climate change 7, 446, 449, see global warning
Coalition for Environmentally Responsible Economies 430
codes of business conduct 307–11
codes of ethics, see codes of business conduct
coercion, as modifier of responsibility 104
coercive power 268
collaboration within the company 271
    necessary for social life 79
collateral effects, morality of 107–8
collective bargaining 344, 360
collusion (price fixing) 397
commercial ethics 381–405

commercial placement, ethics 402–3
commercial promotion, ethics 399–402, 404–5
common good, concept 72
    and sustainability 419
    as reference for the business purpose 245–6
    as social reference 248, 251
    as the purpose of business 244
    principle, the 74, 78–9, 227, 365
    participation on the 72
    based ends of business 245, 248, 251
    based multi-ends 248–52
common values 23
common-sense intuitionism 41
communication ethics 77, 157–8, 252, 277
communication, corporate 87
communities and corporations 414, 419, 425, 431–3
community involvement (of companies), see corporate community involvement
commutative justice 154
companies, humanistic 16
company as a community of persons 236–7
company as social institution 237
company external mission 249–50
company internal mission 250–1
company, see business company
company, views of the 234–5
compassion in leadership 204
compassion 23, 43, 57, 84; *see also* mercy
compensation for damages, see restitution 155
competition, perfect 225–6
competitive advantages 242, 426–7
compliance programmes 474
complicity, see cooperation in wrongdoing
concealing the truth 158, 277
confidential information, definition 165
confidential information, misuse in management 280
confidential information, violation and theft of 163–5
confidentiality 370, see confidential information
conflict of interest companies-governments 427
conflict of interests 167
conflict of interests in management 280
Confucianism 23, 37, 43
Confucius 381
conscientious objection 145
conscious capitalism 241–2
consequences, responsibility for 105–8
consequentialism 42–3, see also utilitarianism

consumer rights 282, 300, 384–5
consumer sovereignty 386–7
consumerism 393–4
contract, honouring 159, 229
contracts, see business contracts
contractualism, as ethical approach 54
Convention on the Rights of the Child 347
Convention Against Corruption (UN) 37, 181
cooperation in wrongdoing 110, 114–16, 145, 177, 273
corporations and governments partnership 425–6
copyright infringement 164
corporate accountability 428–31
corporate citizenship 418–19
corporate community involvement 11, 306, 413, 417, 420–1, 429–30
corporate cooperation with NGOs 427–8
corporate culture, see organizational culture
corporate governance 287–93
    for the common good 287–9
    good ethical practices 289–91
    virtues in 291–2
corporate image 9, 11, 19, 64, 171
corporate involvement in communities 414, 419, 425, 431–3
corporate mission 304–5
corporate philanthropy 413
corporate principles of conduct 230, 315
corporate purpose 304–5
corporate purpose as serving people in a double mission 247–51
corporate reputation 9, 11, 18, 239, 308, 312, 350, 429
corporate responsibilities, existence of 415–16
corporate social performance 417
corporate social responsibility (CSR) 7, 11, 56–7, 101, 237, 409–24, 466, 475
    and sustainability 419–20
    criticisms and responses 413–15
    ethical principles 420–3
    individual principle 422–3
    institutional principle 417, 420
    mainstream approaches 416–19
    organizational principle 421–2
    practical wisdom in 422–3
    scope and order 421–2
    the common good as legitimacy 420
corporate statements 318, see institutional statements
corporate transparency 277

corporate values 305–7
corporate vision 305
corporation, the, see business companies
corporations and law 473
corporations as 'quasi-moral agent' 416
corporations, relationships with governments 424–7
corrective justice 156
corrupted environments 177–8
corruption 271, 426
corruption, conventions against 180–2
corruption, damages of 181–2
corruption, fight against 180–2, 311
corruption, fitting against 180–2, 303, 311
counterfeit 167, 395
courage in leadership 208
courage 24, 27, 36–7, 52, 85–6, 127, 208
creating share value 241
cultural context and ethics 474
cultural diversity 22, 308
cultural relativism 25, 31, 39, 56–7, 474
cultural values 25, 79, 474
culture gap (within organizations) 318
culture of corruption 175
culture of integrity, development 319–20
customer surveillance 368

debt bondage 346
decent work 354–5
deception 50, 133, 157–8, 162, 179, 211, 277–8, 288, 390, 395
deception in marketing 395–405
deceptive advertising 400
deceptive trade practices 375, 385
deceptive tactics in negociation 278
decision-making process 130–2
decision-making 121–149
decision-making, ethical dimension 124–138
decision-making, evaluative criteria 132–6
decision-making, full rationality in 132
decision-making, instrumentality in 134
decision-making, morality of 134
decision-making, practical wisdom in 128
decision-making, relationality in 134
Declaration on Fundamental Principles and Rights at Work 281, 341
deep ecology 447
deforestation 442

deontologism 41
depletion of natural resources 441–443
designing organizations, ethical principles in 324–6
disloyalty 176
despotic anthropocentrism 447
determination in leadership 193, 208, 316
dialogue 9, 25, 39, 301
dialogue-based ethics 47, see Buber and Levinas
dilemmas 135, 144, 475
dilemmas, criteria for solving 135, 144–6
diligence 276
diligence and justice in 168–9, 171
direct voluntary actions 106
discernment 43, 86, 160, 201–2, 354, 401
disclosure of information 158
discourse ethics 44–5
discrimination (employment and occupation) 238, 273, 350–4
discrimination, unfair 350–4
dismissals 254, 345, see lay-offs
distributive justice 154–5
diversity and human dignity 351–2
diversity in the workplace 350
diversity, equity and inclusion (DEI) 351
diversity, equity, inclusion and belonging (DEIB) 351
diversity, managing with justice 353–4
doctrinal advice (responsibility) 109
Donaldson, Tom 44, 240, 243
double effect, principle of the 142–4, 149, (nn. 13, 14), 177, 345
Dow Jones Sustainability Indices (DJSI) 460
Drucker, Peter 193, 221, 245, 272
due process, right to 335, 463
dumping 398
duties, conflict between 53, 117–18
duties, moral 26–7
duties, positive and negative 136
duty *see* moral duty

earnings management 279
ecocentrism 447
ecological actions, precautionary vs proactive 449–51
ecological challenges, business facing to 441–6
ecological ethics 446–8
ecological ethics, definition 446
ecological issues 28

ecological responsibility 101, 437–55
   definition 101
ecology, notion 441
e-commerce, ethics in 403–4
economic laws and their limits 229–30
economic rationality 225
economy for the common good 243
Economy of Communion (EoC) 242–3
ecosystems 70, 157, 441–2, 444–8, 450, 456–8
egalitarianism 273–4
Elkington, John 7, 429
embezzlement 142, 162–3
embezzlement in management 279
emotional intelligence 274, 364
emotional stability 193, 201, 207–8
emotivism 39
employee autonomy 367
   morale 10–11, 30,
   participation 423, 429,
   privacy 345
   remuneration 341–2
   volunteering 431–3
   family responsibilities 352
   engagement in social responsibilities 431–3
   initiatives 235, 271, 275
employees, involvement in community 423, 431–3
energy saving 449–50
energy, non-renewable 443
engagement (relationholders) 356, 360, 370, 418–20, 431, 466–7
ENI 172–3
enlightened self-interest 40, 42
Enron 4–5
entrepreneurship ethics 23
entrusted resources, misuse 163
environment (natural) 6–10, 11–16, 23, 39, 51, 55, 58–9, 64, 74, 81, 84, 98–9, 125, 131–5, 142, 157, 227, 231–3, 250, 280, 282, 437–55
environment (social & cultural) 15, 19, 22–3, 25, 55, 78, 101, 105, 109, 156, 170, 175, 235, 238, 242, 248, 250, 281, 284–6, 294
environmental care 423–4
   ethics *see* ecological ethics
   legislation 463
   proactive strategy 450–1
   responsibility, definition 101
   responsibility, see ecological responsibility
   sustainability 360, 392, 419
Environment Program (UN) 430, 439
Equator Principles 284–5
equitable criteria (distributive justice) 155
equity (justice) 273–4
equity in marketing 308–9
ESG as a reference for investors 459
ESG criteria 239, 289, 458–9
ethical analysis 14–15
ethical culture 474
ethical dilemmas 15
   solving 144–6
ethical duties 26–7
   ethical egoism 42
   evaluation *see* moral judgement
   leadership 195–6
   norms 26–7
   organizational culture, building 319–20
   principles (basic) 73–82
   principles, see moral principles
   relativism 196
   solving conflict between 145–6
   theories, in the Enlightenment 37–8
   theories, ancient and medieval 36–7
   theories, historical development 36–9
   theories, in Postmodernity 38–9
   theory, necessity of a complete 60–62
   training 87, 218–20, 229
   universalism, see Kantian universalism
   values 7, 25–6
ethics and compliance programmes 310–2
ethics and CSR 475
   and cultural context 474
   and sustainability 475
   in business 473
   of encounter 47, see Buber and Levinas
   vs. moral judgments 22
   guide for human excellence 10, 15, 34, 44, 61, 69, 72–3, 85, 83, 92 (n. 83), 121, 151, 154
   a systematic approach to morality 20–1
   business outcomes 8–10
   definition 20
ethnic and racial discrimination 352
ethos 20
eudaimonia 36, 42–3, 52, 68–9, 72

eudemonistic virtue ethics 42–3
Euthyphro dilemma 31 (n. 35)
evaluative criteria in decision-making 132–135
excessive expenses (management) 163
executive compensation, debate on 292–3
exploitative labour 346–9
externalities (economic) 226, 243
extortion 174
extortion, morality 175–8

facilitating payments 174–5
Fageda, La 326–7
fair competition 228–9
fair price 395
fair wage 282, 342, 359
family business 136–8, 210–2, 237, 250, 293
    discrimination 352
        responsibilities 16, 352, 421
        ties and business 51, 53, 55–6, 72, 155
family-work harmonization 78, 147–8, 159, 183, 254, 264–6, 275
favouritism 155, 273–4, 345
Fayol, Henri 271
feminist ethics, see care ethics
feminist advocacy 351
fiduciary duties 114, 140, 143, 146
Fifth Industrial Revolution 374–75
finance, misbehaviours 154–71
financial scandals 4–5
firearms 394
firm, theory of the *see* purpose of business
first do not harm (dictum) 146
first person vs. third person ethics 61
first principle of practical reason, the 73–4
Focolare movement 242
Follett Mary Parker 3, 6, 271–2, 287
Fontrodona, Joan 92 (n. 86), 312
forced labour 56, 346–7
forgiveness in leadership 206
formal organization, see organizational structure
fortitude 36, 81, 85–6, 129
fossil fuels 232–3, 441–4, 446, see carbon print
Foucault, Michel 39
Four Industrial Revolution 325, 373–4
France Télécom 253–5
Frankl, Viktor 409

fraud, definition 162
fraud in food industry 382–3
fraudulent conveyance 161
fraudulent disbursements 163
free market economy and ethics 221–30, see capitalism
freedom of association 344
freedom 51, 132, 135, 160, 224, 324
Freeman, R. Eduard 239–40
Friedman, Milton 229, 238
friendly service 77–8
friendship 19, 37, 42, 68, 71, 166, 172
fully human life, as a basic good of the person 71–2

G20/OECD Principles of Corporate Governance 289
gender discrimination 352
general justice 155
generosity 23, 53, 70, 160, 210, 474
George, Bill 196, 208, 313–16
George's business vision 313–16
gifts and hospitality 175, 183–4
giving in to extortion 175–8
Global Compact 26, 181, 273, 280–2, 312, 341, 344, 346–7, 351, 448, 458
Global Crossing 190
Global Reporting Initiative (GRI) 430–1
global trading 461
global warming 427, 443, 445–6, see climate change
globalization 460–1
governments and cooperations partnership 425–6
Golden Rule 22, 26
golden mean (virtues) 37, 43, 52–3, 86, 206
good behaviour, elements of 125–7
    some basic requirements 154–8
good example, in management 109–10, see role model
good faith 128, 160–2, 166, 226, 277, 279
    abuse of 226
good *see* human good
goods (moral) 25–6
    (basic) of the person 69–72
    principles, virtues, interconnection of 61–2
    types 26
government intervention, see state intervention
government, role in economy 227–30
governmental regulations of economy 228–31

governments, relationships with corporations 424–7
Grameen Bank 244, 456
gratitude in leadership 206
gratitude 41, 175, 201, 206, 210, 236, 448
grease payments, see facilitating payments
greed 5, 190
greenhouse gases 442, 446, see climate change
Greenleaf Robert 197–8
Greenpeace 468
greenwashing 11, 307, 459
grievance procedures 344–6
Grotius, Hugo 45
Guidelines for Consumer Protection (UN) 385
Guiding Principles on business & human rights (UN) 283–4

Habermas, Jürgen 44
habits 27, 68, 82, 105, 275, 340, 345, 357, 392, 399,
hard vs. soft regulation 230–1
heavy metals (pollution) 343, 445–6
hexis, habit in Greek 27
Hilbert, David 210–1
Hinduism 43
homo oeconomicus 235
honesty (marketing) 308
honesty 158
honesty in leadership 206–7
honouring one's word 76, 203
hospitality, as a virtue 23
hospitality, corruption in 175
HP 153
HPH Corp. 411
human action, effects of 132–4
human being, as a whole 12
human being, reductionist view 239
human community 72
human community, business as 111, 237
human dignity 24, 67
human excellence 27, 61, 69
human fulfilment 67–8, 205
human good 61–2, 65, 69, 83, 89; 135, 143, see moral good
human life 36–7, 52, 68
human maturity 203
human needs 76–7, 111, 204, 241, 249
human person 65–7
human quality in dealing with people 272–4

Human Quality Treatment, notion 272–4
human relations 36–37, 230
human relationships 71, 236
human rights 14, 24, 40, 45, 55–7, 67, 76–7, see innate rights
human rights theories 45
Humanism 24
humanistic management 7
humanity, degradation in 240, 357, 361
humanizing technology 374
humanizing technology 374
humans and technology interaction 373–4
Hume, David 38
humility (virtue) 85, 194, 200, 202, 206, 208–10, 316
humility in leadership 194, 200, 202, 206, 208–10, 316
hybrid enterprises 245, 247
hypocrisy 158

IBF Business Service Ltd 153
IBM 6
IG Metall 152
ignorance (in moral responsibility) 103–4, 109, 128, 162, 223
ignorance, abuse of 226
image of God, human being as 64–5, 67
impulsive advice (responsibility) 109
incentives, perverse 167, 223–5, 239, 293–4, 322, 425, 427, 463
inclusion 423–4
indigenous populations 45, 212, 449, 461, 463
indirect voluntary actions 106
Inditex 411
industrial espionage 160, 165
industrial revolution, first 343, 347, 374–75
  fourth 325, 373
  second 325, 373
  third 325, 373
industriousness 200, 208, 275–6, 357
Industry 4.0, see fourth industrial revolution
informal organization, ethics in 323
information technology, ethical 357, 366–8
informed consent 390
injustice, doing vs. suffering (Socrates) 12
innate rights 24, 45, 49, 56, 67, 75–6, 133, 321, 363, 447, *see also* human rights
innate rights, see human rights
insider trading 170–2

institutional (corporate) statements 304–10, 317–19
institutional injustice 59
institutionalizing ethics, scope 303–4
integrative social contracts theory 44
integrity & compliance programmes 172–3, 184, 310–2
integrity as integration of virtues 200
integrity in leadership 9, 200–1
integrity 5, 6, 10, 12, 19
intellectual property, infringement 164
intention, morality of the 141
Inter-American Convention Against Corruption 180
Interfaith Declaration 23
internal goods 12, 25, 43
International Council on Clean Transportation 98
International Labour Organization (ILO) 281, 341, 423
international law 45, 56
International standards for responsible business 280–5
International Standards Organization (ISO) 281–2, 450–1
Internet bubble 5
inter-procedural self 90 (n. 53)
Interquim (company) 431–3
intrinsic ends of the company 247–52
investing, socially responsible 459–60
Islam 23–4, 43, 67, 344
ISO 14001, on environment 450
ISO 26000, on social responsibility 281–2
IT (Information Technology), ethical issues 366–8
IT and employee autonomy 367
    customer surveillance 368
    data privacy and user consent 366
    employees' surveillance 366–7

Jesus Christ 12, 23, 197
John Paul II (Pope) 227, 333, 340, 469, (nn. 5, 8)
Johnson & Johnson, Credo 16–17
Judaism 23, 40, 43
Judeo-Christian tradition 24, 26, 37
judgements of conscience, see moral judgments
justice (and lack of) in management 270–1
    as fairness (Rawls) 45, 55
    in leadership 203
    as a virtue and duty 23–4, 26–7, 36–7, 45–6, 51–3, 55–8, 70–1, 73, 76, 79, 84–6, 127, 129, 154–6

commutative 154
corrective 156
distributive 154–5
general 155
reparative 156–7
restorative 157
retributive 156

Kant, Immanuel 38, 40–1, 45, 67
Kantian ethics 41, 45, 47–8, 50, 52–3, 58, 61, 67, 75
Kantian universalism 47
Kantianism, see Kantian ethics
kickback 152, 174
kindness in leadership 206
knowledge, in responsibility 103–4
Koslowski, Peter 62
Kotter, 191
kyosei 283

labelling, ethics in 396
labour contract 8, 145, 159, 161, 273, 326, 340–1
labour exploitation 34–5
labour rights 341–345
labour unions, *see also* unions
labour, child 347
labour, compulsory labour 346–7
labour, exploitative 346–9
labour, forced 346–7
Lao Tzu 187
law and corporations 473
law, function and limits 229–30
lay-offs 136–7, 142–4, 254, 345
leadership and values in practice 212–13
leadership exemplarity 195, 303
leadership 190–200
    authority in 191–2, 207
    concept of 191–2
    moral character in 193–4
    personality traits 193–4
    relational and ethics 195–8
    self-discipline in 208
    spirituality in 194–5
    theories 194
    virtues in 200–13
    spirituality in 194–5, 197–8
legal duties, see legal obligations
    justice 155

    loopholes 170, 230, 427
        obligations 102, 145, 413
legality vs. morality 21
legitimacy of business 244–8, 270
    ethical 44, 54, 74
    social vs. moral 227
legitimate defence 51, 142–3, 158, 344, 397
Lehman Brothers 222–4
Leo XIII (Pope) 287, 377 (n. 13), 378 (n. 32)
lesser evil, tolerance of 146
Levinas, Emmanuel 47
LGBTQ+ 35, 353
liability 102–3
LIBOR manipulation 7
lies 76–7, 105, 158, 277–8
litigation 58, 167, 308, 335–7
Litton Industries 313
living wage 342
lobbying 426
local communities 392, 419, 438–40, 448, 463
Locke, John 38, 45,
Lockheed 9
love of benevolence 77
loyalty, as a virtue 118, 137, 145, 158–9, 171, 176, 201, 207
    in leadership 207
        as adhesion 9–10, 164–7
        types 158, 200 (n. 22)
Luther King, Martin 197
luxurious offices 279
lying 12, 50–1, 157

Machiavelli, Niccolò 269
Machiavellian, use of power 269–70
Machiavelli Niccolo 269–70
MacIntyre, Alasdair Ch. 33, 43, 52, 62, 69, 243
Madoff scandal 122–4
magnanimity in leadership 210–1
magnanimity 23, 85, 193, 200, 210–1, 305
Malden Mills 136–8
malice 109
malice, avoidance of 23
manager ethics 23
managerial accountability 418
    power 269–72
    stewardship 278–80
    work 272, 275–80
manager's concern for collaborators 274
managing people 269–74

maquiladora system 357–60
Marcel, Gabriel 47
Maritain, Jaques 47, 59, 91 (n. 56), 92 (n. 86)
market economy, its ethical dimension 225–6
market research, ethics in 165, 327, 389–90
marketing 383–4
marketing research 389–90
Marks and Spencer 411
material cooperation in wrongdoing 114–16
maximizing shareholder value 237–9
meaningful work 355–6
Medtronic 304–5
melamine milk scandal 382–3
mental disabilities, employees with 326–7
Merch 252
Merck, Heinrich Emanuel 210
mercy 23, 71, 201, 204
mercy in leadership 204
Metro 411
Michelin, François 63–5
Michelin's vision of business 63–5
microcredit 244, 457, see Yunus
Milgram experiment 113
Mill, John Stuart 38, 42
minimum wage 342
minorities, respect of the 51, 354
misappropriation 152–5
    of corporate funds 142, 279
    of private information 171
    within the company 162–5
misbehaviours in finance 154–71
misrepresentation 160–2, 279, 385, 403
mission (dual) of the business company 249–51
mistreatment of persons 72, 76
mobbing 350
mock-ups (in advertising) 401
moderation 23–24, 36, 53, 68, 72, 85–6, 208, 402, 447, 448, see temperance
Mondragón Corporation 285–7
money laundering 168–9
monopolies 397
monopsonies 397
moral agency 19, 416
    certainty 128
    character in good behaviour 127
    character in leadership 187–212
    character 27, 36–7, 43, 50, 52–3, 59, 84, 114, 125, 127, 187–212

character, shaped by virtues 27, 36–7
conscience 101, 113, 126
development 19, 48, 53, 371
duties 26–7
enhancements 15
evaluation 52, 135, 138–46, 176, 474
goods 25–6, 68–73
hazard 166–7
intention and motivations 139
issues 15
judgement 126
judgments vs. ethics 22
judgments, practical wisdom in 127–30
leadership 193
legitimacy and the common good 78, 227, 270
motivation 126–7
nihilism 39
philosophy 20, 39, 52, 55, see ethics
pluralism 60
principles 26–7
rectitude 86, 104, 117, 126, 128, 203
relativism 25, 31, 39, 43–4, 55, 57, 59–60, 196, 210, 474
responsibility 97–111
sense 19, 110, 158
sensibility 19, 119, 125–6
sentiments 38
standards 474
theology 20
values, see ethical values
voices 21, 128
vs. social legitimacy 227, 417
morality, common insights worldwide 22–3
  human experience of 19–20
  sources 138–42
morals by agreement 44
motivation and virtues 83
motivation, moral 26, 50, 83, 126–7
motivations for undertaking ethical practices 10–12, 19–20
motivations, extrinsic vs. intrinsic 139
multinational corporations (MNC) 425, 449, 457, 461–4
Murphy 309

National Association of Corporate Directors (NACD) (US) 315
natural law theories 45

natural law, realistic (Aquinas) 45, 47
natural resources, overexploitation 238, 393, 419–20, 425, see depletion
negligence, lack of responsibility 106, 109
negotiation 193, 207–8, 344, 403
neighbourly love 23
nepotism 57, 178, 273–4
new organizational forms 225
NGOs 283, 411–13, 415, 422, 428, 430, 441, 445, 456
NGOs, cooperation with business 411–13, 415, 427–8, 442
Nietzsche, Friedrich 39
nihilism, see moral nihilism
Nike 9
noise (pollution) 106, 155, 327, 468
norms, ethical 12, 20–1, 26–7
Northouse, Peter G. 193
nuclear power, controversy 443

object (chosen action), morality of 141–2
object (moral) 138, 141–2, 158, 207, 278
objectivity 202, 390
obsolescence, of the product 394–5
occupational health 342–3
occupational safety 342–3, 410–1
OECD Anti-bribery Convention 181
OECD Guidelines for Multinational Enterprises 281
offensive advertising 401
offshore outsourcing 169, 437, 465
Olympic Games (Athens), bribes 152
obedience in organizations 113, 271
obeying orders, conflicting with ethics 144–5
ontological dignity, of the human being 67
optimism and good humour in leadership 211
organizational care 274
  citizenship behaviour 356
  climate 318
  culture, humanizing 318
  culture, its ethical dimension 316–19
  ethics 13–14
  justice 156–7
  life 206, 312, 231,
  structure, ethics in 320–3
  structure, ethics in 321–3
organizations, see companies
outsourcing 461, 465
ozone-depleting substances 445

packaging 385, 395
pacta sunt servanda (agreements must be kept) 159
Paine 11, 311
Parmalat 264–7
participation principle 80, 324
Pascal, Blas 263
patent infringement 164
paternalism (customers) 387
patience in leadership 208–9
patience 85, 208–9,
payroll fraud 163
peace 23–4, 53, 67, 79
peaceful relations 72, 146
Pérez López 191–2, 197, 204, 243
perfect competition 225–6
performance appraisal 203, 273–4, 321–2
personal values 25, 474
personalist ethics 45–6, 58–9
personalist ethics, ontological 47
personalist ethics, phenomenological-ontological 46–7
personalist principle, the 74–8, 154, 159, 272, 341, 343, 346–7, 385, 390,
person-centred culture 250
persuasion in advertising 399
persuasion, responsibility in 109–10
pesticides 347, 445, 453
Petrick, Joseph A. 201
philanthropy 459
planned obsolescence 395
Plato 20, 36, 72, 93 (note 96)
political contributions of business 426–7
political corruption 384, 426–7
political discrimination 353
political rights 457
pollution 98–9, 133, 142, 144–6, 226, 231–3, 238, 249, 363, 414, 419, 427–9, 444–5
Polo, Leonardo 40, 47, 62
positive discrimination 254
positive organizational virtue ethics 43
potestas vs. auctoritas (power vs. authority) 190–2
poverty alleviation 457–8
power over vs. power with 271–2, see Follett
power, bad use of 264–7, 271, 403
power, in business 267
power, Machiavellian view 270
power, right use of 263–97
power, types of 267–9

practical rationality 35–36, 125, 132, see practical reason
practical reason 27, 69, 73–4, 83
    the first principle of 73–4
practical wisdom 73, 84
    development 128–30
pragmatist ethics 60–1
predatory pricing 398
price fixing 397
    gouging 229, 396–7
    skimming 398
prices, in unfair competition 397
pricing, abuses 395–9
pricing, discriminatory practices 398–9
pricing, predatory 398
pricing, premium 399
pricing, unfair 229, 396
pride 100, 209–10
prima-facie duties 41
primum non nocere (first, do no harm) 146
principal–agent problem 167; *see also* agency theory
principle of the double effect 142–4, 149, (nn. 13, 14), 177, 345
Principles for Responsible Investment (PRI) (UN) 460
Principles of the Caux Round Table 283
privacy, maintaining 390
    respect for 301–2, 345
private information, misappropriation of 171
    property, right of 169, 171, 224
proactive vs reactive strategy 324–325
procedural ethics 44–5, 54–5
    justice 156
procedures, fairness in 345–6
Procter & Gamble 252, 305–6
product stewardship 453
    ethical issues 394–6
    warranties 396
professional secrecy 171–2
profitability of ethics 8–10
profits and ethics 8–9
promises, false 76–7
    keeping 50, 207, 270, 396
property rights 157
protection of personal data 345
prudence 36, 84–6, see practical wisdom
prudential certainty 128
prudential judgement 143–4, 278–9

psychological harassment 350
public relations 11, 279, 292
publicity *see* advertising
puffery 401
purpose of business, views 237–45
    of each company 252–3
    of the firm, see purpose of business
purpose-driven companies 252–3

quality circles 325
Quinn, John F. 201
Qwest 190

R's of waste management 453
racism 59
radioactive contamination 118, 445
Rana Plaza, disaster of 410–2
rational principles 12, see moral principles
rationality (full) in decision-making 130–1
rationality in ethics 37, 54, 58, 66–7
Rawls' theory of justice 45
Rawls, John 45, 270
real goods vs. apparent goods 69
recklessness 37, 85, 104, 105, 109
recycling 423–4, 453
regulations, function and limits 229–30
relational leadership 195–8
relational virtues 84–5
relationholder dialogue 422
relationholder vs. stakeholder 247, 412
relationholders 247–51, 418, 420–2, 427–8, 430–1
    external 248, 250–1
    internal 247, 250–1
relationholder, definition 247
religions on virtue ethics 43
    approaches to business ethics 7, 23, 34
    common values 23, 71
religious and cultural discrimination 353
    duties, respect for 343–44
    motivation 19–20
    spirituality 195
    traditions, on business ethics 20, 22–3, 43
reparative justice 156–7
reports, objectivity in 390
reputation *see* corporate reputation
resilience in leadership 209
resource depletion 441–2, 449, 455, 459
respect for people 75–7

responsibility in the supply chain 7–8, 55, 57, 370, 389, 442–3, 454, 459, 461, 464–5
responsibility, meaning and definition 100
    and moral character 114
    in managerial work 275–8
    antecedent and consequent 102–103
    as attribution 101
    congruent and transcendent 103
    corporate image of 308
    ecological 101
    forms of individual 108–10
    influence of organisational factors 113–14
    legal 101
    modifiers of consent 104–5
    modifiers of knowledge 103–4
    modifiers of 103–5
    organizational influence on 113–14
    personal moral 97–118
    scope 102–3
    social 101
responsible anthropocentrism 447
responsible consumption 8, 393, 455
responsible, of what? 102–3
responsible use of power 269–72
Rest, James 125
restitution 155
restorative justice 157
retaliation 117
retributive justice 156
right to create and join unions 344
right vs. good action 61
righteousness (of moral conscience) 43, 126
rights 174
rights 261–262, 265–267
Rio Declaration on Environment and Development (UN) 281, 448
risks, avoiding 15
role model 109–10, 129, 195, 274, 303,
Roman Catholic Church *see* Catholic Church
Roman law 159
Ross, W. David 41
Royal Dutch Shell 438
Ruggie Framework 283

S&P 500 ESG Index 460
Sabbath day 343–4
safe work 87
safe working conditions 76–7

Sanlu group 382–3
Sant, Roger W. 299
Sarbanes–Oxley Act 5, 190, 289
Sartre, Jean-Paul 39
scandal as leads others into wrongdoing 119
Schein, Edgar H. 317
Scheler, Max 47
secondary effects, see collateral effects
secrets see trade secrets
Securities Industry and Financial Markets Association 122
self-centred attitude 205
self-confidence 193, 209
self-determination 66–7, 69, 70, 83, 102, 416, 447
self-discipline 43, 201, 208
self-esteem 201, 208
self-interest 11, 24, 235, 238–40, 311–12
self-mastery virtues 85
self-possession 102
sense of responsibility 3, 10, 37, 58, 81, 112, 129, 138, 208, 271, 275, 286, 415, 461, 482
sense of service in leadership 204–5
sentiment-based ethics 26
servant leadership 197–8, see TD Industries
sexual harassment 349–50
    object (in advertisement) 401
    offenses 349
    orientation discrimination 353
shareholder activism 294
    approach 237–8, 240–1
shareholders, power and responsibility 293–4
Shaw, Enrique 111–12
Shell Africa 438–40
side effects, see collateral effects
Siemens, accusations of bribery 152–3
sincerity 157–8
Sison, Alejo J. 88 (n. 17), 92 (n. 86)
slavery 42, 56, 76, 346
Smith, Adam 238, 355
sobriety 85, 208
Socrates 12, 20, 270
Social
    actor 147–149, 333
    contract 45, 54, 235–6
    demands, corporate responses 428
    enterprises 244–6, 326–7
    equity 157, 169, 226, 228
    ethics principles 78–80
    justice 156
    pressure 11, 251
    problems 250, 286, 413
    reintegration 423–4
    responsibility of business 413–15
    responsibility, definition 101
    values 24–5, 39, 402
socially responsible investing 459–60
societal business ethics 408–433
society and business relationship 7–8, 11–12, 14, 17, 19
socio-cultural values 79
Socrates 20, 36, 270
soft regulation (civil society) 230–1
soil pollution 445
solidarity in leadership 205
solidarity 53, 58, 71, 79
    principle 74, 79
Solomon, Robert 90 (n. 51), 87 (n. 22), 120 (nn. 16, 17), 200, 207, 257 (n. 25)
Sophists 36
Spaemann, Robert 47, 151, 270
spirituality 59, 73
    in leadership 194–5, 197–8
    in the workplace 340, 370
spontaneous motivation 83, 104–5
SRI, see socially responsible investing
stakeholder view of the firm 235
stakeholder, creating value for 239–40
stakeholder vs. relationholder 247
stakeholders 6, 239–40, 242–3
    managing for 240, 242
state intervention in economy 228, 414, 425
stewardship anthropocentrism 447
stewardship in managing resources 278–80
Stiglitz, Joseph E. 461
stock options 170, 239, 253
Stoic ethics 37–8, 43, 52
Stoic virtue ethics 43
Stormberg (company) 423–4
strategic CSR 416–17
strategy, the ethical dimension of 320–1
strike 344
strike, ethics of 344–5
subjective values 24
subjective/objective meanings of human work 333 239–40, 361

subjectivism 11, 24, 210, 474
subjectivity, of the person 66, 333, 339
subprime crisis 222–4
subsidiarity principle 79–80
suicide, committing 253–5
suppliers 6, 16, 110, 176, 247 see supply chain
supply chain 423–4, 443, 454, 459–60, 464–5
Surgikos 368–70
surveillance of employees 345, 366–7
sustainability 419
sustainability and CSR 419–20
sustainability, encompasses by the common good 419
Sustainable Development Goals 355
sustainable development, broader meaning 419
sustainable development, definition 419
sustainable management 239
sustainability indices 460
sweatshops 342, 348

tax avoidance 168–9, 336
tax evasion 168–70, 178, 427
tax havens 169–70, 265, 427
taxes 155, 168–9
Taylor, Frederick 271
Taylorism 356
TD Industries 198–200
technological surveillance 362–3, 366–7
technology and business development 361–2
technology and human interaction 373–4
technology, ally of work 361–2
    ethics in implementing 364–5
    for the common good 362
    humanizing 374
    upright intention in developing 363
    using it ethically 365
Tellus Institute 430
temperance (virtue), *see* moderation
TEPCO (Japan) 118
terrestrial ecosystems 449
theft 50, 142, 157, 162, 172, 439
thefts by employees 163
third-person ethics 61
Toyota 305
trade secret misappropriation 165
trade unions *see* unions
trademark infringement 164
training programmes on ethics 303

transparency in corporate governance 268
transactional leadership 196
transformational leadership 197
transnational corporations 437, 461–4
transparency (in marketing) 308
transparency 157–8, 168, 170, 180, 182, 201, 206, 242–6
Transparency International 182
transparency, avoiding deceptive tactics in negotiation 278
transparency, conflict of interests 280
transparency, in communications 277
Triple Bottom Line (TBL) 7, 429–30
Triple Font of Morality approach 138–42
trust, development in business 8–10, 13, 17–18, 50, 52, 76–8, 130, 134–5
    abuse of 142
    rebuild 156
trustworthiness 100, 158, 206–7
truth, as a basic good of the person 70
truth, legitimate concealment of 158
truthfulness 157–8
Tyco 9

Uber 334–7
unfair competition 117, 171, 178, 228–9, 321, 395, 397
UNICEF 377 (n. 18)
unions 344–5
United Laboratories 212–13
unity of the virtues 86–7
Universal Declaration of Human Rights (UN) 24, 45, 87, 157, 281, 351
universal norms and principles 17, 21, 24, 38–41
universalism, Kantian 47
US Environmental Protection Agency (EPA) 98
US Foreign Corrupt Practices Act 180
US Securities and Exchange Commission (SEC) 122, 189
US Sentencing Guidelines for Organizations 310
Utilitarianism 41–2, 51–2

values, definition 25–6
values, ethical 7, 25–6
values, subjective and social 24–5
vanity 82, 140, 279, 365
veil of ignorance (Rawls's theory) 45, 55
violence at the workplace 349
virtue ethics, relativist approach 43

virtue, denoting excellence 27
virtue ethics 42–4, 52–4
virtues for trustworthiness 206–6
virtues in leadership 200–2
    conflict between 53
    fundamental 82–6
    globally common 24
    in managerial work 275–9
    in moral evaluation 52
    relational 84–5
    of self-mastery 85
visionary companies 305
visual pollution 444–6
Vitoria, Francisco de 45
Volkswagen, diesel emission test scandal 98–9
voluntariness 103–5, 107–8

wage, fair 282, 342, 359
wage, minimum 342
Wal-Mart 411
waste management 452
water pollution 317, 438–42
water use 228, 249, 396, 426, 442–3, 454, 459, 468
Watergate scandal 180
wealth creation 155, 169, 238–42, 246–7, 412, 450
Weber, Max 271
whistleblowing 116–18
will, consent of 104–54
willpower 37
windfall profits 397
window dressing, see greenwashing 307

wisdom (virtue) 84
wisdom in leadership 201–3
Wojtyla, Karol 48, 59, 74–5, 93 (n. 90), see John Paul II
women 12, 46, 343, 349, 352–4, 355, 373, 375–6
Wood, Donna 417
work, *see also* human work
work conditions 238
    environment 81, 105, 203–5, 227, 254, 301, 309, 349, 367
    inherent dignity of 338–9, 340–1
    managing ethically 338–60
    organization of 356–7
    personalist philosophy on 339
    subjective–objective dimensions 339–40
workers, abuse of, see labour rights
workers' rights, see labour rights
work-family harmony 147–8
working conditions 7, 16, 25, 75–6, 225, 247, 253–5, 282, 325–7, 335–6, 342–3, 346–50, 358
working hours 343
World Bank 182, 445–6, 467
World Commission on Environment and Development (UN) 419
World Health Organization (WHO) 342, 382
WorldCom 190

Yunus, Muhammad 244, 457

Zaleznik, Abraham 191
Zara 411